PERSONNEL ADMINISTRATION TODAY:
Readings and Commentary

PERSONNEL ADMINISTRATION TODAY:
Readings and Commentary

Craig Eric Schneier
College of Business and Management
University of Maryland

Richard W. Beatty
Graduate School of Business Administration
University of Colorado

Addison-Wesley Publishing Company

Reading, Massachusetts
Menlo Park, California • London
Amsterdam • Don Mills, Ontario • Sydney

ISBN 0-201-00503-4
EFGHIJKLM-HA-8987654321

Preface

In a sense this book is an outgrowth of our feeling that both the academic discipline and the profession of personnel administration have had too few resources available in recent years that reflect the complexity and vitality of the field. As in our previously published experiential text, *Personnel Administration: An Experiential/Skill-Building Approach* (Addison-Wesley, 1977), we have attempted to capture in this book the present thrust of personnel, as well as its potential for the future. The book presents a timely and diverse collection of readings selected from books, journals, and other contemporary sources.

Personnel Administration Today follows the same organizational scheme as did our text, *Personnel Administration*. It is intended as a companion volume to the experiential book; together, the books provide a thorough analysis of the field. The text and exercises in *Personnel Administration* are supplemented and reinforced by the more extensive conceptual material presented in this volume. The model of personnel programs explained in the Introduction and depicted in Fig. 1 (p. 3) provides an integrative framework for the readings. We have found this model very effective in pulling together the diverse views and substantive areas dealt with in the book.

Personnel Administration Today was also compiled for use with other personnel texts. To enable readers to coordinate this book with others, we have provided the grid on pages x–xi.

Our audience includes students, as well as professionals in the field. Thus, the selections are balanced between empirical research, conceptual discussions, review and summary articles, and guidelines and suggestions for more effective personnel programs. It is imperative for the serious student of personnel today, whether in the university or in the field, to be conversant with the broad spectrum of literature available. Several criteria guided our selection of the pieces in this volume. We sought articles that were timely, were representative of the range of personnel issues and approaches to human-resource management, and were honest reflections of the current state of the art. In addition, we looked for relevance to all types of organizations, readability, coherence, and excellence in style and organization. The use of various sources, including other texts and periodicals in business, psychology, personnel, law, and social psychology, reflects the eclectic nature of the personnel field and its foundations.

One additional unique feature of this reader: Each major section of the text concludes with an interview. To our knowledge, no other readings book has used this approach. Just before *Personnel Administration Today* went into production, we interviewed well-known leaders in specific topical areas within the field of personnel. These people were most gracious with their time and provided excellent overviews of their area of expertise. The result is an *inside* view of the field of personnel. The comments of our panel of experts lend vitality to the issues discussed elsewhere in the book, for these persons *are* personnel administration. Further, their remarks give us a view of the future of the field and of the challenges those in personnel will face. Their input into this project was invaluable.

In addition to these contributors, we would like to acknowledge the publications and authors who allowed us to reprint their material. Our reviewers, Doug Durand (University of Missouri, St. Louis) and Dave Gray (University of Texas, Arlington), provided us with numerous valuable suggestions. Barbara Leiner assisted ably with the correspondence, administrative duties, and the manuscript preparation. The Faculty Services unit of the College of Business Administration, University of Maryland, also provided administrative assistance, and the staff at Addison-Wesley once again worked its magic in transforming our "mess" into a book. We bear alone, however, the responsibility for any inaccuracies, omissions, or other inadequacies in this book.

College Park, Maryland   CES
Boulder, Colorado   RWB
March 1978

Full Citations for Texts Listed in Grid (pp. x–xi)

1. Anthony, W. P., and E. A. Nicholson. *Management of Human Resources.* Columbus, Ohio: Grid, 1977.
2. Beach, D. S. *Personnel.* 3rd ed. New York: Macmillan, 1975.
3. Beatty, R. W., and C. E. Schneier. *Personnel Administration: An Experiential/ Skill-Building Approach.* Reading, Mass.: Addison-Wesley, 1977.
4. Crane, D. P. *Personnel Management: A Situational Approach.* Belmont, Cal.: Wadsworth, 1974.
5. Chruden, H. J., and A. W. Sherman. *Personnel Management.* 5th ed. Cincinnati: South-Western, 1976.
6. Filippo, E. B. *Principles of Personnel Management.* 4th ed. New York: McGraw-Hill, 1976.
7. French, W. F. *The Personnel Management Process.* 3rd ed. Boston: Houghton Mifflin, 1974.
8. Glueck, W. F. *Personnel: A Diagnostic Approach.* Dallas: BPI, 1974.
9. Jucius, M. J. *Personnel Management.* 8th ed. Homewood, Ill.: Irwin, 1975.
10. Mathis, R. L., and J. H. Jackson. *Personnel: Contemporary Perspectives and Applications.* St. Paul: West, 1976.
11. Megginson, L. C. *Personnel and Human Resources Administration.* 3rd ed. Homewood, Ill.: Irwin, 1977.
12. Miner, J. B., and M. G. Miner. *Personnel and Industrial Relations.* 3rd ed. New York: Macmillan, 1977.
13. Pigors, P., and C. A. Myers. *Personnel Administration.* 8th ed. New York: McGraw-Hill, 1977.
14. Sayles, L. R., and G. Strauss. *Managing Human Resources.* Englewood Cliffs, N.J.: Prentice-Hall, 1977.
15. Sikula, A. F. *Personnel Administration and Human Resources Management.* Santa Barbara, Cal.: Wiley, 1976.
16. Yaney, J. P. *Personnel Management.* Columbus: Merrill, 1975.
17. Yoder, D. *Personnel Management and Industrial Relations.* 6th ed. Englewood Cliffs, N.J.: Prentice-Hall, 1970.

Grid for Use in Coordinating Reading Assignments
in *Personnel Administration Today* with Other Personnel Texts

SECTION IN *PERSONNEL ADMINISTRATION TODAY*

AUTHOR(S) OF TEXT (NUMBERS IN TABLE REFER TO CHAPTERS OF THESE TEXTS)	1: Personnel Administration: The Organizational Function and the Profession	2: Planning and Analysis of Human-Resource Systems	3: Appraising Performance in Organizations	4: Human-Resource Selection and Staffing	5: Training and Development of Human Resources	6: Maintaining and Improving Commitment, Performance, and Productivity	7: Personnel Administration and Human-Resource Management in the Contemporary Environment
1. Anthony and Nicholson	1	4,5		6,10	7,8	4,9	10
2. Beach	1,2,3,4,7,30	8	12	9,10	14,15,16	2,13,17,18, 19,20,21,22, 23,25,26,27, 29	5,6,11,24,28
3. Beatty and Schneier	1	2,3	4,5,6	7,8,9,10	11,12,13	14,15,16,17	18,19
4. Crane	1,2,3,20	4,8		5,6	7,9,10,11	2,8,12,13,14, 15,16	16,17,18,19,20
5. Chruden and Sherman	1,3,4,23,24	2	10	5,6,7	8,9	11,12,13,14, 15,19,20,21, 22	16,17,18,22,24
6. Filippo	1,2,3,4,5,26	6	13	7,8,9	10,11,12	4,12,14,15, 16,17,21,24, 25	22,23,25,26

7. French	1,20,30	10,11	10,15	12,13	16,17,18	6,7,9,19,20,21	8,12,14,22,26
8. Glueck	1,2,3,20	4	9,11	5,6,7,17	8,11,12	9,10,13,14,15,16,19	14,16,17,18,20
9. Jucius	1,2,3,4,5,28	6,7	12,23	6,7,8,9,10	13,14,15	11,16,17,18,19,20,21,22,24,27	19,22,23,24,25,26,27,28
10. Mathis and Jackson	1,2,3,19	4	10	5,6,7	11,12,13	3,8,9,14,15	14,16,17,18,19
11. Megginson	1,2,3,4,5,6,25	7		8,9,10,11	12,13,14,15	15,16,17,18,19,20,23	6,20,21,22,23,24,25
12. Miner and Miner	1,2,3,4,22	6,7,8	8,9	4,5,10,11,12,13	14,15	16,17,18,21	4,5,18,19,20,22
13. Pigors and Myers	1,2,4,23	3,14		9,10,15	3,16	4,5,6,7,11,12,13,17,18,19,20,21	8,11,13,22,23
14. Sayles and Strauss	1,2,3,20	7	13	5,8,10,11	9,12,14	6,15,16,17,18,19	4,10,11,16,20
15. Sikula	1,2,12	5	6	6	7	3,4,8,9,10	11,12
16. Yaney	1	9	10	2,5,6,12		3,4,7,11,13	6,8,12,14,15
17. Yoder	1,2,3,4,5,6,7	8,25	10	9,11,12	13,14,15	4,7,20,21,22,23,24	16,17,18,19,26

Contents

xiii

INTERVIEWS

Introduction

The objective of this book is to present a realistic and timely view of all major aspects of personnel administration or human-resource management. Personnel refers to the entire spectrum of an organization's interaction with its human resources, from its initial recruiting activities to the exit interview or retirement planning process. Personnel administration involves personnel planning and forecasting, appraising human performance, selection and staffing, training and development, and maintenance and improvement of performance and productivity. It is obviously a large and complex field, one that is closely tied to an organization's overall effectiveness.

Personnel administrators in today's organizations face an awesome task. The diversity and technical nature of those programs they administer and the external constraints they face make their job an extremely difficult one. The personnel administrator is responsible not only for the management of his or her subordinates in the personnel department, but also for the design, implementation, and evaluation of the basic human-resource programs which attract, develop, and maintain an organization's most vital asset—its people. In addition, the personnel administrator must interact with line managers and others in the organization, often in an advisory or staff position. Therefore, a delicate interface between the personnel department and employees, managers, unions, and government must be maintained. Further, Equal Employment Opportunity (EEO) legislation, the changing composition of the work force toward more women and professionals, the impact of unionization, and other general economic and technological trends all influence the operation of today's personnel department.

Thus, personnel administrators have begun to assume the power, status, and authority commensurate with the importance of their function. Personnel, however, is still very much an emerging and dynamic academic field and profession. More and more information pertinent to the field is being generated continually by behavioral-science research, and personnel administrators must keep abreast of the flow if they are to maintain their effectiveness. The articles in this volume are a representative sampling of the current literature.

Personnel Administration Today also includes at the end of each section an interview with a key figure in the field. These conversations enable readers to obtain a sense of what those currently engaged in personnel work think of the field, its challenges, and its potential. As noted in the Preface, these interviews *are* personnel administration today.

AN INTEGRATIVE MODEL OF PERSONNEL PROGRAMS

The seven sections of this book reflect the basic programs in personnel or human-resource management. The ultimate objective of personnel programs—the primary criterion for judging their worth—is organizational effectiveness. Each program, policy, or activity of the personnel function must contribute in terms of product or service (i.e., sales volume, cost reduction, persons "educated," programs completed, elections won, etc.) to the results an organization seeks. This contribution to organizational effectiveness is, in the case of personnel, accomplished through the procurement, development, and utilization of human resources.

Figure 1 is a model of this personnel process. The five major functions of the personnel process leading to organizational effectiveness appear in the solid boxes. These, along with the dashed-line box at the top of the figure, represent Sections Two through Seven of the text. Section One, a discussion of the nature of the personnel professional's job, is not included in the figure. So that you may have a better idea of what to expect from the text, let's now take a brief look at each of the seven sections.

Section One, "Personnel Administration: The Organizational Function and the Profession," provides an overview of the academic field of personnel, the profession, and its place in an organization. Personal characteristics that can help personnel managers work effectively with the various groups they encounter and practical suggestions for the administration of personnel programs are discussed. This section sets the stage for what is to follow.

Section Two, "Planning and Analysis of Human-Resource Systems," is the first major category of personnel programs represented by a box in Fig. 1. The placement of this box reflects the fact that these activities occur first in the sequence of major personnel tasks. Planning and forecasting human-resource needs is a prerequisite to decisions on selection, training, and all other personnel decisions. Job analysis and preparation of job descriptions—what people will do in the organization—are also required before individuals can be obtained to fill these positions.

Section Three discusses the next task in the personnel system. "Appraising Performance in Organizations" examines the establishment of standards, or criteria, against which to evaluate performance, as well as the development of various methods to appraise performance. Before a personnel administrator can select the right person for the job, he or she needs to know what the person will be required to do (i.e., a job description) and how to determine when the person has done it correctly (i.e., a set of standards and a method for appraising performance).

After the tasks of planning and criteria definition are completed, the personnel manager is adequately prepared for the procurement process. Section Four, "Human-Resource Selection and Staffing," deals with the various techniques used to make selection decisions, the problems typically encountered, and the technical knowledge required.

Once the procurement phase of human-resource management is accomplished, the next task is to develop those human resources selected to their fullest potential. Section Five, "Training and Development of Human Resources," focuses on providing personnel with the skills, abilities, and

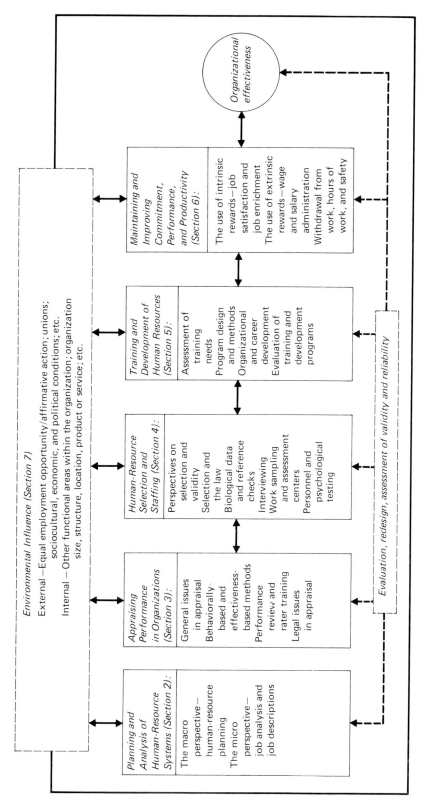

Fig. 1 An integrative model of the personnel process.

Environmental Influence (Section 7)

External—Equal employment opportunity/affirmative action; unions; sociocultural, economic, and political conditions; etc.

Internal—Other functional areas within the organization; organization size, structure, location, product or service; etc.

Organizational effectiveness

Planning and Analysis of Human-Resource Systems (Section 2):

The macro perspective—human-resource planning
The micro perspective—job analysis and job descriptions

Appraising Performance in Organizations (Section 3):

General issues in appraisal
Behaviorally-based and effectiveness-based methods
Performance review and rater training
Legal issues in appraisal

Human-Resource Selection and Staffing (Section 4):

Perspectives on selection and validity
Selection and the law
Biological data and reference checks
Interviewing
Work sampling and assessment centers
Personnel and psychological testing

Training and Development of Human Resources (Section 5):

Assessment of training needs
Program design and methods
Organizational and career development
Evaluation of training and development programs

Maintaining and Improving Commitment, Performance, and Productivity (Section 6):

The use of intrinsic rewards—job satisfaction and job enrichment
The use of extrinsic rewards—wage and salary administration
Withdrawal from work, hours of work, and safety

Evaluation, redesign, assessment of validity and reliability knowledge to perform effectively. The design, implementation, and evaluation of programs to meet this objective are also discussed.

Section Six, "Maintaining and Improving Commitment, Productivity, and Performance," examines the utilization of human resources—the issue of performance improvement. Many different techniques may be used to achieve these ends. Section Six reviews these techniques and provides a basis for understanding their foundations and evaluating their effectiveness.

We noted earlier that the external environment in which the personnel professional operates has changed drastically in recent years. Section Seven, "Personnel Administration and Human-Resource Management in the Contemporary Environment," deals with two aspects of the external environment that have had a major impact on the personnel function—programs related to equal employment opportunity/affirmative action, and the activities of unions. As Fig. 1 depicts, these areas influence *all* of the personnel programs. Hence, each program, if it is to be successful, must be designed with these two factors in mind. In addition, because the entire personnel process is a dynamic one, it requires constant monitoring and redesign, as the feedback lines in Fig. 1 indicate.

Figure 1 is a general integrative model. It is applicable to all types of organizations, as they all must procure, develop, and utilize human resources, no matter what their size, product, or service. The model is sequential and thus reflects the order in which we believe personnel activities normally take place. As you read each section, try to keep this framework in view as a constant reminder that personnel administration is an ongoing, dynamic process whose objective is to contribute to organizational effectiveness.

Personnel Administration: The Organizational Function and the Profession

INTRODUCTION

Section One provides an introduction and an up-to-date view of the role of the personnel administrator and the profession of personnel administration. Few, if any, functional areas within an organization have changed as drastically over the last few decades as personnel. The major determinants of these changes are catalogued by J.B. Miner and M.G. Miner in Part A of this section.

The contemporary role of the personnel administrator is an important one in any organization; the responsibilities are broad and complex. Organization-wide policies and procedures are within the scope of the modern personnel administrator's job, and the working lives of all organization members are touched by personnel decisions. As H.E. Meyer notes in his article in Part B, personnel directors are now "corporate heroes," perhaps on the way to attaining the presidency of their organizations. Meyer's article is testimony to the increased power and prestige many in the profession now enjoy.

Section One presents background material for the more specific discussions that follow in the remaining six sections of the text. In order to appreciate, as well as understand, the design, implementation, and evaluation of specific personnel programs, a sense of the current environment and historical development of the profession and the role of the personnel department is required. The profession is currently on an upswing in terms of status and authority. Speculation on the future of the profession and the role of personnel administrators in organizations is difficult, given the speed of organizational and societal change. However, it seems unlikely that the management of human resources, the major responsibility of those in personnel, will diminish in importance in the future, especially as personnel administrators become increasingly sophisticated in understanding, predicting, and changing human behavior. The future looks challenging, yet bright.

A. PERSONNEL ADMINISTRATION IN CONTEMPORARY ORGANIZATIONS

J.B. Miner

M.G. Miner

The Historical Development of Personnel Management

There are probably few fields of organized human endeavor that have developed in a really pure state, uninfluenced by other areas of knowledge. Sociology was affected by history and social work, psychology developed from a merging of philosophy and physiology, and engineering is primarily an amalgam formed out of the traditional physical sciences, such as physics and chemistry, combined with the demands of the business enterprise. Many other examples could be cited.

Personnel management is no exception. The field as it currently exists represents a crystallization of a variety of historical and contemporary influences, among them economics, psychology, social work, engineering, and accounting. Together these influences have combined in a complex fashion to bring the profession to its current position in the management framework. The purpose of this chapter is to trace these historical roots and show how they have contributed to the growth and current status of personnel management.

In general, it appears that there have been two major traditions or trends within personnel management over the years. One of these, stemming largely from economics and accounting, has emphasized a hardheaded, profit-minded approach to the utilization of human resources; the other, with its origins in social work and certain subfields within psychology, has taken more of a social welfare viewpoint. This duality of approach appears to have hampered the development of the profession within certain segments of American industry, and the signs of the split have still not entirely disappeared (15). The social welfare tradition has been viewed as antithetical to the "real" organizational goal of productivity by many managers both within and outside the personnel field. On the other hand, the feeling among those with a social welfare orientation has been that management generally emphasized productivity and profit at the expense of employee satisfaction.

THE BEGINNINGS

Interest in, and concern with, the utilization and organization of human resources have been in evidence since antiquity (8). The topic appears in the philosophic, religious, and military writings of both ancient and medieval times, and certain aspects of current practice can be traced directly to origins in Europe during the 1400s (13). Yet the history of personnel management as a distinct managerial specialty does not extend back nearly that far. In fact, the field as a separate entity is actually of relatively recent origin. Its development had to await the growth of the business unit and the consequent emergence of at least some degree of managerial specialization. This type of growth did not begin to occur until the years between the close of the Civil War and the early part of the 20th century (6).

It was during this period that a significant increase in the size of the organizational unit began to take place, and it was then that departments devoted to such specialties as finance and accounting, production, and marketing came on the scene. These three were the most common subdivisions at that time. There is no evidence that separate departments devoted to the personnel function were in existence during this post-Civil War period (6).

Scientific management

A small group of managers who were very much concerned with developing techniques for the maximization of the productivity goal through the effective utilization of human resources did begin to emerge, however. These were the industrial engineers, among whom Frederick W. Taylor (19) is perhaps best known. According to these people, the contribution of the human factor to the attainment of high productivity levels could be increased sizably through the appropriate use of selection, training, and monetary incentives.

Although Taylor and the other industrial engineers of the time, such as Frank and Lillian Gilbreth and Henry Gantt, had little interest in the formation of personnel departments as such, they did make a major contribution to that end through their insistence that management must pay attention to such matters as the selection of employees, proper training methods, and the development of appropriate compensation programs. This was in relation to a predominant concern with how machinery might be used most effectively.

The key components of this early industrial engineering approach were the emphasis on identifying the ideal physical conditions and methods of work and the concern with developing monetary incentives for the worker that would be both satisfying and effective. In this way, it was felt that there would be benefits to both the company and the individual. This movement, which was named "scientific management" by Taylor, became an extremely important force in American industry during the latter part of the 19th century and the early 20th century. By the time of World War I, scientific management had spread abroad and was applied to problems of improving productivity in France and England (23).

Scientific management constituted the first real attempt, originating from within management itself, to achieve a means of utilizing human resources that would be optimal from both the company and individual viewpoints. Nevertheless, scientific management was a continuing object of attack by workers and unions for many years, in spite of the fact that it gave important consideration to the welfare of the individual employee (10). Among management scholars, in fact, the motives behind Taylor's approach still are the subject of debate (7).

The labor movement

A second major influence during this period was the growth of the organized labor movement in the United States. Because the new unions were continually making demands for economic concessions from management, the history of the labor movement becomes almost inevitably intertwined with the history of personnel management. To understand the nature of these employee demands, why they became largely economic rather than social in nature, it is necessary to review, at least briefly, the background of unionism in the United States.

A trade-union movement can be found in this country as far back as the late 18th century, when organizations were formed in a number of cities to represent the printers, carpenters, and shoemakers. These unions were local in nature, with few financial resources to call on, although they did resort to strikes on a number of occasions even in those early years (1786, 1799, and 1809). They operated under one major handicap, however, during this period. All unions were considered under the English common law to be conspiracies against the public, because it was presumed that their purpose was to benefit the membership at the expense of society. Not until 1842, in the famous case of *Commonwealth v. Hunt,* did this interpretation of the legal status of trade unionism begin to change. At this time, a precedent was established that a union was no longer illegal in and of itself, but the means that it used to gain its ends (strikes, boycotts, and so on) might well provide a basis for legal action.

As a result of this decision and the rapid industrial expansion of the mid-19th century, the number of trade unions increased significantly, both along the eastern seaboard and in the developing areas around the Great Lakes. By the end of the Civil War, there were approximately 300 local unions, and national organizations had been formed by such groups as the printers, stonecutters, hat finishers, machinists, locomotive engineers, plasterers, cigar makers, and bricklayers.

The next step was the development of some type of national labor federation, and in 1886 a number of unions formed the American Federation of Labor (AFL). In contrast to some earlier, unsuccessful efforts to unify various union groups, undertaken primarily for political purposes of a socialist nature, the AFL was devoted to the purely economic objectives of increased wages and better working conditions and composed largely of unions organized along craft lines (cigar makers, printers, carpenters, and so on). The spokesman for the organization was Samuel Gompers, and under his presidency it grew rapidly in size and solidified its position despite considerable employer opposition. By 1917, total union membership in the United States, most of it within the AFL, was over 3 million. The growth of the union movement during this period produced an increasing concern throughout American industry with questions relating to manpower utilization and with what we would now call personnel policy.

The welfare secretaries

One response to this growth of trade unionism was the emergence of the so-called social, or welfare, secretaries, starting just prior to 1900. Although the major stimulus for the creation of these positions was without doubt management's need to find some means of stemming the union tide, it is also true that employers were increasingly concerned over the growing size of their organizations and the fact that it was becoming more and more difficult to maintain close personal contact with employees.

The welfare secretaries were expected to assist the workers by suggesting improvements in working conditions and in any other way that they could. It is largely from these individuals that the social welfare tradition in personnel management first developed. The welfare secretaries concerned themselves with helping workers with such matters as housing, medical care, educational facilities, and recreational activities, and in the various other areas that have become the province of the social workers of today (20). They were, in actual fact, engaged almost entirely in promoting the organizational maintenance objective, although this was not widely recognized.

The early personnel departments

It was from a merging of these various developments that the first recognizable personnel departments began to appear in the period between the turn of the century and World War I. In 1902, the National Cash Register Company established a Labor Department that was responsible for such matters as wage administration, grievances, employment, sanitary and working conditions, record keeping, and worker improvement (6). Other companies gradually followed suit, and by 1912 the first employment managers association was founded (3). By 1917, this increased to 10 associations, with over 1,000 member companies (21).

Although the work performed in these early departments varied somewhat from company to company, there was a common core of activities that were almost invariably present. These were selection, recruiting, record keeping, training, time and motion studies, welfare, and, generally, union relations. The primary stated goal of the personnel function in this pre-World War I period, as with most other aspects of the business enterprise, appears to have been productivity, or profit. Welfare activities as well as methods improvements were evaluated either explicitly or implicitly in terms of their contribution to this objective. The organizational maintenance goal as such was not widely recognized or accepted, except among a rather limited group of individuals within the personnel area itself.

EARLY INDUSTRIAL PSYCHOLOGY

During this same period, some developments were occurring within certain American universities that were to have a profound impact on the future course of personnel management. The science of psychology had had its beginning on the European continent as a combination of physiology and philosophy. By 1900, it had penetrated the United States and had become well established in a number of major universities. Although originally defined as the study of consciousness, or conscious experience, this emphasis soon began to fade in the utility-minded American environment (4). Men like James Angell and John Dewey at the University of Chicago started to talk about the *uses* of consciousness and its functions. And psychology began to move to a much greater concern with practical problems.

Cattell and Muensterberg

This utilitarian approach was taken up shortly on the East Coast, particularly by James McKeen Cattell at Columbia University and by Hugo Muensterberg at Harvard. Both of these men made significant contributions to early industrial psychology in the period when the possibility of applying the still adolescent science to industrial problems was just beginning to be recognized. Subsequently, their ideas became part of the developing body of knowledge in the field of personnel management as well.

Although Cattell was a psychologist whose early training was in the German laboratories, where a purely descriptive, nonutilitarian approach to the study of conscious experience prevailed, he soon directed his attention almost entirely to ways in which psychology could be of use to society. By 1890, he had coined the term *mental test* and had assumed the chairmanship of the psychology department at Columbia University. During the ensuing years at Columbia, Cattell continued to actively encourage research and interest in the applications of psychology to practical problems. In his later years, he founded the Psychological Corporation, one of the first consulting firms providing psychological services to the business world and a major publisher of psychological tests for industrial use.

In an even more direct line with the development of personnel management are the activities of Hugo Muensterberg at Harvard University. During the first 15 years of the 20th century, Muensterberg developed an extremely active interest in seeking out ways in which psychology could be applied to the problems of business and industry and wrote extensively, expounding his views (16). He was also able to put a number of his ideas to good use within several firms in the Boston area. Perhaps his most famous study involved the development of a selection test for electric-streetcar operators. Throughout Muensterberg's research and writings, a strong emphasis on empirical analysis and statistical validation inheres. This emphasis has now rather thoroughly permeated the methodology of personnel research.

Psychology in World War I

The most historically significant contributions that psychology made to the origins of the personnel field occurred during World War I. Cattell and Muensterberg were important, but it was not until the war period that objective psychological tests were used on a major scale to facilitate the effective utilization of human resources within a large organization.

The U.S. Army was faced with the problem of deciding what to do with the millions of men being drafted into service. Which ones should go to Officer Candidate School, and which ones should get technical training? A special committee of psychologists constructed a short intelligence test known as the Army Alpha. Based on an experimental instrument being developed by Arthur Otis, a Cleveland psychologist, the Alpha was the first group intelligence test and a milestone in the methodology of psychological test construction.

During the course of administering the Army Alpha, it became apparent that a surprisingly large number of recruits were scoring at the zero point or very close to it. Investigation revealed that many of these individuals were illiterate, and that Army Alpha presumed a certain amount of literacy. This led to the construction of a second test, Army Beta, designed specifically to provide information regarding the intelligence of those who were not able to read and write well enough to complete Army Alpha. The new instrument proved invaluable as an aid in the placement of less-well-educated recruits. It subsequently found wide usage in the postwar years in the testing of immigrants who came to the United States with little knowledge of the English language.

THE INTERVAL BETWEEN THE WARS

The 1920s

As a result of steadily increasing growth prior to the war, the success of the Army personnel program, and the general business boom, personnel management grew rapidly during the 1920s. Many companies added personnel departments for the first time, and a number of colleges and universities began to offer training in the area. Personnel consulting firms began to appear, one of the first being the Scott Company, which was formed by a group of people who had worked on the Army Alpha and Beta during the war years. Personnel research studies were initiated in a variety of settings.

The personnel departments of this period looked much like many that exist today. The major areas of specialization were selection, recruiting, training, methods improvement, and employee welfare. The last activity was strongly supported during the 1920s, which often is referred to as the "age of paternalism" in personnel management. One aspect of employee welfare that received special emphasis in this period concerned employee safety and health, which resulted from the recent enactment of state workers' compensation laws (9).

Probably the most important factor contributing to the welfare emphasis was the very intensive campaign that management mounted to discourage the growth of the labor unions. This became possible after the government-sponsored and government-enforced agreements that had been in effect during the war period were permitted to expire. Many companies used both positive incentives, such as benefit and recreation programs, and negative sanctions in their efforts to keep the unions out. This was the period of the so-called yellow-dog contracts, under which the worker agreed, as a condition of employment, not to join a union. At this time also *company unionism* reached its peak. Management-sponsored employee groups of this kind were particularly prevalent in the petroleum industry.

Thus, the welfare programs of the 1920s represented in large part an attempt to eliminate employee dissatisfaction, thereby minimizing the conflict-producing impact of the union movement. But this conflict-reduction objective was not the only one involved here. There was a general feeling, which is still popular in some quarters today, that "a happy employee is a productive employee." Thus, the welfare programs were considered to be good for productivity and were justified as such by the personnel departments of the period.

Toward the end of the 1920s, a series of experiments began at the Hawthorne plant of the Western Electric Company, near Chicago, that was to extend over several years and to have a substantial impact on the field of personnel management. Briefly, these experiments, which have been described and discussed at length in other publications (12, 18, 23), were initiated in order to study the effects of physical factors such as lighting and ventilation on worker productivity. As time went on, it became increasingly apparent that productivity was primarily affected by the emotional state of the employee; by his relationship with other people, particularly those with whom he worked; and by the amount and kind of attention he received from his superiors.

These findings served as the basis for what has since come to be called the *human relations* movement in American industry. For our purposes, however, it is most important that they provided personnel managers with a major justification for their welfare programs. Here was some real evidence that factors in the realm of employee attitudes and motivation did make a difference insofar as performance and productivity and profits were concerned.

The depression years

Whereas the 1920s was a time of growth, the 1930s was just the reverse. With the great reduction in business activity throughout the world came a sharp emphasis on cutbacks and savings (17). Managements were almost universally interested in doing all they could to reduce costs and to eliminate activities that were not absolutely necessary. The welfare programs of personnel management had had some difficulty justifying their existence in times of prosperity; in a time of depression, they were clearly in serious trouble. In many companies, it soon became apparent that they were definitely expendable.

Gradually, therefore, the welfare tradition began to lose out within personnel management, and in many cases whole personnel departments went with it. Those that remained were in most instances rather drastically reoriented and reorganized. The stimulus for this change came in part from government, both federal and state, and in part from the labor unions.

Under the pressures of the depression, a number of laws were passed that placed the unions in a much more advantageous position than that which they had held previously. Among the most important of these were the Norris-La Guardia Act of 1932 and the Wagner Act of 1935. The former drastically limited the use of court injunctions as a method of preventing work stoppages. The Wagner Act went much further and guaranteed the right of workers to organize into labor unions and to bargain collectively with their employers. . . .

The stimulus provided by this new legal environment produced mass unionization drives in a number of industries that had never previously been organized—the automotive, aluminum, and rubber industries, among others. These new unions were in many instances of a very different nature than those that had existed since the 19th century. Increasingly, management found itself faced with demands from *industrial unions* that included all types of workers from a given industry, regardless of specific occupation. Almost all unions, previously, had been of the *craft* variety, containing workers in a single occupation irrespective of the industry in which they worked.

By 1941, the total number of union members had increased from the 1933 low of 2,973,000 to a very respectable 8,614,000 (2), and there were now two major national labor federations, the American Federation of Labor and the Congress of Industrial Organizations (CIO). The former still stressed the old concept of craft unionism, whereas the CIO was made up in large part of a group of industrial unions that had seceded from the AFL in 1935.

As a consequence of this tremendous growth in the size and power of the union movement, major changes had to be made in whatever remnants of the earlier personnel departments remained by the mid-1930s. Increasingly, personnel managers found that they had to concern themselves with developing recommendations and evaluating policies designed to deal with the resurgent labor unions. Individuals with legal training began to find positions in personnel departments, and the attention of the personnel field as a whole became riveted on the labor relations problem.

WORLD WAR II

Although World War I had a sizable impact on the development of personnel management, the significance of World War II was infinitely greater. One reason was that World War II was conducted on a considerably larger scale and, as a result, the need for effective manpower utilization was much more pronounced. Second, the demand was not only greater in a quantitative sense, but more complex in a qualitative sense. Weapons and machinery were of a much more advanced design, and the airplane in particular had introduced a new set of manpower problems.

As in World War I, personnel researchers were called on to help solve the problems of the armed forces in the placement of the vast numbers of draftees and volunteers; the task had become much more complex because of the tremendous increase in the number of technical specialties. The result was a great variety of psychological tests developed to aid in the process of allocating individuals to training programs and to specific duty assignments; many of these tests later were adapted for industry use (1). Military researchers also did considerable work in the applied science of learning and in human engineering as they sought better ways of designing military equipment and more effective ways of teaching people how to use it. Many of the techniques introduced by the armed services subsequently found their way into the business world and had a profound influence on industrial training and management development (13).

For the personnel function, however, the effect of World War II was not limited to developments in the military sector; there was a much more direct impact as the federal government asserted control over various programs relating to personnel management throughout the economy. The activities affected most directly were training and development, which was influenced primarily by the administration of the War Manpower Commission, and compensation and labor relations, which were under the control of the War Labor Board.

Developments in the training field

To meet the need for effective utilization of manpower in the United States, the War Manpower Commission was established to find ways of locating, training, and assigning people with appropriate skills not only for the military, but also for civilian government agencies, business, and agriculture. A major problem was how to train the large numbers of individuals who flocked into the defense plants, many of them women and older people with no factory experience, so they would become satisfactory workers within a relatively short period of time. The problem was complicated by the fact that there was a shortage of experienced instructors to provide the training. The solution was the development of a program of Job Instruction Training (JIT) sessions, conducted by the Commission's Training Within Industry Division, which were highly successful in training inexperienced trainers. The JIT guidelines, using some of the same principles of applied learning theory as those used by the military psychologists, were developed in considerable detail and became the basis of many industrial on-the-job training programs still in use.

A second type of training program that was stimulated by the War was the development program for managers and executives. Under government sponsorship, more than 200 colleges and universities began to offer courses for businessmen on such topics as office management and personnel administration, and in 1943 the Advanced Management Program was established at Harvard. Prior to World War II, the training effort in most companies was limited to manual skills, and many training programs that had existed earlier were abandoned during the depression; by the end of the War, training had become a well-established part of the personnel function (9).

The War Labor Board

At the time of the United States involvement in World War II, the unions were continuing their organizing efforts on a large scale, often with rival unions trying to organize workers at the same plant. Because these jurisdictional disputes were a potential threat to achieving production goals, the mission of the National War Labor Board was to prevent these and other types of labor disputes, a mission in which the Board was highly successful.

It was in the effort to prevent inflation and disputes over wages that the War Labor Board had the most direct impact on personnel management. In the administration of wage and salary controls, the Board exerted authority over all employers with nine or more employees regardless of whether they were represented by a union. Regulations issued by the Board limited the amounts of wage increases employers could grant and also specified what other types of compensation were permissible. One effect of limiting pay increases was that employers increasingly offered extra payments in the form of paid holidays and vacations; it was during this period that these so-called fringe benefits became a major payroll cost for most employers.

For the typical personnel department, the major effect of the War Labor Board's existence was the setting up of a formal wage and salary administration program. Because the Board permitted adjustments without prior approval if they were made under an established plan for wage progression, many companies established such plans for the first time. Just as most companies had no formal training programs before World War II, wage and salary administration programs were also rare but became well established during the wartime period. Two lasting effects of the War Labor Board's regulations are the concepts of adjusting wages to changes in the cost of living and using wage surveys to determine whether the wages paid by one company are fair compared to those paid by other companies (13).

1945-1970: A QUARTER-CENTURY OF GROWTH

The overall impact of World War II on personnel management was that the scope of activities handled by the personnel department increased substantially, and the personnel manager became a much more visible part of the organization. To make sure the company was in compliance with government regulations, and also because of pressures from the unions, personnel administrators increasingly found themselves taking over many responsibilities that traditionally had belonged to the line supervisors. By the end of the war, personnel was recognized and established as a specialized function of management, and the major activities comprising the personnel function as we know it today had been introduced.

The postwar decade

In the postwar period, personnel management had reached what one writer called its "adolescence," with the role of personnel differing widely from one organization to another and no general agreement on what its role should be "when it grows up" (22). However, the decade following the war was a period of almost constant expansion in nearly every segment of the economy, and the field of personnel administration shared in this growth. One result of the continued economic growth in the 1950s was that serious shortages of technical and engineering manpower developed, and personnel people were called upon for solutions to the problem. A solution for many of the nation's large corporations involved extensive college recruiting programs of the kind still found at most large universities.

Labor unrest in the period following World War II was another factor affecting personnel administration. From 1941 to 1945, union membership had increased by 5 million to nearly 13 million; with the end of the war and the end of wage controls, the unions became particularly militant and made increasing demands on industry for health and welfare programs, pensions, and other fringe benefits that were extremely costly to management. Many of these demands were finally granted, but only after extended negotiations and some long and bitter strikes. Public alarm at the obvious power of the unions during this period finally resulted in the enactment of the Taft-Hartley Act to curb the abuses of union power (14). Even with the Taft-Hartley law in effect, unions continued to grow and had more than 17 million members by 1954. In 1955, the 20-year split in the labor movement came to an end when the two major groups of unions united to form the AFL-CIO; despite the merger, however, jurisdictional disputes between unions continued to create problems for management.

Government regulation also continued to have an impact on personnel. Companies were required by law to provide reemployment rights to veterans of both World War II and the Korean conflict, and wage and salary controls were reinstituted in the 1950s, when inflational pressures mounted as a result of the Korean involvement. The combination of manpower shortages, labor relations, and government relations contributed to the increasing influence and expansion of personnel management and also to increasing awareness of organizational maintenance as an important management goal. At the same time, it became apparent that many of the traditional approaches of personnel administrators to the problems of selection and training were no longer viable because of changes in the composition of the work force and in the nature of the work to be done. Compared to earlier generations of workers, the postwar labor force was much better educated and had a much broader spectrum of experiences; increasing numbers of women also were seeking employment in the business world. Technological changes and automated production processes called for quite different skills; extensive retraining often was required, and in many instances companies were completely restructured as a result of technological innovations.

By the mid-1950s, it became clear that the solutions to problems of human resources management could not easily be found in the personnel policies and techniques existing in most companies. Fortunately for management, the academic world had begun to take an interest in questions relating to the management of human resources, and it was from the universities, and particularly from behavioral scientists, that the solutions began to emerge.

The role of the universities

Courses in personnel management at the college level date back to the 1920s in a number of universities, but it was not until the post-World War II period that they became widespread. During this period, there was a sharp increase in the number of courses dealing with manpower utilization and with other aspects of the personnel function, and a major in personnel management was being offered in most schools of business administration. Graduate programs, in particular, were attracting sizable numbers of students.

In conjunction with the increase in course offerings in the personnel area, a second major development was the establishment at a number of universities of various research centers and institutes devoted specifically to the study of manpower problems (13). A few industrial relations centers that were supported primarily by sources outside the universities themselves had been established in the 1930s, but during the 1940s and 1950s nearly 50 research centers were founded, and many of them were financed by university or public funds. Among the first of these were the School of Industrial and Labor Relations at Cornell University (1944), the Institute of Labor and Industrial Relations at the University of Illinois (1946), and the Industrial Relations Center at the University of Minnesota (1945).

Although these centers have been most important in their role as agents in the search for basic knowledge, they have also made a significant contribution in attracting a number of capable individuals to the personnel field. Scholars from a variety of disciplines have been brought together in the industrial relations centers, with the result that a multidimensional approach to the problems of the field has been encouraged. Most prominent among the participants have been economists, psychologists, sociologists, industrial engineers, political scientists, and lawyers. The research emerging from this amalgamation of basic disciplines has proved to be of inestimable value to the practitioners of personnel management.

The impact of behavioral science research

Applications of the results of behavioral science research to the solution of personnel problems began with the work of the psychologists in World War I. During the 1920s many large corporations established personnel research units that set up selection testing and performance appraisal programs similar to the ones that had been so effective in the military. However, the research conducted by these in-house groups was not generally publicized outside the company, so the results did not contribute to the advancement of knowledge in the area.

The Hawthorne studies of the late 1920s, noted earlier, were the first behavioral science studies of industrial workers to receive widespread dissemination, but it was not until the 1940s that they had any real impact on industry. The findings of the Hawthorne researchers, which suggested that a permissive, or democratic, style of leadership was more effective than the traditional authoritarian leadership, received support from another series of studies on leadership techniques conducted by researchers at the University of Iowa under the direction of Kurt Lewin. These and other studies led to a new emphasis in human relations training for supervisors and higher-level managers in programs that were adopted on a large scale in industry during the 1950s.

While the human relations movement obviously was tied to organizational maintenance goals and fostered by the welfare tradition in personnel, it was also argued that productivity goals would be affected positively. According to proponents of the human relations approach, democratic leadership would result in employees who were more satisfied with their jobs and thus would perform more effectively and contribute more to the achievement of the organization's productivity goals. The relationship between employee job satisfaction and productivity became the focus for a vast amount of scientific research in the 1950s and 1960s as it became increasingly clear that the human relations approach does not necessarily result in greater productivity. This relationship still is being investigated, but the consensus at present seems to be that it is possible to improve either productivity or job satisfaction, but not both at the same time (11).

While it is true the behavioral scientists have not solved the productivity-satisfaction dilemma, their efforts have resulted in the development of better techniques and innovative approaches in many areas of personnel practice. In addition to the contributions of those in the academic world, researchers in the employ of major companies have begun to publish much of their research so that others can benefit from their results. Increasingly, however, the researchers are finding that what works in one organization may not be the most effective approach in another; more and more research is being directed to determining what policies and practices will contribute to the most effective utilization of human resources in a specific company.

Professional activities

While developments within the universities and among the behavioral scientists were contributing to the academic respectability of personnel management, significant changes also were taking place for those involved in personnel practice. As more people moved into personnel administration, they began to have an increasing sense of identity and increasing concern over matters of ethical personnel practice. For those in personnel practice, there have been two major areas of expansion in professional activities over the past 20 to 30 years—professional associations and publications.

Among the professional groups in personnel, the largest is the American Society for Personnel Administration, which has grown from fewer than 100 members at its founding in 1948 to nearly 15,000 in 1975. Another group, made up primarily of personnel administrators in the public sector, is the International Personnel Management Association (IPMA), formed in 1973 through a merger of two existing personnel groups oriented toward government and other public institutions. There are also many associations made up of people interested in special areas of personnel, such as the American Society of Training Directors and the American Compensation Association, that have expanded their activities over the years. Two groups that include large numbers of university professors and that have contributed to the advancement of knowledge in the field are the Industrial Relations Research Association, which includes mostly economists and labor relations experts, and the Division of Industrial and Organizational Psychology (Division 14) of the American Psychological Association, which includes personnel researchers from private industry and the government as well as most academics in personnel psychology. All these associations have had a significant impact on personnel management through their meetings, their sponsorship of research projects, and their publications.

Among the most widely read publications in the field, two began in the early 1920s—*Personnel*, which is published bimonthly by the American Management Association, and *Personnel Journal*, a monthly published privately. In the period following World War II, several new publications appeared. Some of these were sponsored by the newly established university centers, such as the quarterly *Industrial and Labor Relations Review*, begun in 1947 by the Cornell School of Industrial and Labor Relations, and *Industrial Relations*, published by the University of California's Institute of Industrial Relations since 1961. In the behavioral sciences, reports of results of personnel research appear in *Personnel Psychology*, published quarterly since 1948; research relevant to personnel also frequently is found in the *Journal of Applied Psychology*, which has been published for more than 50 years by the American Psychological Association. The major personnel associations also have their own periodicals—*The Personnel Administrator*, published by ASPA, and *Public Personnel Management*, published by IPMA. In addition, there are many periodicals for management in general that publish articles relevant for personnel people; the number and scope of these publications also have expanded greatly in the period since World War II.

THE RECENT PAST

In recent years, the growth in personnel management has continued in spite of, or in some cases because of, outside social and economic forces that have created a multitude of problems for management in general. The 1960s witnessed a growth both in numbers of people working in personnel administration and in the level and importance of personnel as an organizational function, and the forecast is that this growth will continue well into the 1980s. One aspect of this growth has been the extension of personnel administration from the large corporations and the federal government to smaller business organizations and to state and local government agencies.

A major factor contributing to the need for even small employers to have a personnel officer is the tremendous increase in laws and government regulations affecting one personnel activity or another that have gone into effect in the last 5 to 10 years. A detailed discussion of the legal influences on personnel in management is presented in Chapter 5; it is important to note, however, that the overall impact of the legislation of recent years has been to bring matters relating to human resources utilization to the attention of the highest levels of management. Achievement of organizational goals, in both productivity and maintenance areas, is directly at stake when a company faces a possible million-dollar lawsuit because of failure to comply with the requirements of legislation, such as that relating to equal employment opportunity.

The expansion in governmental influence on personnel management has resulted in large measure from changing values of society. Increasingly, in recent years, the view has been expressed that management, particularly business management, should concern itself with such matters as social responsibility and service to society (15). Legislation concerning fair employment practices, occupational safety and health, and pollution control represents the government's expanding role in exerting pressure on business and other institutions to act in accordance with society's changing values.

Major changes in personnel practice in areas such as selection and training have resulted from these changes in values and from the efforts of employers to achieve organizational maintenance goals by adapting to society's pressures. Just as results were beginning to be realized in the realm of social responsibility, however, economic difficulties—inflation and recession—beset American industry. By the mid-1970s, productivity and survival once again became the paramount concerns of management, and social goals became a source of conflict; in many companies, programs in the area of social responsibility came to a standstill, at least temporarily (5).

While it is not yet clear what the long-range impact of the current social and economic forces will be as far as personnel management is concerned, the indications are that personnel is more than ever in the forefront of management. People with expertise in solving people problems are being asked to participate in the top-level decision making of today's organizations to a greater extent than ever before.

REFERENCES

1 Bellows, R. *Psychology of Personnel in Business and Industry.* Englewood Cliffs, N.J.: Prentice-Hall, Inc., 1961.

2 Bernstein, I. "The Growth of American Unions." *American Economic Review*, 44 (1954), 303–304.

3 Bloomfield, M. "The Aim and Work of the Employment Managers' Associations." *Annals, American Academy of Political and Social Science*, 65 (1916), 77.

4 Boring, E. J. *A History of Experimental Psychology.* New York: Appleton-Century-Crofts, 1950.

5 Bureau of National Affairs, Inc. "ASPA-BNA Survey No. 29: Economic Pressures and Employee Relations Programs." *Bulletin to Management*, August 14, 1975, Part 2.

6 Eilbert, H. "The Development of Personnel Management in the United States." *Business History Review*, 33 (1959), 345–364.

7 Fry, L. W. "Frederick W. Taylor—Organizational Behaviorist?," in A. G. Bedeian, A. A. Armenakis, W. H. Holley, Jr., and H. S. Feild, Jr., Eds. *Proceedings, Thirty-fifth Annual Meeting of the Academy of Management*, 1975, pp. 1–3.

8 George, C. S. *The History of Management Thought.* Englewood Cliffs, N.J.: Prentice-Hall, Inc., 1972.

9 Kahler, G. E., and A. C. Johnson. *The Development of Personnel Administration, 1923-1945.* Madison, Wis.: Bureau of Business Research and Services, Graduate School of Business (Monograph No. 3), 1971.

10 Kakar, S. *Frederick Taylor: A Study in Personality and Innovation.* Cambridge, Mass.: The MIT Press, 1970.

11 Katzell, R. A., and D. Yankelovich. *Work, Productivity, and Job Satisfaction.* New York: Psychological Corporation, 1975.

12 Landsberger, H. *Hawthorne Revisited.* Ithaca, N.Y.: Cornell University Press, 1958.

13 Ling, C. C. *The Management of Personnel Relations—History and Origins.* Homewood, Ill.: Richard D. Irwin, Inc. 1965.

14 Macdonald, Robert M. "Collective Bargaining in the Postwar Period." *Industrial and Labor Relations Review*, 20 (1967), 553–577. Reprinted in A. N. Nash and J. B. Miner, *Personnel and Labor Relations: An Evolutionary Approach.* New York: Macmillan Publishing Co., Inc., 1973, 414–438.

15 Milton, C. R. *Ethics and Expediency in Personnel Management: A Critical History of Personnel Philosophy.* Columbia, S.C.: University of South Carolina Press, 1970.

16 Muensterberg, H. *Psychology and Industrial Efficiency.* Boston: Houghton Mifflin Company, 1913.

17 Nash, A. N., and J. B. Miner. *Personnel and Labor Relations: An Evolutionary Approach.* New York: Macmillan Publishing Co., Inc., 1973.

18 Roethlisberger, F. J., and W. J. Dickson. *Management and the Worker.* Cambridge, Mass.: Harvard University Press, 1939.

19 Taylor, F. W. *The Principles of Scientific Management.* New York: W. W. Norton & Company, Inc., 1967.

20 "Welfare Work in Company Towns." *Monthly Labor Review,* 25 (1927), 314–321. Reprinted in A. N. Nash and J. B. Miner, *Personnel and Labor Relations: An Evolutionary Approach.* New York: Macmillan Publishing Co., Inc., 1973, pp. 19–25.

21 Willits, J. H. "Development of Employment Managers' Associations." *Monthly Labor Review,* 5 (1917), 497–499.

22 Worthy, James C. "Changing Concepts of the Personnel Function." *Personnel,* 25 (November 1948), 166–175. Reprinted in A. N. Nash and J. B. Miner, *Personnel and Labor Relations: An Evolutionary Approach.* New York: Macmillan Publishing Co., Inc., 1973, pp. 153–163.

23 Wren, D. A. *The Evolution of Management Thought.* New York: The Ronald Press Company, 1972.

FOR DISCUSSION AND REVIEW

1 Briefly explain the impact of the following on the development of personnel management: World War II; early industrial psychology; colleges and universities; and behavioral-science research.

2 Explain how the two traditions of economics and accounting and social work and psychology have shaped the personnel field. Are these two traditions in conflict? Why or why not?

3 One writer has said that personnel reached its adolescence as a field in the post–World War II period. Has it grown up yet? What forces have shaped its growth in the 1960s and 1970s?

Elmer H. Burack

Edwin L. Miller

The Personnel Function in Transition

This article examines some of the steps that should be taken for updating knowledge and approaches of the personnel function in organizations in response to new and growing demands in the public and private sectors of our economy. A parallel theme and need is one of substantial modification of personnel curricula; changes

Reprinted by permission from *California Management Review* 18, no. 3 (Spring 1976): 32–38. © 1976 by the Regents of the University of California.

are needed to prepare students to cope successfully with changing job requirements and new functions within the personnel field or human resource management. This study emerges from the authors' intensive involvement in personnel research, curricula study as a part of a national study group, writings, and professional contacts with clients in business and government.[1]

Various changes in technology, environment, and social attitudes have emerged that dictate substantial modifications in job knowledge and functions for managerial personnel working in functional areas with such descriptions as personnel, industrial relations, and manpower. In turn, shifting organizational needs forecast redevelopment of various educational programs. An important factor here is that the relevance of these understandings apply equally to general management and various specialties. The growing pace of innovation and technological change, combined with increasing institutional size and forms (such as multinationals and conglomerates) and competitive and legislative thrusts, have made business and public-sector activity far more complex than in past years. These have affected career paths, deployment of people, and need for management and technical specialties, to name a few. Also, emerging social trends signal considerable changes in work-related expectations, such as work commitment and life style and including multiple careers and employers, manner of dress, and behavior of work entrants.[2]

Compounding the problems of those who deal with personnel is a vast new body of legislation such as equal employment, manpower, and occupational health and safety acts. Furthermore, difficult planning problems have emerged because of heightened turbulence in the environment from the uncertainties of national and international incidents, scientific innovation, and change itself. Underlying these trends and changes are even more fundamental structural shifts in the character and disposition of the labor force.[3]

By the year 2000, 15 to 20 percent of the American population will be employed in the manufacturing sector of the economy, 30 percent will be employed by the government, and the remaining 50 percent will be employed in services of one type or another.[4] Thus, work-force composition indicates further declines in the manufacturing sectors and continuing growth and attraction of people to the governmental and service sectors. Occupational shifts are also likely for current work-force members.

Importantly, the basis for securing performance will also be changing. Even in the manufacturing sector, where automated facilities have grown in importance, their delicate balance, complexity, and need for continuity place a high premium on human capabilities (training, selection, and motivation). The relative growth in the service and governmental sectors suggests growing dependence on interpersonal processes if productivity gains are to be realized, computer uses notwithstanding.

As the transition in the labor force occurs, different skills and expertise will be required of those persons in (or entering) the contemporary firm who are engaged in the management of human resources as compared to job roles in traditional personnel departments. Personnel maintenance functions increasingly must acknowledge the need for new capabilities in planning and personnel programming technology. Consequently, the educational needs of managers and human resource/personnel specialists are already beginning to differ from the product of many university or college personnel management courses or curricula.

BASES FOR STRATEGIC CHANGES
IN PERSONNEL PLANNING—MANAGEMENT

Four key characterizations concerning personnel activities warrant the attention of policy makers and officers of both private- and public-sector firms.

1 The definition and thrust of personnel administration as a concept and function is undergoing vast modifications in response to a variety of forces and pressures.

2 Personnel as a function is evolving toward a comprehensive resource system both dependent upon and contributing substantially to the various organizational work systems and significantly affecting economic performance, institutional welfare, and employee realizations.

3 Personnel is increasingly exhibiting the potential to make contributions to vital organizational decisions, performances and accomplishments.

4 Of necessity, personnel is moving into higher levels of professional activity; matters confronting it are of higher order of complexity; its affairs are more sensitive; and personnel's tools, appropriately, have grown more sophisticated.

PERSONNEL'S MISSION: CONCEPT AND THRUST

Personnel has moved beyond the traditional functional boundaries where its activities were largely concerned with maintaining people in organizations. It is not that the functions of maintaining people in organizations such as hiring, processing, and keeping records have become less important (Figure 1). Their successful accomplishment is still critical to the ongoing activities of the institution. Yet, as noted previously, the cumulative impact of vast societal changes, legislation, governmental surveillance, and growing need for acceptable social and economic performance have mandated change. Also, the reality of newer life styles, people expectancies, and advanced economic achievement suggests bilateral decisions on the part of individuals and units—such as to join organizations or maintain affiliations—where either party to the decision may opt to withdraw or simply not initiate the relationship.[5]

The figure suggests that various pressures are pushing organizational interests beyond securing and maintaining people to growing concerns with the post-work welfare and the lot of former employees. Disinterest or superficial programming of

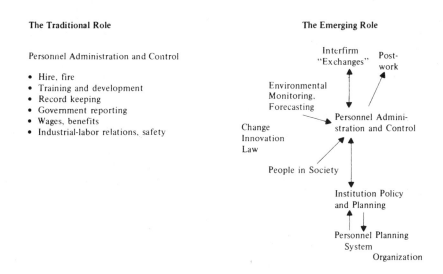

Fig. 1 The personnel function in transition.

various benefits and activities will no longer suffice to meet regulative necessity or socially responsible activity.

The newer profile of personnel administration displays a growing capability and need to plan and mesh with the long-standing planning systems that encompass marketing, financial, and operational concerns. Competitive thrusts and technical innovations portend far more than new packaging, engineering, or merchandising programs. The people component provides an indispensable partner in this game of survival. Personnel specialists must display a high order of analytical ability in providing useful counsel for a wide range of marketing situations or complex sociotechnical problems.[6]

> For example, a large steel firm was confronted with a number of competitive thrusts and technical innovations that led to the need to introduce and formulate a new marketing organization, develop a formal research capability, and introduce several new production systems. Profit objectives and achievement of business plans became dependent on the abilities of key personnel officials to develop a blueprint for manpower development and organizational changes to affectuate planning goals.

In addition, part of the shifting focus of personnel relates to its utilization as an instrument of research in probing difficult organizational problems. Problems of productivity, creativity, and administrative ineptness call forth a posture of inquiry and ability in problem in definition and resolution.[7] A case in point is a recent matter concerning a private university.

> The personnel department had largely concerned itself with routine matters for many years. The growing fabric of legal compliance regarding minority (race and sex) employment and opportunity was acknowledged by officials. But they had little feel for the current state of affairs regarding personnel deployment, let alone how people fared within the system. Several legal suits and adverse publicity in several newspapers demonstrated the vulnerability of institutional practices. Comparatively nominal researching of salary and career development of academic and nonacademic personnel could have easily headed off this situation.

PERSONNEL AS A COMPREHENSIVE RESOURCE SYSTEM

The age of specialization has witnessed the formulation and undertaking of a vast array of activities for securing organizational goals of maintaining people in organization, but the vital interdependency of these undertakings is often overlooked. Thus, compensation, benefits, and programs of employee appraisal may evolve and be highly developed. So, too, many programs of management by objectives and job enrichment have been launched without regard for the critical interdependencies between these.

> A large manufacturer of electronic systems and components maintained a big human relations department with specialists in numerous personnel-related areas. Compensation programming was highly advanced in procedures and specifications, but salaries and promotions were made independent of an employment-performance-assessment program, which never got off the ground. Senior managers had resisted assessment efforts and the program was never fully activated.

Effective personnel work requires a comprehensive programming effort but also necessitates a commensurate display of maturity and understanding to identify needs and integrate these into an organization's planning and administrative systems and successfully launch undertakings.[6]

Comprehensive programming also necessitates an initial awareness of needs. A monitoring and interpretative capability provides the initially vital input of information for exerting a personnel systems effort.

A medium-sized manufacturer and distributor of consumer products possessed a decentralized, multistate operation for the manufacturing of its products. Failure to anticipate the impact of new minimum wage legislation on its cost structure, job rates, and employee motivation led to considerable disruption of its internal operations and poor economic performance before balance could be restored.

Another instance of the critical nature of information inputs and their interpretation concerns a large engineering firm. Here, the need was to "read" important changes in life style; this had an adverse effect on younger engineers' decisions to join and resulted in poorer performance in recruiting efforts. It was incumbent upon personnel in this situation to develop the relevant information and evidence the professional capability to propose modifications in institutional policy and propose programs and strategies to attract younger people to the organization for continuing renewal of its design concept.

Another dimension of personnel's comprehensive effort pertains to the understanding of organizational administration and the behavioral implications of its procedures and actions. Internal programs must be formulated that are responsive to these needs and realities.

A large hospital with many medical and supporting departments continued to place primary responsibility for training with its functional heads. Although these professionals were well qualified in technical skills, many were poor teachers and still fewer members had an understanding of the management or administrative side of their operation and how these tied to other functions and systems of the hospital. Not surprisingly, continuing growth brought disproportionate increases in costs and internal tensions mounted as duplication or lack of execution continued to plague operations.

PERSONNEL, PERFORMANCE, AND ORGANIZATIONAL DECISION MAKING

Human resource-related needs continue to grow more varied and complex as performance must be improved, competing objectives must be resolved, deficiencies clarified and talent identified and developed to meet these needs. It takes little effort to establish the point that compelling payoffs exist where the batting average can be improved in the selection of managerial and supervisory candidates. In one situation with which we are familiar, systematic approaches in employee assessment led to a gain from one of three successful candidates to one of two. Absenteeism, tardiness, drug problems, and turnover require innovative job designs and work-performance-related research that truly reflects system and behavioral insights.

Consistency in performance and equitable treatment indicate the formulation of reward systems where individual and group efforts are tied more closely to performance, compensation, and nonmonetary returns. Individual needs vary greatly such that the development of a more flexible structure of reward and benefits can bolster the recruiting and retention of people. Better approaches in these areas can serve to examine the returns of various undertakings and the possible economics or higher returns through the rebalancing of expenditure programs.

The performance of an organization's decision system, technology aside, is vitally dependent on its human resource members. Facilitating identification of job need and formulation of a manpower data base can prove responsive to the demands of the decision system. Also, these approaches can serve to meet business needs that impose special talent requirements as in venture analysis, multinational operations, and managerial talent for diversification.

PERSONNEL'S GROWING PROFESSIONALIZATION

The growing complexity of personnel functions increasingly signals higher levels of professionalization and sophistication. Growing professionalization indicates expanded needs in terms of perspective, attitude, and tool knowledge. The inclination to utilize and capitalize on various mathematical and statistical approaches, plus the computer, requires a working knowledge of the assumptions, usefulness, and limitations of these approaches. Their use grows more indispensable in career planning, job design, forecasting, planning designs, and productivity approaches. Also, further signs of professionalization are found in the growing criticality of knowledge related to such things as system concepts, newer tools and models for assessment, bases for job evaluation, and incorporation of behavioral models in performance programs.[9]

The leading of personnel's newer activities indicates an important extension and perhaps a redefinition of activity. Experience continues to play a central role in professionalization, but it must be acknowledged that formal education and special training in supportive disciplines are becoming more than a desirable additive. The addition of new responsibilities congenial with the model presented previously and a more appropriate organizational positioning suggesting greater authority and scope of responsibility are concomitant, and indispensable to the realization of personnel's potential.

> The Manpower Division of the National Academy of Management formulated a curriculum study group in 1974 to study personnel-related curricula for undergraduate and graduate programs. New text materials, courses, and greatly modified programs are some of the key ingredients in the report presented to the academicians making up this division.

To meet the changing needs and circumstances of organization, substantive changes in the orientation of personnel specialists, let alone curriculum, faculty preparation, and pedagogical techniques, will be demanded. For example, the descriptive and recipe approaches to personnel or human resource management should be replaced by a more comprehensive approach, which incorporates policy, environment, and people and particularizes these to specific organizational or situational conditions.

The new curriculum should be designed to emphasize the significance of an organization's human resources and the need to develop and utilize these valuable resources more effectively. The perspective of the curriculum should be upon organizational and manpower planning rather than upon a limited emphasis stressing technique. Although there will continue to be a need to familiarize students with the descriptive and recipe approach to personnel or human resource management, the main thrust of the educational program should be more comprehensive in nature. Programs in personnel/human resource management as well as overview courses should increasingly deal with the breadth of processes, structure, and capabilities.

Updating of current department members, acquisition of new personnel specialties, and academic preparation for students interested in the personnel/human resources area will reflect personal development or course work that focuses on four major areas. Figure 2 shows these areas and their interrelationships; they are *the environment, the individual and society, the organization,* and *the public sector.*

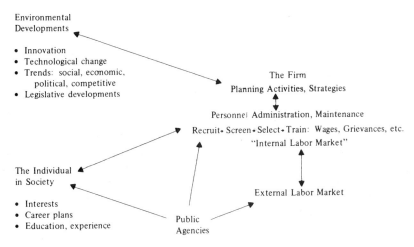

Fig. 2 A personnel/human-resource perspective.

Environment Environmental monitoring, technological forecasting, and interpretation of these events will be critical inputs to the human resource/personnel system. The translation of environmental developments in technical, economic, and social areas will provide key information and data for manpower forecasts and maintenance of an organization's human resources. The monitoring capability need not reside within personnel's functional responsibilities but the information is crucial to human resource designs for the future.

Individual and society The personnel-manpower processes within the organization will of necessity integrate more closely with business planning and strategy processes. Shortages of managerial talent in the prime age level of thirty-five to forty-four, and an increased willingness on the part of many managers and professionals to change employers, if necessary, to facilitate their career development is a force organizations are being forced to contend with. Furthermore, the attitudes of new employees as well as established employees are pressuring management to examine and in many cases to accept obligations to implement meaningful career planning programs, create physically and psychologically healthy work climates, and consider their individual needs, goals, and desires when personnel decisions are made.

Organization Personnel/human resource specialists will increasingly have to take into account the individual himself as a decision unit, as the decisions *to join, to stay,* and *to produce* continue to grow in significance for productivity and desired economic and social performance.

Public sector Educational programming will need to deal explicitly with the public agencies and actions affecting the external labor market (labor supply, wages, and distribution of various professions and job specialists), as well as impinging on the organization and its internal maintenance activities involving recruiting and training, for example. Legislative action, the role of agencies in training and employment preparation, external-internal labor market relationships, and the public sector's role and responsibility in manpower forecasts and analysis are of growing significance for personnel officials and are needed in curriculum design.

In more formal educational programs, the focus will be that of producing graduates who are prepared first with a general management orientation and second with competencies in personnel or human resource specialties. That is, the graduate will be a broad-based individual who understands the dynamics of management and the calculus of organization. The skills and competencies of the personnel or human resource management specialist will complement the graduate's general management perspective.

IMPLICATIONS FOR PERSONNEL/HUMAN RESOURCE SPECIALISTS

We can expect to see several distinct modifications in the personnel/human resource area, and these changes will have significant influence upon the work and the environment in which the personnel/human resource specialist will operate. It is our expectation that the personnel official will move into those types of activities much more closely aligned with contributing to the destiny of the organization. Specifically, we propose the following implications for the personnel/human resource area.

1 Within organizations there will be structural modifications and potential creation of new jobs built around manpower planning, manpower forecasting, career planning, and manpower information systems. Although specific approaches to manpower planning are varied, there is an awareness of the need for planning to enable an "organization to attain its goals and objectives more surely, faster, better, and perhaps cheaper."[10] As a result the personnel/human resource people will have an opportunity to assume a more important role in the management and administration of the organization. No longer will a personnel activity be able to justify itself only on the basis of the number of interviews conducted during the year or the acquisition of watermelons and name tags required for the company's annual picnic. Rather, the personnel/human resource area will be oriented toward planning and policy making in the areas of overall manpower planning, utilization of personnel, development, employment, and compensation. The overriding emphasis of the personnel/human resource area will be less on programs and gadgetry and more on what will actually be required to help the organization meet its goals.

2 As a corollary to the impending structural modifications for the personnel/human resource functional area, there will be an emphasis upon in-house programs focusing on updating personnel's technology for forecasting an organization's human resource needs as well as assessing and evaluating the qualifications of the organization's present workforce. Specifically, the personnel/human resource specialist will be expected to become more sensitive to what operating managers find to work best rather than what is easiest or most comfortable for the personnel function. Thus, there will be increased emphasis placed upon developing employees in ways that are meaningful and challenging to the individual and provide for the future of the organization. The theme must be one in which personnel/human resource officials are concerned with making an organization more effective rather than maintaining an organizational climate or environment that can be objectively justified only on the basis of being familiar and comfortable.

3 Reexamination of personnel's program for maintenance functions and the need to begin to plan the development of a more comprehensive scheme designed to translate the corporate or institutional plans and objectives into future quantitative and qualitative manpower requirements together with plans to fulfill those requirements over both the short and long terms. Those personnel activities concerned with recruiting, employment, compensation, and training must be integrated into the organization's overall planning process. Instead of a melange of

diverse activities or specialties, the personnel department's responsibilities will be regarded as an integral, integrated general management activity responsible for the effective utilization of the organization's human resources, sensitive to the requirements of the organization and committed to making the organization more effective. Specifically, the personnel/human resource function will be directly responsible for coordinating the planning, employment, utilization, and compensation functions so as to maintain an equilibrium between the organization and the external environment.

4 The personnel/human resource specialist will be called upon to assist top management in initiating different organizational approaches to the effective utilization of human resources and the capabilities of the personnel/human resource function. Chief executives of a growing number of organizations are becoming increasingly aware of the significance of their organization's human resources; reviewing the efficient use of the organization's existing manpower at its present level of development; assessing the level of performance of their employees; and concerning themselves with the enhancement of the individual's skills and talents and thus contributing to the productivity and overall contribution of the workforce.

As a result of this interest expressed by chief executives, it becomes increasingly apparent that personnel/human resource specialists have an excellent opportunity to contribute to the growth and success of their organization in still other ways. The personnel specialist must be able to help to identify and ease potential pressure points and adverse trends related to an organization's human resources. For example, the personnel specialist should be able to provide management with the type of counsel and assistance that can help to meet the intense pressure generated by equal employment legislation and affirmative action programs. No longer can equal employment be indiscriminately lumped in with the sundry group of activities included under the rubric of corporate social responsibility. With expanded responsibility in this area it is imperative that personnel people be qualified to provide the advice desperately needed by organizations.

The personnel/human resource function must also be able to spot adverse trends in turnover and absenteeism. Yet responsibility will not end with problem identification. The goal must be to determine the causes of these problems and what's actually needed to help the organization solve its manpower problems. As we see it, the personnel department will become much more creative or proactive in those areas of its responsibilities and the personnel specialist must become involved in providing managers with advice that is workable and useful.

It is our conviction and the role of personnel is changing rapidly and that the responsibilities of the personnel activity are being redefined. The personnel specialist must become increasingly oriented toward growth and efficiency of the organization instead of merely administering traditional personnel activities. This will mean greater emphasis upon planning the structure of the future organization and its personnel requirements, identifying and selecting personnel to meet these expected needs, developing and utilizing the organization's human resources, and assessing and rewarding performance. These activities will be undertaken with the purpose of ensuring growth of both the individual employee and the organization.

To handle these responsibilities, many personnel specialists will be required to engage in professional development, self-renewal types of activities. If personnel departments and specialists fail to meet these challenges, there is the distinct possibility that the personnel function will be relegated to an employee services activity limited to serving the needs of lower-level employees and maintaining those traditional personnel activities. It is our hope that personnel will begin turning its energies toward making the organization more effective now and into the future.

REFERENCES

1 Professor Miller has chaired a national study committee on behalf of the Manpower Division, Academy of Management, of which Professor Burack was a member. In addition, both authors have established continuing contacts with personnel/manpower officials and specialists. Burack has directed several research projects on the personnel function and is president of the Industrial Relations Association of Chicago.

2 Adam Smith, "The Last Days of Cowboy Capitalism," *The Atlantic Monthly* (September 1972), pp. 43–55.

3 D. Zand, "Managing the Knowledge Orientation," in P. Drucker (ed.), *Preparing Tomorrow's Business Leaders Today* (Englewood Cliffs, N.J.: Prentice-Hall, 1969).

4 D. Bell, *Toward the Year 2000: Work in Progress* (Boston: Beacon Press, 1967).

5 An excellent example is in the "Last Days of Cowboy Capitalism," *op. cit.*

6 F. H. Cassell, "Manpower Planning: State of the Art at the Micro Level," *MSU Business Topics* (Autumn, 1973).

7 M. D. Dunnette and B. Bass, "Behavioral Scientists and Personnel Management," *Industrial Relations* (May 1963), pp. 115–130.

8 F. E. Fischer, "The Personnel Function in Tomorrow's Company," *Personnel* vol. 45 (1968), pp. 64–71.

9 *Ibid.*

10 E. Burack, *Strategies for Manpower Planning and Programming* (Morristown, N.J.: General Learning Corporation, 1972).

FOR DISCUSSION AND REVIEW

1 How will the composition of the labor force change by the year 1985? What are the implications of this change for the personnel field?

2 Discuss the authors' description of the "emerging" role of the personnel function. In what ways is it difficult from the "traditional" role?

3 Develop a profile of the characteristics of personnel professionals who would best be able to manage personnel's "emerging" role.

4 Review the authors' four implications for personnel specialists and discuss the crucial role of planning they emphasize.

B. THE PROFESSIONAL PERSONNEL ADMINISTRATOR TODAY

Herbert E. Meyer

Personnel Directors Are the New Corporate Heroes

The personnel department has been represented on many a corporate organization chart as an orphaned box—one that came from nowhere and didn't seem to fit anywhere. To many businessmen, including many chief executives, the people who worked in "personnel" appeared to be a bunch of drones whose apparent missions in life were to create paperwork, recruit secretaries who couldn't type, and send around memos whose impertinence was exceeded only by their irrelevance. As a result of this perception, personnel directors, whatever their individual competence, suffered the *sui generis* image of being good-old-Joe types—harmless chaps who spent their careers worshiping files, arranging company picnics, and generally accomplishing nothing whatsoever of any fundamental importance.

In some cases, this depressing image was accurate. Companies *have* been known to use their personnel departments as a sort of dumping ground for executive misfits, or for burned-out vice presidents who needed just a little while longer on the payroll to be eligible for their pensions. But there have always been some personnel directors who found the job a springboard to higher corporate office, and in some companies the executive in charge of personnel management has traditionally been regarded not as an outcast but as an heir apparent.

The current chairman and chief executive of Delta Airlines, W. T. Beebe, was once Delta's senior vice president for personnel. Both Richard D. Wood, the chairman of Eli Lilly & Co., and one of his predecessors as chief executive served as corporate personnel directors on their way to the top—and a former president had followed the same route. Right now, the top Lilly executive responsible for personnel, Harold M. Wisely, holds the rank of executive vice president and has a seat on the company's board of directors.

A STEP TOWARD THE TOP

In the last few years, many companies have joined Delta and Lilly in putting their personnel departments in the hands of powerful senior executives. That old chestnut about a transfer to personnel being a one-way ticket to oblivion is no longer true. Absolutely no one at First National City Bank viewed it as a setback for Lawrence M. Small when he was transferred from the commercial-banking division to head the personnel division in August, 1974. Indeed, it was universally regarded as one very impressive step up the ladder: the job carries the title of senior vice president, and Small was only thirty-two years old at the time. And at I.B.M., to cite just one other example, the former director of personnel resources, David E. McKinney, is now president of the Information Records Division, an important marketing and manufacturing unit.

Those good-old-Joes of yesteryear would be stunned by the amount of power and prestige today's personnel directors can claim within their companies. At Dow Chemical Co., for example, the man in charge of personnel, Herbert Lyon, reports directly to President Ben Branch, the chief executive. Lyon is a member of Dow's board of directors, and is responsible for, among other things, global product plan-

From *Fortune* 93 (February 1976): 84–88, 140. Reprinted by permission.

ning and corporate administration. At Warnaco Inc., most of the executives promoted to jobs in top management during the last three years were singled out for advancement by John Limpitlaw, the company's vice president for personnel.

The executives who are being put in charge of personnel departments today are hard-driving business managers who speak what they call "bottom-line language"; they are as interested in profits as any other executives. George A. Rieder, senior vice president for personnel at Indiana National Bank in Indianapolis, provides an almost textbook example of how today's personnel executives perceive their role. "I'm not a personnel manager," Rieder says, in a tone of voice conveying scorn for that traditional title. "I'm a business manager with responsibilities for personnel."

Rieder quickly adds that this difference is much more than merely semantic. "It's a difference of style, scope, and approach. I view myself as a businessman first, whose job has as much of an impact on the bottom line around here as anybody else's. To be effective I have got to understand every aspect of my company's business, and I have got to participate actively in major management decisions before they're made." As a senior vice president, Rieder reports to John R. Benbow, the bank's president, and participates actively in day-to-day management of the business.

"GOOD ONES ARE WORTH A LOT"

Salary scales provide a measure of the growing importance of personnel. When the average salaries of executives in different specialties are compared—manufacturing, finance, and so on—personnel directors come out as the lowest paid. But they've begun catching up, because they are getting bigger raises than other executives. According to the American Management Association, the average compensation for personnel directors of industrial companies with sales of $500 million to $1 billion was $61,400 in 1975. Executives in charge of manufacturing for those companies got an average of $83,400, chief financial officers got $103,400, and chief executives $225,700. But since 1970, the average compensation of personnel directors has increased by 20 percent, compared with just 13.5 percent for chief financial officers, 15 percent for manufacturing executives, and 18 percent for chief executives.

It's likely that personnel directors will continue to receive larger raises than other kinds of executives, according to Pearl Meyer, a compensation expert who is executive vice president of Handy Associates. "These poor guys in personnel won't be at the bottom of the scale for too much longer," Mrs. Meyer predicts. "Companies are recognizing that good ones are worth a lot." Last year, when Chase Manhattan Bank went looking for an executive to head its human-resources division (modern corporations don't have personnel departments anymore), the bank put out word that for the right man, it would pay up to $120,000. Chase was obviously not in the market for a mere picnic planner. (The right man turned out to be Alan Lafley, from General Electric.)

Clearly, things are not at all what they used to be in the once dull world of personnel or, if you please, human-resource management. And just as clearly, much of the pressure for change came from the economic environment in which corporations have been operating. As Warnaco's John Limpitlaw points out, "The business climate out there today is a whole lot different from what it was ten years ago." In the economy of the 1970's, just about everybody has found the going tough and profits hard to come by. The cost of labor—union contracts, executive salaries, pension plans, and so on—keeps moving up.

Furthermore, many companies that had expanded geometrically during the 1960's discovered that their acquisition programs had left them with a tangle of incompatible compensation plans, and with scores of highly paid executives who now seemed to be in the wrong jobs or, worse, were superfluous. And with the stock market remaining in the doldrums, stock-option plans that had looked like money machines during the 1960s suddenly seemed most unsatisfactory; new compensation plans had to be devised to keep key executives contented. The job of personnel director took on new dimensions—especially as chief executives began scrambling to minimize the adverse effects of the recession.

Companies eager to increase their worker's productivity—and which were not?—discovered that an alert personnel director was in a unique position to contribute to the company's welfare. For example, George Sherman, the vice president of industrial relations at Cleveland's Midland-Ross Corp., got to wondering just why productivity rates in Japanese factories were so high. He flew to Japan, visited some factories, and concluded that part of the answer lay in the use of committees, made up of both workers and supervisors, that met regularly to hear suggestions for meeting production goals. On his return to the U.S., Sherman got clearance to form Japanese-style committees of workers and supervisors at the company's electrical-equipment plant in Athens, Tennessee. One modification of the Japanese plan involved the offer of a cash bonus to both workers and managers if productivity really did increase beyond the goal set by Midland-Ross. One year and 400 suggestions later, productivity at the Athens plant was up by 15 percent. The company was able to cancel plans to invest $250,000 in added manufacturing capacity, because output increased without it. Now Sherman expects to set up similar committees at other plants.

TIME OFF WHEN IT COUNTS

An idea developed by I.B.M.'s vice president for personnel, Walton Burdick, further illustrates how a personnel executive can help his company, and its workers, through a difficult economic period. Burdick developed a policy allowing I.B.M.'s employees to defer vacation time for as long as they wanted. Postponement was actively urged during years of booming business activity, thus keeping a lid on the number of employees. The payoff for both I.B.M. and its employees came during the past year, when the recession took a bite out of I.B.M.'s production. Workers who had saved up weeks or even months of vacation time were encouraged (rather firmly, one gathers) to use it.

I.B.M. Chairman Frank Cary credits the policy of deferred time off for helping the company get through a rough period without any layoffs. "You can't put a dollar sign on this sort of thing," Cary says. "The real benefit is in terms of morale. Our people know our policies are designed to keep them on the payroll. It makes them a lot more willing to go along with organizational changes we propose from time to time."

Pressure on American corporations from their not-so-silent partner, Uncle Sam, has done a great deal to add luster to the job of personnel director. In the last twenty years, there have been more than a hundred individual pieces of federal legislation directly affecting the relationship between corporations and their employees—e.g., the Work Hours Act of 1962, the Occupational Safety and Health Act of 1970, and the Employees Retirement Income Security Act of 1974. There has been a whole basket of laws and regulations to outlaw discrimination, including the Civil Rights Act of 1960, the Equal Pay Act of 1963, and the Age Discrimination in Employment Act of 1967.

SUITS THAT CONCENTRATE THE MIND

Personnel directors complain that the federal rules and regulations are poorly conceived, sloppily written, and almost impossible to comply with because they change so rapidly. But many of those same personnel directors concede that the federal government's antidiscrimination activities have done wonders for their own prestige and power. To paraphrase Samuel Johnson, there is something about being sued for a lot of money that concentrates a chief executive's mind wonderfully. While some antidiscrimination suits involve just one aggrieved person and not much money, there have also been some class-action suits whose costs to corporations have been considerable. American Telephone & Telegraph Co. has settled two antidiscrimination suits—one for $38 million and another for $25 million—and nine steel companies settled one for a total of $31 million. The threat of class-action suits by aggrieved employees or disgruntled job applicants has made chief executives very much interested in having their personnel directors come up with ways to avoid even the appearance of discrimination. "Boy, do they listen to us now," says one personnel expert rather cheerfully.

In addition to setting affirmative-action goals, such as for the number of women and blacks to be hired during the coming year, and the number to be promoted into various levels of management, personnel directors develop procedures to make sure the goals are reached. That may involve new hiring systems or special training programs for those already hired and marked for fast promotion. Personnel directors must spend a lot of time these days with supervisors at all levels, helping them to meet their targets.

At Chemetron Corp., Melvin Shulman, corporate director of human resources, works directly with Chief Executive John P. Gallagher to set the affirmative-action goals and develop the procedures for reaching them. Then he works with Chemetron's line executives to make sure they understand what those goals are, and also that they understand how serious could be the consequences of failing to reach them. Says Shulman: "I tell them of the possible damage to the company, but in a sense I'm making sure they realize that their own careers here are involved. When they understand how directly the chief executive is involved, and that in effect I'm representing him, they're more than willing to get cracking."

Personnel directors probably would have come in from the cold even without the help of a topsy-turvy economy or a flood of legislation. It would have happened because attitudes within the American corporation itself have been changing steadily for at least a generation—the attitude of chief executives toward their subordinates as well as the attitude of employees at all levels toward the companies for which they work.

It is so commonplace now for chief executives to deliver speeches extolling "people" as their companies most important resource that one tends to dismiss the phrase as cant. For some chief executives, of course, it may be. But a growing number of them really do realize that the quality and morale of their employees can make the difference between success and failure for their companies. One chief executive who is especially articulate on the importance of a company's human resources is Delta Airlines' Tom Beebe. "The name of the game in business today is personnel," he says emphatically. "You can't hope to show a good financial or operating report unless your personnel relations are in order, and I don't care what kind of a company you're running. A chief executive is nothing without his people. You've got to have the right ones in the right jobs for them, and you've got to be sure employees at every level are being paid fairly and being given opportunities for promotion. You can't fool them, and any chief executive who tries is going to hurt himself and his company."

Since Beebe is a former personnel man, there is some temptation to pooh-pooh his views as those of a man loyal to his old specialty. But one cannot argue with success. Delta hasn't had a strike in twenty years, and as airlines go, it is uncommonly profitable.

COURSES FOR THE COMERS

Every chief executive has to be especially concerned about bringing along capable successors. One company that is justifiably famous for the breadth and quality of its management-training programs is I.B.M. Frank Cary works closely with Walton Burdick, the vice president for personnel, to develop those programs and to assign the executive "graduates" to appropriate jobs within I.B.M. "It's the chief executive's responsibility to make sure the company has personnel policies and practices that can select the best people, then train them for management positions," says Cary.

Dresser Industries' senior vice president for industrial relations, Thomas Raleigh, spends a lot of time with President John V. James developing and administering the company's executive-training programs. At the recently established Dresser Leadership Center, a campus-like training center near the company's Dallas headquarters, executives enroll for courses lasting one to four weeks. They take courses in business management, and also study aspects of Dresser's energy-related business that may be unconnected to their immediate assignments. And Raleigh gets a chance to size up Dresser officials who work far from Dallas.

Few personnel managers work only with executives, of course, and the changed attitudes of employees toward their companies present a constant flow of new challenges. Today's blue- and white-collar workers want more from their jobs than just a paycheck; they want satisfaction, and they want to be treated fairly. Specifically, they want a salary that's fair in relation to their co-workers' salaries, and they want a fair chance for promotion that's based on an objective evaluation of their performances rather than the subjective whims of their immediate supervisors, or on their sex or skin color.

When Harold Johnson joined Philadelphia's INA Corp. as vice president for personnel a few months ago—he was formerly with American Medicorp Inc.—the insurance company did not have a fully developed system for setting the salaries of new employees. Nor were there clear ground rules for awarding raises, or for evaluating employee performance. "Things worked pretty much according to the whims of individual supervisors," says Johnson. "There were no company-wide standards at all. The employees were unhappy because they felt their salaries were sometimes unfair, and because they felt top management wasn't aware of the quality work they were doing. And top management needed a tool to help identify the high performers so they could be promoted, or selected for advanced training."

INA Chairman Ralph Saul has ordered Johnson to develop a system to identify the company's most promising executives, and to establish corporate salary scales so that employees in similar jobs will be paid within an established range. Johnson is also devising an evaluation system to assure that raises will be awarded in a consistent way, based on individual performance. Once the system is in effect, Johnson will be responsible for getting supervisors to use it. Saul has told Johnson that the latter's own job performance will be measured in part by how quickly he can get the new pay and evaluation system working.

POWER FOR THE TEAM

In many companies, the personnel director's responsibilities have become so complex that they can only be shouldered by topflight business managers who have the backing of the chief executive. The people who do the job like to say that in the years to come, a tour of duty in the personnel department (more likely the division of human resources) will be mandatory for any executive who aims to be chairman. Though that may prove to be an exaggeration, it is true that more companies are transferring up-and-coming executives into personnel for a while, en route to greater things. Dow Chemical's Herbert Lyon says it's a good thing for personnel departments to have a mix of professional experts, who have worked exclusively in personnel, and generalists who are brought in for a tour of duty from other parts of the company. I.B.M.'s Walton Burdick agrees, and adds that in his view the professional personnel types—of whom he is one—benefit even more than the generalists from having a mix. "It gives the specialists a better sense of what's really going on out there," he explains.

Citibank's Larry Small reflects a perspective common to executives who have moved into personnel but who do not expect to remain in it forever. "I'm not a personnel guy," he says carefully, displaying the annoyance of a man who has explained this to others before and who knows he'll have to explain it again to somebody else. "I'm a businessman—a manager. I just happen to be handling personnel at the moment, because it's a very important part of managing a business today."

As more and more personnel departments become populated with managers like Small, what were once enclaves will increasingly be seen as key corporate divisions. And the executives who run them, whether they are called personnel directors or executive vice presidents for human resources, will finally be recognized for what they now are and what in retrospect they always should have been—power-wielding members of their companies' management teams.

FOR DISCUSSION AND REVIEW

1   Describe how the typical personnel specialist was generally perceived some years ago. What has changed?
2   Why do today's personnel people have more power than personnel staffs had in the past?

John B. Miner

Levels of Motivation to Manage among Personnel and Industrial Relations Managers

A reading of the historical literature in the field of personnel and industrial relations raises serious questions regarding the extent to which managers in this field are primarily interested in managing and are committed to managerial as opposed to other types of goals (Ling, 1965; Milton, 1970; Nash & Miner, 1973). Throughout its history, personnel management has often been identified more strongly with employees than with management, and more strongly with organizational maintenance goals than with making a profit. These orientations are inherent in a number of interpretations of the human relations and participative management viewpoints, both of which have often been embraced by personnel managers; they are also inherent in the current emphasis on a professional commitment to employee-clients and to society as a whole.

In a recent article, Patten (1972) has hypothesized that the net result of these essentially nonmanagerial orientations within the field has been to produce a function staffed by "managers" who lack the will to manage. Although he considers this unfortunate and predicts a change in the future, he nevertheless views the current deficiency in managerial motivation as the major factor keeping personnel and industrial relations managers from achieving their full potential as contributors to the managerial systems of most companies. It is this hypothesis, that personnel and industrial relations managers are lacking in motivation to manage relative to managers in other functional areas, that the present research seeks to test.

METHOD

The measure

The Miner Sentence Completion Scale was used to measure managerial motivation (Miner, 1964). The Miner scale contains 40 items, only 35 of which are scored. The stems were selected so as to hide the true purposes of the measurement. In this sense the Miner scale is a projective measure. A majority of the items refer to situations that are either outside the work environment entirely or not specifically related to the managerial job. As far as can be determined, subjects do not have any idea what the Miner scale measures. Consequently, they are in no position to select their responses so as to present a consciously predetermined picture of their motivation with regard to managerial work.

Each individual response is scored as positive, neutral, or negative in accordance with guidelines and examples which are presented in the *Scoring Guide* (Miner, 1964). The neutral category is used wher, in extending the stem to make a complete sentence, the subject says nothing that would provide an indication of his attitude or motivation with regard to the stem concept.

The subscales of the test are intended to measure the component variables of a role-motivation theory of managerial effectiveness (Miner, 1965b). These subscales

From *Journal of Applied Psychology* 61, no. 4: 419–427. Copyright © 1976 by the American Psychological Association. Reprinted by permission.

The author wishes to thank Barbara Williams for her helpful assistance in connection with the data analyses.

Table 1
Subscales of the Miner Sentence Completion
Scale and Their Interpretation

SUBSCALE	NO. ITEMS	INTERPRETATION OF POSITIVE RESPONSES
Authority figures	5	A desire to meet managerial role requirements in terms of positive relationships with superiors.
Competitive games	5	A desire to engage in competition with peers involving games or sports and thus meet managerial role requirements in this regard.
Competitive situations	5	A desire to engage in competition with peers involving occupational or work-related activities and thus meet managerial role requirements in this regard.
Assertive role	5	A desire to behave in an active and assertive manner involving activities which in this society are often viewed as predominantly masculine and thus to meet managerial role requirements.
Imposing wishes	5	A desire to tell others what to do and to utilize sanctions in influencing others, thus indicating a capacity to fulfill managerial role requirements in relationships with subordinates.
Standing out from group	5	A desire to assume a distinctive position of a unique and highly visible nature in a manner which is role-congruent for the managerial job.
Routine administrative functions	5	A desire to meet managerial role requirements regarding activities often associated with managerial work which are of a day-to-day administrative nature.

are described in Table 1. Subscale scores are obtained by subtracting the total number of negatively scored responses within each set of five items from the number that have been scored positively. In all cases these subscale scores can vary from +5 to −5.

When all of these subscale scores are combined into a single index, the Item Score is obtained. This, of course, can vary from +35 to −35. It reflects the overall positive versus negative trend of the responses to the 35 scorable items, and thus provides a measure of the extent to which an individual is motivated to fulfill the role requirements specified in the theory of managerial effectiveness.

A second comprehensive measure, called the Rare Score, has been developed in accordance with the theory of projective test interpretation (Tomkins & Miner, 1957). The primary requirement of this scoring procedure is that patterns of responses given by a subject be compared against frequencies obtained from a normative group, to determine if a rare pattern (one occurring 5% of the time or less) is present. If a subject gives responses on a particular subscale matching one or more patterns that are rare in the normative group, a +1 or −1 is given as the case may be. The normative group utilized in obtaining this score contained managers drawn from a wide range of functional areas (Miner, 1964).

The reliability of the scoring procedure has been checked by rescoring 20 records at a 4-month interval. Both scorings were done by the author. The average change in either direction on the Item Score was 1.6 per record and in the Rare Score .25. Repeat testings at 2- to 3-month intervals, again with the author doing the scoring, have yielded correlations of .83 for the Item Score and .79 for the Rare Score (Miner, 1965b).

All of the protocols for all samples used in the present study were scored by the author. For eight of these samples this presents no special problem, since the scoring was done prior to the conceptualization of the research. However, in the case of the two primary personnel and industrial relations manager samples, the scoring was done with knowledge of the hypothesis. Thus a check for unconscious bias in favor of the hypothesis is required.

To accomplish this, 15 records were selected at random and submitted to an individual not otherwise involved in the research who had had some prior experience with the test for independent scoring.[1] The resulting Item Scores deviated in one direction or another by 1.60 from those of the author and the Rare Scores by 1.07. The mean Item Score was .40 *lower* and the mean Rare Score .13 *lower*. Individual subscale mean scores varied from .33 higher to .27 lower. Correlations were .91 for the Item Score and .71 for the Rare Score. Subscale correlations ranged from .79 for Standing Out from Group to .96 for Competitive Situations, with a median of .86. Overall there is no basis for concluding that the author's scoring of the personnel and industrial relations manager protocols led to a bias in favor of the hypothesis. What it does appear to have accomplished is a degree of comparability across the 10 samples studied.

Tests of the seminal hypothesis that motivation to manage as measured by the Miner Scale is positively related to *managerial* success as indicated by performance ratings, peer ratings, promotion rates, and managerial level in large hierarchic organizations have consistently produced positive results (Gantz, Erickson, & Stephenson, 1971; Lacey, 1974; Miner, 1965b, 1974a; Steger, Kelley, Chouiniere, & Goldenbaum, 1975). In addition, a sufficient number of these studies are predictive in nature to justify a causal interpretation from motivation to performance. Furthermore, there are a number of studies indicating that the key conditions are *managing* rather than some other type of work (Gantz, Erickson, & Stephenson, 1972; Miner, 1962, 1965a, 1971b) and managing in a *large hierarchic* organization rather than in a small organization with minimal hierarchy (Miner, 1968; Miner, Rizzo, Harlow, & Hill, 1974). To the extent that individuals are aware of the requirements of managerial work in hierarchic organizations and possess the motives required to perform in accordance with them (motivation to manage), they would be expected to seek out managerial positions to satisfy their strong motives. This, too, appears to be true (Miner, 1968; Miner & Smith, 1969). Finally, the Miner scale is positively related to other indexes of managerial talent such as the Kuder Preference Record scale for supervisory interest (Miner, 1960), the Ghiselli Self-Description Inventory measures (Miner, 1976), and the various managerial scales for the Strong Vocational Interest Blank (Gantz et al., 1971). Taken as a whole, the evidence that the Miner scale does measure a construct which is of importance in managerial work is substantial.

Samples

The major source of personnel and industrial relations managers was a national panel used by one of the major reporting services in the area of personnel practices.

---

[1] I am most appreciative of the assistance given by Timothy Singleton, Dean of Men at Georgia State, in rescoring these protocols.

This panel contained 234 managers who were sufficiently senior to have a comprehensive knowledge of personnel practices at their locations. They were employed by business firms with more than 100 employees and, in most cases, had spent the majority of their careers in the personnel field. The range of business types, company size, and geographical locations represented was very broad.

Panel members were contacted by mail and asked to complete the Miner scale. After one follow-up, 101 respondents were obtained. A comparison of respondents and nonrespondents in terms of level of position and company size indicates no significant differences.

Because previous research has consistently shown a positive relationship between managerial motivation scores and managerial level (Miner, 1965b), the 101 subjects were divided into two relatively homogeneous samples in terms of the level of their positions.

Personnel and industrial relations sample—top managers. This sample contained 50 managers who met one of the following criteria: (a) the individual's position title contained the designation vice-president and the position was described by the respondent as being of a top management nature, (b) the individual reported either to the chief executive officer or one level lower and the position was described by the respondent as being of a top management nature, (c) the individual's position title contained the designation of vice-president and the individual reported either to the chief executive officer or one level lower. The relatively few people in this third category described their positions as being at the middle management level. However, they, like the other managers in this sample, met at least two of the three criteria used in defining top management. The data were collected in 1974.

Personnel and industrial relations sample—middle managers. This sample contained the 51 managers who did not meet the criteria for inclusion in the top management sample. Of these, 44 described their position as at the middle management level and 3 as in lower management (first-line supervision). The 4 individuals included here who said they were in top management did not have a vice-presidential title and reported at a relatively low level.

As a check on the extent to which these two primary personnel and industrial relations manager samples could be considered typical, two additional personnel samples were used for comparative purposes. Both of these samples contained a cross-section of personnel and industrial relations managers within a given company component. No attempt was made to control for differences in age, education, and intelligence between these samples and the two primary personnel and industrial relations samples, since these factors have consistently been found to be unrelated to the motivation to manage scores (Miner, 1965b). No doubt age differences will appear at the management level eventually as the college students of the past 10 years, who tend to have relatively low levels of managerial motivation, move up in the management hierarchy (Miner, 1971a, 1974b). However, no such effect is currently in evidence.

Personnel and industrial relations managers—heavy manufacturing company. This sample contained 20 managers from the personnel component of a major division of a heavy manufacturing firm. All levels of management were represented. Average scores for this sample would be expected to be roughly the same as for the primary middle management sample, but below the top management sample. The data were collected in 1974.

Personnel and industrial relations managers—oil company. This sample contained 21 managers from the corporate industrial relations department of a major oil company. All levels of management were represented, the sample being of essentially the same nature as that from the heavy manufacturing company. However, the data were collected in 1957. Thus this sample provides a check on the comparability of findings obtained over a 17-year interval. Assuming comparability, average scores for the oil company sample should approximate those for the middle management and heavy manufacturing samples but fall below those for the top management sample.

In order to establish the relationship between motivation to manage scores of personnel and industrial relations managers and those of managers in general, the two primary personnel samples were compared with six other managerial samples. These represent all the samples that could be constituted from the author's files where homogeneity of managerial level could be established with confidence and where the protocols had been scored by the author. There were no personnel and industrial relations managers in any of these samples. Three of the samples were made up of first-line supervisors and three of middle managers.

Lower level managers—automobile manufacturing company. This sample contained 117 foremen and first-level supervisors from the production, office, and to a lesser degree, sales operations of the company. A wide range of locations and functions are represented; thus the sample is a particularly appropriate one for a comparison with managers in general. The data were collected in 1974.

Lower level managers—oil company. This sample contained 50 foremen and first-level supervisors from various functional areas and locations, drawn from the same oil company as the personnel and industrial relations sample. The sample is of basically the same nature as that from the automobile company but represents a different industry. In addition, the data were collected in 1958–1959. Assuming comparability across industries and over an approximately 16-year time span, the automobile company and oil company subjects would be expected to score at roughly the same level.

Lower level managers—baking company. This sample contained 30 supervisors of route salesmen for a regional baking company. Previous studies have tended to indicate that higher scores can be anticipated in the territorial sales area than in other functional components (Miner, 1965b). This fact, combined with the restricted occupational and geographical range within the baking company sample, make this sample somewhat less valuable for comparative purposes than the preceding two. The data were collected in 1969.

Middle level managers—wood products company. This sample contained 30 regional managers for a major wood products company. The managers all had at least one level of supervision below them. The sample suffers from the fact that all the managers were in the same job. However, they were dispersed throughout the United States. In general, the average scores for this sample would be expected to be above those for lower management samples. The data were collected in 1965.

Middle level managers—oil company. This sample contained 30 managers above the first level from the same company as the two preceding oil company samples. None of the managers were at the top level, but within the middle management

Table 2

Mean Miner Sentence Completion Scale Scores for Various Personnel and
Industrial Relations Manager Samples

MEASURE	TOP MANAGERS ($n=50$)	MIDDLE MANAGERS ($n=51$)	MANUFAC- TURING CO. ($n=20$)	OIL CO. ($n=21$)	F
Item score	4.92	1.28	1.90	2.10	3.17*
Rare score	−.04	−1.55	−.40	−.86	2.83*
Authority figures	1.47	.53	−.10	.86	4.80**
Competitive games	1.55	.51	1.05	.62	2.70*
Competitive situations	−.31	−.45	.40	−.71	1.29
Assertive role	−.29	−.74	−.70	−.52	.66
Imposing wishes	.88	.49	−.20	.76	3.43*
Standing out from group	.98	.98	.80	.90	.12
Routine functions	.63	−.04	.65	.19	1.40

*p .05.
**p .01.

range there was considerable dispersion. Also, a variety of functional areas and geographical locations were represented. The data were collected in 1958–1959. Given the fact that the company, dates of testing, range of functions, and range of locations were essentially constant between this sample and the lower management oil company sample, while managerial level varied, higher scores would definitely be expected from this middle management group. Also, this sample should be generally above other lower management samples and at the same level as other middle management samples, assuming comparability over time.

Middle level managers—department store. This sample contained 37 managers, representing the total managerial component of the store, once first-level supervisors and the store manager were eliminated. Although a number of them were retail sales department managers, a variety of office functions were also included. Again, this sample would be expected to score generally at a level comparable to that of other middle management groups and above lower management samples. The data were collected in 1963, thus placing this sample between the other two middle management samples as to time of testing.

In order to identify significant differences between mean scores for the various samples, the data were first subjected to simple one-way analyses of variance, computed separately for each Miner scale measure. This was done for the four personnel and industrial relations samples as a group and then for the six comparison samples plus the top and middle level personnel and industrial relations samples derived from the national panel. In those instances where the F values achieved significance, t tests were performed to determine whether the particular differences that had been hypothesized were in fact present.

RESULTS

Comparisons involving the four personnel and industrial relations manager samples are given in Table 2. As anticipated, significant differences are present and the two primary samples do differ, with the top managers scoring at a higher level on both total scores and two subscales. In no case do the middle managers have a higher score.

Table 3
Values for Hypothesized Differences Where F Is Significant

| | TOP MANAGERS VS. | | |
MEASURE	MIDDLE MANAGERS	MANUFACTURING CO.	OIL CO.
Item score	3.10**	1.94*	2.17*
Rare score	3.12**	.53	1.37
Authority figures	2.84**	3.59**	1.47
Competitive games	2.73**	1.05	2.09*
Imposing wishes	1.37	2.91**	.37

*p .05.
**p .01.

When the top level personnel and industrial relations managers are compared with the heavy manufacturing company and oil company groups, the results are somewhat less striking, but where significant differences are identified the top managers consistently have higher scores (see Table 3). In contrast, the basic middle management sample shows no clear-cut differences in comparison with either the manufacturing or oil company samples, thus tending to confirm the original interpretation that all three are on the average at the middle management level and that their scores are typical for personnel managers at this level.

The total score differences for the manufacturing company and oil company personnel components do not approximate significance. However, the manufacturing group has a distinctly elevated score on Competitive Situations ($t = 2.19, p<.05$) and a very low score on Imposing Wishes ($t = 2.32, p<.05$). Overall, since these differences tend to cancel each other out, there does appear to be considerable stability of the scores over the 17-year period from 1957 to 1974.

Table 4 compares the two primary personnel and industrial relations manager samples with the three lower management and the three middle management groups, thus permitting a relative slotting of the personnel managers to determine whether their scores are indeed relatively low. Such a slotting requires, however, a degree of homogeneity *within* managerial levels and distinct differences *between* levels for the six comparison samples. As specified by these hypotheses, significant overall F values were obtained for both the total scores and for five of the subscales.

The homogeneity requirement is clearly met among the middle managers. The only significant differences obtained involve the elevated Competitive Situations score of the oil company managers. There are no total score differences and the only two subscale differences (both ps $< .05$) fall within the bounds of what might be expected to occur due to chance alone.

Within the lower management samples there are no significant differences at $p<.05$ between the automobile manufacturing company and the oil company samples. However, the baking company sales supervisors do score above the other two lower management groups. This is true for both total scores and for the Authority Figures subscale. However, other subscale score differences occur only on the comparisons involving the automobile company (Competitive Situations, Assertive Role, Imposing Wishes).

The elevation of the baking company managers' scores is of sufficient magnitude so that they do not differ from any of the middle manager samples on any measures. However, there is clear evidence of differentiation for the other two lower

Table 4
Comparison of Personnel and Industrial Relations Managers with Various Other Managerial Groups

MEASURE	PERSONNEL MANAGERS		LOWER LEVEL MANAGERS			MIDDLE LEVEL MANAGERS			F
	TOP (n=50)	MIDDLE (n=51)	AUTOMOBILE CO. (n=117)	OIL CO. (n=50)	BAKING CO. (n=30)	WOOD PRODUCTS CO. (n=30)	OIL CO. (n=30)	DEPARTMENT STORE (n=37)	
Item score	4.92	1.28	3.07	4.62	7.13	5.90	7.20	5.73	6.23**
Rare score	-.04	-1.55	-.74	-.44	.57	.33	.97	.35	6.53***
Authority figures	1.47	.53	.87	1.18	1.90	1.70	1.33	1.73	4.60**
Competitive games	1.55	.51	1.15	1.14	1.90	1.63	1.97	1.22	2.72***
Competitive situations	-.31	-.45	-.90	-.48	-.17	-.40	.47	-.27	2.79**
Assertive role	-.29	-.74	.14	.52	.90	.30	.67	.70	4.84**
Imposing wishes	.88	.49	.51	.66	1.13	1.00	.73	.54	1.19
Standing out from group	.98	.98	.65	1.08	.73	.83	.97	.76	.81
Routine functions	.63	-.04	.65	.52	.73	.83	1.07	1.05	2.04*

*p .05.
**p .01.

management groups. The automobile company managers are significantly below all three middle manager samples on both total scores and on the Authority Figures and Competitive Situations subscales. They are also lower than the wood products and oil company groups on Competitive Games, the department store managers on Assertive Role, and the wood products company sample on Imposing Wishes.

The comparisons involving the lower level oil company managers and their middle management counterparts are a key consideration insofar as differentiation is concerned. The lower managers do in fact score lower on both total scores, on Competitive Games, and on Competitive Situations. Also, the oil company lower managers are significantly below the other two middle management samples on the Rare Score and below the department store managers on Authority Figures.

The evidence from the six comparison samples, like that from the personnel and industrial relations samples, indicates considerable stability of scores within managerial levels when the different samples are compared with reference to the time of measurement. The middle managerial samples show little variation even though the different samples were tested over a 7-year span. The lower manager samples span 16 years; yet the 1957–1959 and 1974 groups have very similar scores. The intermediate baking company group does vary, but this is more appropriately explained as a function of the particular occupational composition of that sample rather than as a consequence of widespread temporal changes.

With the exception of the baking company first-level supervisors, the comparison samples do appear to meet the requirements for slotting the two primary personnel and industrial relations manager samples (see Table 5). The top level personnel managers score somewhat higher than the lower managers in the automobile company, but otherwise there are few differences in the lower manager comparisons. The one striking exception is the unusually low Assertive Role score in the personnel sample. The comparisons with the middle management samples show some tendency for the top level personnel managers to score below the oil company managers and once again to be low on the Assertive Role subscale.

When the middle level personnel and industrial relations managers are fitted into the comparison groups, they emerge as distinctly below other middle managers and, in fact, even below lower level managers. The same tendency to lower scores on the Assertive Role subscale as found with the top managers is strongly in evidence. But in addition, the middle level personnel managers have low scores on Authority Figures, Competitive Games, and Routine Functions.

A further check on these findings can be obtained by comparing the scores for the oil company personnel managers in Table 2 with those for lower and middle managers in the same company, as given in Table 4. On the two total scores the personnel sample is distinctly lower than the middle managers ($t = 3.42, p < .01$ and $t = 3.19, p < .01$, respectively). They are also lower on Competitive Games ($t = 2.89$, $p < .01$), Competitive Situations ($t = 2.80$, $p < .01$), Assertive Role ($t = 2.77$, $p < .01$), and Routine Functions ($t = 2.06, p < .05$). Only the substitution of a significantly low score on Competitive Situations for that on Authority Figures distinguishes these findings from those obtained with the primary group of middle level personnel managers.

In the oil company the personnel group, which averages out at the middle management level, is not as clearly below the first-line managers as in the previous comparisons. However, the Item Score difference is almost significant at the .05 level ($t = 1.97$) and the Assertive Role difference is once again pronounced ($t = 2.47$, $p < .05$).

Table 5
t Values for Hypothesized Differences Where *F* Is Significant

MEASURE	AUTO	OIL	BAKING	WOOD	OIL	STORE
	TOP PERSONNEL MANAGERS VS.					
	LOWER MANAGERS			**MIDDLE MANAGERS**		
Item score	2.00*	.29	1.98*	.84	1.84*	.75
Rare score	1.94*	.97	1.24	.72	2.00*	.84
Authority figures	2.24*	.90	1.19	.60	.39	.78
Competitive games	1.25	1.18	.84	.22	1.00	.92
Competitive situations	2.00*	.54	.36	.28	1.98*	.10
Assertive role	1.43	2.35*	3.38**	1.34	2.47**	2.77**
Routine functions	.36	.10	.50	.81	1.45	1.43
	MIDDLE PERSONNEL MANAGERS VS.					
	LOWER MANAGERS			**MIDDLE MANAGERS**		
Item score	1.79*	2.88**	4.87**	3.40**	4.16**	3.69**
Rare score	2.17*	2.61**	4.51**	3.51**	4.84**	3.93**
Authority figures	1.42	2.05*	3.88**	3.09**	2.35*	3.69**
Competitive games	1.89*	1.72*	3.18**	3.13**	3.34**	1.84*
Competitive situations	1.44	.09	.65	.13	2.15*	.47
Assertive role	3.03**	3.86**	4.65**	2.51**	3.92**	4.32**
Routine functions	2.46**	1.66	2.01*	2.38**	2.95**	2.97**

*p .05.
**p .01.

DISCUSSION

The data support the hypothesis that motivation to manage is relatively low among personnel and industrial relations managers. At the maximum, middle managers in the field appear to be at the same level as the average first-line supervisor in other functional areas. Top managers appear to fall at a point roughly intermediate between lower and middle level managers in the other areas of the business.

Whether the historical factors noted at the beginning of this article are responsible for this situation cannot be determined from the data available. However, from what is known about age relationships and the long-term predictive validity of the Miner scale (Lacey, 1974; Miner, 1965b), the hypothesis that the field attracts individuals who are relatively low in motivation to manage originally seems much more tenable than the alternative explanation that exposure to personnel and industrial relations work reduces this kind of motivation. Age is unrelated to Miner scale scores in the total group of 101 personnel managers, as it has been in other managerial groups studied, and it can be assumed that the older managers have been in the personnel field longer. Thus, duration of exposure to the work is not likely to determine managerial motivation levels.

The finding of an overall depression in managerial motivation levels is somewhat surprising in view of the fact that the managers picked for top level personnel and industrial relations positions are more strongly motivated. One might have thought that rewarding motivation to manage in this way would have attracted more strongly motivated managers to the field generally. The top managers are not only higher than the middle managers on the two total scores but also on two of the four subscales where the middle level personnel managers turn out to be particularly low relative to managers in other functions. On a third such subscale, Routine Functions, the t value is 2.04 ($p < .05$) even though the overall F in Table 2 is not significant. Only on the Assertive Role measure, among those where the score depression is particularly pronounced, do the two levels of personnel managers clearly fail to differ significantly. A likely explanation is that people are selected for top level positions in the personnel area on the basis of their *managerial* capabilities, and this selection process serves in many cases to compensate partially for the relatively low managerial motivation that seems to characterize the field in general.

In contrast, middle level personnel managers appear to be less positively oriented to authority figures, less competitive in the nonoccupational sphere, less assertive, and less responsible in routine matters than other managers at their level. However, they are equally desirous of standing out in a differentiated manner, of exercising power, and probably of competing in the occupational arena. The very low assertiveness characterizes all four personnel and industrial relations samples and may provide a clue to the processes of occupational choice underlying entry into the field. However, an analysis of the developmental dynamics inherent in the present findings is beyond the capabilities of the data. Also, the data do not permit a determination of whether the motivational patterns identified might not be functional in some way for the total organization.

What does seem clear is that although personnel and industrial relations managers operate within a managerial system where rewards are allocated in relation to managerial motivation, they are somewhat less likely to possess these motivational requirements than other managers around them. This suggests that individuals with relatively high motivation to manage, who wish to achieve the rewards of promotion, might find it advantageous to seek careers in the personnel and industrial relations field at the present time. They would be competing with others who have relatively low managerial motivation levels and thus the chances of moving to the top management level are greater than in many other functional areas.

REFERENCES

Gantz, B. S., Erikson, C. O., & Stephenson, R. W. Measuring the motivation to manage in a research and development population. *Proceedings of the 79th Annual Convention of the American Psychological Association,* 1971, *6,* 129-130. (Summary)

Gantz, B. S., Erikson, C. O., & Stephenson, R. W. Some determinants of promotion in a research and development population. *Proceedings of the 80th Annual Convention of the American Psychological Association,* 1972, *7,* 451-452. (Summary)

Lacey, L. A. Discriminability of the Miner Sentence Completion Scale among supervisory and nonsupervisory scientists and engineers. *Academy of Management Journal,* 1974, *17,* 354-358.

Ling, C. C. *The management of personnel relations: History and origins.* Homewood, Ill.: Irwin, 1965.

Milton, C. R. *Ethics and expediency in personnel management: A critical history of personnel philosophy.* Columbia: University of South Carolina Press. 1970.

Miner, J. B. The Kuder Preference Record in management appraisal. *Personnel Psychology,* 1960, *13,* 187-196.

Miner, J. B. Personality and ability factors in sales performance. *Journal of Applied Psychology,* 1962, *46,* 6-13.

Miner, J. B. *Scoring guide for the Miner Sentence Completion Scale.* New York: Springer, 1964.

Miner, J. B. The prediction of managerial and research success. *Personnel Administration,* 1965, *28,* (5), 12-16. (a)

Miner, J. B. *Studies in management education.* New York: Springer, 1965. (b)

Miner, J. B. The managerial motivation of school administrators. *Educational Administration Quarterly,* 1968, *4,* 55-71.

Miner, J. B. Changes in student attitudes toward bureaucratic role prescriptions during the 1960s. *Administrative Science Quarterly,* 1971, *16,* 351-364. (a)

Miner, J. B. Personality tests as predictors of consulting success. *Personnel Psychology,* 1971, *24,* 191-204. (b)

Miner, J. B. Motivation to manage among women: Studies of business managers and educational administrators. *Journal of Vocational Behavior,* 1974, *5,* 197-208. (a)

Miner, J. B. Student attitudes toward bureaucratic role prescriptions and prospects for managerial talent shortages. *Personnel Psychology,* 1974, *27,* 605-613. (b)

Miner, J. B. Relationships among measures of managerial personality traits. *Journal of Personality Assessment,* in press.

Miner, J. B., Rizzo, J. R., Harlow, D. N., & Hill, J. W. Role motivation theory of managerial effectiveness in simulated organizations of varying degrees of structure. *Journal of Applied Psychology,* 1974, *59,* 31-37.

Miner, J. B., & Smith, N. R. Managerial talent among undergraduate and graduate business students. *Personnel and Guidance Journal,* 1969, *47,* 995-1000.

Nash, A. N., & Miner, J. B. *Personnel and labor relations: An evolutionary approach.* New York: Macmillan, 1973.

Patten, T. H. Personnel administration and the will to manage. *Human Resource Management,* 1972, *11* (3), 4-9.

Steger, J. A., Kelley, W. B., Chouiniere, G., & Goldenbaum, A. A forced choice version of the MSCS and how it discriminates campus leaders and nonleaders. *Academy of Management Journal,* 1975, *18,* 453-460.

Tomkins, S. S., & Miner, J. B. *The Tomkins-Horn Picture Arrangement Test.* New York: Springer, 1957.

FOR DISCUSSION AND REVIEW

1 What is "motivation to manage"? Why would it be an important personal characteristic to measure?

2 In what years were the data collected for the various subsamples used in this study? Would this have an effect on the results obtained? Why or why not?

3 Summarize the results of this study. What implications might it have for personnel as a profession? For the selection of personnel managers?

4 Why does the author suggest that those persons with a high motivation to manage might be wise to seek careers in personnel?

INTERVIEW WITH ROBERT L. BERRA

Robert L. Berra is Vice President–Personnel for Monsanto Company. Born in St. Louis in 1924, Berra was graduated from St. Louis University in 1947 with a B.S. degree in commerce and finance. He received his MBA degree from the Harvard Graduate School of Business.

Berra joined Monsanto Company in 1951 as an assistant training manager and, in 1967, became assistant director of Monsanto's Corporate Personnel Department. After four years with Foremost-McKesson, Inc. as Corporate Vice President of Personnel and Public Relations, he rejoined Monsanto Company as Vice President–Personnel in June of 1974.

Berra is the author of several articles in the area of management and motivation and has served as guest lecturer at a number of universities. He is a current member of the Board of Directors of the American Society for Personnel Administration, and current president of the ASPA Foundation. He serves on the President's Council of St. John's Mercy Medical Center, on the Board of Directors of Psychological Associates, and on the Board of Trustees for the CORO Foundation.

Q What major forces external to the organization have impacted on the personnel administrator's job in the last twenty years? What have been the major forces internal to the organization?

A The major external forces that I've seen impacting the personnel administrator's job in the last several years are centered around two things—the increased legislation emanating from both the federal and state level in such areas as safety, pensions, affirmative actions, etc., and the changing value systems, particularly among the younger generation. I don't mean to imply that either of these forces is bad, just that they are different, and it's important that we, in the profession, learn to adapt our thinking to cope with these changes. The major internal force, I would say, is the increased recognition given by top management to the function. This is due partly to the fact that the pressures being brought to bear on management are in areas where personnel professionals have a relatively high degree of expertise.

Q As you perform your job as Vice President of Personnel in a large and visible corporation, what is (are) your greatest challenge(s)?

A There are a lot of challenges. Which are the most important will vary depending upon the state of evolution of the company and what's happening to the outside world. Right now I'd say that one of the biggest challenges we have is to make sure that we put together an integrated program for directing and motivating our employee group. This involves the setting of goals and standards, rewarding according to performance, and promoting the deserving people. Another very important challenge is how to more effectively utilize those people over age forty-five who have great intelligence and a broad range of knowledge, and, consequently, have a great deal of wisdom to bring to problems that face us. Our job is to find a way to match up this great capability with the opportunity to perform. To the extent that we don't do it, the company is losing a great deal of leverage.

Q How should the performance of a personnel professional be evaluated? How should his or her department's performance be evaluated?

A I'm somewhere between those who figure that you can be completely digital in the evaluation of a personnel department and those who feel that there is no point in even trying. I think we have a responsibility to our management and our stockholders to make sure that what we do has a meaning. And there are ways of measuring the degree of excellence and professionalism. But I think we ought to try to do this measuring in terms of how it affects the total organization. It is not important that the personnel department get credit; it is only important that the total organization move ahead in the direction that is planned. You can still measure functional performance in some very old fashioned ways, such as the ability to attract and hold top caliber people, whether or not there is a line of succession of capable people ready to take over as they are needed, whether or not your benefit programs are cost effective, the degree to which you are able to achieve and sustain a good level of morale. These things can all be measured. So I think that the personnel function should be expected to account for its stewardship. As far as personnel professionals are concerned, you have to measure them on two things, I think—the ability to make good judgments and the ability to get things done. They will not be fully effective unless they can do both.

Q What are the major responsibilities of the administrator of a personnel department?

A The major responsibilities of the administrator of a personnel department vary considerably. It depends upon whether you are talking corporate level, division level, or plant level. Certainly at the corporate level, where I sit now, policy is the main concern. Also important is the coordination from a functional point of view of all those personnel professionals that operate outside of my direct jurisdiction. I have a responsibility to administer my own department just as any other line manager does, but also to supply functional leadership throughout the personnel organization worldwide. I would say that my responsibilities in that regard are no different than those of a general manager or the head of the financial organization, or the chief executive officer. Anyone with administrative responsibilities has to be concerned with planning, organizing, controlling, directing, and, hopefully, innovating.

Q We have heard and read recently of the ever-increasing power people in personnel hold. They no longer simply keep the records and schedule the company picnic. In general, have personnel specialists increased their relative power in organizations recently? Why?

A I really don't like the use of the word "power." I think it is an adjective that we really don't need in the personnel function. What we are after is an opportunity to make things happen, but to make them happen primarily through other people. We only exist because the line at some point in time decides that what they have to do requires so much expertise it can no longer be handled by the individual operating managers. So if we get into a position that it is a matter of our having power, you almost inevitably set up a condition of confrontation. I would much prefer to think that we play a supportive role. We also, of course, have to think in terms of joint accountability where we have an assignment that calls for joint commitment between personnel and the line organization. To the extent that we have proven our professional capability, we indeed do influence what happens in the organization, but we do that only to the extent that we are in continued demand by those who would use us. I think the words "influence" and "impact," even though they are becoming somewhat overused, are much better than power. In these terms I'd say we have indeed made progress. In answer to the question of why, it is, I believe, because the world is becoming more complex. At the same time managements are becoming more sensitive and sophisticated. The need for professional help in the broad area now encompassed by personnel is being more clearly perceived at a time when the capability is maturing. To paraphrase an old chestnut, personnel is a function whose time has come.

Q Personnel still seems to be a staff position. What do you and your staff do to help improve the interface with line managers who often still possess legitimate authority in many human-resource matters?

A We don't fight the business of the line manager possessing the authority in the human-resource matters. In fact, we think it belongs right there with the line managers. We have found over the past few years that we are much more effective as a company when we insist that the line managers do most of the interfacing even in areas that would normally be considered personnel territory. I'm not much of a believer in the ombudsman concept because I think it automatically sets up a counterforce which encourages people to go outside the appropriate lines of authority. I understand that there are times when communications between individuals break down and another route is important. But we find other ways of providing that, which are external to the organization and which are not quite so visible, such as Employee Assistance Programs. As a part of the latter program supervisors encourage their people to get other advice and counsel, but they do it outside the organization so as not to set up two camps inside. Let me reemphasize my strong feeling that the personnel function's objective is to be supportive of line management—not to compete with them.

Q What strikes you about the young people entering the field today? Do they possess adequate backgrounds? What courses of study would you recommend they pursue to prepare themselves while in college? What types of employment would seem to be most beneficial as they prepare for a professional personnel position?

A The young people are very impressive that are coming into the field today. I feel that by and large they are better prepared than we were and I find a great deal of enthusiasm, particularly when I visit the student chapters at our national personnel conference. These young people are dedicated, interested, and very bright. As to the curriculum that I would suggest, I'd probably run a balance of economics and some behavioral-science exposure, certainly some finance, and a bit of liberal arts to give the perspective and background that I think is necessary, particularly as we look to the future. Those things combined with a fairly good understanding of political science would, I think, permit the individual to do a professional job while coping with the increasing intensity of social and economic problems. I certainly feel that the new breed of personnel people have got to have some familiarity with and comfort with numbers as well as an in-depth background in the behavioral sciences. I don't think it makes much difference as to the kind of employment experience the individual has prior to entering personnel. It would be helpful, of course, if during their college careers, they could spend some time working in plants with people on shifts to find out what it is like out there—to sense the way people think. The likelihood that they will have an opportunity to do so once they begin their permanent career is rather slim. Other than this, anything that provides an opportunity to address problems, to be analytical, to make judgments, and to implement is going to be helpful.

Q What personal characteristics are important for the modern personnel professional to possess? In other words, what type of person do you think would have the best chance of success, given the demands of the job?

A Well, I've always thought that the same things that go into making a successful line manager go into making a successful personnel person. I think that they must have a sense of urgency; be articulate and able to communicate; have a sensitivity for the value systems of other people; and be reasonably smart. I don't think a person can get by in the modern world in a major executive position without brain power. They might have to be a little more unobtrusive in their aggressiveness than the true line person, but they've got to move the ball, and they've got to do it in a way that balances the needs of the individuals with the company's objectives and ability to pay.

Q At the higher levels of the organization, those people in personnel are more managers than technicians or specialists. This seems true in other functional areas as well. Can successful managers from other functional areas be successful in personnel, or are there additional factors that come into play in running a human-resource program?

A I think I pretty well answered that in the previous question. I don't see that there is any reason why people can't come across functions and be successful in the personnel area, provided they possess the things I mentioned earlier.

Q I know you are quite familiar with the ASPA accreditation program. What impact do you feel this has had on the profession to date? What impact do you forecast for it?

A I think the ASPA Accreditation Program is a step in the right direction. Whether or not it is successful is going to depend upon a lot of things, including how it is administered, whether or not there is an insistence upon keeping current, the degree to which the testing program sustains its credibility, and whether or not employers consider the standard to be sufficiently broad and stiff. Now there is an argument as to whether the generalist should stress his role as a professional or blend himself into the managerial group. Both are important. It's the difference between being a living part of the organism or being called upon only when the organization gets into trouble, such as a doctor or lawyer would be called upon. When we think of accreditation, we tend to think of the engineer, the doctor, the lawyer who address themselves to specific bodies of knowledge. There are some who feel that the personnel person should be intertwined almost inextricably with the line and, therefore, we should not draw attention to differences; that he or she should be involved at all times, not just when the organization is in trouble; and should be in a position to be anticipatory. But as I say, overall, I think it is a step in the right direction and will result eventually, if not already, in the standards of performance for the profession being raised. And that's what we are all interested in.

Q What do you envision will be important duties of a personnel professional in the future? Earlier we discussed the impacts, from forces both internal and external to the organization, on the personnel administrator's job. What impacts do you see appearing in the future?

A I'll try to answer the second part of this question first. The second part has to do with what impacts, from forces both internal and external to the organization, will affect the personnel administrator's job in the future. So let's talk about the impacts first. Surely the push for more entitlements and more rights by individuals; higher expectation levels resulting from more education and better communication; and more focus on self and more loyalty to self and the profession as opposed to loyalty to the company and the institution are important, readable trends. They will surely make a difference in the way our employees view not only their own lives but the place where they spend the greater part of their waking hours, namely their place of employment. These values, which are different from the pure work ethic that tended to prevail earlier in the century, right up through the fifties, is going to cause some change in the way employers must respond and will certainly have an effect upon policies. Also, the tremendous increase in legislation and government involvement, which I spoke of earlier, will change the dependence of the organization on the personnel organization—it will tend to continue to enhance the value of the function.

I think much more is going to be expected of the chief personnel officer at the corporate level. He's going to have to be more knowledgeable; he's going to have to be more involved in the business itself; he's going to have to understand the long-term direction of the business so that he can help assure that the proper amount of human resources is available to carry out the long-range plans that are being developed. And this leads me into the first part of the question which has to do with forecasting the important duties of the personnel professional in the future. I've got to believe that the ability to think ahead, to anticipate, to help management manage change rather than react to it, are going to be very important characteristics of the personnel administrator of the future.

If the professional happens to be specializing in a particular area of expertise, then I think much more innovation is going to be demanded than in the past and cost/benefit analyses will be a must in evaluating recommended programs.

I think the personnel person of the future is going to have to be capable of understanding the full management spectrum rather than just his or her part, whether he or she is a specialist or administrative generalist. Personnel administrators are going to have to be superknowledgeable in their own field and have a general knowledge of the business as a whole. In addition, they have to have the presence to deal effectively with their peer group in the executive suite and be able to handle effectively the relationships with the outside Board and the other publics with whom they will be expected to relate.

Planning and Analysis of Human-Resource Systems

INTRODUCTION

The first prerequisite to an effective personnel system is planning. The readings in Section Two are divided into two major categories: macro and micro planning activities.

Macro planning refers to human-resource planning and forecasting. Here, as Milkovich and Mahoney indicate, overall organizational objectives are converted into specific personnel actions. The procurement, development, and utilization of human resources depends on the plans the organization has for its future (e.g., growth, relocation, research and development, diversification, merger, contraction, etc.).

Macro planning also involves a methodology for planning and anticipating the costs and benefits of various personnel activities, such as absenteeism and promotions. Macy and Mirvis explain a procedure for attaching economic values to behaviors that can be helpful in planning the personnel programs of an organization because it permits forecasts of the costs involved.

Micro planning and analysis in personnel refers to job analyses and the writing of job descriptions. Job information is systematically assessed and a concise description of the duties, responsibilities, and activities of each job results. The job description, as McCormick notes, has innumerable uses in personnel. It is, in a sense, the source document from which other programs flow. Careful attention to human-resource (macro) and job (micro) planning and analysis results in significant payoffs as the human-resource program is implemented.

A. THE MACRO PERSPECTIVE: HUMAN-RESOURCE PLANNING

George T. Milkovich

Thomas A. Mahoney

Human Resources Planning and PAIR Policy

1.0 INTRODUCTION

PAIR [Personnel Administration and Industrial Relations] management may be defined in many ways. It can be seen as a *"collection" of activities*—for example, "whatever PAIR managers do." In terms of this description, manpower management consists of rather discrete activities or programs, such as college recruiting, labor relations, employee benefits, supervisory training, Equal Employment Opportunity compliance, and compensation. Each of these activities focuses upon a specific subset of PAIR activities, draws upon a subset of theories and research from related disciplines, and is characterized by practices for coping with the major decisions and problems in each component.

The role of manpower management in an organization may also be viewed as consisting primarily of a maintenance and control function. According to such a view, PAIR programs are designed to maintain competitive wage structures and competent internal work forces, to control labor expenses, and to react to such problems as manpower surpluses, civil rights charges, and union pressures. PAIR managers, then, respond to directives from operating managers or other staff personnel and react to human resource problems; they may but do not always look ahead to anticipate impending manpower problems or to foresee and create opportunities to improve manpower utilization.

Finally, manpower management can be viewed as something more than a means of reacting to pressing organization needs or a loose collection of separate programs to maintain and control human resources, but only if guided through appropriate policies. The task of PAIR planning and policy formulation is to ensure that personnel programs are *integrated* into a system which is greater than the "sum of the parts" and to assist the organization to effectively utilize its human resources.[1] Manpower managers, no less than managers of other resources, attest to the importance of policy and planning; they formulate policies and engage in limited planning, but often *without a clear understanding of the role policy and planning can play.*

The total contribution of human resources to an organization depends on establishment of effective manpower plans and policies, and responsibility for ensuring effective plans and policies lies with PAIR managers. Their ability to generate manpower plans and formulate policies will become increasingly vital in a future environment characterized by changing employee values and attitudes; continued enactment and enforcement of PAIR-related legislation; and increased questioning of the role of market forces in allocating income, goods, and services.[2] Pressures to

Reprinted by permission from *Planning and Auditing PAIR*, Volume 4 of the *ASPA Handbook of Personnel and Industrial Relations*, ed. by D. Yoder and H. G. Heneman, Jr., copyright © 1976 by the Bureau of National Affairs, Inc., Washington, D.C. 20037.

[1] Yoder, D., *Personnel Principles and Policies* (6th ed.; Englewood Cliffs, N.J.: Prentice-Hall, 1970).

achieve equal employment opportunities, for example, have demonstrated in recent years that equal employment goals can be achieved only if policies and programs for hiring, placement, promotion, training, and compensation are all coordinated toward the same objectives. This is also true for all other manpower goals.

. . .

5.0 ESSENTIAL ELEMENTS OF PAIR PLANNING

The broad definition of manpower planning given above can be broken down into specific elements in the manpower planning approach (see Figure 1). These are:

- *Determination of manpower objectives* based upon corporate goals for the planning period and external constraints such as socio-legal responsibilities. Organization goals typically relate to production, sales, and financial performance; and related manpower objectives concern output, productivity, and labor-cost objectives for the planning period.

- *Inventory of current manpower status* and projection for the planning period. Relevant dimensions of manpower status are those that bear upon and affect the attainment of manpower objectives—size of labor force, skill distribution, employee earnings, productivity levels.

- *Identification of gaps* between projected manpower status and desired manpower objectives. These gaps normally take the form of a surplus or a shortage of personnel, a surplus or a shortage in specific occupations or skills, lower than desired productivity, and higher than desired labor costs.

- *Generation of alternative PAIR programs* to overcome anticipated manpower gaps. Examples of such alternatives might include recruitment and/or layoff of personnel, redesign of jobs and reorganization of work processes, change in abilities sought in recruits, skill training programs, revision of wage structure and/or system of compensation, and changes in work rules. Certain of these changes may require negotiation with labor unions and revision of current contracts; others may be initiated without negotiation.

- *Evaluation of program alternatives* based upon anticipated costs and benefits. Normally, no suggested alternative can be evaluated without considering its interaction with various PAIR functions. Work rules revisions have implications for contract negotiations and labor relations; changes in the wage structure influence employee development and recruitment of new employees; and reorganization of work processes affects performance motivation and skill distributions. Additionally, PAIR programs may directly influence variables such as size of the labor force and may indirectly influence variables such as motivation, coordination, quality of supervision, and cooperation of labor unions. *These complex interactions point up both the importance of and difficulty in attempting to anticipate consequences of PAIR program alternatives.*

- *Establishment and implementation of overall PAIR program.* A comprehensive PAIR program must be established upon the basis of earlier analysis and then implemented for the planning period.

- *Monitoring and evaluation of feedback* regarding the performance of the program, and revision and alteration of the program and/or objectives as necessary. This stage of monitoring, feedback, and revision ensures that *the planning process is continual and dynamic rather than periodic and formalistic.*

---

[2]   For example, see Galbraith, J. K., *The New Industrial State* (New York: Signet Books, 1967); and Dunnette, M. D., *Work and Nonwork in the Year 2001* (Monterey, Calif.: Brooks/Cole Publishing Co., 1973).

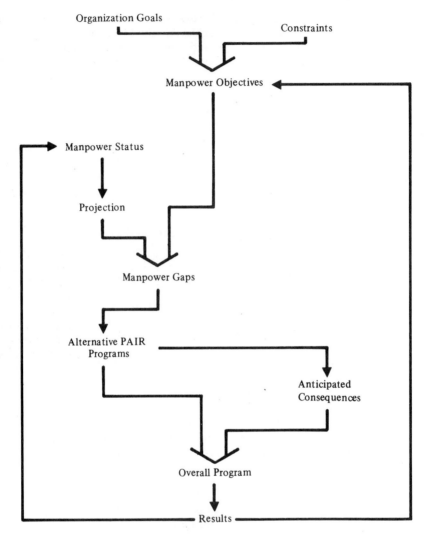

Fig. 1 Manpower planning approach.

6.0 DETERMINING MANPOWER OBJECTIVES

The first step in the manpower planning process involves the specification of manpower objectives. These objectives are derived from several sources; no single source adequately provides them all. Since the quality of manpower planning depends critically upon the objectives specified, it is important that all relevant sources of objectives be considered.

6.1 Sources of manpower objectives

Manpower objectives are derived from sources both within and without the organization. One obvious source lies in organizational objectives—production, marketing, and profit goals. From these goals specific manpower requirements, such as numbers and types of personnel, levels of productivity, and labor costs, may be derived. Another source of manpower objectives lies in PAIR policy statements and their operational implications. For example, the representation and distribution objectives for minority employees may be derived from an organization's EEO policies.

Difficulties identified through evaluation of current and past manpower practices constitute another source of manpower objectives. Analysis of rank and file employee grievances, for instance, may indicate opportunities for improved productivity or labor costs. Some manpower planning specialists argue that analyzing the current manpower situation to identify current problems should be the first step in the planning process. Analysis of *current* manpower practices probably has dominated manpower planning in the past. There is danger, however, in failing to realize that in many cases *future* difficulties can be anticipated and avoided through planning based on analysis of *past* difficulties.

Important external forces influencing manpower objectives include human rights and employee relations legislation and regulation procedures generated by public agencies, industry and labor market trends, union bargaining objectives, and community pressures. Changes in the minimum-wage law, for example, must be monitored and incorporated into manpower goals. This is especially critical for employers with large percentages of employees whose wage rates are at or near the specified minimum.

Finally, manpower objectives should be *anticipatory,* that is, based upon the projection of current trends and the future challenges and opportunities occasioned by these trends. For example, future amendments to pension reform legislation or the extension of human rights legislation to other classes of employees are trends that can be anticipated to directly influence manpower objectives.

6.2 Approaches

Two broad alternatives to manpower planning may be used to establish manpower objectives. These alternatives, which can be labelled (1) top-down (policy) and (2) bottom-up (individualized) approaches, differ both in method of implementation and in the derivation of manpower objectives.

6.21 Top-down approach The "top-down" or "policy" approach to manpower planning depends on the determination of overall organizational goals, which are refined in a means-end chain of relationships through all organizational units. Manpower planning objectives, then, proceed from profit and production planning for the entire organization. The Weyerhauser Corporation's manpower planning model developed by W. R. Maki and shown in Figure 2 illustrates this approach. Overall corporate plans are specified in the first section. Manpower requirements based on these plans are spelled out in the second section. In the third section, projections of current manpower and labor market conditions are analyzed to determine the adequacy of continuing current manpower programs. In the fourth section, this projection is compared with the estimate of needs; deficits as well as excesses are noted; and actions to eliminate each are considered. The quality of current resource utilization is examined and possible changes are considered in the fifth section. In the final sections, programmatic changes are identified as major strategies for achievement of the manpower objectives. *Note that this approach focuses upon overall manpower objectives and performance as well as major programs and policies; it does not consider individual work units or individual employees.* While policies and programs determined in the overall manpower plan will be applied in individual situations, information about individuals is not utilized in the planning process.

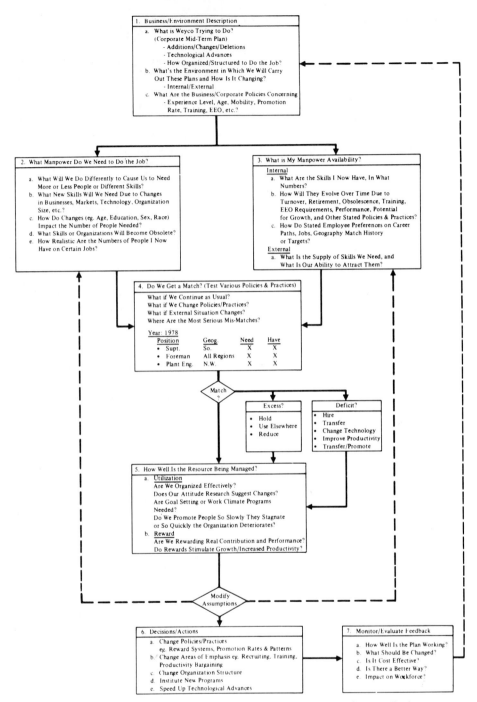

Fig. 2 Human resource planning process (Weyerhauser Corporation).

One advantage of this top-down or policy approach to planning is that it is relatively easy to relate manpower objectives to overall organizational objectives. With the top-down approach it also is easier to interrelate the various manpower programs and policies than to interrelate programs based upon individualized analysis.

6.22 Bottom-up approach The "bottom-up" or "individualized" approach to manpower planning relates to the determination of manpower objectives and plans based upon *analyses of individuals and individual work units* in the organization. Individualized manpower planning begins with the analysis of the individual worker in a particular position, his performance, his skills, and his potential, and proceeds to interrelate and sum the plans for individuals throughout the organization. The overall manpower plan which emerges is an amalgam of individualized plans. One example of this approach is replacement charting and planning (see Figure 3). Individual positions and incumbents within a work unit are analyzed in terms of performance, promotability, and replacement needs. Individual training needs; plans for compensation; and plans for promotion, transfer, and retirement are based upon these analyses. Summation and integration of individualized plans throughout the organization provides the basis for staffing, training, and compensation programs.

The major advantage of the bottom-up approach to manpower planning lies in its link to individualized data; plans are based upon observation of specific individuals performing their tasks. A major disadvantage, however, lies in the difficulty of relating plans based upon individuals to overall organizational objectives relating to production and profit.

6.23 Combined approach While in the past *the bottom-up approach to manpower planning probably has dominated* due to the tradition of industrial psychology and its focus upon individuals, today the top-down or policy approach is becoming more common due to pressures stemming from corporate productivity goals and other factors such as EEO requirements. Clearly both approaches offer advantages, and a simple choice between the two would lose some of the potential offered by both. *A combined approach within the framework of management by objectives probably offers the most potential for the future.* Overall manpower objectives and policies must be determined within the framework of the top-down approach to integrate manpower programs and to relate these programs to total organizational objectives. The translation of these policies into individualized actions, however, requires consideration of individual data and might be accomplished through manpower planning by individual managers in a management-by-objectives framework. Such an approach would require that manpower planning be combined with product and profit planning at the corporate level in order that manpower objectives could be integrated with the product and profit objectives communicated to individual managers for their MBO planning.

6.3 Translating organization objectives into manpower objectives

Profit, production, and labor-cost objectives, must be translated into objectives more closely related to manpower variables. The corporate objective most closely related to manpower variables is productivity; a variety of approaches are employed in the specification of productivity and staffing objectives consistent with production and labor-cost objectives. Figure 4 illustrates an implicit set of relationships between manpower variables often used in the development of operational manpower objectives.[13]

---

[13] The relationships shown in Figure 4 have been incorporated into a computerized manpower simulation model developed by the authors and employed in manpower analysis and planning efforts. See Mahoney, T. A., and Milkovich, G. T., The Use of a Computer Based Simulation in Manpower Management Education, in *Proceedings: Academy of Management Thirty-Fourth Annual Meeting* (1975), pp. 240–243.

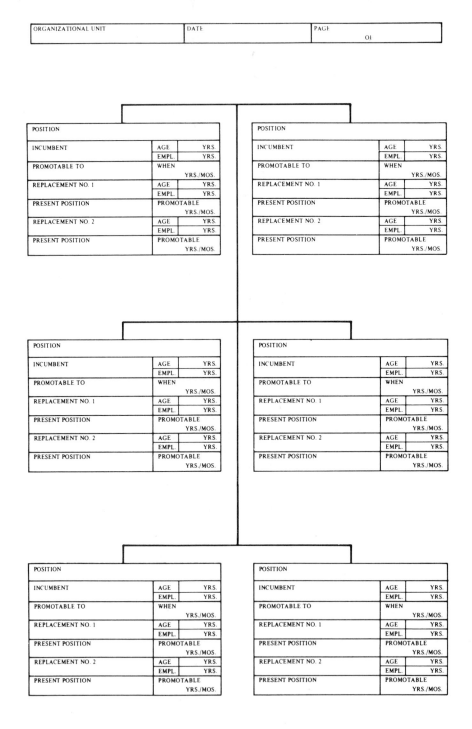

Fig. 3 Employee replacement chart.

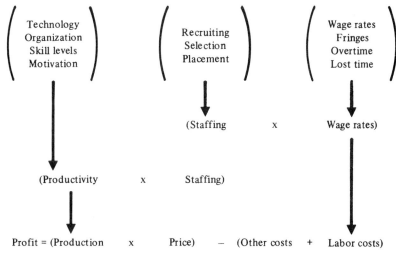

Fig. 4 Relationships of manpower objectives and organization objectives.

Production is viewed as a function of productivity and staffing levels. Labor cost is viewed as a function of wage rates and staffing levels. Productivity is viewed as a function of the technology and capital equipment employed, the organization of tasks and teams, skill levels of employees, and the motivation of the work force. Labor costs are viewed as a function of the basic wage rates, fringe benefits, supplementary compensation, overtime compensation, and lost time due to to absenteeism and tardiness.

Any general model such as this obviously must be *tailored to fit the individual organization;* relationships which are reasonable for one organization may be totally inappropriate for another. However, some such model must be developed and applied in manpower planning to provide order and consistency in analysis.

The first step in application of the general manpower planning model requires development of objectives for productivity, staffing, and labor costs consistent with profit and production goals. Vetter describes one approach to establishment of productivity and staffing objectives in which historical trends in productivity are projected ahead and used as a basis for planning.[14] Because of difficulties in measuring productivity, particularly in a multiproduct organization, Vetter proposes the use of value added in production in the analysis of productivity. Trends in value added per employee are projected ahead and used in the establishment of future objectives and as the basis for determining staffing objectives. An analogous approach is described by Burton of 3M, although he employs a somewhat different measure of productivity.[15] Vincent describes an alternative approach also employing productivity in the determination of manpower objectives in a casualty insurance firm.[16] Productivity levels of agents at different stages of experience are rea-

[14] Vetter, *Manpower Planning for High Talent Personnel* (Ann Arbor: University of Michigan Bureau of Industrial Relations, 1967), pp. 125–162.
[15] Burton, W. W., Forecasting Man-Power Needs—A Tested Formula, in Ewing, D. W. (ed.), *Long Range Planning for Management* (New York: Harpers, 1958), pp. 228–236.
[16] Vincent, N. L., Issues and Problems in Manpower Planning, in *Proceedings of Executive Study Conference* (Princeton, N.J.: Educational Testing Service, 1967).

sonably well established; and, given production objectives, the required mix of agents can be determined. Still another illustration is provided by Doeringer and Piore, who describe the manpower planning of a major electrical equipment manufacturer. In their example, trends in productivity measured in terms of value added and trends in labor cost are both employed in the establishment of staffing objectives related to profit and production objectives.[17] The concept of productivity is vital in manpower planning. The specific measure of productivity appropriate to each organization will vary, as well as will assumptions relating to change in productivity. PAIR professionals should be familar with the range of productivity measures for their organizations and determine through analysis of past relationships the most appropriate measure for the particular circumstances.[18]

Certainly productivity measures are easier to obtain for relatively specific work units, but the integration of manpower objectives into the production and profit planning is more difficult. Gascoigne reports one study in which the experience of individual work units varied considerably and in which a top-down approach to planning would have produced quite different results than a bottom-up approach.[19] It is relatively impossible to determine in advance which approach is most appropriate for any given organization. Both approaches probably ought to be employed at the start.

The identification of relationships between productivity, staffing, and labor costs is more easily approached through statistical analysis than is the identification of relationships between other variables such as organization, skill levels, motivation, and absenteeism. Presently the establishment of objectives relating to the latter variables is much more dependent on hunch, insight, and intuition than on statistical analysis. One approach to manpower planning objectives, presented by Bassett, is objectively—that is, statistically—based, and does attempt to take into account variables such as turnover, overtime scheduling, and absenteeism.[20]

Milkovich, Annoni, and Mahoney have demonstrated the potential applicability of a more subjective approach to manpower planning.[21] In their study, they used a Delphi method of obtaining manpower forecasts from managers and found it more predictive of future staffing than forecasts based upon statistical analysis. Manpower objectives of production, productivity, and labor costs were not made

---

[17]　Doeringer, P. B., Piore, M. J., and Scoville, J. G., Corporate Manpower Forecasting and Planning, *The Conference Board Record,* Aug. 1968, 5 (No. 8), 37–45. Other interesting descriptions of corporate-level forecasting approaches include Packard, K. S., Probabilistic Forecasting of Manpower Requirements. IRE *Transactions on Engineering Management,* Sept. 1962, *EM-8,* 136–138; Geisker, M. A., Manpower Planning: An Emerging Staff Function, *American Management Association Bulletin,* 1967, *101* (No. 1); Bryant, D. T., A Survey of the Development of Manpower Planning Policies, *British Journal of Industrial Relations,* pp. 279–289; and Rudelius, W., Lagged Manpower Relationships in Development Projects, *IEEE Transactions on Engineering Management,* December 1966, *EM-13* (No. 4), 188–195.
[18]　See Greenberg, L., *A Practical Guide to Productivity Measurement* (Washington: Bureau of National Affairs, Inc., 1973); and U.S. Department of Labor, Bureau of Labor Statistics, Meaning and Measurement of Productivity, *BLS Bulletin* 1714, 1971.
[19]　Gascoigne, I. M., Manpower Forecasting at the Enterprise Level, *British Journal of Industrial Relations,* 1968, *6* (No. 1), 94–106.
[20]　Bassett, G. A., Employee Turnover Measurement and Human Resources Accounting, *Human Resources Management,* 1972, *11* (No. 37), 15–23.
[21]　Milkovich, G. T., Annoni, A., and Mahoney, T. A., The Use of the Delphi Procedures in Manpower Forecasting, *Management Science,* 19 (No. 4), 381–388. In essence, the Delphi technique is a set of procedures, originally developed by the Rand Corporation in the late 1940s, with the purpose of obtaining the most reliable consensus of future events from a group of experts.

explicit, however, and managers involved in the forecasts presumably employed subjective assessments in the derivation of their staffing forecasts.

7.0 INVENTORY AND PROJECTION OF MANPOWER STATUS

The inventory and projection of current manpower status into the future requires consideration of two components, the internal and external labor supplies. Planning for the future requires, first, projection of the implications of current practices into the future, and, second, generation of the implications of alternative programs. Both an inventory of internal labor supplies and a forecast of external labor supplies are needed for this planning.

7.1 Manpower inventory

A manpower inventory is a data system which describes the workforce of the organization.[22] Such inventories may be designed for several purposes—monitoring workforce capabilities and performance, identification of employees for promotion, transfer and/or training, and the projection of workforce capabilities. Depending upon the intended purpose, these inventories range from distributions of employees by earnings, age, sex, and race to individualized employee files indicating qualifications for job openings. Employee inventories in the simplest form may consist of personnel files or in more sophisticated form of computerized data banks. The usefulness of any data system for employee inventories depends upon the appropriateness, accessibility and current validity of the data. A simple file system may be adequate for a small, relatively stable organization while a computerized data system with daily processing of changes may be required for a larger, more dynamic organization.

Many systems used for manpower or skills inventories were designed to identify qualified candidates for staff openings. Many of these inventories are usable or readily adaptable for purposes of manpower planning. Ideally, a data system should be designed with its uses in mind; a skills inventory system should be designed to single out data needed for manpower planning. Most inventories used for manpower planning call for information on age, sex, race, tenure, skills, rated potential, rate of compensation, job and organizational assignment, and any other information found useful in predicting turnover, performance, and job moves in the organization.

7.2 Manpower projections

A choice requires some forecast of the consequences of alternatives; forecasts and projections thus are a necessary element in manpower planning. One alternative in any planning situation—to continue without change and to project the current situation into the future—provides a baseline against which alternative actions can be compared. As suggested in Section 6.3 above, a variety of approaches ranging from statistical methods to more subjective and intuitive methods may be used to make projections.

7.21 Variables for projection The number of variables for which projections might be made is endless. A choice of variables must be made based upon overall man-

---

[22] For example, see Murphy, R., A Personalized Skills Inventory: The North American Rockwell Story, in Burack, E. H., and Walker, J. W., *Manpower Planning and Programming*, pp. 206–219.

power objectives and upon the planning model employed. Examples of potentially relevant variables include the following:

- productivity under varying conditions of technology, capital equipment, level of production, and organization;
- manpower skill level and composition under varying conditions of staffing, organization, training, and labor-market supply;
- labor costs under varying conditions of productivity, wage settlements, and labor force composition;
- number and distribution of minority and female employees under varying labor-market conditions, staffing, training, and promotion policies;
- supplies of manpower available for employment under varying labor-market conditions, wage rates, and recruitment policies;
- turnover, absenteeism, and lost time under varying conditions of labor-markets, wage rates, and recruitment policies;
- employee motivation and attitudes under varying conditions of organization, supervision, and labor relations;
- wage rates under varying economic conditions, wage settlements, and alternative strategies of contract negotiation.

Variables are selected for analysis and projection based upon some explicit or implicit model of manpower planning or, as is more commonly the case, upon some assessment of *problem areas.* Attention has been directed in the past toward variables and issues perceived as problems (e.g., turnover, morale, low productivity); the continued development of manpower planning suggests that, in the future, variables and issues will be selected more commonly on the basis of assumed relevance in achieving manpower objectives and will be monitored continuously rather than on an ad hoc basis.[23] Similarly, the continued development of manpower data systems will facilitate such continuous analysis and monitoring of manpower variables. Experiments in the development of human-resource accounting systems currently are directed toward this end.[24]

. . .

7.23 Projection of internal resources Projections of internal manpower resources are necessary in any planning for the future in order to anticipate problems of meeting future needs and to evaluate the possible consequences of alternatives. Some of the projections possible and desirable for different purposes are presented below:

- Projections of age distributions and retirements are useful in the calculation of insurance and retirement costs.
- Projections of sex and racial distributions are relevant in planning for EEOC objectives.
- Projections of distributions of wage rates within rate ranges are useful in estimating costs of wage adjustments.
- Projections of numbers of personnel in different occupations and skill levels are necessary in planning to meet production objectives.
- Projections of absenteeism and days lost are relevant in the determination of required labor force to ensure minimal staffing levels.

---

[23]   The variables used to forecast the quantity and quality of manpower needs vary among organizations. For lists of possible variables, see: Heneman, H. G., and Seltzer, G., pp. 10–13 (see note 6) and Gascoigne, I. M., pp. 95–97 (see note 19).
[24]   Flamholtz, E., *Human Resources Accounting* (Encino, Calif.: Dickenson Publishing Company, 1974).

Projections can be generated for almost any variable; the choice of variable(s) is critical, however. In general, variables selected for projections should "make a difference"; different projection outcomes should be indicative of different problems or required actions.

Approaches to manpower projection, like approaches to manpower planning, range from the summation of individualized projections to projections based upon statistical analysis of manpower data distributions. Individualized projections are exemplified in individual career planning and organizational unit projections for individuals.[25] Thus, for example, occupational and skill projections might be generated through summation of individual plans for training and skill development or through summation of supervisory ratings of promotability. Projections based upon these individualized plans probably have most validity in relatively small organizations or units, while *statistical projections have most validity in relatively large organizations....*

8.0 DESIGNING AND EVALUATING ALTERNATIVE STRATEGIES

The design and evaluation of alternative PAIR strategies in terms of their interrelationships and their impact on organization manpower goals is the weakest link of PAIR practice and the least developed stage of manpower planning. Manpower planning proceeds from the establishment of manpower objectives to the analysis and projection of the organization's current manpower position on these objectives. The differences between these objectives and projections require the design and evaluation of alternative PAIR strategies or actions to achieve these objectives. These strategies encompass the traditional activities and programs of PAIR. Linkages need to be developed between these activities and objectives and PAIR research, theory, and practice.

The wide variety of strategies developed by organizations to achieve manpower objectives are presented and evaluated in other chapters of this volume. This chapter advocates a modeling approach to designing and evaluating strategies to cope with and achieve PAIR objectives.

8.1 Modeling the alternative strategies

A modeling approach to strategy design and evaluation generally involves:

- the specification of manpower objectives, already accomplished in the first stage of planning;
- the identification of the key factors that influence these objectives and the nature of their relationships to the objectives; and
- the development and evaluation of PAIR actions based on their impact on the key factors that influence the organization's manpower objectives.

A generalized modeling approach is illustrated in Figure 7. A variety of manpower objectives (listed in the right column) might be established during the first stages of manpower planning. The next step in modeling is the identification of critical variables (middle column) influencing whatever objective is under consideration. Absenteeism, skill and job match, and effort and motivation, for example, would appear to be critical variables influencing the level of productivity. Finally, strategies for dealing with manpower variables are established (left column). Potential manpower strategies are generated and evaluated in terms of expected impact upon the critical variables and, ultimately, upon the specific manpower objective(s).

---

[25] See Dyer, L. (ed.), *Organizational Careers Research and Practice* (Ithaca, N.Y.: Cornell University, 1975).

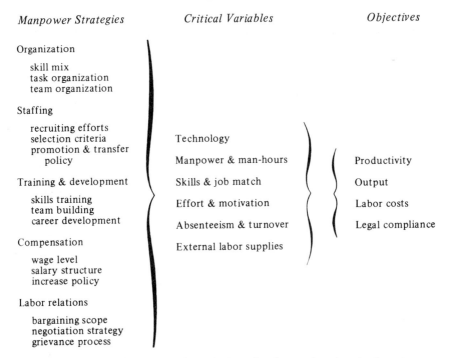

Manpower Strategies   *Critical Variables*   *Objectives*

Organization

    skill mix
    task organization
    team organization

Staffing

    recruiting efforts
    selection criteria
    promotion & transfer
      policy

Training & development

    skills training
    team building
    career development

Compensation

    wage level
    salary structure
    increase policy

Labor relations

    bargaining scope
    negotiation strategy
    grievance process

Technology

Manpower & man-hours

Skills & job match

Effort & motivation

Absenteeism & turnover

External labor supplies

Productivity

Output

Labor costs

Legal compliance

Fig. 7 Modeling approach to strategy development and evaluation.

The modeling approach to manpower planning permits PAIR managers systematically to:

- identify which factors are important in the situation;
- analyze these factors and their interrelationships, especially their impact on goals;
- identify which factors in the model the organization can directly control through its manpower programs and which may lie outside the organization's influence;
- suggest the types of information that should be included in the PAIR information system;
- simulate or test what may occur in the future under varying conditions, thereby *avoiding the trap of basing manpower projections and decisions exclusively on historical relationships.* [35]

. . .

10.0 PAIR PLANNING RESPONSIBILITIES IN THE ORGANIZATION

Effective manpower planning is a major responsibility of PAIR management. The elements making up the planning process are *not simple, clear-cut operations to be*

---

[35] For other discussion and illustrations of the modeling approach to manpower planning, see Benson, R. G., and Klasson, C. R., A Computer Simulation Model for High Talent Personnel, in Burack, E. H., and Walker, J. W. (see note 5); Flast, R. H., A Computer Simulation of a Corporate Employment Office, *Personnel Journal,* Jan. 1974, pp. 52–58; and Charnes, A., et al., A Model and a Program for Manpower Management and Planning, *Management Sciences Research Report* (No. 132; Washington, D.C.: Office of Civilian Manpower Management, Department of the Navy, 1968).

carried out completely by one or a few persons within a specialized unit. These operations require input, decisions, and actions from operations and staff managers in the entire organization, and the PAIR professional must be ready to deal with the process or mechanics of planning and the content or substantive aspects of planning for his particular organization.

10.1 Introduction strategies: technical and organizational competence

There are a variety of approaches for introducing manpower planning into an organization, ranging from installation of a full-scale personnel information system and planning reports to preparation of relatively limited analyses and planning efforts. Both extreme approaches have advantages and disadvantages. Introduction on a large scale of a complete information system with periodic planning reports and analyses can be extremely expensive and is likely to generate more resistance than a smaller, less demanding program. Smaller planning efforts designed in response to recognized needs of the organization often have a greater chance of acceptance than comprehensive large-scale programs. It is not uncommon, for example, to begin PAIR planning with analyses of recruiting sources and the planning of recruiting efforts or with analysis of specific turnover problems and the planning of efforts to affect turnover. A currently recognized need for analysis and monitoring of distributions of minorities and females provides another base for PAIR planning that can be relatively easily accepted by the organization. There are, however, cost disadvantages associated with the project approach to implementation of PAIR planning which must be balanced against other advantages. A large-scale computerized PAIR information system, once installed, can be used to generate reports and analyses far less expensively than manual data analyses prepared for individual projects. In general, development of PAIR planning capabilities is enhanced by early establishment of a complete personnel data system with easy access; and implementation of PAIR efforts to introduce manpower planning into overall corporate planning is enhanced by focusing initially upon relatively small but visible and beneficial projects.

11.0 CONCLUSIONS

PAIR policy and manpower planning are closely related; neither can be considered alone. Policy, viewed generally as a guide for action, becomes more and more specific as the unit of analysis and concern changes from the total organization to the division, department, work group, and individual. Policy enunciated at one level of analysis provides the guidelines for planning actions at the next level of analysis, and these guidelines serve in turn as policy for planning actions at the next level of analysis. *Policy and planning thus are inextricably intertwined in PAIR functioning in an organization.*

Two broad alternative approaches to PAIR planning, a "top-down" and a "bottom-up" approach, have been identified. The top-down approach explicitly provides for integration of PAIR policy and manpower planning; the bottom-up approach links action and planning more closely. Neither approach is adequate alone; rather, both approaches should be employed in the development and implementation of PAIR activities. (See Section 6.2 in this Chapter.)

Manpower planning must be developed as a means of integrating all PAIR functions and activities for the accomplishment of organizational objectives. Manpower strategies normally associated with functional components of the broader PAIR function ought to be analyzed and compared as alternatives, and interactions between strategies ought to be considered in an overall planning effort. Strategies for staffing and recruitment cannot be considered without regard for their implications for organizational structuring, training and development requirements, wage and labor costs, maintenance of union relationships, and objectives regarding minority representation. Manpower planning ought to be viewed as a *framework for the integration of all PAIR activities, not merely as an exercise for analysis of staffing needs.*

The development of PAIR information systems and manpower models is needed to aid in manpower planning and PAIR policy formulation. *PAIR information systems exist in every organization,* often in payroll, personnel files, training records, and files of manpower requisitions and personnel transactions. These data systems could be used much more effectively if organized around a planning function and model. Similarly, *manpower models or representations of anticipated consequences of PAIR actions exist in the minds of all managers.* Each manager is accustomed to anticipating the consequences of PAIR actions.

Manpower modeling is still an art, yet there are a variety of modeling efforts already underway, and certain benefits already have been realized using this approach to planning. Further development of manpower modeling for planning can be expected.

Despite the fact that manpower is the most valuable resource in many organizations, manpower planning and policy formulation often have lagged behind planning and policy formulation for other resources such as investments, capital maintenance and replacement, and raw materials and inventory management. *PAIR administrators face a challenge to develop manpower data systems and modeling and planning efforts to better capitalize upon their organizations' human resources.*

FOR DISCUSSION AND REVIEW

1 Outline the steps in the planning process.
2 How can application of the systems approach enhance the effectiveness of PAIR planning?
3 What data are required to develop a useful manpower plan?
4 What is an employee replacement chart? How is it used in the planning process?
5 What is a manpower inventory? How is it used in the planning process?
6 What problems is one likely to encounter as a plan for future human resources is created?

Barry A. Macy

Philip H. Mirvis

A Methodology for Assessment of Quality of Work Life and Organizational Effectiveness in Behavioral-Economic Terms

The measurement and assessment of work organizations often focuses on gross financial outcomes. Variables commonly used to represent economic effectiveness include the volume of goods or services produced, the cost of output, and the like. For both practicing managers and organizational researchers, however, these gross measures are not sufficient for interpreting financial changes or assessing organizational performance. Indeed, Katzell and Yankelovitch (1975: 99) reported that chief executives and national union leaders hold a broad view of economic effectiveness and regard absenteeism, turnover, work disruptions, and materials handling as important elements of productivity. This paper describes the development of a standardized approach for identifying, defining, and measuring indicators of work performance fitting this broader conception of effectiveness and the methods for expressing these indicators in financial terms. The purpose of the methodology is to complement the usual fiscal evaluations of work organizations with reliable and valid measures pertinent to the longitudinal assessment of organizations.

The importance of standardized assessment has become more salient with the expansion of work humanization or quality of work life experiments and the growth of industrial and governmental interest in this area. Mills (1975) and others have argued that these experiments will improve economic effectiveness. Unfortunately, few evaluation efforts utilize the behavioral and economic criteria necessary to test this contention. An illustration is a recent report (United States Department of Health, Education, and Welfare, 1972) which attempted to make a persuasive case for the economic significance of improvements in the quality of working life. Ash (1972: 600) challenged the findings of this report based upon "the adequacy of the data . . . and the validity of its underlying assumptions." For example, in the 34 case studies cited, absenteeism was measured in 5 studies, turnover was reported in only 3, and the financial assessments were generally not comparable in conceptual definition, breadth of coverage, or specific measurement operations. Therefore, beyond describing the behavioral-economic methodology, this paper illustrates its use in assessing a quality of work life experiment. A longitudinal assessment of an intervention in a Southern manufacturing and assembly plant is reported.

From *Administrative Science Quarterly* 21, no. 2 (June 1976): 212–226. Reprinted by permission.

Prepared in connection with research being conducted in the Quality of Work Program, Survey Research Center, Institute for Social Research at The University of Michigan and supported by the Ford Foundation (Grant No. 740-0430) and the United States Development Administration (Grant No. 99-06-009377) and the National Commission on Productivity. The authors appreciate and acknowledge the initial assistance and support from Neil Q. Herrick during the earlier stages of this research effort. The authors want to thank Stanley E. Seashore, James L. Price, Clayton P. Alderfer, Douglas T. Hall, J. Grant Rhode, Robert J. House, Eric Flamholtz, Thomas W. Ferratt, and the *Administrative Science Quarterly* reviewers for their insightful suggestions and assistance with earlier versions of this paper. Due to equal contribution, this is a coauthored paper.

DEVELOPMENT OF THE METHODOLOGY
Conceptual framework

The conceptual framework underlying this methodology emphasizes the notion that employees' behavior at work results from choices they make: (1) about being available to work (March and Simon, 1958) and (2) about role performance while on the job (Lawler, 1973). It assumes that employees are more likely to come to work and remain in the organization if they obtain satisfaction from their jobs, and that they are likely to put forth more effort and work more effectively if they expect to be rewarded for their efforts and performance.

The employees' satisfaction and reward expectations are influenced by their work environment and the extent to which it provides valued rewards. The work environment includes the employees' jobs, supervisors, and work groups, and the organizational structure and technology. Implicit in this conceptualization is the assumption, supported in the literature (Lawler, 1973; Porter and Steers, 1973), that work behaviors are to some extent intended products or by-products of the socio-technical organization. Thus, quality of work life experiments which alter organizational characteristics and employees' reward expectations should affect their choices in job-related behavior. These choices, however, are moderated by the external labor and production market, technological constraints, and individual differences.

Despite the noncomparability of conceptualization and measurement in other research, there is ample evidence that work experimentation can affect employees' behavior. For example, Hill and Trist (1962), using a similar causal scheme, noted changes in absenteeism, accidents, and productivity in a coal mine following an intervention. Similarly, Rice (1953) found shifts in productivity and equipment damage in a textile mill and Marrow, Bowers, and Seashore (1967) noted improvements in absenteeism and turnover rates and performance versus an engineered standard in a clothing factory. Unfortunately, these studies and others have used only a few behavioral variables. Further, they have not attempted to measure the financial impact of the behavioral changes.

Selecting, defining, and measuring the behaviors

There is some precedent for assessing organizations in behavioral terms. The definitions and measures used, however, have not been standardized and reviews by Price (1972) and Campbell *et al.* (1974) underscore the need for a methodology using a systematic reporting of behavioral outcomes. Herrick (1975), recognizing this need, identified a group of behavioral variables likely to be influenced by work experiments and stimulated the development of the standardized methodology reported here. Macy and Mirvis (1974) proposed three criteria for selecting a behavior for measurement:

1 It had to be defined so that it was significantly affected by the work structure;
2 It has to be measurable and convertible to significant costs to the organization; and
3 The measures and costs of the behaviors had to be mutually exclusive.

Consistent with these criteria, behavioral definitions were devised, distinguishing behaviors such as absence because of jury duty, funerals, maternity, and so on from those related to the work environment. Behaviors like alcohol consumption were omitted, for though potentially related to working conditions, they manifest themselves in the costly behaviors of absenteeism and tardiness.

Four variables were selected relating to member participation: absenteeism, tardiness, turnover, and work stoppages and strikes. Six variables reflecting role performance were chosen: productivity, product or service quality, grievances, accidents and job-related illnesses, unscheduled downtime, and unaccounted-for inventory, material, and supply utilization variances. In constructing the definitions and measures for each behavior, specific conceptual and methodological problems were encountered and should be reviewed.

Absenteeism and tardiness

Of concern when defining absenteeism were the distinct psychological and organizational implications of absences arising from different causes. Involuntary absence (for example, long-term illness) seemed less likely to reflect intentional or unconscious withdrawal from participation in the organization than voluntary absences (for example, absence for personal reasons). Indeed, these two classes of absences correlate differently with various organizational characteristics (Student, 1968; Lyons, 1972). Therefore, voluntary and involuntary absenteeism were distinguished and reported separately. However, since each might be influenced by work experimentation and have a financial effect on the organization, both were included for assessment purposes.

Another problem centered on the measurement of absenteeism. There is contradictory evidence in the literature as to whether absenteeism is best represented in terms of lost time, number of incidences, or an absence rate (Heneman *et al.*, 1961). Latham and Pursell (1975) noted that Huse and Taylor (1962) found intercorrelations between different measures of absenteeism to be quite low, so they suggested computation of an attendance rate as an alternative. In the present research, an absenteeism rate was used, total workforce days absent over total possible workforce days, but this computation can be easily altered to reflect an attendance rate.

Tardiness is analogous to absenteeism in terms of the definition and measurement operations and was treated similarly.

Turnover

Price (1972) defined turnover as movement across the membership boundary of the organization, which excludes promotions and transfers within a firm. In the methodology reported here, voluntary and involuntary turnover were distinguished, predicated on whether or not the employee initiated the action.

Price (1973) reported that measures of turnover generally reflect a "crude separation index" and noted that such measures have been widely criticized. Some alternative measures have included a regeneration rate (McNeil and Thompson, 1971) reflecting the ratio of newcomers to veterans, and a measure of additions to the work force over the total employed (Katzell, Barrett, and Parker, 1961). The measure used in the present study was a turnover rate, total work-force turnovers over the average work-force size (Levine, 1957 and Wright, 1957; Bowers and Seashore, 1966). It was computed on a monthly basis in order to highlight months with significant work-force additions, thus aiding in interpretation of changes in the turnover rate.

Strikes and work stoppages

These vary across organizations in terms of their occurrence and economic impact (Chamberlain and Schilling, 1954). There are no standard conceptual schemes for identifying strikes related to working conditions; though Hyman (1972) and the United States Department of Labor, Bureau of Labor Statistics (1971) provide criteria for distinguishing sanctioned and unsanctioned work stoppages. The measure reported here compared the number of strike days with the total available working days.

Accidents and grievances

These two behaviors are significant indicators of the quality of work life in many organizations, and they often represent substantial costs to an organization (Heinrich, 1941). Student (1968) used the number of reported injuries per work group over the number of group members as an accident rate. Following the introduction of accident reported guidelines (United States Department of Labor, Occupational Safety, and Health Administration (OSHA), 1972), standard reporting categories and measures of major accidents have been devised and were adopted for this methodology. Since firms differ in the extent to which they record minor accidents, this methodology also reported the number of visits and revisits to the plant's first aid facilities and the kinds of injuries that were treated. The minor accident rate was computed using the OSHA formula.

Records of grievances tend to be characteristic to each type of organization (Kaplan, 1950). Labor-management contracts generally define grievable issues and the procedures for resolutions. In this study, grievances were reported as a ratio of individual grievances over the average work-force size. However, this measure treats group grievances as singular ones. Therefore, the methodology can be used to distinguish individual grievances from collective ones.

Productivity measures

Measurement of productivity represents extraordinary problems arising from the uniqueness of performance in many organizations and the idiosyncrasies of their measurement operations. Nevertheless, since the volume of work performance and the quality of the products or services are so central to the assessment of the organization, a serious effort was undertaken to define and incorporate productivity measurement in this present study.

Productivity is best regarded as a family of measures comparing a set of work inputs with a set of work outputs, along with intervening process indicators or activity measures (Stein, 1971; Greenberg, 1973). A number of researchers have used productivity indicators and for measurement purposes, this family of measures can be divided in the following ways. The amount of output is defined as the quantity of goods or services produced. This may be reported as a measure of productivity when compared against inputs, such as man-hours (Katzell, Barrett, and Parker, 1961) or labor costs (Bowers, 1964). It becomes a measure of efficiency when compared against engineered standards. The quality of the output may be reflected as the number of errors (Parker, 1963), product rejects (Beek, 1964), customer returns (Likert and Bowers, 1969), product rework time, and scrap. Such figures, too, may be compared against standards (Student, 1968). Intervening process measures center on downtime (Beek, 1964), unscheduled machine repair, and material, supply, and inventory variation.

The central problem in developing an array of productivity measures is finding a common metric for equating them. Greenberg's (1973) "principle of equivalents" is commonly used. It stated that if one output can be valued, for example in dollars, then dollars can be used to value all other outputs in relative terms. Using this principle, diverse production or service outputs can be brought to a value equivalence and merged in a common scale. The methodology reported here included four productivity indicators measuring productivity, product quality below standard, downtime, and material, supply, and inventory utilization variances all in comparable dollar terms. Appendix A summarizes the general definitions and reporting categories for these performance indicators and the other behavioral variables. Appendix B reports the computational formulas and measures of each.

The 10 variables reported in the methodology will not apply in all organizations. Further, those which do apply may be reported in somewhat different terminology. Indeed, in the demonstration study, voluntary absenteeism and leave days, tardiness, turnover, accidents, grievances, production below standard, and quality below standard were the only measurable variables.

Determining the costs of the behaviors

The expression of behavior in financial terms is not a novel idea. A classic article by Brogden and Taylor (1950) addressed the potential for developing on-the-job performance criteria in cost accounting terms. Predating that was the work of Heinrich (1941) determining the costs of industrial accidents. Rather it is the intention to financially quantify a common set of behavioral and performance outcomes that represents a new undertaking.

Traditional cost accounting reflects the productivity measures in financial terms. Following the introduction of human resource accounting costing guidelines (Brummet, Flamholtz, and Pyle, 1968), the other behaviors could be reported in dollar terms, too (cf. Flamholtz, 1973; Alexander, 1971; Gustafson, 1974; Macy and Mirvis, 1974). To accomplish this, human resource accounting asset and expense models had to be distinguished (Mirvis and Macy, 1976a). Asset models are used to reflect the organization's investment in employees. They are directed toward assessing the value of employees, treating them as capitalized resources. In contrast, expense models are oriented toward measuring the economic effects of employees' behavior. As such, an expense model was used here to financially assess the quality of work life experiment.

To measure the financial effects of employee's behaviors, the cost components associated with each behavior had to be identified and their separate and mutually exclusive dollar values computed. The costs could be conceptualized in two ways. One would reflect outlay costs, such as materials used in training new employees, versus time costs, such as supervisor's time allocated to orienting the new staff members. A second distinction would be between variable, fixed, and opportunity costs. An example of a variable cost would be the overtime expense incurred because of absenteeism, a fixed cost would be the salary and fringe benefits for personnel involved in replacing the absent worker, while an opportunity cost would be the profit lost during the replacement process. Those distinctions are important because only variable costs would be directly related to incidents of behavior. Fixed costs are incurred regardless of behavioral occurrences and opportunity costs are realized only if employees put their free time to productive use.

Each behavior has distinct costs to an organization. Included in the costs of absenteeism, for example, are expenses like fringe benefits, lost efficiency, replacement employees, and overtime. To report these costs for a particular behavior, however, they must be separated from their expense accounts. Appendix C illustrates the decision rules used in measuring the costs of absenteeism. A detailed costing procedure for each behavior is available from the authors.

In order to be comprehensive, all the behavioral costs were measured, but special care was taken not to report a cost component under more than one behavior. For example, if the production losses associated with absenteeism were found, they were reported as absenteeism costs and not included in the production figures.

The preceding pages describe the development of the behavioral-economic methodology. The remainder of this paper illustrates the use of this approach in assessing a quality of work life experiment.

IMPLEMENTATION OF THE METHODOLOGY

Sample

The field researchers, working in a unionized manufacturing and assembly plant in the rural South, XYZ Corporation, relied on historical data for the most part in collecting behavioral and financial information. The plant was located in a small community of approximately 8,000 people. The study covered three years and the average work-force size of hourly personnel for the three periods was 652, 884, and 900 persons and the average wage rate for these persons during the periods was $2.67, $2.83, and $3.24 per hour. The average supervisory rate during this time was $6.47, $8.08, and $8.50 per hour. The XYZ work force was composed of 53 percent black and 47 percent white employees; 66 percent of the hourly staff lacking a high school degree. In addition, 55 percent of the work force was over 30 years of age, and 81 percent were raised on farms. The organization's cost accounting system was a typical one for industrial settings, accumulating costs in direct labor cost centers.

Data collection procedures

The standardized methodology was devised for assessment of change and, where appropriate, interorganizational comparisons. To ensure that collection of the data was consistent with those purposes, standard procedures were developed. First, the organization's data gathering practices were reviewed with their accountants and engineers. Next, the system was examined by the researchers to assess the measurement operations and their compatibility with the standardized methodology. A series of meetings was held, as necessary, with officials of the organization and modifications and supplements to their present system were proposed and implemented. Lastly, organizational personnel were oriented and trained in the use of the recording forms and computational procedures. The experience indicated that this was practical and resulted in unanticipated benefits to the organization in increased efficiency in data gathering.

Records of employees' absenteeism, tardiness, and turnover were maintained in the personnel department. Incidents of these behaviors were grouped into voluntary and involuntary coding categories on the employees' time cards. These variables were recorded at the individual level, but could be aggregated to work group or organizational levels. These measures were suitable for comparison over time, and since they are calculable in most organizations, they could also be used for interorganizational comparisons.

Records of accidents and grievances were also found in the personnel department. Since this data is more characteristic to the firm, it was suitable only for comparison over time.

Productivity data was found in the accounting department. Ideally, this data is recorded in natural units, such as man-hours and units of output. Unfortunately, the site reflected these variables in monetary terms. To use this data for comparison over time, deflation factors had to be constructed expressing productivity in constant dollar terms. Thus, all production figures were reported using base period dollar valuations, controlling for inflation. Productivity and product quality figures were compared against standards developed and periodically updated by the engineering department. They were reported as a variance, the difference between actual productivity and product quality and their respective standards. Production data was available by the work group and organizational level only.

The costs of the other behaviors were calculated by reviewing variable and fixed expense accounts and allocating the costs among the relevant behaviors. Time savings resulting from a reduction of one incident of a behavior were calculated and the profit contribution associated with that time was reported as the opportunity cost. The costing methodology was designed to measure the costs per incident of behavior, thus involving some averaging, since the cost per incident at a low incidence rate may not be the same at a higher rate.

Findings

Table 1 reports the incidents and rates of absenteeism, turnover, tardiness, accidents, and grievances at the plant over the three time periods. The measures are reported in their standard computational forms.

Table 2 reflects the cost per incident and total estimated costs for each behavior measurable at the plant during the three periods. Costs for the last period represent data from only eight months, except for production and quality below standard, so for reporting purposes, year-end projections were computed. The behavioral costs per incident vary due to fluctuations in the work force size and incident rates. The production quality under standard costs is reported in constant dollar terms.

Table 1
Incidents and Rates of Behaviors at XYZ Corporation
1972 to 1975

BEHAVIORS AND PERFORMANCE	PERIOD 1 1972–1973		PERIOD 2 1973–1974		PERIOD 3* 1974–1975	
	NUMBER OF INCIDENTS	RATE (%)	NUMBER OF INCIDENTS	RATE (%)	NUMBER OF INCIDENTS	RATE (%)
Absenteeism*						
Absences	4,420	3.3	9,604	5.19	6,905	3.76
Leave days	—	—	12,486	6.75	13,332	7.25
Accidents						
OSHA						
Hourly work force	251	38.35	316	35.34	208	23.76
Salaried work force	16	17.56	12	10.90	9	7.90
Minor†	3,181	421.80	6,713	706.08	5,559	635.26
Revisits†	1,806	216.99	2,455	258.22	2,028	231.74
Turnover						
Voluntary						
Hourly work force	132	24.10	229	29.59	116	14.57
Salaried work force	18	17.00	29	24.17	4	3.25
Involuntary						
Hourly work force	118	21.40	161	20.80	120	16.08
Salaried work force	—	—	5	4.17	4	3.25
Tardiness‡§	48	8.68	—	—	—	—
Grievances§§	57	10.40	40	5.17	41	5.15

*Actual incidents and rates only for eight month period; projection for the period is reported.
†Hourly work force; leave days were instituted in periods 2 and 3 and are measured and computed as absences.
‡Hourly and salary employees combined.
§This is a daily rate; available only in period 1.
§§Hourly work force.

Table 2
Estimated Costs of Behavior at XYZ Corporation (1972–1975)

BEHAVIORS AND PERFORMANCE	PERIOD 1 1972–1973 ESTIMATED COST PER INCIDENT($)	PERIOD 1 ESTIMATED TOTAL COST($)	PERIOD 2 1973–1974 ESTIMATED COST PER INCIDENT($)	PERIOD 2 ESTIMATED TOTAL COST($)	PERIOD 3 1974–1975 ESTIMATED COST PER INCIDENT($)	PERIOD 3 ESTIMATED TOTAL COST($)
Absenteeism*						
Absences	55.36	$ 286,360	53.15	$ 510,453	62.49	$ 431,494
Leave Days	—	—	55.04	687,229	61.64	821,795
Accidents*						
OSHA	727.39	194,213	698.31	229,046	1,106.52	240,115
Minor	6.64	21,122	5.71	38,331	6.45	35,856
Revisits	6.64	11,992	5.71	14,018	6.45	13,081
Tardiness*†	4.86	56,920	—	—	—	—
Turnover*						
Voluntary	120.59	18,089	131.68	33,973	150.69	18,083
Involuntary	120.59	14,230	131.68	21,859	150.69	18,686
Grievances	32.48	1,851	34.44	1,378	56.10	2,300
Quality below standard‡‡	19,517	663,589	19,517	573,800	19,517	409,857
Production below standard§	22,236	266,838	22,236	335,764	22,236	255,714
Total Costs§§#		$1,535,204		$2,445,851		$2,246,971

*Costs associated with absenteeism, leave days, accidents, turnover and grievances during the last four months of this period are projections. Product quality and production below standard are actual figures.

†Rates and costs for salaried personnel are assumed to be the same as those for hourly employees (period 1: salaried absence costs—$41,669; salaried accident costs—$11,638; salaried tardiness costs—$9,641; salaried turnover costs—$1,829).

‡Average tardiness time was 27 minutes.

‡‡The costs of rejects and scrap was 3.4% of total sales for period 1. Each .1 reduction is valued at $19,517 per incident. Period 2 costs were 2.94% of total sales; period 3 costs were 2.1% of total sales. A constant dollar equivalency of $19,517 was used in periods 2 and 3 to discount inflation. Nondiscounted cost in period 2 was $677,015 ($23,028 per incident); in period 3, nondiscounted cost was $613,970 ($29,237 per incident).

§Plant productivity for period 1 was 88% of standard. The production below standard rate is 12%, thus, a reduction of 1% is valued at $22,236 per incident. Plant productivity in periods 2 and 3 was 84.9% and 88.5% of standard respectively. A constant dollar equivalency of $22,236 was used in periods 2 and 3 to discount inflation. Nondiscounted cost of production below standard in period 2 was $400,567 ($26,528 per incident); in period 3, nondiscounted cost was $405,938 ($25,299 per incident).

§§The total cost in period 1 is $1,470,427 for hourly personnel; $64,777 for salaried personnel.

#The total cost is reflected in standard labor dollars. The estimated cost in real dollar equivalents in period 1: $1,688,724 or 10.4% of sales; in period 2: $2,690,436 or 8.45% of sales; in period 3: $2,471,668 or 10.61% of sales.

The major costs measured for the behaviors are: lost productivity, downtime, salaries and benefits paid, costs of a replacement work force, and other expenses associated with hiring and training new personnel. For example, the cost per incident of absenteeism in period one ($55.36) included downtime ($10.03), fringe benefits paid to the missing worker ($5.12), replacement work force costs ($6.29), and under-absorbed fixed costs ($33.92). The production and quality below standard costs are reported in standard direct labor dollars, costs which do not reflect the profit realizable through customer sales. Indeed, a significant problem in utilizing the behavioral-economic methodology is its dependence on the measurement and accounting systems at the site. Limitations in these systems at the XYZ Corporation precluded the precise allocation of fixed costs across the behaviors, necessitating some estimation of their relative expense. Further, some salaried personnel records were unavailable, so that the fixed costs were not entirely accounted for. Finally, the firm's profit contribution figures were out of date, so no estimates of opportunity costs were computed. The costs reported in Table 2 combine both fixed and variable expenses, and because of the absence of some data, are conservative.

These tables illustrate the feasibility of reporting the rates and costs of employees' behavior over multiple periods. They indicate a sizable reduction in turnover, OSHA accidents and grievances during the experiment. Absenteesim increased, however, as employees in experimental groups seemed to select leave days, rather than a bonus, as a reward for good performance. Product quality improved over the course of the experiment and in the third period, production levels did too (see Figure 1). Any interpretation of these trends is dependent on the reliability and validity of the behavioral and cost figures. Some steps were undertaken to verify the accuracy of these data.

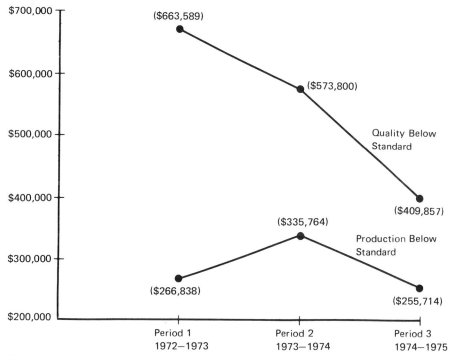

Fig. 1 Quality below standard and production below standard at XYZ Corporation (in dollars).

Reliability and validity

It is difficult to attest to the reliability of the behavioral and financial data (cf. Mirvis and Macy, 1976a). The volume of record keeping suggests that some mistakes were inevitable. On-site sampling procedures were used to check the accuracy of the behavioral data. Time cards were periodically examined and cooperative ventures into this plant were undertaken with union and management officials to ensure that actual production rates were entered into the company records. In addition, extreme variations in trends were discussed with site personnel to determine whether the data were misrecorded.

The reliability of the cost figures was more difficult to check. Financial data is inherently unreliable in the sense that the "true cost" of a behavior is never determinable (Committee on Nonprofit Organizations, American Accounting Association, 1975: 17). Any employee action can result in varied financial effects on the organization. It seemed reasonable, therefore, to measure only the recurring behavioral costs, assuming that the more extreme effects would not be representative. All costs were estimated using generally accepted accounting procedures. When dollar components were based on time estimates, such as the amount of time spent in replacing an absent worker, the judgments of a number of supervisors and hourly workers were pooled.

There was no systematic attempt to assess the validity of the behavioral and cost figures reported here. Other research, however, illustrates possible approaches. Flamholtz (1974) reported finding convergent validity between measures of turnover costs, performance, and compensation; Taylor and Bowers (1972) noted the use of attitudinal data in predicting employees' attendance and performance; Hopwood (1972, 1973) presented examples of these relationships using financial data. Similarly, Miller's (1975) follow-up study of Rice's (1953) intervention illustrated the importance of integrating attitudinal and performance information in assessing work experiments. The central problem in validating behavioral and cost data centers on controlling for nonwork-related variation. As such, variables such as the unemployment rate, inflation rate, utilization of plant capacity, salary changes, and so on should be partialled from the behavioral and production measures before attempting validation.

Nevertheless, some information was garnered bearing on the validity of this data. For example, employee satisfaction is often negatively related to turnover: at the XYZ Corporation, the absence rate was quite low while over 86 percent of the employees reported that they were satisfied with their jobs. Employee productivity is related to reward expectations: at the plant, both productivity and quality were below standard while 63 percent of the employees reported that the output demanded from them would be increased if they did their job well and only 13 percent reported they would receive a bonus or pay increase. Further, 57 percent of the employees reported that their coworkers sometimes worked slowly, badly, or incorrectly on purpose, 39 percent reported that coworkers sometimes damaged the company's products or equipment, and 21 percent noted that coworkers sometimes stole merchandise or equipment from the plant. This data was useful in interpreting some of the behavioral costs. Clearly, in future research the behaviors and costs must be validated through predictive conceptual models.

FUTURE DIRECTIONS

In its present form, the behavioral-economic methodology has wide applications. First, from the viewpoint of the economy, it provides a means for estimating the costs of employee absenteeism, turnover, and so on (Kearns, 1970). Dierkes and

Bauer (1973) suggest such financial measures are important economic and social indicators. Second, the methodology can be used to stimulate interest in quality of work life experiments. Mirvis and Lawler (1976) used this methodology in estimating the cost savings associated with improvements in employee's satisfaction, motivation, and organizational involvement, all concerns in quality of work life experiments. Third, the methodology can be used to assess the costs and benefits of quality of work life experiments (Mirvis and Macy, 1976b), in order to evaluate the cost effectiveness of these programs. Fourth, the behavioral measures can be utilized in the ongoing management of an organization. They have high face validity and can be continuously monitored within the framework of the organization's normal data collection. As such, they can be incorporated into organizational information systems. Fifth, the estimated costs of behaviors can be included in profit-sharing and incentive plans, where financial outcomes are contingent on reduced absenteeism, increased productivity and so on. In the XYZ Corporation, for example, they have initiated a cost-savings program, where employees and management will jointly share the financial benefits associated with increased output and reduced scrap, supply utilization, downtime, and rework. Some of the savings are planned for child care services and social causes.

All of these applications, however, are predicated on the refinement of the methodology. Research is needed to determine whether voluntary absenteeism is more related to the work environment than other absences. The behavioral measures proposed here, and the alternative measures that were discussed, must be empirically tested to determine which best reflects the effect of the working environment on employees. Attention can be given to determine optimal rates of employee behavior. For example, both too little and too much turnover can be costly for the organization. Although the methodology presented here is in its preliminary stages, it has many uses. Research is needed to both revise and refine it for these purposes.

REFERENCES

Alexander, Michael O. (1971). "Investments in people." Canadian Chartered Accountant, July: 1–8.

Ash, Philip (1973). "Review of Work in America." Personnel Psychology, 26: 597–604.

Beek, H. G. (1964). "The influence of assembly line organization on output, quality, and morale." Occupational Psychology, 38: 161–172.

Bowers, David G. (1964). "Organizational control in an insurance company." Sociometry, 27: 230–244.

Bowers, David G., and Stanley E. Seashore (1966). "Predicting organizational effectiveness with a four-factor theory of leadership." Administrative Science Quarterly, 11: 238–263.

Brogden, Hubert E., and Erwin Taylor (1950). "The dollar criterion—applying the cost accounting concept to criterion construction." Personnel Psychology, 3: 133–154.

Brummet, R. Lee, Eric G. Flamholtz, and William C. Pyle (1968). "Human resource measurement—a challenge for accountants." The Accounting Review, April: 217–224.

Campbell, John P., David Bownas, Norman G. Peterson, and Marvin D. Dunnette (1974). The Measurement of Organizational Effectiveness: A Review of Relevant Research and Opinion. Final Technical Report No. TR 75-1, University of Minnesota.

Chamberlain, Neil W., and Jane M. Schilling (1954). The Impact of Strikes. New York: Harper and Brothers.

Committee on Nonprofit Organizations, American Accounting Association
   (1975). "Report of the committee on nonprofit organizations." The Accounting Review, Supplement to Vol. XLX: 3–39.
Dierkes, Mienoff, and Raymond G. Bauer (1973). Corporate Social Accounting.
   New York: Praeger Publishers, Inc.
Flamholtz, Eric G. (1973). "Human resources accounting: measuring positional
   replacement costs." Human Resource Management, spring: 8–16.
_____ (1974). Human Resource Accounting, Encino, CA: Dickenson.
Greenberg, Leon (1973). A Practical Guide to Productivity Measurement. Bureau
   of National Affairs, Inc., Washington, D.C.
Gustafson, H. W. (1974). "Force loss cost analysis." Human Resource Labora-
   tory, Human Resources Development Department, American Telephone and
   Telegraph Company. New York, January.
Heinrich, Herbert W. (1941). Industrial Accident Prevention, New York:
   McGraw-Hill.
Heneman, Herbert G., Jr., Carter Comaford, Judson Jasmin, and Roburta, J.
   Nelson (1961). "Standardized absent rate: a first step toward comparabil-
   ity." Personnel Journal, July–August: 114–115, 127.
Herrick, Neil Q. (1975). The Quality of Work and its Outcomes: Estimating
   Potential Increases in Labor Productivity. Columbus, Ohio: The Academy
   for Contemporary Problems.
Hill, J. M., and E. L. Trist (1962). Industrial Accidents, Sickness, and Other Ab-
   sences. London: Tavistock Institute of Human Relations, Pamphlet No. 4.
Hopwood, Anthony G. (1972). "An empirical study of the role of accounting data
   in performance evaluation." In Empirical Research in Accounting: Selected
   Studies; Supplement to Vol. X, Journal of Accounting Research.
_____ (1973). An Accounting System and Managerial Behavior. Lexington,
   Mass.: Lexington Books, D. C. Heath & Co.
Huse, Edgar F., and Erwin K. Taylor (1962). "The reliability of absence mea-
   sures." Journal of Applied Psychology, 46: 159–160.
Hyman, R. (1972). Strikes. Fontana/Collins: London, England.
Kaplan, A. (1950). Making Grievance Procedures Work, Institute of Industrial
   Relations. University of California, Los Angeles, Los Angeles.
Katzell, Raymond A., Richard Barrett, and Treadway G. Parker (1961). "Job
   satisfaction, job performance, and situational characteristics." Journal of
   Applied Psychology, 45: 65–72.
Katzell, Raymond A., and David Yankelovich and others (1975). Work, Produc-
   tivity, and Job Satisfaction: An Evaluation of Policy-Related Research.
   Final Report to the National Science Foundation, Grant No. SSH 73-07939
   A01. Psychology Department, New York University.
Kearns, J. (1970). "Controlling absenteeism for profit." Personnel Journal, Janu-
   ary.
Latham, Gary P., and Elliott D. Pursell (1975). "Measuring absenteeism from
   the opposite side of the coin." Journal of Applied Psychology, 60: 369–371.
Lawler, Edward E. III (1973). Motivation in Work Organizations. Monterey,
   Calif.: Brooks/Cole Publishing Company.
Levine, Eugene (1957). "Turnover among nursing personnel in general hospitals."
   Hospitals, 31: 50-53, 138–140.
Levine, Eugene, and Stuart Wright (1957). "New ways to measure personnel
   turnover in hospitals." Hospitals, 31: 38–42.

Likert, Rensis, and David G. Bowers (1969). "Organizational theory and human resource accounting." American Psychologist, 24: 585–592.

Lyons, Thomas F. (1972). "Turnover and absenteeism: a review of relationships and shared correlates." Journal of Applied Psychology, 25: 271–281.

McNeil, Kenneth and James D. Thompson (1971). "The regeneration of social organizations." American Sociological Review, 36: 624–637.

Macy, Barry A., and Philip H. Mirvis (1974). Measuring Quality of Work and Organizational Effectiveness in Behavioral-Economic Terms. Paper presented at APA Convention, New Orleans.

March, James O., and Herbert A. Simon (1958). Organizations, New York: Wiley.

Marrow, Alfred J., David G. Bowers, and Stanley E. Seashore (eds.) (1967). Management by Participation. New York: Harper and Row.

Miller, Eric J. (1975). "Socio-technical systems in weaving, 1953–1970: a follow-up study." Human Relations, 28: 349–386.

Mills, Ted (1975). "Human resources—why the new concern." Harvard Business Review, Vol. 53, No. 2.

Mirvis, Philip H., and Edward E. Lawler III (1976). "Measuring the financial impact of employee attitudes." Journal of Applied Psychology, in press.

Mirvis, Philip H. and Macy, Barry A. (1976a). "Human Resource Accounting: A Measurement Perspective," Academy of Management Review (in press).

_____ (1976b). "Accounting for the Costs and Benefits of Human Resource Development Programs: An Interdisciplinary Approach," Accounting, Organizations, and Society (in press).

Parker, Treadway G. (1963). "Relationships Among Measures of Supervisory Behavior, Group Behavior, and Situational Characteristics," Personnel Psychology, 16: 319–334.

Porter, Lyman W., and Richard M. Steers (1973). "Organizational, work, and personal factors in employee turnover and absenteeism." Psychological Bulletin, 80 (3): 151–176.

Price, James L. (1972). Handbook of Organizational Measurement, Lexington, Mass.: D.C. Heath Co.

_____ (1973). The Correlates of Turnover. Department of Sociology, University of Iowa. Working Paper, Series No. 73-1.

Rice, A. K. (1953). "Productivity and social organization in an Indian weaving shed: an examination of some aspects of the socio-technical system of an experimental automatic loom shed." Human Relations, 6: 297–329.

Stein, Herbert (1971). The Meaning of Productivity. Bulletin 1714, United States Department of Labor, September.

Student, Kurt R. (1968). "Supervisory influence and work group performance." Journal of Applied Psychology, 52: 188–194.

Taylor, James C., and David G. Bowers (1972). Survey of Organizations. Ann Arbor, Institute for Social Research, The University of Michigan.

United States Department of Health, Education, and Welfare: Report of a Special Task Force to the Secretary (1972). Work in America. Washington, D.C.: G.P.O.

United States Department of Labor, Bureau of Labor Statistics (1971). Work Stoppage—Selected Periods. January, Washington, D.C.: G.P.O.

United States Department of Labor, Occupational Safety and Health Administration (1972). Recordkeeping Requirements: Form 100, Washington, D.C.: G.P.O.

APPENDIX A: Behavioral Definitions and Recording Categories

Definition	Recording category
Absenteeism: Each absence or illness over four hours	Voluntary: short-term illness (less than three consecutive days), personal business, personal leave day, family illness.
	Involuntary: long-term illness (more than three consecutive days), short-term leave of absence (jury duty, maternity, military), funerals, out-of-plant accidents, lack of work (temporary lay off), presanctioned days off.
Tardiness: Each absence or illness under four hours.	Voluntary: same as absenteeism.
	Involuntary: same as absenteeism.
Turnover: Each departure beyond organizational boundary.	Voluntary: resignation.
	Involuntary: termination, disqualification, requested resignation, long-term leave of absence, permanent lay off, retirement, death.
Strikes and work stoppages: Each day lost due to work strike or stoppage.	Sanctioned: union authorized strike, company authorized lockout.
	Unsanctioned: work slowdown, walkout, sitdown.
Accidents and work related illness: Each recordable injury, illness, or death from a work related accident or from exposure to the work environment.	Major: OSHA accident, illness, or death which results in medical treatment by a physician or registered professional person understanding orders from a physician.
	Minor: Non-OSHA accident or illness which results in one time treatment and subsequent observation not requiring professional care.
Grievance: Written grievance in accordance with labor-management contract.	Stage: recorded by step (first step—arbitration).
Productivity*: Resources used in production of acceptable outputs (comparison of inputs with outputs).	Output: Product or service quantity (units or $).
	Input: Direct and/or Indirect (Labor in hours or $).
Production quality: Resources used in production of unacceptable output.	Resource utilized: Scrap (unacceptable in-plant products in units or $). Customer returns (unacceptable out-of-plant products in units or $). Recoveries (salvageable products in units or $). Rework (additional direct and/or indirect labor in hours or $).
Downtime: Unscheduled breakdown of machinery.	Downtime: duration of breakdown (hours or $).

Inventory, material, and supply variance: Unscheduled resource utilization.

Machine repair: nonpreventative maintenance ($).

Variance: Over-or-under utilization of
supplies, materials, inventory (due to
theft, inefficiency, and so on).

*Reports only labor inputs

APPENDIX B: Behavioral Measures and Computational Formulas

Absenteeism rate* (monthly)	$$\frac{\Sigma \text{ Absence days}}{\text{Average work-force size} \times \text{working days}}$$
Tardiness rate* (monthly)	$$\frac{\Sigma \text{ Tardiness incidents}}{\text{Average work-force size} \times \text{working days}}$$
Turnover rate (monthly)	$$\frac{\Sigma \text{ Turnover incidents}}{\text{Average work-force size}}$$
Strike rate (yearly)	$$\frac{\Sigma \text{ Striking workers} \times \text{ strike days}}{\text{Average work-force size} \times \text{working days}}$$
Accident rate (yearly)	$$\frac{\Sigma \text{ of accidents, illnesses}}{\text{Total yearly hours worked}} \times 200{,}000\dagger$$
Grievance rate (yearly)	Plant: $$\frac{\Sigma \text{ Grievance incidents}}{\text{Average work-force size}}$$ Individual: $$\frac{\Sigma \text{ Aggrieved individuals}}{\text{Average work-force size}}$$
Productivity total	$$\frac{\text{Output of goods or services (units or \$)}}{\text{Direct and/or indirect labor (hours or \$)}}$$
Production below standard	Productivity (actual versus engineered standard)
Product quality total	Scrap + customer returns + rework − recoveries ($)
Product quality below standard	Product quality (actual versus engineered standard)
Downtime	Labor ($) + repair costs or dollar value of replaced equipment ($)
Inventory, supply, and material usage‡	Variance (actual versus standard utilization) ($)

*Sometimes combined as Σ hours missing/average work force size $\times$ working hours
†Base for 100 full-time equivalent workers (40 hours $\times$ 50 weeks)
‡Often subsumed under total productivity below standard figure

APPENDIX C: Measuring the Costs of Absenteeism

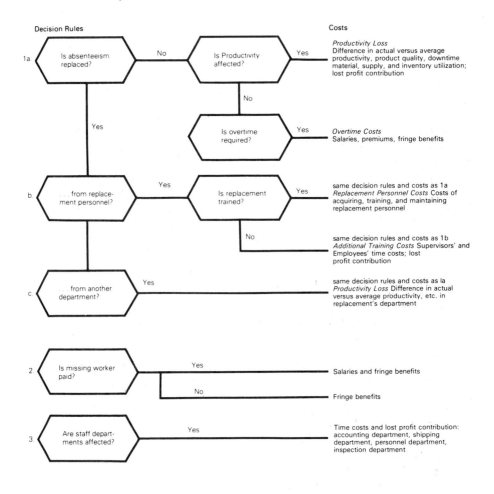

FOR DISCUSSION AND REVIEW

1 What was the objective of this study? What problems complicated the authors' research?
2 Why would it be important for those in personnel to begin to attach economic values to certain behaviors (e.g., tardiness) they are trying to change?
3 What measure of productivity was used in the study? Does this measure apply to all organizations?
4 Summarize the results of the research. Explain what is being shown in Fig. 1.
5 Review the applications of this behavioral-economic methodology.

B. THE MICRO PERSPECTIVE: JOB ANALYSIS AND JOB DESCRIPTIONS

Ernest J. McCormick

Job and Task Analysis

In large part, the entire domain of industrial and organizational psychology and the related aspects of personnel administration and management have their roots in the interface of people with their jobs. The human "problems" in business and industry are reflected to a substantial degree in terms of such criteria as job performance, absenteeism, labor turnover, grievances, job satisfaction, etc. Some of the statistical "variance" of these and other criteria can, of course, be related to any of a number of variables within the work context, such as individual differences, the social and organizational context of work, incentives, and the nature of supervision; but any such listing of possible sources of variance would be incomplete without consideration of the nature of the jobs in question. In more operational terms, the conventional facets of personnel administration and management cover personnel selection and placement, training, personnel appraisal, the establishment of incentive systems (including job evaluation), the establishment of organizational relationships, manning programs, safety programs, etc. To varying degrees these and other management functions are intertwined with the jobs in question. Further, the functions associated with job design, system development, industrial engineering, and human factors engineering also have very direct implications in terms of the nature of human work, and thus should not be carried out in a vacuum, but should be pursued in full recognition of their implications in terms of the nature of the human work activities that would ultimately be influenced by them.

The job-related aspects of these numerous nooks and crannies of the various domains naturally place an emphasis upon the availability of relevant job information that—for the particular purpose in hand—can contribute positively to the problems at hand. The importance of job-related information to these various objectives has, of course, long been recognized, as reflected, for example, by the job-analysis programs of many organizations, the operations of the United States Training and Employment Service (UST&ES), and the research carried out by various organizations, both private and public. If one looks outside the confines of the organization, the implications of job-related information are extended into other areas, such as vocational counseling, educational and training programs, and a wide range of psychological and economic studies that have job-related orientations.

Although various apparent needs for job-related information have stimulated efforts over the years to develop such data, it must be granted that the efforts along these lines have tended to be rather unsystematic and to be more subjective than objective, and have been shrouded in verbiage that does not lend itself to systematic analyses. Certainly for some purposes the conventional approach to job analysis and job description has served (and will continue to serve) very useful purposes. But the widespread implications of job-related data argue for more systematic research approaches to this domain. In this connection, it is encouraging to know that in recent years there have been certain significant efforts

From *Handbook of Industrial and Organizational Psychology,* ed. by Marvin D. Dunnette, © 1976 by Rand McNally College Publishing Company, Chicago. pp. 651–683.

in the direction of the more systematic study of human work, and more systematic approaches to the processes of collection and analysis of job data.

THE COLLECTION OF JOB
AND OCCUPATION INFORMATION

Fundamental to any given purpose that requires job-related information is the need to make some determination as to the type of information to be obtained and the method of so doing. Thus, as one takes something of an overview of the field of job and task analysis, it is appropriate first to consider the processes of collection of job and occupation information, including some of the pros and cons of various such approaches.

ASPECTS OF THE JOB ANALYSIS PROCESS

With some notion as to the purposes of a job analysis program in mind, someone needs to make a determination regarding each of various aspects of the approach to be used in the actual collection of job-related data. There are at least four such aspects, these being set forth in the form of questions as follows:

1 What *type(s)* of information is to be obtained?
2 In what *form* is the information to be obtained (and usually presented)?
3 What *method* of analysis will be used?
4 What *agent* will be used? (Usually the "agent" will be an individual, such as a job analyst, but in isolated circumstances it may be a device, such as a camera.)

Let us touch on these separately, indicating in each instance some of the alternatives.

Type of job analysis information

Following are some of the types of information that might be elicited by job-analysis procedures.

Work activities
Job-oriented activities (description of the work activities performed, expressed in "job" terms, usually indicating what is accomplished, such as galvanizing, weaving, cleaning, etc.; sometimes such activity descriptions also indicate how, why, and when a worker performs an activity; usually the activities are those involving active human participation, but in certain approaches they may characterize machine or system functions)

  Work activities/processes
  Procedures used
  Activity records (films, etc.)
  Personal accountability/responsibility
Worker-oriented activities
  Human behaviors (behaviors performed in work, such as sensing, decision making, performing physical actions, communicating, etc.)
  Elemental motions (such as used in methods analysis)
  Personal job demands (human expenditures involved in work, such as energy expenditure, etc.)

Machines, tools, equipment, and work aids used

Job-related tangibles and intangibles
  Materials processed

Products made
Knowledge dealt with or applied (such as law or chemistry)
Services rendered (such as laundering or repairing)

Work performance
Work measurement (i.e., time taken)
Work standards
Error analysis
Other aspects

Job context
Physical working conditions
Work schedule
Organizational context
Social context
Incentives (financial and nonfinancial)

Personnel requirements
Job-related knowledge/skills (education, training, work experience, etc. required)
Personal attributes (aptitudes, physical characteristics, personality, interests, etc. required)

Form of job analysis information

The form of job analysis information refers essentially to the distinction in terms of its qualitative versus quantitative features, or in some instances in terms of its "degree" along a qualitative-to-quantitative scale.

Qualitative. This end of the scale is characterized by typically verbal, generally narrative, descriptions in the case of certain types of information, such as job content, or qualitative statements about such items of information as working conditions, social context, personnel requirements, etc.

Quantitative. This end of the scale is characterized by the use of "units" of job information, such as: job tasks; specific worker behaviors, such as making color discriminations, handling materials, etc.; oxygen consumption during work; production per unit of time; error rates per unit of time; noise level; size of work group; aptitude test standards; ratings of job characteristics; etc.

Methods of collection of job information

Among the methods of collection of job information are the following:

1 Observation
2 Individual interview (interview with job incumbent)
3 Group interview (interview with several job incumbents as a group)
4 Technical conference (conference with experienced personnel)
5 Questionnaire: structured
6 Questionnaire: open-ended
7 Diary
8 Critical incidents (records of worker behaviors that are "critical" in terms of characterizing very good or very poor job performance)
9 Equipment design information (blueprints and other design data of equipment being developed)

10 Recordings of job activities (films, mechanical recordings of certain job activities, etc.)

11 Records (available records, such as maintenance records, etc.)

Agent used in collecting job information

In most instances the "agent" is an individual, but in some circumstances a device of some sort is used. Following is a listing of possible agents.

Individuals
  Job analyst
  Supervisor
  Incumbent

Devices
  Cameras
  Physiological recording devices
  "Force" platforms (for recording physical movements in three dimensions)
  Other devices

Discussion

One could contemplate other aspects of job information that might also be added to the above list, such as, for example, the level of specificity of the information. (Work activity data, for example, can be characterized in terms of very minute detail, such as elemental motions, or at a very gross level.)

Considering the above four facets, we can envision many combinations thereof, such as (in the most common case) *job-oriented work activities* (type of information) being recorded as *essay descriptions* (qualitative form), on the basis of *observation* (method), by an *analyst* (agent). Needless to say, certain combinations are manifestly impossible; for example, an incumbent, as the agent, obviously cannot use the observation method on himself.

. . .

TASK DESCRIPTION AND ANALYSIS

There are many variants of the processes of task description and analysis, but there is also something of an underlying theme. The theme relates to the dissection of human work into "tasks," and the further analysis thereof. Such dissection is carried out for various purposes, but the dominant objectives are those of training and system development.

Before proceeding, however, let us clarify the distinction that has been made between *task description* and *task analysis.* Miller (1962) makes the point that a task description may be best understood as a statement of requirements, in particular a description of what has to be accomplished. Such description is essentially in "operational" terms, typically describing a physical process, the description specifying such aspects as the cues (or stimuli) which the person should perceive in the task environment and the related responses which he makes. On the other hand, Miller characterizes task analysis in terms of the "behavioral understanding" of the task requirements. As related to possible training objectives, task analysis tends to be focused on the human performance requirements and the skills and knowledges that need to be developed in order for people to be able to perform the task as described.

Task description and analysis in system development

Task description and analysis processes for system development purposes have been used in particular by, or on behalf of, the military services (especially the United States Air Force). In the case of systems being developed, the intent of such programs has been that of "predicting" the job activities of personnel who ultimately would be involved in the operation or maintenance of the system. At various stages during the process, analyses are made on the basis of the features and operational requirements of the system (as it is then envisioned) of the tasks that would be involved. If such analyses indicate that some tasks or combinations thereof could not be performed adequately by personnel, the design of the system may then be modified accordingly. As the system is developed the task description and analysis tends to become more and more definitive until, toward the end of the development process, it becomes essentially a specification of the training for personnel who would be involved in the system.

One point should be added about task description and analysis in this context. Since the "system" does not exist as an entity during this process, and since there are, therefore, no personnel who actually are engaged in the jobs in question (since the jobs actually do not then exist), the task description and analysis must be inferred from an analysis of the physical equipment of the system as it "exists" in the form of drawings, blueprints, and other descriptions, and of any intermediate prototypes or models that may be created. In this frame of reference, the task description and analysis process undergoes a series of "approximations" over time, becoming progressively "closer" to the activities of the "final" system.[3]

Task description and analysis for training

In discussing task description and task analysis in the training context, let us first clarify further the distinction that is commonly made between these two. Cunningham and Duncan (1967) make the point that task description specifies the *terminal* (end-of-course) *performance* of trainees, and thus the *content* of training. On the other hand, task analysis relates to "behavioral categories" that are relevant to learning—behavioral categories, such as identification, short-term and long-term recall, decision making, making multiple discriminations, applying concepts, applying principles and rules, etc. The "learning" conditions that would be optimum for these different behavioral categories presumably would be different for each such category. Because of this tie-in between learning conditions and behavioral categories, task analysis (which is in part directed toward the analysis of tasks in terms of such categories) is then the handmaiden of training *methods*. Training *content* (the focus of task description) typically does not itself provide inklings about appropriate training methods to be used. Rather, the training methods should be predicated upon the "behavioral categories" involved in the activities—and the learning conditions that presumably are optimum for learning the behaviors in question.

---

[3]   The use of task analysis in this context is discussed in more detail in a technical report of the Wright Air Development Division (WADD Technical Report 60-593, December, 1960). As one phase of the development of systems, the Air Force has developed the concept of the *personnel subsystem* that embraces the various aspects of personnel planning for each system. One part of this program consists of developing the Qualitative and Quantitative Personnel Requirements Information (QQPRI), which is substantially based on task analysis information. This program is described further in a report by Demarce, Marks, Smith, and Snyder (1962).

Task description Miller (1962) states the opinion that each *task activity* consists of the following:

1   An indicator on which the activity-relevant indication appears
2   The indication or cue which calls for a response
3   The control object to be activated
4   The activation or manipulation to be made
5   The indication of response adequacy, or feedback

Thus, the *indicator* is in a sense an external source that gives rise to some *indication or cue* to make a response by *activation or manipulation* of some control object, with there being some subsequent indication of *response adequacy or feedback*. The indication to trigger the response may appear all at once, or it may have to be assembled by the human by recall through periods of time. The feedback may be proximal (as by feel of a control) or distal (as by hearing an engine start). The critical features of task description can then be characterized as follows:

Indication (stimulus) → Activation (response) → Feedback

This formulation can be envisioned as the framework for many common activities, such as:

Alarm clock rings → Turn off alarm → Peace and quiet returns

Car approaching from side street → Honk horn → Car stops

This formulation also is fairly straightforward in its application to many types of essentially physical tasks. However, Cunningham and Duncan (1967) call our attention to the fact that, although the formulation is appropriate to most repetitive tasks, there are problems in applying it to some non-repetitive (physical) tasks. (And it might be added, parenthetically, that the problems are magnified in attempting to describe tasks that are more cognitive in nature and in which observable physical activities are nominal.) The difficulties referred to by Cunningham and Duncan relate to both the cues and responses. In some (if not many) industrial jobs, for example, there is no readily identifiable cue to trigger a given response. Rather, the cues may consist of combinations of indications (in some cases distributed through time), but these may be vague and, therefore, defy delineation. Further, Cunningham and Duncan report that, in their efforts to specify the cues used by some workers, they could not identify any objective observable cues and had to resort to teasing out subjective responses from the workers; and in certain instances, they found that such subjectively reported cues were not really the ones used by the workers.

They also report problems in trying to spell out, definitively, in some task descriptions the nature of the response to be made. One facet of the problem relates to the fact that dissimilar but *functionally* equivalent responses may be made on different occasions to the same cue. And in some circumstances, workers were observed to make responses without any preceding cue to trigger it. There also are problems of ambiguity with respect to specifying the nature of the feedback in some tasks.

Although Miller (1962) has taken cognizance of some of these problems, Cunningham and Duncan (1967) argue for a somewhat more flexible approach to task description than that proposed by Miller and others. They propose, in effect, that although it seems sensible to consider each such ingredient, one should not be a slave to the procedures and forms by obediently putting down an "entry" for each such ingredient (if in fact it makes no sense to do so, or if any such entry would be redundant or trivial). They go on to make the point that the fact that the method of observation cannot be applied rigorously to task description does not necessarily mean that such description cannot be rigorous; rather, this argues for recognition of the dependence on the subjective aspects of the process.

Task analysis As indicated above, task analysis is concerned in part with analyzing the behavior components that are involved in tasks, with the view toward developing training methods that are reasonably appropriate to such components. This objective has led to various attempts to develop some taxonomy of tasks or activities. One such scheme proposed by Gagné (1965) is called a cumulative learning sequence, and consists of six categories as follows: (a) stimulus-response connections; (b) chain of relationships (motor or verbal); (c) multiple discriminations; (d) concepts; (e) simple principles or rules; and (f) complex principles or rules. He postulates the notion that this is essentially a hierarchy in the sense that the learning at any given level subsumes learning at the lower levels (with the possible exception of the "chain of relationships"). The potential relevance of such a formulation to training methods can be reflected by the following series of assumptions:

1 Any given task can be characterized in terms of one of these categories.
2 For any given category there is some optimum approach to learning (such as how to learn multiple discriminations, concepts, etc.).
3 Therefore, the specific training method for the task should be predicated on the learning approach that is most relevant for the category that represents the nature of the task.

There are, however, some hitches in this possible approach. Annett and Duncan (1967), for example, express the opinion (somewhat supported by evidence) that Gagné's formulation is not invariably a hierarchy; in other words, learning of, say, simple principles and rules, does not necessarily depend upon learning at each and every lower level in the sequence. And further (and perhaps more basic) it probably can be said that, at this stage of affairs, there is no manifestly optimum learning procedure or approach for each such category of the hierarchy; thus, the bridge between any given category of learning task and a corresponding (optimum) training method is a fairly shaky one.

These and other reflections lead Annett and Duncan to the unsatisfying conclusion that a method of analyzing tasks which reliably prescribes the training procedures required probably does not exist. They go on to suggest that one way of building up such a method would be to begin with a provisional set of categories for which there is some evidence of relatively specific training methods and conditions (such as might now be done in the case of multiple discriminations and chains of relationships). Beyond this, it would be necessary to test the value of providing specific methods and conditions in training people on the various components of real tasks.

The business of the world (including the training business) cannot stop until research provides complete, unambiguous answers. Thus, even though task analysis procedures do not yet lead in all cases to definitive answers to training problems, training must be continued (even if in some instances not as efficiently as might be wished). Hopefully, research might ultimately resolve some of the presently vexing aspects of this problem.

. . .

Listed below is a duty and the tasks which it includes. Check all tasks which you perform. Add any tasks you do which are not listed. Then rate the tasks you have checked.	CHECK	TIME SPENT	IMPORTANCE
H. INSTALLING AND REMOVING AERIAL CABLE SYSTEMS	√ IF DONE	1. Very much below average 2. Below average 3. Slightly below average 4. About average 5. Slightly above average 6. Above average 7. Very much above average	1. Extremely unimportant 2. Very unimportant 3. Unimportant 4. About medium importance 5. Important 6. Very important 7. Extremely important
1. Attach suspension strand to pole			
2. Change and splice lasher wire			
3. Deliver materials to lineman with snatch block and handline			
4. Drill through-bolt holes and secure suspension clamps on poles			
5. Install cable pressurization systems			
6. Install distribution terminals			
7. Install pulling-in line through cable rings			
8. Load and unload cable reels			
9. Load lashing machine with lashing wire			

Fig. 6 Portion of a job inventory for the outside wire and antenna systems career field of the Air Force. (From Morsh and Archer, 1967.)

JOB INVENTORIES

A job inventory (also referred to as a task inventory) is a form of structured job-analysis questionnaire that consists of a listing of tasks, usually the tasks being those which are relevant to the jobs within some occupational area.[4] The "tasks" as incorporated in job inventories usually consist only of a statement of the activity as such, omitting the cues and feedback features as discussed above in task description and analysis. Examples shown later will illustrate their nature. Job inventories usually are completed by incumbents as the basis for reporting some job-related information about the incumbents' positions; however, in some instances they may be completed by someone other than an incumbent, such as by a supervisor (who might thus describe an incumbent's position).

The job inventory technology has been developed over the last several years primarily by the Personnel Division of the Air Force Human Resources Laboratory (Christal, 1969; Morsh, 1969; Morsh & Archer, 1967). However, the methodology has also been adopted by certain other military services both in the United States and elsewhere; and there have been at least a few other organizations—private and governmental—that have used some form of job inventory for research or operational purposes.

---

[4]   The term *check list* has also been used for what is referred to here as a job inventory. Although the term *check list* may be appropriate in some instances, it implies simply a "checking" of items, whereas most job inventories require more elaborate responses, such as ratings.

The nature of job inventories

In its final form, a job inventory usually is characterized by two dominant features, namely, the list of tasks and provision for some response(s).

Task listing The list of tasks included in an inventory typically includes virtually all the tasks that might be performed by incumbents in the occupational field in question. In the military services an occupational field usually embraces a variety of jobs within some relatively broad, but related, domain of work, such as medical services or aircraft maintenance. The tasks usually are grouped within broader categories of duties. An example of part of a job inventory is shown as Figure 6. In final form, an inventory might include anywhere from 100 to 200, up to 400, or 500 or more, tasks.

Responses to job inventories Usually the job incumbent completes an inventory as related to his own position. In a very simple case, he may simply indicate whether he does, or does not, perform a particular task. If this is all that is required, the inventory is, in effect, a simple check list. However, it is usually the practice to ask for further responses to the individual tasks. There are many options in this regard, but they generally are referred to as primary and secondary task rating factors (Morsh & Archer, 1967). The primary task rating factors provide for an indication for each task of the relevance of that task to the position, such as in terms of time, importance to the position, how much "part of the job" the task represents, or how frequently the task is performed.

In connection with reporting time spent, it has been the experience of the Air Force that a relative time-spent scale usually is better than one based on absolute time or percentage of time. The relative time-spent scale used by the Air Force is given below (Morsh & Archer, 1967):

Relative Time-Spent Task Rating Scale

Compared with other tasks you do in your job, the time you spend on the task you are rating is:

1. Very much below average
2. Below average
3. Slightly below average
4. About average
5. Slightly above average
6. Above average
7. Very much above average

Another scale, the Hemphill part-of-job scale, was developed by Hemphill (1959) for use by executives, but has been found to be quite acceptable for use by Air Force officers (Cragun & McCormick, 1967). This scale is shown below in slightly modified form:

Part-of-Job Task Rating Scale

0. Definitely not part of the position
1. Under unusual circumstances is a minor part of position
2.
3.
4. A substantial part of the position
5.
6.
7. A most significant part of the position

In the use of this scale the incumbent is asked to consider and weigh the importance, frequency of occurrence, relevance, or other factors which he thinks will determine the extent to which the task is a "part" of his position.

There are quite a number of secondary rating factors that have been used, most of these eliciting more subjective responses of the incumbent about the task. Some of these are of a continuous nature, and others of a categorical nature. Some examples are listed below (Morsh & Archer, 1967):

1 Continuous variable task rating factors
   a) Complexity of the task
   b) Criticality of task to unit mission
   c) Difficulty of learning the task
   d) Difficulty of learning the task by OJT
   e) Difficulty of task performance
   f) Experience needed for task performance
   g) Extent of training in school or work experience
   h) Satisfaction in performing task
   i) Special training necessary to perform task
   j) Supervision required in task performance
   k) Technical assistance required to perform task
   l) Time spent in task during entire career
   m) Training emphasis task should have
   n) Training required for task performance
2 Categorical variable task rating factors. Method of learning (usually with categories representing different ways of learning the task)
3 Special training required (usually expressed in terms of amount)
4 Task performance (expressed as "can do now" or in terms of time that would be required to learn)

When inventories are completed by someone other than the incumbent (as by a supervisor), the primary rating factors might be used as the basis for eliciting his perception of the position. In addition, he might be asked to use certain of the secondary rating factors. Or he might be asked to use specially adapted scales, including scales for use in evaluation of subordinates, such as relative proficiency or time to learn (to become proficient) as reported by Swanson (1969).

. . .

JOB AND OCCUPATION STRUCTURES

In searching for some order and system in this world of ours, people have developed classifications or taxonomies of biological organisms, of material substances, and (in the domain of human life) of human behavior—even of the jobs and occupations people pursue. A taxonomy of things or phenomena is predicated on manifestations of certain similarities and differences between and among the individual cases being classified. There are various approaches to the development of taxonomies, as discussed by Theologus (1969), these having been developed and applied especially in the biological sciences. Certain of these, specifically the Linnaean and Darwinian approaches, depend heavily upon subjective opinions regarding the bases of classification in the actual classification of specific organisms or objects. On the other hand, numerical taxonomy places emphasis on repeatability and objectivity, thus aiming toward the establishment of classifications based on stable, objectively derived, data bases. Existing taxonomies in the job and occupational area probably have some parallels to these alternative approaches, although the bias proposed here is that of the numerical approach, with its focus on the use of reasonably objective data.

JOB DESCRIPTORS

In any event, the development of job or occupation taxonomies is predicated upon the characteristics of jobs and occupations—whether subjectively judged or quantified. In this connection there are, of course, many different facets or kinds of attributes that conceivably could serve in some way as the basis of a taxonomy for some purpose (Farina, 1969). For our purposes these various characteristics will be referred to as *job descriptors.*

In general, individual job descriptors are of two types—qualitative and quantitative. *Qualitative* descriptors are those which are categorical, or nominal, in nature. Such descriptors either "apply" or "do not apply" to individual jobs. At a very specific level one could thus characterize jobs as to whether they do, or do not, involve out-of-town travel, or reading blueprints, or driving a vehicle; at a grosser level jobs can be characterized in terms of professional, clerical, etc., or on the basis of other broadly conceived classes (although such allocation typically is predicated on the basis of syndromes of more specific descriptors). On the other hand, *quantitative* descriptors are those in which jobs are characterized in terms of degree, such as amount of physical effort required or the amount of time involved in, say, personal contacts. It should be noted that some descriptors can be characterized in either qualitative (i.e., categorical) or quantitative terms.

For purposes of the present discussion some types of job variables will be mentioned, but these will not comprise an exhaustive listing. Before so proceeding, however, two points should be made that are relevant to the discussion of taxonomic approaches mentioned above. In the first place, the possible use of any job descriptor in a taxonomy in some circumstances is based on rational considerations, and in other circumstances is based on quantitative job data. In the second place, the classification or quantification of individual jobs in terms of specific variables can be based on subjective judgments and evaluations, or on essentially objective data or observations relating to the jobs.

Job content

One of the most commonly recognized types of job descriptors is that of job content; that is, the nature of the work activities that incumbents perform. Usually job content is viewed in the framework of job-oriented activities, but it can also be viewed in the framework of worker-oriented activities. Job content, of course, can be characterized at various levels of specificity or generality.

Clerical job functions One example of a systematic analysis of job content variables of a job-oriented nature is reported by Chalupsky (1962). In this study, a check list of thirty-three clerical operations was used in analyzing a sample of 192 jobs. The operations included such items as analyzes, compiles, plans, and translates. The 192 jobs were represented by complete job descriptions provided by the United States Training and Employment Service. A factor analysis of the data resulted in the identification of five factors, as follows: inventory and stockkeeping; supervision; computation and bookkeeping; communication and public relations; and stenography-typing and general clerical. Each of these can be viewed as representing a reasonably stable cluster of the more specific clerical functions which, in the world of work, typically tend to occur in combination with each other. (It might be added that a parallel analysis of the same jobs using a check list of fifty-eight clerical knowledge items resulted in the identification of factors that corresponded very closely with these, except that the last factor was broken down into two, namely, stenography-typing and filing and general clerical.) In this study, the descriptors of job content can be viewed at two levels, namely, at the level of the thirty-three clerical operations and at the level of the several factors.

Work performance factors of health officers As another illustration of the use of factor analysis of job content, Brumback and Vincent (1970) describe a fairly large-scale survey of commissioned officers of the Public Health Service in which 3,719 officers used a job inventory to report their own work activities. The resulting responses were subjected to factor analysis in order to identify the different functional areas of work represented by the sample. A total of twenty-six such functional work areas (i.e., factors) were identified, a few of which were: performing public health inspection and control activities; conducting surveys (such as epidemiological investigations); and preparing and testing samples for contaminants or disease agents.

In large part, this analysis was made with the possible objective in mind of providing a more appropriate basis for personnel appraisal, in particular, one that might be more job-oriented than person-oriented.

Job factors of high-level positions As another illustration of a systematic approach to the study of descriptors of job content, Baehr (1967) carried out a factor analysis of a job analysis questionnaire called the Work Elements Inventory that consisted of 122 "generic" job elements that might be relevant to supervisory, management, sales, and other higher-level positions. The factor analysis was based on data provided by 600 job incumbents who used the inventory to describe their own positions, and generated the factors, here grouped into four areas:

Organization

1 Setting organizational objectives
2 Improving work procedures and practices
3 Promoting safety attitudes and practices
4 Developing and implementing technical ideas

Leadership

5 Judgment and decision making
6 Developing group cooperation and teamwork
7 Coping with difficulties and emergencies

Personnel

8 Developing employee potential
9 Supervisory practices
10 Self-development and improvement

Community

11 Promoting community-organization relations
12 Handling outside contacts

Job dimensions based on PAQ job data Mention was made earlier of the Position Analysis Questionnaire (PAQ). This questionnaire consists of job elements of a worker-oriented nature, that characterize human "behaviors" in jobs. Each such element, of course, can be thought of as a job descriptor by itself. But further, such job elements can be subjected to statistical analyses (such as factor and principal components analyses) to identify broader descriptors. Two such studies have been carried out with PAQ-based data, one reported by Jeanneret and McCormick (1969) using the first form of the PAQ (Form *A*), and the other by Marquardt and McCormick (1973; June 1974). Both of these consisted of principal components analyses of two "sets" of data based on the PAQ, one set dealing with "job data" (data from PAQ analyses of jobs) and the other from "attribute profiles" of the PAQ job elements. (The analyses based on the attribute profiles will be discussed later.) Since the job data study by Marquardt and McCormick (June 1974) was based on the more recent PAQ (Form *B*) and involved a large sample of jobs, the results of this will be presented here. This consisted of principal components analyses of PAQ data for 3,700 jobs. One such analysis, an "overall" or general analysis, was carried out with the ratings for the 3,700 jobs on virtually all of the PAQ job elements (182 job elements). Other analyses were carried out separately for the job elements within each of the six divisions of the PAQ.

The results of these principal components analyses are given in Table 3 in the first column. (Reference will be made to the second column later.) Since it is not feasible here to present the voluminous data on the loadings of the job elements on the components, only the titles of the components are given. These are referred to as job dimensions.

These dimensions can be interpreted as reflecting the "organization" of human job behaviors; that is, the extent to which job behaviors tend to group themselves together in the world of work.

Attribute requirements of jobs
Aside from characterizing jobs in terms of job content descriptors, they can also be characterized in terms of their human "requirements"; that is, the nature (and possibly degree) of the human attributes (qualities, abilities, etc.) that presumably contribute to satisfactory job performance. Such requirements most typically are established for individual jobs on the basis of judgments (such as those of job analysts), but in some instances (and more defensibly) on the basis of statistical validation procedures. However, one would wish for a more analytical approach to this process than has been practiced in the past. In this connection, there is the initial question regarding the identification of the relatively independent attributes that are relevant to job performance. Further, it would be useful to have some well-founded, systematic procedure for specifying the attributes required for various types of human work activity. A couple of probing efforts along these lines will be discussed briefly.

Human abilities in task performance As one such effort, the American Institutes for Research has embarked on a program for the development of a taxonomy of human performance, in particular for providing a unifying set of variables for describing human task performance. (Such a common task-descriptive language would lend itself to various purposes, such as relating human performance in one task to that observed in other tasks, or for applying the results of task-related research to operational tasks.) In this regard, Fleishman (1967)

Table 3
Summary of Job Dimension Titles[a]

JOB DIMENSIONS BASED ON JOB DATA	JOB DIMENSIONS BASED ON ATTRIBUTE PROFILE DATA

Division 1: Information Input

J1-1	Perceptual interpretation	A1-1	Visual input from devices/materials
J1-2	Evaluation of sensory input		
J1-3	Visual input from devices/materials	A1-2	Evaluation of visual input
		A1-3	Perceptual input from processes/events
J1-4	Input from representational sources	A1-4	Verbal/auditory input/interpretation
J1-5	Environmental awareness	A1-5	Non-visual input

Division 2: Mental Processes

J2-6	Decision making	A2-6	Use of job-related knowledge
J2-7	Information processing	A2-7	Information processing

Division 3: Work Output

J3-8	Manual/control activities	A3-8	Manual control/coordination activities.
J3-9	Physical coordination in control/related activities	A3-9	Control/equipment operation
J3-10	General body activity versus sedentary activities	A3-10	General body/handling activities
J3-11	Manipulating/handling activities	A3-11	Use of foot controls
J3-12	Adjusting/operating machines/equipment		
J3-13	Skilled/technical activities		
J3-14	Use of miscellaneous equipment/devices		

Division 4: Relationships with Other Persons

J4-15	Interchange of ideas/judgments/related information	A4-12	Interpersonal communications
J4-16	Supervisory/staff activities	A4-13	Signal/code communications
J4-17	Public/related personal contact	A4-14	Serving/entertaining
J4-18	Communicating instructions/directions/related job information		
J4-19	General personal contact		
J4-20	Job-related communications		

Division 5: Job Context

J5-21	Potentially stressful/unpleasant environment	A5-15	Unpleasant physical environment
J5-22	Potentially hazardous job situations	A5-16	Personally demanding situations
J5-23	Personally demanding situations	A5-17	Hazardous physical environment

JOB DIMENSIONS BASED ON JOB DATA	JOB DIMENSIONS BASED ON ATTRIBUTE PROFILE DATA

Division 6: Other Job Characteristics

J6-24	Attentive job demands	A6-18	Work schedule I
J6-25	Vigilant/discriminating work activities	A6-19	Job responsibility
		A6-20	Routine/Repetitive work activities
J6-26	Structured versus unstructured work activities		
		A6-21	Attentive/discriminating work demands
J6-27	Regular versus irregular work schedule		
		A6-22	Work attire
J6-28	Work/protective versus business clothing	A6-23	Work schedule II
J6-29	Specific versus non-specific clothing		
J6-30	Continuity of work load		

General (G) Dimensions

JG-1	Decision/communication/social responsibilities	(No overall analyses made)
JG-2	Environmental demands/ general body control	
JG-3	Equipment/machine operation	
JG-4	Unnamed	
JG-5	Manual control activities	
JG-6	Office/related activities	
JG-7	Evaluation of sensory input	
JG-8	General/public-related personal contact	
JG-9	Use of technical/related materials	
JG-10	General physical activities versus sedentary activities	
JG-11	Hazardous/personally demanding situations	
JG-12	Attentive/vigilant work activities	
JG-13	Unnamed	
JG-14	Supervision/coordination	

[a]The dimensions based on job data and on attribute profile data are arranged by PAQ division in parallel columns for comparative purposes. Within any given division there may be dimensions based on the two sources which may be identical, or nearly so. However, the ordering and numbering of dimensions within each division is not intended to reflect corresponding dimensions.

differentiates between what he refers to as an *ability* (a general trait of the individual which has been inferred from certain response tendencies) and a *skill* (the level of proficiency on a specific task or group of tasks). He postulates the notion that the development of proficiency (i.e., skill) on any given task is predicated in part on the possession of relevant basic abilities.

As one phase of the research program of the American Institutes of Research, Theologus, Romashko, and Fleishman (1970) crystallized at least a tentative listing of human abilities that have relevance to human task performance, and developed scales for use in classifying tasks in terms of such abilities. An initial listing of fifty such abilities was used, these being based primarily on previous factor analyses of human performance in the sensory, perceptual, cognitive, psychomotor, and physical areas. These were used experimentally in a couple of pilot studies, and were then reduced to thirty-seven, each with its own definition and rating scale.[5] The rating scales consist of seven points, each one having three benchmark tasks to represent specified scale positions as aids in rating other tasks.

As one phase of the study, two groups of raters rated the degree to which each of the thirty-seven abilities was required for performance on each of six hypothetical tasks. The pooled reliability correlations (i.e., intraclass correlations) for groups of ten or twenty raters were about .90 and .91 for the two groups. Although the reliability of ratings of individual raters was fairly modest, the pooled ratings take on very respectable reliability.

Job dimensions based on PAQ attribute data The listing of human abilities developed by Theologus, Romashko, and Fleishman (1970) mentioned above probably reflects about the most adequate inventory of such abilities available, and thus provides a reasonably sound set of descriptors of human abilities for use in characterizing individual tasks or jobs. Aside from the use of these (or other) attributes as descriptors of job requirements, one can also analyze such requirements on an across-job basis. One such approach consisted of a factor analysis based on the "attribute-profiles" of job elements of the PAQ. The attribute profiles were developed on the basis of two studies, one by Mecham and McCormick (1969a) with Form *A* of the PAQ, and the other by Marquardt and McCormick (1972) with Form *B*. In both instances industrial psychologists rated the relevance of seventy-six human attributes to the job elements of the PAQ, using a six-point scale. Most of the thirty-seven abilities reported above by Theologus, Romashko, and Fleishman (1970) were included. There were from eight to eighteen raters per attribute, and the pooled reliability of the ratings was generally in the upper 80s and lower 90s. The attribute profile for a job element consisted of the median ratings for the seventy-six attributes. In the principal components analyses of these profiles, the profiles for the job elements were cor-

---

[5]   These thirty-seven abilities are: (1) Verbal comprehension; (2) Verbal expression; (3) Ideational fluency; (4) Originality; (5) Memorization; (6) Problem sensitivity; (7) Mathematical reasoning; (8) Number facility; (9) Deductive reasoning; (10) Inductive reasoning; (11) Information ordering; (12) Category flexibility; (13) Spatial orientation; (14) Visualization; (15) Speed of closure; (16) Flexibility of closure; (17) Selective attention; (18) Time sharing; (19) Perceptual speed; (20) Static strength; (21) Explosive strength; (22) Dynamic strength; (23) Stamina; (24) Extent flexibility; (25) Dynamic flexibility; (26) Gross body equilibrium; (27) Choice reaction time; (28) Reaction time; (29) Speed of limb movement; (30) Wrist-finger speed; (31) Gross body coordination; (32) Multilimb coordination; (33) Finger dexterity; (34) Manual dexterity; (35) Arm-hand steadiness; (36) Rate control; (37) Control precision.

related. Principal components analyses were carried out separately for the job elements in each of the six divisions of the PAQ.

The results of the principal components analyses are given in the second column of Table 3. These job dimensions can be interpreted as reflecting the extent to which job elements tend to be grouped in terms of their common profiles of attribute requirements. It will be noted in Table 3 that a number of the job dimensions based on the attribute profile data correspond substantially with some of those based on job data (as given in the first column). Such similarities in job dimensions appeared despite the differences in the nature of the input data.

. . .

EXISTING JOB CLASSIFICATION SYSTEMS

Job descriptors serve as the common denominators for bundling jobs together into specific job categories, and in some instances for relating these categories to each other into a total classification system or taxonomy. Some such taxonomies are of a very simple nature, such as the pay-grade structure of individual organizations, as based on job evaluations (in such an instance, the variable in common to those in a particular category is, of course, the pay-grade evaluation). There are, however, certain job classification systems that provide for a systematic organization of all, or many, jobs into a complete structure to serve some purpose or objective. Certain such systems are in operational use, whereas others exist more as formulations for possible specific uses (although the extent of their actual use by an individual organization may not be known). The basis for at least some existing systems is in terms of rational considerations, and the classification of individual jobs in specific categories is essentially subjective. In certain schemes, the structure has been established on the basis of more objective, quantitative data, and the allocation of jobs is accordingly more objective. A few of the better known classification systems will be described briefly.

Bureau of the Census

The United States Bureau of the Census uses an occupational classification system for classifying people in the labor force in terms of present or past occupation. This system consists of ten major occupational categories as follows (United States Bureau of the Census, Population Division, Technical Paper 18, 1968):

1 Professional, technical, and kindred workers
2 Farmers and farm managers
3 Clerical and kindred workers
4 Sales workers
5 Craftsmen, foremen, and kindred workers
6 Operatives and kindred workers
7 Private household workers
8 Service workers, except private household
9 Farm laborers and foremen
10 Laborers, except farm or mine

The Dictionary of Occupational Titles (DOT)

In its operations, the United States Training and Employment Service provides for the classification and coding of applicants and of available positions by the use of an occupational classification system that is incorporated as a part of the *Dictionary of Occupational Titles* (DOT). The major occupational categories are as follows:

1 Professional, technical, and managerial occupations
2 Clerical and sales occupations
3 Service occupations
4 Farming, fishery, forestry, and related occupations
5 Processing occupations
6 Machine trades occupations
7 Bench work occupations
8 Structural work occupations
9 Miscellaneous occupations

Within these occupational categories are less than a hundred occupational divisions (such as occupations in life sciences, computing and account-recording occupations, printing occupations, and packaging and materials-handling occupations); these are identified by a two-digit code. At the next level (a three-digit code) are about 560 more specific occupational groups (such as physicians and surgeons, mail carriers, hoisting and conveying occupations, and tailors and dressmakers). The basis for the occupational groups is essentially that of job content as judged by analysts.

It should be added that the jobs in the *Dictionary of Occupational Titles* are also characterized in terms of other variables, in particular the worker traits mentioned earlier (including training time, aptitudes, interests, temperaments, physical demands, and working conditions), and the relationship with the data, people, and things hierarchies.

A psychological classification of occupations

Another type of occupational classification is that developed over the years by Holland et al. (1970). The classification is based on a theory of personality types. The underlying rationale is that vocational choice, and presumably vocational success, are a function of personality factors, and that personality types are in fact reflected by vocational choice. The initial classification scheme developed in 1959 was essentially of an a priori nature. It has been further developed and tested, and is now reasonably well supported by empirical data. The basic classification is given below:

R: Realistic occupations. (Includes skilled trades, many technical, and some service occupations.)
I: Investigative occupations. (Includes scientific and some technical occupations; this group was originally designated as Intellectual occupations.)
A: Artistic occupations. (Includes artistic, musical, and literary occupations.)
S: Social occupations. (Includes educational and social welfare occupations.)
E: Enterprising occupations. (Includes managerial and sales occupations.)
C: Conventional occupations. (Includes office and clerical occupations.)

The classification system provides for an occupation to be coded in terms of three of these classifications, such as E S C for salesmen; this code means that salesmen resemble people in Enterprising (E) occupations most of all, but they resemble people in Social (S) and Conventional (C) occupations to a lesser degree. Holland et al. (1970) represent the relationships among these classes with a hexagon. The values shown on the lines between the individual classes are correlations (for a sample of 1,234 college students) of their scores on the Vocational Preference

Inventory (VPI), which provides scores reflecting vocational interests as related to the six classes. In general, the hexagon is so presented that close relationships (i.e., higher correlations) are represented by shorter distances, and more distant relationships by longer distances.

A special tabulation of data was carried out at Purdue University for 832 jobs for which Position Analysis Questionnaires (PAQ) were available, to provide the basis for relating such data (actually job dimension scores) to Holland's classification. The resulting analyses, reported by Holland et al. (1970), reflected a reasonable relationship between the PAQ data and Holland's classifications, and also provided the basis for expanding the occupations included in Holland's classification.

CAREER FIELDS

Certain organizations, especially the military services, organize various jobs into career fields or career ladders, in which specific jobs are depicted in something of a pyramid, reflecting the typical, or (more generally) the planned, progression of personnel from lower level up to higher level positions. Each such ladder represents a separate career area, such as electric computer repair, accounting and finance, preventive medicine, and jet engine mechanic.

Since the usual context in which such career fields are used is that in which some "planning" of careers is involved, the development and implementation of such a program requires various analyses and decisions, such as: the identification of the "job types" as they actually exist; the possible restructuring of such job types; the determination of the "level" of each job type; and the possible establishment of sub-areas within which promotional sequences would be expected to take place. In large part, the structuring of a career field must be predicated on rational, judgmental considerations. However, the development of reasonably objective, relevant data can, of course, provide more "substance" on which to base such decisions. For example, the use of job inventories can reflect the (existing) patterns of tasks that occur in positions, and thus contribute to the identification of job types and of relating job types to each other on the career ladder; and systematic job evaluation procedures can aid in the establishment of appropriate levels (and pay grades) for jobs within the ladder.

The concept of career fields and the development of formalized structures that represent typical (or desired) progression ladders has been promulgated primarily by the military services, presumably because of the large number of personnel involved. There are, of course, many occupational areas in civilian life that can be viewed as career fields within which there are common, or rational, progression sequences that have not been formally crystallized; the "formal" recognition of a career field as such is very much a matter of administrative desirability (as in the military services). But whether formally so crystallized or not, the occupational structure in question can serve as a blueprint of typical progression within the occupational domain, and, by implication, aid in career planning, including the implications for desirable training and for planning job experiences to facilitate the occupational development of the individuals in question.

. . .

REFERENCES

Annett, J., & Duncan, K. D. Task analysis and training design. *Occupational Psychology*, 1967, 41, 211-221.

Baehr, M. E. *A Factorial framework for job descriptions for higher-level personnel.* Chicago: Industrial Relations Center, University of Chicago, 1967.

Brumback, G. B., & Vincent, J. W. Factor analysis of work performed data for a sample of administrative, professional, and scientific positions. *Personnel Psychology,* 1970, 23, 101–107.

Chalupsky, A. B. Comparative factor analyses of clerical jobs. *Journal of Applied Psychology,* 1962, 46, 62–66.

Christal, R. E. Comments by the chairman. In *Proceedings of 19. Division of Military Psychology Symposium: Collecting, analyzing, and reporting information describing jobs and occupations.* (77th Annual Convention of the American Psychological Association.) Lackland Air Force Base, Tex.: Personnel Research Division, Air Force Human Resources Laboratory, September, 1969, 77–85.

Cragun, J. R., & McCormick, E. J. *Job inventory information: Task and scale reliabilities and scale interrelationships.* Lackland Air Force Base, Tex.: Personnel Research Laboratory, Aerospace Medical Division, PRL-TR-67-15, November, 1967.

Cunningham, D. J., & Duncan, K. D. Describing non-repetitive tasks for training purposes. *Occupational Psychology,* 1967, 41, 203–210.

Demaree, R. G., Marks, M. R., Smith, W. L., & Snyder, M. T. *Development of qualitative.*

Farina, A. J. Jr. *Development of a taxonomy of human performance: A review of descriptive schemes for human task behavior.* Washington, D.C.: American Institutes for Research, AIR-726-1/69-TR-2, January, 1969.

Fleishman, E. A. Development of a behavior taxonomy for describing human tasks: A correlational-experimental approach. *Journal of Applied Psychology,* 1967, 51, 1–10.

Gagné, R. M. *The conditions of learning.* New York: Holt, Rinehart and Winston, 1965.

Hemphill, J. K. Job descriptions for executives. *Harvard Business Review,* 1959, 37, 55–67.

Herzberg, F. One more time: How do you motivate employees? *Harvard Business Review,* 1968, 46, 53–63.

Holland, J. L. et al. *A psychological classification of occupations.* Baltimore: Center for Social Organization of Schools, Johns Hopkins University, Research Report No. 90, November, 1970.

Jeanneret, P. R., & McCormick, E. J. *The job dimensions of "worker-oriented" job variables and of their attribute profiles as based on data from the Position Analysis Questionnaire.* Lafayette, Ind.: Occupational Research Center, Purdue University, Report No. 2, June, 1969.

Marquardt, L. D., & McCormick, E. J. *Attribute ratings and profiles of job elements of the Position Analysis Questionnaire (PAQ).* Lafayette, Ind.: Occupational Research Center, Department of Psychological Sciences, Purdue University, Report No. 1, 1972.

Marquardt, L. D., & McCormick, E. J. *The job dimensions underlying the job elements of the Position Analysis Questionnair (PAQ), Form B.* Lafayette, Ind.: Occupational Research Center, Department of Psychological Sciences, Purdue University, Report No. 4, June, 1974.

Mecham, R. C., & McCormick, E. J. *The rated attribute requirements of job elements in the Position Analysis Questionnaire.* Lafayette, Ind.: Occupational Research Center, Purdue University, Report No. 1, January, 1969. (a)

Miller, R. B. Task description and analysis. In R. M. Gagné (Ed.), *Psychological principles in system development.* New York: Holt, Rinehart and Winston, 1962.

Morsh, J. E. Collecting, analyzing, and reporting information describing jobs in the United States Air Force. In *Proceedings of 19. Division of Military Psychology Symposium: Collecting, analyzing, and reporting information describing jobs and occupations.* (77th Annual Convention of the American Psychological Association.) Lackland Air Force Base, Tex.: Personnel Research Division, Air Force Human Resources Laboratory, September, 1969.

Morsh, J. E., & Archer, W. B. *Procedural guide for conducting occupational surveys in the United States Air Force.* Lackland Air Force Base, Tex.: Personnel Research Laboratory, Aerospace Medical Division, PRL-TR-67-11, September, 1967.

Swanson, J. B. Job inventory information: Inventory and scale reliability. Unpublished master's thesis, Purdue University, Lafayette, Ind., January, 1969.

Theologus, G. C. *Development of a taxonomy of human performance: A review of biologic taxonomy and classification.* Washington, D.C.: American Institutes for Research, AIR-726-12/69-TR-3, December, 1969.

Theologus, G. C., Romashko, T., & Fleishman, E. A. *Development of a taxonomy of human performance: A feasibility study of ability dimensions for classifying human tasks.* Washington, D.C.: American Institutes for Research, AIR-7-26-1/70-TR-5, January, 1970.

FOR DISCUSSION AND REVIEW

1 Why would the systematic gathering of information about jobs be of use in a personnel system? What are the basic steps in a job analysis?

2 What differentiates task analysis from job analysis? A task description from a job description?

3 What are job inventories? How are they developed and used?

4 What problems might you encounter as you attempted a job and task analysis of a corporate president? A senator? A student?

5 Describe the PAQ and its uses in job analysis.

INTERVIEW WITH GEORGE T. MILKOVICH

George T. Milkovich is a professor in the Industrial Relations Center, Graduate School of Business Administration of the University of Minnesota. Dr. Milkovich received a B.S. from the University of Minnesota in 1963, and went on to earn M.A. and Ph.D. degrees in industrial relations.

Dr. Milkovich is especially interested in the areas of compensation and motivation and human-resource analysis and modeling. He has organized and directed projects related to the development and application of various mathematical approaches to human-resource analysis, forecasting, and planning. Recent work includes the application of markov and semi-markov processes to the study of personnel mobility and the use of simulation to investigate the possible consequences of a variety of personnel strategies. He is currently working on several projects related to the evaluation of affirmative action programs and the application of human-resource models to equal opportunities issues. In addition, Dr. Milkovich has served as a consultant to both public and private organizations on a variety of human-resource issues. He is currently writing a book on compensation management.

Q Can you tell us why forecasting an organization's future human-resource needs can benefit its personnel programs?

A First of all, it's useful to distinguish between human-resource forecasting and planning. Planning is a blend of science and art. It becomes a sequence of forward-looking, goal-directed activities. Human-resource planning incorporates the traditional personnel-administration and industrial-relations functions as strategies designed to achieve human-resource goals. At least we hope they've been designed to achieve these goals. Forecasting, on the other hand, is systemmatic preparation of a statement concerning uncertain or unknown future events. Usually we think of generating forecasts of human-resource requirements, labor costs, turnover, and the like. Forecasting is one component of planning, an important component, but only one aspect of human-resource planning.

Now, your question focused on why generating future human-resource needs can benefit personnel programs. Insofar as these forecasts become part of the organization's human-resource goals, then these goals should direct and drive the personnel programs. For example, if the forecast, based on the firm's sales or market-share goals, points to the need for more chemical engineers with M.S. degrees, and if the forecast is judged as useful by management, then the planners must consider alternative personnel programs that will generate the chemical engineers. These programs may include recruiting from colleges and/or other employers, developing the necessary skills internally, perhaps even acquiring another firm with the pool of necessary talent. So, in sum, forecasts of future resource needs become one input into the determination of the human-resource goals of the organization. The personnel programs should in turn be designed to achieve these goals.

It's important to recognize that there are several types of forecasts in human-resource planning; for example, forecasts may involve requirements, supplies, labor costs, and/or productivity, and they may be generated for varying lengths of time into the future under a variety of assumptions regarding business and socioeconomic conditions.

Now, it seems to me, critical questions for human-resource professionals are: "Why bother forecasting?" or, for that matter, "Why bother with human-resource planning?" Perhaps another way to raise this issue is to ask how personnel programs and activities assist the organization in achieving its objectives.

Q   To what extent is a formalized planning and forecasting system used in today's large organizations?

A   The extent of formalized human-resource planning in large organizations today is difficult to judge. A variety of activities seem to be considered planning; thus, if you ask one firm, they may respond affirmatively because they have a replacement chart or because they once generated a requirements forecast with a regression equation. Certainly the interest in it is high, at least judging by the inquiries I receive. The question may be best answered by someone conducting a survey. Eric Vetter did one several years ago and his text has a copy of his questionnaire. Herb Heneman also did one several years ago. Perhaps the time is ready for one of your students to do it again.

One of the principle reasons for the increased interest in human-resource planning is pressure for affirmative action and equal opportunity. Human-resource professionals are discovering that many of the models and techniques of human-resource planning have great utility in affirmative-action planning. In fact, it is my position that affirmative-action planning is simply part of a sound overall human-resource planning effort.

Q   Are such plans and forecasts viable for the smaller organizations?

A   Certainly planning and forecasting is viable for small organizations. I don't think you need sophisticated mathematical models to get some of the benefits from generating a human-resource plan. A variety of the benefits come from systematically considering the impact of various decisions you are making. Some of these more complex models certainly help us simulate the results of our decisions and provide us with additional insight and additional tools, but certainly the process of planning how to achieve human-resource objectives can benefit small as well as large employers.

Q   Are planning and forecasting functions performed by specialists within personnel departments in large organizations or by the general staff? What specific qualifications, background, and skills would you recommend for the planning and forecasting specialist?

A   Human-resource planning is not necessarily performed in the personnel function; other functions in large organizations, principally the comptroller/ financial and industrial engineering units may do it. For example, we find in the chemicals industry a great deal of work being done in the applied math and the engineering groups; in manufacturing firms it is common for the industrial engineering and operating management to generate manpower plans.

At Bell Labs, for example, some of the operations research staff have very advanced models for human-resource planning and simulation of alternative policies and programs. In Exxon Chemicals the financial group does a considerable amount of the planning, while the employee-relations function simply carries out some of the personnel programs that are generated by the plan. Traditional employee-relations functions in some firms do not seem to be very involved in the plan, except as they are one of the functions that carry out some of the recommendations of the plan. In other organizations you'll find personnel/human-resource departments very involved in human-resource planning.

Regarding some of the specific qualifications and background required, a good human-resource planner needs analytical skills and quantitative skills. A human-resource planner can't just be an employment or compensation specialist. He/she needs good analytical skills as well as being knowledgeable in finance, manufacturing, and human resources.

Now, to be sure, considerable planning could go on inside of the existing personnel functions. In labor relations you certainly plan for a negotiation and in compensation you plan for next year's compensation budget. So planning goes on within each of these functions. I think what we're discussing is planning for the utilization of human resources within the context of the organization's objectives.

Q   Why do you feel our interest in manpower planning has lagged behind an interest in, for example, product planning or financial planning? Are there more variables to consider? Are the variables more complex?

A   Well, I'll say manpower planning really hasn't lagged behind. It's just that personnel people haven't been doing it. As I said before, in many major corporations, the human-resource planning activities have been performed by financial analysts and comptrollers, engineers, and other professionals.

That's one reason why it is lagging in the personnel area. I think another reason why it's lagged behind is that personnel people really haven't been under any pressure to do it. As I said, others are doing it for us. Some personnel professionals may be more comfortable responding to problems rather than anticipating.

Very recently, within the last five years, with affirmative action and EEO pressures, personnel is being required to be a bit more analytical about some of their decisions and about the impact of these decisions. So perhaps some of the renewed interest in human-resource planning, at least among personnel people, can be attributed to the pressures from affirmative action and civil rights requirements.

Are the variables more complex? Not really. If you talk to production planners and financial planners, you'll get the impression that things are pretty complicated there, too.

Finally, I am hopeful that universities and other organizations are beginning to develop and train professionals who have some skills required in human-resource planning. Currently, few universities offer courses in this topic.

Appraising Performance in Organizations

INTRODUCTION

There is probably no program as difficult for many in personnel to implement effectively as performance appraisal. Whether it be the uneasiness resulting from judging others, the hesitation to confront workers with poor performance, or the failure to remove one's biases from the rating process, performance-appraisal systems are frequently troublesome.

Section Three first provides an overview of the major appraisal techniques in an article by Cummings and Schwab. Schneier discusses the impact role prescriptions have on the appraisal process and presents a diagnostic procedure for identifying potentially divergent ratings given by raters of different organizational levels.

Behaviorally based and effectiveness-based appraisal systems, the most commonly used methods, are next discussed. Articles by Kearney and Carroll and Tosi stress the development and implementation of these systems.

Even if a useful appraisal format can be agreed on, the issue of feeding results to ratees remains. Maier's three types of appraisal interviews and Bernardin and Walter's study of rater training both suggest ways to improve the feedback process.

Finally, Holley and Field explain the impact of equal employment opportunity legislation on the appraisal process. As these authors note, courts are increasingly interested in the ability of an organization to demonstrate the validity of its appraisal systems.

A. GENERAL ISSUES IN APPRAISAL

L. L. Cummings

D. P. Schwab

Methods of Appraisal

INTRODUCTION

Over the years a wide variety of appraisal methods have been developed. This proliferation is primarily a result of inadequacies identified in earlier methods. We have already identified the types of inadequacies to be concerned with in our discussions of construct validity and constant and variable errors in the previous chapter.[1] In the present chapter we describe a number of major appraisal methods. These methods can be subsumed under four general headings: (1) comparative procedures, (2) absolute standards, (3) management by objectives, and (4) direct indexes. Our focus will be on describing the various methods and in evaluating their susceptibility to various types of errors. . . .

COMPARATIVE PROCEDURES

Comparative procedures are generally characterized by two features. First, in all cases the evaluation is made by comparing an appraisee against other appraisees on the dimension(s) of interest. Second, this comparison is generally made on one global dimension which seeks to get at the employee's overall effectiveness to the organization. Figure 7.1 provides an illustration of a statement designed to elicit an overall assessment of employee performance. Four popular comparative procedures are: (1) straight ranking, (2) alternative ranking, (3) paired comparison, and (4) forced distribution. The first three procedures are similar in that they all *rank* the appraisees—they are called ranking procedures. The fourth procedure, however, is different and will be discussed apart from the others.

> ". . . consider these people with respect to their overall competence, the effectiveness with which they perform their jobs, their proficiency, their general overall value. Ask yourself such questions as: Which of them is the most successful, most competent, most effective, most valuable of the group? Take into account all elements of successful job performance, such items as knowledge of the job and functions performed, quantity and quality of output, relations with other people—subordinates, equals, superiors, visitors from outside the department or company—ability to get work done, intelligence, interest, response to training, and the like. In other words, which most nearly approximates the ideal, the kind you want more of?"

From T. A. Mahoney, W. W. Sorenson, T. H. Verdee, and A. R. Nash, "Identification and Prediction of Managerial Effectiveness," *Personnel Administration*, Jan.-Feb. 1963, 26, 12-22. Reproduced by permission.

Fig. 7.1 Illustration of a global dimension of effectiveness.

[1]   The material discussed in this chapter is based substantially on information to be found in Dunnette (1966); Flanagan (1949); Guion (1965); McGregor (1960); Tiffin and Mc-Cormick (1965); Whisler and Harper (1962); and Wikstrom (1968).

Ranking procedures

Straight ranking Straight ranking is a very simple procedure involving a comparison of appraisees. In an appraisal context the evaluator is typically asked to consider all of the employees to be appraised and identify the very best performer, the second best, and so on, through all employees to the very poorest. This procedure is a natural one for most evaluators, since we frequently rank people on an informal basis.

Alternative ranking Alternative ranking is a slightly more complex variant of straight ranking. The evaluator is given an alphabetical list of all employees to be ranked and asked to think of the very best employee in the group on the dimension of interest. Following this, he is asked to think of the very poorest employee. Each time a person is identified as best or poorest, his name is removed from the alphabetical list and recorded on a separate ranking. The evaluator can thus alternate between thinking of the best and poorest employee on an increasingly smaller list.

Paired comparison Another common variant of straight ranking is paired comparison. The evaluator compares each employee to be ranked with every other employee, one at a time. An employee's standing in the final ranking is determined by how many times he is chosen over the other employees. Figure 7.2 shows an illustration of the paired comparison technique with four employees (A through D). The circled letters indicate the evaluator's choice of the better employee in each pair. C would thus be ranked highest, followed by A, B, and finally D. In general the number of comparisons to be made is found by the formula $N(N-1)/2$, where N refers to the number of employees to be ranked.

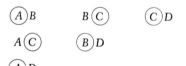

Fig. 7.2 Illustrations of comparisons in paired comparison appraisal technique with four employees.

Evaluation of ranking

Because the evaluator is forced to array appraisees from high to low, ranking procedures are not subject to the interindividual constant errors (leniency, central tendency, and strictness) identified earlier. Likewise, ranking procedures are often satisfactory from the standpoint of obtaining adequate agreement between different rankers. Alternative ranking and, particularly, paired comparisons are good in this respect.

A major limitation of any of the ranking systems described is the fact that employees are generally ranked on only one dimension, usually some global-effectiveness measure. As Dunnette (1966) has pointed out, treating job success as consisting of only one general characteristic is usually unrealistic. Moreover, problems are created because two or more evaluators may not define overall effectiveness in exactly the same way. Indeed, halo error as we defined it earlier may provide the basis for an individual's ranking, although it is impossible to identify when only one dimension is being ranked. If only one characteristic is employed, it is important to define it carefully, as done in Figure 7.1.

A second important limitation of any ranking system results from the difficulty of comparing two or more groups of rankings. For example, it is difficult to combine rankings of employees in two departments because the highest-ranking individual in one department may be only average in the other department. If, however, there are some individuals known by the evaluators in both departments, the rankings can be meaningfully combined (Guion, 1965, pp. 103–4).

A final limitation pertains to the difficulty of using ranking procedures for developmental and feedback purposes. There are two issues involved. The first has to do with the generality of the rankings. Little concrete information for improving performance can be given when only one global dimension is evaluated. The second issue hinges on the comparative aspect of the method. To communicate the comparisons to the appraised employees may well result in dysfunctional, highly personalized discussions about the relative merits of various individuals. This in turn is not likely to lead to increased employee motivation or to specific suggestions for growth and development.

Forced distribution

A forced distribution procedure is a comparative technique that generally overcomes one major limitation of ranking. Specifically, forced distribution methods usually include comparisons on several performance factors rather than on one global dimension. This in turn enables one to identify halo error by examining the similarity of scores given each appraisee across factors.

The term *forced distribution* is used to describe this method because the evaluator is forced to assign a certain portion of his employees to each of several categories on each factor. A typical classification scheme requires the evaluator to rate 10% of the appraisees highest on a factor, 20% above average, 40% average, 20% below average, and 10% lowest. Such a scheme is illustrated in Table 7.1 for groups of 13 and 20 appraisees. By forcing the distribution in this way, interindividual constant errors such as leniency are controlled. Of course, there is always the chance that the appraisees as a group do not conform to whatever distribution is established.[2] This is particularly likely when small groups are being appraised and/or when the group has been successfully preselected for high performance potential.

Table 7.1
Illustration of the Distribution of 13 and 20 Employees
on a Forced Distribution Scale

TOTAL NUMBER OF EMPLOYEES	LOW 10%	NEXT 20%	MIDDLE 40%	NEXT 20%	HIGH 10%
13	1	3	5	3	1
20	2	4	8	4	2

ABSOLUTE STANDARDS

Appraisal systems using absolute standards can generally be differentiated from comparative systems on two points. First, each individual is evaluated against one or several written standards rather than against other employees. Second, several

---

[2]   Ranking methods are subject to an analogous limitation. Specifically, forcing the evaluator to differentiate between all appraisees may be artificial in the sense that some of the appraisees may be equal on the dimension being ranked.

facets of overall performance are generally measured rather than a single global dimension typically measured in comparative procedures.

There are two general absolute standards methods. In the first, evaluators are asked to identify whether the appraisee possesses or does not possess, in a qualitative sense, some performance characteristic. For example, an evaluator may be asked to answer yes or no to the question, "Does the employee present a neat appearance when meeting customers?" Critical incidents, checklists, and forced choice are illustrative of this first procedure. The second method attempts to measure the degree to which each appraisee possesses certain characteristics. Using the example above, the evaluator might be asked to assess on a seven-point scale the degree to which each appraisee presents a neat appearance when meeting customers. Conventional rating procedures and behaviorally anchored rating procedures are illustrative of the second method.

Qualitative methods

Critical incidents We have already briefly mentioned Flanagan's (1949) critical incidents approach when discussing job analysis in Chapter 2. Its use in appraisal involves two major steps. The developmental step stipulates that requirements critical to the successful performance of the task be identified. This information is typically obtained from the supervisors of the employees to be evaluated. They are asked to give illustrations of when their subordinates have been outstandingly successful or unsuccessful on the job.

These incidents are next abstracted into a smaller number of behavioral categories. Kirchner and Dunnette (1957), for example, obtained over one hundred critical incidents for a sales position. These were subsequently condensed into thirteen categories, including: (1) communicating important information to sales managers, (2) initiating new sales approaches, and (3) calling on all accounts.

The implementation step involves giving each evaluator a list of the general categories developed from the procedure described above. He is then expected to record any positive or negative incidents that occur pertaining to the general categories. Incidents thus determined for each employee may serve as a basis for evaluational as well as developmental actions.

Weighted checklist A weighted checklist is developed by first obtaining a number of statements about employee performance on the job to be rated. A comprehensive list of these statements is developed judgmentally by persons familiar with the job. Each statement is then evaluated by a group of persons (e.g., the supervisors of the jobs to be appraised) on how favorable or unfavorable it is for successful performance. This evaluation of items is typically done on a seven- or eleven-point scale, where low values represent unfavorable scores and high values represent favorable scores.

When the judges cannot agree on the favorability of an item for performance, it should be eliminated from the final checklist. Lack of agreement is reflected in the variability of scores assigned to the item by the judges. This variability may be shown in the range or, more appropriately, the standard deviation of the distribution of scores. The remaining items are then "weighted" by the average score obtained from the group evaluations. Table 7.2 provides an illustration of a weighted checklist developed for bake shop managers.

The evaluators are generally given copies of the final checklist that do not contain the weights assigned to each item. Their task is to indicate whether each appraisee does or does not engage in the behavior specified in each item. The ap-

Table 7.2
Illustration of a Weighted Checklist Developed on Bake Shop Managers

ITEM	SCALE VALUE
He occasionally buys some of his competitor's products.	6.8
He never consults with his head salesgirl when making out a bake order.	1.4
He belongs to a local merchants' association.	4.9
He criticizes his employees unnecessarily.	0.8
The window display is usually just fair.	3.1
He enjoys contacting customers personally.	7.4
He does now know how to figure costs of products.	0.6
He lacks a long range viewpoint.	3.5
His products are of uniformly high quality.	8.5
He expects too much of his employees.	2.2
His weekly and monthly reports are sometimes inaccurate.	4.2
He does not always give enough thought to his bake orders.	1.6
He occasionally runs a selling contest among his salesgirls.	6.8
Baking in his shop continues until 2 P.M. or later.	8.2
He keeps complaining about employees but doesn't remedy the situation.	0.9
He has originated one or more workable new formulas.	6.4
He sometimes has an unreasonably large inventory of certain items.	3.3
Employees enjoy working for him.	7.6
He does not delegate enough responsibility to others.	2.8
He has accurately figured the costs of most of his products.	7.8
He wishes he were just a baker.	0.8
His shop is about average in cleanliness.	4.4
He is tardy in making minor repairs in his sales room.	1.9
He periodically samples all of his products for quality.	8.1

From E. B. Knauft, "Construction and Use of Weighted Checklist Ratings Scales for Two Industrial Situations," *Journal of Applied Psychology*, 1948, 32, 63–70. Copyright 1948 by the American Psychological Association and reproduced by permission.

praisee's evaluation is determined by summing the scores of the items that have been checked for him.

Forced choice Forced choice procedures involve a series of groups or clusters of statements about job behavior. Each group generally contains two, three, or four items. The evaluator is asked to choose the item which is most descriptive of the appraisee. When three of four items are included in each group the evaluator may also be asked to identify the least descriptive item.

Items are chosen for inclusion in the clusters subject to two constraints. The first constraint has to do with the items' ability to differentiate between successful and unsuccessful performance (discrimination index). A typical approach has judges evaluate very effective and ineffective performers on the items. Those items that differentiate between the two types of performers are weighted while those items which do not differentiate go unweighted. The second constraint pertains to the items' desirability index. Item desirability refers to the judges' assessment that the statement is a favorable or unfavorable statement to make about a worker.

In constructing clusters of items, an effort is made to equate items on desirability so that the rater cannot bias the ratings for or against any appraisee. Alternatively, an effort is made to have differences in the discrimination indexes so that the resulting instrument differentiates between effective and less effective appraisees.

An illustration using two clusters of two items each is given in Table 7.3. For simplicity assume that both desirability and discrimination are measured on a five-point scale. Note that the two A items are both highly desirable, but that only A_1 substantially differentiates between successful and unsuccessful performers. Both B items have a lower desirability; again only one has a high discrimination index.

Table 7.3
Two Illustrative Forced Choice Clusters

ITEMS	DISCRIMINATION INDEX	DESIRABILITY INDEX
A_1 Turns in work assignments promptly	4.21	4.75
A_2 Is at ease in any situation	0.82	4.72
B_1 Almost always reports for work on time	3.69	3.27
B_2 Makes friends with others easily	0.91	3.30

In using a forced choice procedure of the type illustrated, the evaluator would be given all clusters of items without discrimination or desirability indexes and told to check the item in each cluster most descriptive of the individual being appraised. The individual's evaluation score consists of the sum of the discrimination indexes for the items checked. High scores reflect high performance, while low scores reflect lower performance.[3]

A summary of steps involved in the development of qualitative methods is shown in Figure 7.3.

Quantitative methods

All three of the above procedures employing absolute standards are characterized by the fact that the evaluator must decide if a statement about performance—be it a critical incident, checklist, or forced choice format—applies or does not apply to a particular appraisee; that is, he is asked to make an "all-or-none" judgment. In the present section two methods are described that ask the evaluator to specify the degree to which various statements about performance pertain to the appraisee.

Conventional rating Conventional ratings in their many and varied forms undoubtedly constitute the most popular form of appraisal techniques. This is somewhat curious in view of the fact that ratings, as they are most frequently employed, are subject to a number of important limitations.

Rating scales generally have several statements about employee characteristics or behavior. A continuous or discrete scale is established for each item. Table 7.4 illustrates several types of scaling procedures.

---

[3] For detailed information on the steps involved in constructing forced choice scales, including formulas for calculating desirability and discrimination indexes, see Sisson (1948, pp. 376–80) or Tolle and Murray (1958, pp. 680–84).

Critical Incidents

1. Obtain statements about successful and unsuccessful performance from job incumbents and supervisors.
2. Abstract statements into 10–15 general categories describing job behaviors.
3. Provide evaluator with list of categories to record appropriate behaviors of employees.

Weighted Checklist

1. Obtain statements about job performance from persons unfamiliar with the job.
2. Have judges evaluate favorableness of each statement on a seven- to eleven-point scale.
3. Retain those items on which judges agree on favorableness of item.
4. Provide evaluator with list of retained items to assess employees' performance.

Forced Choice

1. Obtain statements about job performance from persons familiar with the job.
2. Determine items' (a) discrimination index, and (b) desirability index.
3. Develop clusters of items that differ in discrimination, but are similar in desirability.

Fig. 7.3 Summary of steps in the development of qualitative methods.

Table 7.4
Illustrations of Conventional Rating Scaling Formats for a Single Item

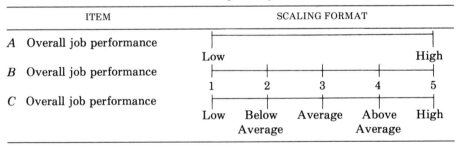

ITEM	SCALING FORMAT
A Overall job performance	Low ⸺⸺⸺⸺⸺⸺⸺ High
B Overall job performance	1 2 3 4 5
C Overall job performance	Low Below Average Average Above Average High

Item *A* is scaled continuously; the evaluator places a check somewhere on the scale to represent his assessment of the appraisee. Item *B* has a numerical discrete scale. Sometimes letters are used instead of numbers. Item *C* is also scaled discretely with adjectives. On the latter two scales the evaluators must check one of the five discrete points.

Discrete scales generally result in greater interrater agreement and hence are preferable to continuous scales. They usually have at least four and sometimes as many as twenty-five points. Too few points to check obviously results in less information about differences between appraisees than the evaluator is capable of providing. On the other hand, too many discrete points asks for finer discriminations than the evaluator can reliably make. Considerable research has been performed on this issue. The results suggest that seven to nine points is about the minimum while up to twenty-five points may be used in some situations. The evidence also suggests that inexperienced evaluators have greater difficulty with more discrete points than do experienced evaluators.

Ratings also vary widely in the number of items they measure. Some seek assessments on as few as two, while others attempt to get information on up to twenty or thirty performance characteristics. Relatively little information is available on the optimum number to include in a rating form. We would obviously expect some differences depending on the type of job being rated. Often, however, an attempt is made to get at more information than evaluators can realistically provide. A relatively small number of items (five to eight) will usually account for most of the relevant job performance information.

Behaviorally anchored rating scales An effort is made through behaviorally anchored rating scales to overcome two methodological problems of conventional ratings. The first has to do with the type of items included in the assessment, while the second deals with the method of scaling the items. These two issues can perhaps best be described by explaining the procedure for developing a behaviorally anchored rating scale.

The first two steps in developing a behaviorally anchored rating scale are identical to the developmental process of the critical incidents procedure discussed earlier. Supervisors are asked to describe examples of when their subordinates have been outstandingly successful or unsuccessful on the job. Second, the incidents are condensed into a smaller number of general categories. In a recent study by Fogli, Hulin, and Blood (1971) on grocery clerks, for example, eight categories were developed. These included such things as (1) knowledge and judgment, (2) skill in human relations, (3) skill in monetary transactions, and (4) observational ability, as well as others.

The third step is somewhat similar to weighting items in the checklist procedure. Judges are asked to rate each critical incident. In the Fogli et al. study, judges were asked to rate each incident on a seven-point poor-good performance scale. Incidents were eliminated when judges were unable to agree on their value as reflected in moderate or large variations in the scores assigned. Frequently mentioned incidents with high interjudge agreement were retained for the final instrument.

The remaining incidents were assigned to their respective general categories (step 2). A scale for each category was developed by ordering the incidents of the category according to their average value assigned by the judges. Figure 7.4 shows an illustration of such a scale obtained from the Fogli et al. study. Note, for example, that the incident "by knowing the price of items, this checker would be expected to look for mismarked items" has an average value of about 6.5 and represents high performance in the knowledge and judgment category.

The evaluator rates each appraisee on each category. The appraisee's evaluation is determined by summing the assigned scores across all general categories. Discussion with the appraisee of specific behaviors checked in the general categories may also serve developmental needs.

Evaluation

Conventional rating is subject to a number of serious limitations. In the first place, its scaling method permits halo error and the interindividual errors of leniency, strictness, and central tendency. The method additionally makes it easy for the evaluator to bias his assessment for or against someone if he chooses. Finally, conventional ratings too often focus on employees' personality characteristics rather than on performance behavior, which is what is really of interest.

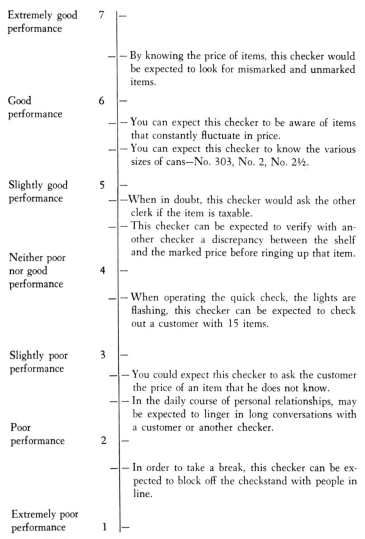

Fig. 7.4 Behaviorally anchored rating scale of grocery clerk's knowledge and judgment. (From L. Fogli, C. L. Hulin, and M. R. Blood, "Development of First-Level Behavioral Job Criteria," *Journal of Applied Psychology*, 1971, 55, 3–8. Copyright © 1971 by the American Psychological Association and reproduced by permission.)

Each of the alternative methods employing absolute standards was designed to correct one or several limitations of conventional rating. Weighted checklist and forced choice procedures, for example, attempt to differentiate between observing behavior and the evaluation of that behavior by keeping the values reflecting the favorability of each item off the appraisal form. Forced choice potentially does this very effectively by additionally equating the items on desirability. These procedures can result in reduced constant errors, particularly interindividual errors such as leniency.

The need to include only valid items in an appraisal form is emphasized in both forced choice and critical incidents (and hence, behaviorally anchored rating scales) procedures. The former method seeks to achieve this by weighting only items that have been shown to differentiate between successful and unsuccessful performers, while the latter method attempts to do so by carefully generalizing from specific illustrations of effective or ineffective performance. These efforts are to be contrasted with conventional rating systems that typically choose items on a wholly judgmental basis.[4]

The critical incidents method also appears to be desirable from the standpoint of providing feedback to the appraisee. The evaluator has specific incidents to communicate with the appraisee. Specific incidents, in turn, are n_ore likely to be agreed upon by both members of the discussion than are the more global assessments of a typical rating procedure. Hence, critical incidents are probably more likely to form a basis for objective and productive communication with the appraisee.

On the other hand, forced choice is a decidedly poorer procedure for feedback purposes. If the procedure has equated the items in each cluster on desirability as it is supposed to, neither the evaluator nor the appraisee has any basis for deciding the observed behavior is superior to behavior which is not observed. The uncertainty induced by equating items on desirability also may make evaluators uncomfortable about using the procedure.

Organizations considering implementing one of the qualitative methods (critical incidents, checklist, or forced choice) must recognize that each involves considerable developmental effort. This effort may be difficult to justify unless the ratings are to be used on a substantial number of employees. Forced choice procedures, in particular, require much input before a usable form is developed. This input frequently may not be justified in view of the limitations of forced choice that we have already discussed.

In several respects the behaviorally anchored approach, although obviously also requiring considerable developmental work, is the most attractive alternative to conventional ratings. It shares with critical incidents the fact that the persons who use the final appraisal forms aid in the forms' development. This, in turn, should aid in gaining commitment to the appraisal program and hence reduce the errors resulting from lack of concern and attention to the program on the part of the evaluators.

The evaluators' participation also aids in developing scales with a high degree of meaning to the users of the instrument. This is borne out by the extremely high degree of interrater agreement obtained on the behaviorally anchored scales developed by Smith and Kendall (1963) and Fogli et al. (1971).

A most promising aspect of the behaviorally anchored approach, however, pertains to its potential value for employee development through a feedback program. Fairly specific employee behavior is pinpointed in the rating process. In addition, by going over each scale the appraisee can be shown the types of highly scored behaviors which are desired by the organization.

---

[4]   It should be noted, however, that the research evidence is not entirely supportive on this point. The voluminous research evidence on the forced choice procedure shows that, at best, it is only moderately superior to alternative appraisal methods as far as validity is concerned (Cozan, 1959, and Zavala, 1965). Almost no direct evidence exists on the validity of the critical incidents or behaviorally anchored rating scales procedures.

MANAGEMENT BY OBJECTIVES

The method

Management by objectives (MBO) has been offered by McGregor (1960) as an alternative to conventional rating and employee comparison systems. It is essentially based on two related concepts: "(1) The clearer the idea one has of what it is one is trying to accomplish, the greater the chances of accomplishing it; and (2) progress can only be measured in terms of what one is trying to make progress toward" (Wikstrom, 1968, p. 2).

An effort to implement these concepts often results in a four-step process. The first step involves defining goals for the employee to accomplish during some specified future time period. These goals may be initially proposed by the subordinate with resulting approval by the superior or by the superior with resulting discussion and acceptance by the subordinate. Advocates of the method stress the need for subordinate participation, regardless of who initiates the process.

Advocates also stress the need to specify goals as quantitatively as possible. In a sales job, for example, specific goals might be set with respect to sales volume, new accounts, customers called on, and so on. A personnel manager may set goals with respect to selection instruments validated, number of employees retrained, and so on. Goal statements may be set for methods or for means of accomplishment as well as for desired outcomes.

The second step consists of the subordinate's carrying out the objectives established. In some respects MBO may make the task easier since the goals to be achieved have presumably been clearly stated in the previous step. This, of course, also suggests that if the goals have been incorrectly specified, the subordinate will likely devote his energies to accomplishing unproductive tasks.

The third step involves an evaluation of the performance against the goals initially established. This step is often begun by a self-appraisal. The subordinate writes a report describing how well he has met his objectives. This appraisal is discussed with the superior. Reasons for goals not being met are analyzed and discussed.

The final step consists of establishing new goals for the subsequent time period. Thus the process repeats itself.

Evaluation

As is fairly obvious from this brief description of the procedure, management by objectives was initiated primarily as a developmental tool rather than an evaluative one. We may note several issues related to the construct validity of MBO and to its use as an evaluative device here.

We might easily have included MBO under our discussion of absolute standards since goals are clearly standards to be accomplished. We devoted a separate section to MBO primarily because, unlike other absolute standards, it sets unique standards for each participant.

This is a potentially valuable innovation. It is consistent, for example, with the implications of our discussion of individual differences in Chapter 2. It is also consistent with the notion that each job requires some unique contribution to achieve the overall objectives of the organization. Thus, the establishment of individualized goals is intuitively appealing in terms of developing a procedure with high construct validity.

Unfortunately, this individualization also creates a problem from an evaluation point of view. Specifically, it is difficult to attach rewards equitably to a MBO system because goals are individualized and because the subordinate plays a key role in the evaluation process. Indeed, to tie rewards directly to MBO may encourage the subordinate to subvert both the goal-setting and performance review aspects of the procedure.

Despite the popularity of MBO, more research is needed investigating its effectiveness.[5] In one study Meyer, Kay, and French (1965) discussed research conducted on MBO at General Electric. They found some support for the notion that participation in the goal-setting phase of MBO resulted in higher subsequent employee performance. Apparently even more important, however, was whether any goals were set at all. This latter finding is consistent with the research being conducted by Locke (1968) that suggests goals are an important determinant of performance.

DIRECT INDEXES

All of the procedures described to this point require that employee performance be evaluated or assessed by someone, even though the evaluator may occasionally be the person engaging in the performance. It is also sometimes possible to obtain information about performance more directly without the necessity of the performance behavior being "filtered" through the evaluative processes of an appraiser. In this section we briefly describe two such direct indexes, measures of productivity and job withdrawal.

Measures of productivity

In some instances it is possible to measure the productivity of an individual directly. These measures are generally aimed at quantity (e.g., hourly units of output, monthly gross sales) or quality (e.g., percent units rejected, scrappage) of output. The actual collection of data will be determined largely by the specific objective to be measured and by the type of output and technology used for producing it. Quality measures, for example, would frequently be obtained from special inspection units established within the organization. Mechanical measurement of quantity may be appropriate for highly standardized operations producing many homogeneous output units. In other situations the accounting department might be the most appropriate source of productivity data.

Obviously, direct measures are obtainable only when the employee produces a distinguishable output. This is generally more typical of blue-collar or managerial workers. Moreover, it is reasonable to use direct measures of the sort described to distribute organizational rewards only if the worker has substantial control over the output measured. It makes little sense to use direct measures to reward an individual if his productivity is largely a function of the contributions of fellow workers, supervision, or the technology of the work place. On the other hand, group productivity data may be very useful for evaluating the supervisor of the work group.

Measures of withdrawal

A special form of productivity is evidenced by actual job attendance. The employee may fail to attend either temporarily (absenteeism) or permanently (turnover). Sometimes the organization chooses to evaluate the individual on the frequency of his absences or the supervisor on the frequency of absences and turnover of his subordinates. Although the two might superficially appear to present no special mea-

---

[5]   For empirical research on the factors influencing the success of a MBO program see: Carroll (1971); Carroll and Tosi (1969a, 1969b, 1970, 1973); Ivancevich, Donnelly, and Lyon (1970); Raia (1965, 1966); Tosi and Carroll (1968, 1969, 1970a, 1970b); Tosi, Rizzo, and Carroll (1970).

surement problems, several issues are involved that can potentially create difficulty.

In measuring turnover, an initial distinction should be made between voluntary (employee-initiated) and involuntary (organization-initiated) turnover. Measures should reflect this distinction, because the causes and consequences of the two are likely to differ. For example, layoffs necessitated by declining sales should be interpreted quite differently than voluntary turnover resulting from dissatisfaction with supervision.

Another distinction should be made for both turnover and absenteeism. Specifically, measures should differentiate between that turnover or absenteeism which is avoidable and that which is unavoidable. Avoidable refers to turnover or absenteeism that might be prevented if the organization changed something about its environment (e.g., its reward system, task design, etc.) Examples are turnover because of dissatisfaction with wages, or absenteeism because one is bored with the job. Unavoidable refers to turnover or absenteeism that neither the organization nor the employee can reasonably prevent. Being drafted into military service is a source of unavoidable turnover, and a nonjob-related accident requiring hospitalization would likely be thought of as unavoidable absenteeism. Again, the distinction is important in terms of causes and consequences.

Evaluation

Direct measures have some distinct advantages and disadvantages relative to the other types of measures. On the positive side, direct measures avoid many of the problems of constant errors discussed in Chapter 6. This is true because direct measures usually avoid the need to have an appraiser evaluate the performance, so that problems of leniency and other forms of constant errors are not likely to arise. Variable errors resulting from disagreements among judges should also be minimized if the procedure to obtain the direct measure is well defined.

Direct measures also sometimes have a high degree of construct validity. This is particularly true on production jobs where the output is clearly definable and where the individual worker is largely responsible for that output on both quality and quantity dimensions. In such cases, the use of indirect measures would be difficult to justify. Most tasks, however, do not have the characteristics just described. Outcomes are often not clearly definable or attributable directly to the individual. In these situations direct measures tend to be deficient indicators of the performance construct.

Of course, even when they are deficient, direct measures can provide valuable information about certain dimensions of performance. For example, it might be appropriate to use an index of subordinate avoidable absenteeism in evaluating a line manager. This could be done within the context of MBO, or comparative or absolute standards systems. On the other hand, we would argue that measures of withdrawal are always deficient taken alone. The danger lies in using the deficient direct measures to the exclusion of other indexes, so that the employer and supervisors alike tend to focus on those subsets of the task that happen to be directly measurable.

SUMMARY

A variety of evaluation procedures have been developed for purposes of appraising employees. Comparative procedures such as ranking, alternative ranking, paired comparison, and forced distribution focus on employee-to-employee assessments. Absolute standards approaches such as critical incidents, checklists, forced choice, conventional rating, and behaviorally anchored rating focus on employee-to-common-standards assessments. MBO focuses on employee-to-specific-objective assessments. Direct indexes focus on objective measures of behavior.

Comparative procedures are relatively easy to develop and use. In addition they often provide adequate agreement between raters. Alternatively, all but forced distribution are frequently, but not necessarily, limited to tapping only an overall measure of organizational contribution. Moreover, the nature of the comparison makes feedback to the appraisee somewhat cumbersome.

It is more difficult to generalize about the various absolute standards methods. Some, like conventional rating, are subject to a wide number of criticisms. Others, like forced choice, presumably protect against certain specific types of constant error, but are subject to a number of other criticisms. The critical incidents and particularly the behaviorally anchored rating scales are potentially desirable from several points of view. Both involve the evaluator's active participation in the development of the instruments, and both focus on relatively specific employee performance behaviors. Behaviorally anchored rating scales additionally require a fairly sophisticated scaling method that appears to result in higher interrater agreement.

Management by objectives appears to be most desirable from a developmental standpoint. Its emphasis on meaningful participation in goal setting, however, seems to limit the procedure to managerial, professional, and certain other types of selling tasks where the job can really vary with the capabilities and interests of the individual. Moreover, its individual orientation has certain limitations in terms of distributing rewards to groups of individuals.

Direct measures of performance are generally most appropriate on jobs with easily definable outcomes. They can, however, often be used in conjunction with indirect measures in other situations.

REFERENCES

Carroll, S. J., and H. L. Tosi. "The Relation of Characteristics of the Review Process as Moderated by Personality and Situational Factors to the Success of the 'Management by Objectives' Approach." *Academy of Management Journal.* 1969, 12, 139–143.

Carroll, S. J., and H. L. Tosi. "The Relationship of Goal Characteristics to the Success of Management by Objectives as Moderated by Personality and Situational Factors." Paper presented at the *American Psychological Association Convention,* 1969.

Carroll, S. J., and H. L. Tosi. "Goal Characteristics and Personality Factors in a Management-by-Objectives Program." *Administrative Science Quarterly.* 1970, 61, 295–305.

Carroll, S. J., and H. L. Tosi. *Management by Objectives: Applications and Research.* Macmillan, 1973.

Cozan, L. W. "Forced-Choice: Better than Other Rating Methods." *Personnel.* 1959, 39, 80–83.

Dunnette, M. D. *Personnel Selection and Placement.* Wadsworth, 1966.

Flanagan, J. C. "A New Approach to Evaluating Personnel." *Personnel.* 1949, 26, 35–42.

Fogli, L., C. L. Hulin, and M. R. Blood. "Development of First-Level Behavioral Job Criteria." *Journal of Applied Psychology.* 1971.

Haynes, M. E. "Improving Performance Through Employee Discussions." *Personnel Journal.* 1970, 49, 138–141.

Kirchner, W. K., and M. D. Dunnette. "Identifying the Critical Factors in Successful Salesmanship." *Personnel.* 1957, 34, 54–59.

Locke, E. A. "Toward a Theory of Task Motivation and Incentive." *Organizational Behavior and Human Performance.* 1968, 3, 157–189.

McGregor, D. *The Human Side of Enterprises.* McGraw-Hill, 1960.

Meyer, H. H., E. Kay, and J. R. French, Jr. "Split Roles in Performance Appraisal." *Harvard Business Review.* 1965, 43, 123–129.

Sisson, E. D. "Forced-Choice—the New Army Rating." *Personnel Psychology.* 1948, 1, 365–381.

Smith, P. C., and L. M. Kendall. "Retranslation of Expectations: An Approach to the Construction of Unambigious Anchors for Rating Scales." *Journal of Applied Psychology.* 1963, 47, 149–155.

Tiffin, J., and E. J. McCormick. *Industrial Psychology,* 5th ed. Prentice-Hall, 1965.

Tolle, E. R., and W. I. Murray. "Forced-Choice: An Improvement in Teacher Rating." *Journal of Educational Research.* 1958, 51 680–685.

Tosi, H. L., and S. J. Carroll. "Managerial Reactions to Management by Objectives." *Academy of Management Journal.* December 1968, 11, 415–426.

Tosi, H. L., and S. J. Carroll. "Some Structural Factors Related to Goal Influence in the Management by Objective Process." *Business Topics.* 1969, 45–50.

Tosi, H. L., and S. J. Carroll. "Management by Objectives." *Personnel Administrative.* 1970, 33, 44–48.

Tosi, H. L., and S. J. Carroll. "Some Factors Affecting the Success of 'Management by Objectives.' " *The Journal of Management Studies.* 1970, 209–223.

Tosi, H. L., J. R. Rizzo, and S. J. Carroll. "Setting Goals in Management by Objectives." *California Management Review.* 1970, 12, 70–78.

Whisler, T. L., and S. F. Harper. (Eds.) *Performance Appraisal: Research and Practice.* Holt, Rinehart and Winston, 1965.

Wikstrom, W. S. *Managing by and with Objectives.* National Industrial Conference Board, Personnel Board, Personnel Policy Study No. 212, 1968.

Zavala, A. "Development of the Forced-Choice Rating Scale Technique." *Psychological Bulletin.* 1965, 63, 117–124.

FOR DISCUSSION AND REVIEW

1 Distinguish between comparative and absolute standard rating procedures.

2 Briefly describe each of the following: straight ranking, paired comparisons, forced distribution, critical incidents, weighted checklists.

3 How is a forced choice rating scale developed?

4 What are the relative advantages and disadvantages of comparative and absolute standard systems? Of conventional ranking? Of MBO?

5 What are direct indexes? How can they be useful in performance appraisal?

Craig Eric Schneier

Multiple Rater Groups and Performance Appraisal

Performance appraisal (PA) is a vital organizational activity in that its results form the rationale for such important personnel decisions as promotion and merit raises. It also serves to pinpoint performance deficiencies that can be removed through training and/or motivational programs. The former objective of a PA system is measurement of performance, while the latter is development and improvement of performance.[1]

Because both the performance measurement and development functions of PA are necessary for organizational success, much has been written concerning the process. One suggestion frequently made urges organizations to use as many raters as possible in their PA systems and to consider the use of raters occupying various roles in relation to a ratee (e.g., subordinate, superior, peer, self, and/or field reviewers from the personnel staff).[2]

But this suggestion raises the following important questions regarding the implementation of PA programs: Are self-ratings generally overinflated? Would subordinate ratings of a superior be too lenient if they were not anonymous because subordinates would fear reprisal? Are peer ratings simply popularity contests? Are ratings by superiors too lenient because rating their people low makes *them* look bad? Do superiors and field reviewers observe ratees' performance too infrequently to obtain a true picture? Finally, should we expect ratings of various groups to agree or disagree, and if they disagree, how can we identify the accurate group?

The purpose of this discussion is to review the advantages and disadvantages of using multiple groups as raters. Most importantly, a set of techniques is explained whereby organizations can assess the perspectives of the potential rater groups, diagnose their degree of difference and similarity, and utilize the results of such a diagnosis to strengthen their PA system.

THE CASE FOR MULTIPLE RATER GROUPS

The use of raters from different groups or roles relative to a ratee, as opposed to relying solely upon superiors' ratings, offers certain potential advantages. First, multiple raters facilitate the generation of a larger data base upon which to make personnel decisions. Second, multiple raters facilitate the identification of any extremely biased or out-of-line ratings. Third, multiple rater groups allow for the assessment of performance from multiple perspectives or vantage points. For example, peers may be in the best position to assess a ratee's competence in interpersonal relations, superiors to assess technical expertise, and subordinates to assess leadership effectiveness. Likewise, field reviewers may be able to give "objective" ratings because they are removed from the superior-subordinate relationship, and self-ratings may be useful for ratees in jobs having no direct supervision. A broader spectrum of performance can thus be tapped by using multiple rater groups.

Fourth, multiple rater groups can be used to assess the reliability (i.e., consistency) of ratings as well as the sensitivity of the rating format. Agreement among different raters would be evidenced of inter-rater reliability. Finally, the use of

From *Public Personnel Management*, January–February 1977, pp. 13–20. Reprinted by permission of the International Personnel Management Association, 1313 East 60th Street, Chicago, Illinois 60637.

multiple rater groups would allow others beside superiors to participate directly in the PA process. This participation can foster a sense of commitment to the system, which may thus be seen as more than mere paperwork invented by the personnel staff. Commitment is a necessary prerequisite for accurate ratings.

MULTIPLE RATER GROUPS:
REASONS FOR DIVERGENT RATINGS

The potential advantages of using multiple rater groups are important; however, in an organization's haste to realize these advantages, it may ignore the reasons for differences in ratings gathered across the various groups. That is, when ratings of different groups are obtained, how should they be used? Often they are simply combined to enlarge the data base. But if rater groups' perspectives toward performance are divergent, such combinations would mask the differences and forfeit the potential benefits the different perspectives offer. Likewise, if perspectives toward performance are divergent across or within rater groups, combining ratings to assess their reliability or the sensitivity of a format would be like mixing apples and oranges. We would not expect the groups to agree and, when disagreements are found, would not know how to distinguish between the biased and the accurate raters.

There are three reasons why ratings from members of different groups would diverge. The extent of these differences can be diagnosed by the techniques described below and can either be lessened by one of several methods or taken into account in a PA system. Either option results in more accurate and useful ratings but also strengthens the PA system.

Perspective toward job performance

Raters from different groups each typically have a different perspective toward job performance based upon their own jobs. Thus, they may not only generate different appraisal criteria but may also weight a set of criteria differently. As noted above, peers often see the interpersonal aspects of job performance as most important since these aspects may influence them on a day-to-day basis. If a co-worker is difficult to work with—is offensive or autocratic—peers may rate him or her low overall. They would thus tend to prefer to use interpersonal criteria and perhaps weight them more heavily in their subjective judgments.

Superiors, on the other hand, may prefer the technical aspects of job performance, or dependability.[3] These impinge most heavily on their jobs. A subordinate who is not dependable (but who may be very personable) would cause problems for a superior and would typically be rated low. If superior *and* peer ratings are used, the criteria upon which the ratings are based may not be seen as equal by the two groups. Unless this divergence in perspective is accounted for as the ratings are made (by allowing each group to develop its own criteria and/or weight them separately), combined ratings would not be expected to converge.

Performance observation frequency

Different groups of raters are likely to have unequal frequencies of observation of a ratee's performance. For example, peers may observe performance over a longer period of time and have very frequent contacts with a ratee, and their ratings may reflect typical performance over an entire review period. Superiors may observe performance only intermittently, perhaps seeing a nonrepresentative sample of performance. This may result in halo, or the coloring of their entire evaluation based upon one or a few either exceptionally good or poor performance episodes. Of course, superiors may also observe primarily during peak periods or when crucial tasks are performed, and the resultant ratings could reflect performance under stress, an important piece of information. If a divergence in observation frequency across rater groups is noted and not remedied (for example, by urging superiors to make anecdotal records of performance over a long period of time), resultant combined ratings of different groups would be based on different samples of performance and thus may not converge.

Expectations due to role prescriptions

Members of different levels each behave according to role prescriptions—normative guidelines for proper behavior. Superiors, for example, attempt to behave like superiors; and it is often taken as a negative remark when someone is said not to "act" like the boss. In the PA setting, various role prescriptions can influence the judgments of raters. Superiors are typically less lenient and have higher expectations for performance due to their traditional roles as critics and evaluators of performance. Peers may be more lenient due to their roles as co-workers, colleagues, and friends. They are in the same boat and would not want to be rated too harshly themselves, so they may be a bit less critical.

Self-ratings are typically least critical.[4] Perhaps due to our selective perception, we tend to forget or repress our shortcomings in order to protect our favorable self-images. We may rationalize away the blame for poor performance to others ("Marketing gave me inflated sales forecasts!"), to the environment ("That machine never did work right!"), or to the tasks themselves ("This job is too much for any one person to do well!").

These divergent perspectives due to role prescriptions lead to different standards in rating. Thus, what the ratee may perceive as excellent performance, the peer may perceive as good performance and the superior may perceive as only fair performance. To combine ratings without accounting for, or changing, such divergent standards (perhaps by setting explicit, unambiguous definitions of various degrees of performance and communicating them to all raters) would be to ignore such real differences among raters, which could result in erroneous ratings.

DIAGNOSING DIFFERENCES AMONG RATER GROUPS

In order to account for the three types of differences across potential rater groups noted above, the extent of such differences must be assessed. This can be done by using three different data gathering techniques, each meant to assess one of the potential differences.

1 *Generating separate sets of criteria.* In order to assess their differences in perspective toward the job, each rater group could be called upon independently to generate its own set of appraisal criteria, criteria definitions, and weights to denote their relative importance. If the lists generally overlap, the perspectives among the different groups would be convergent enough to allow them to use the same set of criteria meaningfully, and combined ratings would thus be appropriate.

If there are notable differences among the criteria or their weights across groups, these can either be resolved through intergroup consensus and discussion aimed at compromise, decided by management and communicated to all groups, or taken into account in the ratings. In regard to the last alternative, suppose groups of peer raters and of superior raters substantially agree on six criteria while each feels a different three should also be used. The vantage points of each group can be effectively utilized by allowing both groups to give ratings on the six common criteria and each group to give ratings on its own additional three.

2 *Assessing observational frequencies.* The following procedure is used to assess the frequency with which members of each group have observed the behavior of ratees. First, groups each generate sets of critical incidents or behavioral statements[5] illustrative of various levels of performance on each appraisal criteria. Critical incidents are brief anecdotes of very effective or very ineffective behavior (*e.g.*, a description of effective behavior required to handle a customer complaint). Behavioral statements are statements of job incumbents' actual behavior (*e.g.*, "files reports with Director every six months," "inspects financial records," or "repairs machines when needed"). These should be written for each criteria to be used in PA (*e.g.*, leadership, work quality, dependability, report writing, cooperation, technical ability, etc.) and for different levels of performance (*e.g.*, excellent, good, fair, poor).

Next, the incidents and/or statements are edited and redundancies are removed. Then they are ordered by job dimension, or the performance criteria they were meant to illustrate, and each potential rater notes his or her perception of how frequently each behavior occurs among the entire group of ratees in a three- or six-month period. A five-point scale can be used. Figure 1 presents a form useful for this activity.

The mean frequencies for each behavior are calculated for each rater group. If the means are generally agreeable,[6] it can be inferred that members of the groups recall the behaviors as occurring equally often and hence have observed performance with similar frequency. Any notable discrepancies can be dealt with either by removing those particular aspects of performance from the appraisal process, by allowing only the group with the highest frequency of observation to evaluate those behaviors, or by allowing all groups to evaluate, but weighting their evaluations in proportion to their relative observation frequency. Other remedies include allowing for more frequent observation time of certain groups, urging certain raters to keep anecdotal records to augment their recall over periods of time between performance reviews, and setting up fixed observation intervals.

3 *Assessing differences in perspectives toward performance.* Differences in perspectives toward performance can also be assessed by utilizing critical incidents or behavioral statements (Figure 1). The incidents or statements are again placed on a sheet grouped according to the criterion for which they were written. Raters each then note what degree of performance on that criterion each of the specific behaviors illustrate by using a seven- or nine-point scale of values (*e.g.*, excellent performance to unacceptable performance). Figure 2 shows a form effective for this purpose. It is important that each performance criterion have a range of behaviors associated with it in order to observe the variance in degree of performance. If some criteria have only a few behaviors and/or have only ones that, upon reading, obviously illustrate either very good or very poor performance, additional behaviors should be written.

The mean scale values given to each behavior by the members of each rater group can then be computed and compared. Similar means indicate agreement across groups as to standards for performance, and thus their ratings could be combined fairly. Divergent means indicate different perspectives. Standard deviations for behaviors could also be calculated and would give evidence of degree of agreement *within* each group. If large standard deviations are found, it can be inferred that since the dispersion of the group was large, its members disagree regarding the value of the behavior.

Perhaps the superior group felt a certain behavior was evidence of only good performance (*e.g.*, mean scale value = 5.5), while the peer group felt it was evidence of excellent performance (*e.g.*, mean scale value = 6.9). The groups would be using

PERCEIVED FREQUENCY OF OCCURRENCE

INCIDENTS/BEHAVIORAL STATEMENTS	1 NEVER	2 ONCE OR TWICE PER MONTH	3 ONCE OR TWICE PER WEEK	4 ONCE OR TWICE PER DAY	5 SEVERAL TIMES PER DAY
1.					
2.					
3.					
4.					
etc.					

Fig. 1 Form for diagnosing potential raters' frequency of performance observation.

LEVEL OF PERFORMANCE ILLUSTRATED

INCIDENTS/BEHAVIORAL STATEMENTS	1 EXCELLENT	2 VERY GOOD	3 GOOD	4 AVERAGE	5 POOR	6 VERY POOR	7 UNACCEPT-ABLE
1.							
2.							
3.							
4.							
etc.							

Fig. 2 Form for diagnosing potential raters' perspectives toward performance.

different standards in this case, and their ratings would not be comparable. A single set of scale values could be decided upon and communicated to all raters, a compromise set could be used, or the different perspectives could be weighted in the final ratings. Raters could also be trained in workshops designed to explain the nature of leniency (or strictness) response set errors and their consequences in ratings in order to remove some divergence in scale values. Most importantly, however, the process described here would make explicit the perspectives different rater groups have.[7]

BENEFITS FOR THE APPRAISAL SYSTEM

The techniques explained above for diagnosing the degree of divergence between rater groups have, as their primary advantage, the facilitation of PA systems that are able to reap the benefits of using multiple rater groups. If no divergence among rater groups is found using these techniques, their ratings can be combined meaningfully to augment the PA data base, assess interrater reliability, and identify heavily biased raters. Where divergence is found in perspectives across groups, it can be used to enlarge the domain of criteria or of specific behaviors used in PA as each rater group is used to evaluate only those criteria for which it has meaningful information.

The divergent vantage points of different groups are thus used effectively rather than repressed in an attempt to gather data from as many raters as possible. Perspectives of any group that are based upon erroneous or scarce information or that are inconsistent with organizational objectives can be identified through these diagnostic procedures and hence changed through rater training, feedback of information, group discussion and compromise, or other means.

General benefits

However, in addition to these primary benefits, the diagnostic procedures explained above have several secondary benefits that also improve the PA system. By simply assessing the perspectives of various rater groups as a prerequisite to using them as actual raters, their participation in the PA system and hence their commitment is gained. As with most organizational programs, people take them seriously and take responsibility for making them effective through a feeling of ownership fostered by soliciting their participation.

The process of allowing different groups each to identify the PA criteria and weight them aids in the development of a set of criteria that tap all meaningful aspects of performance. Communicating the set of criteria developed by a group of supervisors for their subordinates to those subordinates is often itself an eye-opener. Subordinates are often surprised to see the criteria their superiors are using. Comparing lists of criteria across groups helps remove ambiguity felt in many jobs regarding what the required duties are.

Scaling specific behaviors as to degree of performance they illustrate identifies areas in which performance standards are either ambiguous, nonexistent, or conflict among potential raters. Expectations held by superiors can be fed back to subordinates to reduce role ambiguity and anxiety. The resultant scale values are themselves essentially a set of specific performance standards. Rater deficiencies, such as leniency or stereotyping, can also be identified through the scaling process.

Performance appraisal and the law

The behaviors or incidents developed in the manner described above can be used to help make PA formats less subjective and more job-related. With more frequency, courts are beginning to require that selection techniques be validated against a job-related, accurate PA system. In addition, any decisions based on PA data, such as promotions or layoffs, are in possible violation of EEO laws if they are not based upon a very specific, job-related PA system. The following statement illustrates this requirement:

> Using performance ratings for determining personnel layoffs was found to be in violation of Title VII of the Civil Rights Act when an employer failed to validate the appraisal methods according to EEOC guidelines. The evaluations were judged invalid because they were based on subjective observations (two or three evaluators did not observe the employee on a daily basis), evaluations were not administered and scored under controlled and standardized conditions.... The courts ordered the company to reinstate the employees with nominal back pay and required the company not to use performance ratings until they had been validated.[8]

This statement not only emphasizes the importance of job-related evaluations but also of assessing the frequency of performance observation for each rater. The diagnostic procedure explained above in Figure 1 can facilitate such an assessment. An appraisal system using actual job behaviors or incidents as its base goes a long way toward satisfying the courts' requirements and thus provides a safer system upon which to validate selection techniques.

In conclusion, this discussion has presented the potential advantages of using raters from multiple groups in PA as well as three reasons why these groups' ratings may typically diverge. These reasons were differences in perspectives toward the job, differences in frequency of observation of ratee performance, and different perspectives toward performance due to role prescriptions. As these differences occur, the practice of combining ratings of various groups may be harmful to a PA system as it masks true differences across the groups and thus denies the use of their respective vantage points in rating. Techniques were described whereby the degree of each of these differences can be diagnosed accurately and in a practical manner and incorporated into a PA system. The resultant PA system is more objective and job-related and better able to comply with anti-discrimination legislation.

Performance appraisal is one of the most vital yet complex organizational activities related to public personnel management. It is vital due to the importance of decisions that hinge on its results; it is complex because it not only effects all other human resource programs (*e.g.*, wage and salary administration, training and development, selection and placement) but also because, at bottom, it relies so heavily on human judgment. Reducing the bias, error, inconsistency, and anxiety associated with the process of people judging others is a key to any effective PA system. Adopting a policy of using raters from different groups can facilitate effective PA's, but the full range of assumptions and consequences of such a policy must be diagnosed and built into the operational PA system in order to reap its full potential.

NOTES

1 L. L. Cummings and D. P. Schwab, *Performance in Organizations* (Glenview, Illinois: Scott, Foresman and Co., 1973).

2 See, for example, R. S. Barrett, *Performance Rating* (Chicago: Science Research Associates, Inc., 1966); J. P. Campbell *et al. Managerial Behavior, Performance and Effectiveness* (New York City: McGraw-Hill Book Company, 1970); W. L. French, *The Personnel Management Process* (Boston: Houghton Mifflin Company, 1974); M. E. Haynes, "Improving Performance

Through Employee Discussions," *Personnel Journal,* 49 (1970), pp. 138–141; and E. E. Lawler, "The Multitrait—Multirater Approach to Measuring Managerial Job Performance," *Journal of Applied Psychology,* 51 (1967), pp. 369–381.

3   Such an occurrence has been substantiated in several research studies. See, for example, W. Borman, "The Ratings of Inidviduals in Organizations: An Alternate Approach," *Organizational Behavior and Human Performance,* 12 (1974), pp. 105–124.

4   For research results supporting these statements, see R. J. Klimoski and M. London, "Role of the Rater in Performance Appraisal," *Journal of Applied Psychology,* 59 (1974), pp. 445–451; G. C. Thornton, "The Relationship Between Supervisory and Self-Appraisals of Executive Performance," *Personnel Psychology,* 21 (1968), pp. 441–451; S. Zedeck *et al.,* "Development of Behaviorally Anchored Rating Scales as a Function of Organizational Level," *Journal of Applied Psychology,* 59 (1974), pp. 249–252.

5   A detailed discussion of the entire process of developing behavioral statements is contained in Richard W. Beatty and Craig Eric Schneier, *Personnel Administration: An Experiential/Skill Building Approach* (Reading, Massachusetts: Addison-Wesley Publishing Co., Inc., forthcoming). Critical incidents are discussed in W. K. Kirchner and M. D. Dunnette, "Identifying the Critical Factors in Successful Salesmanship," *Personnel,* 34 (1957), pp. 54–59.

6   Statistical procedures for assessing whether mean differences are statistically significant or due merely to chance, such as the *t*-test, can be found in any introductory statistics text.

7   The process described here for generating behavioral statements or critical incidents can be used as part of a complete behaviorally anchored rating scale PA system. For discussions of the development, uses, and advantages of such a system, see Campbell *et al., op. cit.;* Cummings and Schwab, *op. cit.;* and Beatty and Schneier, *op. cit.*

8   See W. H. Holley and H. S. Feild, "Performance Appraisal and the Law," Labor Law Journal, 26 (1975), p. 428, which cites the relevant court cases.

FOR DISCUSSION AND REVIEW

1   What are the potential advantages of using multiple rater groups?
2   How can role prescriptions determine a person's judgment of others when appraising their performance?
3   Outline the author's solution to the multiple rater/role prescription problem. What are the benefits of such a solution?
4   How could the problem of divergent perspectives toward performance across organizational levels impact on the legality of appraisal systems from an equal-employment-opportunity perspective?

B. BEHAVIORALLY BASED AND EFFECTIVENESS-BASED APPRAISAL METHODS

William J. Kearney

The Value of Behaviorally Based Performance Appraisals

Employee performance appraisal is typically considered by managers to be necessary, but difficult and usually unpleasant. Such appraisals seem to promise so much for the effective and efficient functioning of organizations, yet they often deliver so little. At times, they create as many problems, or more, than they solve; the aftereffects often defeat their purposes, and the residue of ill feeling lingers on and on.

A review of the literature on performance appraisal instruments suggests the following:

- Much effort has been devoted to developing or refining a single appraisal system to serve both judgmental and developmental needs.
- An appraisal instrument which will cover many different jobs and more than one organization level is still being sought.
- Most appraisal instruments are based on the assumption that it is easy to determine how performance might be improved.
- A pervasive assumption is that good performance is due almost exclusively to individual effort, and other factors play a very minor role.
- Appraisal instruments show an overriding concern for eliminating appraiser bias and achieving objectivity.
- Inexpensive appraisal instruments are preferable to more expensive ones.

A SINGLE APPRAISAL SYSTEM

Even if we recognize only two categories of appraisal needs, judgmental and developmental, it should be clear that a single instrument cannot satisfy both if the data requirements are different. Organizations obviously must have some basis on which to make important human resource decisions. For example, suppose there are several candidates eligible for promotion but a limited number of positions available. Who is to be promoted? Again, assume there are limited funds for raises and there are several people with expectations for more money. Who should receive raises and how much should be given? Or, suppose the staff must be reduced. Who should be released first?

These are important and tough problems which require *judgmental* decisions, and managers need an appraisal instrument to help make the decisions. The final judgments reflect an evaluation of a person's performance, but typically there is little follow-up of a remedial nature to benefit the individual. Data necessary to help *improve* performance are often not generated by appraisal instruments which are designed primarily to judge results or achievements. It is up to the worker and the supervisor to identify effective means of getting results.

However, employees often need to have behavioral guidelines to improve performance. These guidelines must be specific, goal oriented, job related, and within an individual's control. Appraisal instruments that concentrate on personality

From *Business Horizons* 19, no. 3 (June 1976): 75–83. Copyright © 1976, by the Foundation for the School of Business at Indiana University. Reprinted with permission.

traits (industriousness, responsibility) and getting results (management by objectives) offer little help in the way of specifying to the individual controllable behavior that improves performance. Appraisal instruments that seek to provide data indicating how performance might be improved, and for which remedial prescriptions are behaviorally based, are *developmental.* Such performance data facilitate developmental decisions. Judgmental and developmental needs are typically not met equally well by a single appraisal instrument. In the past, judgmental needs have prevailed in the design and use of appraisal instruments.

A GENERALIZED INSTRUMENT

Time and money are needed to construct and administer valid and reliable performance appraisal instruments. When an organization attempts to do an outstanding job and incurs considerable expense, it desires to spread these costs by using the instrument in several jobs and at more than one organization level. Also, a common appraisal instrument is easier for all to use once the mechanics of it are understood. Yet these advantages are offset by sacrificing specificity in isolating important determinants of performance or results for a job or job category. Thus, whatever one gains in generality comes at the cost of precision; whatever one gains in precision comes at the cost of generality. This is a basic dilemma in performance appraisal systems that must be kept in mind.

IDENTIFYING EFFECTIVE BEHAVIORS

Many appraisal instruments do not direct the individual to specific ways of improving performance. The assumption seems to be that if a person knows where he stands, the way to improvement is self-evident and appropriate new behavior is not only clear but will be forthcoming. Yet performance appraisal instruments seldom differentiate between behaviors that lead to results and behaviors that do not. That is, the process or means of achieving results is not identified. If this were so, many of the problems in the aftermath of performance appraisal would be eliminated. It is not a case, usually, of a person knowing how to be more effective and being unwilling, but rather it is a matter of not knowing the more effective behaviors. If performance appraisal is to improve individual performance, the instrument must show how to get results.

One false assumption in most performance appraisal instruments is that results achieved are almost exclusively the product of a person's individual effort. For example, a person's effectiveness may be influenced by environmental factors over which he has little control. These environmental factors may fluctuate to help him look good at times, and at other times may make him look bad. Thus, the economy itself or variation in the quality of raw materials may determine effectiveness as much as the effort expended. Appraisal instruments that are used to dispense rewards and make recommendations on improving performance should identify those things over which an individual has control and can change.

A key factor in motivation is establishing a close link between performance and reward. Performance appraisal instruments that fail to relate individual contributions to results and differentiate between effective and less effective behavior fail to establish a link between performance and reward. Additionally, they fail to provide important data for managers interested in helping their subordinates improve. The fact that the relationship between individual behavior and results is not a direct, one-to-one relationship needs to be recognized more clearly.

CONCERN WITH OBJECTIVITY

Performance appraisal instruments go to great lengths to eliminate appraiser bias. The development of such instruments seems to follow closely the efforts to eliminate a variety of errors such as halo effect, leniency and central tendency. Indeed, various techniques to guard against these errors were often the precipitating factor in the development of new instruments. Unfortunately, almost lost in this concern is proper attention to two fundamental questions about the purpose of any appraisal instrument: (1) Does it generate information that helps in an important judgmental decision? (2) Does it generate developmental information that can help an individual change his job behavior to get better results in the future? Though the concern over bias is well founded, it should not overshadow these two important questions which are the mainspring of performance appraisal.

COST OF APPRAISALS

Organizations much prefer inexpensive performance appraisal instruments to more expensive ones. This is understandable. After all, performance appraisal is a peripheral matter in many organizations, and costs can be reduced there without noticeable effects. Also, just about anyone who has been involved in performance appraisal has some bad feelings about it. But the inexpensive performance appraisal system often leads to the problems and negative feelings that are found in far too many organizations. Our myopia on costs hides the fact that a well-designed appraisal system may deliver far more than it costs by improving judgmental and developmental decisions regarding human resources, and may avoid most of the negative aftereffects that linger on. Costs must be balanced against returns.

BEHAVIORALLY BASED SCALES

No single system can deal effectively with all of the problems encountered in performance appraisal. Behaviorally based performance appraisal is no exception. However, it deals more adequately with the assignment than most other systems, such as trait rating, ranking, forced distribution, critical incidents and management by objectives. The major characteristics that distinguish behaviorally based performance appraisal are these:

- It emphasizes development goals.
- It is job specific.
- It identifies definite, observable and measurable behavior.
- It differentiates between behavior, performance and effectiveness (results).

... Emphasize development

Substantial improvement in performance appraisal is achieved by the adoption of management by objectives (MBO). MBO identifies what is important in organizations—results. It involves goal setting, participation of subordinates and feedback on performance. Perhaps the major factor in its successful application is the system's focus on a well-defined goal; the results desired are clearly specified. People either achieve results or they do not. Either way, they know where they stand. Judgmental decisions are easier under an MBO system, and data are there to support such decisions. However, when individuals do not achieve the desired results, the reason is not always clear. MBO does not produce information on how people do or do not get results; that is, what behaviors are more effective and others less so. It only tells what happened. Behaviorally based performance appraisal is an important supplement to MBO because it attempts to get at the *how* of performance. It identifies effective behaviors known to produce consistently superior performance leading to results against which actual behavior may be compared. Hence, it is an especially powerful developmental tool.

... Are job specific

Behaviorally based performance instruments are tailored to the characteristics of a job or job family. They pinpoint explicit behaviors that are critical to effective performance, thereby providing job-based information to individuals that will lead to getting results. Most appraisal instruments are designed to cover a broad category of jobs. Since they are neither derived from nor tailored to a specific job, they cannot provide the developmental help found in behavioral scales.

... Use observable behavior

Behavioral scales identify the critical areas of performance for a job, and describe more effective and less effective job behaviors in getting results. Moreover, appraisers record the specific, observable job behavior of the worker and compare it to behaviors listed on the scale. The outcome is a comparison of actual behavior with behavior previously determined to be more or less effective. Subordinates and managers alike can then see the difference between what behavior occurs and what should occur. Moreover, subordinates know exactly how they should behave to be more effective. Most present-day appraisal systems do not provide these all-important diagnostic data.

... Make important distinctions

Behaviorally based performance appraisals make important distinctions between behavior, performance and effectiveness.

> *Behavior* is simply what people do in the course of work (e.g., dictating letters, giving directions, sweeping the floor, etc.). *Performance* is behavior that has been evaluated (i.e., measured) in terms of its contribution to the goals of the organization. Finally, *effectiveness* refers to some summary index of organizational outcomes for which an individual is at least partially responsible, such as unit profit, unit turnover, amount produced, sales, salary level, or level reached in the organization. The crucial distinction between performance and effectiveness is that the latter does not refer to behavior directly but rather is a function of additional factors not under the control of the individual (e.g., state of the economy, nepotism, quality of raw materials, etc.)[1]

Behavioral scales concentrate on behavior and performance since these are controllable by the individual. In addition to human behavior and performance, effectiveness is a product of other factors. If more effective behaviors can be distinguished from the less effective, and if individuals adopt those behaviors that are more effective, their performance will most likely lead to the desired results. Behavioral scales, then, attempt to enhance the individual's control over result-producing behavior. Most other appraisal instruments do not make these crucial distinctions between behavior, performance and effectiveness.

---

[1]   John P. Campbell, Marvin D. Dunnette, Richard D. Arvey and Lowell V. Hellervik, "The Development and Evaluation of Behaviorally Based Rating Scales," *Journal of Applied Psychology* (February 1973), p. 15.

CONSTRUCTING THE SCALE

The development of a behaviorally based performance appraisal instrument is accomplished in the following steps.

1 Identify the jobs to which the instrument will be applied, because the supervisors or managers of those positions will develop and use the instrument to evaluate their subordinates' performance.

2 Ask the managers to write several (five to ten) specific statements that reflect particularly effective performance on the part of subordinates occupying the positions being studied. Then have them write statements reflecting ineffective performance. These statements are to be drawn from the managers' own experiences and are to be examples of actual observed behavior of those who are or have been employed in the jobs being studied.

3 To begin the process of translating the statements of effective and ineffective performance into scales, the scale designers sort each statement into a homogeneous category which reflects a common performance dimension. Any statements that are vague, unobservable or duplications should be omitted at this point.

4 Only statements describing extremely effective or ineffective performance have thus far been gathered. Now, managers should be asked to write statements describing specific, observable behavior that falls between the extremes on each performance dimension. This step will establish a continuum of job-based behavior from very effective to very ineffective. Again, statements that are duplicates, vague or unobservable should be removed.

5 Last is the retranslation or cross checking phase. Working from the several homogeneous categories of behavior developed by the scale designers in the initial translation, managers are asked to sort each specific behavioral statement into the category it most clearly fits. They should then scale each behavioral statement in its category on a seven or nine point scale (one=most ineffective and seven or nine=most effective). Behavioral statements which are assigned to a category by at least 75% of the respondents will be retained, since at this level the statement is interpreted in a consistent way. With respect to scaling, the means and standard deviations should be calculated for all of the items rated by the managers. This is done to identify and retain those statements for which there is high agreement among the managers on the scale value of the behavioral statement. Typically, if the standard deviation of the item is less than 1.5, the item is retained.[2]

Examples of scaled statements along performance dimensions are shown in Figures 1 and 2. A complete behaviorally based performance instrument would contain approximately ten or twelve such scale dimensions.

Administration of the instrument is very similar to that of the critical incidents technique. In order to overcome the limitations of recall and the tendency for humans to stress recent events, the manager who is appraising his subordinates should regularly observe and record examples of their behavior in the form of behavioral statements reflecting observed job performance. Such behavior is expressed in brief statements much like those contained in the scaled job dimensions. If performance appraisal occurs yearly or every six months, the manager should space out instances when subordinates will be observed briefly so that a representative sample of job performance is obtained. The time allocation for observation of a subordinate may be as short as two or three minutes.

---

[2]   Ibid., p. 16.

	Could be expected to exchange a blouse purchased in a distant town and to impress the customer so much that she would buy three dresses and three pairs of shoes.
Could be expected to smooth things over beautifully with an irate customer who returned a sweater with a hole in it and turn her into a satisfied customer.	
	Could be expected to be friendly and tactful and to agree to reline a coat for a customer who wants a new coat because the lining had worn out in "only" two years.
Could be expected to courteously exchange a pair of gloves that are too small.	
	Could be expected to handle the after-Christmas rush of refunds and exchanges in a reasonable manner.
Could be expected to make a refund for a sweater only if the customer insists.	
	Could be expected to be quite abrupt with customers who want to exchange merchandise for a different color or style.
Could be expected to tell a customer that a "six-week-old" order could not be changed even though the merchandise had actually been ordered only two weeks previously.	
	Could be expected to tell a customer who tried to return a shirt bought in Hawaii that a store in the States had no use for a Hawaiian shirt.

Fig. 1 Department manager job behavior rating scale for the dimension "handling customer complaints and making adjustments." (From John P. Campbell, Marvin D. Dunnette, Edward E. Lawler III, Karl E. Weick, Jr., *Managerial Behavior, Performance, and Effectiveness.* Copyright 1970 by the McGraw-Hill Book Company. Used with permission of McGraw-Hill Book Company.)

As the appraisal period draws near, the manager should refer to the diary of observations. Each statement is assigned to the dimension it most closely fits, and is scaled on the seven or nine point scale, again on the basis of closeness of fit to the statements originally placed on the scale. After all statements reflecting observed job performance have been scaled, the mean scale value should be calculated for each job dimension and recorded on a summary sheet. Thus, specific, observed behavior concerning job performance is then available for use in feedback to the subordinates. Just as important, data are available for developmental purposes which indicate how subordinates can improve their performance, because more effective behaviors in important job performance dimensions are indicated as well as those which are less effective.

ADVANTAGES, LIMITATIONS, COST

Several advantages over other appraisal methods are to be found in a behaviorally anchored performance appraisal instrument. First, appraisals are based on samples

Could be expected never to be late in meeting deadlines, no matter how unusual the circumstances.

Could be expected to meet deadlines comfortably by delegating the writing of an unusually high number of orders to two highly rated selling associates.

Could be expected always to get his associates' work schedules made out on time.

Could be expected to fail to schedule additional help to complete orders on time.

Could be expected to offer to do the orders at home after failing to get them out on the deadline day.

Could be expected to meet seasonal ordering deadlines within a reasonable length of time.

Could be expected to be late all the time on weekly buys for his department.

Could be expected to disregard due dates in ordering and run out of a major line in his department.

Could be expected to leave order forms in his desk drawer for several weeks even when they had been given to him by the buyer after calling his attention to short supplies and due dates for orders.

Fig. 2 Department manager job behavior rating scale for the dimension "meeting day-to-day deadlines." (From John P. Campbell, Marvin D. Dunnette, Edward E. Lawler III, Karl E. Weick, Jr., *Managerial Behavior, Performance, and Effectiveness.* Copyright 1970 by the McGraw-Hill Book Company. Used with permission of McGraw-Hill Book Company.)

of actual observed behavior taken at regular intervals. There is no attempt to focus on personality traits, which are not only hard to define and measure, but which may be rated in different ways by various appraisers. Moreover, traits may be difficult to change even if carefully identified and their relationship to performance is questionable.

Second, behavioral data gathered in the appraisal process indicate what behaviors have led to specific results, and more effective behaviors can be identified for the purpose of helping the manager improve output. This is usually not the case with trait rating, forced distribution, narratives, MBO and most other appraisal systems. While MBO has the distinct advantage of being results-oriented and indicates whether or not a manager has achieved preset goals, decidedly less information is generated concerning the more effective and less effective behaviors that lead to goal achievement.

Third, the appraisal instrument is used by those who developed it. The process of concentrating attention in the design stage on defining effective and ineffective performance encourages precision in definition and care in measurement, as well as more care in later observations of employee performance. Thus, managers become more discriminating in their observations.

Fourth, the process of generating the behaviorally anchored scale has several important spin-offs. The behavioral statements might be used as criteria to evaluate predictors for selection and promotion decisions. Or, they could serve as the basis for a management training program, with most ineffective behaviors being discouraged and most effective behaviors being reinforced as they occur in the development process.

Fifth, behaviorally based performance appraisal can provide a check on the understanding of policies at the organizational level to which they are applied. In step five of constructing the scale, the behavioral statements that do not enjoy high agreement among the raters are discarded. Yet these items are an important data source for the organization. If any of them concern policies, it is clear there is confusion over them. Therefore, the policies must be clarified so that the preferred behavior is identified and encouraged.[3] Last, we should not overlook the opportunity behaviorally based performance appraisal presents for increased communications with employees at the outset of their employment, or at the beginning of a new position. Such an appraisal system points out to the person before work begins critical areas of performance that will be judged.[4]

Behaviorally based performance appraisal, like every other appraisal system, has its limitations or drawbacks. The most important practical ones center around the conditions for its use. There must be several managers available to develop the scales. A dozen managers would be a minimum to generate sufficient data, sort the behaviors and then scale them. There must be a large number of subordinates performing the job for which more and less effective behaviors are to be identified and scales developed. The development of behaviorally anchored performance scales is time consuming and expensive. Since the scales are tailored to a specific job, a large number of people should be engaged in a given job so that the costs of design and construction can be spread widely. Last, managers who use the scales must have the opportunity on a systematic basis to observe the behavior of their subordinates.

The cost of developing behaviorally based performance appraisals is largely in the time managers are away from their other duties during the design and construction phase. Also, during initial adoption, a consultant may be hired to introduce the system, answer questions and provide guidance on the first scales. Two and a half or three days should be allowed for the development of the instrument. Since the cost of the system is largely in the managers' time, the total can be quickly calculated. The cost can easily appear to be quite high, and therefore discouraging, especially when the returns or benefits are not as easily quantified and totaled. Keep in mind, however, that a well-designed and administered MBO system is likely to be no less expensive. Inexpensive appraisal systems are fictitiously inexpensive. In reality, they often generate inaccurate and irrelevant data that can mislead management. If managers wish to have appraisal systems that produce useful data that can be used with confidence, they must expect to make a reasonable expenditure to generate such data.

No single appraisal system is equally effective in satisfying all appraisal needs. All have their strong and weak points. Those that require little time and effort, and that are inexpensive, usually offer little help in making important decisions about human resource utilization, or provide little direction in developing human resources. MBO and its focus on results has been a big step forward for employee

---

[3]   Milton R. Blood, "Spin-Offs from Behavioral Expectation Scale Procedures," *Journal of Applied Psychology* (August 1974), pp. 513–515.

[4]   James G. Goodale, "How to Improve Ratings of Employee Performance," *The Canadian Personnel and Industrial Relations Journal* (January 1975), pp. 20–24.

appraisal. There is little question that in performing a job, results are what count. Yet, in spite of the logic of MBO and its ability to target the proper focus of appraisal, it often does not provide a key ingredient in helping employees improve their ability to get results. MBO tells us whether or not an employee gets results. It does not tell us much about how the results were achieved, or more important, what behaviors are associated with getting results.

Behaviorally based performance appraisal is designed for that purpose. It is an important supplement to results-oriented appraisal. It recognizes that results are not solely determined by an individual's performance. Behaviorally based performance appraisal pinpoints the individual's contribution to results since it focuses on specific behaviors that are controllable. Inherent in behaviorally based appraisal is the generation of specific job-centered prescriptions for improving performance. No other appraisal instrument provides developmental data in such a direct and practical manner.

FOR DISCUSSION AND REVIEW

1 What are the two major objectives of an appraisal system? Why is it difficult for one system to meet both?
2 Review the key characteristics of behaviorally based scales that distinguish them from other types of scales.
3 Explain, sequentially, the procedure for designing a set of behaviorally based scales.
4 What are the disadvantages of these scales? Why might they be costly to develop and use?

S. J. Carroll, Jr.

H. L. Tosi

Implementation of MBO

SOME ORGANIZATIONAL CONSIDERATIONS

Some broad-policy problems must be resolved before MBO can effectively be implemented. For example, MBO must be integrated with the other components of the formal structure, such as the subsystems of budgeting, man-power planning, appraisal, and development. If such compatibility does not exist, several problems may arise in the future, as in the case study of an English firm cited earlier, in which there was no integration of the subsystems with the MBO program.[1]

There must be some consideration given to the manner in which goal setting will take place. Some advocates of MBO would argue for a fairly formalized and scheduled series of meetings between superiors and subordinates to ensure that the conditions for effective goal setting are present. Others argue that goal set-ting should be the responsibility of the superior and the subordinate and that how it is done should be left to them.

Such mechanistic questions as the following: What kind of appraisal forms are to be used? How are they to be used? Should the interview between the boss and the subordinate be the primary vehicle for the evaluation, or should the eva-luation be recorded on some form? must be resolved. More important, however is the answer to the question: What should be the content of the interview? Meyer, Kay, and French suggested the separation of discussions about performance from salary considerations.[2] Also in an English case study, the separation of per-formance review from the establishment of merit pay increases seemed to result in fewer problems.[3] However, when performance and compensation are discussed separately, it becomes very difficult for the individual to link performance with salary and promotion, thus potentially reducing the effectiveness of salary as an incentive. Previous research has shown that managers who perceive a relation-ship between performance and the reward system perform at a higher level.[4] Thus, if management prefers to link incentives and performance, goal accom-plishment and salary can be considered at the same time.

Frequency of performance appraisal is an important issue. There should be at least one required annual performance review. This should be supplemented with intermittent reviews. Our research suggests that the frequency of perfor-mance review is related to many positive managerial attitudes and to higher per-formance.

Once an individual's performance has been evaluated and discussed exten-sively with him, how much of the information gleaned from this process needs to be submitted to higher levels of management, recorded in his personnel file, and made generally available to others in the organization? What information should be provided to the subordinate? Such information may have substantial impact on an individual's future in the organization and must be handled with care.

In the event that a manager lacks the necessary skills to set goals or ap-praise performance, will some sort of training effort be available? Or should the development of these skills be the responsibility of one's immediate superior? If there are deficiencies, especially in goal setting, the whole MBO process breaks down. Because this skill is so critical to the success of MBO, its development should be provided for either by training or intensive coaching.

Once major goal areas have been set at the top-management level, the free-dom of action that lower and middle managers have in choosing their own goals should be interfered with only when necessary. However, if the original goals have been formally recorded, a change in them should be made formally. Other-wise, at the end of the appraisal period, goals that are no longer relevant will still be listed on a form, and a manager may well become uneasy. In later periods when the form on which the original goals were recorded is examined by others, a manager might be evaluated as a failure because he did not achieve those parti-cular goals.

The answers to all these questions will serve as a guide in the implementa-tion of MBO and are problems that top management must contend with before attempting to implement any type of formal MBO system.

MANAGERIAL RESISTANCE TO MBO

Individuals may not be fully receptive to a formal MBO program. Although most managers no doubt feel that the philosophy of MBO is an important one—one that they believe that they use—a formal program will cause some problems and encounter some managerial resistance to change. Some of the problems are those discussed in Chapter 2. In addition, there were also some subtle indications of resistance to MBO in the interview study described in that chapter, although most of these were encountered in such a way that they were difficult to document.

Time expenditures

"I've always managed this way. Why do I have to spend time in training? Why do I need to write these goals? My people know what is expected." Comments such as these indicate that some managers feel that the determination of objectives takes an unreasonable amount of time. There is little question that the development and statement of objectives and subsequent programs of action will take a great deal of a manager's effort and time. When a formal MBO program is used, the manager must communicate the goals and objectives of the organization. These must be developed and prepared in such a way that they can be clearly stated to his subordinates, as well as to his superiors. This means that a manager will be forced to spend time, which may be in very short supply for him, to prepare his objectives and to assist his subordinates in preparing their objectives in such a way as to facilitate communication.

Subordinate deficiencies

Another problem is that some managers may not believe their subordinates capable of using MBO because they lack the adequate decision discretion necessary to participate effectively in MBO or are not competent enough to make the proper decisions. However, what is more likely to be the case is that managers who resist MBO are either underestimating the competence of their subordinates or rationalizing their own unwillingness to allow additional subordinate involvement and participation.

Erosion of authority

Because of subordinate participation in setting objectives, a superior may feel that he is losing some control, that his authority is being eroded. This concern probably arises from a lack of understanding of the relationship among participation, discretion, and decision parameters. To participate means that an individual has influence on the decision. If subordinates do, in fact, participate in decision making, their input should be valued and used when appropriate. Essentially, the subordinate must have some discretion to act in the area in which he is participating. (Discretion can come either from a general policy or from the delegation of responsibility and authority by a superior.) However, in some cases, it may not be appropriate for the subordinate to influence the decision, for instance, parameters such as budget limitations imposed by top management may make certain decisions nonnegotiable. What is of utmost importance in this case is that the subordinate know what these nonnegotiable areas are. In this way, there is better understanding between the superior and the subordinate as to which areas the subordinate may participate in, and which areas he cannot participate in.

Lack of planning ability

MBO forces managers, especially at the top levels, to look ahead to the future. In two organizations studied, the authors found a great deal of reluctance on the part of certain high-level but very disorganized managers to look ahead and establish specific objectives for their organizational units. As MBO forces an analysis of the future, managers who are reluctant to do this may resist MBO.

Status of the group proposing the program

In the University of Kentucky studies cited earlier, a new MBO program was more successful when it was initiated by the top-management group than when it was initiated by the personnel department.[5] Certainly perceptions of the initiator will influence acceptance. Initiators of any new program who are perceived by others to be of low status, low competence, untrustworthy, or who are disliked because of past behavior will have difficulty in gaining acceptance for their suggested programs.

MBO as a "club"

Some managers feel that MBO is a club used by the organization or superiors to compel them to perform at higher levels than they are able to. In an unpublished study, Stein, who interviewed several hundred managers participating in an MBO program[6] found that a manager may feel that he is forced to commit himself to unrealistic or undesirable goals simply because he is unable to argue effectively against such goals.

The MBO cycle and work cycle

Other planning and work cycles may not be compatible with the formal MBO cycle. For example, sometimes there will be scheduled evaluations whose dates may not coincide with the planning and control cycles of the various units in the organization. The end of the fiscal year may be the time specified for the annual performance evaluation under MBO, but some units may be operating on a calendar-year basis. This means that different goal-setting and evaluation cycles would be appropriate for them. Different cycles must be taken into account.

Dislike of the performance review requirements

When MBO is implemented, the intended review and feedback may not take place as needed or required. Many managers make the mistaken assumption that when they interact with their subordinates, the subordinates receive feedback about their performance. Such is not the case. When goals are set in MBO, they represent a statement of the superior's expectation of the subordinate's work and provide the subordinate with guidelines delineating his responsibilities and activities. Having these stated in "objective form" leads the individual to expect some feedback. When performance feedback is not forthcoming, particularly with respect to goals set, he may be somewhat upset, frustrated, and concerned with how he is being evaluated. Therefore, if MBO does create an expectancy for feedback, we must ensure that it occurs *and that the subordinate perceives it as feedback.* Some managers dislike the face-to-face discussion of performance with their subordinates. One manager interviewed by one of the authors indicated that he hated to review performance with his subordinates. This activity caused him considerable discomfort and was decidedly unpleasant to him. He did not like the MBO program, preferring instead the old performance review program, which involved using groups of superiors from several levels to review the performance of engineering personnel. Obviously he liked the group evaluation because he could share responsibility for his judgments and suggestions.

Paper-work problems

In our research we have found paper work to be an irritant for a certain number of managers. There is no doubt that more work is involved for the MBO manager. Goals and evaluations should be documented, which means additional forms. Becoming bogged down in paper work does reduce time for other managerial activities. However, it is possible that the paper-work syndrome is simply the easiest rationalization for failing to use MBO. Furthermore, it has been our experience that this is only an initial response. Later, managers are more willing to use the MBO system and prepare a goal statement, if the program is implemented with the true support and assistance of top management.

IMPLEMENTATION OF MBO

To implement MBO, an integrated, well-designed program should be developed that will enhance the chances of MBO's acceptance by managers and will contribute to its effectiveness. Like any new program, MBO must be fully understood; managers must know why and how it works. In addition, they must both be motivated to use it and have the ability to implement it. The implementation effort should take place in at least three stages: learning, implementation, and follow-up.

The learning phase

There are some important skills that managers must develop before they can use MBO effectively. In addition, there are various types of information that will facilitate its use. The following areas are of utmost importance and must be covered in the "learning phase."

What MBO is Managers must know as much as possible about MBO and its value. Emphasis must be placed on the planning aspect as well as on the goal-setting and appraisal dimensions of MBO. In the learning phase, theory and practice should be tied together. Managers should examine the value of participation, feedback, and goal-setting and learn how these relate to performance and satisfaction on the job. The details of goal setting in the organization must be discussed, in addition to the sequencing of goal-setting and evaluation activities. These can be tied in with other organizational activities, such as budgeting, performance evaluation, salary, and promotional review.

The management philosophy and MBO Managers must know how MBO fits into the general philosophical framework of management in the organization. This is especially important because MBO and top-management philosophy must be consistent. Simply verbalizing support for MBO is not enough to ensure its implementation. However, the process of thinking through the relationship between MBO and management philosophy, especially by top management, forces the kind of commitment and decisions that must be made prior to implementing MBO. Managers, especially those at the higher levels, are also forced to become aware of the problems that will be encountered in the future and, more importantly, to think of specific ways to resolve these problems.

Goal setting Managers should know in what ways the general objectives of the organization can be broken down into meaningful objectives for lower-level units. Translation of general objectives into operational terms for lower levels must be part of the training effort. For example, objectives can be viewed as means-end chains to show that the goals and objectives of one unit are the means used by a higher-level unit to achieve its objectives. An understanding of means-end chains is thus helpful in the determination of lower-unit objectives.

Certain training techniques, such as the problem-solving methods of Kepner and Tregoe, and Maier, may be very helpful in goal setting.[7] After all, goals may be viewed as a type of problem to be solved, and the ability to define well the problems to be solved can facilitate the development of various solution strategies.

Managers must know the difference between objectively and subjectively measured goals. This becomes especially acute in the appraisal process and in the development of performance measures, as the nature of the performance standards will have an impact on managerial performance. Because grave misunderstanding can result from using poorly developed and understood performance standards as a basis for evaluation, managers must know the difficulties in the development of effective evaluation criteria.

Appraisal Part of the training should focus on appraisal. Role playing can make managers more aware of the difficulty of conducting appraisal interviews. For example, defensiveness resulting from criticism can be brought out more directly when experienced in role playing. Using the appropriate training methods, managers can learn techniques to reduce defensiveness in the appraisal process.

Summary Once these subject areas have been covered in detail, managers are in a better position to know the relationship between MBO and their job. This understanding, developed through active participation and involvement in the learning phase, will facilitate the use of MBO on the job.

An external consultant might be extremely helpful in this phase of the introduction. The practicing manager probably has neither the time nor the inclination to develop an understanding and explanation of the underlying theory of MBO; he is more concerned with practice. The consultant can bring to bear experiences and skills in training managers to use MBO, and can make certain that the manager is exposed to both the positive and negative aspects of MBO.

Training for MBO, however, may cause some of the resistance to it. As many managers may believe that they use it already or that another approach is more effective for them, training is directed at changing a managerial style. This means that the training process must allow the participants the opportunity to practice the skills, assess them, and ultimately arrive at their own judgment regarding the advantages of MBO. Thus, extensive time during the program should be devoted not only to the discussion of how MBO works but to the opportunity to understand the benefits derived from it as well as the typical problems encountered with it.

Essentially, the learning process described so far will increase knowledge of MBO and develop basic skills, but it cannot guarantee that MBO will be used effectively on the job. Thus, the learning phase represents only the first step. Because implementation occurs on the job, the organization's environment must be supportive of the MBO process. That is, the ideas developed in the learning phase must be consistent with existing norms that underlie the superior-subordinate relationship and the managerial philosophy that generally permeates the organization. These, and the decisions and policies resulting from them, will have the most substantial effect on whether managers use MBO effectively and their attitudes toward it. If managers find that the reward system pays off for behavior other than that recommended in the objectives process, MBO will achieve only secondary status. If it is not part of the ongoing system of the organization, it will be shoved aside and viewed as a useless appendage to the manager's job. He will view it as excessive paper work, to be completed only because the personnel department requires it. If this is his perception, MBO will be relatively valueless to him.

The implementation of MBO

As stated above, the developmental experiences described in the learning phase will probably expose the manager adequately to the theory of MBO and provide some basic practice in its requisite skills, but the key to successful implementation is the use of MBO by top management. Verbal support is not enough to get managers at lower levels to use the system. Because they are unlikely to use it unless their superiors use it, it may be necessary to implement MBO in a relatively structured fashion.

The statement of goals The most fundamental problem to be resolved is the definition of the organization's objectives. These must be defined as clearly as possible and then stated both as desired results and as the general plans and programs to achieve them. If not, individuals at lower levels will be unable to determine how they can contribute to the goals. The determination of organizational objectives will be one of the most valuable contributions of MBO, as it forces top management to review and assess the objectives of the firm and state them in an operational fashion.

Goals cannot be stated in simple, general terms. For instance, it is not enough to state that we want to be the "leader in the field." An operational definition of what leadership in the field means must be developed. Is it measured by increased market penetration? If so, how much? Is it the rate of new product introduction for the following year? Broad philosophical statements of abstract ends may be relatively meaningless to lower-level managers—one reason it is important that the organizational goals be the subject of intense concern at the top level.

The cascading process The responsibility, of course, for developing these goals is top management's—probably the chief executive's. He may do it in conjunction with the board of directors or a group of vice-presidents at the level below him. Once the goals and general plans have been developed, they must be clearly communicated to the next-lower levels. This can be done by a series of cascading meetings. The cascading process in nothing more than a set of meetings between the superior and his work group to deal with the objectives of the boss.

First, the corporate executive officer determines his objectives and general program. Then he meets with all his immediate subordinates, including staff and operating executives in charge of major divisions. At this meeting he defines his objectives and plans for the group. Essentially, this is a statement of what he believes to be the major activities and goal areas for the following year. The purpose of this meeting, especially for the subordinate, is informational.

At the meeting, subordinates should be given the opportunity to increase their understanding of how the chief executive sees the direction, goals, and plans of the company through a free flow of information about objectives. Negotiable and nonnegotiable areas and plans should also be discussed, as these will become operating constraints for lower-level managers. At this meeting, there is only slight emphasis on the specific goals and objectives of the subordinates.

From the information received at this group meeting, each manager should develop a plan of action, goals, and appropriate performance measures for each relevant organizational objective in his own unit or division. Then, in a private meeting with the chief executive officer, each manager undertakes to make an assessment of his own goals and what he will do to achieve them. When these goals and specific plans of action are agreed upon, precise goals and ways of achieving them will exist for two levels of management.

Once an executive at the second level knows what his objectives are, he schedules a meeting with his operating and staff personnel. At this meeting, he makes known to that group the goals and action plans that he has agreed to with his boss. This group meeting is essentially an informational one, at which subordinates should be encouraged to ask questions and engage in discussion that will help them understand the kinds of commitments that have been made to the higher level. The subordinate can then make a more accurate assessment of his discretion areas. He will know those areas in which he can make decisions, in addition to those that are nonnegotiable, nondecision-making areas for him.

After this group meeting, each third-level executive individually prepares a set of action plans and objectives for himself and his unit, and then meets individually with his superior. At this time the superior and the subordinate agree upon the goals, activities, and criteria for assessment of success.

When some consensus has been reached and the executive has his set of goals, he should then schedule a meeting with his subordinates and the process described above continues. This cascading process should proceed to the lowest level of the organization feasible. At each succeedingly lower level, the range of individual discretion will, of course, become less and less, as an individual at the lower level will have more of his activities specified for him. This may mean that for the lowest operating managerial level, the meetings are essentially communicational in nature. The subordinate may be given a fairly well-developed set of operating measures and action plans that he must implement. The nature of the organizational beast is such that these managers must operate within tighter organizational constraints than managers at higher levels.

Some difficult problems must be resolved in this cascading process, or else there will be a breakdown in MBO. The first one is timing. For the cascading process to occur effectively, the meetings between superiors and subordinates should be fairly tightly scheduled; otherwise, the goal setting process may extend over a long period of time. Weeks or months could be spent in refining the general organizational goals to meaningful operational components for managers of lower levels. We therefore suggest that a specific period be devoted toward goal setting—perhaps the two-week period immediately following the final budget determination for the following fiscal year. If managers know that a particular time is scheduled for goal setting, they can schedule other commitments appropriately so as to be available to engage in that activity.

Another problem is the amount of individual time involved in the determination of objectives and action plans. We have already noted that one general complaint voiced by managers is that MBO takes what they regard as an inordinate amount of time. Perhaps they are already burdened with too many activities. It is our contention, however, that MBO is a way to be an effective manager. Therefore, managers must either find the time or make it.

Another important problem is the possibility of a break in the goal-setting chain. If, at any level, a manager fails to set goals, those at lower levels cannot effectively use MBO. This is perhaps the primary reason that goal setting should be done during a specific time. Managers can then be held accountable for setting goals. As a matter of fact, one goal that might be set for all managers by their superiors is to have goals set for subordinate groups. Their success in this area can be verified later in the evaluation of performance. Managers can be asked to bring with them to the evaluation discussion the goal statements developed earlier with their subordinates.

The evaluation of performance Our research suggests that managers feel that they do not receive adequate performance review and feedback.[8] On the other hand, most managers would argue that they supply subordinates with adequate information on performance. They say, for example: "I hold a group meeting every Monday morning to discuss the past week's results," or "I sit with my subordinates at least once a week and talk with them about their progress." This is not the kind of review and feedback activity necessary to make MBO effective because subordinates generally do not regard these activities as feedback. Group meetings are usually situations in which there is limited specific information given to any one individual about his performance. (If such specific information were given in a group meeting, it would probably arouse intense defensiveness of those in attendance.) General meetings are usually viewed by subordinates as situations in which the manager, seeking solutions, presents his own problems to his work group. The review and feedback process should be more personalized—one in which the managers and subordinates operate on one-to-one basis.

In most organizations at least one annual performance review is required. The reason, normally, is to provide data on promotability and appraisal for personnel records, in addition to the desire to convey performance review information to individuals. Our data suggest that one meeting a year is not frequent enough; more frequent feedback is necessary for positive results of MBO.[9] Therefore, intermediate review meetings should be scheduled.

More meetings will undoubtedly take more of the manager's time. But we would argue that this is his job, his responsibility. These intermediate review sessions might be held on a quarterly basis, or perhaps more frequently or randomly through the period. They would no doubt be more effective if they took place at the end of some major activity. For instance, if one of the major components of a subordinate's objectives is to complete a subtask at the end of a specified time, say three months, the intermediate review session should be held at the end of the three-month period. It should be clearly stated that the intermediate review session is a ·review session at which progress can be reviewed, problems solved, and some assistance given to the subordinate in working toward his goals. These intermediate sessions will provide an opportunity for both positive feedback, such as praise and recognition, and negative feedback.

It is our contention that there must be some formal mechanism to ensure that appraisal occurs. For example, the personnel department can develop some sort of monitoring system, through which the department operates as a support unit for facilitating the appraisal process rather than requiring it to meet formal requirements. Otherwise, managers may feel that reviews are conducted primarily for providing information to the personnel department rather than for the appraisal of subordinates.

The follow-up

After the MBO program has been formally implemented and is in operation, some assessment should be made of how it is used by managers. Undoubtedly, problems will occur that need to be discovered and resolved.

There should be constant ongoing discussion with managers about difficulties with forms, format, and other specific problems of goal setting or appraisal. There is also the need for a well-conceived, formal follow-up evaluation. This formal evaluation—in which there is an examination of the goal-setting process, generally recurring problems with MBO, suggested changes, and the manager's reaction to the program—should probably occur about eighteen months after the program has been formally instituted.

A follow-up may be helpful in uncovering some important problems. For instance, it may help to pinpoint whether the goal-setting and evaluation processes have broken down in any of the departments. If so, action can be taken to reinforce goal setting, and pressure can be brought to bear on those managers who are not using the MBO process. If this is not desirable, a fairly extensive general educational effort can be undertaken to make these managers aware of the value of MBO.

The follow-up will uncover cases in which MBO is incompatible with other systems. For instance, where there are discrepancies between the compensation program and MBO, they will be highlighted in the follow-up study. Constant monitoring of MBO is important because of the benefits to be derived from altering the program to fit the needs of the managers.

It is our feeling that it will take approximately three to five years to build an MBO process into an organization such that it becomes part of the managerial style and philosophy. Follow-up evaluation of the process is necessary to facilitate this integration, as it is only then that the process can be tailored to the needs of the company and the philosophy of the management.

The use of consultants The external consultant will be of importance in performing this auditing function. In this capacity, he may investigate areas in which the program, once implemented, needs to be changed and improved.

SUMMARY

In this chapter we have described the mechanics for implementing MBO and presented research results about MBO in action. Specifically, attention has been directed to those problems of getting managers to understand this approach and to use it. We have not dealt at length with the nature of forms or the specific types of reporting mechanisms to be used in MBO. These should be developed individually to meet the needs of each organization.

Some will argue that our strategy for implementation is an intensively formalized, rigid one. There is no doubt that such is the case. However, it is our experience that unless it is implemented in this manner, MBO is unlikely to be broadly used throughout the organization in its first stages. If formal requirements are not imposed on managers, they will continue to operate in a style and fashion they believe to be appropriate.

Without an implementation process, such as we described above, we do not believe that MBO will be effectively implemented. This is not to say that it cannot work any other way. It is certainly more desirable that MBO become an integrated part of the managerial style and philosophy in the company than not. But we think that this is most likely to happen if there is a fairly well disciplined, formal MBO effort. Perhaps the implementation process that we have described will allow those managers who use it to see its benefits and facilitate their adoption of the process.

The most important key to the implementation of MBO is its use by top management. This is not a system to be used solely by subordinates. To us, there is little question that the participation by top management in MBO is the fundamental factor that governs the effective implementation of such a system, as participation is the best indicator of top-management support. The earlier discussion of our research suggests that satisfaction with MBO is positively related to the manner in which the subordinate feels that MBO is supported, that is, used, by the boss. We believe our research to be strong evidence of the link between managerial support and the degree of acceptance of MBO by an individual. Only when each level of management reinforces the use of MBO for lower levels by using it itself are there any real benefits.

NOTES

1 Wickens, J. D. "Management by Objectives: An Appraisal," *Journal of Management Studies*, 5 (1968), 365–379.

2 Meyer, H. H., E. Kay, and J. R. P. French, Jr. "Split Roles in Performance Appraisal," *Harvard Business Review*, 43 (1965), 123–129.

3 Preston, S. J. "J. Stone's Management by Objectives," *Personnel* (London) 1 (1968), 22–25.

4 Porter, L., and E. Lawler III. *Managerial Attitudes and Performance.* Homewood, Ill.: Irwin, 1968.

5 Ivancevich, J. M., J. H. Donnelly, and L. Lyon. "A Study of the Impact of Management by Objectives on Perceived Need Satisfaction," *Personnel Psychology*, 23 (1970), 139–151.

6 Stein, C. I. Personal communication, Carroll I. Stein and Associates, Minneapolis, Minn., July, 1970.

7 Kepner, C. H., and B. B. Tregoe. *The Rational Manager: A Systematic Approach to Problem Solving and Decision Making.* New York: McGraw-Hill, 1965. Maier, N. R. *Problem Solving Discussions and Conferences: Leadership Methods and Skills.* New York: McGraw-Hill, 1963.

8 Tosi, H. L., Jr., and S. J. Carroll, Jr. "Managerial Reaction to Management by Objectives," *Academy of Management Journal*, 11 (1968), 415–425.

9 Carroll, S. J., Jr., and H. L. Tosi, Jr. "The Relationship of Characteristics of the Review Process as Moderated by Personality and Situational Factors to the Success of the 'Management by Objectives' Approach," *Proceedings, Academy of Mnaagement*, 1969.

FOR DISCUSSION AND REVIEW

1 Review the reasons for managerial resistance to MBO.

2 Outline the MBO implementation process. What suggestions are offered to improve the effectiveness of this process?

3 Why is the setting of specific goals so difficult for many organizations?

4 Briefly outline the results of the studies discussed by the authors. Why do you feel these studies were effective?

C. PERFORMANCE REVIEW AND RATER TRAINING

N. R. F. Maier

Three Methods with Specific Objectives

The three interview methods used in this book have specific and slightly different objectives. The differences are highly important to determine the skills required by an interviewer, and to a great extent the methods need different skills from the interviewer's repertoire, as a very unique interaction sequence characterizes each of the methods. This qualitative difference makes the skill requirements for each interview specific to the method. The three appraisal interview methods described and demonstrated in this book are Tell and Sell, Tell and Listen, and Problem-Solving.

THE TELL AND SELL METHOD

Objectives

The initial objective of the Tell and Sell method is to communicate the employee's evaluation as accurately as possible. The accuracy and fairness of the evaluation are assumed. The supervisor must (a) let the employee know how he is doing; (b) gain the employee's acceptance of the evaluation; and (c) have the employee agree to follow a plan for improvement. The three objectives seem, at first glance, to be consistent with each other and attainable through a single method.

If it is also assumed that a person has a desire to correct his faults, that the judgment of the superior is acceptable to the subordinate, and that the subordinate has the ability to change in the direction specified, it is reasonable to suppose that the desired objectives can be achieved. However, it is not uncommon for subordinates to think that supervisors expectations are unreasonable and their criticisms are unjustified or to think that the methods of work suggested are inefficient. It may not be reasonable, either, to expect a person to improve just because he wishes he could. Abilities to make wise decisions, to be patient, to get along with people, to conduct conferences, and to stand up under strain may be sought, but may not be subject to voluntary control, although abilities such as getting to work on time, turning in honest expense accounts, and doing more work are usually considered to be matters of volition. However, even some of these may require more than the desire to change them, and frequently they are as much a problem of emotional adjustment as of motivation. Emotional maladjustment may require therapy, and improper attempts on the part of an employer to make improvements may aggravate rather than correct the condition.

For purposes of discussion, we will assume that extreme and difficult cases are exceptions and that the interviewer has to deal with management personnel who probably are above average in their ability to take criticism.

Skill requirements

The skills required for success in the Tell and Sell interview are considerable. They include the ability to persuade the person to change in the prescribed manner (and this may require the development of new needs in the person), as well as an ability

Reprinted from Norman R. F. Maier, *The Appraisal Interview: Three Basic Approaches* (La Jolla, Ca.: University Associates, 1976). Used with permission.

to make use of the kinds of incentives that motivate each particular individual. The salesperson must know a client in order to influence him, and selling an evaluation makes the same demands on a supervisor who attempts to upgrade an employee.

The method is especially difficult if the supervisor encounters resistance. Because the interviewing supervisor sees himself as doing something for the good of the employee, failure on the part of the latter to appreciate this gesture places the supervisor on the defensive, and from this point on, the situation becomes strained or deteriorates into obvious hostility. This result, of course, is not part of the interviewing plan, and yet it sometimes happens despite anything the interviewer can do.

Usually, however, the employee senses the supervisor's increased aggression before actual hostility is apparent and refrains from questioning the evaluation. The passive resistance and verbal agreement that follow are often seen by the interviewer as acceptance of the evaluation. A failure to allow the subordinate to discuss the evaluation introduces a different difficulty. When the subordinate ceases to talk, the supervisor feels more obligated to talk and, consequently, lectures or preaches. This is something the supervisor does not plan to do during the session, and yet he may find himself dominating the discussion and unable to stop.

Potential reactions

Defensive feelings Whether expressed through docility or overt behavior, defensive feelings are a natural reaction to the Tell and Sell interview situation, because the supervisor is cast in the role of a judge who has the diagnosis and the remedy. However, the person who is being judged is motivated to make as good a showing as possible. The employee would like to conceal any weaknesses and, if he feels the criticism is severe or the praise faint, is inclined to protest. If the criticism appears unjust (and this is bound to happen because the judge never knows all the circumstances and provocations) defensive responses are impossible to repress.

Face saving Once the subordinate questions the superior's evaluation, a face-saving situation is created and, unless the interviewer is very patient or something happens to break the chain of events that naturally comes from this type of conflict, the relationship continues to deteriorate. Without unusual interviewing skill or a salvaging event, someone must lose face. Because the superior usually has some degree of power, it is the subordinate who invariably learns to give in. Actually, subordinates often can develop a degree of insensitivity and not become unduly disturbed by criticism on these occasions. The employee's viewpoint can be expressed as "everybody gets criticized during appraisal interviews, so you just take it with a grain of salt." Some interviewers attempt to comfort their subordinates by saying that they themselves are also evaluated and criticized.

Motivational factors

Although an appraisal interview of the Tell and Sell type may be unpleasant for both parties, this does not mean that it lacks merit. It may be that correction is necessarily unpleasant. Most of us can recall ways in which we have discarded faults because of criticisms that once were painful. There is no question but that faulty behavior can be inhibited or replaced when someone points out a better way. The crucial issue is to find the most effective way or the most dependable approach. Both training and motivation are essential to any change.

When an employee lacks the ability to do a job in the way a superior desires, the problem is whether to train or transfer. If the person is worthy of being developed on the present job, then the interviewer needs to clarify the job demands so that the subordinate knows what is expected. He also must indicate where and how the subordinate can acquire the desired knowledge or skills.

Because people usually want to do a job in an effective way and behave in the proper fashion, there is motivation to adopt correct methods and habits. Even approval from the boss may be an important source of motivation.

Sometimes, however, employees have their own views about a job or are inclined to continue as they have previously because they do not wish to show a lack of ability to change. If employees have "bad habits" or are negligent in certain respects, they may resist the change because the undesirable behavior is attractive to them. Whenever one kind of behavior is more attractive to an employee than another, motivational conditions must change to produce a modification. One way to make the old behavior unattractive is to use punishment and threats of discharge. This is similar to removing an undesirable growth through surgery. The *operative* approach is unpleasant for the employee, who must either do without the desired behavior or suffer undesirable consequences.

A second method is to make another behavior attractive by rewarding it or promising a better future for the person if a given change is made. This is the *substitution* approach and it is usually more pleasant and effective than the *operative* approach, not only because the threat of punishment is unnecessary, but also because an alternative is supplied. For example, a child's emotional disturbance will be reduced if a toy that has been removed is replaced by another, and a smoker will find it somewhat easier to give up cigarettes by substituting gum. However, something pleasant (a reward) must be added to the alternative to make the choice attractive and voluntary.

Both approaches require that an external motivating factor be added to one of the alternatives; a negative incentive (punishment) must be connected with the undesirable behavior, or a positive incentive (reward) must be connected with the acceptable alternative. This form of motivation is *extrinsic*, or external to the activity itself, in contrast to *intrinsic* motivation, where the activity itself is satisfying and is chosen for its own sake (e.g., the motivation for walking to reach a restaurant is extrinsic; the motivation for walking for pleasure is intrinsic). When extrinsic motivation is used to correct behavior, the new way is not accepted for its own sake, but for the products of the activity. Undoubtedly, if an employer knows an employee's needs, he can find highly effective incentives, but such an approach can only lead to extrinsic forms of motivation.

Because of the limited motivation and the defensive attitudes that are aroused, the Tell and Sell method lacks effectiveness. A selling situation permits two possibilities: either the product is bought or it is not, although the product may be accepted with limited enthusiasm. Frequently, the subordinate buys the evaluation, or says he does, in order to get out of the interview situation. Regardless of the degree of acceptance a subordinate has for a supervisor's judgment or plan, a selling situation permits only two possibilities: continue as before or change to the superior's plan. However, plans for improving a work situation and ways of dealing with a behavior problem can seldom be reduced to two possibilities.

When to use tell and sell

Favorable conditions No plan can be expected to be satisfactory in all situations, and an approach that is effective in one situation may fail in another. The Tell and Sell method has its greatest potential with young and/or new employees, who may be inexperienced and insecure and want the advice and assurance of an authority figure. The superior is likely to be respected, not only because of position, but also because knowledge and experience are so obviously greater. To a considerable degree, this same favorable condition prevails when the employee is new on an assignment; mutually recognized inexperience with a given assignment of any kind tends to assure a favorable reaction to the Tell and Sell method.

Individual differences also play a part in reactions to the Tell and Sell method. Persons who are easygoing, uncritical, and somewhat unimaginative, and who accept authoritarian leadership should be most able to profit from the method.

From a company's point of view, it is an efficient method, providing it works. It takes less time to present an evaluation than to discuss one and, if the person interviewed accepts the presentation, a fairly complete evaluation can be covered in fifteen minutes. However, if the subordinate resists the appraisal, the time required may be considerable.

Unfavorable conditions Although the Tell and Sell method may produce positive results under favorable conditions, it also may be harmful. The method becomes undesirable if the harmful effects exceed the gains. For this reason, an interviewer must examine the possible gains in light of the price that must be paid for them.

When subordinates perceive appraisals as unfair, they may feel unappreciated and think that their interests and those of the company are no longer the same. Loyalty depends on *mutual interests* and both supervisors and the company may lose employee's loyalties in the process of conducting appraisal interviews.

If the exchange becomes personal, face-saving problems come up; these may extend beyond an interview and strain the day-to-day relationship between superior and subordinate. If each finds the relationship unpleasant and stressful, these feelings depress job satisfaction for both.

The greatest risk, particularly where appraisals include middle and top management, occurs when the subordinate accepts the judgment of the superior and tries to please him rather than give his own best thinking to the job. Every language has a word for a "yes man" and no superior wishes to develop one, yet the Tell and Sell method is bound to encourage this kind of reaction. Using the method, the superior assumes that he knows best; he is the parental figure and the dispenser of rewards and punishments. An executive who relies on Tell and Sell expects employees to want to please him, and they soon learn to know what is expected of them. Often, they compete with each other to gain favors. Although the boss may ask subordinates to make independent judgments and take the initiative, the fact that the boss appraises and recommends motivates the weaker among them to find out what the boss wants and then do it his way. Even adopting the boss's manners and dress can forestall criticism, because no executive can criticize a person for following in his footsteps. Dependent and docile behavior is likely to be developed in those with whom the method works best; individualistic and rebellious behavior may be produced in those who are least able to profit. Neither extreme is desirable.

Underlying organizational philosophy Organizations vary in the extent to which they are conservative at one extreme and receptive to new methods, fads, and ideas at the other. When decisions are made from the top down, it is difficult for anything new to enter the organization, except at the top. New values can enter the organization if top personnel are recruited from outside, but this requires overcoming resistance to change down the line. Because the Tell and Sell interview is a form of downward communication that makes no provision for upward communication, the perpetuation of existing values is one of its pronounced effects. Although changes can occur effectively when initiated from the top or when approved by the proper superiors, methods for stimulating and discovering new ideas are not built into the plan. The Tell and Sell method of developing employees promotes conservatism rather than change, and insofar as conservatism has merit, the Tell and Sell method is effective in assuring it.

THE TELL AND LISTEN METHOD

Objectives

The Tell and Listen method is somewhat unnatural for an interviewer and he often views it with skepticism because he must be a bit ambiguous about authority to use it. The general idea of the Tell and Listen interview is to communicate the evaluation to the employee and then wait for a response. This means that the interviewer covers the strong and weak points of a subordinate's job performance during the first part of the interview and avoids interruption and controversy by postponing any points of disagreement for later consideration. The second part of the interview is devoted to thoroughly exploring the subordinate's feelings about the evaluation. The superior is still in the role of a judge, but he always listens to disagreement and defensive behavior without attempting to refute any statements. Actually, the interviewer encourages the employee to disagree and to express feelings, because he sees the objective as not only to communicate an appraisal, but also to allow the release of feelings aroused by the evaluation. The value of catharsis, that the verbal expression or release of frustrated feelings tends to reduce or remove them, is assumed.

Skill requirements

Accepting defensive reactions Initially, reactions to the Tell and Listen method are similar to those for the Tell and Sell method because both begin with the presentation of the evaluation. However, they differ radically in the way disagreement and resistance are handled. Instead of dominating the discussion to clarify his views, the interviewer encourages the subordinate to disagree with the evaluation and to relate his own feelings. Thus, the interviewer is a nondirective counselor (Rogers, 1942) during the second part of the interview.

The skills of the Tell and Listen approach are (a) *active listening*—to refrain from talking and to accept and try to understand the employee's attitudes and feelings; (b) effective *use of pauses*—to wait patiently and avoid embarrassment, knowing that a pause will cause the other person to talk; (c) *reflection of feelings*—to respond to feelings to show understanding; and (d) *summarizing of feelings*—to indicate progress, to show understanding, and to point up aspects of the problem, as well as to wrap up the interview. None of these skills requires that the interviewer either agree or disagree with what is said. Rather, he strives to communicate that he understands the subordinate's position; he entertains the possibility that the evaluation may be unjust and even incorrect; and he reveals that he wants the employee to take from the appraisal only ideas that may be helpful.

Potential reactions

Face saving reduced Because it is assumed at the outset that there are two sides to the appraisal, face-saving issues are not aggravated and the superior is not caught in a situation where he feels the need to defend his evaluation. He does not expect the subordinate to agree and is not disappointed when the employee resists. The unpleasant aspects of the appraisal interview are reduced when the superior has a method for dealing with defensive responses and when he is in a better position to understand and respect feelings. For this reason, the manager who is able to practice the Tell and Listen method is less inclined to avoid appraisal interviews than is the Tell and Sell interviewer, who may be overanxious and overprepared to fend off signs of resistance.

Motivational factors

The motivational factors in the Tell and Listen interview are complex. Fears of reprisal and of displeasing the superior are reduced, so most motivational factors associated with fear of displeasing the superior are weakened, if not lost. Unadaptive defensive behavior fanned in part by these same fears is also reduced. Thus, *resistance to change* is overcome or reduced by the counseling process, and the desire to change to avoid displeasing the boss is sacrificed. Which of these two opposed motivations is of greater value undoubtedly varies from one individual to another.

The positive motivation that is created by having a pleasant experience with the boss is undoubtedly greater for the Tell and Listen type of interview than for the Tell and Sell type, because the former reduces any hostility that may have been engendered. In addition, it makes the subordinate feel accepted and even important. This is conducive to the formation of a constructive attitude—so essential to growth. A subordinate is more likely to want to please a supervisor he likes than one he fears. When fear is the dominant motive, a person, at best, shies away from wrongdoing but does not extend himself to perform beyond the call of duty.

Up to this point, the motivational factors discussed have been *extrinsic*—that is, the incentives lie outside the job activity but the task or work itself has not been made more interesting, although some increase in job satisfaction may come about. Interest in a job depends on the work itself and on the social climate in which it is performed. An employee who likes the boss will find the job more satisfying than an employee who fears or dislikes the boss. Other employees also influence job interest, and a supervisor who respects and knows how to deal with feelings is able to reduce strains in interpersonal relationships and create a relaxed and friendly social climate. Any change in job interest represents a form of *intrinsic motivation.*

A more important intrinsic motivation is present if the interview results in (a) solving some job problems; (b) clarifying certain misunderstandings between supervisor and subordinate; or (c) solving a personal problem. The motivational possibilities vary from individual to individual and are greater when an employee's performance shows deficiencies that can be corrected.

If the superior listens and learns from the interview, additional intrinsic motivational gains are possible. The superior can modify job assignments and expectations; alter his evaluation; perceive the subordinate's job differently; and discover his own negligence in training and assisting. These gains tend to depend upon an exceptional interviewer, however, because the appraisal has been made prior to the interview and a previous commitment reduces the interviewer's ability to see inaccuracies or injustices in the appraisal (Maier, 1973a).

When to use tell and listen

Favorable and unfavorable results The result that the Tell and Listen interview is most likely to produce is a good relationship between superior and subordinate during the interview. The employee is likely to leave with a positive feeling and with a favorable attitude toward the supervisor. He is likely to regard the interview as worthwhile and feel important to the company as an individual. The superior can profit from what he learns about the employee's needs and aspirations and should not be misled by a defensive attitude or feelings expressed emotionally.

There is a risk, however, that the interview may not achieve its first objective, letting the employee know where he stands. Although the employee may change, depending on new insights, he is not likely to discover ways to improve the job. An employee may leave the interview with satisfaction, but not necessarily with a program for developing on the job.

Underlying organizational philosophy The values promoted by the Tell and Listen interview are tolerance and respect for the dignity of the individual. Any supervisor who tries to understand a subordinate's viewpoint experiences an increased respect for the employee, so the method tends to make management personnel employee minded rather than production minded. Because supervisors who are employee centered tend, in general, to stimulate higher morale than others (Katz, Maccoby, & Morse, 1950) this influence may be a constructive one. However, simply because high morale and higher productivity frequently are related, it does not mean that there may not be variations in productivity among groups that have equally high morale.

The fact that the interviewer may profit from the appraisal interview is one of the greatest potential values of the Tell and Listen method. Change initiated from below can occur because a subordinate is able to influence a superior's views on how the job may be improved by changes in (a) supervision; (b) work methods; (c) job assignments; and (d) job expectations. Very often the people who supervise the work of others once performed the jobs of those they now supervise. This causes them to expect the job to be performed much as they themselves did it (Read, 1962). Because individuals differ, and times as well as jobs change, this expectation may be unreasonable, impractical, or biased—yet it is most understandable. The expectations of a superior, under the best circumstances, tend to restrict freedom, stifle initiative, and inhibit improvements that have their origin with subordinates. Although some of the loss in new ideas from below may be recaptured by suggestion boxes, it is important not to stifle new ideas through an appraisal program that was designed to develop employees. A supervisor who listens and learns may encourage upward communication in deed as well as in word; the belief that constructive forces for change can come from below may be an important part of organizational philosophy.

THE PROBLEM-SOLVING METHOD

Objectives

The Problem-Solving approach to an appraisal interview is a product of the author's research on problem solving and his studies of executive development. Of the three methods presented in this book, it deviates the most from commonly held management views. It is the only method that takes the interviewer out of the role of a judge and makes him a helper. Although the interviewer may always wish to be a helper to a subordinate, he can not escape retaining the role of a judge in the other two types of interview because the process of appraising is inconsistent with helping. Because an appraisal, by its nature, is an evaluation or judgment, it may appear that the purpose of the interview has been lost if the evaluation is not directly communicated to the subordinate. However, the development of the employee's performance often is the primary reason for conducting an appraisal interview and this objective may be lost in the process of communicating the evaluation directly.

Although the two methods discussed in the preceding sections communicate the appraisal to the subordinate, they do not assume his understanding and acceptance. The Problem-Solving approach, in contrast, has no provision for communicating the appraisal, and indeed it may not be essential to do so. If the appraisal is required for other purposes, it may be desirable to delay making it until after the interview.

The soundness of having the development of the employee's performance serve as the objective of the interview is apparent; this establishes a *mutual interest* between the interviewer and his subordinate. Both would like the employee to improve on the job and both would agree that the boss could assist in this improvement. When the subordinate accepts the supervisor as a helper, he is more willing to describe the nature of his difficulties. When the boss passes judgment on job performance, however, the interests conflict. The employee wants to impress his boss favorably and is motivated to cover up any weaknesses. The interviewer, on the other hand, would like to avoid being deceived and is inclined to discuss weaknesses that have come to his attention. The mutual interest factor in the traditional appraisal interview, therefore, is present only as long as the employee's merits are extolled and ends when the interviewer indicates that he is not satisfied.

Because job performance can also be improved by changes in the job itself, problem solving places attention on the situation, not on the individual. Subordinates are not on the defensive when discussing how their jobs can be made more satisfying and efficient. "Changing the job" explores an entirely different dimension of job performance and avoids the implication that individuals must change, which invariably leads to defensiveness.

Another way to improve job performance is to change the nature of the supervision. Superiors have great influence on the productivity of their subordinates, but subordinates are reluctant to be critical of their superior's style of supervision. Discussion of job-related factors can reveal problems in this area.

The Problem-Solving approach may show four ways in which the performance of subordinates can improve: (1) changing the subordinate's behavior; (2) changing the job duties or the job procedure; (3) changing jobs; and (4) changing the pattern of supervision. The Tell and Sell and the Tell and Listen approaches tend to limit improvement to the first of these four changes and this change is often least acceptable to the subordinate.

Essential attitudes

Although the objective of the Problem-Solving approach is improved job performance, the interviewer can not specify the area in which this development should take place because this constitutes diagnosis and judgment. The interviewer must limit his influence to stimulating thinking, rather than supplying remedies or solutions. He must be willing to accept for consideration all ideas on job improvement that the employee brings up. It is his function to discover the subordinate's interests so that he can respond to them and cause the employee to examine himself and his job duties. To accomplish these things, the interviewer must forget his own viewpoint and try to see the job as the employee sees it. If the employee's ideas seem impractical, the interviewer should explore the views expressed more thoroughly, using questions to learn more specifically what the employee has in mind. Often the ideas that are difficult to accept are ones that are misunderstood or viewed with a different mental set. Each person speaks from his own frame of reference, but each listener has a different frame of reference. Communication is faulty until the backgrounds, attitudes, and experience of each are mutually understood.

When the interviewer finds that a subordinate's thinking is naive and in need of upgrading, he must be willing to assume that a problem-solving discussion is the best way to stimulate growth and sophistication. If an employee can grow in this way, it is never necessary that he know he has had weaknesses and faults. The process may be analogous to the training of children; to learn to be graceful and skilled, they never need to know that they once were gawky and uncoordinated. As a matter of fact, they might improve more if left to themselves and not exposed to too much faultfinding. These assumptions are not easily converted to practice, largely because discriminating adults are so concerned with the faults they observe that it is difficult for them to suppress comments and advice. Wisdom and experience can be a handicap to an individual who directs the work of others, unless he knows how to share them in an acceptable manner.

Problem-solving behavior is characterized by the exploration and evaluation of a variety of solutions. It is inhibited whenever one person feels threatened by an evaluation, because this directs attention to the person rather than the situation. When people are placed in the spotlight, they are motivated to hide defects and alerted to protect themselves. Defensive behaviors are attempts to justify old behaviors, and as long as people defend their past actions they are not searching for new or better ways to perform. If an evaluation is very threatening it may induce frustration, which not only arouses hostile and childish behavior, but also promotes stubbornness. These behavior characteristics also delay problem solving because they are in direct opposition to rational thinking.

Skill requirements

The skills associated with the Problem-Solving approach are consistent with the nondirective procedures discussed in connection with the Tell and Listen method: listening, accepting, and responding to feelings. The interviewer needs to be especially alert and notice any expression of concern during the introductory period. A remark such as, "Well, this is the day we get overhauled, I suppose," should be answered with a statement such as, "You consider these interviews somewhat rough on people in some ways, I suppose."

However, the objective of the Problem-Solving interview is to go beyond an interest in the subordinate's feelings. As soon as he is ready to discuss the job situation (and this may be at the very outset if the employee is not anxious about the interview), the interviewer can ask questions about the job. Such questions are directive in order to channel the subject of conversation, but nondirective about feelings that an employee can express.

In some situations, the employee's job description should be explored and its importance discussd. The interviewer may find differences in perceptions of what the job is that may account for some of the unfavorable points in the evaluation. For example, the interviewer may be surprised to learn that the subordinate sees the job as "getting an assignment finished on time, regardless of the feelings of others" and that he has this mistaken emphasis because of a previous reprimand. These differences should be passed over and should serve to enlighten the interviewer about misunderstandings and the need for better job descriptions, training, or communication.

In the typical appraisal interview with an employee of long standing, the job analysis may be omitted because it can be assumed that this understanding has been accomplished with previous interviews. The employee can be asked to review the year's progress and discuss the problems, needs, innovations, satisfactions, and dissatisfactions he has encountered. The idea is to make this interview the employee's opportunity to get the boss's ear.

To help a subordinate talk freely, it is desirable for the superior to consider all problems the employee wishes to raise. Restating ideas in somewhat different words is an effective way for the interviewer to test his understanding, and it demonstrates that the superior is interested in considering changes that are important to the subordinate. An interviewer need not agree or disagree with ideas to accept them. Understanding or accepting ideas is an important neutral position between agreeing and disagreeing.

When the employee's ideas are numerous, it may be wise for a supervisor to jot them down so they can be referred to later. Making a record of ideas is an act of accepting and considering without taking a stand for or against. Later, these same ideas can be evaluated to pick out the best ones.

Skillful questioning is an effective way for an interviewer to stimulate a subordinate to evaluate his own ideas. Questions should not be used to put an employee on the spot or indicate the weakness of a plan, but should indicate that the listener wants to hear the complete story. The following examples illustrate stimulating exploratory questions:

• Can this plan of yours deal with an emergency situation, in case one arose?
• Would you have other people at your level participate in the plan?
• Could your own employees be induced to go along with the change?
• What kinds of problems do you anticipate with a changing market?
• Have you examined the plan from the point of view of quality control?

Nonthreatening exploratory questions are effective for drawing an employee out and making him think more clearly; in addition, they may serve to direct attention to areas that have been overlooked. The last two questions above are examples of broad questions, and the first three stimulate more detailed examination of a delineated area.

Skillful summarizing serves a variety of purposes, and opportunities for useful summaries usually occur several times during an appraisal interview. Effective summaries may be used to accomplish the following:

1 To restate the points already covered in a broader sense;
2 To demonstrate that the interviewer understands the ideas expressed up to the point at which the summary occurs;
3 To facilitate communication by creating opportunities to check and refine ideas; and
4 To separate what has been covered from the problems that remain unexplored.

The effective *use of pauses* is one of the most subtle skills and is useful in connection with the Problem-Solving method, as well as the Tell and Listen method. Ideas require thought, and if the interviewer interrupts the employee he disturbs a train of thought. By waiting patiently he gives the subordinate time to explore and evaluate. This is in contrast to the cross-examination some interviewers practice.

Motivational factors

Problems offer opportunities to explore the unknown, and their solutions lead to new experiences. The statement of a problem can cause a group to engage in a lively problem-solving discussion. Curiosity is a strong drive and, as long as fear is not aroused, it leads to exploratory behavior. Children, for example, have a strong motivation to explore their surroundings when they are in a free and secure environment, but the exploration ceases when danger or threats of punishment are introduced. If a subordinate is free to analyze the job and expects to have an influence on any improvements that are made, he is immediately motivated to think constructively, rather than defensively. Some *extrinsic* motivational factors, such as gaining approval or avoiding failure, may be present, but essentially the problem-solving activity itself has interest value and is a form of *intrinsic* motivation. Intrinsic motivation is present in many of the things we like to do and is an important aspect of play. If intrinsic motivation could be made a larger part of the job, then work would become more like play and the problem of gaining acceptance of any changes would be nonexistent because employees would be carrying out their own solutions.

Sources of job satisfaction An examination and a re-evaluation of the job description are bound to suggest some changes, because there always are aspects of the job that give more satisfaction (or less dissatisfaction) than others. Usually, how to maximize the best features and how to minimize the poorer ones are topics of mutual interest for the interviewer and the subordinate.

When the job itself is a topic for consideration, it is apparent that there are four distinctly different ways in which job satisfaction may be improved. These are (a) the job itself may be reorganized, enlarged, subdivided, or rescheduled; (b) the subordinate's perception of the job and the meanings of its various aspects may be changed; (c) the superior's understanding of the job problems may be increased so that he will relate differently to his subordinates, supply assistance in the form that is needed, or improve communication; and (d) the opportunity may be created for solving problems that are of a group nature, involving all of the subordinates who report to the interviewer.

When to use problem solving

Favorable and unfavorable results Since problem solving can lead to so many different approaches to job satisfaction, improvement seems possible for every employee. If no acceptable solutions come under discussion, the interviewer can ask questions to explore various possibilities and a selection can be made in terms of practicality and interest. If the goal of the interview is to experiment and to improve the job situation in line with the employee's wishes, then problem solving gives good assurance that a change in the desired direction will occur.

If the subordinate recommends changes that conflict with the goals of the company or the superior, the superior may respond by asking how the change can take place without being unfair to other employees or without violating company objectives. Invariably, such questions lead to further clarification. Superiors often turn down suggestions prematurely because they see obstacles in the path of the change, but if an obstacle is discussed, ways to avoid it may be discovered or the subordinate may realize that he has overlooked certain consequences of a new plan. Ideas that seem impractical can be tabled for future consideration and the exploration can be directed to other topics. An interview can give considerable satisfaction, even if only one of many new ideas can be implemented.

If a subordinate has no ideas and fails to respond to the Problem-Solving approach, it may assumed that this method has failed, but this does not preclude use of one of the other two methods.

Underlying organizational philosophy One of the unique advantages of the Problem-Solving approach is that it affords both participants a highly favorable oppor-

METHOD	TELL AND SELL	TELL AND LISTEN	PROBLEM-SOLVING
Objectives	To communicate evaluation To persuade employee to improve	To communicate evaluation To release defensive feelings	To stimulate growth and development in employee
Psychological assumptions	Employee desires to correct weaknesses if he knows them Any person can improve if he so chooses A superior is qualified to evaluate a subordinate	People will change if defensive feelings are removed	Growth can occur without correcting faults Discussing job problems leads to improved performance
Role of interviewer	Judge	Judge	Helper
Attitude of interviewer	People profit from criticism and appreciate help	One can respect the feelings of others if one understands them	Discussion develops new ideas and mutual interests
Skills of interviewer	Salesmanship Patience	Listening and reflecting feelings Summarizing	Listening and reflecting feelings Reflecting ideas Using exploratory questions Summarizing
Reactions of employee	Suppresses defensive behavior Attempts to cover hostility	Expresses defensive behavior Feels accepted	Problem-solving behavior
Employee's motivation for change	Use of positive or negative incentives or both Extrinsic: motivation is added to the job itself	Resistance to change reduced Positive incentive Extrinsic and some intrinsic motivation	Increased freedom Increased responsibility Intrinsic motivation—interest is inherent in the task
Possible gains	Success most probable when employee respects interviewer	Employee develops favorable attitude toward superior, which increases probability of success	Almost assured of improvement in some respect
Risks of interviewer	Loss of loyalty Inhibition of independent judgment Face-saving problems created	Need for change may not be developed	Employee may lack ideas Change may be other than what superior had in mind
Probable results	Perpetuates existing practices and values	Permits interviewer to change his views in light of employee's responses Some upward communication	Both learn, because experience and views are pooled Change is facilitated

Fig. 1. Comparisons among three types of appraisal interviews.

tunity to learn and communicate. Usually, training and developing others is a one-way process: the superior gives knowledge and know-how, and the subordinate receives them. The Problem-Solving approach, like the Tell and Listen method, offers the interviewer an opportunity to learn because it stimulates upward communication. Unlike Tell and Listen, Problem-Solving also creates a climate for high-quality decisions and changes because it pools the thinking of those most likely to have supplementary experiences. The Problem-Solving approach allows an interviewer not only to remove sources of frustration through *listening* skills, but to activate or stimulate change through discussion of a problem.

The interviewer is most likely to have the proper attitude for effective problem solving if he understands that effective plans, decisions, and ideas must be not only factually sound, but also acceptable to the persons who must implement them. This attitude encourages an interviewer to respect the problem-solving ability of each subordinate and to place mutual interests above personal interests. A favorable opportunity to explore a problem with an experienced and understanding superior can stimulate a subordinate's thinking and lead to increased job interest, as well as to a better utilization of a subordinate's talents.

The Problem-Solving method cuts across barriers created by rank and places the attention on mutual interests, rather than on prerogatives, status, and personality clashes. To use the method an interviewer assumes that change is an essential part of an organization and that participation in change is essential to healthy growth.

Fig. 1 (p. 163) outlines the three types of appraisal interviews described on previous pages and compares them on ten different variables. Because the psychological assumptions vary considerably from one method to another, quite different outcomes may result from their use, as discussed previously.

As shown in the figure, the underlying psychological assumptions differ for each type of interview and seem to be dependent on the desired objectives. The objectives an interviewer has determine the role he will play and the role he feels he must play determines the attitude he will have, as well as which skills he will use. The interviewer's attitudes and skills, in turn, influence the interviewee's reactions to the situation and his desire to change. How the latter reacts determines the possible gains and the probable results of a given interview situation. All these things also depend, in part, on the personalities of the participants. All aspects must be studied carefully before an interviewer decides which method to use in a given situation. His decision may also be influenced by whether he wishes to perpetuate existing organizational values or to stimulate initiative from below.

FOR DISCUSSION AND REVIEW

1   Distinguish between the three types of appraisal interviews.
2   What are the assumptions, skills required, and motivational factors of each type of interview?
3   Why is the problem-solving interview recommended by the author?

H. John Bernardin
C. S. Walter

Effects of Rater Training and Diary-Keeping on Psychometric Error in Ratings

Behavioral expectation scales (BES) have become a popular form of performance appraisal in recent years. In his appraisal of BES, Dunnette (1966) states that the method shows "great promise for overcoming many of the problems and potential errors believed so long to be inherent in most systems of behavior observation" (p. 105). Indeed, the intuitive appeal of the method (Zedeck, Jacobs, & Kafry, 1976) leads one to expect that common psychometric problems would be alleviated. Empirical testing has shown that BES have generally performed no better or worse than other types of scales (Bernardin, in press; Bernardin, Alvares, & Cranny, 1976; Borman & Vallon, 1974; Burnaska & Hollman, 1974). Two exceptions are studies by Campbell, Dunnette, Arvey, and Hellervik (1973) and Borman and Dunnette (1975).

Among the more common hypotheses for the inconsistent performance of BES are (a) developmental, procedural, or format differences in the scales themselves (Bernardin, Alvares, & Cranny, 1976; Burnaska & Hollman, 1974) and (b) the lack of training or preparedness of raters in using the rather complicated scales (Borman, 1975; Borman & Dunnette, 1975). Research has found the first hypothesis to be at least tenable, if not conclusive (Bernardin, LaShells, Smith, & Alvares, 1976). A thorough assessment of the second hypothesis has yet to be made. It is the purpose of the present study to test the effects of training and rater preparedness on psychometric error with BES.

Previous research with other rating formats concludes that psychometric error can be reduced with training. In a survey of the literature, Brown (1968) reported that raters benefit from training when it includes (a) practice with the specific scales (Wakeley, 1961), (b) discussion of errors in rating by the raters (Levine & Butler, 1952), and (c) special emphasis on the importance of trait differentiation (Taylor & Hastman, 1956).

Recent studies corroborate the second and third of Brown's (1968) conclusions. Latham, Wexley, and Pursell (1975) measured the effects of training designed specifically to alleviate problems of contrast and halo errors. In a well-controlled simulation, both errors were significantly reduced as a function of the training.

The only study dealing specifically with the effects of training on error with BES (Borman, 1975) revealed that a 5-minute training session significantly reduced halo in ratings of hypothetical supervisors. Borman does point out, however, that halo is still quite pervasive after training.

The suggestion made by Brown (1968) that practice be implemented with the specific rating scale is related to the recommendation by Guion (1965) that a diary method of performance appraisal be used. The diary method entails the recording of critical behaviors observed by the rater throughout the appraisal period. Such a procedure would facilitate better discrimination across dimensions (i.e., less halo) and provide for a more behavioral basis of appraisal. Bernardin, LaShells, Smith, & Alvares (1976) concluded that the best response format for the BES was the recording and rating of new critical incidents by the ratee on each dimension. The dimen-

From *Journal of Applied Psychology* 62, no. 1: 550–555. Copyright © 1977 by the American Psychological Association. Reprinted by permission.

sion rating is then compiled by averaging the ratings of these newly scaled incidents. Such a procedure resulted in significantly less leniency error and halo effect than the more common procedure for BES rating. Based on consolidation of the results of the above study with the recommendations of Brown (1968) and Guion (1965), the use of the actual BES as a context for observation during the appraisal period seems to be a good strategy.

It is hypothesized that the use of the BES as a context for observation, plus a training session designed specifically to make the rater aware of psychometric error (as per Borman, 1975), will result in less psychometric error than other conditions of training or no training at all.

The psychometric considerations in this study were interrater reliability, leniency error, halo effect, and discrimination across ratees. Interrater reliability was defined as the degree of agreement between raters on several dimensions for each ratee. Leniency error was defined as a shift in mean ratings from the midpoint of the scale in the favorable direction (Sharon & Bartlett, 1969). Halo effect was defined as the standard deviation across dimensions of a rater's rating of a particular ratee. Level of ratee discrimination was defined as a difference in standard deviations of ratings on each dimension, with higher standard deviations representing greater discrimination (Barrett, Taylor, Parker, & Martens, 1958).

HYPOTHESES

Based on Brown's (1968) recommendations regarding training and on Guion's (1965) suggestions regarding diary-keeping, the following predictions can be made: (a) ratings from the group who receive training on psychometric error and who are exposed to the BES prior to and during observation will have significantly less halo and leniency error than ratings from groups without such training or exposure; (b) ratings from the above group will have significantly greater interrater reliability and discrimination across ratees than ratings from the other groups; (c) ratings from a group trained on psychometric error prior to observation will have less halo effect and leniency error than ratings from groups without such training; (d) ratings from a group trained in psychometric error immediately prior to observation will have less halo effect and leniency error than ratings from a group without such training.

METHOD

Sample

Raters in the study were 156 students of 13 different instructors of a general psychology course. Students fulfilled the experiment-participation requirements of the course by participating in this study. Students were randomly assigned to one of four experimental groups. For each instructor of the course there were three raters from each of the experimental groups. The number of total students in the participating classes ranged from 26 to 38. Ratings of the instructor were taken in the 10th week of a 10-week semester.

Group 1 received 1 hour of training in the 1st week of the semester on the various types of psychometric error such as halo effect, leniency error, and contrast error. This training involved definitions, graphic illustrations, and examples of the errors. Students were also given copies of the seven BES to be used in the 10th week of the semester to evaluate the instructor. They were asked to maintain an observational diary for their instructor by recording observed critical incidents on the

BES throughout the semester as they pertained to the seven dimensions of performance. It was pointed out that the diary would be collected and checked at the end of the semester. Thus, the three recommendations by Brown (1968), mentioned above, were implemented for Group 1.

Group 2 received the identical training on the various types of psychometric errors as Group 1, also in the 1st week of the semester. The seven dimensions of teacher performance measured on the BES were also discussed, and students were instructed to observe the instructor throughout the semester with these considerations in mind. These students, however, did not see the BES. Group 3 received the identical training on psychometric error and participated in a similar discussion on the 7 dimensions of performance as did Groups 1 and 2. Their training and discussion took place in the 10th week of the semester, immediately prior to the evaluation of the instructors. Group 4 received no training prior to the period of evaluation, but brief mention was made of halo error and leniency effort in the written instructions of the evaluation form.

BES development

The BES for instructors were developed according to the procedures recommended by Bernardin, LaShells, Smith, and Alvares (1976). Thus (a) dimensions were written and clarified by the student population; (b) critical incidents were written for each dimension; (c) a new group of students "retranslated" incidents back into dimensions. Incidents that were retranslated correctly 80% of the time or more were retained; (d) a new group of students rated each surviving incident on its relative desirability for the dimension to which it belonged (on a scale from 1 to 7); (e) those incidents with standard deviations of 2.0 or below were retained; (f) of the items surviving the standard deviation criterion, those that would provide anchors at relatively equal intervals through the 7-point scale continuum were retained. While this procedure is very similar to that which was recommended by Smith and Kendall (1963), alternative procedures have been used (Campbell et al., 1973). Campbell et al. (1973) reversed Steps a and b listed above. In the present study there were 118 students who participated in the development of the BES. None of these students participated in later phases of this study.

The final BES were comprised of seven performance dimensions: instructor knowledge, testing procedures, student-teacher relations, organizational skills, communication skills, subject relevance, and utility of assignments.

Instructor evaluation

As per Bernardin, LaShells, Smith, and Alvares (1976), all participants were given the BES and asked to evaluate their instructor by writing and rating a minimum of three "typical" critical incidents for each dimension. The mean of the ratings of the new critical incidents was then taken as the rating on each dimension.

RESULTS

Group 1: diary-keeping

Diaries maintained by members of Group 1 were collected after the evaluations. The average number of critical incidents written per dimension was 3.9. Only 3 of the 39 members of Group 1 turned in diaries that were unquestionably of poor quality (less than 3 incidents recorded on each dimension and most incidents of an ambiguous nature). After making their evaluations, raters in Group 1 were asked to indicate how helpful the diaries were for evaluating their instructor. A 7-point Likert-type scale ranging from not helpful at all to very helpful was the rating instrument, and the mean rating was 5.9.

Leniency effect

Means and standard deviations on each of the seven performance dimensions for all groups are presented in Table 1. The maximum possible rating was 7.0.

Table 1
Means and Standard Deviations on Performance Dimensions for Each Group

CONDITION	DIMENSION[a]						
	1	2	3	4	5	6	7
Group 1							
M	4.33	4.62	4.16	4.21	4.97	4.61	4.04
SD	1.12	1.06	.94	1.01	1.21	1.14	.94
Group 2							
M	4.49	4.79	4.41	4.14	4.99	4.77	4.38
SD	1.29	1.24	.86	1.14	1.12	1.12	1.05
Group 3							
M	4.51	4.73	4.67	4.38	5.12	4.69	4.64
SD	1.01	.81	1.16	1.16	.96	1.04	.99
Group 4							
M	4.62	4.91	4.72	4.37	5.17	4.92	4.72
SD	1.07	1.04	1.09	.93	1.20	1.01	.87

[a]Performance dimensions were as follows: 1=communication skills; 2=organizational skills; 3=student–teacher relations; 4=testing procedures; 5=instructor knowledge; 6=subject relevance; 7=utility of assignments.

Table 1 shows that mean ratings from Group 1 fall closer to the scale midpoint (4.0) on six of the seven scales than ratings from Groups 2, 3, and 4. To test for differences between means, the 13 ratee means were compared as a function of rater group and dimension in a Group $\times$ Dimension $\times$ Ratee ($4 \times 17 \times 13$) analysis of variance design. A significant group effect was found, $F(3, 36) = 4.47, p < .01$. Multiple comparisons of group means revealed the following significant differences between groups: 1 and 2, $p < .05$; 1 and 3, $p < .01$; 1 and 4, $p < .01$; and 2 and 4, $p < .05$.

Interrater reliability

Interrater reliability was derived by taking the standard deviation of the three ratings on each dimension for each ratee. This procedure was followed for each of the four experimental groups. The standard deviations were then taken as data points in a $4 \times 7 \times 13$ analysis of variance. Results revealed a significant group effect, $F(3, 36) = 3.29, p < .05$. In multiple comparisons of mean standard deviations, only Groups 1 and 2 ($p < .05$) were significantly different from each other.

Halo effect

As the conventional index of halo could not be assessed (correlations between dimensions with ratees as data points), the following procedure was followed: The standard deviation was calculated for each rater across the seven dimensions. Thus, 39 standard deviations were calculated for each group. A low standard deviation was interpreted as a high degree of halo and vice versa. Mean standard deviations for Groups 1-4, were 1.59, 1.27, 1.15, and 1.06, respectively.

The 39 standard deviations for each group were used as data points in a simple one-way analysis of variance. Again, a significant difference was found between means. $F(3, 152)=4.69$, $p <.01$. Multiple comparisons (t-tests for differences among several means) revealed the following significant differences between groups: 1 and 2, $p <.01$; 1 and 3, $p <.01$; 1 and 4, $p <.01$; 2 and 3, $p <.05$; 2 and 4, $p <.05$; 3 and 4, $p <.05$.

Discrimination across ratees

In order to compare ratee discrimination for each of the groups, the following procedures were followed. First, a mean rating on each dimension was computed for each ratee. Thus, there were seven mean ratings on each of the 13 ratees for the four groups. Next, the standard deviations of these 13 mean ratings on each dimension were calculated for the four groups. The seven standard deviations were then used as data points in a simple one-way analysis of variance. No significant difference was found between groups in assessing discrimination across ratees, F (3, 24) = 1.82, ns.

DISCUSSION

Results support the recommendations made by Brown (1968) and Guion (1965) and other recent research regarding the effects of training in reducing psychometric error. In this study the group who had received psychometric training and exposure to the evaluation scale prior to and during observation showed significantly less leniency error and halo effect than all other groups. Interrater reliability was also higher for Group 1 than for Group 2. Also, based on the survey data collected after evaluations, it appears that members of Group 1 thought the diary method to be helpful in the rating process.

The differences in psychometric properties of ratings from Groups 1 and 2 illustrate the importance of familiarization with the scales. Prior knowledge of the important dimensions, plus scaled, specific behavioral examples, apparently provided a relevant and useful context for observation and subsequent evaluation. The recommendation by Smith and Kendall (1963) to bring appraisal into closer correspondence to observation was thus applied. The psychometric superiority of ratings from Group 2 supports the recommendations made by Borman and Dunnette (1975) to get raters to "observe work-related behavior more systematically and representatively" (p. 565).

A comment is also warranted about the overall performance of BES in view of the new rating system of recording and scaling new incidents, as per Bernardin, LaShells, Smith, and Alvares (1976). With this procedure, as in Bernardin, in press, leniency error and halo effect were less than the errors reported in studies using different rating procedures with BES. The two most recent comparisons of ratings from other formats are Borman and Dunnette (1975) and Bernardin, Alvares, and Cranny (1976). Additionally, with this procedure, ratees receive specific examples of their perceived good and bad behaviors. This "spin-off" (Blood, 1974) cannot be discounted, since the major purpose of most appraisal systems is to ultimately improve performance (Beatty, Schneier, & Beatty, Note 1). In this respect, specific behavioral feedback on one's performance would certainly be preferable to mere numbers.

Results from this study also support the Borman and Dunnette (1975) recommendation that one receive extensive training with BES. Subjects in Groups 1, 2, and 3 were all clearly superior to those in Group 4, who received only cursory mention of psychometric error.

A possible limitation on the generalizability of these findings may be the special sample of raters. The combined effects of demand characteristics and "forced" and close observation may account for some of the variance between groups. These characteristics are not common to the normal supervisor—subordinate situation. Thus, until there is a field test of the above hypotheses, results should be interpreted cautiously.

At least for this sample, results indicate that raters should receive training in performance appraisal and potential psychometric error prior to observation of the ratee. Additionally, the use of the actual BES during the appraisal period as a context for observation and diary-keeping appears to enhance rating quality.

REFERENCE NOTE

1 Beatty, R. W., Schneier, C. E., & Beatty, J. R. *An empirical investigation of perceptions of ratee behavior frequency and ratee behavior change using behaviorally anchored rating scales (BARS)*. Unpublished manuscript, 1976.

REFERENCES

Barrett, R. S., Taylor, E. K., Parker, J. W., & Martens, W. L. Rating scale content: I. Scale information and supervisory ratings. *Personnel Psychology*, 1958, *11*, 333–346.

Bernardin, H. J. Behavioral expectation scales versus summated scales: A fair comparison. *Journal of Applied Psychology*, in press.

Bernardin, H. J., Alvares, K. M., & Cranny, C. J. A recomparison of behavioral expectation scales to summated scales. *Journal of Applied Psychology*, 1976, *61*, 564–570.

Bernardin, H. J., LaShells, M. B., Smith, P. C., & Alvares, K. M. Behavioral expectation scales: Effects of developmental procedures and formats. *Journal of Applied Psychology*, 1976, *61*, 75–79.

Blood, M. R. Spin-offs from behavioral expectation scale procedures. *Journal of Applied Psychology*, 1974, 59, 515–517.

Borman, W. C. Effects of instructions to avoid halo error on reliability and validity of performance evaluation ratings. *Journal of Applied Psychology*, 1975, *60*, 556–560.

Borman, W. C., & Dunnette, M. D. Behavior-based versus trait-oriented performance ratings: An empirical study. *Journal of Applied Psychology*, 1975, *60*, 561–565.

Borman, W. C., & Vallon, W. R. A view of what can happen when behavioral expectation scales are developed in one setting and used in another. *Journal of Applied Psychology*, 1974, *59*, 197–201.

Brown, E. M. Influence of training, method, and relationship on the halo effect. *Journal of Applied Psychology*, 1968, *52*, 195–199.

Burnaska, R. F., & Hollman, T. D. An empirical comparison of the relative effects of rater response biases on three rating scale formats. *Journal of Applied Psychology*, 1976, *59*, 307–312.

Campbell, J. P., Dunnette, M. D., Arvey, R. D., & Hellervik, L. V. The development and evaluation of behaviorally based rating scales. *Journal of Applied Psychology*, 1973, *57*, 15–22.

Dunnette, M. D. *Personnel selection and placement*. Belmont, Calif.: Wadsworth, 1966.

Guion, R. M. *Personnel testing.* New York: McGraw-Hill, 1965.

Latham, G. P., Wexley, K. N., & Pursell, E. D. Training managers to minimize rating errors in the observation of behavior. *Journal of Applied Psychology,* 1975, *60,* 550–555.

Levine, J., & Butler, J. Lecture vs. group decision in changing behavior. *Journal of Applied Psychology,* 1952, *36,* 29–33.

Sharon, A. T., & Bartlett, C. J. Effect of instructional conditions in producing leniency on two types of rating scales. *Personnel Psychology,* 1969, *22,* 251–263.

Smith, P. C., & Kendall, L. M. Retranslation of expectations: An approach to the construction of unambiguous anchors for rating scales. *Journal of Applied Psychology,* 1963, *47,* 149–155.

Taylor, E. K., & Hastman, R. Relation of format and administration to the characteristics of graphic rating scales. *Personnel Psychology,* 1956, *9,* 181–206.

Wakeley, J. H. *The effects of specific training on accuracy in judging others.* Unpublished doctoral dissertation, Michigan State University, 1961.

Zedeck, S., Jacobs, R., & Kafry, D. Behavioral expectations: Development of parallel forms and analysis of scale assumptions. *Journal of Applied Psychology,* 1976, *61,* 112–115.

FOR DISCUSSION AND REVIEW

1 What are the psychometric errors of leniency, halo, and failure to discriminate across ratees?

2 Define interrater reliability and explain how this was ascertained in the study.

3 What conclusions were drawn from this study? What do these conclusions imply?

D. LEGAL ISSUES IN APPRAISAL

William H. Holley

Hubert S. Feild

Performance Appraisal and the Law

In today's economic environment, personnel productivity, efficiency, and account-ability have emerged as subjects of considerable interest to both public and private employers. Every organization aspires to develop management systems that contri-bute toward the objectives of productivity improvement and cost efficiency while at the same time rewarding its employees for high levels of effective performance. Per-formance appraisal or evaluation is one such system which serves as a basis for this commitment to organizational objectives and establishing personnel accountabil-ity. However, in order to insure that the performance appraisal system meets its ob-jectives while complying with EEOC, OFCC, and court requirements, more efforts and research must be devoted to the design of valid or job-related instruments and methods of performance appraisal. Without valid appraisal systems, the costs to an organization, both internal and external, may easily become exorbitant.

An intricate part of the overall performance evaluation system is the ratings given by supervisors and used by management in making personnel decisions, e.g., layoffs, promotions, transfers. Presently, performance ratings are receiving more than just a passing interest from the EEOC, OFCC, and the courts because often they contain bias, are not reliable, and are not demonstrably job-related.[1] As such, they do not meet the requirements and standards of the EEOC, OFCC, or other in-vestigative agencies. Yet, as ironic as it may seem, supervisory ratings of employee performance are commonly used as the performance measure or criterion in test validation studies.[2]

Industrial psychologists, through various methods such as behavioral expec-tancy rating scales and other critical incident techniques, have minimized some of the subjectivity of supervisory ratings in performance appraisal and have suc-ceeded in screening out some of the grossest aspects. However, a problem with ratings remains where there may be racial or sexual prejudice, conscious or uncon-scious, on the part of the supervisor.[3] Serious legal questions are being raised con-cerning the use of ratings in personnel decision-making.

USE OF PERFORMANCE APPRAISAL SYSTEMS

Compliance with EEOC and OFCC standards and requirements would not be such a widespread problem if evaluation systems were not so common in industry and government. A national study of 139 companies by the Bureau of National Affairs showed that performance appraisal systems using ratings were quited prevalent

From *Labor Law Journal*, July 1975, pp. 423–430. Reprinted by permission.

[1]   H. G. Heneman, "Research Roundup," *The Personnel Administrator*, XIX (July–August, 1974), p. 49.

[2]   R. M. Guion, *Personnel Testing* (New York: McGraw-Hill Book Company, 1965), p. 96.

[3]   G. Cooper and R. Sobol, "Seniority and Testing Under Fair Employment Laws: A General Approach to Objective Criteria of Hiring and Promotion," *Harvard Law Review*, LXXXII, (August, 1969) pp. 1662–1663.

across a variety of job levels in industry.[4] Over 90 percent of the companies surveyed had formal performance evaluation programs for their supervisors, middle managers, and professional/technical personnel. Eight out of 10 companies had programs for their office and sales personnel, while 59 percent included their production workers in their performance appraisal programs. A recent survey of state personnel directors showed that almost 80 percent of the states had state-wide appraisal programs using some form of personnel rating.[5]

Table 1 summarizes the factors commonly used to appraise employees in industry and state government. It is interesting to note that many of the factors entail subjective judgments (e.g., personal traits). With such widespread application of appraisal systems and the employment of ratings for factors such as those in Table 1, it can only be an understatement that much research on performance appraisal remains to be done.

Table 1
Percentage of Employers Using Selected Factors
in Appraising Employee Performance

FACTOR	PRIVATE INDUSTRY[a]		STATE GOVERNMENT[b]
	MFG.	NONMFG.	
Managerial skills (knowledge, experience, ability to organize, etc.)	80	87	74
Achievement of goals (completion of programs, costs, production, etc.)	81	87	26
Job behaviors (as related to job duties)	64	65	80
Personal traits (attitudes, intelligence, dependability, etc.)	61	65	80
Potential (capacity to develop and advance, etc.)	58	61	8

[a]Based on a study of 139 firms by the Bureau of National Affairs, *Managerial Performance Appraisal Programs,* Washington, D.C., 1974, pp. 4-5.
[b]Based on a study of 24 systems by H. S. Feild and W. H. Holley, "Performance Appraisal in Public Employment: An Analysis of State-Wide Practices," *Public Personnel Management,* 1975 (in press).

The potential of the problem multiplies when one considers the purposes for which performance ratings are used in the private and public sectors. Table 2 reflects the purposes of their use in private industry and state governments. Since they serve as a basis for making these personnel decisions (e.g., layoffs, promotions), performance ratings must comply with legal requirements.

EEOC GUIDELINES

The legal aspects of performance appraisal systems are reflected in the EEOC "Guidelines on Employee Selection Procedures," the requirements for establishing a prima facie case in shifting the burden of proof, and recent court cases regarding the use of performance ratings.

---

[4] *Management Performance Appraisal Programs* (Washington: The Bureau of National Affairs, 1974), p. 2.
[5] Ibid.

Table 2
Percentage of Employers Using Performance Appraisal
Systems for Selected Purposes

FACTOR	PRIVATE INDUSTRY[c]	STATE GOVERNMENT[b]
Promotion	73	58[d]
Layoffs	27	
Discharge	46	
Wage and salary decisions	69	39
Training and development	61	38
Manpower planning and utilization	e	46

[b]Based on a study of 24 systems by H. S. Feild and W. H. Holley, "Performance Appraisal in Public Employment: An Analysis of State-Wide Practices," *Public Personnel Management*, 1975 (in press).
[c]Based on a study of 166 firms by the National Industrial Conference Board, "Personnel Practices in Factory and Office: Manufacturing," *Studies in Personnel Policy*, 1964, No. 194, p. 17.
[d]The categories of promotion, layoffs, and discharge were combined in the survey of state governments.
[e]Not reported.

Several sections of the "Guidelines on Employee Selection Procedures" published in the *Federal Register* have a direct bearing on the use of performance ratings. In particular, these sections include the definition of a "test," requirements for use of selection techniques other than tests, and minimum standards for validation. Although by title the Guidelines sound as if they apply only to tests commonly used in employee selection, it will be seen that they apply to any formal or informal device used to evaluate employees for such diverse purposes as layoffs, transfers, promotions, and salary adjustments.

For the purposes of the EEOC and the OFCC, a "test" is defined as ". . . any paper-and-pencil or performance measure used as a basis for any employment decision [which] . . . includes all formal, scored, quantified or standardized techniques of assessing job suitability including . . . specific or disqualifying personal history or background requirements, specific educational or work history requirements, scored interviews, biographical information blanks, interviewer's rating scales, scored application forms, etc"[6] In this sense, the definition of a test as used in the Guidelines is not limited solely to the measurement of cognitive areas such as abilities, aptitudes, and intelligence, but is extended into noncognitive domains as well, such as interests, attitudes, personality, and biographical data.

In extending the jurisdictional purview of the EEOC and the OFCC to cover personnel devices other than tests to assure compliance with the Equal Employment Opportunity Act and Executive Orders 11246 and 11375, the requirements for such techniques are also specified. "Selection techniques other than tests . . . may be improperly used so as to have the effect of discriminating against minority groups. Such techniques include, but are not restricted to, unscored or casual interviews and unscored application forms. Where there are data suggesting

---

[6]   U.S. Government, "Guidelines on Employee Selection Procedures." *Federal Register*, XXXV, (August 1, 1970), 12333.

employment discrimination, the person may be called upon to present evidence concerning the validity of his unscored procedures as well as any tests which may be used."[7]

The Guidelines also present additional evidence that performance appraisal methods are covered in their standards for use. "The work behaviors or other criteria of employee adequacy which the test is intended to predict or identify must be fully described; and additionally, in the case of rating techniques, the appraisal form(s) and instructions to the rater(s) must be included as a part of the validation evidence. Such criteria may include measures other than actual work proficiency, such as training time, supervisory ratings, regularity of attendance, and tenure. Whatever criteria are used they must represent major or critical work behaviors as revealed by careful job analyses.

"In view of the possibility bias inherent in subjective evaluations, supervisory rating techniques should be carefully developed and the ratings should be closely examined for evidence of bias. In addition, minorities might obtain unfairly low performance criterion scores for reasons other than supervisors' prejudice, as, when as new employees, they have had less opportunities to learn job skills. The general point is that all criteria need to be examined to insure freedom from factors which would unfairly depress the scores of minority groups."[8]

Most formal performance evaluation systems rely on paper-and-pencil measures to review employees' job performance (e.g., ratings). These reviews are then used for personnel decision-making and/or test validation purposes. It is therefore reasonable to conclude that performance appraisal systems fall under the purview of the EEOC. As will be seen, recent court cases support this contention.

PRIMA FACIE CASE AND BURDEN OF PROOF

The requirements for establishing a prima facie case and shifting the burden of proof are critical elements to understanding the legal processes in equal employment opportunity cases. To investigate the issues regarding a prima facie case and the burden of proof, the most reliable sources are the Supreme Court decisions and their interpretations by the lower courts. In *Griggs v. Duke Power Company*, the Court was specific in its position as it noted that ". . . Congress has placed on the employer the burden of showing that any given requirement must have a manifest relationship to the employment in question."[9]

Later, in 1972, the Supreme Court clarified its position further in *McDonnell Douglas Corporation v. Green*. "The complainant in a Title VII trial must carry the initial burden under the statute of establishing a prima facie case of racial discrimination. This may be done by showing (i) that he belongs to a racial minority; (ii) that he applied and was qualified for a job for which the employer was seeking applicants, (iii) that despite his qualifications, he was rejected, and (iv) that, after his rejection, the position remained open and the employer continued to seek applicants from persons of complainants' qualifications. [Once the prima facie case is established,] the burden then must shift to the employer to articulate more legitimate, nondiscriminatory reasons for the respondent's rejection."[10]

Other cases have shown that evidence of discrimination alone will establish a

---

[7]   Ibid., p. 12336.
[8]   Ibid., p. 12334.
[9]   *Griggs* v. *Duke Power Company*, 401 U.S. 424 (1971). 3 EPD ¶ 8137.
[10]   *McDonnell Douglas Corporation* v. *Green*, 411 U.S. 792 (1972), 5 EPD ¶ 8607.

prima facie case of discrimination, and statistical data may not be needed.[11] In addition, lower courts have approved other ways to establish a prima facie case. In *Carter v. Gallagher*,[12] statistics showing that a certain group performed more poorly than others on a test was accepted as prima facie evidence. In *Western Addition Community Organization v. Alioto*,[13] a comparison of the percentage of a particular minority group among those employed by the defendant with the percentage of that minority group in the general population established a prima facie case. Lastly, in *Chance v. Board of Examiners*,[14] a comparison of the racial composition of the defendant's work force with that of a similarly situated work force was successfully used as evidence.

COURT CASES ADDRESSING PERFORMANCE APPRAISAL

For years the courts obviously considered performance rating systems as serving an accepted and legitimate function within the overall personnel management system. In fact, it was not until the 1970's that performance rating systems began to fall from grace. Coupled with the close reading of the Guidelines, the employer's burden to show validity of personnel devices, and a more thorough investigation into the implementation and administration of performance rating systems, the courts, the EEOC, and OFCC have become highly critical of performance ratings and the manner in which they have been utilized.

The following cases indicate that performance appraisal results have been "inappropriately" used by employers in personnel decision-making and that legal consequences await the employer found to be in violation.

A municipal police department violated the Civil Rights Act of 1866 and 1871 and the Equal Protection Clause of the 14th Amendment when several black patrolmen were not promoted to sergeant. The court found that the regular service ratings of job performance were discriminatory and a special service rating of applicants for promotion had racial effects (two Negroes who passed the promotion exam received a greater drop in their regular service ratings than white officers who also passed the exam). As a remedy, the judge required that evaluations be performed on a six-month basis, ratings be retained even though the person is not seeking promotion, potential for serving in the next rank be evaluated, explanations for any market discrepancies between evaluation for promotion and regular service ratings be given, special ratings be performed by five persons, two of which were to be selected by the ratee, and raters support their evaluations with narrative reasons for their judgments.[15]

A municipal fire department violated the Equal Protection Clause of the 14th Amendment by not proving that either the efficiency rating system or the use of seniority credits for promotion was necessary to the conduct of business of the department. The discrimination violation included: time-in-grade requirements to determine eligibility to take the exam, application of performance ratings differently for blacks, and penalizing effects of seniority credits to blacks. To correct the violation, the promotion list was voided and the defendant was required to design an effi-

---

[11]   "Employment Testing: The Aftermath of *Griggs* v. *Duke Power Company.*" *Columbia Law Review*, LXXII, (May, 1972), p. 912.

[12]   *Carter* v. *Gallagher*, 3 FEP 900 (1971), 3 EPD ¶ 8205.

[13]   *Western Addition Community Organization* v. *Alioto*, 330 F. Supp. 536 (1972), 3 EPD ¶ 8327.

[14]   *Chance* v. *Board of Examiners*, 330 F. Supp. 213 (1972), 4 EPD ¶ 7600.

[15]   *Allen* v. *City of Mobile*, 331 F. Supp. 1134 (1971), 4 EPD ¶ 7582.

ciency rating system which would insure that blacks and whites were equally graded.[16]

A state-wide cooperative extension service was found in violation of the law when its evaluation instrument to appraise performance discriminated against black employees in that evaluations were made by subjective judgments, scores of black employees averaged less than those of white employees, the evaluation instrument was not based on job analysis, and no data were presented to demonstrate that the evaluation instrument was a valid predictor of employee job performance. This organization was required to employ qualified blacks in substantial numbers at all levels without delay and the court warned that lack of reasonable success would cause more stringent relief.[17]

PROMOTION AND TRANSFER

Two similar cases found employer discrimination in violation of Title VII of the Civil Rights Act. Neither employer was able to show that promotion and transfer procedures did not discriminate against black hourly employees. The court found the following as a basis for discrimination: recommendations by foremen were based on standards which were vague and subjective and were made without written instructions concerning qualifications necessary for promotion, hourly employees were not notified of promotional opportunities or the qualifications necessary for promotion, and no safeguards to overt discriminatory practices were designed.

As an affirmative action, one company was required to offer training programs to upgrade personnel, to provide foremen with written instructions delineating objective criteria and specific qualifications necessary for promotion and/or transfer, and to establish a committee of managers to insure that no one was denied consideration for promotion or transfer.[18] The other company was ordered to post announcements of pre-foremen training classes, to post notices of qualifications required for salaried positions, and to insure that every hourly-rated employee was considered for salaried employment when a position was available.[19]

Using performance ratings for determining personnel layoffs was found to be in violation of Title VII of the Civil Rights Act when an employer failed to validate the appraisal methods according to EEOC guidelines. The evaluations were judged invalid because they were based on subjective observations (two of three evaluators did not observe the employee on a daily basis), evaluations were not administered and scored under controlled and standardized conditions, and a disproportionate number of Spanish workers were laid off. The court ordered the company to reinstate the employees with nominal back pay and required the company not to use performance ratings until they had been validated.[20]

VALIDATION OF TESTS USING RATINGS

The court agreed wth an EEOC ruling that an employer did not appropriately validate a selection test when it used ratings based on subjective and vague factors as

---

[16]   *Harper* v. *Mayor and City Council of Baltimore*, 359 F. Supp. 1187, (1973), 5 EPD ¶ 2650.

[17]   *Wade* v. *Mississippi Cooperative Extension Service*, 372 F. Supp. 126, (1974), 7 EPD ¶ 9186.

[18]   *Baxter* v. *Savannah Sugar Refining Company*. (DC Ga. 1972). 5 EPD ¶ 8009.

[19]   *Rowe* v. *General Motors Corp.*, 457 F. Supp. 348, (1972), 4 EPD ¶ 7687.

[20]   *Brito, et al.* v. *Zia Company*, 478 F. 2d 1200. (1973), 5 EPD ¶ 8626.

the criteria for validation. Further, the employer did not comply with EEOC guidelines when it did not base the performance ratings on job analysis. As a result, the employer was enjoined from continuing the use of the selection test, and was required to provide back pay to the employees and pay their attorney fees.[21]

These case analyses reveal that inappropriate use of evaluations may occur for any one or more of the following reasons:

1 the performance rating method has not been shown to be job-related or valid;
2 the content of the performance rating method has not been developed from thorough job analyses;
3 raters have not been able to consistently observe the ratees performing their work;
4 ratings have been based on raters' evaluations of subjective or vague factors;
5 racial, sexual, etc. biases of raters may have influenced the ratings given to ratees;
6 ratings have not been collected and scored under standardized conditions.

Although these six reasons are not meant to be mutually exclusive nor exhaustive, they do point out specific considerations to be given when using performance appraisals in personnel decision-making.

CONCLUSIONS

As noted earlier, performance evaluation systems have enjoyed extensive application in both public and private organizations for a multitude of purposes, ranging from serving as a basis for promoting employees to serving as a criterion in test validation studies. Recently, however, serious legal questions have been raised concerning their use. In fact, of the available evidence to date, a significant number of cases brought to the courts involving performance evaluations have found them to be in violation of equal employment guidelines. Given the widespread use of these methods, the purposes for which they are used, and results of recent court cases, employers utilizing such data for personnel decisions may be in a precarious position. Thus, much research remains to be undertaken on the applicability of performance evaluation.

Clearly, a first step in this direction must be in terms of the validation of the methods used in performance evaluation. In previous years, performance ratings were used as a criterion for evaluating the validity of predictors such as tests. Now, however, criteria are needed for validating ratings used in performance evaluation. Establishing empirical concurrent or predictive validity of ratings is likely to be quite difficult and, in some cases, perhaps impossible. Content validity, on the other hand, seems to be a reasonable step toward a validation effort.[22]

---

[21] *Moody* v. *Albemarle Paper Co.*, 474 F. 2d 134 (CA-4, 1973), 5 EPD ¶ 8470. On June 25, 1975, the U.S. Supreme Court affirmed the decision of the Court of Appeals (Nos. 74-389 and 74-428). The Court concluded: " . . . [We] agree with the Court of Appeals that the District Court erred in concluding that Albemarle had proved the job relatedness of its testing program and that the respondents were consequently not entitled to equitable relief. The outright reversal by the Court of Appeals implied that an injunction should immediately issue against all use of testing at the plant. Because of the particular circumstances of this case, however, it appears that the more prudent course is to leave to the District Court the precise fashioning of the necessary relief in the first instance."

[22] See, for example, S. J. Mussio and M. K. Smith, *Content Validity: A Procedural Manual*, Chicago: International Personnel Management Association, undated; Selection Consulting Center, *Content Validity Manual*, Sacramento, California: Selection Consulting Center, undated; and R. M. Guion, "Content Validity Conference," *The Industrial Psychologist*, XII (December, 1974), p. 18.

Newer evaluation techniques utilizing ratings must also be developed. Behavioral expectancy rating scales using specific job behaviors rather than subjective traits hold some promise.[23] These scales, however, are usually job-specific and may be difficult to develop and apply in organizations having many different jobs. Techniques based on management-by-objectives (MBO), where measurable standards or objectives are set and the employee is judged on goal performance, represent another promising approach. An MBO program seems to be particularly relevant for managerial personnel, but often has limited application to non-managerial jobs. Other techniques which base the ratings on output or quotas show possibilities but comprehensive job analyses must precede their development. Regardless of the methods employed, the introduction of these newer evaluation techniques must be centered on research of the viability and effectiveness of the methods, and this research must be conducted within the framework of EEOC, OFCC, and court requirements.

FOR DISCUSSION AND REVIEW

1 In general, what impact have equal-employment-opportunity laws had on performance appraisals?
2 Why is a performance appraisal a test?
3 Review the relevance of the *Moody* versus *Albemarle* case for performance appraisal and equal employment opportunity.
4 Summarize how, according to EEO laws, performance appraisals may be inappropriately used.
5 How might MBO be a potentially illegal appraisal system?

---

[23]   J. P. Campbell, M. D. Dunnette, R. D. Arvey, and H. V. Hellervik, "The Development and Evaluation of Behaviorally Based Rating Scales," *Journal of Applied Psychology*, LVII (July–August, 1973), pp. 15–22.

INTERVIEW WITH GEORGE S. ODIORNE

Dr. Odiorne is Professor of Management and former Dean at the University of Massachusetts in Amherst. He received a B.A. from Rutgers and an MBA and Ph.D from New York University. Prior to joining the staff at the University of Massachusetts, Dr. Odiorne was Dean of the College of Business at the University of Utah and Director of the Bureau of Industrial Relations at the University of Michigan.

Dr. Odiorne has also held positions with General Mills, American Management Association, and American Can Company and been a consultant to the Ford Motor Company, Honeywell, General Motors, Aetna Life Insurance Company, and other major American corporations. In addition, he has written several books on management and personnel.

Q You have been involved in the area of performance appraisal for several years, as a teacher, consultant, researcher, and author. What has changed over the years? What is currently being done in organizations that is new?

A Constant change is the rule for performance appraisal. In its beginnings, appraisal was *merit rating* of employees, generally hourly rated and clerical, for the purpose of allocating pay increases. Then it moved into supervisory performance and the emphasis moved from personality to skills —from trustworthy, loyal, helpful, etc. to organizing ability, planning ability, and similar skill areas. This was amended when the subjects being appraised were executives and middle managers. In such instances, the shortcomings of prior systems became apparent, and the emphasis shifted to *results.*

Most current innovations in appraisal seem to be centered around better ways of assessing goals and results, for they have become the criteria of success. This has produced some sticky problems in defining success, in determining whether it is attributable to the person or to his or her situation.

Q What basic differences do you see between managerial and nonmanagerial appraisal systems?

A The major emphasis in nonmanagerial appraisals is on *activity* and its forms, while the major emphasis in technical and managerial jobs centers around *outputs.*

Q What impact has EEO and the ever-increasing number of women in the work force had on the appraisal systems in most organizations? Are there differences between men's appraisal of men and of women in the same jobs? How can biases in this area be overcome? Have the *EEOC Guidelines* removed some of the subjectivity from ratings?

A EEO taught most of us that prior personality-based systems of appraisal, testing, and the like were often culture biased and therefore not valid for all populations. Goals-and-results-centered appraisals seem to stand up better, for it is performance against objectives which stands the test of objectivity.

Most of our biases are unconscious, or readily rationalized into such a condition. Over time and with persistence, however, a constant reiteration of the question, "What kind of a job did the person do?" makes performance, not sex or race, the crucial criterion.

Q Much of the current empirical research on appraisal systems is pretty sophisticated stuff—psychometric properties of scales, response-set errors, etc. Has this research filtered into the organization's personnel department? What positive consequences of recent appraisal research have you seen in applied settings?

A Most of the behavioral research being done hasn't been converted into use yet. This is rather heartening in many ways, for it indicates that the universities are ahead of the corporations and government agencies in technique and theory. Once a major evolutionary stage has been reached, it takes considerable testing, research, problem solving, and innovation to perfect the system. For example, Peter Drucker and Doug McGregor are often cited as the originators of the concept and philosophy of MBO, but it was E. A. Locke's dozen or more scientific research studies which *proved* that it works the way its conceptualizers had said that it would work. I suspect that many more people know Drucker's name than Locke's, but he represents the finest tradition of academic research and in many ways represents the new academic theorist.

Still another function is required, a converter and carrier, perhaps even persuader, who carries the ideas and findings to industry through widely sold books, speeches, and executive development programs. This is a function which I have worked at with MBO. It's analogous to the engineer who converts good theory into useful products.

Q Are some people better than others at judging their subordinates' performance? Are there differences over and above bias that have to do with ability in interpersonal situations?

A Clearly some people are far better than others at judging subordinates. Those who are naturally empathetic do a better job. Also, there are those who have a long personal acquaintance with the other person, and this is the best basis for judgment, prediction, and assessment. Behavior in mature persons is often persistent and therefore can reasonably be assumed to follow a pattern, although we still get surprises, both pleasant and unpleasant, from time to time. It is this persistence which permits us to use scientific methods of study, prediction, analysis, and control. Another kind of person, then, who is good in judging people is a skilled technician in assessment who relies on statistical tendencies.

A cautionary note is needed, however. None of the systems is infallible and even the most scientific method should be reviewed with St. Augustine's maxim in mind that "there are hidden deeps in people" which we can never fully plumb. This is especially true in individual cases between boss and subordinate. One of the bosses' functions is to develop and enlarge people working for them, and such changes should be sought, hoped for, and noted when they occur.

Q How can the subjectivity in ratings be alleviated? Is this a practical objective? Many people have argued that subjectivity could be lessened by using performance-based (e.g., work quality) as opposed to personality-based (e.g., initiative) appraisal criteria. Yet recent surveys indicate trait ratings are typically preferred. Are personal criteria too subjective? Please comment.

A There are three ways in which subjectivity can be managed, but none that eliminates it. The first is to have a policy which describes the desired way and also the undesired way. The second is extensive training in how to do performance reviews, with some role play and feedback. The third is for another party at a higher level to review the ratings for equity of treatment and consistency of standards. All of these are time consuming and expensive.

The criteria used in ratings should be treated as measures of *utility* of the job being done and the contribution of the person. Measurement of utility is best done when we rely first on objective measures, then on statistical ratios and the like, and only as a last resort when others fail to apply subjective standards.

The big pitfall in personal and subjective ratings is that they conceal bias, hunch, discrimination, or even self dealing by the rater.

Q I know that one of your major areas of interest and expertise has been MBO. Since you began working with this appraisal tool, how has it changed inapplication? Do you feel MBO has been a particularly effective appraisal system over the years? Why or why not?

A MBO started out in General Motors as a way of allocating executive bonuses. That application persists, and recent studies by the Conference Board report that about half of the executive bonus plans are based upon MBO in some form. It then moved into the general appraisal area. In part this was in response to the strong criticism which came about against personality-based management systems. Popular books damning conformity and false scientism, the organization man and the like led to a revulsion against personality assessment as an invasion of privacy. From this it evolved into a general system of managing, especially into planning and budgeting. It is today the predominant method of appraisal, but pockets of other systems, including no appraisal system at all, persist.

The research evidence shows that MBO does change behavior, that it sorts out people into performance-centered versus non-performance-centered people, that it tends to bring self-reliant people to the fore. It has some self-fulfilling characteristics. If it is vigilantly applied, it works to produce the effects sought.

Q It seems as if everyone is using MBO, running workshops on it for managers, writing articles extolling its virtues, etc. Has MBO been oversold? Is it a fad? Have the basic ideas been changed in the innumerable varieties available tcday? Does the old adage, "A little knowledge is a dangerous thing," hold for MBO?

A Fads by definition extinguish themselves after the initial burst of enthusiasm. MBO has had many faddish moments, and in some organizations it worked like any fad. The test of whether or not it is a passing fancy is determined by the extent to which it is used. Dr. Bruce Kirchoff has defined four tests of whether or not you have MBO: a policy statement favoring it or requiring it, a responsible person to administer it, continuing training, and regular improvements. Adding variations and improvements doesn't prove its weaknesses but its strengths and diversity.

The "magical interview" aspects which construe MBO to be two interviews, one at the beginning of the year and another at the end by bosses and subordinates, will extinguish themselves. MBO is not an addition to anybody's job but a way of doing it.

Q Critics have argued that too big an emphasis on results, which they feel is often a consequence of MBO, can reinforce managers for engaging in behaviors which may produce short-run results but have long-term negative effects. How would you respond to this argument?

A This is a valid argument and led to a response which has moved MBO into a multiyear, or long-range planning, model. I suggest that MBO has two facets: Management by Anticipation for staff and executive jobs, and Management by Commitment for operating jobs. An organization needs both, and this division of labor is necessary to make it work. Otherwise people will work very hard doing things right rather than doing the right things. Orville Beal, former President of the Prudential, once stated that "purposes flow down and methods must flow up" for MBO to work.

     I see more of a trend toward requiring some mention of *constraints* when defining goals, lest people achieve narrow goals at the expense of overall organizational performance, or their fellow employees.

     Recent research into job design suggests that there will be more attention to job structure and content in future goal-setting practices. Some bosses have experimented with negotiating a suitable management style with their subordinates to avoid this dilemma.

Q The joint goal-setting phase of MBO, as well as the performance-review phase, require sincere participation on the part of the rater. How does an authoritarian manager operate here? Isn't honest participation difficult to come by in this setting? What can be done to help an authoritative manager to elicit subordinates' participation in goal setting?

A MBO permits participative management, and tends to bring it about, but there are many organizations where the culture and style, as well as the expectations of people, are that an autocratic style will prevail. Clarity of goals in this environment can be produced, and where that is understood by all, it produces good organizational performance. MBO doesn't demand or require participative management, and should not be equated to participative management as being one and the same. MBO makes it easy, natural, and, in time, will produce a Likert's system 3.

     Autocratic managers don't change their behavior from persuasion or evidence, except where they try something and it works. Occasionally a well-placed retirement or funeral is necessary.

Q How does an appraisal in general, and an MBO system in particular, impact other personnel programs, such as training and selection? What can be done to enhance cooperation between the programs?

A As you know, I have a book called *Personnel Administration by Objectives* which goes over all of the personnel functions from the objectives viewpoint. It suggests that a modern personnel department will select by objectives (define goals before assembling applicants), train by objectives, administer salaries by objectives, discipline by objectives. In short, you manage by objectives.

     The difficulty comes in the traditional personnel program in which people are clinging fiercely to the methods of the thirties, the forties, and the fifties in subprograms. In selection many firms still adhere to 1920s methods. In training they still "run programs" without the faintest idea of intent and behavior change sought or achieved.

My experience has been that one of the major obstacles to a well-developed MBO program in some firms has been the immense resistance of the personnel department to change to current behavioral findings, or even the needs of their employers.

Q   Do very many organizations actually tie their rewards (promotions, salaries, etc.) to performance-appraisal scores? Why or why not? Would you be in favor of determining the size of a bonus by the degree to which a person attained their objectives? What would be the disadvantages of such a system?

A   My estimate is that 50 percent of the firms have objectives-centered bonus plans, merit rating plans, or compensation plans. The Conference Board and others have reported similar levels. In the hourly rated jobs, industrial engineering standards comprise the major basis for merit rating, including incentive pay plans.

Q   Performance appraisal is useful not only for the measurement, but also for the development, of performance. Yet feedback is often so general and subjective, or omitted altogether, as to disallow any improvement. What appraisal techniques can help here?

A   Feedback is so crucial to making MBO work that a whole area of study is emerging in ways of making job feedback more effective. Basically it breaks into three kinds of feedback: from the job itself, from periodic reviews by the boss, and from continual feedback from clients, peers, and the like.

Jobs and how they feed back information to their incumbents comprise a frontier. We are constantly getting information about our performance from the physical surroundings ("Why don't they give engineers more privacy to write reports?") and from our clients. Many jobs by their design and structure tell the incumbent: "Don't do me right." One of the areas in which MBO will lead to changed job design is in arranging the work environment so that desirable performance will produce favorable consequences for the person in the job, rather than the opposite.

This doesn't eliminate the annual performance review, but changes its context. People should see the review as forward looking: not "Where did you fail?" but "How could you do an even better job?" The major behavioral effect from performance review comes from the immediate feedback on the job while you are doing it. The annual review merely helps you set better goals for the future.

Q   What do you see in the future regarding executive appraisal systems? Will MBO remain popular? Why? What place is appraisal likely to have in the personnel department ten years from now?

A   I think there will be more group appraisals, and more self-appraisals. Self-appraisals, reviewed by a boss, have a more important behavior-change effect, for they draw on our natural tendency to be self-rewarders and self-punishers. They also clarify our goals more precisely.

At an organizational level the program review and program assessment will emerge more heavily in the future. We'll be seeing more program audits, environmental audits, and the like. This will have a strong impact upon individual goals, especially in staff jobs.

Q What new knowledge, perhaps gained through research, would be useful in improving the appraisal process?

A The research frontiers seem to lie in job design. The old-fashioned industrial engineering department will be revised into a new kind of department to build motivation, feedback, and behavioral factors into the job and not just elimination of cost—although that's not unimportant. Some other topics will be behavior modification through MBO ideas, new ways of handling face-to-face relations, new ways of organizing teams and companies, new kinds of management information systems, and new kinds of program audits and individual self-audits.

Human-Resource Selection and Staffing

INTRODUCTION

Of the many personnel activities, selection and staffing programs probably receive the most publicity today. In large part, this reflects not only the importance of the hiring process, but also the influence of equal-employment-opportunity (EEO) legislation.

Korman's review of concurrent- and predictive-validity models in Part A provides information essential for anyone connected with hiring today. Part B, on selection and the law, presents another topic vital at present. Here, the major EEO and related laws, guidelines, executive orders, and so forth are explained clearly by Higgins. However, the rapidly changing nature of EEO legislation, new court decisions, and hence new required practices preclude any article on these topics from being timely for long. The most recent sources thus must always be consulted before decisions are made.

Section Four next focuses, in Parts C through F, on each of the four major selection techniques or classes of predictors—biographical data, interviewing, work samples and simulations, and tests. England's discussion of the weighted application blank details an excellent procedure for validating this predictor. Martin's refreshingly candid comments place the subjectivity of the interview in a new light, while Schmitt's review of research tells us what has been learned over the years. The utility of assessment centers and work samples as providers of data to augment other predictors is explained by Kraut and Campion, respectively. Tests, the final selection technique examined, have caused an enormous amount of frustration and confusion over the years for those in personnel. Robertson's timely piece explains the legal constraints on testing as a personnel selection tool.

A. PERSPECTIVES ON SELECTION AND VALIDITY

John P. Wanous

Tell It Like It Is at Realistic Job Previews

In analyzing the recruitment process, industrial psychologists traditionally have focused attention on how companies select new employees. More recently, however, organizational behaviorists have taken a hard look at how applicants choose one organization over others, and old assumptions about how new employees should be recruited are being questioned.

The traditional approach to recruitment and selection views the applicant as passive rather than active. An individual is typically selected for a job on the basis of tests, interviews, and background information. Almost completely ignored in the process is the organizational choice made by the applicant—how and why he showed up in the first place. To obtain a favorable selection ratio—that is, a large number of applications in relation to the number of job openings—companies sometimes present themselves to potential new employees in a more favorable light than the facts justify. In the end, this kind of policy can produce dysfunctional results, costly to both the organization and the employee.

Recent research suggests, however, that recruitment can be made more effective through the use of *realistic job previews* (RJP), an atypical, untraditional approach that stresses efforts to communicate—before an applicant's acceptance of a job offer—what organizational life will actually be like on the job. A study conducted by the author at Southern New England Telephone Company and related research by others at Prudential Insurance Company, the U.S. Military Academy, and Texas Instruments utilized the RJP approach to recruitment. Major findings from these studies show:

- Newly hired employees who received realistic job previews have greater job survival than those hired by traditional recruiting methods.
- Employees hired after RJPs indicate higher job satisfaction.
- An RJP can "set" the job expectations of new employees at realistic levels.
- RJPs do not reduce the flow of highly capable applicants.

WHY TRADITIONAL RECRUITMENT PRACTICES NEED REEXAMINATION

Traditional recruitment practice is characterized by its emphasis on having the organization "look good" to potential employees, usually to attract a large pool of job applicants so that a cream-of-the-crop selection may be made.

In selecting employees, most organizations try to match individual and organization. This usually means selection of those who the employer predicts will be good *performers.* Selection according to who also will be a good risk on turnover or absenteeism is sometimes considered, but this factor typically plays second fiddle to selection based on job performance predictions.

This approach deserves reexamination, however, because it has hidden costs and because of laws now controlling personnel selection and recruitment.

1 *Emphasis on expected job performance as the dominant—almost exclusive—criterion in selection overlooks possible turnover costs resulting from mismatches between the employee and the organization.* The forces influencing performance on the job and those influencing an individual to remain on the job have important distinctions. Job performance generally is considered to be influenced by an individual's abilities and his motivation, that is, his need to achieve. On the other hand, a person's tendency to remain in the organization is seen as a result of that person's need fulfillment, for example, satisfying his need for security, and resulting job satisfaction.

2 *In most organizations highest turnover occurs among newly hired employees—those in their first six months on the job.* Employees new to the job and organization have a higher turnover rate than those with more experience in the organization because they may simply be "testing out" the new environment to see if it suits their particular needs. And their "test" may be necessitated by the company's practice of overselling the attractiveness of jobs during the recruitment process.

Much research, spanning 40 years or more, shows that the higher the job satisfaction, the lower the turnover. But the relationship between job satisfaction and job performance is much less clearly understood and has been the focus of controversy over the years among both researchers and theorists in the field.

Selecting new employees on the basis of performance criteria thus will not necessarily result in long-tenure employees. In fact, it is not unusual to find that the best job performers are high-turnover employees because of the thrust of their upward mobility internally or in other organizations.

Careful attention must be paid, therefore, to the results desired in organizational recruitment and selection. For example, companies risk increased turnover problems if they elect to:

- Select new employees exclusively in terms of the company's interests rather than in terms of the balanced interests of both the company and the employee.
- Present the organization in overly attractive terms to encourage people to apply for jobs.
- Select new employees only on the basis of matching limited performance requirements to individual capabilities rather than on the basis of both performance and satisfaction requirements and capabilities.

Companies that cannot shift their personnel policies to recognize the interests of their employees may face personnel costs stemming from high turnover caused by mismatches between an individual's desires for human need satisfaction and the organization's capacity to fulfill these needs.

THE RJP: WHAT IS IT AND HOW DOES IT WORK?

A realistic job preview should be given to an applicant before the job offer has been accepted. It should try to communicate important information to the potential employee—especially information that is closely tied to employee satisfactions and dissatisfactions.

But just what is "reality," and how can it be designed into a job preview?

It must be understood that an RJP is not an indictment of a particular job nor does it exclude positive information. An RJP must be balanced to include important facets of a particular job (and the organization) that the typical employee experiences as satisfying and those that are commonly dissatisfying. The final balance between positive and negative characteristics will vary, depending on the

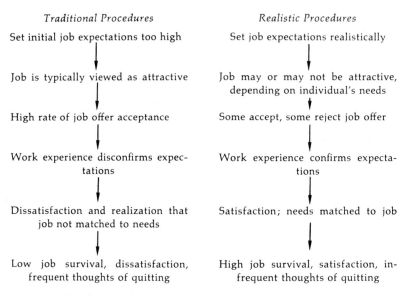

Fig. 1 Typical consequences of job preview procedures.

nature of the job in question. Figure 1 illustrates RJP logic and the rationale underlying the research findings.

Impact of the traditional approach

The traditional job preview is not a homogeneous procedure. Organizations recruit new employees in a variety of ways, ranging from systematic attempts to "sell" the organization to the individual (via advertising techniques) to informal, unsystematic distribution of information given in the course of testing, interviewing, and selecting. Although there are wide degrees of conscious intent to sell an organization and widely varying methods for doing so, there is the common thread that an organization almost always presents itself attractively to outsiders who may become new employees.

Thus it often turns out that recruits have unrealistic initial expectations of what the job and the company are like. If these expectations, unrealistic as they may be, approach the recruit's personal preferences or desires, he is likely to conclude that the organization is an attractive place to work.

But what happens after a period of on-the-job experience? Typical reactions are disappointment and dissatisfaction because the initial expectations have not been realized. The employee probably will conclude the job is really not matched to his needs, and since this mismatch was not discovered until after work began, there is a good chance he may quit—or if the labor market is tight, he may stay on the job as a dissatisfied worker, think often about quitting, and be absent often.

Impact of a realistic preview

An RJP also "sets" the initial expectations of recruits, but in this case they are realistic expectations. To avoid pitfalls of the traditional preview, an RJP provides important job information—both positive and negative—completely and without bias. Thus when an individual compares his realistic expectations about the job and organization to his own desires, an appropriate organizational choice (or self-selection) can be made.

If the RJP as an impact on the individual's organizational choice, then those who actually go to work will tend to be better matched to the new environment than those recruited via the traditional procedure. This combination of "inoculating" the individual against disappointment and the more effective organizational choices typically results in greater job survival, higher job satisfaction, and fewer thoughts of quitting.

AN EXPERIMENT: RJP VS. THE TRADITIONAL

The author's study of RJP versus the traditional job preview involved a sample of about 80 female telephone operators at several employment offices of Southern New England Telephone Company.

Prior to the study, which covered a period of about nine months, the overall turnover rate for operators varied between 30 and 40 percent per year. But for operators in their first six months on the job, the rate often rose to 100 percent or higher.

To compare the effects of the two contrasting job preview approaches, the previews were presented to job candidates in the form of 15-minute films shown on portable units in each employment office. Figure 2 shows the sequence of events in this experiment for each job preview approach as well as the typical sequence used prior to the experiment. Applicants were assigned at random to the preview groups.

PREEXPERIMENT	REALISTIC EXPERIMENT	TRADITIONAL EXPERIMENT
Receptionist	Receptionist	Receptionist
Initial interview	Initial interview	Initial interview
	Questionnaire 1	*Questionnaire 1*
Testing, medical questionnaire	Testing, medical questionnaire	Testing, medical questionnaire
Application blank	Application blank	Application blank
Selection interview	Selection interview	Selection interview
	Realistic film	*Traditional film*
	Questionnaire 2	*Questionnaire 2*
Job visit	Job visit	Job visit
Training	Training	Training
Work experience	Work—1 month: *Questionnaire 3*	Work—1 month: *Questionnaire 3*
	Work—3 months: *Questionnaire 4*	Work—3 months: *Questionnaire 4*

Fig. 2 Selection procedures for operators.

The operator applicants also were asked to complete several questionnaires designed (1) to measure the impact of each preview on *initial expectations*, (2) to obtain a measurement of each individual's own *job preferences*, and (3) to assess *on-the-job satisfaction* and thoughts of quitting after some work experience.

The traditional preview film used in the experiment existed prior to the study. Dealing with the operator's job, it had been used in high school recruiting and in several other ways, but it never had been systematically applied as a job preview for all candidates on a regular basis.

Figure 3 shows some of the major differences between the preview films, but as a chart, it captures only part of the "flavor" of the sequences. Subjective impressions of company managers and colleagues of the author indicate that this RJP was about 60–40 negative in balance. Compared to the traditional preview film, this was quite a difference.

OVERLAP BETWEEN FILMS

---

1. Customers can be quite unfriendly at times
2. Work is fast paced
3. Some operators receive satisfaction from helping out customers
4. Action sequences of operators at work:
   a. emergency call
   b. "wise guy" calling operator
   c. credit card call
   d. overseas call
   e. directory assistance operators at work
   f. "nasty" customer calling operator
5. Dealing with others (customers, co-workers) is a large part of the job

---

NONOVERLAP CHARACTERISTICS

Realistic Film
1. Lack of variety
2. Job is routine; may become boring
3. Close supervision; little freedom
4. Limited opportunity to make friends
5. Receive criticism for bad performance, but no praise when deserved
6. Challenging initially, but once learned is easy and not challenging

Traditional Film
1. Everyone seems happy at work
2. Exciting work
3. Important work
4. Challenging work

Fig. 3 Job characteristics emphasized by each job preview film.

WHAT THE STUDY SHOWED

In terms of "job survival" (being on the job three months after starting to work), 62 percent of the realistic group of newly hired operators survived compared to 50 percent of the traditional group. This was similar to other research studies of the RJP concept.

For example, the first study of life insurance agents found a difference of 68 percent survival for the realistic group compared to 53 percent for the traditional after a period of five months. In a second study the difference was 71 percent vs. 57 percent survival over a six-month period.

The original West Point study found that 91 percent of the first-year cadets survived who received a realistic booklet before choosing to accept the appointment. Of those who received the traditional material from West Point, 86 percent survived the first year. A second West Point study analyzed the effects of an RJP booklet on voluntary resignations during the summer training period prior to the first year at West Point. Of those receiving the RJP, 94 percent survived as compared to only 88.5 percent of a control group, which had no such preview.

The study at Texas Instruments was not a job preview but an on-the-job first-day indoctrination and did not report job survival data. But, in every case, to my knowledge, the RJP has increased job survival over traditional methods of recruitment.

In addition to higher job survival rates, members of the realistic group in the telephone study indicated higher job satisfaction after three months on the job and had thought much less about quitting after one month. The basis for these attitudes appears to be in the gap between expectations created by the traditional preview and the reality of being an operator.

Figure 4 charts a typical attitude pattern that emphasizes the sharp contrast between preview expectations and on-the-job reality for traditional and realistic groups.

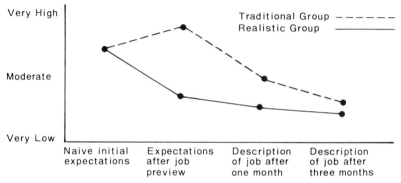

Fig. 4 How attitudes about work change.

Along with assessing the impact of an RJP on end-result variables, it was important to understand why an RJP "works." The questionnaire administered *before* job previews measured "naive, initial job expectations," but the results of the post-preview questionnaire showed clearly that the expectations of those who received the traditional preview were raised, and the expectations of the RJP group were significantly lowered. For example, a sampling of the questionnaire tabulations shows that expectations particularly affected by RJPs included:

- Receiving praise for doing a good job.
- Having freedom to use one's own judgment.
- Making use of one's abilities and using one's own methods.
- Feelings of accomplishment from the job.
- Whether supervisors handle employees well.

The preview films did not touch all facets of the operator's job, just some of the most important. Thus some questions showed no differences between the two groups because the films included nothing pertaining to them. But while lowering certain expectations in comparison to the traditional job preview, the effect of realism was selective because it only affected expectations included in the previews and did not spill over to others.

Contrary to predictions, the realistic preview made no noticeable impact on actual job decisions; the effect of an RJP on applicants' organizational choices did not materialize. Only two out of about 80 applicants refused offers, and the fact that job-offer acceptances were not influenced could be one reason why job survival rates were not even further apart.

Two explanations seem reasonable. First, the study was conducted during a period of high and sharply increasing unemployment. Second, the job previews occurred "late" in the sequence of events in the recruitment and selection process. Each applicant involved in the study had made considerable personal effort to obtain a job—making trips to the employment office, taking tests and interviews, and so forth. Research data show that the more effort individuals put forth, the more attractive the object of their effort becomes. Thus it was quite possible that the operators hired had made some type of advance psychological commitment to accept if a job offer were made.

FUTURE USE OF REALISTIC JOB PREVIEWS

The results of the telephone operator study suggest the following guidelines for implementation of RJPs as an ongoing personnel procedure.

Diagnose the situation Before adopting an RJP policy, thoroughly diagnose the jobs to be considered for an RJP. Check on job-survival-rate data. Are the rates high or low? What is the rate pattern? How does it vary in relation to job experience?

If a job survival problem involving new employees is indicated, make a hard, objective assessment of job characteristics and other information given to recruits to ensure the validity of the data. For example, in identifying all facets of a particular job, a variety of data sources should be tapped. When diagnosing the nature of job information given to recruits, check all potential sources. Then compare these two assessments to determine whether any root problems can be corrected by using an RJP.

The medium may be the message An effective RJP must realistically depict the important facets of a particular work environment. The study of telephone operators showed that the job visit portion of the recruitment and selection process did not fully communicate the job to an unfamiliar person. A short snatch of the action in an operator's workroom did not accurately reflect the long-term reactions of boredom and lack of autonomy that many operators experience.

Although the job visit was intended to be a realistic preview, it probably had the effect of enhancing the attractiveness of this job. In a film format the long-run reactions to his job were portrayed by experienced telephone operators who talked about them.

In contrast to the above example where the medium (film) turned out to affect the message, there are counter examples. The studies at Prudential and West Point used booklets effectively. The Texas Instruments' first-day "realistic orientation" used a small group of peers to set initial expectations and reduce first-day anxiety.

Use previews early rather than late An RJP can function in two ways:

- As a "screening device" to help job candidates decide for themselves on their organizational choices.
  As an "inoculation" against disappointment with the realities of organizational life.

Early use of the RJP in the recruitment/selection/placement process could be difficult, however, because of the costs involved in adding it to standard personnel operating procedures. Thus it may be less expensive to wait until after the first few selection hurdles have thinned the list of applicants. In some situations there even may be a tradeoff between maximum influence on the organizational choice process and the costs of administration, as in the telephone operator study. In any case, whether used early or late, the effectiveness of an RJP to inoculate new employees against disappointment seems unimpaired.

High unemployment rates may affect outcomes Because of the distinction between an RJP's effect on organizational choice versus its value as an inoculation, high unemployment may reduce the impact of an RJP on organizational choices. It has the same effect as that of an RJP administered too late, that is, after psychological commitment to accept a job offer has developed.

Is an RJP limited to a certain type of job? As we have seen, realistic previews have been used successfully on a variety of jobs in differing organizations. How far one can generalize from this is not completely clear. It seems reasonable, however, to assume that RJPs will be effective for a number of entry-level jobs—whether in white collar insurance sales or as a telephone operator. But in the end, each job situation must be analyzed to assess the potential usefulness of the RJP approach.

FOR DISCUSSION AND REVIEW

1   Define a realistic job preview. Why are traditional methods of recruitment criticized?
2   What are the typical consequences of traditional and realistic job previews?
3   Review the results of the research the author describes. What are the implications of this research?
4   What medium is recommended for use in realistic previews?

A. K. Korman

Personnel Selection: The Traditional Models

Most psychologists would probably agree that industrial psychology, as a profession devoted to assisting in the achievement of organizational and individual objectives in the world of work, has its greatest historical support in and still continues to be prominently identified with the personnel selection process. It is in the development and refinement of procedures and methodology relating to the question of the basis on which individuals shall be chosen for roles in the organization that industrial psychology first developed as a recognizable entity and it is in this area that many practitioners continue to work today, at least on a part-time basis.

However, although there is this historical tradition of psychological concern and although there are many individuals who continue to work in this area on a pragmatic, everyday basis, the process of personnel selection and the development of appropriate methodologies relating to it is by no means a closed, decided proce-

From Abraham K. Korman, *Industrial and Organizational Psychology,* © 1971, pp. 178–204. Reprinted by permission of Prentice-Hall, Inc., Englewood Cliffs, New Jersey.

dure. On the contrary, recent years have seen a variety of controversies ranging from civil-rights questions to matters of "privacy" to an attack on the entire philosophy underlying the personnel selection process itself. In this chapter . . . we shall concern ourselves with the various questions relating to personnel selection, its degree of contribution to organizational success, and the benefits and problems which have resulted from such contributions. Finally, we shall also discuss how these contributions may be likely to change in the future.

THE TRADITIONAL PERSONNEL SELECTION MODEL: PREDICTIVE VALIDITY

The major contributions which industrial psychology has made to the personnel selection process have been in two areas. One has been the development of psychological measures which predict job performance and which are available to the employing company prior to the time of hiring or rejecting, while the second has concerned itself with the development of appropriate methodologies for evaluating whether or not a given predictor is actually operating effectively, i.e., whether it is predicting the behavior which it should be predicting. Information relating to these two questions has then generally been reported to management, to be used by them in their judgment and decision making in the way they see most fit. In this chapter we shall concern ourselves with the latter contribution by industrial psychologists. . . .

Until recent years the latter interest and concern by industrial psychologists took a relatively standardized form, i.e, those who were interested in developing effective selection procedures did pretty much the same thing, no matter what type of company they worked for.[1] This procedure, which we shall call the "traditional personnel selection model," will be discussed below as a series of steps. As we go through it the reader will see that it makes a lot of sense and that it appears to be a highly appropriate procedure to be used in personnel selection, and, in many respects, it is. However, a more searching examination, as we shall find, indicates that the picture is not all that good and that this traditional model contains within it a series of assumptions about the nature of work and human characteristics that in today's society are, sometimes (not always), dubious at best. Hence, recent years have seen a number of suggested revisions of this traditional model, and it is these revisions with their associated benefits and disadvantages which we shall discuss in Chapter 9.

Step 1—the job analysis

The traditional personnel selection model has as its first step the study of the characteristics and required behaviors of the job for which the selection process is being undertaken. It is obvious, of course, that one must have some understanding of the nature of the job one wishes to select for, since not to know this would reduce all selection to a purely random, chance basis. The procedure for finding out this information (which also has value for various other organizational functions such as training, job transfer, and performance appraisal) is known as a "job analysis," and it consists, usually, of a description of the various behaviors, characteristics, and abilities required of the occupant of that job. The ways in which this information is

---

[1]   Due to Civil Service regulations the comments which we shall make in the chapter are, in general, not applicable to government organizations.

obtained varies with the company, the job, the occupant, etc., but in essence there are two major procedures.

One way is to ask the current job occupant to describe what he does, either subjectively or along some defined dimensions. This method has some advantages. It elicits worker cooperation by bringing him in on the decision making and possibly enhances his self-esteem (with consequent implications for performance) at the same time. A second advantage is, of course, that the job occupant probably knows the job better than anybody else. At the same time, however, there is the disadvantage that the job occupant will probably be most motivated to distort, either consciously or unconsciously, his description in a favored direction. Furthermore, there is another disadvantage to this procedure in that the occupant may not be psychologically, educationally, or emotionally equipped to write an accurate description of his job duties.

Similar advantages and disadvantages attach themselves to the other major job analysis method, that of "observation." Analyzing a job by observation has the advantage of eliminating "faking" to a great extent since an observer should generally be more objective. Furthermore, the observer will also usually be a "qualified" recorder. However, the first advantage could be illusory in that the job occupant may fake his performance, either consciously or subconsciously, if someone is watching him. In addition, a second possible disadvantage is that this procedure is completely inappropriate for mental "thinking" jobs and for jobs which involve a long period of time before a specific job activity is finished. (The analogy here is between the division manager who might be working on a decentralization plan taking five years as opposed to the mechanical repetitive job.) Since these "long-cycle" types of jobs are becoming increasingly the norm in our society, we might expect to see a decrease in the method of "observation" in job analysis as time goes on.

Besides the advantages and disadvantages of each of these procedures, there are problems in job analysis which are common to both (and, in fact, to any observational system involving the rating of such social objects as jobs and people, as we shall point out in our later discussion on performance appraisal methods). One set of these problems has been called the "judgment" errors and can be summarized as follows:

1 *The "halo" error:* This is the tendency to allow one characteristic of a rating object to dominate ratings along other dimensions of the object being rated. An example of this is when we are more likely to attribute intellectual qualities to a person who wears glasses than a person who does not.
2 *The "central tendency" error:* This is the tendency to rate all rating objects around the "middle" or mean of a rating continuum and not to use the extremes.
3 *The "leniency" error:* This is the tendency to rate all social objects in a relatively favorable manner and not to attribute negative aspects to them.

While there are other kinds of judgment errors besides these, these are probably the most important. How one overcomes them is a different problem, however, and about this there is little agreement. In fact there are some who argue that these may not be errors at all and that one of the only reasons they are considered as such is due to the stubborn refusal of psychologists to admit that (1) some kinds of human behavior may not be distributed according to the normal bell-shaped curve (i.e., in some cases, all people might be "good") and (2) some people may actually have all their characteristics integrally a function of their main characteristic (i.e., the halo error is not an error). This seems an extreme position to take, however. Suffice to say for our purposes here that these behaviors are probably "errors" in the traditional sense but their importance and possible remedial actions will probably vary according to the given situation.

A second problem of perhaps more serious impact in job analysis is how one incorporates into a description of a job's characteristics some recognition of the fact that jobs are becoming increasingly of the type whereby the behaviors that are engaged in cannot be specified in advance but result from the characteristics of the person who happens to fulfill the role at that particular time. For example, let us look at the differences between a management role and the role of a sewing-machine operator in a dress factory. It is much simpler to specify in advance what the behavior of the latter should be than the former. In fact, it is probably very much the case that the essence of the managerial role is success in the ability to handle problems which cannot be specified or "programmed" in advance. While this difference in potential specificity of roles was always a problem for job analysts, its significance is increasing greatly because more jobs in our automated society are becoming increasingly like that of the sewing-machine operator.

It should be emphasized that we are not suggesting that we do away with the job analysis as an aid in the selection (and other manpower utilization) program. This is clearly an impossibility, since the alternative is chaos. However, it is to suggest that this is a significant problem which must be taken into account in future job analysis research.

Step 2—hypothesis development

The second step in the traditional model is derived from the job analysis, with this step consisting, essentially, of hypothesis generation as to the kinds of individuals who would be most likely to fit the behavioral demands of the job. This step can be a subjective one based on a subjective appraisal of the job analysis information. Hence, it can be highly dependent on the cognitive characteristics of the person developing the hypotheses. Unfortunately, we know little about the kinds of people who would be particularly good at this type of thing. Such recognition of this situation is, undoubtedly, one of the reasons the more common procedure in job analysis has been to describe jobs in terms of more objective psychological dimensions and then to verify such descriptions by either (1) testing job occupants with unambiguous tests of these dimensions or (2) getting qualified interjudge agreement as to the importance of the dimensions for the given job. Due to the difficulty of getting tests which are unambiguous measures of simple psychological dimensions, particularly in nonability areas, the latter verification procedure is the more common one today.

A good example of the kinds of dimensions by which jobs may be described and compared to one another in terms of the requirements they call for is seen in Table 8.1. This summarizes some recent work by McCormick and his co-workers (cf. McCormick, Cunningham, and Gordon, 1967). Since these dimensions can be used in varying quantities to describe a variety of different jobs. It is obvious that this project has great potential for assisting in such personnel activities as selection, job promotions, transfers, training, etc.

Step 3—predictor development

Once the relevant psychological and behavior variables have been hypothesized, it is time for the third step. This consists of deciding how one is to measure individual differences in job applicants on the relevant variables. The most important problem is that it is important that one choose a measure which actually measures the relevant psychological variable which one is proposing as being demanded by the job.

Table 8.1

Dimensions of Job Behavior and Examples

---

1 *Decision making and communication activities:*
   Develops budgets; supervises management personnel; verbal presentations; forecasts needs; variety of communications; personnel decisions

2 *Hierarchical person-to-person interaction:*
   Instructs; supervises students, trainees, patients, subordinates, etc.; issues directives; schedules work of others; interchanges information with prospective employees, students, or trainees

3 *Skilled physical activities:*
   Skill of hand tool usage; number of hand tools used; finger manipulation; estimates size

4 *Mental vs. physical activites:*
   Positive loadings—deals with data; interprets information; intelligence; uses mathematics; clerical tasks
   Negative loadings—manual force; moves objects by hand; deals with things

5 *Responsible personal contact:*
   Persuades; interchanges information with customers, clients, patients, etc.; distractions from people seeking or giving information

6 *General physical activities:*
   Adjustment to the vertical; climbing; balancing; general physical coordination

7 *Unpleasant vs. pleasant working conditions:*
   Uncomfortable atmosphere; unclean environment

8 *Decisions affecting people:*
   Personnel decisions (promotions, transfers, hiring, etc.)

9 *Varied intellectual vs. structured activities:*
   Positive loadings—interpretation of information; intelligence; usage of mathematics; occupation prestige
   Negative loadings—high job structure; repetitiveness; deals with things

10 *Supervisory activities:*
    Supervises others; issues directives; number of people supervised

11 *Man-machine control activities:*
    Control operations; monitors work process; interpretation of information; responsible for physical assets

12 *Planning and decision making:*
    Uniqueness of decisions; time span of decisions; forecasts needs; develops methods

13 *Skilled manual activities:*
    Skill of hand tool usage; finger manipulation; number of hand tools used

14 *Intellectual vs. physical activities*
    Positive loadings—"thinking" (vs. "doing"); occupation prestige
    Negative loadings—activity domain—things; repetitiveness; job structure

15 *Body-balancing activities:*
    Adjustment to the vertical; balancing; climbing

16 *Physical vs. sendentary activities:*
    Positive loadings—standing; general force; manual force
    Negative loadings—activity domain—data

17 *Clerical activities:*
    Clerical tasks (filing, typing, shorthand, etc.)

Table 8.1 cont'd.

18 *Knee-bending activities:*
Crawling; kneeling, stooping
19 *Informative communications:*
Giving information; instructing; issuing directives; verbal communications
20 *Communication of data:*
Reporting; activity domain—data; interchange of information; written communication
21 *Persuasive communications:*
Persuading; verbal presentations; negotiating
22 *Public contact activities:*
Publicizing; information interchange with public
23 *White- vs. blue-collar situations:*
Positive loadings—wearing presentable clothing; social obligations; occupational prestige
Negative loadings—receiving hourly and/or overtime pay; receives close supervision
24 *Job security vs. performance-dependent income:*
Positive loadings—job security; occupational prestige
Negative loadings—receives tips, commissions, hourly pay, and/or overtime pay
25 *Apparel: Optional vs. work clothes:*
Positive loading—wears special working clothes
Negative loading—dress left to incumbent's discretion
26 *Apparel: Formal vs. optional:*
Positive loadings—wears presentable clothing; social obligations; occupational prestige
Negative loading—dress left to incumbent's discretion
27 *Apparel: Specific uniform:*
Wears specific uniform
28 *Hourly pay vs. salary:*
Positive loading—regular salary
Negative loading—hourly pay; overtime pay
29 *Annoying environment:*
Noise; uncomfortable atmosphere; poor illumination; cramped work space

Source: E. J. McCormick, J. W. Cunningham, C. G. Gordon: Job dimensions based on factorial analyses of worker-oriented job variables. *Personnel Psychology*, 1967, *20*, 417–30.

The reasons for this are simple. If the chosen measure is not an actual measure of the relevant variable, two possible problems develop, depending on whether or not the measure is actually related to job performance. First, we may reject a good hypothesis as to the cause of good job performance in a given job and not know it. Hence, whatever else we eventually learn about the job in terms of selection and training, such knowledge must always be incomplete, perhaps seriously so. Suppose, however, that the "mistake" works; i.e., suppose we have hypothesized "sociability" as an important variable but have measured "anxiety" by mistake (without knowing it) and "anxiety" does actually predict job performance. It does not matter, the "practical" man says, that it does not measure what it is supposed to measure, since it predicts job performance and hence can be used for selection.

The answer to this is that this is a wasteful, shortsighted, uneconomical attitude.[2] One reason this is so can be seen if we assume that the relevant important psychological variable is "sociability" (when it is really "anxiety"). First, all of the recommendations for managerial action in training, development, appraisal, and promotion which would follow from such a successful prediction would be based on a mistaken, erroneous belief. A second reason this attitude is an impractical one relates to the fact that jobs do change, and sometimes a variable which used to predict performance no longer does. Hence, if we find that our measure of sociability (which is really anxiety) no longer predicts job performance, we shall start looking for new predictors eliminating sociability, although a good measure of sociability might now be a good predictor on the changed job.

How does one decide, then, when a measure is actually a measure of the desired variable? The best process for this is a procedure known as "construct validity," consisting basically of looking at all the relationships which the proposed measure of the variable has with other measured variables and then deciding whether or not these observed relationships are consistent with what they should be if the measure was really measuring what it says it is. (The judgment is, of course, a subjective one and hence must be a result of the knowledge and skills of the person making the judgment). As an example, let us look at Table 8.2, where we have listed the results of a construct validity study of a scale known as the Ghiselli Self-Assurance Scale. Defined as a measure of the extent to which people see themselves as "competent, need satisfying, and able to deal with their problems," it can be seen in this table that the relationships with other variables are about as they should be, given this kind of definition. Were they not of this nature, then we would have a basis for inferring that the scale was not a measure of what it claimed to be.

It should be noted that the process of establishing the construct validity of an instrument is a never-ending one and that we must continually be concerned with obtaining new information on the construct validity of our instrument since the more we know about it, the more we can have confidence that we are actually measuring what we claim we are measuring. In this sense, then, the development of the construct validity of an instrument is similar to the testing of the utility of a theory. In both cases, however, as we have emphasized throughout this book, great practical benefits ensue.

What kinds of predictors are typically chosen? As indicated above and as we shall discuss in Chapter 10, the development of measures of characteristics that will be good predictors of performance has been a primary concern of industrial psychologists with the result that a wide variety of different measures may be used. Briefly, we may summarize them into the following categories (others besides these are possible):

1 *Ability tests:* These consist of measures of verbal and other abilities of the type discussed in Chapter 4.
2 *Objective personality tests:* These are measures of personality characteristics which have a relatively structured format; i.e., the individual respondent describes himself along dimensions defined by the test constructor rather than along dimensions defined by himself.
3 *Projective personality tests:* These are measures of personality characteristics

---

[2]   Actually, this was also the implicit attitude of some practical industrial psychologists for many years. Even these, however, paid lip service to our step 3, even if they did not follow it very often.

Table 8.2
Relationships between Ghiselli Self-Assurance Scale
and Other Psychological Measures

NATURE OF SAMPLE	MEASURE	N	MEAN OF "HIGHS"[a]	N	MEAN OF "LOWS"	SIGNIFI-CANCE LEVEL[b]
Engineering students	Gough Adjective Checklist— *Self-Confidence Scale*	14	52.60	20	46.60	.05
Industrial foremen	Miner *Sentence Completion Scale* (a projective test of organizational power orientation)	10	4.70	12	.60	.05
Business students	Crites *Need for Social Service* (Likert-type scale)	35	5.77	36	7.97	.05
Business students	Crites *Need for Job Freedom* (Likert-type scale)	35	9.60	36	8.22	.10
Industrial foremen	Biographical data frequency with which parents supervised their jobs and tasks (lower score = greater frequency of supervision)	15	2.93	23	2.30	.05
Industrial foremen	Biographical data frequency with which they argued with their parents during teens (higher score = greater frequency of arguments)	15	2.73	23	2.34	.05
Liberal arts students	Marlow-Crowne SD Scale[c]	89		$r=.16$		No score
Business students	Bass *Self-Orientation* (forced-choice tetrads)	20	27.10	15	24.06	.10

Source: A Korman: Task success, task popularity and self-esteem as influences on task liking. *Journal of Applied Psychology,* 1968, *52,* 484–90. Copyright 1968 by the American Psychological Association, and reproduced by permission.
[a]Division between "highs" and "lows" was based on the median of national norms.
[b]All significance tests are two-tailed.
[c]I am indebted to Mrs. Virginia Dunda and Mr. Charles Miller for these data.

which have an unstructured format and which allow the individual to respond along any dimension which he wishes and which he constructs.

4 *Objective life-history items:* These consist of questions concerning relatively objective characteristics of a person's school, work, and personal background; the rationale for these is that they are measures of various attitudinal and personal characteristics of the individual which are not measured by other means.

5 *Interviews and other judgmental assessments:* These consist of judgments by various individuals as to the extent to which the individual possesses the behavioral characteristics which are felt to be necessary for adequate job performance.

Which of these are the best? As we shall see later, this is a multidimensional question, with the answer depending on the criteria used, the occupations involved, various ethical problems, theoretical measurement problems, etc. To some extent, it is even a meaningless question since such a question implies that one may have a choice in the given situation. Yet, this may not be the case.

For example, the best predictors of job performance have consistently been ability tests. However, just as consistently, it has also been shown that their predictive effectiveness will reach only a certain point and that it is necessary to use personality test variables if one wishes to predict performance more accurately above this point, even though personality tests are generally not as effective predictors as ability tests (Guion and Gottier, 1965).

For these reasons, then, our later procedure will be not to bother to make any comparative claims as to the relative fruitfulness of these kinds of measures, since all have their uses in given situations and all must be improved to the greatest extent possible. Their usefulness depends on the given prediction situation and the given prediction problem, and they must be evaluated as such, a procedure which constitutes the basis for our discussion here. (It should be noted, however, that there may be different ethical problems involved with each of these measures, a point we shall discuss later.)

Step 4—administration of predictors to applicant sample

Once the measures of the relevant behaviors have been decided upon, they are administered to the applicants for the job in question. However, the measures are *not* used as a basis for selection at this time. Rather, the applicants are then selected for the job in question on the basis of whatever procedures for this process are existing at that time. The scores on the hypothesized predictor measures are filed away at this time, to be utilized in connection with step 5.

The reasoning behind this procedure can be explained quite simply. Thus, if we use the hypothesized measure as a basis for hiring, then we shall never know what the job performance would have been of those individuals with the predictor scores who were not hired. That is, if the company were to take in only those with high scores, then we would not know the eventual performance of those with low scores and vice versa. The problem is, of course, that the unselected group might have been better in job performance than the selected; something we could not know unless we gave them the opportunity.

Step 5—relate predictor test scores to measure of job performance

After the applicants have been hired and been on the job for a long enough period of time to get some meaningful measure of differences in job performance, the first critical point in this process is reached. This is to relate scores on the predictor variable to the measure of job performance, i.e., the criterion.

There are two major problems which are of concern here. First, what measures of relationship should be used, and what are the advantages and disadvantages of each of these measures? Second, how shall we interpret the results found in terms of their practical significance for organizational action? These are the questions we shall attempt to answer here, discussing both where we have only *one* predictor variable for each applicant and where we have more than one predictor variable for each person.

1 The correlation coefficient Undoubtedly, the most popular method for describing the relationship between two variables that has been utilized in personnel selection research has been the correlation coefficient, or r, the basic mechanics of which we have described in an earlier part of this book. The reasons for this are several. First, there is the element of familiarity, i.e., most industrial psychologists are quite familiar with it, having studied it as part of their graduate training. Second, it is a convenient way of summarizing a relationship into one general descriptive term. Hence, when we say that a correlation is .60, it is agreed that this means something different than when we say a correlation is .10 or $-.35$. A third reason for the great utilization of the correlation coefficient is that there is a considerable amount of theory developed around it, theory concerned with how much confidence we can have in certain obtained results, given certain assumptions. Thus, because the theory concerning the correlation coefficient is well developed, we are able to specify, given certain assumptions, the likelihood that our results are not due to "chance" or "unstable" factors and we can also estimate the degree to which our specifications will be in error. Related to both this reason and the second is a fourth advantage of using the correlation coefficient as a measure of a relationship and that is that the actual r obtained is directly convertible into a measure of predictive accuracy, the purpose of the whole selection mechanism process. Finally, and this should not be underestimated, a fifth reason for the frequent use of r is that it constitutes part of the "mystique" of the industrial psychologist as opposed to the typical manager and thus enables the former to "look good" in this sense. This is, of course, not necessarily an advantage of r except for the benefit of the psychologist.

These advantages hold whether we are concerned with the situation when we have only one predictor variable for each applicant or, the far more common case, when we are concerned with more than one predictor in a given selection situation. In the latter situation, the correlation coefficient which is used is called the multiple correlation coefficient, as opposed to the "simple r," the measure used in the case where there is only one predictor variable. The two can be distinguished in this way:

1 For the case of one predictor—one criterion, we correlate the two variables X (the predictor) and Y (the criterion) using the appropriate formula.[3]
2 For the case of multiple predictors—one criterion, the procedure can be outlined conceptually as follows:[4]
  a) Assume four predictor variables, X_1, X_2, X_3, and X_4, and one criterion variable, Y.
  b) All the predictor variables are correlated with the criterion variable and with each other.
  c) Each predictor variable is then weighted by a statistical procedure according to the degree of its intercorrelations with the criterion and with the

---

[3]   See any standard statistics textbook.
[4]   The reader may consult any standard statistics textbook for a discussion of the statistical equations of multiple r.

other predictor variables; the higher the correlation with the criterion and the lower the correlation with the other predictors, the greater the weight that specific variable has for predicting that criterion.

d) The absolute sum of these weights are then converted, again statistically, into a correlation coefficient called the multiple r which is then interpretable along the *same* scale as the regular r. In other words it has the same range from -1.00 to $+1.00$, an r of 0.00 means no relationship between the two variables, and so on. In this case, of course, the X or predictor variable is not a single variable, but a weighted composite of the four predictor variables, with each individual's score on this composite being the average of his scores on each of the predictor variables, corrected by the weight for the variables. An example of this procedure is given in Figure 8.6.

The last statement does point to one difference between the simple and multiple r which the reader should keep in mind and which does limit to an extent the general equating of the two we have made here. This difference results because the weighting system used in developing the multiple correlation is based on *maximizing* the correlation between the predictors and criterion and all variables are weighted on this basis, whether the scores that are being weighted are based on real, valid differences between people or on chance, accidental influences on the scores. The problem is that these chance, accidental scores are counted only if they add to the level of the correlation coefficient. They are *not* counted if they decrease this level; rather, they are ignored. It is for this reason that the multiple r has a general tendency to be too high, given the nature of the scores involved. Hence, it is even more necessary in the case where the multiple r is used that the step we have called "cross-validation," which we shall discuss later, be employed.

This is not the only disadvantage in the use of r or even the most serious, since there are other problems in utilizing this procedure as a way of determining the relationship between a hypothesized predictor of job behavior and an actual measure of job behavior. One of these problems stems from the fact that r measures the extent to which two variables order a group of people similarly. The greater the similarity in ordering, the higher the r, and the greater the discrepancy in ordering of the individuals, the lower the r. The latter aspect is particularly important, since such discrepancies in ordering have a negative effect on r, no matter what levels of the variables we are talking about, even though in many selection situations there may be some discrepancies which are more important than others. For example, let us look at (a) in Figure 8.1. In this case, let X be a predictor (either a simple predictor or a weighted composite such as in the multiple r) and Y be *actual* job behavior, i.e., the kind of work the person will actually do. Now look at (b) and (c), both of which give examples of different kinds of predictors (X_1 and X_2) and levels of job behaviors which each predicts (Y_1 and Y_2). Both X_1 and X_2 make the same level of error and both show equal correlations with actual job performance (Y); yet X_1 is much more useful than X_2 since it errs at a level which is unimportant (i.e., high in the distribution where everybody performs well), whereas X_2 errs at a crucial point in the distribution (i.e., it predicts a poor performer to perform well and a good performer to perform poorly).

Another problem with the use of correlation as a measure of a relationship is that it assumes that a straight line best describes the relationship between the two sets of pairs [see (a) in Figure 8.1 for a good example]. Yet, it is conceivable that some predictors would not be linearly related to the criterion but curvilinearly. For example, let us suppose that we wish to use a test of intelligence to predict performance as a department store sales clerk. One might certainly assume that at least a

| | (a) | | (b) | | (c) | |
	X	Y	X_1	Y_1	X_2	Y_2
Individual A	10	18	10	16	10	18
B	9	16	9	18	9	16
C	8	14	8	18	8	12
Acceptable job behavior ($Y = 14$ or more)						
Unacceptable job behavior						
D	7	12	7	12	7	14
E	6	10	6	10	6	10
F	5	8	5	8	5	8

Figure 8.1

certain level of intelligence is required to write sales slips, take returns, etc. Hence one would predict a positive correlation between intelligence and performance, or would one? Would this relationship also be so once we sampled above the average in intelligence? Would it not be just as likely here that the relationship would turn negative, since high-intelligence people would become bored with the job? If this were so, then the relationship would be a U-shaped one, as in Figure 8.2. While most relationships studied in industry have been found to be linear ones, the possibility of the kinds of relationships we have hypothesized here has made psychologists increasingly wary of a blind use of r without the specific prediction situation.

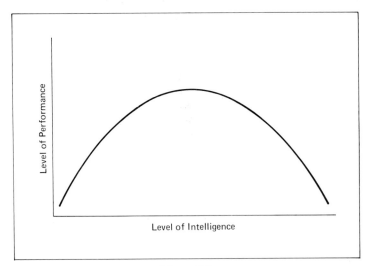

Figure 8.2

A third problem with the use of r concerns how one actually interprets the actual figures obtained. There are two problems here. One is the tendency of some to interpret r as the proportion of predictive accuracy; e.g., an r of $+.50$ is twice as accurate as an r of $+.25$. This is *not* so. The most that can be said in this respect is that r^2's can be compared with one another. That is, an r of .50 is equal to an r^2 of .25 ($.50 \times .50$) and an r of .70 is equal to an r^2 of .49 ($.70 \times .70$), and the latter "explains" or is about twice as useful as the former. However, for the r figure itself, about all that can be said is that an r of .50 is greater than an r of .30 and so on. The second problem is the interpretation of the actual level of r itself. How much confidence can we have in it as being (1) useful in prediction and (2) a consistent, reliable relationship? Theoretically, this is a function of (1) the size of the obtained correlation and (2) the sample size. Thus, various formulas are available which provide us with a guide for determining whether a given correlation is "significant" or not (i.e., whether it is as a result of chance fluctuation or whether it really does seem to indicate a true relationship between variables). To an overwhelming extent industrial psychologists have used this concept of significance, as defined by statistical theory, as their guide to evaluating their obtained correlations for importance. There have been some objections to this, however, with the major one being that a "significant" correlation (i.e., one cited as being a "real" relationship between a given predictor and a measure of job behavior) may actually be one that is very small in actual size, if it is based on a large enough sample size. For example, a correlation of .10, based on a sample of 400 is "significant" at the .05 level of probability (i.e., there is less than 5% chance that this relationship could have occurred by chance alone, given the size of the obtained relationship and the sample size). Since this correlation is only equal to about 1% of predictive accuracy $(r^2 = .10 \times .10)$, we can see why there have been some complaints about this concept of statistically defined significance. Surely being able to improve the accuracy in prediction 1% hardly seems "significant"! As a result, Dunnette and Kirchner (1965), among others, have argued that the correlations obtained in prediction studies should be evaluated in terms of practical rather than statistical significance. While this is a laudable argument with which the author is in agreement, it must be admitted that how one translates practical significance into guides for decision making is still a question.

Perhaps the only way of even approaching some kind of meaningful judgment as to whether a given correlation is of practical significance is to view it in terms of the specifics of a given situation since it is these specifics which may play an important part in determining whether or not to use selection instruments at all. For example, let us contrast the sets of situations given in Figure 8.3.

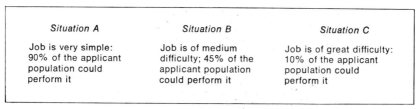

Situation A	*Situation B*	*Situation C*
Job is very simple: 90% of the applicant population could perform it	Job is of medium difficulty; 45% of the applicant population could perform it	Job is of great difficulty: 10% of the applicant population could perform it

Figure 8.3

Let us assume that we do not have any selection instruments at all and we hire all people who apply for each job; that is, we predict that *all* will succeed. The number of mistakes in prediction we shall make are as follows:

Situation A = 10% (the base rate of success is 90%)
Situation B = 55% (the base rate of success is 45%)
Situation C = 90% (the base rate of success is 10%)

Hence, if a test is to be of practical usefulness, its correlation coefficient must be higher in situation A than in situation B and much higher than in situation C, since our accuracy of prediction is so much higher in the former than the latter without the use of any selection instruments at all. (It is for this reason that selection instruments are often utilized in managerial and high-level selection which would be considered to be too low to be of practical usefulness when dealing with lower-level employees.) This, then, is one factor which enables us to interpret when a correlation coefficient is practically useful.

A second factor of significance is the selection ratio. Consider the situation where we need select only 1 of 100 applicants for a job, as opposed to one where we must select 50 of 100. Since in the first case we can take only the best, a selection instrument does not have to be very accurate in increasing our ability to predict job behavior over chance levels. It only has to be a little bit better than chance in order to help us in picking out the best person for the job. On the other hand, this is not the case in the latter situation, where we must pick out 50 and where, hence, the selection instrument must be high to be useful. The former case is called a "low selection ratio" situation and the latter, of course, a "high selection ratio" situation.

These two factors, then, the "base rate of success" (or "difficulty level" of the job) and the selection ratio in the given situation, are the major guides we have in determining the practical usefulness of a given selection instrument for any given selection question. The two are combined in making a judgment as to whether the obtained correlation coefficient is a useful one or not. To show how this may be done, Ghiselli and Brown (1955) have suggested the principles indicated in Table 8.3. (Note that "validity" in Table 8.3 means the correlation coefficient between the predictor and the criterion.)

2 Simple and multiple cut-off systems To overcome some of the weaknesses of the correlation coefficient as a way of describing the relationship between the hypothesized predictors of job behavior and actual job behavior, an increasing number of psychologists have suggested the use of simple and multiple cut-off systems. These, in essence, are expectancy charts and/or tables which depict the level of job performance which is to be expected from any given level of predictor scores; cut-offs can then be developed both for simple and multiple predictors which will maximize the level of performance. An example of a simple predictor expectancy chart is given in Figure 8.4.

Although the cut-off methods do not provide convenient summary figures for describing the obtained relationships, a look at this chart indicates the obvious advantages which account for its increasing usage. It is clear and easy to interpret, thus overcoming the resistance to the correlation coefficient as a medium of communication which is frequently found among nonpsychologically trained people. A second advantage is perhaps a more technically important one in that it can be keyed to any type of relationship, linear or curvilinear, better than the correlation coefficient. Consider the example given in Figure 8.5.

If we were to compute the correlation coefficient between these variables, it would probably not be a high one due to the lack of variation in criterion performance for all those with predictor scores of 7 or above. Hence, we might discard this predictor if we were using correlation analysis. On the other hand, if we were using a cut-off system, we would have perfect prediction if we selected all those with predictor scores of 7 or more and rejected those with scores of 6 or less.

The comparative discussion is somewhat analogous but does get more complex when we talk about situations where there are multiple predictors. To review our previous comments, the reader will recall that in the multiple r situation the various predictor variables are weighted in terms of their relationships to the criterion. In essence, each individual is then assigned a score based on his scores on the predictor

Table 8.3

Usefulness of Selection Devices When Related to Validity,
Selection Ratio, and Job Difficulty

The higher the validity of the selection device, the larger will be the proportion of selected persons who turn out to be satisfactory (e.g., with a selection ratio and job difficulty of 50%, a validity of .75 will yield 77% satisfactory workers. Under these same conditions a validity of .25 will yield only 58% satisfactory workers).

The smaller the proportion of candidates selected, the larger will be the proportion of selected persons who turn out to be satisfactory (e.g., with a validity of .50 and a job difficulty of 50%, a selection ratio of 20% will yield 78% satisfactory workers, whereas a selection ratio of 80% will yield only 57% satisfactory workers).

The easier the job, the larger will be the proportion of selected persons who turn out to be satisfactory (e.g., with a validity of .50 and a selection ratio of 50%, a job with a base success level of 80% will yield 91% satisfactory workers, but one with a base success level of 20% will yield only 31% satisfactory workers).

A selection device of lower validity when coupled with a lower selection ratio may be as effective as, or more effective than, a device of higher validity which is coupled with a higher selection ratio (e.g., for a job of 50% difficulty, with a validity of .25 and a selection ratio of 20%, the yield of successful workers will be 64%. In a job of equal difficulty, but with a validity of .75 and a selection ratio of 80%, the yield of successful workers will be 61%).

A selection device of lower validity when applied to an easier job may be as effective as, or more effective than, one of higher validity which is applied to a harder job (e.g., with a selection ratio of 50%, a validity of .25, and a job difficulty of 80%, the yield of successful workers will be 86%. With a selection ratio of 50%, a validity of .75, and a job difficulty of 20%, the yield of successful workers will only be 37%.

Source: E. Ghiselli and C. W. Brown: *Personnel and industrial psychology.* New York: McGraw-Hill, 1955.

variables, corrected by the weights for each variable. Consider Figure 8.6, taken from our example in Figure 8.4.

One aspect which is immediately apparent and which is crucial to our discussion is that there is a variety of ways by which a person may derive a given X score on the composite variable. Hence, person A gets a score of 62 by being high on variables 2 and 3, even though he is only medium on variable 1. On the other hand, individual E is high on variable 1 but he is considerably lower on variables 2 and 3. In other words, E has "compensated" for being low on variable 2 by being higher on variable 1. This principle of "compensation" and of there being alternative ways to derive high predictor scores is the essence of the multiple correlation system.

Suppose, now, that we wanted to use a multiple cut-off system. How would this operate? Using the same sample, suppose we found that the following cut-offs for each of the variables led to the highest level of predicted performance:

Cut-off levels

Variable $X_1 = 9$ or more
Variable $X_2 = 6$ or more
Variable $X_3 = 3$ or more

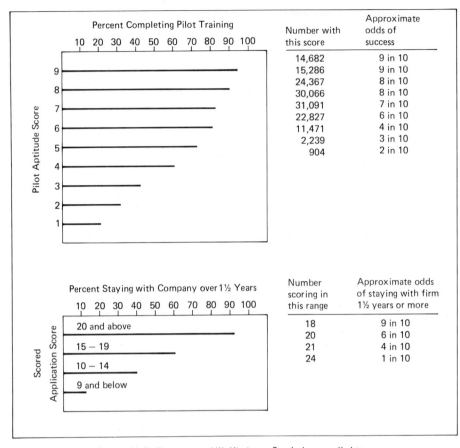

Percent Completing Pilot Training	Number with this score	Approximate odds of success
(Pilot Aptitude Score 9)	14,682	9 in 10
	15,286	9 in 10
(8)	24,367	8 in 10
	30,066	8 in 10
(7)	31,091	7 in 10
	22,827	6 in 10
(6)	11,471	4 in 10
(5)	2,239	3 in 10
	904	2 in 10

Percent Staying with Company over 1½ Years	Number scoring in this range	Approximate odds of staying with firm 1½ years or more
20 and above	18	9 in 10
15 − 19	20	6 in 10
10 − 14	21	4 in 10
9 and below	24	1 in 10

Source: M. D. Dunnette and W. Kirchner: *Psychology applied to business and industry.* New York: Appleton-Century-Crofts, 1965.

Fig. 8.4 Examples of simple cut-off systems relating test scores to job behavior. (a) Chart showing relation between pilot aptitude score and successful completion of pilot training (Psychological activities in training command AAF. *Psychological Bulletin*, 1945, 42, 46). (b) Chart showing relation between biographical "score" and length of service for female office employees (Development of a weighted application blank to aid in the selection of office employees, *Research Report No. 7,* Personnel Research, 3M Co., 1956).

Predictor X	Criterion Y
10	25
9	25
8	25
7	25
Acceptable performance	Unacceptable performance
6	20
5	18
4	16
3	14

Figure 8.5

					Composite predictor	
Predictors						
	Variables					
	X_1	X_2	X_3	X_4	*Composite predictor*	
Individual weights	3	2	1	0	*score (i.e., the X vari-*	*Level necessary*
					able in the multiple	*for hiring*
Applicants					*correlation equation)*	*decision = 55*
A	10	12	8	9	62	Hire
B	6	7	15	9	47	Reject
C	13	3	11	15	56	Hire
D	9	6	8	4	47	Reject
E	13	10	3	8	62	Hire

Figure 8.6

According to these levels, using our previous examples, the following decisions would be made:

Individual A = Hire
Individual B = Reject
Individual C = Reject
Individual D = Hire
Individual E = Hire

Hence, we see that requiring each individual to be above a given level on all predictors, as in the multiple cut-off system, leads to different decisions than when we allow a person to compensate for being low on one predictor by being extra high on the other.

Which system is a better one? There is, of course, no simple answer to this. It depends on the situation. In some prediction situations it would seem that we can safely allow compensation and use the multiple *r* method, given the other advantages we have previously mentioned. However, it is also apparent that cut-offs may be necessary on some variables in that a low score on that given predictor cannot be compensated for by high scores on any other predictor. An example of this concerns the necessity of visual acuity for being a dentist. Unless the dentist has a high level of visual acuity, any other ability of his, verbal, manipulative, or otherwise, is not likely to be of use or value to him.

Hence, perhaps the best approach to use in the multiple predictor situation is a combination of the multiple cut-off and multiple correlation methods. The first step would be to use the multiple cut-off method for those variables where a minimum level is considered necessary and select people on that basis. After this is done, the multiple *r* method should be used with the remaining predictors in order to select from those remaining after the initial cut-off is made.

Step 6—cross validation

The next step in the traditional personnel selection model depends on whether or not the results in step 5 look promising. Assuming that they do, the next step is to *repeat the entire procedure*, utilizing the same job, same measure of performance, same kinds of applicants, etc. The reason for this kind of procedure relates to the essentially conservative nature of the scientific endeavor in that it is felt that despite proper precautions of the type we have discussed, it is always conceivable that a single obtained result, no matter how positive the relationship, could always occur on the basis of chance factors alone. Hence, to have greater confidence in the results, one should always replicate or repeat the study. This is the purpose of the cross-validation step.

Unfortunately, it is often the case that the results of step 5 are not promising enough to continue to the cross-validation attempt. In this case, there is nothing else to do according to the traditional personnel selection model but start all over again.

Step 7—recommendation for selection

Finally, the last step in the procedure, assuming that step 6 works out, is to make recommendations for selection. The essential problem here is to develop a procedure as to the kinds of scores which will be acceptable for selection and to set up guidelines for the administration of such recommendations. Often such recommended guidelines may take the form of the tables given in Figure 8.4 with the desired scores outlined in some manner. Since this whole procedure is one that depends very much on the specifics of a given situation, we shall not bother to discuss it further here.

This, then, is the traditional personnel selection procedure in outline form. Its advantages are that it is statistically based, it attempts to limit human error, and it provides checks on the various steps along the way. Hence, it should work well, and it does *when* the implicit assumptions involved in it are met. However, the problem has been that these assumptions are being met less and less in today's world and new models and procedures in personnel selection of the type we shall describe in Chapter 9 are becoming necessary in some situations. In addition, these revised models have been designed to meet other problems which seem to be increasingly common in the process of personnel selection. Let us see, then, what some of these assumptions and problems of the traditional model are.

The first major assumption which underlies the procedures in this model is what seems to be a belief in a "static" world relating to both jobs and people. Very clearly, there is a strong assumption here that the kinds of people who apply for a given job will not change over time, nor will the characteristics of the job. Is this a reasonable assumption? It probably was in the days when our predominant organized work force consisted of blue-collar individuals engaged in semiskilled, manual factory employment, but these jobs are increasingly less the case today. We now have more white-collar than blue-collar employed people and the discrepancy is increasing all the time. Since white-collar work is generally less routinized than factory work, the opportunities for innovation and job change by particular job occupants is much greater. Furthermore, an increasing number of white-collar workers are in jobs where the opportunity for job innovation and self-expression are expressly engineered into the job. In this class we may put such positions as research and managerial personnel, among others. Clearly, the assumption of the static nature of the job is difficult to meet here, and, if it is, it is done at so high a level of abstract behavioral dimensions as to make it meaningless as a guideline to specific selection.

A related argument can be made for the assumption as to the similarity of applicant populations. We live in a dynamic society and we are constantly being subjected to various legal, social, and ethical constraints on our behavior, constraints which are always changing. A good example of this is the greatly increased concern with minority-group employment and utilization, the implications for selection, training, and development of which we shall discuss in more detail later. Suffice it to say at this point that it should be obvious to all but the densest that a large company in a downtown metropolitan area is proceeding in a somewhat foolhardy manner if it assumes, without checking, that its applicant pool, particularly for low-level positions, is equivalent psychologically to the type of applicants the company had 10 or even 5 years ago.

The second major problem with this model is a fairly obvious one, that of sample size. It is clearly the case that one cannot apply procedure unless we have a considerable number of people doing the same job, with this not changing over time. Again, one can see the remains here of a way of thinking about jobs which was adequate for the industrial world of 20 to 30 years ago but which is increasingly less so. The very essence of managerial, technical, and much other white-collar employment is their very "uniqueness" and the fact that they, and only they, do that type of work in the organization. While there are many jobs where this assumption still holds, it is obvious that there are many where it does not, and personnel selection procedures must be revised to take this into account.

A third problem is also a relatively obvious one and that is the amount of time involved. To develop a set of predictor instruments utilizing the traditional personnel selection model, a longitudinal study must be undertaken with *no* guarantee that the attempt will be a successful one (see step 6). This, of course, makes it a problem to sell to management.

A fourth and final problem with the procedure is not quite as obvious as this but is potentially a far more serious one. This has to do with the very clear assumption in this procedure that when we find a set of predictors of job behavior these will be equally applicable to all individuals applying for that job in terms of determining success on the job. In other words, it is assumed that if a person is to succeed on a job it is because he has the required amount of that given characteristic, and if he is to fail it is because he lacks the characteristic. There is no acknowledgment anywhere that some small subgroup of the population might succeed on the job for a different reason, and, hence, these people's unique characteristics that would enable them to succeed on the job would not be taken into account.

Consider the following:

1 100 girls apply for a position as salesgirl.
2 67 of these girls would use perseverance as a method of job behavior if they were hired; none would use tact.
3 33 of these girls would use tact as a method of job behavior; none would use perseverance.

If all these girls were thrown into the same applicant pool and analyzed as a group, then the psychological variable which would come out as being of greatest predictive importance would be perseverance. Hence, all the girls who would use tact as a way of succeeding and who would succeed, if given the opportunity, are being prevented from doing so. This is unfair to these applicants since it prevents them from obtaining a job in which they would be successful. In addition, it is also unfair to the organization, since the relationship that is obtained is lower than it would be if just the 67 girls were analyzed.

This question and the increasing recognition of the fact that people may use different routes to job success have become of great importance in recent years as a result of two factors. First, there has been a great increase in the number of jobs which allow personal innovation and differing ways of succeeding. For example, to assume that one may succeed as a research personnel psychologist only by performing experiments in the area of training and development is a foolish and dangerous process since the individual interested in personnel selection might develop a procedure of far greater benefit if given the opportunity. A second factor is that industry is becoming increasingly concerned with the utilization of culturally deprived groups such as Blacks and Latin Americans in occupations where they were never utilized previously. The problem here is that there is some evidence which suggests that different cultural groups may succeed in various achievement situations for different reasons. Consider Table 8.4, in which we have summarized several studies of both academic and work performance (Green and Farquahr, 1965; Kirkpatrick, et al., 1968). The differing patterns of correlation coefficients for differing racial groups seem to support quite strongly the notion that individuals may use different patterns of variables in order to achieve effective performance and that groups with these differing tendencies may be identified *prior* to selection. The process of doing this is known as the "moderator variable" approach to personnel selection, since it involves choosing a variable (in this case race) which "moderates" or "determines" how two other variables might be related (e.g., aptitude and work achievement).

Table 8.4
Difference in Validity According to Race

A. CORRELATIONS BETWEEN APTITUDE AND M-SCALE SUBTESTS WITH
GRADE-POINT AVERAGE AS A FUNCTION OF RACE AND SEX

SAMPLE		APTITUDE AND M-SCALE SUBTESTS CORRELATED WITH GRADE-POINT AVERAGE					
RACE AND SEX	VERBAL APTITUDE	GSCI	HTI	PJCS	WRL	M TOTAL	N
Negro							
Male	−.01	.26[a]	.14	.30[a]	.36[a]	.37[a]	104
Female	.25[a]	.46[a]	.40[a]	.34[a]	.64[a]	.55[a]	129
White							
Male	.62[a]	.50[a]	.42[a]	.32[a]	.51[a]	.50[a]	254
Female	.21[a]	.21[a]	.29[a]	.18[a]	.34[a]	.43[a]	261

B.

PREDICTOR	GROUP	CORRELATIONS WITH OVERALL JOB EFFECTIVENESS
Numerical test	Total	.29[a]
	White (N=39)	.32[a]
	Negro (N=33)	.21
Coding test	Total	.19
	White	.04
	Negro	.48[b]
Total score	Total	.34[b]
	White	.24
	Negro	.47[b]

Sources: (A) R. L. Green and W. Farquahr: Negro academic motivation and scholastic achievement. *Journal of Educational Psychology,* 1965, *56,* 241–43. Copyright 1965 by the American Psychological Association, and reproduced by permission. (B) Reprinted by permission of New York University Press from *Testing and fair employment: Fairness and validity of personnel tests for different ethnic groups,* by James J. Kirkpatrick, Robert B. Ewen, Richard S. Barrett, and Raymond A. Katzell. © 1968 by New York University.

Note: Abbreviations used: GSCI, Generalized Situational Choice Inventory; PJCS, Preferred Job Characteristic Scale.
[a]$p < .05.$
[a]$p < .01.$

THE CONCURRENT VALIDITY MODEL

The first major revision to be made in the traditional personnel selection model is, in some respects, not a revision at all, since its historical antecedents are at least as old. In addition, it is probably more commonly used in the industrial situation than is the traditional selection model. The reason for this is that its major purpose is to eliminate what is practically the most frustrating aspect of the traditional model, the delay between the administration of the predictor measures and the collection of job behavior measures. In essence, the concurrent validity model differs from the traditional model (which we call "predictive validity") in that it utilizes present, already working groups of employees as test groups upon which to determine whether given variables are related to job performance. In other words the procedure is very much the same as the traditional approach except that the hypothesized predictors of successful job performance are administered to those already on the job for whom job performance data are immediately available. If the expected relationships occur and are replicated in a cross-validation relationship and so on, then the measures are recommended for administrative use in selection procedures.

There is little doubt that it is because this procedure overcomes the time problem inherent in the traditional model that it became the most popular method for developing selection instruments in industrial situations. Yet, there are some who feel that despite this enormous benefit of the concurrent validity model, this advantage, when weighed in the balance, does not compensate for the very serious disadvantages entailed, disadvantages which include almost all of those in the traditional model plus several that are unique to it alone. These additional disadvantages, we shall see, are so serious that some have argued the concurrent validity procedure should be used only as a hypothesis generator, not as a hypothesis tester (Guion, 1965).

In addition to the fact that the concurrent validity procedure makes the same assumptions as the traditional model as to the static nature of the job, the constant large influx of applicants with similar characteristics, and the necessity for large numbers of individuals performing the same job, this procedure also makes the following crucial assumptions:

1 The motivational determinants of responding to a possible selection instrument such as personality tests, attitude questionnaires, etc., are the same for those already on the job as for those applying for the job.
2 Scores on a potential predictor of job behavior are not related in any systematic manner to experience on the job.

It is quite obvious that these are two very important assumptions, violations of which would destroy the validity of this whole procedure. How often are they violated? There is little systematic evidence available, but it would appear that this would depend to a great extent on the instruments being studied. For example, there are studies on record where various kinds of leadership attitudes have been studied via a concurrent validity procedure and then recommended for administrative use in selection. It seems hard to believe that attitudes in this area are not reflecting organizational experience to a great extent. Similarly, when a person with union security is asked about his motivational characteristics, it is hard to believe that the psychological determinants of his answers are similar to those of a person who has been out of work for several months.

There is a third problem associated with the concurrent validity procedure, and that is a technical one. Consider the situation where an organization has a job category involving 40 positions but which now has 5 available openings. Who are the 35 currently on the job? Technically, they are a subgroup of those who were originally hired for that position, differing from the 5 who left in that they remained on the job. Now if we assume that, in general, the person who stays on the job or who is not fired is more competent than the one who quits or is fired, then the 35 now on the job would, in general, show less variation in job performance than the original unrestricted group of 40. If this were so, then it would be harder to find any correlation between predictor and job performance, since a correlation measures the similarity in variation between two variables and one of the variables does not have much variation. This, in turn, would depress the level of the correlation to a level perhaps lower than it would be if we had used it in a predictive validity situation.

SUMMARY

Industrial and organizational psychology has its historical beginnings as an aid to management in the selection of workers likely to be more capable in their job duties. In this process its major focuses have been in the development of a methodology for the evaluation of selection tools and the development of the selection tool itself.

Despite such historical antecedents, the field is by no means a settled one, and there is great ferment today as to the selection process, its rationale, its methods, and even its desirability. In this chapter we began our discussion of the personnel selection process by discussing and outlining the original achievement of the industrial and organizational psychologist in this area. This achievement, as we have seen, consisted primarily of the development of a rigorous methodology, quantitatively based, for the evaluation of selection tools, an achievement which became of significant value to large numbers of organizations.

Unfortunately, however, this methodology has always involved certain assumptions about the nature of organizations and the nature of the world surrounding the organization, assumptions which are increasingly difficult to meet in today's world, for at least some organizations. Hence, while this is still an appropriate methodology for personnel selection tool evaluation in many organizations and is so utilized, it is not for others. Thus, alternative procedures have been and are being developed.

REFERENCES

Dunnette, M., and Kirchner, W. *Psychology applied to business and industry.* New York: Appleton, 1965.

Ghiselli, E., and Brown, C. *Personnel and industrial psychology,* 2nd ed. New York: McGraw-Hill, 1955.

Green, R. L., and Farquahr, W. Negro academic motivation and scholastic achievement. *Journal of Educational Psychology,* 1965, *56,* 241–43.

Guion, R. M. *Personnel testing.* New York: McGraw-Hill, 1965.

Guion, R., and Gottier, R. F. Validity of personnel measures in personnel selection. *Personnel Psychology,* 1965, *18,* 135–64.

Kirkpatrick, J. J., Ewen, R. B., Barrett, R. S., and Katzell, R. A. *Testing and fair employment: Fairness and validity of personnel tests for different ethnic groups.* New York: New York University Press, 1968.

McCormick, E. J., Cunningham, J. W., and Gordon, C. G. Job dimensions based on factorial analyses of worker-oriented variables. *Personnel Psychology,* 1967, *20,* 417–30.

FOR DISCUSSION AND REVIEW

1 Explain the predictive and concurrent validity models.
2 Trace the steps required in demonstrating both predictive and concurrent validities. Cite advantages and disadvantages of each.
3 How is the correlation coefficient used in the selection models?
4 What is the difference between simple and multiple cut-off scores?
5 Explain cross validation. Why is it recommended?

B. SELECTION AND THE LAW

James M. Higgins

A Manager's Guide to the Equal Employment Opportunity Laws

While equal employment opportunity (EEO) has been required by law for several years, it is apparent that most organizations have only recently begun to seriously respond to the EEO requirements with which they are confronted. In defense of those required to provide equal employment opportunity, their EEO compliance efforts are made inordinately difficult by the fact that there are no less than six major federal laws related to EEO as well as various and differing state and local laws. In addition, there are numerous federal, state and local agencies which enforce these laws and these agencies frequently have varying compliance requirements. Moreover, these agencies often change the requirements which they stress as being most important. To further complicate the situation, there is no central governmental unit which controls the overall EEO program nor one which provides organizations and their managers with systematic information related to the total requirements of the EEO program. As a result, organizations must seek compliance information from several sources, information which is often in different formats and inconsistent in its treatment of essential issues. It is the purpose of this article to provide the manager with a guide to these essential issues, a guide presented in a consistent manner.

In order to better understand and comply with EEO requirements it is appropriate to view them in light of their historical perspective. To begin, equal employment opportunity is only one of five major issues involved in the civil rights movement. Voting rights, equal education, fair housing, and public accommodation are the other major issues. With the exception of public accommodation, these problem areas have yet to be completely resolved.[1] Secondly, it is clear from the history of legislative and executive activity preceeding Federal EEO laws that the Congress and various Presidents were reluctant to initiate dramatic action on EEO issues. It is evident that they were finally prompted to act primarily as the result of civil unrest among the minorities and women who eventually became protected by the laws and the Presidential Executive Orders. As a result of this reluctance, the laws and Executive Orders addressing EEO issues while varied in thrust, share a common ambiguity. In fact, the Federal EEO laws and the Presidential Executive Orders were stated so vaguely that it has taken several years for them to become translated into specific requirements by the appointed enforcement agencies. These agency requirements, in turn, have had to be ruled upon by the courts before they could be given much credence by subject organization. These factors, combined with inherent weaknesses in the enforcement powers of the agencies, an inadequate administration of the enforcement effort and the almost total lack of coordination of interagency activity have contributed to the insufficient compliance responses observed in many organizations subject to these laws. While changes have been made to strengthen the EEO laws and the powers of the major enforcement agencies as well as to streamline administrative efforts, a recent Civil Rights

From *Personnel Journal* 55 (August 1976): 406–418. Reprinted with permission of *Personnel Journal,* copyright © August 1976, July 1971.

Commission study characterized the Federal program as "fundamentally inadequate."[2] However, it should be noted that the Federal enforcement effort has been gaining momentum in recent months. Almost all Federal enforcement agencies have increased their enforcement efforts and several have made impressive gains in achieving equal employment opportunity for protected class members.

THE MANAGER'S GUIDE

The following paragraphs contain 25 questions and their answers. Each question is related to a key area of EEO compliance. These questions and their answers provide a framework which can be used by managers for the purposes of understanding and complying with the requirements for all of the major EEO laws, especially Title VII of the Civil Rights Act of 1964 and the principal Executive Orders. Both public and private employment practices are considered but the major emphasis is upon private employment situations. In addition, for explanatory purposes, certain requirements not directly related to employment are discussed. These requirements are primarily those contained in Title VII, the subjects of which are union membership, joint apprenticeship training program composition, and employment agency referrals. Not all requirements reviewed are applicable to every organization nor are all requirements presented. Rather, only the major provisions of these laws are discussed. Further, enforcement agency guidelines and organizational administrative relationships are subject to occasional change. As a result, certain information presented here may also change.

1. What are the equal employment opportunity laws with which an organization must be concerned?

A. Title VII of the Civil Rights Act of 1964 as amended by the Equal Employment Opportunity Act of 1972.

B. Presidential Executive Orders 11246, 11375, 11141, 11478, 11758.

C. Equal Pay Act of 1963 as amended by the Education Amendments of 1972.

D. Age Discrimination in Employment Act of 1967.

E. Sections 500 and 503 of the Rehabilitation Act Amendments of 1974.[3]

F. The National Labor Relations Act of 1947 (Taft-Hartley) as amended by the Labor-Management Reporting and Disclosure Act of 1959 (Landrum-Griffin).[4]

G. Other Federal Laws.[5]

H. Various State and Local Laws.[6]

2. For what situations in which discrimination might occur does each law apply?

A. Title VII
 • All conditions of employment and related personnel practices, union membership, joint apprenticeship training program composition, union hiring hall and employment agency referrals

B. Executive Orders
 • All conditions of employment and related personnel practices

C. Equal Pay Act
 • Compensation (base pay, raises, overtime, bonuses, commissions)

D. Age Discrimination Act
 • All conditions of employment and related personnel practices, union membership, employment agency referrals

E. Rehabilitation Act
 • All conditions of employment and related personnel practices

F. NLRA
  - Union representation of all employees, employee rights in relations with union and employer

3. **Upon what basis is discrimination considered illegal by each law?**

A. Title VII
  - Race, Color, Sex, Religion, National Origin
    1. Race—while reporting requirements designate the following as being of specific concern: Blacks, Asian Americans, Americans, American Indians, Spanish Surnamed Americans, all races, including Whites, are in fact protected by Title VII.

B. Executive Orders
  - 11246: Race, Color, Religion, National Origin
    1. Race—all races are protected as in Title VII.
  - 11375: Sex (amended 11246 to include sex)
  - 11141: Age (no specified ages) This order has received little Federal emphasis and is not discussed from this point forward.
  - 11478: Race, Color, Sex, Religion, National Origin.
    Supersedes 11246, 11375, provisions for Federal Government.
  - 11758: Mental and Physical Handicaps (from this point forward, this Executive Order is discussed under Rehabilitation Act).

C. Equal Pay Act
  - Sex, where jobs require equal skills, effort and responsibility and are performed under similar working conditions

D. Age Discrimination Act.
  - Age (40–65)

E. Rehabilitation Act, Executive Order 11758
  - Mental and Physical Handicaps

F. NLRA
  - When a union breaches its duty of fair representation, or if a company commits a derivative violation by condoning this action, then an individual can claim discrimination against either or both based on membership in one of the previously referenced protected classes, i.e., race, sex, color, etc.

4. **Who is required to obey each law?**

A. Title VII
  1. Employers with fifteen or more employees
  2. Unions with fifteen or more members
  3. Joint apprenticeship training programs
  4. Employment agencies, including union hiring halls
  5. Federal, state and local government subunits
  6. Institutions of higher education

B. Executive Orders, 11246, 11375
  - First and second tier Federal government contractors and subcontractors; Construction contractors are handled very differently from supply & service contractors. Unless otherwise indicated, comments on 11246 and 11375 refer to supply and service contractors only[7] 11478
  - Federal Government agencies and U.S. Postal Service

C. Equal Pay Act
  - Employers subject to Fair Labor Standards Act of 1938 to which this act is an amendment, i.e., employers "engaged in commerce or in the production of goods for commerce" interpreted broadly; As the result of the 1972

amendment the Equal Pay Act now covers employees in executive, administrative, professional and outside salesforce categories, employees in most state and local governments, hospitals, and schools.

D. Age Discrimination Act
1. Employers with twenty or more employees
2. Unions with twenty-five or more members
3. Employment agencies
4. Federal, state and local government subunits

E. Sec. 500 Rehabilitation Act
- Federal Government Sec. 503 Rehabilitation Act, Executive Order 11758
- Federal Government contractors and subcontractors, including construction contractors

F. NLRA
- Essentially, any employer or union in the private sector engaged in interstate trade or commerce (meeting certain other requirements)

5. Who enforces each law?

A. Title VII
- Equal Employment Opportunity Commission (EEOC) except for Federal Government which is enforced by the individual agencies with final authority resting with the U.S. Civil Service Commission

B. Executive Orders
11246, 11375
- Office of Federal Contract Compliance (OFCC) and the contracting Federal Agencies 11478
- Individual agencies and U.S. Civil Service Commission

C. Equal Pay Act
- Wage and Hour Division of the U.S. Department of Labor

D. Age Discrimination Act
- Wage and Hour Division of the U.S. Department of Labor for employers, unions, employment agencies, State and Local Governments
- Individual agencies and U.S. Civil Service Commission for Federal Government

E. Rehabilitation Act,
Executive Order 11758
- Office of Federal Contract Compliance (OFCC), and to a minor extent, the contracting agencies

F. NLRA
- National Labor Relations Board

6. How may an individual who believes he has been discriminated against initiate enforcement agency action?[8]

A. Title VII
- File a complaint with the EEOC or where applicable with a state EEO agency;
- Federal employees must first talk with agency EEO counselor, then may file a complaint with agency.

B. Executive Orders,
11246, 11375
- File a complaint with the contracting Federal agency, the OFCC or EEOC, or state EEO agency

- Federal employees must first talk with agency EEO counselor, then may file a complaint with agency.
C. Equal Pay Act
  - File a complaint with the Wage and Hour Division of the U.S. Department of Labor
D. Age Discrimination Act
  - File a complaint with the Wage and Hour Division of the U.S. Department of Labor
  - Federal employees must first talk with agency EEO counselor, then may file a complaint with agency.
E. Rehabilitation Act, Executive Order 11758
  - File a complaint with the OFCC; these may be referred to the contracting agency
F. NLRA
  - File a charge with the National Labor Relations Board

7. What other actions may an individual who believes he has been discriminated against take to attempt to rectify this situation?

A. Title VII
  - May ultimately file individual or class action suit in Federal District Court;
  - Federal employees may appeal to the agency chief, to the U.S. Civil Service Commission Appeals and Review Board, or file civil action in Federal District Court
B. Executive Orders
   11246, 11375
  - Normally if an individual is dissatisfied with OFCC actions, he will go to EEOC procedures which ultimately could lead to filing suit in Federal District Court, but EEOC procedures are in fact available simultaneously with OFCC procedures
    11478
  - Federal employees may appeal to the agency chief, to the U.S. Civil Service Commission Appeals and Review Board or file civil action in Federal District Court.
C. Equal Pay Act
  - May file suit individually or collectively in State or Federal District Court
D. Age Discrimination Act
  - May file suit individually or collectively in State or Federal District Court, but first must notify Secretary of Labor
  - Federal employees may appeal to the agency chief or to U.S. Civil Service Commission Appeals and Review Board
E. Rehabilitation Act
   Executive Order 11758
  - Hearing at Assistant Secretary of Labor Level, may file suit in Federal District Court
F. NLRA
  - If dissatisfied with NLRA actions, may go to EEOC procedures which ultimately could lead to filing suit in Federal District Court, may in fact go to the EEOC and to NLRA provisions at same time or only to EEOC

From this point forward, the emphasis is on private employment situations. Thus, Title VII and Age Discrimination Act comments, unless otherwise indicated, do not discuss Federal Employment situations and the Executive Order section considers only Executive Orders 11246 and 11375.

8. May the applicable enforcement agency initiate its own investigations and if so, why?

A. Title VII

- No. The EEOC can only activate its enforcement mechanism as the result of an individual complaint. However, once it begins an investigation, it may discover other acts of discrimination against which it may take action.

B. Executive Orders, 11246, 11375

- Yes. The OFCC (or contracting agency) is charged with monitoring affirmative action programs. They can perform on site or off site inspections as they deem necessary.

C. Equal Pay Act

- Yes. The Wage and Hour Division may investigate, gather data, enter establishments, obtain records as is necessary to insure compliance with the Equal Pay Act.

D. Age Discrimination Act

- Yes. The Wage and Hour Division may investigate, gather data, enter establishments, obtain records as is necessary to insure compliance with the Age Act.

E. Rehabilitation Act
Executive Order 11758

- Yes. Primarily where the contractor has not included the required affirmative action clause, but also as is necessary in order to obtain compliance.

F. NLRA

- Yes. But unless discrimination is open and blatant, it is extremely unlikely that they would do so.

9. What is the typical pattern of events once an agency has initiated its enforcement mechanisms?

A. Title VII

- EEOC investigation; finding of probable causes; conciliation efforts; court suit by EEOC, U.S. Attorney General or individual. Conciliation is the major weapon.

B. Executive Orders, 11246, 11375

- OFCC or contracting agency investigations; conciliation hearings; show cause notice; sanctions, such as loss of contract. Severe sanctions are rarely used.

C. Equal Pay Act

- Wage and Hour Division investigation or conciliation (not required by law); court suit; injunction. Most complaints are settled without litigation.

D. Age Discrimination Act

- Wage and Hour Division investigation; conciliation (required by law); court suit; injunction. Most complaints are settled without litigation.

E. Rehabilitation Act
Executive Order 11758

- OFCC hearings; conciliation; sanction, such as loss of contract. Severe sanctions are rarely used.

F. NLRA

- Agency will send investigator. Upon completion of investigation, if the investigator reports findings of likely discrimination, the agency will sue the defendant.

10. What are the possible penalties associated with noncompliance? (For Employers)
  A. Title VII
    1. Voluntary conciliation agreement—EEOC determination of personnel policies and Affirmative Action Program contents as designated; ratio hiring of minorities and women; back pay, hiring, promotion and seniority settlements.
    2. Court Ordered involuntary action—Affirmative Action Program (AAP) contents and personnel policies as designated; ratio hiring as required; back pay, hiring, promotion and seniority settlements as deemed appropriate.
  B. Executive Orders
     11246, 11375
    1. Voluntary conciliation agreement—OFCC modifications of AAP; OFCC determination of personnel policies; ratio hiring of minorities and women; back pay, hiring, promotion and seniority settlements.
    2. Failure of Conciliation—withholding of progress payments, suspension or cancellation of contracts.
  C. Equal Pay Act
    1. Voluntary conciliation agreements—back pay settlements; modification of personnel practices.
    2. Court Ordered Involuntary Action—back pay plus when suit is brought by individual, it may result in liquidated damages. The courts can order any other appropriate action to rectify the situation.
    3. Willful violation is punishable criminally—fines up to $10,000 may be levied. Second convictions may result in imprisonment.
    4. Injunctions may be issued (including against unions).
  D. Age Discrimination Act
    1. Voluntary conciliation agreements—back pay settlements; modification of personnel practices.
    2. Court Ordered Involuntary Action—back pay plus when suit is brought by individual it may result in liquidated damages. (Only if an employer willfully violated the law.) Courts may order other appropriate action.
    3. Willful violation is punishable criminally—fines up to $10,000 may be levied. Second convictions may result in imprisonment.
    4. Injunctions may be issued (including against unions).
  E. Rehabilitation Act
     Executive Order 11758
    1. Voluntary conciliation agreements—modification of personnel practices.
    2. Failure of conciliation—withholding of progress payments, suspension or cancellation of contract.
  F. NLRA
    • Cease and desist orders.

11. What exceptions exist to this law? (For Employers)
  A. Title VII
    • Bona Fide Occupational Qualifications (BEOQ) for sex, religion and national origin; "compelling business necessity"; compensation differentials resulting from merit, incentive or seniority systems if such are not based on discrimination; certain other exemptions for private membership clubs, purposes of national security, allowances of preferences for Indians, allowances for exclusion of communists, allowances for preferences of veterans.

B. Executive Orders
   11246, 11375
   - Contracts less than $10,000 (except bills of lading) do not have to include equal opportunity clause.
   - Employees with contracts for less than $50,000 and fewer than fifty employees are not required to have written Affirmative Action Programs (AAP); but these employers are still required to have AAP. Miscellaneous minor exemptions.
C. Equal Pay Act
   - Differentials in pay resulting from a seniority system, a merit system, a system measuring earnings by quantity or quality of production; any other factor except sex. (Systems must be written and formal.)
D. Age Discrimination Act
   - BFOQ for age; bona fide seniority systems; bona fide apprenticeship programs, reasonable factors other than age.
E. Rehabilitation Act
   Executive Order 11758
   - Contracts less than $2,500 are not required to include affirmative action clause; undue "hardship" caused by accommodation to the handicaps; certain other exemptions related to affirmative action program and annual report.
F. NLRA
   - Essentially none.

12. What records should be kept?

1. Employers
A. Title VII[9] and
B. Executive Orders
   11246, 11375
   - The Affirmative Action Program; EEO policy statements; work force composition by race and sex by job classification—for departments and for the organization in total; applicant flow data by race and sex; promotion and transfer data by race and sex; training data by race and sex; termination data by race and sex; equal pay analysis by race and sex by job classification; EEO grievances and formal complaints filed and their resolutions; utilization (workforce) analysis computations; test validity and reliability studies; notification of affirmative action programs to employment agencies, unions, suppliers; maternity leave policy; EEO training program contents; internal control reports; applications; test results; advertisements; employee benefit plans; recuitment program activity including places visited; seniority lists; current collective bargaining agreements; job descriptions and specifications; affirmative action program goals and progress analysis; where applicable, lists of those seeking admission to joint apprenticeship training programs, and, in general, any personnel practice records.
C. Equal Pay Act
   - Employee's name, address, sex, occupation; records related to employees' wages, job classifications, hours, terms and conditions of employment; all records which relate to the determination of wages, certain collective bargaining agreements; an equal pay analysis is advisable.

D. Age Discrimination Act
- Personal data on employees—name, address, date of birth, occupation, pay information, etc.; data related to hiring, promotion, transfer, training, lay-off, discharge, termination, recruitment correspondence; test results; physician exam results; advertisements; benefit plans, etc. Any other records as deemed appropriate.

E. Rehabilitation Act
Executive Order 11758
- The Affirmative Action Program; records that are necessary for filing annual reports to OFCC; other records necessary for compliance.

F. NLRA
- Only those normally required by this Act.

2. Unions
A. Title VII
- Records that are necessary for the filing of the EEO-3 report and where applicable, lists of those seeking admission to joint apprenticeship training programs, copies of collective bargaining agreements. If a complaint is filed, required to keep all "relevant" records.

D. Age Discrimination Act
- Members and applicants names, addresses, date of birth.

3. Apprenticeship Training Programs
A. Title VII
- Records that are necessary for the filing of the EEO-2-E report, and where applicable, lists of those seeking admission to joint apprenticeship training programs. If a complaint is filed, required to keep all "relevant" records.

4. Employment Agencies
A. Title VII
- If a complaint is filed, required to keep all "relevant" records.

D. Age Discrimination Act
- Personal information for referrals and applicants for referral including test scores, etc.

5. Federal, State and Local Governments
- Records that are necessary for the filing of internal Federal reports or the EEO-4 or EEO-5 reports.

6. Institutions of Higher Learning
- Records that are necessary for the filing of the EEO-6 report.

13. What reports must be filed?

A. Title VII
1. Employers—EEO-1, EEO-5, EEO-2-E
2. Unions—EEO-3, EEO-1
3. Joint Apprenticeship Training Committees—EEO-2
4. Employment Agencies—only EEO-1 or EEO-2, as employer or union, nothing as an employment agency.
5. Federal Government Units—various internal reports. Each agency required to have AAP which is monitored by the U.S. Civil Service Commission. State and Local Governments—EEO-4, Primary and Secondary Schools —EEO-5.
6. Institutions of Higher Education—EEO-6

B. Executive Orders
11246, 11375
- Employers—EEO-1 (supply and services)

E. Rehabilitation Act
- Employers Annual Report to OFCC where contract is greater than $500,000 and calls for performance in 90 or more days.

F. NLRA
- None

14. What have been the enforcement agencies' strategies?

A. Title VII
- The EEOC has concentrated lately on securing massive conciliation agreements with the larger, more visible firms such as AT&T and industry agreements such as that with the steel industry. Smaller firms remain virtually untouched except for the complaint process. Currently they are committed to reducing the complaint backlog. They attempt to have complainant reconcile with his organization if at all possible to reduce backlog of complaints.

B. Executive Orders
11246, 11375
- Its strategy in the nonconstruction area is largely one of securing massive conciliation agreements and of delegating AAP compliance monitoring to the contracting agencies. Complaints are usually not handled on an individual basis and are passed on to the EEOC. With respect to construction contractors, it has engineered the previously referred to "home town" plans. Discussion with an OFCC representative indicates a hoped for computer analysis of contractor AAP's and EEO-1's but this has yet to materialize.

C. Equal Pay Act
- The Labor Department has responded to complaints.

D. Age Discrimination Act
- The Labor Department has responded to complaints.

E. Rehabilitation Act
Executive Order 11758
- Not much visible effort to date.

F. NLRA
- None.

Note: The EEOC, the OFCC, the other applicable divisions of the Department of Labor, and the Federal Agencies are all undermanned, and rely extensively on fear of punishment as a motivator for those they regulate. Both the volume and seriousness of complaints call attention to the worst offenders. Action is prioritized.

15. How effective have the enforcement agencies' efforts been?

A. Title VII
- Lately the EEOC has been effective in gaining impressive conciliation agreements with AT&T and the steel industy. The EEOC was granted the right to sue in its own name in the 1972 amendments and as a result has been perceived as more potent by the firms it regulates. Increased, but still insufficient, manpower has also helped. Overall, the EEOC seems to have very little impact on smaller employers, perhaps only marginal impact on most employers. The EEOC still has a serious backlog of complaints, reach two years in some districts.

B. Executive Orders
11246, 11375
- The OFCC has shared responsibility with the EEOC for the major concilia-

tions. Several major contractors have been changed significantly, but in sum, the OFCC has been only marginally effective. The OFCC has a very small staff. The contracting agencies have assigned few personnel to the tasks of monitoring Affirmative Action Programs.

C. Equal Pay Act
  • The Department of Labor has prosecuted this act very rigorously and rather successfully.
D. Age Discimination Act
  • The Department of Labor has reacted to complaints. More effort is currently being placed on remedying this type of discrimination, but past activities have been limited.
E. Rehabilitation Act
  Executive Order 11758
  • This program is just commencing on a serious level.
F. NLRA
  • No apparent impact. Relatively few complaints have occurred.

16. What are key enforcement agency problems?

1. Manpower—None of the agencies has sufficient manpower to adequately carry out its assigned tasks. With current Federal budget limitations, increases in manpower appear improbable.
2. Lack of coordination of requirements among the enforcement agencies—A few efforts have been made to coordinate activities, but these have not provided the unified effort believed necessary. A recent Civil Rights Commission report was especially critical of this situation.[10]
3. Internal strife has unsettled some of the agencies, especially the EEOC.

From this point forward, the questions refer to Title VII and Executive Orders 11246 and 11375 only.

17. What is the difference between equal employment opportunity and affirmative action?

Equal employment opportunity is just that. Namely, anyone regardless of race, color, sex, religion, national origin, age, or handicaps has an equal chance for a job based on qualifications and predicted performance in that job.

Affirmative Action goes beyond equal opportunity and requires the employer to make an extra effort to hire and promote those in the protected classes with the implied provision that the most important "qualification" is membership in the protected classes.

18. What are revised orders numbers 4 and 14 and what are their principal provisions?

Revised Order Number 4 contains the OFCC's instructions for the design, implementation and control of the nonconstruction contractor's Affirmative Action Program.

Revised Order Number 14 contains the OFCC's checklists for usage by contracting Federal agencies in auditing non-construction contractor's Affirmative Action Programs. Both off-site and on-site audit checklists are detailed.

19. What is an Affirmative Action Program (AAP) and what are it's major components?

An Affirmative Action Program is a requirement of the OFCC for complying with Executive Orders 11246 and 11375, and a requirement of the Employment Standards Administration for complying with the Rehabilitation Act. The EEOC has taken the position that an AAP is a vital ingredient, but on a voluntary basis, for complying with Title VII. The AAP is an employer generated plan for EEO compliance and should be designed to provide for EEO in all personnel practices as well as address the issues of top management support, the assignment of program responsibility and the control of program results. The major target of the EEOC's and OFCC's AAP's policies is racial and sexual discrimination. The OFCC and EEOC requirements for an AAP are rigorous and include: an analysis of workforce composition, i.e., utilization or workforce analysis; employment goal setting; examinations of recruitment, selection, testing, transfers, training, promotion, layoff, recall, seniority, termination, control reports, etc. Similar but less detailed requirements are necessary for the AAP for the Rehabilitation Act. Most commonly this phrase refers to requirements for the Executive Orders to Title VII.

20. What is utilization analysis? (workforce analysis) What is employment goal setting and how is it accomplished?

Utilization or workforce analysis is the process of determining whether or not minorities and women are being employed by the organization in the appropriate numbers within all job classifications. Utilization analysis is a three step process. First, the organization must determine how many minorities and women should be employed by job classification in total and by department according to a complex series of factors which include minority and female: percentages of the population and workforce, unemployment rates, skills availabilities, training possibilities both internal and external, and internal promotional possibilities. In step three, the organization begins by comparing these two figures. Normally minorities and women will be underutilized, especially in managerial, technical and professional job classifications. Next the organization must establish employment goals for minorities and females. Using the figures derived above in combination with its normal employment planning process, the organization establishes hiring, training, and promotional goals for minorities and women for five and one year periods while considering the expansion and contraction of the firm's employment level as well as transfer, training, and promotion potentials.[11]

21. What are the principal guidelines which have been made available by the EEOC and OFCC?

	EEOC	OFCC
Discrimination		
related to: Sex	Yes	Yes
Religion	Yes	Yes
National origin	Yes	Yes
Selection procedures	Yes	Yes
Records and reports	Yes	Yes
Procedural regulations	Yes	Yes
Availability of enforcement		
Agency records	Yes	Yes
Pre-employment inquiries	Yes	Yes
Overall affirmative action		
program	Yes	Yes
Obligations of contractors		Yes
Audit checklists		Yes

22. How are statistics used in an investigation?

Statistics can be used in two ways. First, appropriate documentary (comparative) statistical data must be available for inspection for all validation and reliability studies of tests. Secondly, demographic (population) statistics can be used by complainants and investigators to show that insufficient numbers of protected class members are employed in various job classifications and thereby establish a "prima facie" case of discrimination.[12]

23. What are the primary personnel practices which have been affected by EEO and how have they been affected?

Recruitment—Active recruitment of those in the protected classes especially minorities and females, is required. Movement of organizational facilities must be assessed for impacts on minority employment levels. Advertisements must be adapted to legal requirements.

Selection for Hiring—Testing is the key concern. Interviews and application blanks as well as paper and pencil and skills tests, must be made valid and reliable. Job descriptions, job specifications and performance appraisals must also be analyzed for relevance.[13] Of special concern are education and experience requirements set at too high a level.

Selection For: Transfer, Training, Promotion, Layoff, Recall, Termination—Special efforts must be made to train and promote minorities and women. Forms are available through the EEOC for analyzing training, promotion, and termination practices. Of special interest to the EEOC and OFCC are upward mobility and seniority. Performance appraisals as predictors of performance at higher levels will undoubtedly come under close scrutiny in the near future.

Pay and Benefits—Equal pay for equal work is carefully observed. Benefits must be equal. Performance appraisals as determinants of pay must be made unbiased.

Other Working Conditions—Discriminatory working conditions are not allowable.

24. What is "reverse discrimination" and is it legal?

Reverse discrimination is preference for those in the protected classes as opposed to equal opportunity. Its legality is debatable. There are contradictory provisions regarding such preferences in Title VII.[14] The OFCC states that it should not occur, yet one of its chief representatives has suggested that it is a favored solution for low levels of protected class member employment.[15] Contrastingly, the U.S. Supreme Court has noted, "Congress has not commanded that the less qualified be preferred over the better qualified simply because of minority origins. Far from disparaging job qualifications as such, Congress has made such qualifications the controlling factor. . . ."[16] Since contradictory decisions on reverse discrimination have been issued by lower courts, the Supreme Court will probably have to settle this issue.

25. What is an appropriate EEO strategy?

For the employing organizations: Get serious about EEO. Assign personnel full time to this program and give them the authority to carry out its requirements. Hire expert assistance, i.e., a management consultant, in the formative stages and during times of turmoil. Do not hesitate to seek expert legal advice. Secure top management support for the program. Follow the EEOC and OFCC guidelines for Affirmative Action Programs. Seek results not just activity. Keep abreast of changes in the law and especially changes in the case law. The price of non-compliance can be extremely costly, not only in terms of the outright settlement amounts, but legal and administrative costs as well.

For the individual manager: The manager must follow his organization's program but this must be balanced against moral conviction. The individual manager should become familiar with specific relevant requirements. These are available through the personnel department, but are also available through the appropriate enforcement agencies. The principal areas in which the individual manager becomes involved are these: *Selection interviews:* The questions which can be asked are much more limited than they were before EEO. Questions related to protected class membership are generally inappropriate. A structured interview is more valid than an unstructured one. *Performance appraisals:* Underlying biases against protected class members must be eliminated. *Upward mobility:* Extra efforts must be given to promoting protected class members, especially minorities and females. These include training, transfers, and other forms of development: *Layoff, recall, termination:* Seniority has been a primary concern of all EEO agencies. The legal findings are varied. Your organization should have a strategy in this area. *Goals:* You may be required to assist in establishing employment goals for protected class members. *Reports:* You may be required to submit any number of reports in support of EEO. *Subordinate behavior:* The reaction of white males may approach "backlash." Some protected class members are difficult to manage and many require more understanding than do members of the majority. The best in humanistic management is required.

An important point to remember is this: If you are prejudiced, that is your business, but if you, as a manager, allow this prejudice to become discrimination on the job, then that is your employer's business. And if as a result of your discrimination you cost the employer money, it may just cost you your job.

REFERENCES

1   Hart, Phillip A. "Notre Dame Law School Civil Rights Lectures," *Notre Dame Lawyer,* XLIX, (October, 1973), pp. 5–45.

2   Civil Rights Commission, *The Federal Civil Rights Enforcement Effort-1974,* Volume V, Civil Rights Commission, Washington, D.C., 1973, p. i.

3   Sec. 500 of the Rehabilitation Act covers Federal Government employment situations and is not discussed here in detail. Future comments refer only to Sec. 503 and more specifically to provisions required by Presidential Executive Order 11758 which is the major private sector implementation mechanism of this law.

4   While Taft-Hartley was not drafted as a civil rights law, certain of its provisions provide the plaintiff with quick, low cost relief measures. These provisions have tremendous potential and therefore Taft-Hartley is included in this discussion.

5   While these laws may have substantial impact on a few court cases, they are not sufficiently demanding of most organizations to make their inclusion in this discussion particularly relevant.

6   Most state and local laws parallel federal laws. Therefore, because of the variations in state and local law coverages plus the fact that federal law has precedent over state and local laws except in rare situations in which state and local laws are more demanding, state and local laws will not be discussed in the following paragraphs.

7   Construction contractors are handled through "home town plans." These plans are negotiated Affirmative Action Programs involving various community contractors, Federal Agencies, the OFCC, and representatives of the protected classes, usually minorities.

8 Employees may of course first file a complaint with their employer. Failing this, other actions may be taken.

9 Technically, under Title VII, employers are not required to keep records unless a complaint is filed. If a complaint is filed an employer must keep all "relevant" records. The items listed here are suggested as relevant and appropriate to providing evidence if necessary. It is recommended that employers keep these records even if a complaint is not filed. The apparent attitude of most federal enforcement agencies is that you are guilty unless you can prove your innocence. This you establish through records.

10 Civil Rights Commission, *op. cit.*

11 For a more detailed discussion of how to accomplish these activities, see, Higgins, James M., "The Complicated Process of Establishing Goals for Equal Employment Opportunity Programs," *Personnel Journal*, (December, 1975), pp. 631–637.

12 William Byrd Fryer, "Employment Discrimination: Statistics and Preference Under Title VII," *Virginia Law Review*, Volume 59, Number 3, (March, 1973), p. 466.

13 Relevance refers to the degree to which success on the job as conceived is related to success on the job as measured either in performance appraisals or in job specifications, i.e., the perceived traits, abilities, and other requirements of the individual who is sought to fill a position opening.

14 Sections 703(a) and 703(j) versus Section 706(g), Title VII, "Civil Rights Act of 1964."

15 41 CFR 60-2.30; William J. Kilberg, at that time Associate Solicitor for Labor Relations and Civil Rights, U.S. Department of Labor, has stated that where discrimination exists and no other remedy is available, then " . . . temporary preferential hiring is legal and appropriate." Daniel Seiligman, "How 'Equal Opportunity' Turned into Employment Quotas," *Fortune* (March, 1973), p. 167.

16 Griggs v. Duke Power Co., (SupCt 1971), 3, Bureau of National Affairs, Fair Employment Practices, Cases 177.

FOR DISCUSSION AND REVIEW

1 Why is it difficult for organizations to obtain information on EEO compliance?

2 State the major EEO laws. What types of employers are exempt from each?

3 What actions can a person who believes he or she has been discriminated against take?

4 Trace the typical pattern of events which may occur once an agency has initiated its enforcement mechanisms.

5 Review the records employers should keep regarding EEO.

6 What is utilization or workforce analysis?

James Ledvinka, APD

Robert D. Gatewood

EEO Issues with Pre-Employment Inquiries

The past few years have been a time of concern over the legal vulnerability of employment practices, including employment applications and other pre-employment inquires.[1] Warnings in business periodicals and lists of "taboo" questions in the popular press[2] have led to vague feelings of uneasiness over the use of these inquiries to obtain information on applications.

This article reviews the problems of pre-employment inquiries and gives some specific recommendations for developing a defensible procedure. It is not an attempt to give specific legal advice, but to distill the opinions of various regulatory agency staff, labor lawyers and other EEO specialists into a usable set of general guidelines.

LEGAL STATUS OF PRE-EMPLOYMENT INQUIRIES

Federal EEO laws do not directly prohibit employers from asking *anything*. But several states do and the U.S. Equal Employment Opportunity Commission looks with suspicion on certain types of inquiries—even when they are asked innocently by employers. So the matter of pre-employment inquiries should be of concern to all.

Table 1 lists the states that have fair employment practice laws governing pre-employment inquiries. Some of those states restrict virtually any questions relating to race, religion, sex and the like, even the most indirect ones. Other states are less restrictive. Moreover, some states exempt questions that are asked for EEO record-keeping purposes, while others do not. The safest course is to seek out information on the specific prohibitions of any state listed in Table 1.[3]

Table 1
States with Fair Employment Laws
Governing Pre-Employment Inquiries

Arizona	New Jersey
California	New Mexico
Delaware	New York
Hawaii	Ohio
Illinois	Oregon
Kansas	Pennsylvania
Massachusetts	Rhode Island
Michigan	Utah
Minnesota	Washington
Missouri	West Virginia

One rule of thumb will serve for state and federal law alike: any question that tends to identify an applicant as a member of a protected group, or any question that tends on the average to disfavor members of a protected group, is a problem

The Personnel Administrator 22, no. 2 (February 1977): 22–26. Reprinted by permission.

question. "Protected groups" cover a wide variety of categories nowadays: race, sex, religion, national origin, age, the handicapped, disabled veterans and Vietnam-era veterans. If an employer asks any question that in any manner affects a protected group disproportionately, EEOC and the contract compliance agencies may view it as evidence that the employer is guilty of discrimination. In such cases, the burden of proof falls upon the employer to justify such questions.

The justification is stringent. Technically, the same EEOC selection guidelines that have made it so hard to justify standardized tests apply with equal force to other screening devices, including pre-employment inquiries. Thus, EEOC considers it necessary to demonstrate the job relatedness of pre-employment inquiries. While some people may not share EEOC's view concerning the scope of their guidelines, several courts have concurred with EEOC in this matter.[4] Besides, the job-relatedness requirement is well established by now, so employers who wish to avoid conflict with EEOC should scrutinize their questions carefully.

SOME PROBLEM QUESTIONS[5]

While it is impossible to enumerate all the pre-employment questions that could possibly give rise to EEO problems, some commonplace ones deserve mention. Many of them have already been eliminated by some employers; all of them have been identified as potentially troublesome by EEO attorneys and others knowledgeable in EEO matters:

1 *Marital status* (including husband's name). EEOC treats these questions with suspicion because of the possibility that an employer could use them to discriminate against women on the basis of their marital status.[6] It would be difficult to show the relevancy of this inquiry to job qualifications for either sex.

2 *Height and weight.* This inquiry is a problem because of the possibility that employers would use it to discriminate against women on the basis of their personal appearance—also because minimum height and weight requirements tend to discriminate against protected groups of smaller average stature (women, Orientals, Mexican-Americans, etc).[7] However, there may be some positions for which a height requirement may be justified—for example, if the job involved operating a machine of a certain height and platforms or other arrangements could not be made to allow operation by shorter individuals.

3 *Hair and eye color.* These may suggest an applicant's race and they are very difficult to justify as job related.

4 *Child care.* (including ages of children, questions about what arrangements have been made for child care, etc.). In the past, these have been used to exclude women with preschool-aged children or young children in general.[8] Besides, they tend to fall disproportionately on protected groups that have more children on the average. If such questions must be asked, the application form should emphasize that answers are required of both male and female applicants.

5 *Availability for Saturday or Sunday work.* Such questions may tend to discriminate against applicants whose religion prohibits Saturday or Sunday work. EEO laws require that a reasonable effort be made to accommodate an applicant's religious practices, unless it would create an "undue hardship on the conduct of the employer's business".[9] This may mean that the employer would have to change work schedules, trade shifts and make other alterations in the work routine. But it does *not* mean that an employer has to put up with a situation where it can be documented that the employee's absence significantly impedes the operation of the organization.

6 *Credit, garnishment, home ownership, etc.* These questions often have a greater impact on minority applicants than others. Despite the inconvenience of garnishments for the employer, courts have ruled that garnishment disqualification of minority applicants constitutes a violation of Title VII of the 1964 Civil Rights Act.[10]

7 *Arrests, less than honorable discharges and convictions.* These questions also often have a greater impact on minority applications than others. Arrest questions have been recognized as a problem for some time, the argument being that an arrest is no indication of guilt. As for convictions, EEOC recognizes the employer's right to exclude those convicted of certain crimes from certain jobs, but discourages the automatic rejection of an application because of a criminal record. The courts have supported this position.[11]

8 *National origin* (place of birth, "are you a naturalized citizen?", etc.). While the Supreme Court has conceded that a policy of favoring U.S. citizens is not necessarily a violation of the 1964 Civil Rights Act, disfavoring foreign-born applicants has been interpreted to be a violation of the 1866 Civil Rights Act.[12] Thus questions regarding place of birth or questions designed to distinguish between native citizens and naturalized ones are difficult to defend.

9 *Relatives or friends working for company.* This becomes a problem when the employer has a workforce in which protected groups are underrepresented. In such cases, a question about friends or relatives might reflect a preference for friends or relatives of present employees—or it might be taken that way by applicants from protected groups. Again, it falls to the employer to show the need for such a question.

10 *Age.* While most applications ask for it, it seems like an obvious red flag to someone looking for age discrimination. The Age Discrimination in Employment Act protects those between the ages of 40 and 65; refusal to hire those younger or older is not prohibited. Nevertheless, the question is sensitive enough that some experts advise asking date of birth instead of age—a query that has lower visibility.

11 *Education.* The most famous Supreme Court EEO case, *Griggs v. Duke Power Co.*,[13] struck down not only tests but also educational requirements that had an adverse impact on blacks and were not required by business necessity. Yet no one doubts the relevance of certain kinds of educational experience for certain kinds of jobs. It is important, though, to give credit where credit is due: give consideration to education that is not acquired through the normal middle-class channels. Thus the application might be phrased in a way that invites applicants to list educational experiences such as on-the-job training, vocational school, equivalency diplomas and informal job-related experiences. Also, to avoid reliance on those conventional badges of educational attainment that often serve as block to minorities, the application might ask the applicant to circle years of schooling rather than list diplomas or degrees.

PROBLEM OF SUBJECTIVITY

Another concern is the use to which screening information is put. Some screenings call for the interviewer to judge the applicant's personal characteristics. It is not unusual to find places for the interviewer to rate "tact," "judgment," "grooming," "initiative" and the like. These are basically subjective judgments and they may well have adverse impact on protected groups.

Similarly, there is concern over the subjective use of objective information. It is subjective judgment to base a hiring decision on an objective criterion such as ex-

perience without a careful study of that criterion's relationship to the job in question. Such a decision would be just as vulnerable to legal attack as a decision made
on the basis of a test score, an interviewer's casual appraisal, or anything else. Recently, more attention has been paid to possible EEO conflicts with those sorts of
subjective judgments about applicants.[14] While employers are turning away from
objective selection methods such as tests in an effort to avoid legal problems, the
courts have been declaring subjective methods to be unlawful when they operate to
exclude protected groups disproportionately.

WEIGHTED APPLICATION BLANKS

To solve the subjectivity problems, some organizations have turned to the weighted
application blank,[15] a useful device if some potential hazards are avoided. The
weighted application method does the same thing with biographical information
that test validation does with ability or aptitude information. Basically the method
assigns numbers to the information according to its statistical relationship with an
organizational performance variable (such as job performance, absenteeism, turnover, etc.) For instance, if employees with military service had significantly lower
absenteeism than those without, the military service variable would be given a high
numerical weight; if there were no difference in absenteeism, no weight would be
given.

Once the appropriate information on the application is given numerical
weights, the weights are added to yield an application blank "score" that can be
treated much as a test score is treated in hiring applicants. If the relationship between application items and the performance variable holds up over time for applicants who are hired, the whole procedure has a degree of "criterion validity" that
few other screening methods can claim.

However there are a number of potentially serious drawbacks that accompany
the development and use of this technique. For one, there is some doubt whether the
"content validity" of the method is sufficient to legitimate the method without
further justification.[16] While a weighted application question may be *statistically*
related to an outcome variable, it may not be *logically* related to anything of significance. For instance, an item asking for hobbies might for some unknown reason
correlate with stenographers' job performance, but a manager would be at a loss to
point out any logical relationship between that item and the job.

Another EEO-related issue has to do with the generalizability of the weighted
application items across different racial or ethnic groups. One study reported little
carryover between groups on the items identified for use in selection.[17] Different
questions predicted well for different groups. This raises the possibility that
separate weighted application blanks would have to be developed for each group.

Furthermore, some have questioned the accuracy of the information given by
potential employees on application forms. One study found that a large percentage
of organizations do not seek complete verification of information obtained on application forms.[18] This becomes important in light of another study's finding that in 57
percent of the cases there was disagreement between the applicant and previous
employers as to duration of previous employment and previous salary earned.
Applicants usually overestimated both.[19]

Finally, there is the question of whether the relationship between the weighted
application questions and performance holds up over time. One study reported that
changes in the employment situation reduced the validity of the weighted application over time.[20] In other cases, chance seems to account for the impressive rela-

tionship between questions and performance; a repeat validity study with another group of employees may well show no relationship.[21]

WHAT TO DO

Strictly speaking, no precaution can guarantee that an employer will stay out of trouble with pre-employment inquiries; there is always an element of legal risk. Nevertheless, there are steps that can be taken to make pre-employment inquiries more defensible to EEOC and more effective for meeting organizational objectives.

1 *Pinpoint any question that might possibly tend to: (a) Identify* an applicant as a member of a protected group; (b) *Disqualify* or disfavor an applicant of a protected group.

2 *Decide whether there is sufficient justification for such questions.* Are they related to the jobs being applied for? Do the advantages of using the question outweigh the risks? Do you think you could defend it against a charge of discrimination?

3 *When questionable inquiries must be made, indicate on the application form that they will not be used to discriminate.* Applications frequently include footnotes stating that age and sex-related questions would not be used to discriminate against any applicant. The same approach could be used with any problem question that an employer decides is necessary to ask. For example, if criminal convictions are asked about, the application could state that a criminal record would not mean that the applicant is automatically disqualified. Another example would be if birth date is requested, the application could point out that the company complies with the Age Discrimination Act.

4 *Consider a two-phase inquiry: pre-hiring and post-hiring.* Some information is needed to make a hiring decision, but much of the suspect information can wait until after the applicant has been hired. The latter category often includes questions that are used for insurance and retirement benefits purposes, such as age, dependents and marital status. By waiting to gather this information until after the hiring decision is made, the employer can do much to avoid the appearance of impropriety.

5 *Keep a separate file of race and sex information needed for EEO recordkeeping.* This way the employer can maintain the statistics he needs for affirmative action planning with less likelihood that an EEO compliance agency will infer that race or sex affected the hiring decision. Race and sex information can be collected before hiring in most states, but it should *not* be coded on the application form—that has already been a factor in one court decision against an employer.

6 *Try to minimize subjectivity and intuitive judgments that cannot be defended on the basis of a relationship to job performance.* Make the relative importance of information explicit and decision rules clear.

7 *If you use a weighted application blank to minimize subjectivity, make sure that:*
- Individual items are related to skills identified in a job analysis.
- Protected groups are adequately represented in the sample on which the weighted application is developed.
- The procedure is double-checked on another sample to see if they differentiate high and low groups in this sample also.
- The procedure is re-analyzed periodically to make sure the validity remains adequate.

REFERENCES

1 Many individuals provided helpful comments and information in the prepara-
   tion of this article: Donald R. Stacy of Kilpatrick, Cody, Rogers, McClatchey
   & Regenstein in Atlanta; Edward Katze of Constangy, Brooks & Smith in
   Atlanta; David Copus of the Equal Employment Opportunity Commission's
   Washington office; W. D. Buel of Byron Harless, Reid, Hite & Associates in
   Tampa, Florida; and others. The authors, however, are responsible for the
   use made of those ideas in this article.

2 For example, see *Business Week*, May 26, 1975.

3 An excellent source of information on state fair employment practice laws is
   Employment Practices Guide, vol. 3, published by Commerce Clearing House
   in Chicago.

4 For a good review, see Donald R. Stacy, "Subjective Criteria in Employment
   Decisions Under Title VII," *Georgia Law Review*, 1976, vol. 10, no. 3,
   pp. 737-752 (esp. 747-748).

5 Various lists are provided by law firms, state fair employment practice
   agencies and corporate personnel offices. This section was taken in part from
   a list provided by Constangy, Brooks & Smith in Atlanta.

6 *Sprogis* v. *United Air Lines*, 444 F.2d 1197 (7th. Cir. 1971).

7 *Laffey* v. *Northwest Airlines, Inc.*, 366 F. Supp. 763 (U.S. Dist. Ct., D.C.,
   1973); *Smith* v. *City of East Cleveland*, 520 F.2d 492 (6th Cir., 1975); and
   other cases.

8 *Phillips* v. *Martin-Marietta*, 400 U.S. 542 (U.S. Sup. Ct., 1971).

9 Title VII of the 1964 Civil Rights Act, Sec. 701j (42 U.S.C. sec. 2000e (j)).

10 *Wallace* v. *Debron*, 494 F.2d 674 (8th Cir., 1974); *Johnson* v. *Pike Corp.*, 332
   F. Supp. 490 (U.S. Dist. Ct., Calif., 1971).

11 *Green* v. *Missouri-Pacific R.R. Co.*, 523 F.2d 1290 (8th Cir., 1975); *Gregory* v.
   Litton Systems, 472 F.2d 631 (9th Cir., 1972).

12 *Espinoza* v. *Farah Manufacturing Co.*, 414 U.S. 811 (U.S. Sup. Ct., 1973),
   but see *Guerra* v. *Manchester Terminal Corp.*, 498 F.2d 641 (5th Cir., 1974)
   for a somewhat different picture of this area.

13 401 U.S. 424 (1971).

14 See Stacy (note 4 above); and Robert D. Gatewood and James Ledvinka,
   "Selection Interviewing and EEO: Mandate for Objectivity," *The Personnel
   Administrator*, May 1976, vol. 21, no. 4, pp. 15-18.

15 For a summary of this area, see G. W. England, *Development and Use of
   Weighted Application Blanks*. Industrial Relations Center, University of
   Minnesota, 1971.

16 L. Pace and L. F. Schoenfeldt, "Are Weighted Application Blanks Legal?"
   Personnel Psychology, in press.

17 D. Toole, J. Gavin, L. Murdy, and S. Sells, "The Differential Validity of
   Personality, Personal History, and Aptitute Data for Minority and Non-
   minority Employees," *Personnel Psychology*, 1972, vol. 25, pp. 661-672.

18 G. Beason and J. Belt, "Verifying Applicant's Backgrounds," *Personnel
   Journal*, 1976, vol. 55, no. 7, pp. 354-348.

19 I. Goldstein, "The Application Blank: How Honest Are the Responses?"
   Journal of Applied Psychology, 1971, vol. 55, no. 5, pp. 491-492.

20 D. Roach, "Double Cross-Validation of a Weighted Application Blank Over
   Time," *Journal of Applied Psychology*, 1971, vol. 55, no. 2, pp. 157-160.

21 D. Schwab and R. Oliver, "Predicting Tenure with Biographical Data: Ex-
   huming Buried Evidence," *Personnel Psychology*, 1974, vol. 27, pp. 125-128.

FOR DISCUSSION AND REVIEW

1 What general rule can be used as a guideline for pre-employment inquiries in order to help ensure their legality?
2 Specifically what types of inquiries may be illegal? Why?
3 Review the suggestions made by the authors to improve the legality and effectiveness of preemployment inquiries.

C. BIOLOGICAL DATA AND REFERENCE CHECKS

Irwin L. Goldstein

The Application Blank: How Honest Are the Responses?[1]

Many recent studies (Fleishman & Berniger, 1960; Scott & Johnson, 1967) have demonstrated that the application blank can be used to successfully predict tenure on the job. Scott and Johnson have especially noted the feasibility of employing the application blank in low-skilled occupations. Recently, a firm that was cooperating with the investigator on a research project questioned the honesty of the responses given by the applicants applying for jobs as nurses aides. The honesty of the replies is an issue aside from the question of validity since it is possible to predict from most any set of data. In any case, a search of the literature did not disclose any studies that had collected data reflecting on the honesty of the application blank responses.

Several studies, however, have questioned the accuracy of data collected in the interview. A study by Keating, Paterson, and Stone (1950) found that the correlations between reports on wages, and duration of employment were above .90. Another study by Weiss and Dawis (1960) discovered poorer agreement for a sample of 91 physically handicapped persons. The information varied in accuracy from 0% invalid information for reports on sex to 55% on the questions of receiving assistance. Essentially, invalid information was found for substantial numbers of persons (over 20% of the sample) on questions related to previous education, age at disablement, received assistance, job title, pay, and length of employment.

Blum and Naylor (1968) have suggested that the interview results in a face-to-face pressure that might cause a respondent to stretch the truth. In addition, prospective employees might be more likely to respond honestly on the application blank when their responses are actually recorded in their own handwriting. The present study examined the data recorded on the application blank for a sample of 111 applicants.

METHOD

The original sample consisted of 173 persons with the final sample equalling 111 persons for whom matching application blank data and previous employer responses were available. The application blanks were filled out by persons applying for positions as nurses aides in a group of nursing homes owned by the same corporation in a large east coast city. The blanks were collected during the period from September 1, 1968, to June 1, 1969. A form was filled out for each of these individuals with the following items listed: name, address, dates employed by last employer, and position previously held. The information for these items was obtained from the completed application blank. This form was sent to the employer listed by the applicant as the last place they were employed. The following information was requested from the previous employer: marital status, position held,

From *Journal of Applied Psychology* 55, no. 5 (1971): 491–492. Copyright © 1971 by the American Psychological Association. Reprinted by permission.

[1] Arnold Richman's aid in collecting the data from the application blanks is gratefully acknowledged. The author also wishes to thank William Mobley and Sharon Dorfman for their analyses and comments about the data.

dates of employment, salary of employee, and why the employee left. The previous employer was requested to draw a line through the item if he did not have the requested information. He was also asked to return the questionnaire and indicate "not employed by us" if he had never employed the applicant. The previous employers were assured of the confidentiality of the individual pieces of information as well as their firms' anonymity. They were also assured that their information would not affect the employment of the individuals concerned.

RESULTS AND DISCUSSION

The data generally indicate a substantial number of discrepancies between the employee's application blank responses and the responses of the previous employer. The interpretation of these data does require a note of caution. In this study, two sets of responses are being compared, and the true state of the world is not available. It is possible that some of the previous employer's responses are in error. As the discussion proceeds, however, it will become apparent from some of the directions of the differences that the most parsimonious explanation seems to point to a bias on the part of the applicant.

For the 111 employers who responded to the survey, 15% (17 respondents) indicated that the applicant had never worked for them. Married females who may have been previously employed under their maiden name were excluded from this count. Those applicants ($N=94$) whom the employer indicated had worked for their firm were included in the rest of the analyses. Information that was left blank by the applicant or the employer (e.g., in some cases salary disclosure was against company policy) reduced the N for the various categories. Also, in some cases, the respondent used completely different scales (i.e., pay per week versus pay per hour without the number of hours per week being stated). In these cases, or in any other case in which the responses could not be reconciled, the data were not used in these analyses. This was done in order to avoid, wherever possible, reported differences where none might exist.

The largest amount of agreement between the applicant and the previous employer occurred on the topic of the previous position held. There were only five clear discrepancies. Considering that the applicant was applying for a position as an aide in a nursing home, which is an unskilled low socioeconomic-status job, the applicant would be hard pressed to indicate that he or she had previously held a job substantially different from the job being considered. The category with the next highest percentage disagreement was the reason(s) for leaving. In the 63 cases in which the data were comparable, 25% were in disagreement. These are cases in which there were clear-cut differences. For example, the previous employer stated that the applicant was dismissed because of a violation of the company's rules, while the applicant stated that he left because the pay was too low.

The categories in which the discrepancies were largest were the duration of previous employment and the previous salary earned. As far as duration of employment, there was 57% disagreement. Since this category (as well as the salary data to be discussed next) provided information that permitted an assessment of the degree of overestimation or underestimation, the normal approximation to the binomial was used to test the significance. In the duration of employment data, the applicant's response, as compared with the previous employer, overestimated the amount of time spent on the job in 39 of the 46 cases ($z=4.57$, $p<.01$, two-tailed test). For the six cases in which the applicant underestimated the time spent on the job, the average underestimation equalled 3 mo. per person. Most of that total resulted from one person who underestimated the time he spent on the job by one year. For those who overestimated, the average overestimation was 16 months. An inspection of the data indicates that the average overestimation was not raised substantially by a few applicants but, rather, occurred across most of the applicants.

It was difficult to analyze the degree of estimation data for salaries because the types of differences were more complicated. In the 43 cases in which there was disagreement, there were 18 instances where the applicant and previous employer disagreed on the mode of payment. Most often, the previous employer indicated that the applicant worked on a piece-rate basis while the employees indicated they worked on a dollar-per-hour basis. For the 25 instances in which the data could be compared, the applicant overstated his salary in 18 instances ($z = 4.56$, $p < .05$, two-tailed test).

In summary, there were a substantial number of discrepancies between the applicant's responses and those answers provided by the previous employers. It is interesting to note that this was not true of all applicants. Of the 94 employees that were reported by the previous employer as having been employed, 31 sets of data were in complete agreement. Thus, the remaining 63 employees disagreed with the previous employers on two of the four categories (previous position held, duration of employment, previous salary earned, reason for leaving) that were examined.

These data suggest that inaccurate information is likely to appear on the application blank as well as in the interview. The same face-to-face pressure that Blum and Naylor (1968) discuss in their analysis of the interview situation probably does not exist in the context of the application blank. The pressure to obtain a job, however, may be equally demanding in both situations. The interview data indicate that two of the responses with the most inaccurate information are duration of previous employment and previous salary earned. The data in this note on application blanks indicate that the largest discrepancies also occurred in these two categories.

REFERENCES

Blum, M. L., & Naylor, J. C. *Industrial psychology.* New York: Harper & Row, 1968.

Fleishman, E. A., & Berniger, J. One way to reduce office turnover. *Personnel,* 1960, 37, 63–69.

Keating, E., Paterson, D. G., & Stone, C. H. Validity of work histories obtained by interview. *Journal of Applied Psychology,* 1950, 34, 6–11.

Scott, R. D., & Johnson, R. W. Use of the weighted application blank in selecting unskilled employees. *Journal of Applied Psychology,* 1967, 51, 393–395.

Weiss, D. J., & Dawis, R. V. An objective validation of factual interview data. *Journal of Applied Psychology,* 1960, 44, 381–385.

FOR DISCUSSION AND REVIEW

1 Explain the study's objectives, method, and results.
2 Why do you feel discrepancies or inaccuracies were found in application-blank information?
3 What implications might this research have for selection systems?

George W. England

Development and Use
of Weighted Application Blanks

PART I: INTRODUCTION

The continuing importance of selection and placement decisions to individuals, employers, and society is highlighted when we are reminded that over thirty million job changes take place each year at an estimated annual cost to industry of more than ten billion dollars. The cost to society and to individuals when selection and placement errors are frequent is incalculable but unquestionably large. It is little wonder that we have been willing to try almost anything to do a better job. In the 1920's, standard methods of selection were based primarily on letters of application in the applicant's own handwriting (graphology, a pseudo-science was in vogue); submission of a photograph (physiognomy, another pseudo-science was also in vogue); the interview in chaotic form; and unstandardized letters of recommendation. Evaluation of these methods showed that they improved predictions of subsequent job success by no more than two or three per cent above chance.[1]

Real progress has been made since then. Selection methods have been improved by developing better measures of job success, standardizing the interview, standardizing blanks for obtaining recommendations, introducing a wide variety of psychological tests into the employment process and by making application blank information more useful through quantification. We have also increased our understanding of the complexities involved in making predictions about how well individuals will perform specific jobs in a given organization. England and Paterson (1960) illustrated the role of selection and placement instruments to be that shown in Figure 1. Such a schema clearly recognizes that it is the complex relationships between person characteristics, job characteristics and organizational setting characteristics that selection and placement efforts must work through. Very straight forward notions such as predictor criterion relations often hide more than they reveal in terms of understanding. Dunnette (1963, 1966) has further specified the com-

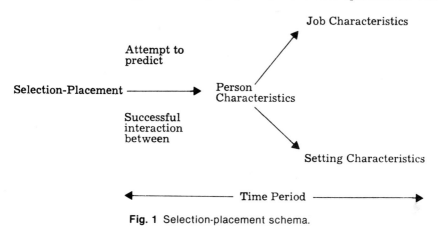

Fig. 1 Selection-placement schema.

Excerpted from *Development and Use of Weighted Application Blanks*, Rev. ed., Bulletin 55, Industrial Relations Center, University of Minnesota, 1971. Reprinted by permission.

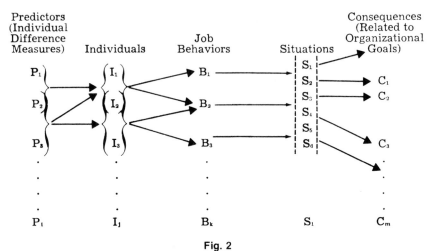

Fig. 2
A model for test validation and selection research as indicated by Dunnette.

plexities of real prediction situations in his model for test validation and selection research as shown in Figure 2.

The brackets and arrows serve as reminders of the many possibilities for different prediction strategies that should be considered in any personnel selection or test validation study. The brackets in the diagram signify different groupings of tests for different groups of persons, depending upon the patterns of job behavior to be predicted. The arrows in the diagram show that different avenues based on various groupings of predictors, persons, and behaviors may be utilized. For example, predictors P_2 and P_3 might be tried for individuals I_2 and I_3 or for individuals I_1 and I_2, but they probably would yield differentially accurate predictions for different job behaviors. The diagram also portrays the possibility of different job behaviors leading to various organizational consequences depending upon differing situational contexts. Thus, the prediction model calls attention to the likelihood of complex interactions between predictor groupings, groups or types of individuals, job behavior patterns, and broadly defined organizational consequences. Moreover, the model makes explicit the necessity for predicting actual job behavior and studying it in the context of different job situations rather than simply contrasting groups formed on the basis of overall organizational outcomes.

Selection research, based on this model, becomes a series of investigations designed to discover the optimal groupings or subsets of predictors, persons, job behaviors, and situations within which to study patterns of predictability and to validate and cross-validate prediction strategies. As we have said, most previous selection research has been rather fixedly concerned with predicting organizational consequences directly without first seeking to learn the nature of possible linkages between such consequences and all that goes before in the model—notably the patterns of situational circumstances and the possible differences in job behavior. Our model implies no lessening of interest in predicting organizational outcomes but it does direct research efforts toward a more careful analysis of their behavioral and situational correlates with the hope of understanding these organizational outcomes better, and of predicting them more accurately.

Three major characteristics stand out when we study the improvement in selection over the past forty years. First, it seems that we have done a better job of selecting as our methods have become more standardized. We have, in effect, directed more effort and research toward determining "what we should know about people" and then planned standardized ways of obtaining and using this information. Secondly, our selection methods have become more effective as we have been able to express them in numerical terms (quantification). Finally, we would expect further improvements as understanding directs our approaches and methods toward better approximation of the actual level of complexity found in the real world.

The intelligent development of weighted application blanks (WAB), continues to rely on the three hallmarks of progress in selection: standardization, quantification and understanding.

The rationale behind WAB development can be outlined as follows:

1 Personal history information such as age, years of education, previous occupations, and marital status represent important aspects of a person's total background and should be useful in selection. The major assumption is that how one will behave in the future is best predicted by how one has behaved in the past or by characteristics associated with past behavior.

2 Certain aspects of a person's total background should be related to whether or not he will be successful in a specific position. Numerous studies have shown that information contained in application blanks is predictive in selecting employees for certain types of positions. Personal factors such as age, years of education, previous occupations, and marital status have been found to be correlated with indicators of desirable employee behavior (length of service, supervisory ratings, sales volume, and average salary increase).

3 A way of determining which aspects of a person's total background are important for a given occupation is needed. The WAB technique identifies those items on an application blank which differentiate between groups of desirable and undesirable employees in a given occupation.

4 A way of combining the important aspects of a person's total background is needed so we can predict whether or not he is likely to be successful in a given occupation. By determining the predictive power of each application blank item, it is possible to assign numerical weights or scores to each possible answer. Weights for these items may then be totaled for each individual and a minimum total score established, which, if used at the time of hiring, will eliminate the maximum number of undesirable candidates with a minimum loss of desirable candidates.

The WAB technique, then, provides one systematic method for determining which personal factors are important in specific occupations and how to use them in selection. Use of the WAB technique in the employment process permits rapid screening of applicants by means of a simple scoring of the application blank. WAB results also can be used in combination with test and interview information to further improve screening and placement.

This technique is applicable in any organization having a relatively large number of employees doing similar kinds of work and for whom fairly adequate records are available. It seems particularly valuable for use with positions requiring long and costly training periods, positions where the turnover rate is abnormally high, or in situations where large numbers of applicants are seeking few positions. Already it has proved useful in the selection of managers, supervisors, production workers, clerical workers, cab drivers, sales personnel, engineers, and military personnel.

Development of weights for the application blank does not need to be a long, expensive, complicated process requiring the services of a specialized consultant.

There is no reason why the job cannot be undertaken successfully by any trained member of the company's personnel department staff once he has learned the fundamentals of the technique. No complicated statistic formulas need be involved—just simple arithmetic and a fair amount of clerical aptitude. Ordinarily the process for one type of job can be completed and ready for trial use in as little as 100 working hours, with possibilities of reduction in hiring costs which may repay many times over the original investment in research.

These materials have been prepared to present step-by-step methods which have been found successful in developing weights for an application blank. An attempt is made to present the material in such a way that it may serve as a practical guide to persons who may wish to develop similar weights applicable to their specific local situations. To illustrate the details of the method, an actual study is presented in part. This study concerned department store saleswomen where turnover was the major problem. The intent of the study was to develop a scoring system for the application blank which would indicate whether or not applicants were likely to remain with the company for relatively long time periods. Therefore, length of service was used as the criterion or measure of employee desirability.

Seven major steps will be considered in detail in the following sections. These steps cover the major decisions which must be made in developing a WAB and can be listed as follows:

1   Choosing the criterion
2   Identifying criterion groups
3   Selecting application blank items to be analyzed
4   Specifying item response categories to be used in the analysis
5   Determining item weights
6   Applying weights to the holdout groups
7   Setting cutting scores for selection

PART II: PROCEDURES

Developing weights for the application blank is accomplished by a systematic method of determining what application blank item responses were given more frequently by applicants who proved to be desirable employees and, at the same time, were given less frequently by applicants who proved to be undesirable employees. To be useful in the selection process, the personal history responses which are compared are those obtained at time of hiring. This is done by comparing item by item the application blanks of a group of desirable employees with those of a group of undesirable employees. In order to select these two groups for comparison, one must have some index or criterion of desirability. One must decide what employee performance characteristic he wishes most to identify.

Choosing the criterion

It is often helpful in selecting a criterion of success to consider what characteristics have been most frequently lacking in employees hired by existing techniques. Perhaps the major problem has been in selecting employees who are proficient in their work. If so, the best accessible measure of job proficiency should be the criterion. On the other hand, turnover rather than job performance may be the most pressing problem. In this case, length of service would be the most appropriate criterion. Table 1 lists the types of criteria which are most commonly reported in the literature on weighted application blank studies.

. . .

Table 1

Criteria Used in Weighted Application Blank Studies

1 Length of service
2 Absenteeism
3 School grades
4 Rate of salary increase over a period of time (salary of present job minus salary of first job ever held, divided by the number of years worked).

Identifying criterion groups

After a criterion has been selected, it is necessary to form two criterion groups (a *high criterion group*—representing desirable employees and a *low criterion group* —representing undesirable employees). It is recommended that these two criterion groups be as large as possible, and that no study be undertaken without, at the minimum, 75 in each of the two groups.

Each criterion group is further separated into a weighting group and a holdout group. The weighting groups are used to identify and weight personal history items which differentiate between desirable and undesirable employees. Each weighting group (high and low) should contain at least 50 individuals. The holdout groups (high and low) are used in evaluating the effectiveness of the WAB and for setting cutting scores to be used in later application of the technique in selection. Each holdout group should contain at least 25 individuals. Figure 3 illustrates the formation of these groups. . . .

Selecting application blank items to be analyzed

The type and number of items which can be analyzed will depend on the content of the application blank used by the organization in which the study is undertaken. Sometimes additional items can be secured from other personnel records filled out at the time of hiring, provided such records are available for all individuals in the criterion groups.

Table 2 lists a wide variety of items which have been found to be predictive of "job success" for different types of jobs.

Specifying item response categories

Names and item responses from the application blanks of all persons in the weighting groups should be recorded on ruled work sheets, using separate sheets for the high and low groups. For the most part, this will be a simple matter of transferring responses from application blank to the appropriate square on the work sheet.

In some cases, however, it may be desirable to translate data into more useable terms. For example, if the application blank shows date of birth, this should be subtracted from date of application and recorded on the work sheet in the form of age at the time of application. Likewise, if the amount of previous experience in the type of work under study is wanted, it may be necessary to draw this information from several places in the applicant's work history and to do a little simple addition in order to arrive at a single figure for the work sheet.

In cases of omitted responses, some standard no-answer entry should be adopted on the work sheets, such as the letters N.A. or a diagonal line through the square.

For some items, suitable response categories to be used in calculation of weights will be obvious. This is particularly true of items which automatically elicit

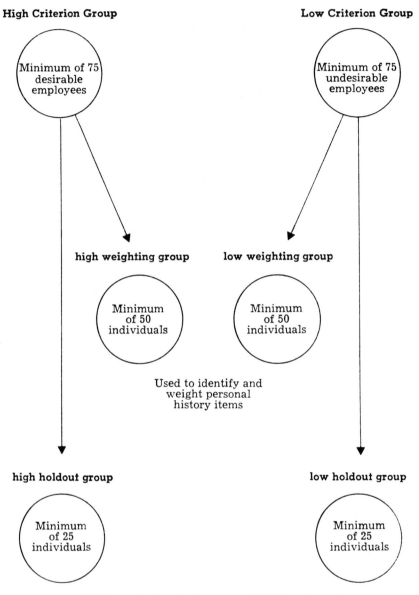

Fig. 3 Use of criterion groups.

Table 2
Personal History Items Found to Be Predictive of "Job Success"

PERSONAL

1. Age
2. Age at hiring
3. Marital status
4. Number of years married
5. Dependents, number of
6. Children, number of
7. Age when first child born
8. Physical health
9. Recent illnesses, operations
10. Time lost from job for certain previous period (last 2 years, etc.)
11. Living conditions, general
12. Domicile, whether alone, rooming house, keep own house, etc.
13. Residence, location of
14. Size of home town
15. Number of times moved in recent period
16. Length of time at last address
17. Nationality*
18. Birth place*
19. Weight and height
20. Sex

BACKGROUND, GENERAL

21. Occupation of father
22. Occupation of mother
23. Occupation of brothers, sisters, other relatives
24. Military service and rank
25. Military discharge record
26. Early family responsibility
27. Parental family adjustment
28. Professionally successful parents
29. Stable or transient home life
30. Wife does not work outside home

EDUCATION

31. Education
32. Educational level of wife
33. Educational level of family, relatives
34. Education finances—extent of dependence on parents
35. Type of course studied—grammar school
36. Major field of study—high school
37. Specific courses taken in high school or college
38. Subjects liked, disliked in high school
39. Years since leaving high school
40. Type of school attended, private/state
41. College grades
42. Scholarship level, grammar school and high school
43. Graduated at early age compared with classmates

Table 2 cont'd

EMPLOYMENT EXPERIENCE

44. Educational—vocational consistency
45. Previous occupations (general type of work)
46. Held job in high school (type of job)
47. Number of previous jobs
48. Specific work experience (specific jobs)
49. Previous selling experience
50. Previous life insurance sales experience
51. Total length of work experience (total years, months)
52. Being in business for self
53. Previous employee of company now considering application
54. Seniority in present employment
55. Tenure on previous job
56. Employment status at time of application (employed, unemployed)
57. Reason for quitting last job
58. Length of time unemployed
59. Previous salary earned, or salary earned at present employment

SKILLS

60. Ability to read blueprints
61. Does repair work on own car
62. Amount of previous training for applicant job
63. Amount of previous training for any other job
64. Possesses specific skills required for job
65. Number of machines that a person can operate

SOCIOECONOMIC LEVEL—FINANCIAL STATUS

66. Financial responsibility
67. Number of creditors
68. Number of accounts with finance companies
69. Number of accounts with stores
70. Amount loan as a proportion of total income
71. Monthly mortgage payment
72. Highest pay received
73. Debts
74. Net worth
75. Savings
76. Amount of life insurance carried
77. Amount of other insurance carried
78. Kinds of and number of investments
79. Real estate owned (own home, etc.)
80. Owns automobile
81. Make, age of auto owned
82. Owns furniture
83. Has telephone in home
84. Minimum current living expenses
85. Salary requests, limits set for accepting job
86. Earnings expected (in future, 2 yrs., 5 yrs., etc.)

Table 2 cont'd

SOCIAL

87. Club memberships (social, community, campus, high school)
88. Frequency of attendance at group meetings
89. Offices held in clubs
90. Experience as a group leader
91. Church membership

INTERESTS

92. Prefer outside to inside labor
93. Hobbies
94. Number of hobbies
95. Specific type of hobbies, leisure time activities preferred
96. Sports
97. Number of sports active in
98. Most important source of entertainment

PERSONAL CHARACTERISTICS, ATTITUDES EXPRESSED

99. Willingness to relocate or transfer
100. Confidence (as expressed by applicant)
101. Basic personality needs (5 types) as expressed by applicant in reply to question on application blank
102. Drive
103. Stated job preferences

MISCELLANEOUS

104. Time taken for hiring negotiations between applicant and company
105. Former employer's estimate of applicant
106. Interviewer's estimate of applicant's success, based on health, social personality, relationships, etc.
107. Source of reference to company for job application
108. Has relatives or acquaintances presently working for company
109. Number of character references listed
110. Availability for entire season of work stated
111. Availability—can start immediately, can't start immediately
112. Manner of filling out application blank (time taken, method used, way information stated, etc.)
113. Restrictions on hours available for duty

---

*Some items may violate fair employment practice legislation.

a limited number of possible answers, discrete in nature. Marital status, for example, is an easy item to categorize. Any person can be classified as either single, married, divorced, separated, or widowed.

Continuous variables, on the other hand, such as age and length of residence are somewhat more difficult to classify. With items of this nature, one of three types of classification is most frequently used. These may be described as equal frequency classes, equal interval classes and maximum weight classes. Using the variable of age, each method is illustrated:

1 *The method of equal frequency classes* divides the responses of the combined weighting groups into four or five classes with an approximately equal number of individuals in each class. The age data shown in columns 2 and 3 of Table 5 would appear as follows:

AGE	GROUP I HIGH WEIGHTING GROUP	GROUP II LOW WEIGHTING GROUP	CLASS TOTALS
Under 23	9	46	55
24–32	15	39	54
33–48	40	16	56
Over 48	48	11	59
No answer	0	0	0

2 *The method of equal interval classes* classifies age into five or ten year intervals. Five year intervals are used in Table 5 with the exception of the "under 20" group and the "over 40" group.

AGE	GROUP I HIGH WEIGHTING GROUP	GROUP II LOW WEIGHTING GROUP
Under 20	30	32
20–40	35	30
Over 40	35	38
Total N	100	100

3 *The method of maximum weight classes* is essentially one of trial and error to determine what response categories or interval limits best bring out differences between the groups. The following *hypothetical* example partially illustrates this method. The first trial sets up age categories of under 20, 20–40, and over 40.

	AGE	GROUP I HIGH WEIGHTING GROUP	GROUP II LOW WEIGHTING GROUP
	Under 20	30	32
	20–40	35	30
Over	41–50	5	33
40	Over 50	30	5
	Total N	100	100

Working out the weighting procedure (see next section) would show that age was not a significant variable and should not be used. However, if the "over 40" class actually had the following distribution, the age variable should be weighted for prediction.

Table 5
Sample Weighting Work Sheet

RESPONSE CATEGORY COLUMNS: 1	NUMBER RESPONDING		PERCENT RESPONDING*		COL. 4 MINUS COL. 5	NET WEIGHT	ASSIGNED WEIGHT
	GROUP I– HIGH WEIGHTING GROUP	GROUP II– LOW WEIGHTING GROUP	GROUP I– HIGH WEIGHTING GROUP	GROUP II– LOW WEIGHTING GROUP			
	2	3	4	5	6	7	8
AGE							
Under 20	6	28	5%	25%	–20%	–6	0
20–25	7	42	6	38	–32	–9	0
26–30	7	12	6	11	–5	–2	1
31–35	7	6	6	5	1	0	1
36–40	17	8	15	7	8	2	1
Over 40	68	16	61	14	47	12	2
No answer	0	0					
	112	112	99%*	100%			
MARITAL STATUS							
Single	30	53	27%	47%	–20%	–4	0
Married	45	49	40	44	–4	–1	1
Divorced or separated	9	6	8	5	3	1	1
Widowed	28	4	25	4	21	6	2
No answer	0	0					
	112	112	100%	100%			
NUMBER OF DEPENDENT CHILDREN							
None	79	96	70%	86%	–16%	–4	0
One	20	9	18	8	10	2	1
Two or more	13	7	12	6	6	2	1
No answer	0	0					
	112	112	100%	100%			

*Percentages have been rounded to the nearest whole percent. For this reason, they do not always total exactly 100%.

Obviously, the distinction between age 41–50 and over 50 is one that is desirable to make. While such sharp reversals as illustrated rarely occur in practice, the trial and error process is a way of detecting such differences. The danger in using strictly a trial and error method is that many chance differences between the two groups may be weighted. These differences will increase the separation of the original groups but may not remain as stable differences which are useful in later application.

On balance, it seems most useful to categorize continuous variables following the method of equal frequency classes, but to check for reversals within each class. If reversals are found which would change the weighting and are based on the responses of at least ten people in an interval, the classes should be changed. . . .

Determining item weights

In order to determine whether or not desirable workers respond to certain items in a way different from that of undesirable workers, information from response work sheets #1 and 2 must be drawn together for comparison on a third work sheet similar to the one shown in Table 5. Appropriate response categories for each item are listed in the first column on Table 5, and the number of persons from the high and low weighting groups whose responses fall into each of these categories is recorded in columns 2 and 3.

After the number of persons from each weighting group whose responses fall into each category have been recorded in Table 5, these numbers are converted to percentages for each group, as shown in columns 4 and 5. The percentages for Group II (Low Weighting Group) are then subtracted from the corresponding percentages for Group I (High Weighting Group) and the differences recorded in column 6, using the appropriate sign, plus or minus. For example, in Table 5 it may be seen that the age category "under 20" includes 5% of Group I and 25% of Group II. Subtracting the percentages for Group II (25%) from the percentage for Group I (5%) gives a minus 20%, and this difference has been recorded in column 6. . . .

Any item which has the same assigned weight for every response category does not differentiate between the high and low weighting groups and should be discarded.

For the three items illustrated in Table 5, adequate responses were available for every person in both criterion groups. There were no omissions. However, in cases where there are persons who have given no answer or inadequate answers on a particular item, the usual procedure is to eliminate these persons from the calculation of weights for that item, and thus to work with a reduced number of subjects. For example, if five individuals in Group I and twelve individuals in Group II had not given their ages, weights for the age item would have been standardized on the remaining 107 subjects in Group I as compared with the remaining 100 in Group II. The percentages in columns 4 and 5 of Table 5 would then have been calculated on the basis of total groups of 107 and 100, rather than 112 and 112. Of course, if the weighting groups are small to begin with and the proportion of "no answer" responses is large for a specific item, it may be necessary to discard the item altogether.

. . .

REFERENCES

Dunnette, M. D. A Modified Model for Test Validation and Selection Research. *Journal of Applied Psychology.* Vol. 47, 1963, pp. 317–323.

Dunnette, M. D. *Personnel Selection and Placement.* Belmont, California: Wadsworth Publishing Co., Inc., 1966.

England, G. W. and D. G. Paterson. Selection and Placement—The Past Ten Years. In Industrial Relations Reseach Association *Employment Relations Research: A Summary and Appraisal.* New York: Harper & Brothers, 1960.

FOR DISCUSSION AND REVIEW

1 What is a weighted application blank (WAB)? How does it differ from traditional application blanks in appearance and in use?
2 Outline the steps required to develop a WAB.
3 What factors should be considered in choosing the criterion, the criterion groups, and the biographical items?
4 Briefly review how item weights can be chosen for the WAB.

Allan N. Nash

Stephen J. Carroll, Jr.

A Hard Look at the Reference Check: Its Modest Worth Can Be Improved

Virtually all employers use the reference check as part of their selection process. There are two basic types of references: the character reference, typically obtained from a friend or relative of the applicant, and the previous employer reference, which is most widely used in the industrial situation. One survey found that 90 percent of all responding employers contacted former employers of their job applicants.[1]

The reference check with former employers has two purposes. It is used to check the validity of information given by the job applicant on the application blank, and it is used to predict success on the new job. The second purpose seems to be more important since several research studies have indicated that job applicants rarely lie when filling out an application blank.[2] Most of the organizations that contact former employers believe that they obtain useful information. For example, one survey reports that 76 percent of responding companies believed that their selection procedures would suffer if written references were not available to them.[3]

HOW VALUABLE ARE REFERENCES?

Despite this widespread acceptance of references by employers, a survey we have made of the ten most widely used personnel management and employee selection textbooks indicates that the writers of these books believe that the reference check does not provide enough valid information to be of practical value. In addition, a

---

From *Business Horizons,* October 1970, pp. 43–49. Copyright © 1970 by the Foundation for the School of Business at Indiana University. Reprinted by permission.

[1]   W. A. Spriegel and V. A. James, "Trends in Recruitment and Selection Practice," *Personnel,* VI (1958), pp. 35–45.

[2]   For example, D. Yoder, H. Henemen, J. Turnbull, and C. Stone, *Handbook of Personnel Management and Labor Relations* (New York: McGraw-Hill Book Company, 1958), pp. 8–17.

[3]   J. N. Mosel and H. W. Goheen, "Use of the ERQ in Hiring," *Personnel Journal,* XXXVI (1958B), pp. 338–40.

number of research studies have examined the effectiveness or validity of the reference check in predicting job performance. In the most extensive study of this type, Mosel and Goheen compared the information in reference checks obtained for 1,193 civil service employees in twelve skilled occupations with specially devised performance ratings made by their present supervisors.[4] The information analyzed dealt with occupational ability, character and reputation, and employability. The reference check information showed no consistent or sizable relationship with present job success (no relationships were higher than a correlation of $r = +.29$ and most were near zero).

Another study in a nonindustrial setting collected references from many sources for 508 school teachers.[5] These references were correlated to various ratings of teaching effectiveness in the first year in the new teaching position. The references were generally unpredictive of teaching effectiveness (average correlation was $r = .13$). References were most predictive when they were completed by the last supervisor of the teacher in a teaching position, but the relationship here was modest ($r = .23$). Still another study examined the relationship of references received for Peace Corps candidates with ratings of their performance in overseas positions. Again the relationship was modest.

REFERENCE CHECK PROBLEMS

The rate of return

The reference check, unlike other selection approaches, has the problem of the response rate. If previous employers exercise their right to reject a reference request for a former employee, the employing organization must get along without this information. There are little data available to indicate what the rate of return is likely to be. Mosel and Goheen report a 56 percent return for 4,000 reference questionnaires sent out be a federal government agency for twelve skilled occupations, and a 64 percent rate of return for 16,000 questionnaires sent out for professional and semiprofessional groups.[6]

Research conducted by the present authors indicates that the method used to solicit the reference checks can substantially influence the response rate. Nearly 85 percent of written, objective, one-page questionnaires were completed and returned by former employers of more than a hundred 1967–68 clerical applicants at the University of Maryland. However, this was achieved after a previous effort had resulted in a return rate of only 35 percent. The first approach involved a mimeographed form letter requesting cooperation, a stamped addressed envelope, and a copy of the questionnaire. A switch was made to an individually typed letter with basically the same content sent out under the title "Director of Personnel" and signed in ink by one of the authors. The response rate improved after this change was made. However, this approach was not nearly as successful in obtaining a satisfactory return rate when it was used for former employers of maintenance and custodial applicants at the university.

The finding that the method used has differential effects depending on the occupation involved is consistent with findings reported by Mosel and Goheen, who

---

[4]   J. N. Mosel and H. W. Goheen, "The Validity of the Employment Recommendation Questionnaire in Personnel Selection: Skilled Trades," *Personnel Psychology*, XL (1958A), pp. 481–90.
[5]   R. C. Browning, "Validity of Reference Ratings from Previous Employers," *Personnel Psychology*, XXI (1968), pp. 389–93.
[6]   Mosel and Goheen, "The Validity of . . . , pp. 481–90.

also found a higher response rate for applicants for higher level jobs. It now appears that, with care, a high rate of return can be obtained for reference checks for job applicants, and that somewhat higher rates of return can be expected for occupations at higher levels.

However, a fairly recent development may reduce the rate of return for reference checks in the future. Several management reporting services have described a case in which a company was successfully sued when it failed to keep a reference confidential, but referred to a negative one it had received as reason for rejecting an applicant.[7] It is conceivable that this may frighten personnel departments into adopting a policy prohibiting company managers from filling out reference requests.

The leniency problem

An adequate response rate, of course, does not mean that the references received are of much value in making employment decisions about job applicants. The research study conducted by Mosel and Goheen indicate that employers may be reluctant to furnish other employers with negative information about former employees. For this reason, the reference check generally lacks high validity. On a four-category scale (poor, satisfactory, good, and outstanding), they found almost 92 percent of the responses were either good or outstanding when occupational ability was being rated, and about 95 percent when character and reputation were being rated. Over 97 percent of their respondents said they would reemploy the applicant.

These findings may be distorted somewhat by unique circumstances existing in that study. First, it is possible that the typical government reference form and the impersonal manner of collecting references contribute to an indifferent attitude on the part of the reference giver. It is also possible that the typical reference giver does not mind passing off a borderline employee onto the government as much as he might to a smaller less bureaucratic private organization, which might send him a critical follow-up comment if the recommended applicant does not live up to his reference. The reference giver probably feels that the government is less likely to send such a follow-up, especially if the reference is sent to a department or institution rather than a specific person, as is usually the case. He may even feel that the government can better absorb such an employee. The feeling may exist that the bureaucracy has more than its share of similar kinds of people anyhow, and "one more won't hurt it."

Evidence collected by the authors in conducting a study of the predictive validity of a new type of reference check (forced choice) for clerical employees also suggests that the degree of leniency in the Mosel and Goheen results is not necessarily to be expected in industrial application. Notes and comments frequently written in the margin of a new forced-choice reference form being tested, which included only pairs of positive-sounding statements, suggested that a significant minority of reference givers would have checked negative statements if they had been given the opportunity to do so on the form. A small pilot study attempted to test this proposition.[8] In this study, seven personnel managers were contacted and asked to provide the names of at least two former employees "who were borderline performers at best." The personnel managers furnished these names along with the names of the immediate supervisors of these employees. A reference form and letter soliciting

---

[7]   *White Collar Management* (New York: Man and Manager, Inc., 1967).
[8]   Allan N. Nash, "A Methodological Suggestion for Constructing Forced Choice Scales," *Experimental Journal of the APA* (1970).

cooperation was sent to each former supervisor of the inferior employee. Fifteen reference check forms were sent out and thirteen were returned, of which eleven had negative statements checked for the employee in question. This study indicates that supervisors, when asked to give a reference for a former relatively unsatisfactory employee, were willing to make negative comments.

Results of an older study by Bingham in which one-hundred sales managers were surveyed also supports this contention.[9] He found that although 85 percent of them said they would give the former employee the benefit of the doubt in writing letters of recommendation, 39 percent also said they would point out the man's failings and weaknesses as well as his strong points.

Characteristics of the reference giver

A few studies suggest that there are marked differences in the validity of references depending on who gives them and the relationship of the giver to the applicant. For example, the studies by Mosel and Goheen and Browning indicated that references from immediate supervisors are somewhat more valid than those from other sources, including various character sources not related to the job. Browning also found that the most recent immediate supervisor was better than an older one. Kornhauser found references given by former teachers and employers were better at predicting academic success than references given by a group of friends and professional acquaintants, which is similar to findings reported above by Mosel and Goheen and Browning. Yoder suggests that the reference is most useful if the job being sought is similar to jobs previously held.[10]

Data collected by the authors in a study of a forced-choice reference check also support the theory that the nature of the reference giver may affect the validity of the references. We found the following personal characteristics to be important.

First, leniency seems related to the sex of the reference giver. Women tended to be more lenient than men in rating both former employees and present employees. In this situation, the women were rating women. This finding is congruent with previous research, which indicates that individuals of a particular sex are more lenient in rating members of their own sex.[11] However, in this study the men rating women held higher and more responsible jobs than the women rating women.

Second, the usefulness of the reference depends on how much the reference giver knows about the applicant. We found that references given by a supervisor for a job applicant who had performed nonclerical work were not predictive of success in doing clerical work in another organization. This supports the suggestion of Yoder that references from former employers should be discounted unless the work done in the old job is similar to the work to be done on the new job. We also found that references received for former employees who had held their old jobs for less than two months were unpredictive of performance on the second job. This may have occurred not only because of sketchy information, but also because of a tendency for former supervisors to be disgusted with previous employees who quit shortly after being hired.

Third, references given by a person in a foreign country were not predictive of performance on a job in this country. In addition, references given by a supervisor

---

[9]   W. V. Bingham, "The Three Functions of the Interview in Employment," *Management Review*, VX (1926), p. 36.

[10]   D. Yoder, *Personnel Management and Industrial Relations* (5th ed.; Englewood Cliffs, N.J.: Prentice-Hall, Inc., 1962), p. 346.

[11]   Stephen J. Carroll and Allan N. Nash, "The Evaluation of Performance," unpublished manuscript, 1970.

of one race were not predictive of job performance as rated by a supervisor on the new job of another race. This was especially true when the applicant was of the same race as the reference giver but of a different race from the supervisor evaluating his performance on the new job. This finding is congruent with that in other studies, which generally show that individuals have a tendency to rate members of their own race higher than they rate members of another race.

In general, then, it does appear that the characteristics of the reference giver must be considered in deciding how reliable their references are. References are probably more accurate if received from immediate supervisors who supervised the applicant for a considerable length of time in a job similar to that for which the applicant is being considered. References received from supervisors of the same sex, race, or country of origin as the applicant are likely to be more favorable than performance ratings by a supervisor of a different sex, race, or country of origin.

Method of obtaining references

References can be obtained from former employers by letter, telephone, and the use of specially structured objective type questionnaires or field investigations which use interviews to collect information from the reference givers. It is not known what percentage of all employers use these alternative methods, but one survey indicated that about 50 percent of all firms require some type of written recommendation.

The majority of authors in the field suggest that the telephone check is better than a written reference considering cost, accuracy, and time. With the telephone check, one is reasonably certain that the reference giver is the person named as the reference and not some secretary or clerk. The reference can also be obtained quickly and inexpensively. In addition, some feel that the reference giver finds it more difficult to stretch the truth about a job applicant in oral conversation than he would in providing the reference in writing. Also, oral answers may contain hesitations and voice inflections that can be revealing as to what the reference giver really thinks about the person under consideration. The reference giver may feel more secure in making negative statements informally than he would in making them formally in a written reference check. Despite these apparent advantages of the telephone check no research study has demonstrated its superiority over the other methods of obtaining references.

The field investigation, which involves interviewing reference givers in their homes or places of employment, has some of the obvious advantages of the telephone check. One can be certain the named reference is involved in the check, and the oral conversation may reveal information that might not be presented in written form. However, the field investigation is obviously considerably more expensive and time consuming than the telephone check. One study compared the field investigation with the written reference check.

In this study, written reference questionnaires and field investigation reports were obtained for 109 applicants for three professional jobs in the federal service.[12] Each field investigation consisted of from three to six interviews with individuals who knew the applicants. Only a moderate relationship was established between ratings made of the applicants on the basis of these two different types of reference checks. An investigation was also made of the success of these methods in identifying applicants who were ineligible for employment in the federal service because of alcoholism, homosexuality, or gross incompetence. Only the field investigation

---

[12]   J. N. Mosel and H. W. Goheen, "The Employment Recommendation Questionnaire: Validity of Different Types of References," *Personnel Psychology.* XII (1959), pp. 469–77.

identified the seven individuals who were not acceptable for these reasons. The written reference form did not identify these individuals primarily because written references were not sent in by the persons who were sent questionnaires. Perhaps, however, the telephone check could collect the information on such clearly disqualified applicants under the standards used, since the problem of nonresponse is greatly reduced under this method. The telephone check would be far cheaper and less time consuming than the field investigation. A research study should be conducted in this area, perhaps by the federal goverment which obviously spends a great deal of money on field investigations.

The disadvantages of the written reference questionnaire have already been discussed; it is subject to the problems of poor response and to low validity because of the problem of leniency. Our research has shown the poor response problem can be reduced considerably by the use of individually typed and signed letters. We also have developed a new type of reference check questionnaire to eliminate or alleviate the problem of low validity due to the error of leniency. The new check incorporates the forced-choice format developed for the prediction of promotability in the armed forces in the mid-1940's.[13]

The forced-choice method was introduced in order to eliminate or reduce the error of leniency in ratings of performance. The rater is presented with a group of behavioral statements. Such statements may be in groups of two, three, or four. Through a fairly complex research procedure, it is determined how well each behavioral statement used in the form predicts success in a particular job and also how favorable each statement sounds to the raters using the form. The behavioral statements are grouped so that they are similar to other statements in their group with respect to "apparent" favorability, but differ from the other statements in their group with respect to ability to predict success in a particular job. The rater is asked to choose the statement(s) from a group of statements that most apply to the person being rated. Thus the rater is forced to choose from among alternative behavioral statements.

We have developed forced-choice rating forms for both maintenance workers and for clerical workers, but only the form for the clerical workers was tested in order to establish its validity. The form consists of twenty-four pairs of behavioral statements descriptive of clerical workers. All the statements were constructed in a positive manner because of the apparent desire of reference givers to give positive references. The pairs of statements are constructed so that the two statements in each pair sound equally favorable, are equally characteristic of clerical workers in general, but differ in their ability to predict success in clerical work. The form was developed for clerical workers in an electronics firm in Baltimore and then was tested at the University of Maryland. The test involved the use of forced-choice reference checks completed by former employers of applicants for clerical jobs at the university. These reference checks were then put aside and not examined until the 122 clerical workers studied had been on the job for at least four months; they were then rated by the supervisors with respect to many aspects of their over-all work performance.

It was found that when the reference giver on the previous job had adequate time to observe the worker and was of the same sex, race, and nationality as the supervisor on the new job, and where the old and new jobs were similar in content,

[13]   Allan N. Nash and Stephen J. Carroll, Jr., "Improving the Validity of a Forced Choice Reference Check with Rater and Job Characteristics Moderators," *Proceedings of the 78th Annual Convention*, American Psychological Association, 1970, pp. 577–78.

the forced choice reference check was quite highly predictive of success (r = + .64 between reference check scores and performance ratings).

IMPROVING USEFULNESS OF THE REFERENCE CHECK

The research indicates that organizations can improve the usefulness of the reference check in selecting organizational personnel by following certain suggestions derived from this research.

Survey only previous supervisors of the job applicant. The research indicates that only references from former supervisors of the job applicant are predictive of success on a new job. Less valid references are provided by friends, neighbors, and other organizational personnel in the old organization such as coworkers and higher level organizational personnel who were not in immediate contact with the applicant.

Consider the characteristics of the immediate supervisor giving the reference. References from supervisors who have not had adequate opportunity to observe the job performance of the applicant are less predictive of job success than references from supervisors who have had an adequate observational opportunity. In addition, references from supervisors on previous jobs differing in sex, country of employment, or race from supervisors on the prospective job are less predictive of job success than when these supervisors are similar.

Use individually typed letters to request the reference. Our research indicated that a return of 85 percent can be obtained with individually typed letters.

Choose the appropriate method. There are several alternative methods of obtaining references, including the written reference form, a forced-choice variation of this developed by the authors, the telephone check, and the field investigation. Research has established that the forced-choice reference check format can be predictive of job success. Research can be carried out by organizations themselves on the relative validity of the other reference check methods. The personnel department should find it easy to compare, in a systematic way, alternative reference check methods for the various types of employees the organization employs. Certainly such research would be worthwhile considering the cost, time, and present usefulness of reference check methods.

FOR DISCUSSION AND REVIEW

1 What are the objectives of the reference check? How often is it used?
2 Review the problems encountered with the reference check.
3 Why are the typical references so lenient?
4 How do the characteristics of the reference giver influence the references?
5 Describe the advantages of a forced-choice reference check.

D. INTERVIEWING

Robert A. Martin

Confessions of an Interviewer

Most of the corporate recruiters with whom I've had contact are decent, well-intentioned people. But I've yet to meet anyone, including myself, who knows what he (or she) is doing. Many interviewers seem to have an absolute faith in their omniscience, but I suspect that their "perceptiveness" is based more upon preconceived, untested assumptions than upon objectively derived data.

This unscientific approach to the process of selecting employees saddens me. All my life I've accepted, as an unassailable truism, the bromide that "people are our most important asset." Yet I know that many major companies spend more money researching what kind of paint to use for their buildings than they do trying to determine how to recognize and measure talent.

When I bemoan my own inadequacies in such matters to my colleagues, I am, more often than not, rewarded with the bemused sympathy of a master for his servant. I would urge more of my associates to consider the virtue of humility. A humble person is more susceptible to a reexamination of his beliefs and practices. The following quotation, from *The Selection Process* by Milton Mandell, by far the best book on employment practices I have ever encountered, is a classic:

"Many reasons can be advanced for the need of humility among interviewers—just one should be sufficient. The interviewer is trying to obtain in 20 to 60 minutes an accurate understanding of a lifetime of thousands of experiences producing attitudes, motivations, and behavior which, in many cases, are unknown to the applicant himself and which are modified at different times and in different places. Humility motivates the interviewer to avoid hasty judgments, to obtain the evaluations of others in order to check his own conclusions, to improve his skill and knowledge as much as possible, to use other selection devices to contribute to the accuracy of selection, to limit the interview to those factors which can be appraised adequately, and to omit from it those factors which should be measured by other methods." Now that we are all properly humble and open-minded about our beliefs, it might be appropriate to examine those considered to be the most sacrosanct.

It is assumed, first of all, that students who graduate with high grade-point averages are the most intelligent, and therefore the only ones capable of meeting the company's standards. Grades are perhaps the most tenaciously clung to predictor of managerial success. Many major companies use the 3.0 grade-point cutoff as the keystone of their recruiting program.

It is a difficult nut to crack. But let's examine some of the evidence to see if grades are really a reliable predictor of success on the job. Possibly the best-known study on this subject was made by Bell Laboratories in 1962. The company analyzed the records of 17,000 employees who had graduated from college prior to 1950, in order to relate college achievement to progress in management.

The survey found that salary progress was positively correlated with class rank in college, with the college's academic quality, and with extracurricular achievement. At the same time, it found that students who supported themselves in college did not do significantly better in salary, and that undergraduate major made no difference.

The report cautioned: "It would, of course, be a mistake to apply the indices of this study—rank in college, quality of college, and campus achievement—in a blind, mechanical way. Even of the men who stood near the top on all three characteristics, a significant minority have not performed with distinction in business." Conversely, a significant minority of those who did not perform with distinction in college did achieve distinction in business.

In 1957 Purdue University conducted a survey of its engineering graduates since the class of 1911. From 3,799 usable replies the survey concluded that high scholastic achievement is positively correlated with attainment of positions in management, with membership in professional societies, with number of patents, and with salary. The survey also found that doctorates are positively correlated with salary, though M.S. degrees are not. Again, the study cautioned against applying its conclusions too strictly. It emphasized that some of even the lowest decile graduates advanced to the top salary levels (9 percent compared to 25 percent for top decile graduates).

Other recent studies dispute even the mild correlation that these surveys found between job success and various individual achievements. A recently released study done at the University of Utah concluded that "there is almost no relationship between the grades a student gets in medical school and his competence and success in medical practice." No one was more astounded by this finding than the leader of the research team, Dr. Philip B. Price. "It is a shocking finding to a medical educator like myself who has spent his professional life selecting applicants for admission to medical school," he said.

In another study Dr. Eli Ginzberg examined the records of 342 graduate students in various fields who had won fellowships to Columbia University between 1944 and 1950. Ginzberg and his associates set out to learn how successful those graduates had become 15 years after they had completed their fellowships. Their surprising discovery was: "Those who had graduated from college with honors, who had won scholastic medals, who had been on dean's lists, who had been elected to Phi Beta Kappa, were more likely to be in the lower professional performance levels than in the top levels."

In spite of these findings, far too many hiring supervisors continue to proudly insist upon high grades, "good schools," and other questionable criteria for their prospective employees. The corporate effort, in this era of social responsibility, toward understanding "our most important asset" has been almost nonexistent. I would like to see all major corporations establish permanent research departments, staffed by competent people, who would investigate the critical problem of what constitutes valid and reliable predictors of job success. I suspect we would find that those predictors vary among industries, occupations, supervisors, and managerial philosophies.

I am not against high grades. I am appreciative of the hard work and/or intelligence and/or test-taking ability that is required to achieve them. All things being equal, I would choose an A student over a C student. But I don't think an applicant should be recommended for employment simply because of high grades or rejected because of low grades. Success is too dependent upon such other factors as dedication, perseverance, personality, specialized abilities, and so on.

Are there any factors that can be shown to bear a consistent relationship to job success? In an attempt to answer this question, a couple of years ago at the Hughes

Aircraft Company we conducted an informal seminar for supervisors who had a reasonable amount of interviewing experience.

We formed two classes, of 24 people each, which met independently for two days. The first assignment was simply to list all possible predictors of job success. A total of 48 were named, ranging from scholastic performance to marital status, hobbies, and motivation.

Next, the two classes were asked to discuss each predictor. The participants were encouraged to champion their favored predictors with as much vehemence as the sensitivities of the others would allow. The results of these discussions were predictable. The hallowed assumptions could not withstand critical analysis and the actual experiences of others. In particular, the sacrosanct grades and "good schools" predictors took a shellacking.

Each group then selected, independently, the ten predictors they considered to be the most important. After comparing and consolidating the resulting two lists, we were able to come up with a list of six general employment predictors. Ranked in order of importance, they are:

1 Specific abilities
2 Ambition
3 Maturely directed energy
4 Ability to communicate
5 General intelligence and knowledge
6 Integrity.

The specific ranking is less important than the recognition that there are a number of factors that should be considered when evaluating an applicant for employment. We agreed that the importance of grades and schools should be downplayed, though certainly not ignored. And we agreed that, although specific abilities are important, they are not the deciding factor with most hires. No longer should I hear such laments as "Martin, Martin, how many times do I have to tell you? I don't need guys experienced in designing the leading edges of turbine blades—I need guys with *trailing* edge experience."

Another workshop I participated in that attempted to determine the most reliable predictors of job success was even less successful. Three years ago at an Employment Managers Association conference, more than 100 employment managers, representing many of the major corporations of the country, attempted to reach some conclusions on this subject in a day-long workshop.

We discussed our experiences with most of the traditional predictors of job success—grades, school quality, extracurricular activities, number of dependents, rate of job change, level of degree, references, interview comments, and so forth.

Every one of us had pet predictors that we proudly offered to the workshop. But every one of them was shot down with humiliating finality. None could stand up under scrutiny.

It was a disillusioning experience. By the end of the day we had reached one unanimous conclusion. We agreed that only one employment predictor does have significant value: the interviewer's gut feeling.

Admittedly, that's a pretty unsatisfactory conclusion to come to in this age of science. Gut feeling takes into account a wide variety of tangible and intangible elements—including the person's appearance, demeanor, ability to express himself, and so on. The resulting overall thumbs-up or thumbs-down feeling is what, according to the recruiters, correlates most often with managerial success.

The implications of this conclusion are important—especially for employers under pressure from the government to provide equal employment opportunity to minorities and women. No longer can they rationalize their possibly discriminatory hiring decisions on the basis of grades or any other single criterion. They must recognize and take into account the entire range of qualifications that a job candidate brings to the interview.

FOR DISCUSSION AND REVIEW

1 Discuss the general conclusions of the research cited in the article.
2 Why are interviews such a subjective selection technique?
3 What can be done to improve the interview's validity?

Neal Schmitt

Social and Situational Determinants of Interview Decisions: Implications for the Employment Interview

During the last 25 years, four separate reviews of research on the interview have appeared (Mayfield, 1964; Ulrich and Trumbo, 1965; Wagner, 1949; and Wright, 1969). Each of these reviews discussed dozens of studies and concluded that the interview as employed in many employment situations lacks both reliability and validity. However, the interview continues to be a popular selection tool. Evidence of this popularity is the continued proliferation of how-to-interview manuals (e.g., Morgan and Cogger, 1972) despite a call for a moratorium (England and Paterson, 1970).

The importance of understanding the interview is underscored by this continued widespread use and the EEOC guidelines on employment procedures (*Federal Register*, Vol. 35, Pt. 1607, Aug. 1, 1970). It has become increasingly evident that employers are legally responsible for showing that their selection process (including interviews) is job related. Since the last review of the employment interview literature (Wright, 1969), a good deal of the research has focused on the determination of the factors which affect the decision-making process in the interview reflecting both earlier disillusionment with reliability and validity data and the desire to understand the interview process itself. Recent studies have tended to be microanalytic and experimental rather than correlational (Wright, 1969).

While knowledge concerning the interview has definitely been enhanced since Wright's review, the generalizability of these artificial and microanalytic studies to real employment situations remains unestablished. In addition, their importance relative to the validity of the interview decision is largely unexamined.

It is the purpose of the present paper to (1) reexamine the conclusions and problems of the interview as the earlier reviewers perceived them; (2) review the research

---

From *Personnel Psychology* 29 (1976): 79–101. Copyright © 1976, by Personnel Psychology, Inc. Reprinted by permission.

developments of the past six years and relate them to earlier research; (3) attempt to integrate these studies; (4) describe problems in current research and important persistent questions.

MAJOR CONCLUSIONS OF PREVIOUS REVIEWS

In 1949, Wagner published a comprehensive review of employment interview research. He located 106 articles dealing with this topic but only 25 of these articles reported any quantitative information about the value of the interview in selection. Reliability coefficients for 174 sets of ratings and 96 different traits ranged from .23 to .97 for ratings of specific traits and $-.20$ to .85 for ratings of overall ability. Intelligence was the only trait consistently rated with high reliability. Validity and reliability was satisfactory for only one area—that of sociability ($r_{xx} = .87$, $r_{xy} = .37$ and .22).

Wagner (1949) also stated that reliability and validity may be highly specific to situations and interviewers and that reliability could be enhanced if standardized forms were used to elicit and record interview data. The prevailing attitude, though, was that more and more of the factors formerly measured in the interview were better handled by tests.

Perhaps the most interesting part of Wagner's review was his examination of the information processing capacity of the interviewer. Wagner suggested that for predictive purposes, the information obtained from an interview should be statistically combined with other data. He stated, as did Sawyer (1966), that the interviewer may be effective in eliciting information not available elsewhere, but that the interviewer is incapable of effectively weighting and combining this and other information.

Mayfield (1964) also noted the lack of confirmed validity of the interview and the abundance of opinion articles and reports of uncontrolled observations. Mayfield maintained that two new research approaches to the interview would be useful. First, the emphasis should be on the process of decision making as it occurs in the selection interview rather than on the results of the interview. That is, the focus should be on the variables affecting interview decisions. Secondly, this decision-making process may be studied most adequately by dividing the interview into small units and conducting controlled studies on one or two variables at a time. The research of Mayfield and Carlson and their colleagues (Carlson, Thayer, Mayfield, and Peterson, 1971) has followed this 'microanalytic' approach and will be discussed later in this paper.

Mayfield also felt that previous research supported several general statements. Most important of these statements are the following: (1) interview validities are low even for highly reliable interviews; (2) structured interviews are more reliable; (3) interviewers who are consistent in their treatment of interviewees are still inconsistent in their interpretation of data obtained; (4) interviewer attitudes bias their judgments; (5) decisions are made early in the interview; and (6) intelligence is the trait most validly estimated by an interview, but the interview information adds nothing to test data.

Ulrich and Trumbo (1965) agreed with earlier reviewers concerning the dearth of encouraging evidence on the reliability and validity of the interview. And, they posed an additional problem for the interview—that of its functional validity. Noting the expense of the interview, they felt research should be conducted which separates the predictive validity obtained from the interview from that obtained from other sources. Ulrich and Trumbo concluded that the variables having to do with personal relations and motivation were the two areas which contributed most to interviewer decisions and which possessed the most validity. Like Mayfield (1964), Ulrich and Trumbo (1965) believed interview research should be restricted to one or two areas as part of a sequential testing procedure. They also felt that research designed to increase understanding of the interview as a decision-making process and as interpersonal communication would be most promising.

Wright's review (1969) offered three comprehensive recommendations. Unlike Mayfield (1964) and Ulrich and Trumbo (1965), Wright argued that 'macroanalytic' research designs which deal with the interview as a totality, be used more frequently than microanalytic experimental research. Wright maintained that research such as that suggested by Mayfield (1964) would result in fragmentation to the point of meaninglessness. Wright also stated that a multidisciplinary model would both stimulate research and lead to greater understanding of the interviewer's intuition. Finally, he commented that as increased knowledge concerning the selection interview is obtained, computer analysis of stimulated interview responses will become useful in the study of decision making.

The most significant advance in interview research during the time span covered by Wright (1969) was conducted by Webster (1964). Concerned with the problem of decision making in the interview, Webster and his colleagues utilized personnel officers, enlisted men, and recruits of the Canadian Army. Their series of investigations resulted in several significant findings, each of which has led to a series of subsequent research.

DECISION MAKING IN THE INTERVIEW

The major portion of the research reported in the last six years deals with the variables first suggested by the research of Webster and his colleagues (1964). This research has been organized around the specific variables which were the focus of these research efforts and is summarized in Table 1.

Negative-positive nature of information

Springbett (1958) sought to determine the relation between an interviewer's final decision (hire-reject) and the kind and order of presentation of information in an interview. Early impressions played a dominant role in interviews; an interviewer reached a final decision an average of four minutes after the interview began. The interview also appeared to be primarily a search for negative information, as indicated by the finding that just one unfavorable rating (trait) resulted in a reject decision in 90% of the cases. Hollmann (1972) has criticized Springbett's (1958) and Bolster and Springbett's (1961) rating scales in that the base rate of success in the interviewee population was greater than 50%. Consequently, the rejection part of the scale had larger scale units than the hire part of the scale.

Hollmann (1972) used the degree and direction of the difference between the base rate and assigned probability of success for each informational unit (units were extracted from Hakel and Dunnette, 1970) to obtain an index of the predictive utility of an information unit for a particular interviewer. Experienced interviewers were then asked to make multiple evaluations of applicants after each new information unit was presented. Analyzing shifts in ratings with new information, Hollmann (1972) concluded that interviewers appropriately weight negative information but do not weight positive information heavily enough. Hollmann (1972) also noted that interviewers' positive stereotypes of applicants were not well differentiated, i.e., interviewers could explain why an applicant was not likely to be a good employee but not why he might be satisfactory. Webster (1964), in attempting to explain the same phenomenon, suggested that interviewers only receive feedback

Table 1
Experimental Studies of Decision Making in the Interview

VARIABLES	STUDIES	CONCLUSIONS
1. Negative-positive nature of information	Springbett (1958) Bolster & Springbett (1961) Hollmann (1972)	All three studies agree that negative and positive information are processed differently. Springbett and Bolster & Springbett (1961) maintain negative information is weighted too heavily; Hollmann concludes negative information is weighted appropriately, but positive information is not weighted heavily enough.
2. Temporal placement of information	Blakeney & MacNaughton (1971) Johns (1975) Peters & Terborg (1975) Farr (1973) Springbett (1958) Anderson (1960) Crowell (1961)	The early studies found primacy effects; Blakeney and MacNaughton reported negligible primacy effects and Farr (1973) reported recency effects. Peters and Terborg (1975) found favorable-unfavorable information sequence resulted in better applicant ratings than an unfavorable-favorable sequence. Solution may be an attention hypothesis which suggests interviewers use the information they are forced to attend to.
3. Interviewer stereotypes	Sydiaha (1959, 1961) Bolster & Springbett (1961) Rowe (1963) Mayfield & Carlson (1966) Hakel, Hollmann, & Dunnette (1970) London & Hakel (1974) Hakel (1971)	Interviewers seem to have a common "ideal" applicant against which interviewees are evaluated though this generalized applicant may be the effect of halo (Hakel & Dunnette, 1970). Mayfield & Carlson (1966) also suggest that the "ideal" applicant may be at least partially specific or unique to the interviewer and Hakel, Hollmann & Dunnette (1970) found evidence for two clusters of stereotypes.
4. Job information	Langdale & Weitz (1973) Weiner & Schneiderman (1974)	Job information is utilized by interviewers and serves to decrease the effect of irrelevant information for both experienced and inexperienced interviewers.

VARIABLES	STUDIES	CONCLUSIONS
5. Individual differences	Dobmeyer (1970) Valenzi & Andrews (1973) Rowe (1963)	There are wide individual differences and little or no configurality in cue utilization by interviewers. In addition, interviewers are unable to give an accurate verbal statement of their cue utilization policies.
6. Visual cues	Washburn & Hakel (1973)	Visual cues were more important than verbal; their interaction was most responsible for ratings.
7. Attitudinal and racial similarity	Baskett (1973) Rand & Wexley (1975) Ledvinka (1971, 1972, 1973) Sattler (1970) Wexley & Nemeroff (1975) Peters & Terborg (1975) Frank & Hackman (1975)	Baskett (1973) reported that applicants' perceived similarity to the interviewer resulted in higher judgments concerning their competency and recommended salary, but no greater likelihood of recommended employment. Subsequent investigators have confirmed the effect of attitude similarity on interview ratings. Ledvinka reported that black interviewers were more likely to elicit responses of job rejection from black interviewees than were white interviewers in exit interviews.
8. Sex	Cohen & Bunker (1975) Dipboye, Fromkin & Wiback (1975)	Similarity of sex appears to have some minimal effect on job resume ratings though Cohen and Bunker (1975) suggest sexual discrimination of a type that assigns individuals to sex role congruent jobs.
9. Contrast effects	Carlson (1968, 1970) Hakel, Ohnesorge & Dunnette (1970) Rowe (1967) Wexley, Yukl, Kovacs & Sanders (1972) Wexley, Sanders & Yukl (1973); Landy & Bates (1973) Latham, Wexley & Pursell (1975)	The majority of these studies found that an applicant's rating is at least partially dependent on the other individuals being rated at the same time. Landy & Bates (1973) and Hakel et al. (1970) have found the contrast effect to be minimal and Lathan et al. found a workshop successful in the elimination of several rating errors including that of contrast effects.

Table 1 cont'd

VARIABLES	STUDIES	CONCLUSIONS
10. Interviewer experience	Carlson (1967a)	Reliability of interview data was not greater for experienced interviewers, but the stress for quotas impaired the judgments of inexperienced interviewers more than it did the experienced interviewers in the sense that inexperienced interviewers were more likely to accept bad applicants.
11. Type of information	Carlson (1967b)	Personal history information had a greater effect on interview judgments than photographs of the interviewee. A photograph had its greatest effect on the final rating when it complemented personal history information.
12. Accuracy of interviewer as measured by number of factual questions he is able to answer	Carlson (1967a)	More accurate raters used a structured guide, were more variable in their ratings, and tended to rate lower.
13. Structure of interview	Schwab & Henneman (1969) (Carlson, Schwab & Henneman (1970)	Structured interviews result in greater inter-interviewer reliability than interviews conducted without a guide.

from employers about bad employees and consequently learn to utilize negative information more appropriately.

Blakeney and MacNaughton (1971) attempted to assess the effect of temporal placement of unfavorable information in the interview. One hundred twenty-six management science students evaluated tape-recorded interviews in which unfavorable information had been placed at different points. Variance due to placement and the content area of negative information were both found to be negligible.

Farr (1973) constructed eight hypothetical secretarial applicants (from Hakel and Dunnette's items, 1970) manipulating the order of presentation of positive and negative information as well as impressionistic versus factual information. The order in which positive information was received accounted for most of the variance with a recency effect of information favorability being significant for all dependent variables. Impressionistic information was more important than factual information in determining the evaluation of sociability. Farr (1973) explained some of his results on the basis of an attention hypothesis, i.e., if interviewers are asked to make evaluations after each unit of information they will change their minds; if asked to make only one decision, they make up their minds early and then lose attention. This hypothesis is also supported by Peters and Terborg (1975) who found that the sequencing of unfavorable and favorable information had no effect when job resumes were evaluated with job information provided to the interviewers. Furthermore, Johns (1975) found interviewers who chose the order in which they evaluated applicant information to be less competent (as measured by agreement between actual and linearly combined predicted evaluations) than interviewers who received information in a random order. Johns (1975) felt interviewers who chose the order of informational input engaged in a relatively haphazard attempt to utilize information they were given later in the sequence.

This interpretation would also appear to be supported by two earlier studies at McGill (Anderson, 1960; and Crowell, 1961). Anderson found that interviewers spend more time talking when they form a favorable decision, though the total length of time of the interview and the interviewee's speech time remain constant. The interviewer, then, apparently talks a lot to those applicants he likes either to sell them on his company or to gather information to confirm his decision. Crowell (1961), like Farr (1973), showed that interviewers' decisions change as they receive more fragments of information.

It appears, then, that primacy and recency effects can be overcome if an experimenter controls the information presented. This could also be the reason standardized interviews are typically more reliable. A standardized interview form, consistently found to be more reliable than an open-ended interview, (Mayfield, 1964; Schwab and Henneman, 1969; Ulrich and Trumbo, 1965; Wagner, 1949; Wright, 1969), may force the interviewer to be attentive and enhance his agreement with other raters. Of course, this does not mean that validity will necessarily be enhanced.

Interviewer stereotypes

Sydiaha (1959, 1961) and Bolster and Springbett (1961) maintained that interviewers possess stereotypes of idealized successful applicants against which real applicants are judged as to their suitability for hiring. Sydiaha asked four interviewers to Q-sort 120 descriptive items concerning their applicability to recruits and make a decision to hire or reject the applicant. After the study, the interviewers sorted the statements to describe an ideal recruit. Item analysis of the 120 statements against the hire-reject criterion yielded a 67-item key which was cross-validated on a second set of applicants by the same interviewers with the resulting $r = .85$. Using the same key with different applicants and interviewers yielded an r of .80. Also the intercorrelations between different interviewers' ideal recruits ranged from .56 to .98; the median was .81. Sydiaha concluded that personnel interviewers tend to attach the same importance to systematic information such as test data and that they tend to support their decisions by referring to the same stereotype of a good applicant. The problem with Sydiaha's research, as Hakel and Dunnette (1970) suggest, is that the interviewer is probably choosing favorable sounding statements to describe the candidates he accepts. It would be more profitable to learn what these interviewers weighted in reaching their decision.

Hakel, Hollmann, and Dunnette (1970) examined the question of how accurately interviewers can identify the stereotype associated with an ideal job applicant. A forced choice stereotype accuracy test was developed to determine the accuracy with which employment interviewers, Certified Public Accountants, and students could identify the interests of accountants. Though all three groups were equally accurate in identifying CPA interests as evaluated by the number of correct interest choices, there were two distinct clusters, one of CPAs and the other containing employment interviewers, students and four older CPAs. If these stereotypes are important in hiring decisions, then who is hired will depend on who does the interviewing. Whose stereotype is correct would depend on its relationship to job-relevant variables, which is yet another, but equally important, question.

The power of halo or stereotype was further documented by Hakel (1971) who found that a highly structured interview with scaled-expectation rating scales produced no greater interrater agreement than reported in Wagner's review (1949). A control group would have made the evaluation of the structure and rating scales in this study more appropriate.

Rowe (1963) used 30 favorable and 30 unfavorable statements from Sydiaha's list to construct 100 different hypothetical applicants (3 favorable and 3 unfavorable items described all 100). One hundred forty-six interviewers were then asked to hire or reject each of the hypothetical persons. Though there was little or no disagreement as to the favorability of the items, there were marked differences in the pattern of accept-reject decisions and these differences were related to interviewer characteristics. Three of the 146 accepted over 80%; while 40 of 146 accepted less than 20%. The more experienced interviewers tended to accept fewer candidates and their decisions reflected more accurately the consensus. Less experienced interviewers had a more positive view of unfavorable statements than did the more experienced interviewers.

Like Hakel, et al. (1970), Mayfield and Carlson (1966) agree that interviewers formed stereotypes, but they believe that these stereotypes were at least partially peculiar to interviewers. That is, there may be a general factor responsible for interview ratings, but there is also a specific rater effect.

Finally, London and Hakel (1974) have shown that induced stereotypes diminish or are altered by information as the rater continues to evaluate an application. However, real interviewer stereotypes, if they exist, could be more permanent than those experimentally produced in a laboratory.

Job information

Langdale and Weitz (1973) showed that with greater information about the job to be filled, interrater reliability increased; no difference due to the experience of the interviewer was found. Using hypothetical applicants constructed from Hakel and Dunnette's list (1970), Wiener and Schneiderman (1974) found that interviewers made extensive use of job information. Use of job information decreased the effect of irrelevant attributes on decisions but did not eliminate it. As in the Langdale and Weitz study, use of job information was not enhanced by experience in interviewing.

Individual differences in the decision process

Two studies concerned themselves with the utilization of cues by individual interviewers. Dobmeyer (1970), using an ANOVA design, reported that 35 campus recruiters made little or no configural use of cues and that the individual recruiters differed widely in cue utilization practices.

The low interrater reliability that has characterized overall suitability ratings in the interview means that interviewers must be weighting information differently in the interview. Hakel, Dobmeyer, and Dunnette (1970) compared students and interviewers' evaluations of resumes that described 24 applicants in terms of three levels of academic standing, two levels of experience, and two levels of interest. Analyses of variance and examination of interaction effects for student and interviewer raters revealed that interviewers gave much lower ratings to resumés describing students of low and average academic standing while students more heavily weighted job experience. The study provides evidence for differential weighting of content categories and differences between groups of raters. The differences between groups of raters as well as the low interrater reliability (.48) of the student group relative to the interviewer group (.68) would argue for use of studies of actual interviewers. The implications of the study are clear, but even more important are analyses of individual raters and the determination of their weighting strategies which was also the concern of an investigation by Valenzi and Andrews (1973).

Valenzi and Andrews (1973) had four placement interviewers rate 243 secretarial job applicants on the basis of five kinds of informational cues. Again, there were wide individual differences in cue utilization resulting in substantial disagreement on applicant ratings. Like Dobmeyer's subjects, Valenzi and Andrews's subjects made little or no configural use of cues. Valenzi and Andrews also collected verbal reports from the interviewers as to how they thought they were weighting cues and found serious discrepancies between the interviewer's intended cue weights and his actual cue weights. It should be noted that this phenomenon was also discussed by Wagner (1949) in his review.

If an investigator could establish that the interviewer's actual or intended weights or some other set of weights was job related, it would be better to allow the interviewer to continue collecting the interview information and then statistically combine the data using the optimal set of weights. Statistical weights are not necessarily unambiguous (Darlington, 1968); however, policy capturing research has generally affirmed their superiority with respect to actual human judgments (Dawes, 1971).

Visual cues

A number of studies have investigated various postural and facial cues in a variety of social interaction situations including the interview (Dittman, 1962; Ekman, 1964; and Matarazzo, Wiens, and Saslow, 1965). One study (Washburn and Hakel, 1973) was specifically concerned with the employment interview. Two simulated campus interviews were videotaped in which students acted the roles of either an enthusiastic (gesturing, smiling, eye contact) or unenthusiastic campus recruiter and an applicant for a sales position. Observers received video only or a transcript of the interview or the actual audiovisual tape. Observers consistently gave higher ratings to the applicants interviewed by the enthusiastic interviewers. Results also indicated that visual cues were more important than verbal and that a combination of visual and verbal cues was maximally responsible for obtained differences in ratings.

Attitudinal, sexual, and racial similarity

Baskett (1973) asked 51 student subjects to evaluate candidates for a vice-presidency on the basis of 10 attitude statements manipulated so as to be either 20% or 80% similar to the subject. High, medium, and low competency was also manipulated by the description of the job applicant. Similar applicants were perceived as more competent, but no more likely to be recommended for a job than dissimilar applicants. However, similar applicants were deemed more worthy of a higher salary. Peters and Terborg (1975) found that perceived attitude similarity not only affected evaluations of job resumés, but also was resistant to the addition of job related information to use as a standard for evaluation. Rand and Wexley (1975) and Wexley and Nemeroff (1975) have further documented the importance of attitudinal and racial similarity in the determination of interviewer evaluations. However, Frank and Herman (1975) have questioned the generality of the effect of interviewer-interviewee similarity. For three different interviewers, they found a near zero correlation, a moderately positive one and a high positive relationship between interviewee similarity and interviewer favorableness to the interviewee.

Ledvinka (1971, 1972, 1973) and Sattler (1970) have produced evidence that an observer's race affects the behavior of the person being observed in an interview. For example, Ledvinka (1973) found that in exit interviews, black interviewers elicited significantly more reasons involving a rejection of the job or a rejection of the worker by an employer than did white interviewers. A rejection was operationally defined as having been fired or having quit a job. According to Ledvinka (1972), one of the "rules" of interracial behavior is that blacks should not express interracial conflict or hostility to whites or white institutions (work). Ledvinka feels that this fact has practical importance for the black interviewee because his "rejections" become part of his work record.

Dipboye, Fromkin, and Wiback (1975) have shown that male interviewer subjects discriminated against unattractive applicants and females when evaluating job resumés. Eta square values for sex main effects and interactions were not greater than .01 in any case, however. Cohen and Bunker (1975) found more subtle sex discrimination among job recruiters at two university placement centers. Significantly more females than males were recommended for hiring for an editorial assistant position, while significantly more males were recommended for a personnel technician job. Both males and females were more likely to be recommended for traditionally role-congruent jobs though other qualifications were constant.

Contrast effects

Several studies (Carlson, 1968, 1970; Hakel, Ohnesorge and Dunnette, 1970; Rowe, 1967; Wexley, Yukl, Kovacs, and Sanders, 1972; and Wexley, Sanders and Yukl, 1973) have supported the idea that at least part of an interviewee's rating was due to the quality of the interviewees immediately preceding him. Utilizing college student interviewers, the Wexley, et al. study (1973) attempted to overcome these contrast effects through various methods. Wexley et al. (1972) found that when an average applicant was preceded by two highly qualified or poorly qualified candidates, 80% of the variance in the average candidates' ratings was accounted for by contrast effects. Warning interviewer subjects about contrast effects reduced this contrast variance to 64%; use of an anchor on the rating scale reduced the contrast variance to 62%; with a week-long workshop, the variance dropped to 3%. In effect, Wexley et al. (1972) accepted the null hypothesis that contrast effects no longer existed. Latham, Wexley, and Pursell (1975) assigned 60 managers to a control group, group discussion training, or a videotape workshop session in an effort to eliminate rating errors. Six months after the training sessions, group discussion participants still committed first impression errors, the control group still rated applicants like themselves higher, and committed halo and contrast errors, while the videotape workshop participants committed none of these errors.

Landy and Bates (1973), criticizing the Hakel et al. study (1970) specifically, questioned the existence of contrast effects. Their criticisms were two-fold: lack of realism in the experimental situation and the practical significance of the effect. Landy and Bates found that when actual interviewers were given resumés to rate, they found the resumés unrealistic and the hire-reject criterion unsatisfactory. More realistic according to actual interviewers would be the decision to invite an applicant for a plant visit. When these changes were made and actual interviewers served as subjects, contrast effects were not found. Landy and Bates' criticism and their data is supporting evidence for Wright's reservations concerning microanalytic studies of the interview. However, Hakel et al. (1970) did employ real interviewers and also suggested that the effect was trivial ($\eta^2 = .02$). In addition, Landy and Bates (1973) employed sequences of resumés which included the test resumé type earlier in the sequence.

Structured interview guides

Two studies (Schwab and Henneman, 1969; and Carlson, Schwab and Henneman, 1970) have reconfirmed that use of a structured interview guide increases inter-interviewer agreement.

Miscellaneous

Carlson, Thayer, Mayfield, and Peterson (1971) reported a series of studies of the microanalytic type (some of these were already alluded to) which yield information about the effect of several variables on interview decisions. These investigators found the reliability of interview data was no greater for experienced interviewers, but the stress for quotas impaired the decisions of inexperienced interviewers more than the decisions of experienced interviewers (Carlson, 1967a). The inexperienced interviewer faced with quotas was more likely to accept less qualified individuals that his experienced counterpart. Personal history information was more important than appearance (photographs), but personal appearance had more influence when it complemented the personal history information (Carlson, 1967b). Carlson (1967a) also reported that the average number of factual questions an interviewer was able to answer correctly immediately after an interview was 50%. The more accurate raters used a structured guide, were more variable in their ratings, and tended to rate lower.

It is apparent that Webster's book (1964) has stimulated a great deal of research, but that there remain unanswered questions and ambiguities with respect to almost all variables. For example, Table 1 shows conflicting results with respect to the negative-positive nature of the information obtained in the interview, temporal placement of interview information, interviewer stereotypes, and contrast effects. What still is required, and especially important in studies of this type, is an integrative model (Wright, 1969) or at least an intergrated attack on the interview. An attempt to organize the research in a coherent form and present an hypothesized sequence of casual effects is presented in Figure 1.

A model for interview research

Represented in Figure 1 are all the major classes of variables which have been the object of most of the research efforts bearing on decision making in the interview. The directionality of the arrows in the figure is intended to represent an hypothesized causative effect. There is evidence for some of these hypothesized relationships in the studies cited in Table 1, and more broadly, in social and industrial psychology. The influence of socio-cultural variables on the attitudes, motivations, and expectations of adults is well established. That some of these background variables have been found related to interview outcome (Ledvinka, 1971, 1972, 1973; Sattler, 1970; Cohen and Bunker, 1975; Dipboye, Fromkin, and Wiback, 1975) is perhaps due to their influence on attitudinal and motivational variables which in turn influence both interviewer and interviewee behavior and decisions. Background variables may have an influence on interviewer decisions because they are taken as indications of attitudinal similarity and the capacity to "fit in" (Carlson, 1967a). An even larger volume of research has found attitudinal similarity (Baskett, 1973; Frank and Herman, 1975; Peters & Terborg, 1975) and interviewer stereotypes (Bolster and Springbett, 1961; Mayfield and Carlson, 1966; Rowe, 1963; Sydiaha,

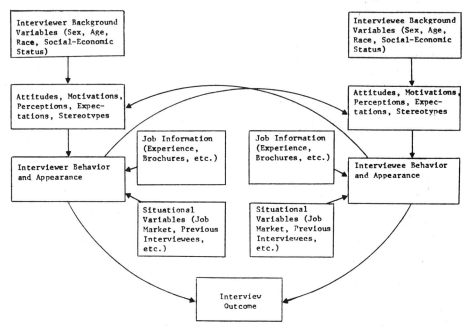

Fig. 1 Determinants of interview outcome.

1959, 1961) related to interviewer's decisions and at least one study has shown that job expectations and valences for rewards are different for culturally advantaged and disadvantaged groups (Arvey and Mussio, 1974). The effect of job information appears to aid interviewers in focusing on important information (Langdale and Weitz, 1973; Weiner and Schneiderman, 1974). The amount of job information an interviewer is able to present to an applicant also appears to have an influence on an interviewee's favorable response to the interview (Schmitt and Coyle, in press). Table 1 indicates that a variety of situational variables-temporal placement of information, favorability of immediately preceding applicants and the stress for quotas-have some effect on interview outcome. It is reasonable to expect an interviewee to be influenced by the geographical location of a prospective employer, personal reports concerning the company, as well as company literature. Finally, it would seem plausible that both interviewee and interviewer behavior in the interview is interpreted in light of both parties' attitudes and expectations and that these interpretations affect subsequent interview behaviors.

The proposed model is consistent with the research reviewed in this paper, but the causal sequence it implies remains relatively untested. Future research could also be directed to the specification of the relative influence of these factors. When appropriate, further research to eliminate or minimize undesirable factors (Latham, Wexley, and Pursell, 1975) should lead to increased reliability and validity. Clearly suggested by the model is research directed to ascertaining what kinds of individual backgrounds will result in attitudes and expectations that imply a given set of responses to an interview situation. The research reviewed in this section establishes the selection interview outcome as the result of a social psychological interaction. Participants' actions and decisions in the interview will be affected by variables similar to those which would affect them elsewhere in their lives. Inclusion or exclusion of those variables should be contingent on their job relevance, but first these variables must be understood. Research of the last ten years has begun to delineate what variables are important, but has done little in the way of evaluating their effect on validity.

UTILITY OF THE INTERVIEW

Two studies (Grant and Bray, 1969; and Carlson, 1971) were found which addressed themselves to the unique contributions of the interview in the employment decision (Ulrich & Trumbo, 1965). Grant and Bray (1969) were concerned with the contribution of interview information to assessment center ratings and the relationship of these interview variables to management progress. Though not bearing directly on the relative contribution of the interview, Grant and Bray's results indicated that judgments of career motivation, work motivation and control of feelings were influenced by the interview. Also, reliable information was obtained on a wide variety of personal characteristics, and this information was a valid predictor of salary progress (coefficients ranged from −.36 to .50; one-half of the 36 validities were significant).

In a simulated employment interview setting, Carlson (1971) requested life insurance agency managers to rate eight hypothetical applicants described with various combinations of favorable and unfavorable information and test results from the Aptitude Index Battery. This battery had been validated, and the raters were aware of the validity data. Test results accounted for 14% of the variance in ratings; the favorability of test items, 12%; and the interaction of amount and type of personal history information, 11%. Carlson concluded that the impact of test results can be altered by subjective personal information especially when that information is negative. London and Hakel (1974) found a similar effect when favorable or unfavorable test scores followed favorable or unfavorable verbal descriptions. Subjects tended not to be affected by verbal descriptions when test scores were low; when verbal descriptions were bad, test scores did affect ratings. Though neither study reports comparative validity data, they suggest that interviewers use the information from interviews to make decisions. Whether their combination of information from tests and interviews is appropriate in a job-related sense was not evaluated.

The question of the functional utility of the interview posed by Ulrich and Trumbo (1965) has not been answered nor has it received much attention.

DECISION OF THE INTERVIEWEE

Largely neglected by researchers interested in the interview process has been the decision making the interviewee does after or during the interview. Models of the interview process (Hakel and Dunnette, 1970; Cannell and Kahn, 1968) including that depicted in Figure 1 include the interviewee component. Alderfer and McCord (1970) hypothesized that interpersonal satisfaction in the interview would be related in the applicant's acceptance of a job. One hundred-twelve MBAs were asked to answer a series of questions about the worst, the average, and the best interview they have had. In addition, the subjects were asked to rate what a desirable job meant to them in terms of satisfaction. The applicants gave higher probabilities of accepting a job offer after interviews by companies in which they had an interest in receiving an offer, where the interviewer was seen as showing interest and concern for them, and where the interviewer discussed the careers of other MBAs in his company.

Another interesting area of applied research bearing on the interviewee has focused on the hard-to-employ. Venardos and Harris (1973) showed that the use of videotape interviews and role playing as job interview training procedures produced significant improvements in interview skills as compared with previous performance and an attention-placebo group. Similarly, Barbee and Keil (1973) used videotape feedback, behavior modification and counseling to train disadvantaged applicants to take more active roles in interviews. The trainees not only took more active roles but were judged more favorably for doing so.

INTERPERSONAL PERCEPTION MODEL

Perhaps the most ambitious recent research attempt is that reported by Hakel and Dunnette (1970). These researchers viewed the interview process as a case of information processing in interpersonal perception. They proposed a series of correlative and experimental studies to investigate the factors affecting the accuracy of predictions based upon interview data and to determine how the accuracy of these predictions could be increased. As a first step in this process, Hakel and Dunnette developed a set of instruments—checklists for Describing Job Applicants—for seven different occupational categories. The items focused on what the applicant did and said, his characteristics, and the impression he created. The checklist items were rated by a large number of interviewers as to their favorability, frequency of occurrence, and importance. These items have served as a basis for several investigators to construct hypothetical applicants with various characteristics (Farr, 1973; Hollman, 1972; Wiener and Schneiderman, 1974).

In a related study, Hakel and Schuh (1971) identified checklist elements which were common to seven occupational categories. The items fell into two content clusters. The first was a personal relations group which corroborates Ulrich and Trumbo's contention (1965) that sociability is best assessed via interview data. The second content category Hakel and Schuh labeled the "good citizen" category. It contains items referring to the applicants' dependability, conscientiousness, stability, etc. Hakel and Schuh's data indicate that these attributes are relatively universal in their frequency, importance, and favorability. A logical next step is the further clarification of these elements and their influence on the decisions an interviewer makes and their relationship to job performance criteria.

CONCLUSIONS AND PERSISTENT PROBLEMS

Perhaps the most dramatic change in the articles discussed in this paper and outlined in Table 1, as compared with the earlier reviews, is the number of articles characterized by (1) an emphasis on decision making in the interview or at least an investigation of one or more factors on an interview decision; (2) the number of experimental studies on the interview; and (3) the microanalytic nature of these studies (Wright, 1969). These studies have illustrated the importance of many variables other than what the applicant says or does (e.g., the situation, interviewer characteristics) which affect the interviewer's decision. Nevertheless, with the possible exception of the Carlson-Mayfield work and the work of Hakel and his colleagues, these studies suffer from a lack of integration. Equally important are questions concerning their generalizability. Carlson (1971, p. 71) has stated that "a great deal of caution is necessary in extending the conclusion of laboratory experiments of theoretical interest to applied settings where the goal may be similar, but the task and tools used to perform the task are different." The threat to generalizability which results from use of college students as evaluators of resumés or interviewers may be exaggerated. In reviewing six studies, Bernstein, Hakel, and Harlan (1975) found no significant differences between employment interviewers and college students with respect to variances, intercorrelations, interrater agreement, and main effects due to independent variables. However, college students do tend to be more lenient in their ratings. Dipboye, Fromkin, and Wiback (1975) also found no differences between employment interviewers and students except for student leniency.

The studies reviewed in this paper have tended to stress what is wrong with the interview decision. More needs to be done to ascertain if and why interview decisions are correct. Likewise, research should be directed toward identification of the variables which are best and most consistently evaluated by the employment interview. Likely possibilities are the variables suggested by Ulrich and Trumbo (1965) and Hakel and Schuh (1971). Combining interview ratings of these variables with test data in the prediction of criteria should answer some of the questions regarding the employment interviews' functional utility. A court case addressed to this issue is almost inevitable, as was noted in the introduction to this paper. Also, as the Valenzi and Andrews study (1973) indicates, and the lack of interviewer agreement attests to, there are individual differences in decision making in the interview. More attention should be given to the nature of these individual differences.

The paucity of research on the impact of the interview on the interviewee also represents a definite liability as far as knowledge concerning the interview process is concerned. Alderfer and McCord (1970) represents the only study investigating the effect of various interview factors on the applicants' decision to accept a job. This should be an area of concern for employers attempting to attract high quality applicants in a tight labor market. The volunteer Army, for example, should be able to apply many of the findings from research such as this. Certainly consumer research suggests many hypotheses to be studied in this area: what types of motivators are effective, what types of interviewers are effective with certain groups of interviewees, etc. These interviewer-interviewee interactions will certainly have an effect on both parties' decision regarding the interview.

In conclusion, there is not much in the research of the last half dozen years to bolster the confidence of a personnel interviewer concerned with the reliability and validity of his decisions. There is a good deal of evidence concerning the influence of variables which may make his decision both less reliable and valid. The following suggestions for the practicing personnel interviewer would appear reasonable. First, use of a structured interview guide will improve interviewer reliability. Simply recording information and then returning to it later to make ratings or recommendations may serve to remove some of the order effects, over weighting of negative information, and contrast effects which may act to diminish the relevance of interview outcomes. Second, knowing the requirements of the job you are interviewing for should help to focus on relevant information. Third, interviewer training to avoid bias in ratings may be appropriate though not much effort has been directed toward this problem or the evaluation of such training. Fourth, the interviewee is also forming an impression of the interviewer and even when he/she is not an acceptable candidate the interview may be employed effectively as a public relations vehicle. Fifth, interpersonal skills and motivation are perhaps best evaluated by the interview; consequently, the interview is likely to prove to be an effective selection device when these elements are also required for effective job performance. Sixth, allowing the applicant time to talk will make rapid first impressions less likely and provide a larger behavior sample. Seventh, interviewer training with minorities may increase the ability to relate, though again, this training rarely exists and has never been evaluated. At any rate, periodic checks on number of minorities hired or recommended along with the jobs they are recommended for may alert one to possible bias. Eighth, attention should be directed to an evaluation of the purpose of the interview, i.e., whether it is intended to select on a given number of variables, whether it is an initial screening device, or whether it is primarily educational. Finally, it is certainly repetitious to state this, but research should still be directed to determining what variables are reliably, validly, and uniquely assessed in the selection interview and that research can best be conducted with the cooperation of personnel interviewers.

REFERENCES

Alderfer, C. P. and McCord, C. G. Personal and situational factors in the recruitment interview. *Journal of Applied Psychology*, 1970, 54, 377–385.

Anderson, C. W. The relation between speaking times and decision in the employment interview. *Journal of Applied Psychology*, 1960, 44, 267–268.

Arvey, R. D. and Mussio, S. J. Job expectations and valences of job rewards for culturally disadvantaged and advantaged clerical employees. *Journal of Applied Psychology*, 1974, 59, 230–232.

Barbee, J. R. and Keil, E. C. Experimental techniques of job interview training for the disadvantaged: videotape feedback, behavior modification, and microcounseling. *Journal of Applied Psychology*, 1973, 58, 209–213.

Baskett, C. D. Interview decisions as determined by competency and attitude similarity. *Journal of Applied Psychology*, 1973, 57, 343–345.

Bernstein, V., Hakel, M. D., and Harlan, A. The college student as interviewer: A threat to generalizability? *Journal of Applied Psychology*, 1975, 60, 266–268.

Blakeney, R. N. and MacNaughton, J. F. Effects of temporal placement of unfavorable information on decision making during the selection interview. *Journal of Applied Psychology*, 1971, 55, 138–142.

Bolster, B. I. and Springbett, B. M. The reaction of interviewers to favorable and unfavorable information. *Journal of Applied Psychology*, 1961, 45, 97–103.

Cannell, C. F. and Kahn, R. L. Interviewing. In G. Lindzey & E. Aronson (Eds.), *The Handbook of Social Psychology* (Vol. II). Reading, Mass.: Addison-Wesley, 1968.

Carlson, R. E. Selection interview decisions: the effect of interviewer experience, relative quota situation, and applicant sample on interviewer decisions. *Personnel Psychology*, 1967, 20, 259–280. (a)

Carlson, R. E. The relative influence of appearance and factual written information on an interviewer's final rating. *Journal of Applied Psychology*, 1967, 51, 461–468. (b)

Carlson, R. E. Selection interview decisions: The effect of mode of applicant presentation on some outcome measures. *Personnel Psychology*, 1968, 21, 193–207.

Carlson, R. E. Effects of applicant sample on ratings of valid information in an employment setting. *Journal of Applied Psychology*, 1970, 54, 217–222.

Carlson, R. E. Effect of interview information in altering valid impressions. *Journal of Applied Psychology*, 1971, 55, 66–72.

Carlson, R. E., Schwab, D. P., and Henneman, H. G. Agreement among selection interview styles. *Journal of Applied Psychology*, 1970, 5, 8–17.

Carlson, R. E., Thayer, P. W., Mayfield, E. C., and Peterson, D. A. Research on the selection interview. *Personnel Journal*, 1971, 50, 268–275.

Cohen, S. L., & Bunker, K. A. Subtle effects on sex role stereotypes on recruiters' hiring decisions. *Journal of Applied Psychology*, 1975, 60, 566–572.

Crowell, A. H. Decision sequences in perception. Unpublished doctoral dissertation. McGill University, 1961.

Darlington, R. B. Multiple regression in psychological research and practice. *Psychological Bulletin*, 1968, 69, 161–182.

Dawes, R. M. A case study of graduate admissions: application of three principles of human decision making. *American Psychologist*, 1971, 26, 180–188.

Dipboye, R. L., Fromkin, H. L., and Wiback, K. Relative importance of applicant sex, attractiveness, and scholastic standing in evaluation of job applicant resumés. *Journal of Applied Psychology*, 1975, 60, 39–43.

Dittman, A. T. The relationship between body movements and moods in interviews. *Journal of Applied Psychology*, 1962, 26, 480.

Dobmeyer, T. W. Modes of information utilization by employment interviewers in suitability ratings of hypothetical job applicants. Paper presented at Midwestern Psychological Convention, Cincinnati, 1970.

Ekman, P. Body position, facial expression, and verbal behavior during interviews. *Journal of Abnormal and Social Psychology*, 1964, 68, 295–301.

England, G. W., & Patterson, D. G. Selection and placement—the past ten years. In H. G. Henneman, Jr. et al. (Eds.), *Employment relations research: A summary and appraisal.* New York: Harpers, 1970.

Farr, J. L. Response requirements and primacy-recency effects in a simulated selection interview. *Journal of Applied Psychology*, 1973, 57, 228–233.

Frank, L. L. and Hackman, J. R. Effects of interviewer-interviewee similarity an interviewer objectivity in college admissions interviews. *Journal of Applied Psychology*, 1975, 60, 356–360.

Grant, D. L. and Bray, D. W. Contributions of the interview to assessment of management potential. *Journal of Applied Psychology*, 1969, 53, 24–34.

Hakel, M. D. Similarity of post-interview trait rating intercorrelations as a contributor to interrater agreement in a structured employment interview. *Journal of Applied Psychology*, 1971, 55, 443–448.

Hakel, M. D., Dobmeyer, T. W., and Dunnette, M. D. Relative importance of three content dimensions in overall suitability ratings of job applicants' resumés. *Journal of Applied Psychology*, 1970, 54, 65–71.

Hakel, M. D., Hollman, T. D., and Dunnette, M. D. Accuracy of interviewers, certified public accountants, and students in identifying the interests of accountants. *Journal of Applied Psychology*, 1970, 54, 115–119.

Hakel, M. D. and Dunnette, M. D. *Checklists for describing job applicants.* Minneapolis: University of Minnesota, 1970.

Hakel, M. D., Ohnesorge, J. P., and Dunnette, M. D. Interviewer evaluations of job applicants' resumés as a function of the qualification of the immediately preceding applicants. *Journal of Applied Psychology*, 1970, 54, 27–30.

Hakel, M. D. and Schuh, A. J. Job applicant attributes judged important across seven divergent occupations. *Personnel Psychology*, 1971, 24, 45–52.

Hollman, T. D. Employment interviewers' errors in processing positive and negative information. *Journal of Applied Psychology*, 1972, 56, 130–134.

Johns, G. Effects of informational order and frequency of applicant evaluation upon linear information-processing competence of interviewers. *Journal of Applied Psychology*, 1975, 60, 427–433.

Landy, F. J. and Bates, F. Another look at contrast effects in the employment interview. *Journal of Applied Psychology*, 1973, 58, 141–144.

Langdale, J. A. and Weitz, J. Estimating the influence of job information on interviewer agreement. *Journal of Applied Psychology*, 1973, 57, 23–27.

Latham, G. P., Wexley, K. N., and Pursell, E. D. Training managers to minimize rating errors in the observation of behavior. *Journal of Applied Psychology*, 1975, 60, 550–555.

Ledvinka, J. Race of interviewer and the language elaboration of black interviewees. *Journal of Social Issues*, 1971, 27, 185–197.

Ledvinka, J. The intrusion of race: Black responses to a white observer. *Social Science Quarterly*, 1972, 52, 907–920.

Ledvinka, J. Race of employment interviewer and reasons given by job seekers for leaving their jobs. *Journal of Applied Psychology*, 1973, 58, 362–364.

London, M., and Hakel, M. D. Effects of applicant stereotypes, order, and information on interview impressions. *Journal of Applied Psychology*, 1974, 59, 157–162.

Matarazzo, J. D., Weins, A. N., and Saslow, G. Studies of interview speech behavior. In L. Krasner & L. P. Ullman (Eds.), *Research in behavior modification*. New York: Holt, 1965.

Mayfield, E. C. The selection interview: A reevaluation of published research. *Personnel Psychology*, 1964, 17, 239–260.

Mayfield, E. C. Carlson, R. E. Selection interview decisions: first results from a long-term research project. *Personnel Psychology*, 1966, 19, 41–55.

Morgan, H. and Cogger, J. *The interviewer's manual.* New York: Psychological Corporation, 1972.

Peters, L. H. and Terborg, J. R. The effects of temporal placement of unfavorable information and of attitude similarity on personnel selection decisions. *Organizational Behavior and Human Performance*, 1975, 13, 279–293.

Rand, T. M. and Wexley, K. N. A demonstration of the Byrne similarity hypothesis in simulated employment interviews. *Psychological Reports*, 1975, 36, 535–544.

Rowe, P. M. Individual differences in selection decisions. *Journal of Applied Psychology*, 1963, 47, 304–307.

Rowe, P. M. Order effects in assessment decisions. *Journal of Applied Psychology*, 1967, 51, 13–22.

Sattler, J. M. Racial "experimenter effects" in experimentation, testing, interviewing, and psychotherapy. *Psychological Bulletin*, 1970, 73, 137–160.

Sawyer, J. Measurement and prediction, clinical, and statistical. *Psychological Bulletin*, 1966, 66, 178–200.

Schmitt, N. and Coyle, B. W. Applicant decisions in the interview. *Journal of Applied Psychology*, in press.

Schwab, D. P. and Henneman, H. G. Relationship between interview structure and interinterviewer reliability in an employment situation. *Journal of Applied Psychology*, 1969, 53, 214–217.

Springbett, B. M. Factors affecting the final decision in the employment interview. *Canadian Journal of Psychology*, 1958, 12, 13–22.

Sydiaha, D. On the equivalence of clinical and statistical methods. *Journal of Applied Psychology*, 1959, 43, 395–401.

Sydiaha, D. Bales' interaction process analysis of personnel selection interviews. *Journal of Applied Psychology*, 1961, 45, 393–401.

Ulrich, L. and Trumbo, D. The selection interview since 1949. *Psychological Bulletin*, 1965, 63, 100–116.

Valenzi, E. and Andrews, I. R. Individual differences in the decision process of employment interviewers. *Journal of Applied Psychology*, 1973, 58, 49–53.

Venardos, M. G. and Harris, M. B. Job interview training with rehabilitation clients: A comparison of videotape and role playing procedures. *Journal of Applied Psychology*, 1973, 58, 365-367.

Wagner, R. The employment interview: A critical summary. *Personnel Psychology*, 1949, 2, 17-46.

Washburn, P. V. and Hakel, M. D. Visual cues and verbal content as influences on impressions after simlated employment interviews. *Journal of Applied Psychology*, 1973, 58, 137-140.

Webster, E. C. *Decision making in the employment interview.* Montreal: Eagle, 1964.

Wexley, K. N. and Nemeroff, W. F. Effects of racial prejudice, race of applicant, and biographical similarity on interviewer evaluations of job applicants. *Journal of Social and Behavioral Sciences*, 1974, 20, 66-78.

Wexley, K. N., Sanders, R. E., and Yukl, G. A. Training interviewers to eliminate contrast effects in employment interviews. *Journal of Applied Psychology*, 1973, 57, 233-236.

Wexley, K. N., Yukl, G. A., Kovacs, S. Z., and Sanders, R. E. Importance of contrast effects in employment interviews. *Journal of Applied Psychology*, 1972, 56, 45-48.

Wiener, Y. and Schneiderman, M. L. Use of job information as a criterion in employment decisions of interviewers. *Journal of Applied Psychology*, 1974, 59, 699-704.

Wright, O. R., Jr. Summary of research on the selection interview since 1964. *Personnel Psychology*, 1969, 22, 391-413.

FOR DISCUSSION AND REVIEW

1 Summarize the major conclusions of previous reviews on the interview process.

2 What aspects of the interview process have been researched to date? What aspects have been neglected in research?

3 Explain similarity and contrast effects in the interview. Explain the interpersonal perception model of the interview process.

4 Review the author's conclusions regarding the interview.

E. WORK SAMPLING
AND ASSESSMENT CENTERS

James E. Campion

Work Sampling for Personnel Selection[1]

In a recent article Wernimont and Campbell (1968) proposed a new strategy for personnel selection. They argue that it would be beneficial in test validation to adopt a model that emphasizes samples of work behavior as predictors of future work behavior. Wernimont and Campbell prefer this behavioral consistency model to the classical model which focuses on the use of tests as signs of predispositions to behave in certain ways on the job. They assert that pursuing the behavioral consistency approach and making test content more relevant to work would have several immediate advantages, such as diminishing the problem of faking or response sets and reducing charges of discrimination and invasion of privacy in testing.

Initial applications in field settings have shown promise. For example, assessment center research (Bray & Campbell, 1968; Bray & Grant, 1966; Hinrichs, 1969) with simulation exercises has been successful in demonstrating the advantages of the consistency approach in selecting managers. Furthermore, Hinrichs (1970), in a controlled laboratory setting, found that the most precise predictors of proficiency in a rotary pursuit task were apparatus tests which closely resembled this psychomotor task.

These initial findings seem promising and suggest that the concept of behavioral consistency may have considerable applied value. However, before this concept can be translated into a useful strategy for the practitioner, additional work is needed to develop guidelines for constructing work sample measures. In particular, the lack of guidelines for behavioral sampling seems to be a major obstacle to wider use of the consistency approach. The present research was designed to examine the effectiveness of one sampling strategy. Specifically, a modified version of Smith and Kendall's (1963) retranslation method was used to provide a framework for behavioral sampling, and concurrent test validation data were used to determine the utility of this methodology.

METHOD
Sample characteristics
The sample consisted of 34 male (32 Caucasian, 1 Negro, 1 Latin) maintenance mechanics (Dictionary of Occupational Titles, Job Code 638.28) employed by a food processing company located in a large Southwestern city. Their ages varied between 23 and 47 yr., with an average age of 35.8 yr. Educational attainment varied between 10 and 16 yr., with an average level of 12.4 yr. Their job tenure varied between 9 and 139 mo. with an average of 32.3 mo.

Development of work sample
The development of the work sample measure required a thorough examination of the job. This information was obtained from several technical conferences with a

From *Journal of Applied Psychology* 56, no. 1: 40–44. Copyright © 1972 by the American Psychological Association. Reprinted by permission.

[1] This research was partially supported by University of Houston Faculty Research Support Program Grant RIG 7016, which the author gratefully acknowledges. In addition, the author wishes to thank Elizabeth C. Freihoff for her assistance in this research.

group of job experts. These job experts were an industrial engineer, who was an assistant to the plant maintenance superintendent, and three foremen, who were responsible for supervising the work of the maintenance mechanics. These conferences progressed through several stages, each of which was designed to achieve a specific objective.

Stage 1. In the first stage the experts were requested to list all possible tasks that maintenance mechanics were required to perform in the company; and for each task they were asked to indicate frequency of performance and to evaluate its relative importance to the job.

Stage 2. In the second stage these experts, plus a member of the personnel department, were requested to provide another task listing based upon the previous work experiences of their maintenance mechanic applicants. All five members who participated in this conference were responsible for screening applicants for maintenance mechanic work.

Stage 3. In the third stage the objective was to delineate the crucial dimensions of work behavior for maintenance mechanics. A modified version of Smith and Kendall's (1963) retranslation technique was used. First, the group of experts listed the major dimensions of work behavior that they felt discriminated between effective and ineffective performance on the job. Second, each expert independently generated behavioral incidents to illustrate performance on each dimension. The procedures followed in this step adhere generally with the guidelines provided by Flanagan (1954) for use with his critical-incident technique. Following this, the experts pooled their information, discussed differences, and decided that there were two critical dimensions of work behavior for maintenance mechanics: use of tools, and accuracy of work. Speed of work also was suggested as a major factor of work behavior; however, the experts eliminated it due to a lack of agreement on choice of behavioral incidents to illustrate it.

Stage 4. In the next stage tasks were selected as possible work sample measures. It was important that the tasks selected were representative of the tasks performed by the maintenance mechanics in the plant, but they could not be unique to this plant. They also had to make them appropriate for the job applicants. These two requirements were satisfied by considering as possible job sample measures only those tasks which were common to the lists obtained in Stages 1 and 2. In addition, each job sample task had to meet two other requirements. Each task had to provide a situation where the opportunities were maximal for the examinee to exhibit behaviors relevant to use of tools and accuracy of work. Also, the behaviors elicited by the job sample tasks had to be the kind that a test administrator could reliably record.[2]

Based on the above criteria, four tasks were selected: installing pulleys and belts, disassembling and repairing a gearbox, installing and aligning a motor, and pressing a bushing into a sprocket and reaming it to fit a shaft.

Stage 5. In the final stage these four tasks were broken down into the steps logically required to complete them. Each step was then analyzed in detail, in order to determine the various approaches a job applicant might follow. The recordable behaviors associated with these approaches were specified and weights assigned to them based on their correctness as judged by the job experts. This resulted in a list of possible behaviors associated with each step in task performance, with every

---

[2]   Of course, reliability is essentially an empirical matter. Unfortunately, the author was not able to convince company officials that it would be worth the added expenses of retesting or of using two test administrators.

behavior assigned a weight for scoring purposes. Thus, the recording form was in a checklist format which required that the test administrator simply describe rather than evaluate the job applicant's behavior. The applicant's responses were later evaluated by adding the weights associated with the behaviors marked on the checklist.

Test instructions were written for the examiner to read. A set of tools and materials were selected that maximized the opportunity for the unqualified examinee to respond inappropriately. The tools and materials, the manner in which they were displayed, and the time given examinees to study them were standardized. All testing was done in the same test administration room, with only the examiner and examinee present. Four hours were allotted for test administration.

Example items and their corresponding weights are as follows:

	Scoring
Installing pulleys and belts	weights

1. Checks key before installing against:
    ____shaft   2
    ____pulley   2
    ____neither   0

Disassembling and repairing a gear box

10. Removes old bearing with:
    ____press and driver   3
    ____bearing puller   2
    ____gear puller   1
    ____other   0

Installing and aligning a motor

1. Measures radial misalignment with:
    ____dial indicator   10
    ____straight edge   3
    ____feel   1
    ____visual or other   0

Pressing a bushing into sprocket and reaming to fit a shaft

4. Checks internal diameter of bushing against shaft diameter:
    ____visually   1
    ____hole gauge and micrometers   3
    ____Vernier calipers   2
    ____scale   1
    ____does not check   0

Paper-and-pencil measures

Scores on a battery of paper-and-pencil tests were also available for all members of the validation sample. These tests were: the Test of Mechanical Comprehension, Form AA (published by the Psychological Corporation); the Wonderlic Personnel Test, Form D (published by E. F. Wonderlic); and the Short Employment Tests (published by the Psychological Corporation).

The standard deviation on the Test of Mechanical Comprehension was restricted. This was due to the mechanics having been preselected, based upon their performance on this test. The cutting score was 44. The other tests were required of all employees but were ignored in selecting craft personnel.

Criteria

The criteria were collected employing the paired comparison method. The three foremen who had participated in the technical conferences as experts were asked to evaluate their subordinates on each of the following factors: use of tools, accuracy of work, and overall mechanical ability. Each mechanic was evaluated by the foreman who was most familiar with his work performance.

Data collection procedure

Concurrent validation data were collected in three stages. First, criteria information was obtained from the foremen. Second, performance on the paper-and-pencil measures was collected from personnel records. Last, the work sample test was administered to the 34 maintenance mechanics. A test administrator was hired from an outside consulting firm, in order to prevent contamination between predictor and criterion measures. The means, standard deviations, and intercorrelations for the criteria, paper-and-pencil tests, and the work sample measures are presented in Tables 1, 2, and 3, respectively.

Table 1
Means, Standard Deviations, and Intercorrelations for Criteria Measures

| | | | INTERCORRELATIONS | |
| | | | ACCURACY OF WORK | OVERALL MECHANICAL ABILITY |
MEASURE	$\overline{X}$	SD		
Use of tools	51.6	13.3	.72	.67
Accuracy of work	51.3	13.7		.87
Overall mechanical ability	50.2	14.1		

Table 2
Means, Standard Deviations, and Intercorrelations for Paper-and-Pencil Measures

| | | | INTERCORRELATIONS | | | |
| | | | | SHORT EMPLOYMENT TESTS | | |
MEASURE	$\overline{X}$	SD	WONDERLIC PERSONNEL TEST	VERBAL	NUMERICAL	CLERICAL APTITUDE
Test of Mechanical Comprehension (Form AA)	50.9	4.0	.56	.24	.15	.26
Wonderlic Personnel Test (Form D)	23.8	5.9		.62	.37	.50
Short Employment Tests:						
Verbal	23.6	9.5			.10	.22
Numerical	46.6	17.2				.62
Clerical aptitude	33.3	11.0				

Table 3
Means, Standard Deviations, and Intercorrelations for Work Sample Measures

| | | | INTERCORRELATIONS | | | |
PART	$\overline{X}$	SD	B	C	D	TOTAL
A. Installing pulleys and belts	60.3	15.8	.25	.01	.16	.63
B. Disassembling and repairing a gearbox	62.9	12.9		.11	.27	.64
C. Installing and repairing a motor	71.1	11.2			.07	.42
D. Pressing a bushing into sprocket and reaming to fit a shaft	51.5	19.0				.70
Total	246.2	36.5				

RESULTS

Examination of Table 4 indicates that the mechanics' performance on the work sample measure was in all instances significantly and positively related to their foreman's evaluations of their work performance, whereas, none of the 15 validity coefficients computed for the paper-and-pencil tests reached acceptable levels of statistical significance. As noted above, the validity coefficients for the Test of Mechanical Comprehension are difficult to interpret due to its being employed in selecting the mechanics in the validation sample. Normative data describing the standard deviation for a similar group of mechanics who had not been preselected on this test variable were not available. Consequently, the validity coefficients could not be corrected for restriction of range on the predictor.

Table 4
Correlations Between Predictor and Criterion Variables

VARIABLE	USE OF TOOLS	ACCURACY OF WORK	OVERALL MECHANICAL ABILITY
Work sample[a]	.66**	.42*	.46**
Test of Mechanical Comprehension (Form AA)	.08	−.04	−.21
Wonderlic Personnel Test (Form D)	−.23	−.19	−.32
Short Employment Tests:			
Verbal	−.24	−.02	−.04
Numerical	.07	−.13	−.10
Clerical aptitude	−.03	−.19	−.09

[a]Performance on the work sample measure and mechanic work experience at this company were insignificantly correlated at −.27.
*$p < .05$.
**$p < .01$.

DISCUSSION

The approach developed here evolved from a need to solve a specific selection problem. The personnel decision was either to hire or reject. The applicants were being considered for only one position, and whether or not they were hired depended upon whether or not they possessed the appropriate work skills. It was assumed that the applicant population included persons with previous work experience that qualified them for the present job opening. A possible shortcoming of these findings is that the concurrent validities found for the experienced, employed mechanics may or may not accurately reflect predictive validity for less experienced applicants for mechanic work. This question can only be definitely answered with data obtained from predictive validation studies. However, as noted in Table 4, performance on the work sample measure and mechanic work experience were insignificantly correlated ($-.27$) for this sample.

The significant validity coefficients for the work sample measure support the Wernimont and Campbell (1968) assertions regarding the utility of the behavioral consistency approach. Furthermore, these positive findings suggest that the work sampling methodology developed here may provide useful guidelines for constructing work samples in other areas of personnel decision making.

For example, consider the situation where job applicants cannot be presumed to possess any of the prerequisite work skills for the job and, therefore, are first placed in training programs. Here, selection into training is usually based on general ability measures. This seems to be the correct strategy, for these instruments have been shown to work best for predicting training criteria in industrial settings (Brown & Ghiselli, 1952; Ghiselli, 1966). However, future decisions in the sequence concerning who should continue training or who should graduate from training may be more appropriately attacked within the behavioral consistency model. Fleishman's (1957, 1967) research on individual differences in learning is relevant here. This research has shown that ability requirements for task performance change over the training period. Particularly relevant is his finding that general ability measures predict performance during early stages of training, whereas, performance variance in the later stages is increasingly a function of habits and skills required in the task itself.

Consequently, the behavioral consistency approach has implications for sequential strategies of personnel decision making as well. Work sample measures for these decisions would be embedded in the training program. Whether the training is on the job or in the classroom, the goal would be to incorporate, early in training, exercises that maximize the opportunity for the trainees to exhibit behavior judged important for later job success. Thus, candidates with low probabilities of later success could be eliminated or rerouted to other training programs.

In summary, it seems that several aspects of personnel decision making could be affected by a strategy that used a behavioral consistency approach to determine a candidate's qualifications and/or deficiencies in hiring or promoting him.

REFERENCES

Bray, D. W., & Campbell, R. J. Selection of salesmen by means of an assessment center. *Journal of Applied Psychology*, 1968, 52, 36–41.

Bray, D. W., & Grant, D. L. The assessment center in the measurement of potential for business management. *Psychological Monographs*, 1966, 80 (17, Whole No. 625).

Brown, C. W., & Ghiselli, E. E. The relationship between the predictive power of aptitude tests for trainability and for job proficiency. *Journal of Applied Psychology*, 1952, **36**, 370–377.

Flanagan, J. C. The critical incident technique. *Psychological Bulletin*, 1954, **51**, 327–358.

Fleishman, E. A. A comparative study of aptitude patterns in unskilled and skilled psychomotor performance. *Journal of Applied Psychology*, 1957, **41**, 263–272.

Fleishman, E. A. Individual differences and motor learning. In R. M. Gagne (Ed.), *Learning and individual differences.* Columbus, Ohio: Merrill, 1967.

Ghiselli, E. E. *The validity of aptitude tests.* New York: Wiley, 1966.

Hinrichs, J. R. Comparison of "real life" assessments of management potential with situational exercises, paper-and-pencil ability tests, and personality inventories. *Journal of Applied Psychology*, 1969, **53**, 425–432.

Hinrichs, J. R. Ability correlates in learning a psychomotor task. *Journal of Applied Psychology*, 1970, **54**, 56–64.

Smith, P., & Kendall, L. N. Retranslation of expectations: An approach to the construction of unambiguous anchors for rating scales. *Journal of Applied Psychology*, 1963, **47**, 149–155.

Wernimont, P. F., & Campbell, J. Signs, samples, and criteria. *Journal of Applied Psychology*, 1968, **52**, 372–376.

FOR DISCUSSION AND REVIEW

1 What is a work sample? How is it related to the "behavioral consistency" approach?
2 Review the method and procedures of this study. What was done?
3 State the results of the study. How would you explain these results?
4 What implications does the use of work samples have for personnel selection?

Allen I. Kraut

New Frontiers for Assessment Centers

The assessment center method has become one of the most powerful techniques available for identification of management potential. During the last six years, its use has spread to hundreds of business and government organizations, and there are many reasons for believing that this trend represents much more than just a passing fad. But, at the same time, serious concerns about the nature and validity of this technique have been raised by many interested parties, reflecting a need for a set of minimal professional standards for users of assessment centers.

Chaired by Dr. Joseph L. Moses of American Telephone and Telegraph Company, a group of professionals actively engaged in the assessment center method recently developed and issued a set of guidelines entitled "Standards and Ethical

Reprinted by permission of the publisher from *Personnel* 53, no. 4 (July-August 1975), © 1975 by AMACOM, a division of American Management Associations.

Considerations for Assessment Center Operations." These guidelines were endorsed in 1975 by the Third International Congress on the Assessment Center Method. More recently, they were admitted into evidence in the first court test of assessment center reliability, in which the city of Omaha was upheld in its use of the method (Berry, Stokes, and Lant v. City of Omaha).

WHAT IS AN ASSESSMENT CENTER?

An assessment center can be described as a multimethod, multitrait, and even multimedia technique (see box, pages 292–293). Essentially, it is a series of individual and group exercises in which a number of candidates participate while being observed by several specially trained judges. The exercises are simulations of managerial tasks designed to test various managerial skills. They include written materials as well as behavioral simulations.

A typical example of an individual exercise is an "in-basket," which simulates the correspondence that managers may find on their desks after being away for a week or so. The items may be complex or simple, important or pedestrian, and candidates are assessed according to how well they handle them. For instance, do they set priorities? Do they delegate properly? Do they use good judgment in disposing of the items?

A "leaderless group discussion" is a typical example of a group exercise. In one popular version, a group of six participants is asked to boost a different candidate for promotion; at the same time, each is instructed to help the group as a whole arrive at a good decision. Thus managerial candidates can be judged on qualities such as oral communication and persuasiveness, sensitivity to others, interpersonal skills, and leadership in a group situation.

Most assessment centers have developed additional exercises and have tailored them to the needs of their own organizations. In addition, many programs use individual interviews and psychological tests. On the average, application of assessment procedures takes about two full days.

VARIETY OF USES

When one considers the variety of organizations in which assessment centers have been used and the variety of needs that this method can fulfill, it should not be surprising that it has been put to several different uses. Paramount among these has been the selection of people with greater ability for promotion to management. Similarly, it has been used to help identify people with management potential early in their careers.

In some organizations, however, assessment center results are not used simply for "go" or "no go" decisions but for the placement of individuals in positions that will use their talents and provide development essential for a meaningful, long-term career. In fact, some organizations use assessment programs exclusively for personal development in order to help people diagnose their competencies and to help improve them.

IS THE METHOD VALID?

The validity of the assessment center method has been the subject of a large number of studies. Of these, the monumental "Management Progress Study" conducted by Douglas Bray and his associates at AT&T is perhaps the best known and best documented. They assessed several hundred first-line managers using non-company psychologists, locked up the data (which was never seen by AT&T offi-

What an assessment center is . . .

The Task Force on Development of Assessment Center Standards has recommended that a program be considered an assessment center only if it meets the following minimum requirements:

1 Multiple assessment techniques must be used. At least one of these techniques must be a simulation. (A *simulation* is an exercise or technique designed to elicit behaviors related to dimensions of performance on the job by requiring the participant to respond behaviorally to situational stimuli. The stimuli present in a simulation parallel or resemble stimuli in the work situation.)

2 Multiple assessors must be used. These assessors must receive training prior to participating in a center.

3 Judgments resulting in an outcome (that is, recommendation for promotion, specific training, or development) must be based on pooling information from assessors and techniques.

4 An overall evaluation of behavior must be made by assessors at a separate time from observation of behavior.

5 Simulation exercises are used. These exercises are developed to tap a variety of predetermined behaviors and have been pretested prior to use to ensure that the techniques provide reliable, objective, and relevant behavioral information for the organization in question.

6 The dimensions, attributes, characteristics, or qualities evaluated by the assessment center are determined by an analysis of relevant job behaviors.

---

cials), and ten years later checked the accuracy of their predictions about who would reach middle-management levels. Sixty-four percent of those predicted to achieve this level actually did so, compared with only 32 percent of those who were predicted not to reach this level.

In a study of several hundred sales representatives of office equipment who attended an operational assessment center program, I (with Grant Scott) found that high-rated participants were three times as likely as low-rated participants to be promoted to higher levels of management during the following few years. Even more dramatic, we found that low-rated individuals who went on to management jobs were more likely to be demoted. During the several years following the assessment center program, one-third of the people were promoted into the first level of management. Of these, only 4 percent of the high-rated people were later demoted, compared with 20 percent of the low-rated people.

Further, recent research by James Huck and Douglas Bray indicates that the assessment center method predicts job performance in an equally valid way for members of different minority groups. In fact, AT&T recently entered into a consent decree with the federal government to use assessment centers as a means of judging management potential of women to facilitate their upgrading. Thus, government officials seem to have tacitly approved the use of assessment centers as a tool for affirmative action. And the results at AT&T have been very promising; of more than 1,000 female supervisors assessed in this way, 42 percent have been judged to have the potential for middle-management positions.

HIGHLY REGARDED

The validity of the assessment center method should come as no surprise when its advantages over a traditional promotion system are considered. For example, in a

7 The techniques used in the assessment center are designed to provide information that is used in evaluating the dimensions, attributes, or qualities previously determined.

... and is not

The following activities *do not* constitute an assessment center:

1 Panel interviews or a series of sequential interviews as the sole technique.
2 Reliance on a specific technique (regardless of whether a simulation or not) as the sole basis for evaluation.
3 Using only a test battery composed of a number of pencil and paper measures, regardless of whether judgments are made by a statistical or judgmental pooling of scores.
4 Single assessor assessment (measurement by one individual using a variety of techniques such as pencil and paper tests, interviews, personality measures, or simulations).
5 Use of several simulations with more than one assessor where there is no pooling of data (that is, each assessor prepares a report on performance in an exercise, and individual, unintegrated reports are used as the final product of the center).
6 A physical location labeled as an "assessment center" that does not conform to the requirements noted above.

typical assessment center program, multiple observers—chosen from managers two levels above the candidates being assessed—judge performance as opposed to a single, immediate superior. In addition, they assess candidates in a setting conducive to attentive observation, usually after receiving systematic training in what behaviors to observe in judging managerial potential (see box on page 295). Further, assessment center observers judge candidates in similar situations and use common standards to measure their performance in simulations of potential management jobs, not in their current jobs.

A recent review by William Dodd of the reactions of participants and observers to assessment center experiences shows that both groups were very positive about assessment centers. Both cited their virtue of appearing to tap management abilities in useful ways and of helping to select individuals for promotion. What's more, even those assessees who knew they had done poorly in an assessment center program shared these positive sentiments.

THE COST/BENEFIT ISSUE

Despite some of the obvious advantages and successes of the assessment center method, a number of questions still remain. One key question often raised concerns the value added by assessment center programs to existing selection and placement systems, or, in other words, the issue of costs versus benefits.

A general estimate has been made by Huck of the contribution of the assessment center approach compared with more traditional methods. By combining a series of independent studies, he estimated that the probability of selecting an above-average performer is 15 percent if individuals are chosen at random. Using traditional management-nomination techniques raises this probability to 35 percent. However, if a rating of "acceptable" in an assessment center program is combined with management recommendations, the probability of selecting an above-average performer increases to 76 percent, or over twice the probability using only traditional management-nomination techniques.

To some people, the cost of assessment center programs seems expensive. A figure commonly mentioned is about $500 per participant. Actually, most of this cost is made up of expenses for travel and room and board. Naturally, these costs can vary greatly, but in general, it's safe to say that the cost of an assessment center program is about the same as the cost of a management development program run under similar circumstances.

Costs are relative to the value of the information and the use to which such information is put. They must be weighed against the consequences of a poor decision. The information from an assessment center will be relatively more valuable when the performance of the person in a particular job really makes a big difference and when an ample number of candidates for such a job are available. As many executives recognize, merely picking the best salesman to be a sales manager may result simultaneously in the loss of a good salesman and the gain of a poor manager. And in some circumstances, where law or custom forbid, the removal of an inadequate manager may be very difficult and costly.

Still, it is highly desirable to get some hard figures on the amount of savings that can be achieved with the use of this method. One estimate, made by Logan Cheek in the selection of sales managers at Xerox, indicated that a net benefit of more than $4.9 million could be achieved for a cost of about $340,000. The exact cost/benefit ratio will, of course, vary with each situation.

IMPACT ON THE REST OF THE SYSTEM

An assessment center cannot be established in a vacuum. It becomes part of the organizational system for dealing with the identification and development of management talent. In planning and implementing an assessment center program, other parts of the system have to be considered.

Top management must be committed to the assessment center concept in order for it to succeed. Part of the plan for gaining an intelligent commitment should include an understanding of where a program will fit into and supplement the existing promotion system. Its impact on management-replacement-planning systems, existing appraisal programs, current methods of using promotion lists or promotion review boards, and related areas must be considered.

One of the key systems to consider is the motivational system of employees and existing managers. For example, if it is important for an organization to honor effective performance in the current job or to consider seniority, these requirements should be built into the minimum qualifications necessary to attend an assessment center. If it is important to maintain management responsibility in selecting and promoting individuals, the use of assessment center results should be monitored to ensure that these data are used in decision making merely as an additional input to managers' considerations of a subordinate's previous performance, experience, and education; qualifications of other candidates; and the needs of the particular opening.

The assessment center approach is not for all organizations. It may not be acceptable for philosophical reasons or for potential value. In some situations, such as conditions of rapid growth or geographical dispersion, assessment center data will be of greater value than in situations where these conditions are not present.

Minimum training requirements for assessors*

Assessors should receive sufficient training to enable them to evaluate intelligently the behaviors measurd in the center. "Sufficient training" will vary from organization to organization and is a function of many factors including:

- The length of time an individual serves as an assessor.
- The frequency of individual participation as an assessor.
- The amount of time devoted to assessor training.
- The qualifications and expertise of the assessment center trainer.
- The assessment experience of other staff members.
- The use of professionals (licensed or certified psychologists) as assessors.

Whatever the approach to assessor training, the essential goal is attaining accurate assessor judgments. A variety of training approaches can be used, as long as it can be demonstrated that accurate assessor judgments are obtained. The following minimum training is required:

- Knowledge of the assessment techniques used. This may include, for example, the kinds of behaviors elicited by each technique, relevant dimensions to be observed, expected or typical behaviors, and examples or samples of actual behaviors.
- Knowledge of the assessment dimensions. This may include, for example, definitions of dimensions, relationship to other dimensions, relationship to job performance, and examples of effective and ineffective performance.
- Knowledge of behavior observation and recording, including the forms used by the center.
- Knowledge of evaluation and rating procedures, including how data are integrated by the assessment center staff.
- Knowledge of assessment policies and practices of the organization, including restrictions on how assessment data are to be used.
- Knowledge of feedback procedures where appropriate.

Recommended by the Task Force on Development of Assessment Center Standards. Copies of the standards are available from Dr. Joseph L. Moses, manager-personnel research, AT&T, 195 Broadway, New York, New York 10007.

SOME POTENTIAL PITFALLS

In all of the above applications, we must remember that the assessment center method represents a selection technique and, therefore, we should be concerned about its actual and demonstrated validity. Like other selection techniques, this one cannot be simply taken over and applied unthinkingly in another situation, with the hope that it will succeed as it has elsewhere. For this program to work, it is necessary to develop a clear understanding of the job requirements for the position to which we are predicting, to develop or adapt the exercises that will tap the required abilities, to ensure that we measure these qualities reliably through rigorous application of the technique, and to check the success of our predictions to determine the degree of validity the technique has in each particular situation.

It is equally important to check the reaction of participants and observers in each program and the various parts of the program. This can be done most simply by standardized questionnaires. In beginning programs, it may be more valuable to get this feedback through open-ended personal interviews.

A VALUABLE ADDITION

My experience in introducing the assessment center method in several countries outside the United States indicates that this technique can be used successfully in many other cultures. Nevertheless, an assessment center must be tailored to each culture, to each organization, and to each job family for which it is being used. This is necessary not only for providing face validity but also for improving the real accuracy of predictions.

The assessment center technique seems to have a number of advantages, logically and empirically, over other forms of evaluation such as paper and pencil tests and individual clinical evaluations. If it is combined with ongoing programs of recruitment, replacement, development, and coaching of job performance, it is likely to be a valuable addition to our techniques for identifying and selecting management potential. The increased use of this technique and the diversity of applications being developed are evidence that the assessment center technique is here to stay, and we should make the most of it.

FOR DISCUSSION AND REVIEW

1 Exactly what is an assessment center?
2 Why are assessment centers useful in selection, as opposed to more traditional techniques?
3 How is the validity of an assessment center checked? What has been the record of assessment centers regarding validity?
4 What criteria should be used to select assessors?
5 For what types and sizes of organizations would assessment centers seem to be most useful?

F. PERSONNEL AND PSYCHOLOGICAL TESTING

David E. Robertson

Update on Testing and Equal Opportunity

About two years ago, an article appeared in this journal outlining some of the critical current problems concerning employment testing and alleged discrimination (*Personnel Journal*, January 1975).[1] The issues discussed in this article apparently struck a responsive chord with practitioners and interested observers, because the author has received correspondence concerning the article from scores of readers across the nation and two foreign countries. A follow-up report seems appropriate to discuss a number of newly emerging questions raised by readers, and to point out some apparent changes in judicial interpretations that have developed in this rapidly changing field in recent months. Two communications received by the author provide considerable reassurance that there are many people in the profession trying to keep their testing programs up to date and lawful, in spite of all the confusion that characterizes the field today. The situation hasn't improved much in the past two years and practitioners are still struggling with a complex assortment of guidelines and court rulings that are difficult to interpret.

For those who may not be familiar with the employment testing controversy, a brief review is in order. Title VII of the 1964 Civil Rights Act forbids discrimination in employment, even though section 703 (h) of this act specifically approves the use of "professionally developed ability tests," provided that such tests are not "designed, intended, or used to discriminate because of race, color, religion, sex, or national origin."[2] In order to properly enforce this section, the Equal Employment Opportunity Commission found it necessary to develop a set of guidelines describing how employment tests can be discriminatory and explaining in detail how tests should be validated to prove that scores are related to job success.[3] Shortly after these guidelines were issued, the Supreme Court, in the landmark case of Griggs v. Duke Power,[4] established a legal framework for employment testing bias and cited with approval the psychometric procedures contained in the guidelines. In the Griggs case, the Court chose to ignore that portion of 703(h) referring to the employer's intent or motivation, and specified that the controlling factor governing lawfulness was the effect or impact of an employment practice without regard to whether or not the employer intended to discriminate.[5] In a recent decision, the Supreme Court departed from this position, as we shall see.

The legal status of employment tests has become so complicated now that many employers have taken the easy road out and suspended their use even before the tests have been challenged. Those who continue testing have had to become familiar with not only the guidelines issued by the EEOC and, in some cases, the Office of Federal Contract Compliance (OFCC),[6] but also the latest EEOC decisions and court rulings. Of the various forces affecting employment testing in the past few years, court rulings have proven to be the least predictable.

Five issues will be discussed in this article: 1. employer motivation, 2. criteria selection, 3. content and construct validity, 4. differential validity, and 5. burden of proof. These topics were selected either because practitioners have raised questions

From *Personnel Journal* 56, no. 3 (March 1977). Copyright © March 1977 by *Personnel Journal*. Reprinted by permission.

about them or because they were pivotal issues in federal district or Supreme Court cases that have been decided in the last five years since Griggs.

EMPLOYER MOTIVATION

Until very recently, the cases being decided in the courts were consistent with the Griggs decision. Any employment practice with a discriminatory effect was judged unlawful, regardless of whether or not the employer intended to discriminate. A few months ago, however, the Supreme Court, in a 7-2 decision, took the first clear departure from Griggs by giving weight to the employer's motives in the Washington vs. Davis case. This case involved alleged discrimination resulting from use of an employment test in the selection of police recruits for the District of Columbia.[7] Discrimination was alleged because 57% of all black applicants had failed an employment test, as compared with only 13% of the white applicants. The court held that the test is not unlawful merely because it places a substantially disproportionate burden on members of a particular race. A "racially discriminatory purpose" had not been proven, and the employers affirmative efforts to recruit black officers "negated any inference that the defendent discriminated on the basis of race, notwithstanding the disproportionate impact of the test on Negro applicants."[8]

What made this case different and caused the reversal? There seem to be at least two factors. First, the class action suit was technically filed alleging discrimination against blacks in violation of the Due Process clause of the Fifth Amendment, rather than the Civil Rights Act of 1964, because public employees were not brought under Title VII of the 1964 Act until 1972 and the case had been initiated several years earlier.[9] It appears that the court has ruled that conduct which is presumably forbidden by Title VII is not necessarily prohibited by the Constitution, and in the future it is uncertain as to whether this precedent will breathe new life into the importance of employer intent in other civil rights cases.[10]

The second factor that makes this case different from preceding cases is that the employment test in question was Test No. 21, a widely used U.S. Civil Service Commission Test. Had the Supreme Court declared that Test 21 unfairly discriminates and enjoined its further use, a wedge would have been driven into the entire Civil Service Testing Program. Test 21 passed the Griggs standard of being "job related" by successfully predicting the applicants' achievement in Recruit School, even though it had been determined that this test would not necessarily predict success once a patrolman is on the job. This brings us to a second troublesome issue that seems to cloud the testing scene, the issue of criteria selection.

CRITERIA SELECTION

The Griggs rule that a test must be "job related" means that the test scores must not only correlate with some criterion or criteria measures of job success but that the criteria measures themselves must be important delineators of job success.

What is job success and how is it measured? Let's take the job of a law enforcement officer. A policeman must learn and understand a myriad of regulations, statutes, and judicial rulings and be able to apply them. He must have sufficient verbal ability to prepare clear and concise reports and be sufficiently articulate when testifying in court. The officer's competency is governed by much more than the ability to swing a nightstick. The job behaviors required for successful performance are thus very complex, yet the criteria that psychologists will ordinarily use, criteria such as supervisors' ratings, salary, absenteeism, turnover, etc.,[11] are themselves imperfect measures of success and usually rather simple composites of standard data whose main virtue is that it is readily available. While the relationship between the test scores or predictors and the criterion measure is defined precisely by the EEOC Guidelines, and is measured statistically, the relationship between the criterion measures and the ultimate criterion (job success) is a subjective or qualitative judgement and is therefore open to interpretation by laymen.

Until recent months, tests that merely predict training success as opposed to job success were not considered properly validated.[12] In the selection of police recruits, for example, employers had not been successful in suggesting achievement in Recruit School as an appropriate substitute for on-the-job behavioral criteria.[13] All of this may be changing, however, if the previously cited Washington v. Davis case becomes a viable precedent for Title VII litigation. In the Davis decision, the Supreme Court agreed with the Federal District Judge that "a positive relationship between the test and training course performance was sufficient to validate the former, wholly aside from its possible relationship to actual performance as a police officer."[14] As reasoning for the relaxation of standards, the Supreme Court pointed out that Civil Service Commission instructions explicitly suggest "success in training" as an appropriate criterion. Practitioners would be well advised to move with caution in this area until the applicable administrative and judicial policies are determined. The complex and sometimes subjective nature of criteria construction is paralleled by another issue requiring qualitative or subjective judgment, the issue of whether content and construct validity can be appropriately substituted for predictive validity.

CONSTRUCT AND CONTENT VALIDITY

The EEOC and the Courts have, in general, permitted either "content" or "construct" validity to be used in some instances as a permissible substitute for "empirical" validity, but only where it was allegedly not feasible or practical to prove empirical validity.[15] A test is said to have "construct" validity when it has proven to measure specific theoretical constructs or traits such as intelligence, mechanical aptitude, or clerical aptitude which are necessary for successful job performance.[16] A test is said to have "content validity" if it contains a representative sampling of tasks which closely approximate the tasks to be performed on the job, such as a typing speed test for secretarial candidates.[17]

The problem here is that construct validity involves the subjective evaluation of more than a single validity co-efficient and content validity is not even expressed statistically, so it comes down to a qualitative judgment as to whether or not a test has this characteristic. While experienced psychometricians can deal with the complexities of these determinations, there has been little hesitation on the part of EEOC examiners and judges to plunge into the field and make their own determinations. The untrained person is likely to decide subjectively whether test content seems reasonable, and there have surely been cases where tests were evaluated on nothing more than "face validity."[18] In one recent instance, for example, a judge attached an entire test to his dissenting opinion as an exhibit, apparently in support of his argument that the test was job related.[19] In addition to the various types of validity examined in this section, there is one other type which deserves special attention, mainly because its existence tends to create more problems than it solves. We are referring to differential validity.

DIFFERENTIAL VALIDITY

The problem of differential validity has been recognized by drafters of the EEOC Guidelines, but there are still apparently great differences of opinion as to whether or not the solutions specified in the Guidelines are appropriate. A test is said to be differentially valid if it does not predict equally well for different subgroups of the same population.[20] The EEOC Guidelines recognize this possibility by providing that where "technically feasible," employment tests should be validated separately for each cultural subgroup.[21] It is not uncommon for white applicants to score higher than minority applicants on an employment test, even though there may be no differences among these subgroups on criteria performance. Psychologists are not concerned with differences among subgroups in test performance unless such scores do not equally predict criteria performance.

If a test underpredicts or overpredicts for particular groups, does this mean an employer is obliged to use a double standard in grading tests and establish two or more sets of cutoff scores so that the tests will be equally predictive among various cultural subgroups? From a technical standpoint, this would seem to be the case, but certainly Title VII would prohibit such dual standards.[22] As a practical matter, it is unlikely that the EEOC and the courts would be tolerant of an employer who would require blacks to achieve higher scores than whites, yet there are tests that consistently underpredict job performance for whites,[23] tests that would theoretically require either upward adjustment of scores or lowering of cutoffs for this group.

This potentially very serious problem has not been resolved as yet, partly because in recent years a number of well respected psychologists have maintained that there is no such thing as differential validity or that proper criterion selection virtually eliminates the problem. Bray and Moses, for example, write that "as a general rule most studies showing lack of differential validity have used better than average criterion measures, while most of the studies supporting differential validity rely on subjective, poorly determined rating criteria."[24] Recent research seems to suggest that differential validity is mostly an illusion,[25] yet the EEOC Guidelines still call for separate validation of each subgroup. If the practitioner follows the EEOC guidelines and validates separately for each subgroup, it is likely that occasional cases of differential validity will continue to arise, despite the claims of some critics that any test that is valid for the whole will be valid for all subgroups. While the issue of differential validity continues to boil, the related issue of burden of proof seems to be at least partly settled.

BURDEN OF PROOF

In alleged discrimination cases, is it the employee's obligation to prove that he was discriminated against or is it the employer's obligation to show that his employment practices are *not* discriminatory? This seems like such a fundamental question, yet there is apparently still some misunderstanding concerning these basic responsibilities. The answer to the question depends partially on the timing. At the outset, it is clear that the initial burden to show a discriminatory effect is on the party challenging the job qualification.[26] To prove that a test unfairly discriminates against a minority group typically requires the challenging party to produce comparative percentage pass rate figures that are clearly disproportionate. In one case in the south, for example, it was shown that 58% of the whites obtained passing scores on a particular test, as compared with only 6% of the blacks.[27] Ordinarily the differences are not so extreme, and in some cases blacks have outscored whites, but the general pattern of lower scores by educationally or culturally disadvantaged groups is well recognized. There are no specific minimums necessary to initiate action, only enough differences so that minority group members are being disqualified at a "substantially higher rate than other groups of applicants."[28] Proof of the discriminatory impact of an employment test by showing a disparity in pass-fail rates or by showing disparity between the percentage of minority employees in the organization and the percentage of minority members in the community is legally sufficient cause to shift the burden of proving that the test is "job related" to the employer.[29] At this point, the heavy burden of showing this relationship is transferred to the employer and it is his obligation to prove that the employment test scores bear a demonstrable relationship to successful job performance. In other words, the employer must provide validation study data showing that the disproportionate impact, which the challenging party has demonstrated produces differences in test performance, will also result in corresponding differences in criteria performance and that the criteria measures selected are closely related to those factors which are truly important to job success. After the charge has been made that the test discriminates, it is the employer's obligation to show that the test discriminates fairly, that is, on the basis of merit rather than race, color, religion, sex or national origin.

CONCLUSIONS

This concludes a brief review of some of the vexing issues arising from the current controversy in employment testing. The situation has not improved much recently, but there are some hopeful signs on the horizon. For those who believe that the institution of employment testing is worth preserving, it is encouraging that in a number of recent cases, the courts have upheld tests by not enjoining their use, even in some instances where the employer's actions were found to be discriminatory.[30] In at least one recent instance, the Court spoke favorably of an employer's efforts through testing to "modestly upgrade the communicative abilities of its employees rather than to be satisfied with some lower level competence."[31] In the same case, the employer's motivation or intent was taken into account in determining the legality of allegedly discriminatory testing practices. It seems eminently reasonable to this author that an employer's conduct be judged in its totality rather than as isolated specific actions without context or purpose.[32] Finally, we can find encouragement in that, while quota systems are still being imposed as solutions for some cases of alleged testing discrimination, courts seem to be imposing such systems less often and there are even occasional recent instances where quotas designed to eliminate discrimination have themselves been judged to be discriminatory.[33] Perhaps it will be recognized soon that equality of opportunity in employment was the intent and purpose of Title VII and not equality of result. It is only through truly "colorblind" selection procedures founded on the principle of merit that we can achieve this desired goal.

REFERENCES

1 David E. Robertson, "Employment Testing and Discrimination," *Personnel Journal,* Vol. 54, No. 1 (January 1975), pp. 18–21.
2 Civil Rights Act of 1964, Title VII, Section 703(h). This section was proposed by Senator Tower to guarantee that tests with a legitimate business purpose would not be ruled unlawful as they had been in another recently concluded case.
3 Equal Employment Opportunity Commission, "Guidelines on Employee Selection Procedures," 35 Fed. Reg. 1233 (29 C.F.R. Sec. 1607.1–1607.14 1971). This is a more detailed version than the original guidelines which were published as an EEOC announcement on August 24, 1966.

4 Griggs v. Duke Power Co., 401 U.S. 424 (1971), or see *Employment Practices Decisions*, Volume 3, Chicago, Commerce Clearing House, Inc., 1971, pp. 6430–6436.

5 The opinion was advanced that "good intent or absence of discriminatory intent does not redeem employment procedures or testing mechanisms that operate as 'built-in headwinds' for minority groups." See *U.S. Supreme Court Reports*, 28 L Ed 2d 160 (1971).

6 Government contractors are required to conform with guidelines issued by the Office of Federal Contract Compliance (OFCC), "Testing and Selecting Employees by Government Contractors," 41 C.F.R. 60-3.

7 Washington v. Davis 96 S. Ct. 2040 (1976). This decision reversed the judgment of the Court of Appeals.

8 Washington v. Davis 96 S. Ct. at 2042 (1976). Lower courts had been less favorably disposed toward the employer's efforts. Noting that the employer "quite commendably" had increased the proportion of black officers, the District Court advanced the opinion that appropriate selection procedures would have resulted in even a greater improvement in the percentage. Davis v. Washington 512 F.2d 961 (1975).

9 In discussing the applicable legal standard the Federal District Court pointed out in Davis v. Washington 512 F.2d 958 n.2 (1975) that, "The many decisions disposing of employment discrimination claims on constitutional grounds have made no distinction between the constitutional standard and the statutory standard under Title VII, e.g., Davis v. Washington, 352 F. Supp. at 191; Bridgeport Guardians v. Civil Serv. Commn, 482 F.2d 1333 (3d Cir. 1972); Fowler v. Schwarzwalder, 351 F. Supp. 721 (D Minn. 1972). The Supreme Court, however, ruled that only the constitutional standard should be applied. Davis v. Washington 96 S. Ct. 2040 (1976).

10 Justice Brennan and Justice Marshall, in their dissenting opinion, warned that, "Today's result will prove particularly unfortunate if it is extended to govern Title VII cases," 96 S. Ct. at 2062 (1976).

11 The most frequently used criterion is "supervisor's ratings," according to one research study. David E. Robertson, "The Validation of Personnel Employment Tests, "*Marquette Business Review*, Vol. 16, No. 3 (Fall 1972), p. 123.

12 In many cases the apparent value of tests in predicting training success is spurious in that training success is measured by scores on other paper and pencil tests. In order for tests to be meaningfully evaluated, training success must be measured by some sort of performance evaluation which demonstrates whether high scorers on the original test are actually able to learn more quickly or more effectively to perform the job or jobs in question, rather than simply to score well on a subsequent test." George Cooper and Richard B. Sobol "Seniority and Testing Under Fair Employment Laws: A General Approach to Objective Criteria of Hiring and Promotion," *Harvard Law Review*, Vol. 82, No. 8, June 1969, p. 1649.

13 See, for example, Pennsylvania v. O'Neill, 348 F. Supp 1084; Officers for Justice v. Civil Serv. Common, 371 F. Supp. 1337; Smith v. East Cleveland, 363 F. Supp. 1148.

14 Washington v. Davis 96 S. Ct. at 2053 (1976).

15 We hold that construct validity may be considered only after a showing that it is unfeasible to undertake proof of empirical validity." Douglas v. Hampton 512 F.2d. at 986. The EEOC guidelines at section 1607.5 (a) (1971) also refer to this requirement.

16 Anne Anastasi, *Psychological Testing* 3d ed., New York; Macmillan, 1968, p. 114.

17 Anastasi, op. cit., p. 100.

18 A test can have "face validity" and *appear* to be a valid measure of job content to the untrained observer without properly sampling the critical skills. Content and face validity are frequently confused.

19 Davis v. Washington 512 F.2d at 967 (1975).

20 For an extended discussion of the legal implications of differential validity, see Hugh Steven Wilson, "A Second Look at Griggs v. Duke Power Company: Ruminations on Job Testing, Discrimination, and the Role of the Federal Courts," *Virginia Law Review*, Vol. 58 (1972), pp. 869–871. The term "differential validity" in this context refers to subgroup differences in validity coefficients, not the desirable differences in correlations between test scores and separate criteria to be predicted.

21 It is often not "technically feasible" because of insufficient numbers of minority members for statistical analysis. EEOC Guidelines, Section 1607.4, 35 Fed. Reg. 1233, 1971.

22 Wilson, op. cit., p. 870.

23 Grand and Bray, "Validation of Employment Tests for Telephone Company Installation and Repair Occupations," *Journal of Applied Psychology*, Vol. 54 (1970), p. 7.

24 D. W. Bray and J. L. Moses, "Personnel Selection," *Annual Review of Psychology*, Vol. 23 (1972), pp. 545–76.

25 F. L. Schmidt, J. C. Bernen, and J. E. Hunter, "Racial Difference in Validity of Employment Tests: Reality or Illusion?" *Journal of Applied Psychology*, Vol. 58 (1973), pp. 5–9.

26 Coopersmith v. Roudebush 517 F.2d at 822 (1975); Shack v. Southworth 521 F.2d at 53 (1975).

27 Cooper and Sobol, op. cit., p. 1641.

28 Coopersmith v. Roudebush 517 F.2d at 822 (1975). For an extended discussion of the necessity for statistical proof in alleging that employment practices are discriminatory, see Alfred W. Blumrosen, "Strangers in Paradise: Griggs v. Duke Power Co., and the Concept of Employment Discrimination," *Michigan Law Review*, Vol. 71, No. 1, November 1972, pp. 59–110 at p. 91.

29 Davis v. Washington 512 F.2d at 957 (1975). Note that this opinion suggests that *either* contingency is sufficient to shift the burden of proof.

30 See, for example, NAACP v. Allen 340 F. Supp. at 706 (1972); Stevenson v. International Paper Company 516 F.2d at 116 (1975).

31 Washington v. Davis 96 S. Ct. at 2050 (1976).

32 For an extended discussion of the intent to discriminate, see Philip Ash, "The Implications of the Civil Rights Act of 1964 for Psychological Assessment in Industry," *American Psychologist*, Vol. 21, No. 8 (August, 1966), pp. 797–803.

33 See, for example, a recent ruling of the Appellate Division of the Superior Court in Trenton, New Jersey that a quota system imposed by the state Division of Civil Rights on the Montclair Fire Department was discriminatory. The decision issued on May 13, 1975 by Judge Joseph Halpern noted that a quota system as a remedy "piles discrimination on top of discrimination."

FOR DISCUSSION AND REVIEW

1 Explain the court case that signaled a departure from the Griggs decision and identify this departure.
2 How does criteria selection influence the legality of tests? What is the rationale behind using success in training as a criteria?
3 Define differential validity. What is the serious practical consequence of requiring higher scores for blacks?
4 When is the burden of proof transferred to the employer in a testing discrimination case?

INTERVIEW WITH JAMES C. SHARF

Since 1974, James C. Sharf has been Staff Psychologist for the Office of Research, Equal Employment Opportunity Commission. In the spring of 1977, he was appointed to the President's Reorganization Project, Reorganization of the Executive Office.

Mr. Sharf received a B.S. from Dickinson College in 1965 and an M.S. and Ph.D. in organizational psychology from the University of Tennessee in 1970. He was assistant director of placement at the University of Tennessee from 1967 to 1970, and was later an assistant professor and adjunct professor in the School of Business Administration, American University. Mr. Sharf is a member of the American Psychological Association, American Society for Training and Development, and American Association for the Advancement of Science.

Q In what way are civil-rights laws and continuing litigation likely to impact on the personnel manager of the future?

A It would be well to remember that implicit in any personnel decision is the notion of predicting performance—that is, prediction of how an individual will perform in a new situation. It is my belief that the impact of Title VII will be to remove this prediction from an implicit "I know one when I see one" type of hunch to more rigorous efforts to document that standards used in making personnel decisions are in fact job related.

Q What are the major problems of defending an alleged discriminatory selection procedure in court?

A While the psychologist doing validation research takes individual differences in skills and abilities as a given, the plaintiff's attorney in challenging differences in selection rates on the basis of race and/or sex assumes that all applicants are equally qualified for all jobs. As a consequence of *Griggs,* the industrial psychologist who defends a selection procedure in litigation is placed in the position of demonstrating two things. First, it must be established to the satisfaction of the court that the selection procedure is job related. Secondly, it must be demonstrated that the abilities measured by the job-related selection procedure are not equally distributed in the various applicant populations. This tension between psychology and the law in a large measure defines one of the major dimensions of the civil-rights fair-employment dilemma.

Q How have employers dealt with this dilemma in the past?

A One way employers have dealt with this dilemma is to do away with objective selection procedures altogether. The introduction of subjective procedures such as the interview, however, virtually eliminate the possibility of making valid selection decisions much less of demonstrating that an alleged discriminatory selection procedure is in fact job related.

Another alternative has been to use hiring "goals" in which comparable hiring rates for minorities, nonminorities, males and females are juggled. The notion that equal employment in terms of the numbers of various classes is actually a popular misconception. It stems partly from the willingness of the courts to remedy past discrimination by applying numerical "goals" as part of the relief afforded members of the affected class. For example, if an employer's hiring rates and work force have reflected parity with the labor market in terms of the number of minorities and nonminorities, males and females, the employer generally has not had to answer to charges of reverse discrimination.

Q What will the impact of "reverse discrimination" cases such as *Bakke* have?

A Even though the case was brought under the Equal Protection clause of the Fourteenth Amendment (and not Title VII), a reverse discrimination case such as *Bakke*, which involves the selection of academically less-qualified candidates on racial grounds, could dampen the popularity of using numerical hiring goals. In addition, the issue of job performance rather than group preference may assume new importance as a result of such cases. Ever since the Supreme Court chose to declare the similar *DeFunis* case moot, the clock on voluntary affirmative action has been ticking.

Q What is the controversy surrounding the *Bakke* case?

A There are several reasons why the *Bakke* case is particularly vexing to the civil-rights community and why the University of California Regents have been criticized for appealing this case. First, the University did not challenge Bakke's contention that race was considered as part of its special admissions program. Secondly, there had been no prior history of discrimination by the University. Neither did the University claim that it had practiced prior discrimination in its admissions programs nor had either of the lower courts found prior discrimination in the University's admissions practices. Thirdly, the University acknowledged that Bakke was better qualified than those minorities admitted both years Bakke applied, but nevertheless rejected him. In short, there seemed to be no legal basis for the University's special admissions effort other than the recognition that the use of traditional selection standards qualified all too few minorities. Without a prior history of discrimination established in a legal proceding resulting in the award of numerical goals as relief, there was no legally defensible basis for a voluntarily assumed affirmative-action effort. The issue comes down to whether the University of California can legally justify a preferential system of admissions which uses race as one of the admissions standards.

Q What are the prospects for personnel management?

A The long-range goal of meeting an employer's business and fair employment objectives will not be met simply by adjusting selection rates, but by improving the job relatedness of standards used in making personnel decisions. This means that employers should expect to use more objective employment selection procedures and to perform validation studies showing that such objective standards are job related, thereby meeting their own business necessity of hiring those who can perform the job, as well as complying with the objectives of the fair employment laws. Obviously, the serious student of contemporary personnel practices who is knowledgeable of both case law and job-relatedness standards will increasingly be a valuable asset to any organization.

Training and Development of Human Resources

INTRODUCTION

Even if effective selection decisions are made, persons entering an organization seldom have all the necessary skills, abilities, and knowledge to perform optimally. Thus, a training and development program is mandatory, if not to improve present job performance, then to ready workers for added responsibility in the future. Section Five is divided into four parts: assessing training needs, designing training programs, organization and career development, and evaluating training programs. These are, sequentially, the activities recommended to improve performance through training.

Once the needs of trainees are identified through the types of analyses Bass and Vaughan describe, the program can be designed to meet these needs. Several methods and techniques are available and Hinrichs's framework is useful for sorting them out.

Organizational development (OD) and career development are two areas within the general purview of training which receive considerable attention today. Huse has provided a framework to catalogue and thereby clarify the basic OD techniques. However, as Huse notes, behind each technique is a set of values that argues for its use. The controversy in the OD field often rests on the divergent values of its practitioners and hence their disagreement as to the utility of various approaches. The complexities associated with implementing an OD technique, coupled with the innumerable variables that could influence its effectiveness, would seem to indicate that any one of the techniques could be useful, given the proper conditions. Thus, diagnosis of the situation is crucial.

Hall and Hall point out the major recent advances in career development, a field combining vocational guidance and psychology with training and development. In today's organizations, characterized often by a high amount of competition, the managing of one's career is vital to obtain certain individual objectives.

Finally, Goldstein reviews the training evaluation process and discusses the design of evaluation research. This aspect of training is often neglected, yet data from a rigorous evaluation are essential in order to redesign programs or substitute others for them if they are judged to be faulty.

A. ASSESSMENT OF TRAINING NEEDS

B. M. Bass

J. A. Vaughan

Assessing Training Needs

"Bill," said a company president to his training director, "I ran into Jack Phillips at the club yesterday and he told me all the salesmen at his firm have been getting the Dartaway Sales Training Program. He thinks it does them a lot of good. Maybe we ought to try the Dartaway Program in one of our divisions to see how our men like it."

In this offhand way many training programs get their start in a company. But whether the training is necessary and, if so, what kind are matters that need much more systematic and careful analysis.

In any assessment of training needs, one seeks the answers to these two questions: *Who, if anyone, needs training? What training do they need?* The questions themselves are simple, but obtaining good answers to them is one of the most difficult and most important aspects of the total training process. There are at least three kinds of analyses that should be performed in seeking the answers: organization analysis, job analysis, and manpower analysis (McGehee and Thayer, 88).

ORGANIZATION ANALYSIS

Organization analysis involves a study of the entire organization—its objectives, its resources, the allocation of these resources in meeting its objectives, and the total socioeconomic-technological environment within which the organization exists. This kind of analysis helps answer the question of what is to be taught in terms of broad content areas. In so doing, it largely determines the training philosophy for the entire organization.

The first step in an organization analysis for training purposes is to obtain a clear understanding of both short- and long-term goals. Long-term objectives need to be established in broad areas for the entire company; next, specific goals and strategies should be stated for the various components of the company (divisions, departments, sections—down to the lowest subgroup) as a means of achieving these broad objectives. Because of the constantly changing nature of the business environment, this process is continuous. Objectives must be regularly reviewed and modified in accordance with this changing environment. Short-term goals and strategies may change radically from one review to the next; but if the long-term goals are the result of careful thought, they will help stabilize company training plans, since they will change much less rapidly than will short-term goals. One of the major limiting factors of this approach to date has been the seeming inability to translate many general objectives into more detailed and specific operational targets.

A second step in an organization analysis is an inventory of the company's attempts to meet goals through its human and physical production resources.

Various efficiency indexes can be derived to determine the adequacy of specific work flows, so that a detailed examination of the inputs and outputs of the total system is possible. The focus, of course, will be on the human contribution to these indexes. Although in the past the human inputs were measured—or, rather estimated—in terms of physical exertion, it is now clear that the psychological costs of the job as reflected in individual feelings, beliefs, emotions, and attitudes must be included as more precise measuring factors. Automation and information technology have already brought about significant changes in the nature of these costs in many companies, as employees now find themselves having significant interactions with *machines* as well as other men. Managers relating to a computer may present a completely different kind of problem from that faced by the worker relating to an automated (controlled) production line.

The final step is an examination of the business enterprise as an organization operating in a distinct social, economic, and political environment, which it can usually influence to some extent, but not control. A business enterprise is more than a collection of buildings, physical equipment, materials, and people. It is a social organization and, as such, involves the employees' awareness of belonging to an identifiable group, their dynamic interaction among members of the group, and the nonmembers' perception of the group as a group. Thus, an organization is said to have a certain "climate," which influences and in turn is influenced by the total environment of the organization.

The climate of an organization is, in essence, a reflection of its members' attitudes toward various aspects of work, supervision, company procedures, goals and objectives, and membership in the organization. These attitudes are *learned*; they are a product of the members' experiences both within and outside the work environment. Thus, a training program may be designed to effect certain changes in the organizational climate; however, the change process is a two-way street, since the prevailing organizational climate—especially the attitudes towards employee development—will largely determine the training program's success.

For instance, in management development, training is primarily considered a line responsibility. A man's boss is his main teacher. The staff expert can only help and advise (Haire, 49). Yet, operational demands too often leave line management little time to do a good job of developing subordinates. Moreover, the subordinate may be superior in every respect to the man who is supposed to be developing him. Or the boss may be insecure and afraid to develop subordinates. Actually, few managers are in a position to observe their subordinates as they perform their jobs with the result that they are seldom able to coach them effectively (Taylor, 121).

Numerous studies show that lack of management support for the objectives of a particular training program reduces or eliminates its potential for serving the company. For example, management development is likely to be given short shrift if a company's board of directors is more interested in maintaining current dividends than in holding a top position in the industry twenty years hence (Taylor, 121). In the same way, formal training is likely to be ineffective if the course work runs counter to management ideology. In one study, foremen from two divisions of a large company were given supervisory training. In the first division, employees, after their training, showed increased satisfaction with their supervisors. Three foremen from this division said, in turn, that they had received considerable encouragement from their bosses. In the second division, employees expressed a greater dissatisfaction with their foremen following training; these supervisors reported that they had not been encouraged by their bosses (Hariton, 52).

At International Harvester, foremen who received two weeks of training designed to increase consideration for their subordinates all showed improvement in
attitudes toward consideration immediately following the training program. However, six months later, only those foremen who believed their bosses wanted them
to be considerate maintained their new attitudes towards their staffs (Fleishman,
38). A deterioration in human relations also resulted when a supervisory training
program came into conflict with union norms, when recruitment for the program
was poor, and when the program itself became a matter of indoctrinating a captive
audience rather than educating individuals (Form and Form, 42).

Ideally, the attitudes and actions of higher-level management need to be consistent with the course content of the supervisory training program. Top management
needs exposure to the program and its objectives, so that it will actively support
them as well as reinforce what is learned in the training program (Mahler, 81). One
of the most common suggestions arising at the end of the typical supervisory training program is, "I sure wish my boss could take this program; he needs it more than
I did."

Often, training must be supported by other company actions to bring about desired changes. For instance, a supervisory training program directed at reducing
employee absenteeism achieved this goal when supervisors at the end of their training received uniform data about the absences of their own personnel (Mann and
Sparling, 83).

Another important consideration, particularly in management development, is
a company's need to project the major trends in what it will require during the
careers of its current management force. Current training programs and plans for
subsequent management-development programs must consider the changes taking
place in business management. They must also pay increased attention to how to
apply the physical and social sciences to business administration, to the nonmarket
responsibilities of management, to long-range planning for the successful administration of technically advanced industries, and to the different types of careers for
management trainees in the same firm (Kirkpatrick, 66).

JOB ANALYSIS

Job analysis for training purposes involves a careful study of jobs within an organization in a further effort to define the specific content of training. It requires an
orderly, systematic collection of data about the job or position; and its purpose is to
spell out, in as much detail as possible, what tasks constitute the job, how they are
to be performed, and what behavior (skills, knowledge, and attitudes) the jobholder
must have to perform certain specified tasks (McGehee and Thayer, 88).

Job analyses are fairly straightforward for production and other lower-level
jobs in an organization, though they become increasingly complex as an individual
moves to higher levels with less clearly defined duties and responsibilities. An
expert can analyze the job of, say, a semiskilled machine operator with relative ease
by following a standardized procedure: observing the operator at work, reading the
manual describing the work, actually performing the job, and asking the operator
questions about the job.

In the collection of job information for the purpose of formulating training programs, particular attention must be focused on performance standards required of
employees, the tasks in which they will be engaged, the methods they will use on the
job, and, most important, the way they have learned these methods (McGehee and
Thayer, 88).

Especially in developing programs that train workers to place complex equipment in operation and then maintain it analysts must consider the component tasks the operators must learn to complete the final performance.

For the purposes of analyzing the need for training, many different ways of collecting job information are available. These include the following:

1 Observations. (Were there obvious evidences of production inefficiency, such as excessive tool breakage, failure to meet schedules, too much scrap, poor methods, wasted time, large number of grievances, high absenteeism, and excessive turnover? Were there dramatic incidences on the part of individuals or a group that reveal poor personnel relationships, emotionally charged attitudes, frustrations, lack of understanding, or personal limitations? Do these situations imply training needs?)

2 Management requests for training of employees.

3 Interviews with supervisors and top management personnel to accumulate information about production problems, as well as interviews with employees concerning problems encountered in production or areas in which they feel they need training.

4 Group conferences with interdepartmental groups and training advisory committees to discuss organizational objectives, major operational problems, plans for meeting objectives, and areas in which training could be of value.

5 Comparative studies of good versus poor employees to underline the bases for differentiating successful from unsuccessful performance.

6 Questionnaire surveys.

7 Tests or examinations of job knowledge of current employees; analyses of samples of their work.

8 Supervisors' reports on the performance of employees.

9 Personnel records.

10 Business and production reports (ASTD Research Committee, 4).

11 Review of literature concerning the job.

12 Actually performing the job.

For most of the jobs in an organization, then, one can follow relatively standardized procedures and obtain very satisfactory job analyses. On the other hand, an analysis of a vice president's job is not so simple. Much of the vice president's time may be spent in interpersonal interaction and thinking, so that it is extremely difficult—often impossible—to determine by observation when he is working on a specific task. The complex and ambiguous nature of the managerial function makes it difficult for the manager to describe just what he does, how he does it, and when he does it. Furthermore, it is impractical to have someone perform the vice president's job for analytical purposes.

The knowledge that job analysis of managerial positions is extremely difficult should not deter us from seeking better ways to perform these analyses. From those performed to date, we have a fairly clear picture of the general characteristics of the manager's job. For example, the typical manager is a solver of unprogramed problems; in other words, the problems he must solve constantly change, and he deals largely with unknowns rather than knowns. He must perform a wide variety of functions, including planning, coordinating, evaluating, negotiating, supervising, and investigating. He must be skilled then, in gathering information, defining problems, searching for alternative solutions, and translating his understanding into decisions for action and ultimately into action itself. The organizational setting in which he works makes his position unique. Typically, he operates from a power position in a pyramidal structure. He is blessed (or cursed) with varying amounts of authority over others, though he is peculiarly dependent on those beneath him even while seeming to be independent. From a somewhat delicate position, then, he must perform his functions through his influence on other people.

His job is further complicated in that the typical manager is not the *top* manager; he is dependent not only on his subordinates but also on his peers and superiors. (For a summary of the manager's man-in-the-middle dilemma, see Bass and Vaughan, 9). In a sense, he is always an apprentice to someone and must deal with difficulties from above and below, as well as all around him (Leavitt, 71). Finally, he is a *teacher* and therefore needs a clear understanding of the significant principles of learning involved in developing subordinates.

MANPOWER ANALYSIS

Manpower analysis focuses on the individual in a given job, rather than on the job itself. Three basic issues are involved in a manpower analysis for training purposes.

First, through appropriate observation, supervisory evaluation, and diagnostic testing, we need to determine whether performance is substandard and training is needed. Second, we need to know whether current employees are capable of training, and we need to know the specific areas in which they may require training, in order to minimize training time. Finally, we need to ask whether current employees with substandard performances can improve their work through appropriate training or should be transferred to make room for those who can already do the job. At the same time, we must consider whether engineering modifications in the job may bring employee performance up to standard, whether, instead, new equipment or processes may be the solution, or whether training seems the wisest course.

Job-knowledge tests, work samples, diagnostic psychological tests, and performance reports provide the kind of information we need to help us choose from the above possibilities. Through such means, for example, 21 textile operators could be consistently identified the second week on the job as either fast or slow in performance. Thus, low aptitude learners or those needing more training could be isolated (McGehee, 86).

When the executives of a marketing firm became disturbed by reports on their salesmen's ability to calculate percentage discounts and markups for their customers, they arranged for the "hundred-problem arithmetic test" (Schorling, Clark and Potter, 108) to be given to approximately 300 of the men. While no correlation was found between their rated merit as salesmen and their ability to add, subtract, multiply, divide, or calculate decimals, fractions, or percentages, their inadequacy in at least some of the areas diagnosed confirmed management's concern. Half of the examinees needed help in addition, subtraction, multiplication, and division while nearly three fourths were below any minimal standard of proficiency in calculating fractions, percentages, and decimals.

Moreover, a sizable group of men had performances so low that they could deal with only the simplest numbers and do no multiplying or dividing at all. As an alternative to training the latter group, it was thought that it might be more feasible to provide them with computational aids of a very simple and clear nature so they could systematically figure discounts and markups. The diagnostic program, then, led to a recommendation for remedial training for many—but not all—of the salesmen, as well as a recommendation for the development of special slide rules and audio-visual aids so that those for whom training might be ineffectual could still be brought up to standard performance (Bruedner, 23).

A comparable diagnostic program was set up for blue-collar workers on 24 work stations at a plant whose management was concerned about its employees' lack of skill in using precision measuring instruments. Approximately every three months, employees were sent to the testing center at which, depending on particular job classification, each was tested in the use of the instruments he employed in his own work. His proficiency in using these instruments on each of a set of job samples was examined. Following inspection, employees lacking skill on a particular instrument were asked to attend a class designed to retrain them in its use (Lawshe, 68).

At the management level, diagnosis mainly takes the form of "readings" or evaluations by superiors and staff personnel. For example, at RCA Victor (Camden Division, New Jersey), appraisals by a management committee of each individual executive lead to a specific statement of development needs. This statement, in turn, leads to a tailor-made development program for the particular executive.

REVIEW AND REVISION OF THE TRAINING PROGRAM

If the training program is to remain current and viable, then the three kinds of analyses described above must be carried on continuously. The very essence of organizational life is change; thus a training program must be reviewed constantly and revised in the light of changes in a company's resources, its objectives, its internal organizational climate, and the total environment within which it operates. Furthermore, these analyses, to be effective, cannot be done in an "armchair" manner; they must be integrated in a carefully designed and carefully executed research program.

Although this kind of program is expensive to pursue in the higher levels of an organization and often produces far from ideal results, there is still reason to be optimistic. Despite the erratic growth of knowledge concerning management, a substantial amount of it has been developed. Each of the fundamental and classic disciplines such as psychology, sociology, mathematics, statistics, and economics has contributed modern analytical tools that are directly applicable to the study of management and its organization. In addition, many newer disciplines—such as operations research and systems analysis—have added to this body of knowledge. Although a widely accepted scientific doctrine of management cannot be described in more than general terms, there is, at least, this core of analytical methods and tools, which was founded in basic disciplines and tested in actual management settings. The intelligent use of these methods, however, demands a well-grounded, basic education that will help the manager recognize their operational limits and adapt them to the particular conditions of many different business decisions.

REFERENCES

ASTD Research Committee, 1953. Madison, Wisconsin.

Bass, B. M., and Vaughan, J. A. Experimenting with the man-in-the-middle of the organization. Paper presented at Ford Foundation Seminar on Social Science of Organization, Univ. of Pittsburgh, June 1962.

Bruedner, L. J. *Diagnostic tests and self-helps in arithmetic.* Los Angeles: California Test Bureau, 1955.

Fleishman, E. A. Leadership climate, human relations training and supervisory behavior. *Personnel Psychol.*, 1953, 6, 205–222.

Form, W. H., and Form, A. L. Unanticipated results of a foreman training program. *Personnel J.*, 1953, 32, 207–212.

Haire, M. Some problems of industrial training. *J. soc. Issues*, 1948, 4, 41–47.

Hariton, T. Conditions influencing the effect of training foremen in human rela-
    tions principles. Doctoral dissertation. Ann Arbor: Univ. of Michigan, 1951.
Kirkpatrick, F. H. Collegiate business education in the next quarter century.
    West Virginia Univ. bus. econ. Stud. (No. 4), 1958, 5.
Lawshe, Jr., C. H. Training operative personnel. *J. consult. Psychol.,* 1944, 8,
    154–159.
Leavitt, H. J. *Managerial psychology.* Chicago: Univ. of Chicago Press, 1958.
Mahler, W. Trends in management training. In Dooher, M. J. (Ed.), *The develop-
    ment of executive talent.* New York: American Management Assn., 1952.
Mann, F. C., and Sparling, J. E. Changing absence rates. *Personnel,* 1956, 32,
    392–408.
McGehee, W. Cutting training waste. *Personnel Psychol.,* 1948, 1, 331–340.
McGehee, W., and Thayer, P. W. *Training in business and industry.* New York:
    McGraw-Hill, 1961.
Schorling, R., Clark, J. R., and Potter, M. A. *Hundred-problem arithmetic test.*
    Yonkers, N.Y.: World, Book, 1938.
Taylor, E. K. Review of *Developing Executive Skills. Personnel Psychol.,* 1958,
    11, 605–609.

FOR DISCUSSION AND REVIEW

1 What are the benefits of a thorough assessment of training needs?
2 Explain the steps in an organization analysis and in a manpower analysis.
3 How would information gathered from the three types of analyses
   recommended in the article be used in the design of training programs?

B. PROGRAM DESIGN AND METHODS

J. R. Hinrichs

Training Techniques

TRAINING TECHNIQUES

Having determined the nature of tasks (terminal behaviors) desired as a result of training and of the component tasks which make up these terminal behaviors, the next concern of a training department is to determine which techniques to use in the training program in order to optimize learning (achieve the greatest amount of learning with minimum expenditure of time and money). We have already touched on the major problems in making such a determination, and it would now be appropriate to review some of the main techniques available to training departments in making this decision.

There are few books on training which fail to describe in some detail the major techniques currently being used. Therefore, we do not intend to give these techniques more than outline coverage in the discussion which follows.

The prevalent training techniques tend to group themselves into three categories, based upon their most common usage. We have given them labels of:

1 *Content* techniques of training, which are designed to impart substantive knowledge or information on a cognitive level.
2 *Process* techniques, mainly intended to change attitudes, develop awareness of self and others, and impact the trainee's interpersonal skills.
3 *Mixed* training techniques, which may have both an information transmitting function as well as an attitude change function.

The literature on training reports little comparative research on the various techniques which is useful in deciding which techniques to use to achieve which specific objectives. Most of the evaluation is based on logical analysis or common sense. It is in this area, in addition to the area of task analysis, in which there is the greatest need for systematic research in an effort to build a true psychology of industrial training.

McGehee and Thayer (1961) outline a number of criteria which have to be weighed in deciding upon techniques for achieving various objectives. These include:

1. The kinds of behavior to be acquired (motor skills, concepts, verbal skills, attitudes, etc.).
2. The number of employees to be trained.
3. The ability level of trainees.
4. Individual differences among trainees.
5. Cost in relation to various factors.
6. The incorporation of alleged learning principles such as motivation, opportunity for practice, reinforcement, knowledge of results, meaningfulness, and overlearning. (McGehee & Thayer, 1961, pp. 195–196)

We would certainly add to this list previous experience based upon systematic evaluation of the results achieved by different techniques within the milieu of the specific organization.

Content-oriented techniques

We have included under the general framework of content techniques designed to impart knowledge the techniques of lecture, audiovisual aids, programmed instruction (PI), and computer-assisted instruction (CAI).

Lecture technique The lecture technique is familiar to everyone, at least everyone who has attended some kind of formal schooling. Almost universally it has been criticized in discussions of training techniques. For example, Korman (1971) outlines the major problems with the lecture method as:

1 It perpetuates the authority structure of traditional organizations with implications of negative behavior. Korman suggests that the degree to which learning is not self-controlled is a negative contributor to performance (Pressey, 1965).

2 Except in the area of cognitive knowledge and conceptual principles, there is probably limited potential transfer from the lecture to the actual skills required to do the job.

3 The high verbal and symbolic requirements of the lecture method may be threatening or incapable of being handled by people with low verbal or symbolic experience or aptitude. Individuals from relatively deprived educational, social, and economic backgrounds may have more difficulty than those from higher levels in learning through the lecture procedure. Where there are language barriers, as in an international group of trainees, the lecture method may be relatively ineffective.

4 The lecture method does not permit individualized training based upon individual differences in ability, interests, and personality. Similarly, the lecture method is not flexible to provide feedback and reinforcement systematically to trainees.

Despite all these problems, however, the lecture method is still widely used in industry, in large measure probably because of widespread familiarly with it from its use in the general educational system. Patten (1971) points out that it is frequently used effectively when skilled lecturers are employed and where it is appropriate. It also can be economical. He emphasizes the necessity for a question and answer period following the lecture. The lecture should rarely be relied upon as the sole method of instruction; it can have some utility as a preliminary training method to provide cognitive awareness prior to skills training, particularly where the instructor possesses significant knowledge about the topic not otherwise accessible to the trainees.

Audiovisual techniques The use of various audiovisual devices is usually included in the list of training techniques. Actually, these should probably not be thought of as stand-alone techniques, as in practice they are usually used as supplements or aids in conjunction with other approaches to the training process. Audiovisual devices include the old standbys of films, slides, filmstrips, records, flannel boards, etc. Use of such training equipment received a big spurt during World War II when there was a need to train large numbers of military and civilian personnel, a shortage of qualified instructors, and a need for a certain amount of uniformity in the training. Now such equipment is part and parcel of any training effort.

Some of these training aids, films, or records, have many of the disadvantages of the lecture. They treat trainees as a passive audience. At the same time, however, they "capture" experts in a topical area to ensure the quality and correctness of the material presented. In the area of films particularly, extensive research has isolated many technical considerations which are important for effectiveness. Professional guidance and assistance should certainly be sought in the preparation of films (McGehee & Thayer, 1961, p. 194).

Recent new technologies such as tape cassettes and television can be thought of as an extension of traditional technologies, though they present some very important new possibilities when used in a feedback mode. Although tapes and TV are used to present content, the ability to individualize immediate feedback can be a powerful tool in process-oriented training, for example in demonstrating the implications of particular trainee behaviors.

The big benefits of audiovisual aids are the ability to cover large numbers of trainees, relatively low costs per trainee, uniformity of training content, and the variety which can be built into the training context through their use. They are being employed as supplements to training efforts ranging all the way from traditional lectures to highly unstructured encounter groups.

Auto-instructional technologies Among the newest content-oriented training techniques which have received a great deal of attention are two which are beamed specifically at self-instruction: programmed instruction (PI) and computer-assisted instruction (CAI). In focusing on these new approaches, however, we should not lose sight of the fact that auto-instructional techniques are probably the oldest form of instructional procedures; probably more learning takes place simply by reading an appropriate book than by any other technology.

However, the new technologies of programmed instruction and CAI provide an exciting extension to this procedure. Programmed instruction burst on the training scene in the late 1950s and was immediately followed by exuberant predictions of fantastic results and a rash of applications and "teaching machine" hardware. Two major approaches to PI have been employed:

1 Linear programs which progress in a regular stepwise fashion through the instructional material ensuring positive reinforcement and gradual building of competence and achievement.

2 Branching techniques which selectively lead the trainee into subroutines when he demonstrates problems in mastering the materials. The key features in PI have been fully described in several texts and will not be repeated in detail here (see, for example, Foundation for Research on Human Behavior, 1961).

Advocates of the approach point out that programmed instruction, when carefully done, has a number of very strong arguments in its favor:

1 It involves the trainee by requiring active response.

2 It is individualized and self-paced rather than under the authoritarian control of a trainer.

3 Knowledge of results can provide immediate reinforcement for correct responses in a non-threatening (private) manner.

4 Challenge and interest can be built into the learning sequence by branching techniques and humorous or unexpected responses within the programmed format.

5 Updating and revision of the program can be done at will, based upon data and experience acquired through use.

6 Perhaps most important, writing the program requires careful organization and pre-study of the content of what is to be included, optimum sequencing of the content, and testing—a process which should precede all training program designs but which seldom does.

In view of all these positive factors, it is not surprising that PI has found significant utility in many instances, both in the academic community and in industry. The major positive effects seem to be in savings in training time although some industrial studies have demonstrated enhanced performance as a result of training under PI versus traditional lecture procedures (Goldberg, Dawson, & Barrett, 1964; Hedberg, Steffen, & Baxter, 1965; Hughes & McNamara, 1961).

However, PI is not a panacea. It is costly, appropriate to a somewhat limited range of training objectives where content is clear and objectives readily identifiable, and because of its low social involvement probably of limited use where one of the training objectives is the facilitation of social interaction. A recent extensive review of research evaluating PI versus other training methodologies (Nash, Muczyk, & Vettori, 1971) suggests that in view of the high costs of preparing program texts a more rigorous criterion of "practical superiority" rather than statistical should be applied in evaluating PI. Under this criterion there is little indicated superiority in learning and retention for PI; and the time savings may be an artifact of self-pacing versus a controlled learning environment, rather than a result of the PI methodology. This review suggests considerable caution in the decision to develop PI materials. However, PI has found considerable use among the array of training techniques.

Computer-assisted instruction (CAI) is a logical extension of the PI methodology. CAI puts the learning program in storage in a computer system and fosters training through interaction between the trainee and the system. Seltzer (1971) describes uses of CAI for drill and practice, tutorial instruction, and dialogue. He debates the utility of CAI in specific areas on considerations of whether or not the computer can do better than more traditional methods, and whether or not there are less expensive ways to achieve the same goals.

On balance, Seltzer concludes:

1   The high costs of CAI will probably limit its utility.
2   It is not clear that it presents any significant improvement over the more traditional modes of drill and practice.
3   The technology for using the computer in a true dialogue mode of instruction is not sufficiently advanced.
4   There are probably some instances in which the potential power of the technique in the tutorial mode would justify its use.

Two other approaches to the use of the computer in an interactive setting show it to be clearly superior to other procedures. These are for information storage and retrieval of large scale data banks and libraries and for simulations and gaming in various models of real world situations.

Research studies done in industry comparing CAI with PI suggest that there may be savings in time with CAI, but it is unclear whether there are significant differences in performance or achievement (Schwartz & Haskell, 1966; Schwartz & Long, 1967). There is need for additional research in this area.

A study of auto-instructional techniques in vigilance training not involving either PI or CAI (Attwood & Wiener, 1969) suggests several possible reasons for the effectiveness of the approach. Primarily, Attwood and Wiener suggest that self-control over the training sequence makes the task more interesting and involving. Also, in the interaction with hardware they suggest there is a "pin-ball machine effect" increasing the trainee's motivation to perform, with the sole reward being knowledge of results and self-satisfaction in performance. Particularly for learning a dull task like vigilance, anything which can inject "fun" into the situation should have a positive effect.

Mixed techniques

There are a number of commonly used training techniques which may be used to impart both substantive knowledge or content as well as to achieve some of the objectives set for the more process-oriented techniques: attitude change, awareness, interpersonal effectiveness. These include techniques such as conference methods, case studies, simulators and games, and various on-the-job techniques.

Conference discussion techniques According to a recent survey of training practices, the conference or discussion technique ranks high in terms of frequency of use (Utgaard & Dawis, 1970). The conference or discussion technique contains a number of elements which should make it superior to the pure lecture or auto-instructional techniques:

1 It can engender considerable involvement of the trainees with an increase in motivation to understand the concepts under discussion and the desire to participate.
2 It provides an opportunity for clarification of any misunderstandings.
3 Feedback is possible either from the conference leader or from the other participants which can serve as a powerful reward or punishment.

Conference techniques may be used both for enhancing the understanding of conceptual and cognitive information and for the development of attitudes among the trainees. Because of this potential multiple use, we have included it among the "mixed" techniques.

Most of the people who advocate the conference technique do so primarily based upon an intuitive feeling of its superiority over the lecture technique, its degree of widespread use, and its relative ease of implementation, rather than on rigorously controlled research studies evaluating its effectiveness. Bass and Vaughan (1966, p. 98) cite one study which demonstrated greater behavioral change—less error in a performance rating task among a management population—as a result of training by the conference method in comparison with a control group and a group trained by the lecture method.

Several problems are prevalent in the use of the conference or discussion technique. First of all, it is limited to use by relatively small groups. Secondly, in practice, conference sessions are often poorly organized, and as Planty, McCord, and Efferson (1948, p. 182) point out, the conference can become "a conversational boat ride on uncharted seas to an unknown port." Finally, effective conference leadership requires considerable skill and finesse, particularly when the conference is used in a "process" mode. Skill is required to ensure that all trainees have an opportunity to participate, that diverging points of view are fully aired, that feedback from the group is not unduly punitive for diverging points of view, and that the discussion does in fact proceed toward some predetermined objective rather than wandering aimlessly.

Case study/incident process The case study method is one which has a long history of use in certain academic settings, but has also found extensive use in industrial training. As Patten (1971, p. 144) points out "using cases on an intermittent basis is perhaps the easiest way to make the transition from traditional cognitive styles of learning in orthodox training classrooms to more dynamic learner-involved participatory and existential styles of learning." The case is essentially a description of some area of activity with which it is hoped the trainees will become familiar. Through study and analysis of the case and discussion, it is hoped that the trainees' behavior will be impacted in several ways. First of all, case study requires understanding, logical thinking, and analysis on the part of trainees. It often forces the trainee to extrapolate from incomplete information and to develop the implications of a situation presented in the case. Frequently, judgment and decision making are entailed, as there is usually not one single best solution to the case. Finally, through discussion of implications and consequences, the trainees receive feedback about the appropriateness of their analysis and decision making. Thus, case study analysis can be a dynamic and involving learning experience, useful both for imparting substantive knowledge about an area of concern as well as for teaching approaches to decision making and problem solving.

The incident process is similar to the case study, except that only a limited scenario is presented initially, and the trainees must develop the pertinent information about the case through a series of questions and answers with the trainer. The trainer provides only information specifically requested by the trainees.

There are several pitfalls inherent in the case process. First of all, it is difficult to know just how much information to include in the case; if too much detail is provided it becomes unwieldy; if it is too limited, the situation seems overly artificial and the necessary information for a fully balanced judgment is not available. Also, the role of the discussion leader is extremely important. Without active leadership there is a tendency for case analysis to become solution-oriented rather than understanding-oriented, for participants to concentrate on finding fault with the positions of others and for the analysis to be relatively superficial. Very little conclusive research on the utility of the case method is reported in the literature.

Simulations One of the long-standing "principles" of training, which has both research justification and considerable common sense appeal, is the concept that practice on a task requiring behaviors as near as possible to those that will be used in the final task will enhance transfer of skills from the training to the job situation and will be an efficient means for carrying out the training. This is the rationale behind the use of simulators.

Simulators are in wide use in many kinds of training requiring the acquisition of motor skills. They have also been widely used in instances which have to couple motor and cognitive skills into total performance. For example, a significant part of the training for aviators, submarine officers, or other military personnel involves simulators. A major component of training for astronauts involves complex and ingenious simulators of the space environment in which they will operate. Simulators of various kinds are also used in a variety of industrial training situations. Most of the research on such "hardware" simulators has been carried out for the military (Valverde & Youngs, 1969).

The simulation approach is particularly useful where there are complex interdependencies among groups of people and hardware and considerable teamwork required for effective operation. Boguslaw and Porter (1965) describe the major considerations in the design of team training for effective performance in complex systems. Their frame of reference is primarily from the military.

In recent years, simulators have found increasing use in non-motor skill areas. Specifically, business games may be thought of as simulations of the operation of an enterprise. Here trainees manipulate a model of an organization or some component part of an organization to try to maximize certain outcomes. Various degrees of competition between teams of trainees may be built into these exercises. Business games, if they entail any degree of complexity, almost always utilize a computer to carry out the simulation.

Such games have a number of appealing aspects which suggest they may be very useful for training. Depending upon the degree to which they mirror real life organizations, they should provide for considerable transfer from the training to the job situation. They are dynamic and permit one to see the consequences of his decisions. At the same time they are non-punitive, in that mistakes or bad decisions will not result in actual loss, as a mistake made by an astronaut in a simulator will not result in his actually crashing on the moon. Games are intrinsically motivating and often build up a high level of involvement. They may also deal with a variety of factors important to the total management situation and thus impart understanding of finance, personnel, manufacturing, distribution, etc.

Some of the problems with business games are that:

1 They often do not encourage or allow normal approaches, but limit behavior to those progammed in the situation.

2 Trainees may become too involved in the game per se and neglect to critique the effectiveness of their behavior.

3 There is a tendency to "lock in" to whatever strategy proves effective in order to "win the game," rather than experimenting.

4 There may be some question of the degree of realism of the gaming situation as well as of the degree to which the game situation is related to the trainees' at-home situation.

5 Participation in the game may be costly, particularly where extensive computer time is entailed.

The in-basket is a specialized form of simulator which can be thought of as a cross between a case study and a game. The trainee works through a pile of typical correspondence and responds to the problems which are raised in a fashion supposedly modeling the kind of behavior needed in a real life situation.

Perhaps because of the "face validity" of many simulators and the extent to which they are employed for specific training objectives, there is a surprising absence of conclusively controlled research to test their effectiveness or to identify general principles for their design. The exception is some of the hardware oriented research conducted for the military.

On-the-job training techniques There are a host of techniques which are essentially designed to enhance learning while the trainee is actually performing in the job setting. It should not be too surprising that these techniques are among those cited as being most frequently used in a recent survey of training practices (Utgaard & Dawis, 1970). Examples of on-the-job approaches are:

1 *Job instruction training* essentially is the process of having a trainer explain the job to the trainee, observe his performance, and provide feedback about his performance. It is a straightforward process of breaking a new employee in on a new job, and is the most frequently used technique.

2 *Orientation training* is merely a systematic effort to ensure that a new employee has all of the basic information he needs to function effectively.

3 *Apprentice training* is like a period of internship in which the trainee works under the guidance of an experienced supervisor for a specified period of time before achieving journeyman status.

4 *Performance appraisals* in many organizations fulfill a training and development function by providing feedback about the appropriateness of on-the-job behavior and performance.

5 *Coaching* is the process of ensuring that training and learning occur in the day-to-day man-manager relationship.

6 *Job rotation* is widely used in management development as a technique to systematically ensure that trainees are exposed to a variety of organizational functions.

7 *Assistantships* or various committee assignments similarly are used to provide personnel development.

All of these on-the-job techniques are based upon the philosophy that people learn a job best by doing it. However, this conclusion may or may not be justified, and there are a number of obvious problems with many of the on-the-job programs:

1 They may be inefficient, resulting in low productivity and waste.

2 There may be low involvement of the trainee in the training process, particularly in a program like job rotation in which he is not an incumbent in the job for a long enough period to really learn very much and is not motivated to dig in because he knows he will move on in the near future.

3 The quality of instruction diffused through an on-the-job situation may be less competent than instruction concentrated in the training department.

4 Too often in the on-the-job situation training takes second place to getting the job out.

However, in spite of these drawbacks on-the-job techniques are probably the most widely used approaches to training in industry today. Probably because they seem so "common-sensical" and easy to use, there has been little research on the effectiveness of these procedures. One study (Goodacre, 1963), which attempted to sort out the effects of a revision in the performance appraisal system, on-the-job coaching, and special instruction in enhancing man-management practices, was confounded with essentially very ambiguous results.

Process-oriented techniques

We have included under the category of process oriented techniques a number of approaches which are distinguished by heavy reliance upon the interaction among trainees. The major emphasis without exception is on behavioral or attitudinal change, rather than on imparting cognitive knowledge. Such processes are used for developing interpersonal insights—awareness of self and of others—for changing attitudes and for practice in human relations skills, such as leadership or the interview.

Role playing Role playing techniques have their origin in psychotherapy, but have found wide use in industrial settings for imparting sales, leadership, and interviewing skills, as well as other skills. The essence of role playing is to create a realistic situation, as in the case study approach, and then have the trainees assume the parts of specific personalities in the situation. The success of the technique depends heavily upon the extent to which the individual throws himself into the role, rather than merely acting. Then, the participants in the role playing interact to solve the problem presented in the case. In the process, they receive considerable feedback about the impact of their behaviors from other members of the role playing session. Advocates of role playing say that it is highly involving, that the cases can be meaningful if carefully developed, and that it provides practice in personal interaction and problem solving which can closely simulate real life conditions.

On the negative side (1) there is danger that trainees will feel that the role playing exercise is childish, (2) they may revert to overacting and neglect focusing on the problem solving, (3) the trainer has no control over the immediate reinforcement or rewards which are in the hands of other trainees in the interaction process, and (4) the technique is somewhat limited in the number of people that can be involved, is time consuming, and relatively expensive.

Research on the effectiveness of role playing shows that it can be useful in increasing the supervisor's sensitivity to an employee's feelings when used in conjunction with case study and adequate discussion (Lawshe, Bolda, & Brune, 1959). It has also been determined that the strength of prior attitudes about role playing is an important determiner of the degree of attitude change. There is a greater degree of attitude change when people play roles at variance with their own points of view, and greater acceptance of the technique when they are placed in roles which are congruent with their original view (Elbing, 1967).

Sensitivity training The training area which has probably received more attention than any other in recent years is sensitivity or T-group training. The approach has increased in attention and its use has evolved and developed since the mid-1940s. Along with the increasing use of the technique, there has been a growing volume of research attempting to evaluate the effectiveness of T-group training.

A detailed description of all the purposes which have been attempted to be served by T-group training is beyond the scope of this chapter. A list of the most common T-group objectives has been synthesized from much of the literature by Campbell, Dunnette, Lawler, and Weick (1970, p. 239) and includes the following:

1. To give the trainee an understanding of how and why he acts toward other people as he does and of the way in which he affects them.
2. To provide some insights into why other people act the way they do.
3. To teach the participants how to "listen," that is, actually hear what other people are saying rather than concentrating on a reply.
4. To provide insights concerning how groups operate and what sorts of processes groups go through under certain conditions.
5. To foster an increased tolerance and understanding of the behavior of others.
6. To provide a setting in which an individual can try out new ways of interacting with people and receive feedback as to how these new ways affect them.

The classical model of the T-group is one of a meeting without an agenda in which participants discuss questions dealing with the "here and now" of the group process. The discussion explores why participants behave the way they do, how they perceive one another, and the feelings and emotions which are generated in the interaction process. The discussion is steered away from cognitive or intellectual aspects of problems and from prior or future events and concentrates instead on the behavioral processes operating at the moment.

Over the years, a variety of modifications and extensions of this basic model have developed to the point where at the present time there is certainly no single monolithic model for the T-group. These include such things as grid training, instrumented laboratories, mini-labs, marathon labs, etc.

The T-group experience is designed to be highly involving for the trainee. He becomes personally involved in what is going on as it deals with many aspects of his basic personality. He is highly motivated to participate. The only problem is that it is not always clear what the motivation is for that participation—whether it is to improve his interpersonal skills for the job situation or to defend his self-concept. Another problem with T-groups is that only small numbers of trainees can be included and the process is relatively expensive. Also, reinforcement of behavior comes from the group and is not controlled in any systematic fashion by the trainer.

Finally, but not least, there may be a considerable amount of psychological stress associated with the T-group experience, and instances of breakdown and severe trauma have been recorded.

House (1967) lists a number of issues which must be considered in the choice to use T-group training.

1. Are the changes that T-group training induces the kind required for more effective leadership behavior?
2. Can the organization tolerate the changes in the individual if the T-group is successful?
3. Can the candidate tolerate the anxiety involved in the T-group process?
4. What are the credentials of the T-group leaders?

House lists a number of ethical considerations including questions of organizational concern for personal well-being, privacy, forced attendance, and extent of organizational responsibility if an employee experiences emotional collapse as a result of participation in a T-group.

There have been several extensive reviews of research evaluating sensitivity training (Campbell & Dunnette, 1968; House, 1967). The reviews outline that there are considerable problems in undertaking effective research in such nebulous areas as sensitivity training and that most of the studies vary widely in quality and degree of control employed. Campbell and Dunnette (1968) conclude that in terms of external criteria of behavioral change on the job, T-group training probably does have an impact. Several studies do seem to demonstrate that participants exhibit changed behavior when back on the job. Such behavioral changes, however, have not been tied to changes in organizational effectiveness by the research studies reviewed. Also, most changes in behavior are individual and unique, making it difficult to assess any common trends of effectiveness out of the T-group experience. As a generalization, the research suggests that people who are motivated to change become most involved in the program and in fact do change; on the other hand, it is clear that many people do not become involved and do not change their behaviors. On the internal level, the extent to which self-perceptions and personality are changed as a result of T-group exposure is not clear.

Modeling Recently there has been put together a management skills training procedure which links several approaches into a coordinated learning system (Goldstein & Sorcher, 1974). The key component is modeling of the behaviors to be learned using film or video. The focus is on supervisory behaviors in interpersonal situations, and the sequence of learning activities includes:

1   a clear statement of the behaviors to be applied
2   a filmed model or demonstration situation of the skills being applied
3   practice through role playing for each trainee
4   social reinforcement of correct behaviors, in the practice situation, and
5   planning by each trainee in how to transfer the skills back to his or her specific job situation.

The technique appears to have great promise, based upon initial evaluation of results.

. . .

REFERENCES

Attwood, D. A., & Wiener, E. L. Automated instruction for vigilance training. *Journal of Applied Psychology*, 1969, 53, 218–223.

Bass, B. M. & Vaughan, J. A. *Training in industry: The management of learning.* Belmont Calif.: Wadsworth Publishing, 1966, 164 pages.

Boguslaw, R., & Porter, E. H. Team functions and training. Chapter II in R. M. Gagné (Ed.), *Psychological principles in system development.* New York: Holt, Rinehart and Winston, 1965, 387–416.

Campbell, J. P., & Dunnette, M. D. Effectiveness of T-group experiences in managerial training and development. *Psychological Bulletin,* 1968, 70, 73–104.

Campbell, J. P., Dunnette, M. D., Lawler, E. E. III, & Weick, K. E. Jr. *Managerial behavior, performance, and effectiveness.* New York: McGraw-Hill, 1970, 546 pages.

Elbing, A. O. Jr. The influence of prior attitudes on role-playing results. *Personnel Psychology,* 1967, 20, 309–321.

Foundation for Research on Human Behavior. *Programmed learning: Evolving principles and industrial applications.* Ann Arbor: University of Michigan, 1961, 179 pages.

Goldberg, M. H., Dawson, R. I., & Barrett, R. S. Comparison of programmed and conventional instruction methods. *Journal of Applied Psychology,* 1964, 48, 110–114.

Goldstein, A. P., & Sorcher, M. *Changing supervisor behavior.* New York: Pergamon Press, 1974, 90 pages.

Goodacre, D. M. Stimulating improved man management. *Personnel Psychology,* 1963, 16, 133–143.

Hedberg, R., Steffen, H., & Baxer, B. Insurance fundamentals: A programmed text versus a conventional text. *Personnel Psychology,* 1965, 18, 165–172.

House, R. J. Leadership training: Some dysfunctional consequences. *Administrative Science Quarterly,* 1968, 12, 556–571.

Hughes, J. L., & McNamara, W. J. A comparative study of programmed and conventional instruction in industry. *Journal of Applied Psychology,* 1961, 45, 225–231.

Korman, A. K. *Industrial and organizational psychology.* Englewood Cliffs, N.J.: Prentice-Hall, 1971, 398 pages.

Lawshe, C. H. Jr., Bolda, R. A., & Brune, R. L. Studies in management training evaluation. Chapter II. The effects of exposures to role playing. *Journal of Applied Psychology,* 1959, 43, 287–292.

McGehee, W., & Thayer, P. W. *Training in business and industry.* New York: Wiley, 1961, 305 pages.

Nash, A. N., Muczyk, J. P., & Vettori, F. L. The relative practical effectiveness of programmed instruction. *Personnel Psychology,* 1971, 24, 397–418.

Patten, T. H. Jr. *Manpower planning and the development of human resources.* New York: Wiley, 1971, 737 pages.

Planty, E. G., McCord, W. S., & Efferson, C. A. *Training employees and managers.* New York: Ronald Press, 1948, 278 pages.

Pressey, S. C. Two basic neglected psychoeducational problems. *American Psychologist,* 1965, 20, 391–395.

Schwartz, H. A., & Haskell, R. J. Jr. A study of computer-assisted instruction in industrial training. *Journal of Applied Psychology,* 1966, 50, 360–363.

Schwartz, H. A., & Long, H. S. A study of remote industrial training via computer-assisted instruction. *Journal of Applied Psychology,* 1967, 51, 11–16.

Seltzer, R. A. Computer-assisted instruction: What it can and cannot do. *American Psychologist,* 1971, 26, 373–377.

Utgaard, S. B., & Dawis, R. V. The most frequently used training techniques. *Training and Development Journal,* 1970, 24, 40–43.

Valverde, H. H., & Youngs, E. J. *Annotated bibliography of the training research division reports, 1950–1969.* Wright-Patterson Air Force Base, Ohio: Air Force Human Resources Laboratory, Air Force Systems Command, 1969, 199 pages.

FOR DISCUSSION AND REVIEW

1   What are the basic differences between content-oriented techniques, process-oriented techniques, and mixed techniques? Give examples of techniques in each category.
2   What are the advantages and disadvantages of the lecture? The case study? Sensitivity training?
3   What factors should be considered as on-the-job training techniques are applied?

Craig Eric Schneier

Training and Development Programs: What Learning Theory and Research Have to Offer

There is little debate among those interested in training and development in organizations that the principles of learning are basic to their programs' design and implementation. This view is evidenced by the fact that training has been equated with learning (e.g. Blumenfeld and Holland, 1971), and that many proponents of Organizational Development, notably those favoring laboratory training techniques, have stressed "learning to learn" as a primary objective (e.g. Golembiewski, 1972).

Recently, various authors have used learning theory and research effectively in their discussions of training and development programs. Such concepts as anxiety, punishment, and reinforcement are used to help evaluate training experiences. Schrank (1971) has used some learning theory research to help emphasize the degree of similarity between the teacher-pupil role and the supervisor-subordinate role. He has also shed some light on the importance of the teacher's role in determining the pupil's learning success. At least one learning theory, operant theory, has recently been explored as to its application to a wide variety of training and development problems (Murphy, 1972; Beatty and Schneier, 1972).

Despite this sampling of useful ideas generated from learning theory and a widespread recognition that training and development programs are primarily learning processes, there is still much validity in the following remarks by Goldstein and Sorcher (1972, p. 37):

> Management training—in its several underlying philosophies, its specific conceptualizations and its concrete techniques—is a human learning process. Yet almost without exception, there has been remarkably little reliance in the devel-

opment and implementation of management training on this vast and relevant body of research literature.

We agree with the statement that there are principles of various learning theories and findings from empirical research that are still relatively unknown and/or not utilized by specialists in training and development. While there is considerable disagreement among the experts as to which one of the several learning theories best explains the human learning process, many principles which logically follow from the various theories are supported by a considerable body of research. Obviously, not all of this research was performed with managers, or even with adults in work situations, but so much of it has been substantiated time and again that the findings are generally agreed upon in the literature.

This article will state some of these principles and findings which are thought to be useful in all phases of training and development programs. The statements will be grouped under the learning environment, the role of the teacher/trainer, characteristics of the learner, basic processes in the human learning activity, reinforcement and punishment, retention and transfer of learning, and practice.*

It will be stressed that these seven categories form the interdependent considerations in the design, implementation, and evaluation of effective training and development programs, that they represent the sources of possible contingencies to be dealt with in each unique learning situation, and that they form the conceptual base for many important organizational training and development programs, such as MBO, skill training, and performance appraisals.

PRINCIPLES AND FINDINGS FROM LEARNING THEORY AND RESEARCH

I. The learning environment

1 Objectives and success criteria for the learning program should be specified and communicated to all learners before the program begins (see V-7).

2 Tests of the learner's progress should be scheduled. If a learner is not ready for a test, he should continue practicing. The learner should have an idea of the types of questions or activities that will be on the test. The "ordeal" aspect of testing should be eliminated.

3 Tasks should be broken into component behaviors that can be learned directly. The behaviors should be sequenced in order of increasing difficulty toward a final target behavior (see V-5).

4 The value of teaching machines and programmed learning devices lies in their ability to help sequence learning, to allow the learner to progress at his own pace, and to help control attention by focusing the learner on the stimuli; their value does not lie in their gadgetry or hardware.

5 To measure learning, note observational changes in the frequencies of desired behavioral responses, not necessarily in the strength of responses, in intentions, or in attitudes. Baseline frequencies of behavior must, therefore, be established prior to the learning situation in order to note the differential effects of learning.

6 "Whole" presentation is usually better than "part" presentation. Therefore, give the learner a "feel" for the total task initially.

---

* For a more detailed explanation of these principles and findings, the reader is referred to any of the works on learning cited in the references.

7 Learning can and does take place in every context, not only in specified locations and in formal programs. Undesirable and desirable behaviors learned in these "informal" settings should be noted.

II. The role of the teacher/trainer

1 Teachers learn a great deal about their learners when they are actually teaching and given responsibility. Having students act as teachers in some situations increases their ability to learn, as well as their empathy for other teachers.

2 The teacher conditions emotional reactions in the learning program, as well as behavioral responses and should, therefore, attempt to condition favorable reactions to himself and to the subject matter.

3 The teacher establishes objectives, methods, sequences, and time limits in learning programs with varying degrees of participation by the learner. The teacher's knowledge of the learner, the situation, and the content of the learning program is vital for specifying both the proper methods and the appropriate degree of learner participation in each learning program.

III. The characteristics of the learner

1 People not only learn at different rates, but each person brings a different emotional state or temperament to the learning situation (see II-2). Assessment of temperament facilitates a more effective choice of teaching strategies.

2 The motivational level of the learner is relevant to the type and amount of stimuli to which he will respond. Whether he finds the learning intrinsically or extrinsically rewarding (i.e. instrumental for internally mediated or externally mediated rewards), should be considered. The needs the learner has unsatisfied as he enters the learning program are also relevant.

3 Each learner's prior conditioning or learning background will influence the amount, frequency, and type of reinforcement and punishment which will be most effective, as well as the method of stimuli presentation (e.g. visual, auditory).

4 Individual learners should be encouraged to learn the skills or behaviors of which they are capable and in which they are interested. They should be able to specialize and demonstrate expertise in at least one area in order to take pride in their accomplishments.

IV. Basic processes in the human learning activity

1 Interest and attention come from successful experiences. These, in turn, facilitate learning as they are seen as rewarding experiences.

2 Attention and curiosity in learning are best facilitated by the use of moderate (not too high nor too low) levels of arousal, curiosity, or anxiety.

3 Learning can occur when the learner merely observes. Active participation is not always necessary, unless motor skills are being taught.

4 Learners should not leave the learning setting after giving incorrect responses. Final responses should always be correct.

5 There are several ways to learn: trial and error, perception-organization-insight, and modeling another's behavior, are all effective under certain conditions.

6 Learning usually progresses to a point and then levels off. This leveling (a "plateau" in a "learning curve") may be due to the fact that incorrect responses are being reduced or that small simple steps in learning were learned rapidly and now as

the small steps are combined into complex tasks, learning slows. Incentives added in the "plateau" stage are helpful.

7 If motor responses are to be learned, verbal guidance, practice, and a favorable, supportive environment are helpful. If ideas or concepts are to be learned, active participation and the formation of meaningful associations between the new material and more familiar material are helpful.

8 Learning can be inhibited and therefore proper responses decreased if too much repetition or fatigue is evidenced (see VII-3).

9 Avoidance learning occurs when fear is felt and a response is made to eliminate the fear. This fear-avoiding response is often reinforced, and it therefore has little chance of being eliminated, as it is needed to avoid aversive stimuli (see V-2). To eliminate avoidance behaviors, the aversive stimuli must be removed.

10 Incidental learning is learning that remains dormant until the occasion for its demonstration arises (e.g. curiosity is stimulated or reinforcement is powerful enough to elicit the response) (see VI-1).

11 Imitation requires that the learner is directly reinforced for matching a model's behavior. "Matched dependence" occurs when the learner models a model. "Same behavior" occurs when two learners respond to the same stimulus, not to each other. Vicarious learning is matching the behavior of another without receiving direct or immediate reinforcement from the model.

12 Complex human learning includes a proper degree of discrimination and generalization. Discrimination requires distinguishing between quite similar stimuli which require *different* responses. Generalization requires noting that similar, but not exactly the same stimuli often require the *same* response.

13 Attitudes can be learned and reinforced in much the same way as behavior is reinforced.

V. Reinforcement and punishment

1 The "Law of Effect" states that behavior that is reinforced will increase in probability of future occurrence. A reinforcer is, therefore, any object or event that *strengthens* the probability of future occurrence of behavior.

2 Punishment occurs when the probability of a response is *weakened* by an object or event. Punishment leads to escape and avoidance behaviors, as well as frustration.

3 Secondary reinforcers (e.g. money) are those objects or events which are linked to or instrumental for receiving other primary reinforcers (e.g. food) and so also take on reinforcing properties themselves. The many effective secondary reinforcers should be identified and used.

4 Undesired behaviors can be extinguished if they are simply not reinforced and not punished, but ignored.

5 "Shaping" behavior occurs when desired responses are observed which are approximates of a target behavior, and are reinforced. The responses are continually reinforced as they become closer and closer to the target, until the target is imitated.

6 For punishment and reinforcement to be effective, they must be dispensed immediately and be appropriate in intensity for the particular response they follow.

7 Knowledge of results of performance is basic to learning and is often a reinforcer. It provides necessary feedback for corrective action, and should be related to

goal levels which are predetermined standards of performance communicated to and understood by the learner.

8 A harder, more intense response will not be elicited unless a more intense, more powerful reinforcer is given.

9 If reinforcement is dispensed on a variable ratio schedule (after a random and changing number of responses unknown to the learner), behavior will be most difficult to extinguish. The variable ratio is thus more effective in sustaining desired responses than either a continuous reinforcement schedule (each desired response rewarded) or fixed interval reinforcement schedule (reinforcement given after the passage of an interval of time, e.g. weekly).

10 Social reinforcement (e.g. approval, status given by others) can be effective in controlling behavior, depending upon the environment and personal attractions.

11 The personality and position of the reinforcing/punishing agent influences the effectiveness of the reinforcement or punishment he dispenses. Therefore, it is not only that he dispenses rewards, but his manner, sincerity, and tone in these instances that is noticed by the learner.

VI. Retention and transfer of learning

1 In transferring learning, the teacher/trainer should be aware of latent learning and offer reinforcement to prompt the demonstration of such learning.

2 Time does not cause forgetting per se; it merely allows for interfering learning processes to occur between what was learned and the time recall is desired.

3 Retroactive inhibition refers to the interference of new material on the ability to recall older material. Proactive inhibition occurs when old material interferes with the learning of new material. At times, therefore, it is wise to almost over-learn or repeat some material many times.

4 Some learned material is not recalled, as it is repressed in the subconscious of the learner because its overt demonstration is deemed to be harmful to the learner.

5 Identical stimuli presented in the learning and application settings should result in positive transfer. The learning of principles that apply across situations also aids in transfer of learning.

6 Transfer is aided if responses are given in situations which are similar to those which will be encountered in the post-learning environment.

7 Transfer is aided if the learner is able to demonstrate generalization (see IV-12).

8 Retention is strengthened if a variable-ratio reinforcement schedule is followed (see V-10).

VII. Practice

1 The learner must be encouraged (i.e. reinforced) to take practice seriously.

2 Practice should include responses to different stimuli than those encountered in learning, but which may be encountered in actual application (see IV-12).

3 Distributed, rather than massed practice with frequent short rests, is usually optimal.

USES OF THE PRINCIPLES AND FINDINGS

It is obvious that while not all of these findings and principles from learning theory and research are applicable to each type of training and development program, some are of obvious use. Depending on the type of program, exigencies of time and cost, and the characteristics of the trainees and trainers, some will be more relevant than others. Furthermore, the seven categories are not meant to be entirely separate. Many items necessarily overlap. The most important aspect of the categories is their *interdependent* nature. Program developers can benefit from some consideration of each category.

As with so many aspects of organizations, the effective design and implementation of training and development programs depend largely on the recognition of the contingencies the data from the seven categories present to the specialist. In each particular instance, the categories come together in a unique way to form a complex learning situation or set of contingencies to be managed. The use of a particular type of training program can depend upon the characteristics of the trainees, which can depend upon the learning environment and learning content, which may depend upon the role of the trainer, and so on. It can thus be seen that each of the seven categories may influence, or be contingent upon, any or all of the others in any given learning situation. The training and development specialist's success in facilitating learning will, therefore, depend in large part on his ability to properly *diagnose* a situation and then develop the most effective learning strategies for that situation. In the diagnostic phase of the facilitation of learning in organizations, the seven categories represent the possible sources of data which can be gathered regarding a training situation (e.g. data regarding the environment, the trainer, the trainees, etc.) (see Figure 1).

After the diagnosis is completed, the actual *design* of a particular program or learning strategy can begin. The statements in each category can be scanned for their relevance to a specific type of strategy, such as programmed instruction, lectures, modeling, etc. For example, if a "skill" training program is required, statements concerning practice, knowledge of results, and reinforcement schedules would be helpful. Following design, the *implementation* of the strategy can be aided by the statements, as they suggest points to be noted which can deter or facilitate implementation in a particular situation. For example, as category three notes, certain characteristics of the learner are vital considerations which would make some strategies more effective than others. The last stage in training and development work is *evaluation* of the strategy and possible *redesign*. This stage can be aided as the seven categories again present the sources of probable success or failure.

The principles and findings from learning theory and research have been presented as an initial list compiled to help those engaged in training and development programs become aware of the scope of the learning literature which is applicable to their programs. The list is also designed for use in the following stages of training and development work: diagnosis of the learning situation, design of the learning strategy, implementation of the strategy, and evaluation and possible redesign. The seven categories are offered as possible sources of data which combine to form each particular training and development situation. Data gathered from the seven categories can facilitate a more rigorous diagnostic effort on the part of the training and development specialist. This diagnosis aids in tying the unique learning situation faced by the specialist to the learning strategy most amenable to that situation. Particular statements within the categories can also be scanned as to their obvious use as guides in implementing specific programs such as MBO, skill training, performance appraisals, and the many other training and development programs which are designed to facilitate learning in organization settings.

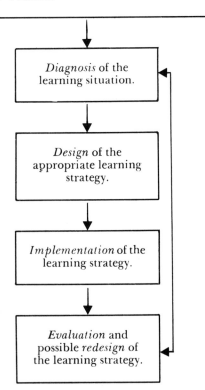

CATEGORIES OF DATA IN THE
LEARNING SITUATION

    I.   The learning environment.
   II.   The role of the teacher/trainer.
  III.   The characteristics of the learner.
  IV.   Basic processes in the human learn-
        ing activity.
   V.   Reinforcement and punishment.
  VI.   Retention and transfer of learning.
 VII.   Practice.

Diagnosis of the learning situation.

Design of the appropriate learning strategy.

Implementation of the learning strategy.

Evaluation and possible *redesign* of the learning strategy.

Figure 1

REFERENCES

Bass, B., and Vaughan, J. *Training in Industry: The Management of Learning.*
    Belmont, California: Wadsworth, 1968.
Beatty, R. W., and Schneier, Craig Eric. "Training the Hard-Core Unemployed
    through Positive Reinforcement." *Human Resource Management,* Winter
    1972, 11(4), pp. 11–17.
Berrelson, B., and Steiner, G. *Human Behavior.* New York: Harcourt Brace,
    1967.
Blumenfeld, W. A., and Holland, M. C. "A Model for the Empirical Evaluation
    of Training Effectiveness." *Personnel Journal,* Aug. 1971, 50(8), pp. 634–40.

Bugelski, B. R. *The Psychology of Teaching,* second edition. Indianapolis: Bobbs-Merrill, 1971.

Goldstein, A. P., and Sorcher, M. "Changing Managerial Behavior by Applied Learning Techniques." *Training and Development Journal,* Mar. 1973, 27(2), pp. 36-9.

Golembiewski, R. T. *Renewing Organizations; The Laboratory Approach to Planned Change.* Itasca, Ill.: Peacock, 1972.

Hilgard, E. R., and Bower, G. H. *Theories of Learning,* third edition. New York: Appleton Century Crofts, 1966.

Logan, F. A. *Fundamentals of Learning and Motivation.* Dubuque, Iowa: Wm. Brown, 1970.

Murphy, J. "Is It Skinner or Nothing?" *Training and Development Journal,* Feb. 1972, 26(2), pp. 2-9.

Schrank, W. R. "Three Experiments in Education." *Personnel Journal,* Sept. 1971, 50(9), pp. 702-4.

Skinner, B. F. *The Technology of Teaching.* New York: Appleton Century Crofts, 1968.

Staats, A. W., and Staats, C. K. *Complex Human Behavior: A Systematic Extension of Learning Principles.* New York: Holt, 1963.

FOR DISCUSSION AND REVIEW

1 Why would learning-theory principles and research seem to be relevant for training programs?

2 What would be useful to know about the learning environment before designing a training program?

3 Explain the author's model of the training and development process (Fig. 1).

C. ORGANIZATIONAL DEVELOPMENT AND CAREER DEVELOPMENT

E. E. Huse

Organization Development: Theory, Values, and Approaches

INTRODUCTION

Having described the concept of "systems," we can now go more deeply into the underlying theory and assumptions of OD. As an evolving and rapidly growing discipline, OD has had successes as well as failures; problems as well as praise. This chapter has three main purposes. The first is to describe some of the current problems with OD. The second is to examine some of the issues in OD. The third is to introduce the typology, or series of change strategies, that will be used in later chapters of this book.

What are some of the unresolved problems in OD? First, we do not really have a good understanding of theory in this area. Motivational theory as it applies to individuals is unclear and as a result, the general theory behind OD is not as strong as might be hoped. We know, for example, that certain strategies work in given situations, but we are not certain exactly why they work. Therefore, we need better and more innovative approaches to research design in OD. A third problem is the differing values and norms of change agents. Most change agents have a set of values, but these are not always explicit and may well vary from one practitioner to another. Fourth, there is the issue of when participation should be used and under what conditions it is most likely to be successful.

What are some of the issues in OD? Among the issues is the problem of power, which until recently has been avoided by many OD practitioners. Another issue concerns the appropriate level of intervention into the client system and, indeed, identifying the client. In addition, there are a number of ethical considerations.

Perhaps the most important section of this chapter is the description of a typology of change strategies, or interventions. . . . This typology of OD interventions is arranged in descending order of focus on the individual. At the highest level of intervention, operations analysis, little direct attention is paid *to* the individual as such, although the individual may be highly affected *by* the change. For example, redesigning an organization according to some newly developed concepts of organization design may affect the individual greatly, but the direct focus is on the total organization or appropriate subsystem rather than on the individual. At each "deeper" level of intervention, more attention is paid to the individual until, at the deepest level, the focus is primarily on the individual, with little focus on the organization as such.

Theory of organization development: the state of the art

Many OD programs have shown excellent *results*, although the underlying reasons, theory, are not as clear. Although OD is based on "behavioral science knowledge," that knowledge is still incomplete. Barnes says, "Despite the common occurrence of organizational change, its dynamics and underlying processes are understood in only rough, ill-defined ways."[1] The process of organizational change involves multiple, complex sets of variables whose interaction, identity, and impact vary from one situation to another. Furthermore, although we can think about a systems model at this level of complexity, we lack the technology to accurately identify, isolate, and measure the variables that go into such a model. However, as Sashkin points out, there is a growing body of literature that has added to our knowledge of theory in the field.[2] For example, about a decade and a half ago, Lippitt, Watson, and Westley published the first theoretical and applied approach to planned change.[3] Sashkin concludes, "While there is much more work needed, in both theory and practice, the state of the art of integration of this body of knowledge is not much, if at all, behind that of other areas in psychology or psychology as a whole.[4]

Burke points out that although the field of OD is in a fluid state and is continually changing and developing, at least 15 books on the theory of OD have been published in the last 15 years.[5] Among the most notable authors in this area are Argyris,[6] Beckhard,[7] Bennis,[8] Blake and Mouton,[9] Hornstein, Bunker, Burke, Gindes, and Lewicki,[10] Lawrence and Lorsch,[11] Likert,[12] Lippitt,[13] Marrow, Bowers, and Seashore,[14] Margulies and Raia,[15] Schein,[16] and Walton.[17] Burke further points out that at least 50 books have been written on the topic of OD. Because of the enormous number of articles that have been written, he does not even attempt to reference them.

We have already discussed the difficulty of using a systems approach to social systems, particularly with regard to the identification, measurement, and interaction of the multiple variables involved. In addition, we can identify at least six additional problems with OD theory: (1) underlying assumptions about people; (2) the concept of the individual vs. the group; (3) differing values and norms of change agents; (4) conditions for participation; (5) other variables in the social system; and (6) approaches to research design.

Underlying assumptions about people

The state of the art of current theories of individual motivation is mixed. There is no one, acceptable theory of motivation to which everybody subscribes. The pages of professional journals are filled with attack and counterattack regarding different theories. Without a good, well-understood, clear, concise theory of individual motivation, it is difficult to build a metatheory which takes into account individual motives, needs, wants, and desires. Although most OD practitioners believe that humans seek greater achievement and strive for more responsibility, challenge, and self-actualization, not everybody agrees with this concept. Certainly, the behavioral modification theorists would see humans as responding to conditioning rather than achieving growth through free choice.

The concept of the individual vs. the group

Here, again, there is basic disagreement. Most OD practitioners believe that the work group, not the individual, is the primary focus for change. Indeed, we have a great deal of evidence that the work group does have an important influence on individual members. However, some OD practitioners believe that the individual should be the primary target of change. Others believe that the main focus should be on overall organizational redesign. It seems necessary to do a better job of articulating the circumstances under which the individual, the group, and/or the total social system should be the primary focus for change. As of now, the best evidence is that the primary work group appears to be the best focus for planned change, but this is probably not true for all cases in all situations.

Differing values and norms of change agents

Every change agent has a normative, conceptual model of the ideal organization. Frequently, these conceptual models vary considerably from change agent to change agent. Further the change agent's model is frequently at variance with the model that the manager (or the worker) has. Tichy, *et al.*, have developed a method to enable consultants and clients to make their models more explicit and, therefore, more available to open, honest, evaluation, and comparison of the models.[18]

Conditions for participation

Many, but not all, OD practitioners value participation and stress the importance of participation under almost every conceivable circumstance. Although strong emphasis has been placed on the *value* of participation, there has also been a great deal of controversy about where, when, and how it is helpful. For example, in reviewing the literature on participation, White and Ruh cited the conflicting studies and failure to replicate results. They address themselves to a key issue: Do all employees desire participation, or does the personal value system of the individual have a moderating effect? Some research indicates that only workers with higher-order needs value participation and that many "alienated" workers or workers from particular subcultures do not value participation. Their study of 2755 employees in six manufacturing organizations found that the employees had a consistently positive reaction between job attitudes and participation in decision making. They found no support "for the hypothesized moderating effects of values on the relationships between participation and job attitudes. Possible methodological weaknesses are discussed, as well as the implication of these and other negative findings . . ."[19]

In spite of the research (pro and con) on participation and just as once the terms "OD" and "T-group" were almost synonymous, so now the terms "OD" and "participation" or "participative management" are almost synonymous in the minds of many people, including both OD practitioners and managers. However, as Sashkin and Frohman point out, participation involves at least two basic concepts: participation as a *method* for bringing about change and participation as a *goal* of change. They indicate that although increased participation of all employees *in* bringing about change is a basic, laudable element of OD, it is not necessarily a part of OD theory or practice. (Certainly, as we will see later, some practitioners would disagree with that statement.) After a lengthy review of the research studies, they concluded that "perhaps the greatest research need is the more precise determination of when participation should be the *aim* of OD, as well as the method."[20]

Sashkin has done a great deal of thinking about participation and has articulated some of the theoretical issues perhaps as clearly as anyone else has. The following is a paraphrase of some of his thinking.[21] The various approaches to participation do not differentiate among participation in change, in goal setting, in problem solving, and in decision making. Although these activities are related, they are quite different from one another.

A second issue is that the effects of participation have not been clearly identified. Increased effectiveness of participation can result from: better information, which can increase the quality of problem solutions, goals, and decisions; greater commitment, which means greater acceptance of the changes, solutions, goals, or decisions; and greater adaptiveness, since the participants learn to use new processes in making changes, arriving at solutions, and in determining goals or decisions.

A third issue mentioned by Sashkin is that we have not sufficiently traced through the results of different methods of participation, which can involve individuals, dyads, groups, or entire organizations. These methods seem to work in different ways for different needs, such as task completion, control over work behavior, and/or improving co-worker relationships. Finally, he notes that the contingency relationship of the change method or approach and the change-goal congruence has not been worked on at all. To remedy this lack, Sashkin is developing a "systematic contingency analysis which should prove valuable in guiding future research and application."[22]

. . .

ISSUES, VALUES, AND ETHICS IN ORGANIZATION DEVELOPMENT

There has been a growing amount of concern about the assumptions and values underlying OD, including philosophical issues such as the nature of power, normative values, and ethical considerations of the change agent. According to Burke, there are at least four areas in which OD, as currently practiced, has limitations.[30] The first is the domain of OD itself. Does it include management by objectives? Career development? Which interventions are OD processes and which are not? The second, and perhaps more important, issue is that OD does not deal effectively with power and the use of power. For example, there is little about the OD process that helps minorities gain more for themselves in the way of greater recognition or better promotion opportunities. The third area of limitation is that managers tend to think in short-term time frames, whereas most OD interventions occur over extended periods of time. For example, Walton and Warwick indicate that one of the problems with the Department of State's OD effort from 1965 to 1967 was the failure of the change agents to recognize that the tenure of executives in the department is only about two years.[31] The fourth limitation of OD is that the technologies and practices have gone "ahead" of the basic theory. In other words, although much actual work is being done in OD, little of it advances the theoretical framework of OD.

THE PROBLEM OF POWER

The problem of power in relation to OD is being attacked both philosophically and pragmatically. On the philosophical side, a number of people are questioning whether the OD practitioner is not tacitly accepting the nature of the overall system. For example, Ross takes OD practitioners to task for remaining silent about some elements of their value system, pointing out that "the OD professional is either unconcerned with, or supportive of (in value terms), what the client organization actually does."[32] Arguing that OD practitioners ignore the purpose of the organization, he says that it makes little difference if an organization making magnesium bombs or napalm is managed benignly or despotically and that the attempt to meet the needs of both the individual and the organization is only a matter of "making some people happier at the job of making others richer."[33] For him, no amount of current OD work would overcome the basic characteristics of capitalism which include competition, power, privilege, and wealth.

. . .

Level of intervention

Critical to the success of any OD effort is the selection of an appropriate level of intervention, which of course depends on the diagnosis of the problem. Selection of an appropriate level of intervention is closely related to both the concept of power and the change agent's own norms and values. For example, the depth of intervention will depend on management's awareness that a problem exists and willingness to undertake the change effort. If the problem is diagnosed as one of structural design, the depth of the interventional strategy may require more than the interpersonal learnings so frequently emphasized in OD, which brings us to the second aspect of selecting an appropriate level of intervention—the change agent's personal norms and values.

Most OD practitioners tend to emphasize interpersonal relationships in change efforts, e.g., sensitivity training, or the T-group. Therefore, the change agent's own values may dictate the use of a favorite tool, or technique, for accomplishing organizational change. In turn, this technique may dictate the level of intervention selected. It is obvious, therefore, that the diagnostic stage of an OD program is highly important, for unless the consultant is highly sensitive to the state of readiness for change in the organization, its prevailing culture, and the expectations of the client system, he may impose his own value systems on the client system. . . .

Who is the client?

Most OD consultants consider the entire social system to be their client—that they are working for the total organization rather than for the individual manager. Nevertheless, they are paid as management consultants and may find themselves in a real role conflict as to just who the client is. In a very thought-provoking article, Argyris describes two cases in which the consultants violated their own norms of openness and authenticity. In the first case, which involved the use and feedback of information gathered through questionnaires and interviews, one of the department heads became angry and defensive during the feedback process. In turn, the consultants were not open about their own concern and frustration. As Argyris points out, the immediate "payoff" for the consultants was that they remained in the "good graces" of the plant manager.[46] However, this was accomplished at a cost, since the plant manager had proof that the consultants did not practice what they preached, but instead accepted the norms and values of the client system. Much the same thing happened in the second case. Although the consultants became accepted "by *becoming a part* of the client system,"[47] they were never accepted as consultants whose values and effectiveness the client system thought worthy of serious exploration.

The issue of values and norms

As we indicated earlier, there is no such thing as a value-free society. For example, millions of American citizens cannot understand the Chinese philosophy of government, and millions of Chinese cannot understand the American system. There is room for legitimate argument and debate about values and norms, particularly at the level of the behavioral sciences, since the generation of knowledge about human behavior results in the development of sets of norms and values. Part of the question here is the issue of where these norms and values come from. As Argyris points out, "To repeat, all descriptive concepts, once they are used to organize reality and guide behavior, become normative."[48] He goes on to describe the "theory of rational man" and the necessity for many "human relations" theorists to deal more directly with the rational side of man, including both intellectual and cognitive variables. At the same time, he makes a strong case that theorists who stress the "rationality" of man must also give more attention to attitudes and feelings, making a strong plea to the "rational-man theorists to consider more seriously the information coming from behavioral science research."[49]

However, the article has a deeper significance in terms of his statement that a descriptive concept *becomes a norm* once it is used to guide behavior and organize reality. This occurs in two ways. If people follow through on the implications of descriptive generalizations, those generalizations become normative. Argyris cites the case of a black militant who used the hypothesis that frustration leads to aggression as a way of explaining and justifying his behavior. Since he was frustrated, he *should* become aggressive. Second, if we describe something in a generalized way, this description of what "is" becomes a self-fulfilling prophecy.

Ethical considerations

In the preceding section, we talked about ethical considerations primarily in terms of power. There are other ethical considerations as well, even though, in a sense, they are all related to power.

Selection of the proper level of intervention Frequently, as we have indicated before, the change agent has a favorite tool or technique which he likes to use under any and all circumstances. The T-group has been one of the most used (and misused) of all of the intervention techniques. As the popularity of the T-group wanes, other "fads" or "panaceas" emerge. The current buzz-words are either "job enrichment" or "transactional analysis." Developing contingency theories of leadership and organizational design raises the question of whether there is "one best way" to manage. Important here is the problem of doing a good job of diagnosis, bearing in mind that a change in one subsystem will have ramifications throughout the entire system.

Freedom to become involved The need for more information and freedom to become involved if desired is true at all levels of the intervention typology. In job enrichment, which is relatively impersonal, the individual who wants a routine, repetitive job should be allowed to perform that kind of job. At the same time, the individual who wants to take on more challenging work should also have that freedom. However, freedom to make a choice implies knowledge about the event. This is particularly true as we move into the deeper, more interpersonal levels of intervention, such as sensitivity training.

Most individuals who get involved in sensitivity training have little knowledge about what the process is, what it involves, and the nature and consequences of the process. A classic case is that described by Kuriloff and Atkins, who used the T-group approach to improve interpersonal relationships and skills.[52] After five months as president of a small manufacturing firm, Kuriloff decided to begin the T-group. Subordinates were told that they had an opportunity to go through five days of special training, although there is little evidence that the T-group was clearly described. The subordinates were also told that "attendance is voluntary, and if you choose not to come, it won't be held against you."[53] However, the wording, at least as given in the article, indicates that the subordinates actually regarded the invitation as a command performance.

Hans, the production manager, declined to participate. During the first two days, there was a great deal of discussion about his absence and how to pressure him into coming to the training session. When he did appear, on the third day, he was submitted to a great deal of pressure since, in his absence, he had been harshly criticized for being a relentless, unfeeling, Nazi-like person. In the session, he finally talked about his own background, suffering, and experience, which allowed others to sympathize and empathize with him. However, it is clear from the article that there was a great deal of coercion, manipulation, and other subtle tactics designed to "force" people to open up.

The issue of manipulation The case just described shows strong elements of manipulation: first, to get the top management into the training session; second, to get Hans involved; and third, efforts by the trainer to keep people from remaining silent. In discussing the value dilemmas of the change agent, Kelman discusses the problem of manipulation, pointing out that behavior change "inevitably involves some degree of manipulation and control, and at least an implicit imposition of the change agent's values on the client or the person he is influencing."[54] As he points out, this places the change agent on two horns of a dilemma: (1) any attempt to change is in itself a change and thereby a manipulation, no matter how slight; (2) there exists no formula or method to structure a change situation so that such manipulation can be totally absent. To attack the first aspect of the dilemma, Kelman would stress freedom of choice, seeing any action that limits freedom of choice as being ethically ambiguous or worse. To attack the second aspect, Kelman feels that the change agent must remain keenly aware of his own value systems and alert to the possibility that he is imposing, rather than exposing, the values he holds. In other words, one way out of the dilemma is to make the change effort as open as possible, with the *free consent and knowledge of the individuals involved.*

Lippitt helps alleviate the dilemma of the change process by describing some of the assumptions underlying what he calls "organization renewal."

a   There are human problems in today's organizations which are unavoidable, since they involve varying degrees of interpersonal and intergroup tension.

b   It is better to solve such human problems than to allow them to remain unsolved.

c   Trial-and-error processes used in the past are no longer adequate, and we need to use behavioral science for the deliberate attempt at solving these problems.

d   Principles of ethical control have, as their most promising source, our system of democratic and scientific values.

Further, the process should be collaborative and, ideally, should involve all the people involved in the change. The process should also be experimental and should be addressed to helping the people themselves to become more competent and able to handle their own problems and develop solutions. "The idea is not to get away from problems, which is to get away from reality, but rather to know better how to confront, diagnose and solve problems."[55]

Competence Certainly, any practitioner in any professional field should remain within the limits of his competence and not make exaggerated claims about what OD or any particular OD technique can do for the organization or the individual. Toward this end, the American Psychological Association publishes a set of ethical principles.[56] Established in 1971, the International Association of Applied Social Scientists, Inc., is striving to promote ethical standards as well as to accredit practitioners. Further, as Walton points out, the major journal of OD, *The Journal of Applied Behavioral Science*, regularly publishes case studies of OD interventions and quite specifically asks the authors to clearly articulate the values and norms underlying their work. The invited comments on these detailed accounts frequently discuss ethical problems.[57]

A final note on ethics After reviewing a number of OD interventions, Walton [58] concluded that ethical issues could arise from five types of inconsistencies:

a   Between the goals and strategies of the organization and the practitioner's values and norms.

b   Between managerial actions that the change agent's interventions are associated with and the practitioner's concepts of fairness and justification.
c   Between the consequences of the practitioner's interventions and his personal value system.
d   Between the actual behavior and actions of the practitioner and the professional standards which normally cover the professional client relationship.
e   Between the consequences of the interventions and the values which are generally attributed to the practice of OD.

A TYPOLOGY OF OD INTERVENTIONS

This section is important because it describes a variety of OD techniques or interventions. Here, we will summarize different techniques or interventions in terms of their depth, from relatively impersonal to highly personal. [See Fig. 1]. . . .

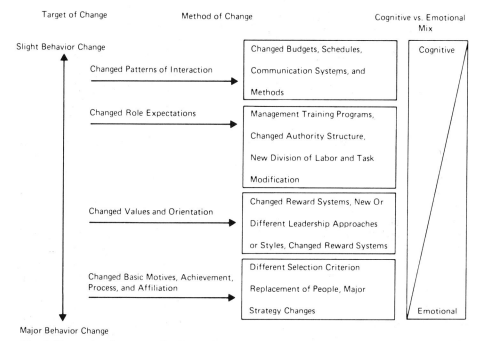

Fig. 1 Elements of an organizational development program. (Adapted from P. Lawrence and J. Lorsch, *Developing Organizations: Diagnosis and Actions*, Reading, Mass.: Addison-Wesley, 1969, p. 87.)

The more impersonal, superficial approaches are less central to the individual and are less likely to cause either psychological harm or good. The deeper the level, the more direct the impact on the individual for either good or bad. As a result, Harrison suggests two basic criteria for selecting the appropriate depth of intervention: *"first, to intervene at a level no deeper than that required to produce enduring solutions to the problems at hand; and second, to intervene at a level no deeper than that at which the energy and resources of the client can be committed to problem solving and to change."*[66]

Harrison also makes a distinction between two types of consultants—those whose approach is based on analyzing and trying to overcome the resistance of the client and those whose approach is to work with the client on the client's "felt needs." It is his belief that the "resistance-centered" change agent usually tries to get the client system to work at a depth at which it is uncomfortable and sees the client's resistance as being a defense against admitting "real" needs and problems. This approach comes basically from clinicians and is characteristic of those who tend to specialize in such techniques as T-groups and encounter groups. The "needs-centered" consultant, by contrast, works within the established organizational climate, although he does not necessarily accept the current climate as being the proper one for the organization to have. Nevertheless, he tends to start where people are, not where he thinks they should be.

Table 1 shows a continuum from the highly impersonalized intervention approach to highly personalized, individual-centered intervention approaches. In later chapters of this book, we will use Harrison's typology to classify and describe different OD techniques, approaches, or interventions, starting with the more impersonal approaches, such as organization design, through more personalized interventions, including laboratory, or sensitivity, training and encounter groups. Following systems theory, Harrison lists five strategies of interventions, successively "deeper" than the others in terms of the *overt emotional involvement* of the individual involved in the change process.

Table 1
A Typology of Change According to Depth of Intervention

SYSTEMWIDE APPROACHES
Contingency theories of organizational design
Survey feedback
Organizational confrontation meetings
Grid organizational development (The six-phase Grid OD program covers almost
    every level, but it is placed here for the sake of convenience and clarity, since it
    does not involve a total, systemwide effort.)

Individual/organizational interfaces

Job design
Decision centers
Role analysis
Management by Objectives

Concern with personal work style

Process consultation
Third-party intervention
Team building
Family group diagnostic meeting
Family group team building meeting
Improving interdepartmental/intergroup intervention

Intrapersonal analysis and relationships

Life and career-planning interventions
Laboratory training
Encounter groups
Personal consultation

Operations analysis

At this level, we are concerned with the functions and roles that need to be performed in the organization as opposed to individual motivation, attitudes, and values. Here, the focus is on specifying the power, resources, and tasks to be performed and includes defining jobs for individuals and work groups in the organization.

This level is highly dependent on the structural design of the organization and can be used to ensure that the structure of the organization fits its environment. If there is a proper organizational "fit" between the two, individuals are more likely to achieve a sense of competence and satisfaction from performing the job. As Morse and Lorsch indicate, individuals can have a sense of competence and achieve high motivation in a highly bureaucratic organization, provided there is a good organizational "fit."[67]

Controlling and evaluating individual performance and behavior

Harrison's second level of intervention is concerned with the selection, placement, training, and appraisal of individuals according to job design and other structural characteristics. The focus is on observable performance rather than on the personal characteristics of the individual. It is clear that individual motivation is involved and that individuals and groups have "feelings" about appraisal, selection, and job design, but the focus is on the *observable*. Change attempts can include both external rewards and punishment, e.g., promotions, salary increases, and transfers, as well as internal rewards, e.g., greater job satisfaction. Job enrichment and management by objectives are two intervention techniques used at this level of change strategy.

This level of intervention strategy may well be applicable to all types of organizations, although it may be most useful in systems or subsystems in which external rewards are important. It may not be as effective in areas such as research and development, areas in which the scientists already have a high degree of freedom and autonomy.

Concern with work style

At this level of Harrison's typology, the primary focus is on working relationships which frequently require negotiation or bargaining between groups and individuals with regard to feelings, attitudes, and sentiments. It includes such "human" areas as the extent to which the individual does or does not delegate authority, the degree of worker collaboration or competition with others on work-related issues, and the way in which the individual does or does not communicate information to others.

Interventions at this "depth" may involve attempts to change behavior in work relationships among individuals and/or groups. An intervention at this level also involves the satisfaction or dissatisfaction that the members of the organization obtain from the work behavior of others. Intervention at this level may require interpersonal or intergroup negotiation and bargaining and can result in changes in group norms about collaboration, communications, and ways of resolving present or future conflicts. These interventions are probably more effective in organizations which exist in an uncertain environment, in which organizational policies, rules, and procedures are not tightly defined, and in which the informal organization is more important than the formal organization. By the same token, interventions at this level, e.g., team building, resolving intergroup conflict, and the like, may be less effective in relatively rigid, bureaucratic systems or subsystems existing in a relatively stable, certain, and known environment.

Interpersonal relationships

According to Harrison's typology, the deepest level of relationships examines the individual's deepest attitudes and values about his own functioning and identity. At this level, the focus is on increasing the range of personal experience and knowledge that the individual can bring into awareness and cope with. The intervention strategy may be on a one-to-one basis or on a group basis, such as T-groups or marathon sessions. The strategy of intervention at this level is more appropriate when the individual is less dependent on bureaucratic rewards and pressures and more likely to seek internal and self-determined rewards which increase his sense of self-worth, competence, and autonomy.

To some extent, we can question the placement of particular intervention techniques at any particular place on the continuum. For instance, Grid OD has a number of phases. The earlier phases really involve both intrapersonal analysis and concern with personal work styles, whereas the later phases are concerned more with the total organization. However, since Grid OD is designed as a formal, highly instrumented intervention technique, it is placed under the category of "System-wide Approaches." The same issue can be raised with the "survey feedback" technique. At times, a change agent doing process consultation may use a short questionnaire to help a group diagnose its current state, a technique described by Schein.[68] In these instances, the questionnaire is given, scored immediately, and then discussed in the group to help it get a better feeling of its current effectiveness and possible blockages.

As used in Table 1, the term "survey feedback" refers to approaches used by such people as Likert and Bowers in organizations such as the Institute for Social Research at the University of Michigan, which uses a highly standardized questionnaire developed and modified over a number of years. The questionnaire is administered either to a large social system or to relatively large subsystems and then systematically "fed back" in small groups with a change agent present to assist in identifying problems and helping the group begin to solve them.

In other words, Table 1 shows a list of OD interventions, or techniques, which range from the more superficial, impersonal to the deeper, more personal in terms of the feelings and attitudes of the individual. This is not to indicate that feelings and attitudes are not involved at *all* levels—they are. The important issue and difference is the *degree of focus*. The deeper the level, the more directly the focus is on the feelings and attitudes of the individual.

Table 1 should not be interpreted as indicating that one, and only one, technique should be used at a time. A combination of change methods of interventions is frequently necessary. "Survey feedback," although it appears under systemwide approaches, actually works best with a modified form of process consultation. . . .

CONCLUSION

In this chapter, we have examined a number of the theoretical underpinnings of OD. As a rapidly growing discipline, OD still has a number of unresolved problems, and better, more clearly defined research is needed to bring OD from its current form as an "art" to a more scientific discipline.

We then examined some of the values and issues in OD, showing that OD, at least in the minds of some, does not deal adequately with issues such as power and that OD needs to become more interdisciplinary in nature. We also examined the issue of ethics, the use of information, and value judgments held by many OD practitioners.

In the final section, we outlined a number of different OD techniques or interventions, placing them on a continuum of *depth* of intervention. This typology will be followed in later chapters of this book. Our purpose in briefly describing them here was to provide a brief overview and introduction in order to put the most widely used interventions into an overall perspective.

REFERENCES

1 L. Barnes, "Approaches to Organizational Change," in W. Bennis, K. Benne, and R. Chin, eds., *The Planning of Change*, New York: Holt, Rinehart and Winston, 1969, p. 79.

2 M. Sashkin, "Organization Development Pro and Con I. Organization Development Practices," *Professional Psychology*, (May 1973), pp. 187–194.

3 R. Lippitt, J. Watson, and B. Westley, *The Dynamics of Planned Change*, New York: Harcourt, Brace and World, 1958.

4 M. Sashkin, *op. cit.*, p. 188.

5 W. Burke, "Organization Development Pro and Con II. Organization Development," *Professional Psychology*, (May 1973), p. 194.

6 C. Argyris, *Intervention Theory and Method*, Reading, Mass.: Addison-Wesley, 1970; *Management and Organizational Development*, New York: McGraw-Hill, 1971.

7 R. Beckhard, *Organization Development—Strategies and Models*, Reading, Mass.: Addison-Wesley, 1969.

8 W. G. Bennis, *Changing Organizations*, New York: McGraw-Hill, 1966; *Organization Development: Its Nature, Origins, and Prospects*, Reading, Mass.: Addison-Wesley, 1969.

9 R. R. Blake and J. S. Mouton, *Corporate Excellence Through Grid Organization Development*, Houston: Gulf Publishing, 1968.

10 H. A. Hornstein, B. B. Bunker, W. W. Burke, M. Gindes, and R. J. Lewicki, *Social Interventions: A Behavioral Science Approach*, New York: Free Press, 1971.

11 P. R. Lawrence and J. W. Lorsch, *Developing Organizations: Diagnosis and Action*, Reading, Mass.: Addison-Wesley, 1969.

12 R. Likert, *The Human Organization*, New York: McGraw-Hill, 1967.

13 G. L. Lippitt, *Organization Renewal*, New York: Appleton-Century-Crofts, 1969.

14 A. J. Marrow, D. G. Bowers, and S. E. Seashore, *Management by Participation*, New York: Harper & Row, 1967.

15 N. Margulies and A. P. Raia, *Organizational Development: Values, Process and Technology*, New York: McGraw-Hill, 1972.

16 E. H. Schein, *Process Consultation: Its Role in Organization Development*, Reading, Mass.: Addison-Wesley, 1969.

17 R. E. Walton, *Interpersonal Peacemaking: Confrontations and Third-Party Consultation*, Reading Mass.: Addison-Wesley, 1969.

18 N. Tichy, H. Hornstein, and J. Wisberg, "Organization Diagnosis and Intervention Strategies: Developing Emergent Pragmatic Theories of Change." Paper presented at the New Technology in Organization Development Conference, NTL Institute, New Orleans, February 18–19, 1974.

19 J. White and R. Ruh, "Effects of Personal Values on the Relationship between Participation and Job Attitudes," *Administrative Science Quarterly*, **18**, 4, (December 1973), p. 506.

20   M. Sashkin and M. Frohman, "Participation as a Factor in Organization Development." Undated manuscript, p. 11.

21   M. Sashkin, "Participation in Organizations, A Contingency Analysis." Paper presented at the Michigan Psychological Association, Eastern Michigan University, April 5, 1974.

. . .

30   W. Burke, *op. cit.*

31   R. Walton and D. Warwick, "The Ethics of Organization Development," *Journal of Applied Behavioral Science*, **9**, 6 (November/December 1973), pp. 681–699.

32   R. Ross, "Comment on Two Preceding Articles, OD for Whom?" *Journal of Applied Behavioral Science*, **7**, 5 (September/October 1971), p. 581.

33   *Ibid.*, p. 583.

. . .

46   C. Argyris, "Explorations in Consulting-Client Relationships," *Human Organization*, **20**, 3 (1961), p. 123.

47   *Ibid.*, p. 126.

48   C. Argyris, "Some Limits of Rational Man Organizational Theory," *Public Administration Review*, **33**, 3 (May/June 1973), p. 265.

49   *Ibid.*, p. 254.

. . .

52   A. Kuriloff and S. Atkins, "T-Group for a Work Team," *Journal of Applied Behavioral Science*, **2**, 1 (January/February 1966), pp. 63–93.

53   *Ibid.*, p. 67.

54   H. Kelman, "Manipulation of Human Behavior: An Ethical Dilemma for the Social Scientist," in W. Bennis, K. Berne, and R. Chin, eds. *The Planning of Change*, 2d ed., New York: Holt, Rinehart and Winston, 1969, p. 584.

55   G. L. Lippitt, *op. cit.*, p. 172.

56   American Psychological Association, *Ethical Principles in the Conduct of Research with Human Participants*, Washington, D.C., 1973.

57   R. Walton, "Ethical Issues in the Practice of Organizational Development," Harvard Graduate School of Business Administration, Working Paper #1840, May 1973.

58   *Ibid.*

. . .

65   R. Harrison, "Choosing the Depth of Organizational Intervention," *Journal of Applied Behavioral Science*, **6**, 2 (April/May/June 1970), pp. 181–202.

66   *Ibid.*, p. 201.

67   J. Morse and J. Lorsch, "Beyond Theory Y," *Harvard Business Review*, **48**, 3 (May–June 1970), pp. 61–68.

68   E. Schein, *op. cit.*, pp. 42–43.

FOR DISCUSSION AND REVIEW

1   Huse reviews several important issues related to OD. What is his conclusion regarding the current state of the art?

2   Why is the notion of power relevant to OD?

3   What factors would determine the level of intervention of an OD effort? What are the different levels of intervention?

4 Summarize the ethical issues facing an OD person, as discussed by the author.

5 How could the typology of OD interventions be useful to a practicing OD specialist?

6 What problems does the academic discipline of OD face? What problems does the applied technology of OD face?

Douglas T. Hall

Francine S. Hall

What's New in Career Management

In many organizations, the largest item in the corporate budget consists of wages and salaries. For this reason, financial problems that dictate cost reductions and increased efficiency usually boil down to problems of personnel and human resource management. Therefore, more creative, flexible, and efficient utilization of human resources through better corporate career planning can be a powerful means of dealing with some of the current headaches of managing a stable or shrinking organization in a stagnant economy. In this article, we will review some current (and probably all-too-familiar) human-resource management problems and report on how some organizations are coping with them through creative techniques for career management. We will also point out what is being neglected in the area of career development. And we will conclude with some general principles about how to make corporate career planning more effective.

PROBLEM 1: HOW CAN WE REDUCE
TURNOVER AMONG RECENTLY HIRED EMPLOYEES?

Students often graduate from college or business school with unrealistically high expectations about the amount of challenge and responsibility they will find in their first job. Then they are put through a job-rotation training program or into a fairly undemanding entry-level job, and they get turned off. They experience "reality shock." The result is low morale, low productivity, and high turnover. Some companies lose as many as one-third or one-half of their new recruits in the first year or two of employment. One company was hiring 130 people at one time in order to have 30 at the end of the first year!

The cost of turnover is tremendous, especially among professionals and management candidates. Michael Alexander, of Touche, Ross & Co., calculated in 1973 that the total cost (including recruiting expenses, training, reduced performance during orientation, and so on) of replacing a manager was $25,000 to $30,000. After three years of inflation, that figure might be closer to $40,000. Therefore, if your company hires 100 new MBAs this year and loses 25 of them in the first year, that first year of "reality shock" may be adding $1,000,000 annually to your operating expenses.

Obviously, then, you can save a lot of money by managing the entry and first year of new employees in a more satisfying way. As companies like AT&T and General Electric have found, making initial jobs more challenging and "stretching"

Reprinted by permission of the publisher from *Organizational Dynamics* 4 (Summer 1976), © 1976 by AMACOM, a division of American Management Associations.

not only decreases turnover, but also improves long-term career performance. In one study of two AT&T operating companies, David E. Berlew and Douglas T. Hall (1966) found that management trainees who received the most challenging first-year jobs were the most successful performers five to seven years later.

Select a challenging first job Granted, then, that one answer to Problem One is to make the first job more challenging. Just how do you go about it? First, instead of simply putting the new employee into any open job, give the matter more careful thought. If more than one job assignment is available, purposely slot the new employee into the most demanding one. "But," you ask, "how can I be sure he or she can handle it?" Good question; obviously, you can't be sure. However, our research shows that managers are quite conservative on this issue and usually err in the direction of making the first assignment too easy. This may eliminate the possibility of failure, but it also prevents the employee from achieving *pshchological success*, the exhilarating sense of accomplishment that results only from achieving a task that entailed a reasonable probability of failure. More likely than not, the new recruit will perform well in a tough assignment—especially if you are available to provide help and support when needed.

Provide job enrichment A second way of enhancing the first job is to provide a measure of job enrichment. How? Add more responsibility to the job, give the new employee increased authority, and let the new person deal directly with clients and customers (not through you); if new employees are doing special projects and making recommendations to you, let them follow through and implement these ideas. AT&T is currently training supervisors of certain new employees in the skills of job enrichment as a way of making initial jobs more of a "stretching" experience.

Assign the new recruit to demanding bosses A third way of improving the first job is to give more care and thought to selecting the supervisor to whom you assign the new recruit. As J. Sterling Livingston has shown, there is a "Pygmalion effect" in the relationship between a new employee and his or her boss. The more the boss expects and the more confident and supportive the boss is of the new employee, the better the recruit will perform. So don't assign a new employee to a "dead wood," undemanding, or unsupportive supervisor. Choose high-performing supervisors who will set high standards for the new employee during the critical, formative first year.

Give realistic job previews If it's not possible to upgrade the first job experience, the opposite strategy is to provide the employee with realistic expectations during the recruiting process. Several organizations (Prudential Insurance Company, Texas Instruments, the Southern New England Telephone Company, and the U.S. Military Academy) have employed *realistic job previews* (RJPs) in the form of booklets, films, visits, or talks that convey not only the positive side of organizational life, but some of the problems and frustrations as well (example: the close supervision, lack of variety, limited socializing opportunities, and criticism experienced by telephone operators).

"But we'll never be able to hire anyone if we tell them the bad news about the job," you may be thinking. Research by John Wanous and others has shown, however, that these fears are unjustified. The recruitment rate is the same for people receiving RJPs as for those who get the more traditional one-sided information.

The big return comes later, after the person starts work: Among the recipients of RJPs, turnover and dissatisfaction are significantly lower than for people on the receiving end of traditional job previews. So to retain more of your new recruits, as the (now somewhat dated) saying goes, "Tell it like it really is!"

A somewhat different form of the RJP has been experimentally introduced into management classrooms at the University of Wisconsin–Parkside in cooperation with the Goodyear Tire and Rubber Company's North Chicago Hose Plant. When a new recruit reacted to his first job with, "We never learned this in a classroom!" training manager Ernie LaBrecque gradually began to bring supervisors into Parkside's classes on a regular basis. The purpose is quite simple: to provide tomorrow's hires with first-hand knowledge of what to expect.

While the Parkside–Goodyear efforts have been limited, the model has significant potential for companies that recruit on a regular basis at particular universities. Not only are business leaders generally welcome in classes, but the opportunity to establish an ongoing relationship has obvious mutual benefits.

PROBLEM 2: HOW CAN WE QUICKLY DEVELOP HIGH-POTENTIAL CANDIDATES (ESPECIALLY WOMEN AND MINORITIES) FOR MANAGEMENT POSITIONS?

The problem of identifying and selecting high-potential management candidates has been well researched over the years and is pretty well understood. Job sampling and other ways of simulating management jobs, such as assessment centers, have been shown to be effective though expensive ways of identifying managerial talent. The real problem is how we can best *train and develop* these promising candidates once they are identified.

Assessment centers for development Assessment centers were originally developed for selection purposes, to identify high-potential candidates for hiring or promotion. When used for selection purposes, the results of the assessment process are used by managers responsible for these personnel decisions and are often not fed back to the employee. More recently, however, assessment centers have also been used successfully for employee development. When they are used in this way, the emphasis is on feedback of results to the employee following the assessment experience. In a feedback session, a trained staff member points out the candidate's strong and weak points, illustrating them with examples of the candidate's behavior in the assessment activities. After the employee understands and accepts the feedback, the discussion turns to counseling and planning for future training experiences and developmental assignments that would lead to a particular target job in management.

Many companies, viewing the results of the assessment center experience as classified information, are reluctant to feed back this information to the employee. This secrecy represents a waste of extremely valuable developmental input, particularly in view of the high cost of putting the employee through the two- or three-day experience. Such secrecy also probably leads the candidate to develop unrealistically high expectations (as in the first job). If, on the other hand, assessment results are used for feedback and career counseling, several benefits are reaped: (1) The candidate's expectations are more realistic; (2) the candidate is helped in overcoming weaknesses; (3) the candidate has a specific career plan; and (4) the company is viewed as a partner rather than an adversary in career planning, something better calculated to result in career satisfaction.

Job pathing The AT&T research cited earlier showed the impact the first job can have on the employee's development. A logical extension of this idea is that a *se-*

quence of jobs can have even greater effects on the person's career growth. In fact, we would argue that *carefully sequenced job assignments have greater impact on a person's development than any other kind of training experience.* Job requirements demand that a person learn certain job-related skills. Training programs, by contrast, by and large do not demand learning. Job activities and job-related learning are by definition integrated into the ongoing work environment, whereas off-the-job training programs are often hard to reconcile with the "back home" job environment.

The critical factors in using jobs for developmental purposes are to identify (1) the skills and experience a person needs to reach a certain target job and (2) which jobs, in what sequence, will provide these skills and experiences in small enough increments so the person will not be overwhelmed, but in large enough jumps so that the person is always being stretched—thus minimizing career time to reach the target job.

One large retailing organization, for example, is undertaking just such a job-pathing program in an attempt to reduce the amount of time it takes to "grow" a store manager. Conventional wisdom in the organization is that it takes around fifteen years, but initial experiences with careful job plotting indicate that it can probably be done in five. Another widely held belief in this organization is that there are one or two main paths to the store manager's position. Yet examination of several alternative paths, which are quite feasible but for some reason never used, indicates that the company has more flexibility in plotting career paths than it is currently using. Plotting paths through several different functions makes it possible to grow "broader" managers.

Talent development among hourly employees Several existing methods of developing managerial talent among hourly workers may need to be reexamined in light of the need to comply with legislation on equal employment opportunity. Companies are beginning to address the question: "How can we attract a substantial number of women and minorities into these presupervisory programs?" To answer this question, some have begun to assess employee *perceptions* of upward mobility opportunities, organizational barriers to or support mechanisms for upward mobility, and the self-perceptions and role perceptions held by women and minorities. When, for example, a plant manager in a brewing company queried a woman on the reasons she *resisted* the opportunity to move into management, she replied, "I thought a production supervisor had to be a 'Two-Ton Tony.' " Obviously, this woman's resistance stemmed at least in part from the discrepancy between her perception of the role requirements and her self-image.

Another approach has been the use of in-service training institutes conducted by professional or trade organizations. While these are common in manufacturing (the Midwest Manufacturing Association, for example, has sponsored numerous "certificate" programs), organizations such as the National Association of Banking Women are also seeking ways of developing their numbers. Frequently, women and minorities view the opportunity for training through these associations as being less competitive and more supportive than company-sponsored programs.

PROBLEM 3: HOW CAN WE INCREASE PROMOTION OPPORTUNITIES IN A STABLE OR CONTRACTING ORGANIZATION?

For many organizations, the current push for career development, especially for women and minority candidates, comes in an economic period when career growth is hardest to provide: a period of corporate slow-down or retrenchment. When many new management positions are opening up in an organization, career opportunities abound; when they dry up, career advancement requires more careful planning. How can we make the most of these declining opportunities?

Cross-functional moves One developmental method is the cross-functional or lateral transfer. Such rotational transfers may occur often at the beginning of a person's career. After a certain point, however, organizations tend to keep people in a particular functional area in which they can become highly trained and specialized and spend enough time to pay off the company's investment. In the long run, this policy leads to obsolescence; the person who is not forced to learn about new areas from time to time ends up stale, bored, and increasingly less creative and productive. Cross-functional transfers throughout the career keep a person fresh and open to new learning and give him or her a broader perspective on the company as a whole.

An example of this sort of transfer occurred at Union Carbide, where three executive vice-presidents traded jobs. The reason for the move was to give each one a better "big picture" view of the total organization and prepare them better for the presidency. One of the men, Warren M. Anderson, explained the value of the move in an article in *Business Week* (July 14, 1975, pp. 82, 84):

> We were a holding company until the mid 1950s, and you could count on your fingers the number of people who moved from division to division. You grow up in a division, and you get about four miles tall but not very broad. . . . Everybody had sneered at lateral transfers. Now, they can point to us. I feel this gives me a chance to see the whole business.

Job pathing enables us to identify jobs *at the same organizational level* that demand more skills in certain areas than do other jobs. Thus the great potential of lateral moves for development is more effectively tapped. After two people trade jobs, as one retailing organization found, it is possible for each to end up in a more demanding position!

A critical issue in any kind of lateral move is how the transfer decision is made. When personnel staff specialists make the decisions, the moves may make good, sound technical sense—but may be unacceptable to the bosses of the people to be moved. Also, this kind of decision-making process implies that career planning is purely a staff function, and not the manager's job.

Management-personnel committees One way of getting managers more involved in career planning is through the mechanism of management-personnel committees. In this structure, which is employed by the Southern New England Telephone Company (SNET), each personnel committee is made up of managers from all the functions at the same level of management. Each committee meets once every week or two to decide what transfers will be made between their departments among people who report to them. They also make recommendations on promotions. Employees are assessed in terms of their management potential, ranging from Category 1 (high-level potential) to Category 6 (not promotable even if the company is on the verge of going out of business).

According to Robert Neal, director of human resources development for SNET, this process results in a high quality of personnel decisions and in personnel actions that generally are well accepted by those affected—both the bosses and the transferred employees. The process does deal with tough issues of bargaining ("I'll take one from your Category 5, but let's agree in writing that you'll take him back in two years"). Actual contracts are written and signed, in much the way that "player swaps" are handled in professional sports. Another benefit of this system, according to Neal, is that a "Cat. 5" in one department—say, marketing—may blossom into a "Cat. 2" in traffic. Employees are periodically reassessed in light of *recent* performance, since these transfers enable an employee to demonstrate potential that might otherwise have been hidden forever if he or she had stayed in one function or department.

One disadvantage of this process, of course, is that like most committee structures, it takes a fair amount of time. However, the benefits seem to justfiy the time invested. Another management "plus" of this system is that the managers who serve on personnel committees develop a greater identification with the company as a whole. The decision process involved forces them to rise above their own department loyalties and look at decisions from a broader perspective. The rate of interfunctional movement has increased from 5 percent of all transfers in 1968 to 50 percent now.

Whenever we discuss developmental lateral moves with executives, the response is usually surprisingly strong, either pro or cons. Some people see it as a radical, impractical idea because the need for retraining would be great, as would the organizational risk of having managers who are inexperienced in their new function or department. Lateral moves also buck a common norm in many organizations—namely, that the only good move is a promotion. Other managers report that they are beginning to experiment with cross-functional moves, and their experiences are generally favorable. Still others report they have never really thought about cross-functional moves, but they get very excited about this "creative new idea." There is nothing new or creative about lateral moves, however; the fact is that in many companies promotion policies are simply taken for granted, like "organization wallpaper," when they might quite easily and profitably be changed.

Fallback positions   One risk of a cross-functional transfer or promotion, especially when it occurs at a senior level, is that the person may fail in the new job simply because it's too demanding. Because many organizations are reluctant to move people down a level, there is some risk that the cross-functional transferee may become stuck in a position beyond his or her level of competence—the Peter Principle in action.

A novel way of reducing this risk in a high-level job move is to identify a fallback position into which the person can move if he or she is not successful after promotion or transfer. The fallback position assures the person of a position equal in status and pay to his or her original job if things don't work out in the new one. Establishing a fallback position in advance lets everyone involved know that (1) there is some risk in the promotion or transfer, (2) the company is willing to accept some of the responsibility for it, and (3) moving into the fallback position does not constitute failure. As a result, the ratchet effect of upward-only movement is partially eliminated, and the organization's degree of freedom in manpower planning is substantially increased.

Consider this illustration of the fallback-position concept: In the Heublein organization, one management-information systems expert was moved to finance, and a human-resources specialist was transferred to a job in production management. Without the fallback position, neither person might have been willing to take the risk. With it, people who have become highly specialized (perhaps overspecialized) can be helped to work their way back into general management. Among the other companies that have employed fallback positions are Procter and Gamble. Continental Can, and Lehman Brothers *(Business Week,* September 28, 1974).

Downward transfers More dramatic than the establishment of fallback positions is the policy of legitimizing downward transfers (demotions). Being able to move people down as well as up introduces considerably more flexibility in manpower planning. As organizational growth decreases, and as more people elect to "stay put" in their present job (or are compelled to), the result could be corporate stagnation—with few people entering or leaving the organization. To maintain flexibility, therefore, new ways of creating internal mobility become critical. For every person moved downward, a shot at a promotion is created for numerous people below this level. Where there is a policy against moving people down, the only way a vacancy could open up would be through retirement or death (assuming no organizational growth or turnover).

The problem with downward transfers, obviously, is the strong norm in our society against moving down. Moving up is good, moving laterally is suspect, and moving down spells *failure*.

The upward-mobility norm is a tough one to buck, but it is being challenged on several fronts:

1 As concern over the quality of life increases, more people are turning down promotions or accepting lower-level jobs in order to move to or to stay in such desirable geographical areas as San Diego, Minneapolis, Atlanta, and Seattle. When, for example, the department of psychology at San Diego State University advertised an opening for an assistant professor (a position generally filled by someone fresh out of graduate school), the department received many applications from full professors and department chairmen who were willing to move down in order to live in San Diego.

2 Realizing that growth opportunities are becoming more limited, people are willing to move down into a new area or company as a possible base from which to move up later on.

3 Given the option of being terminated or being demoted, people are often willing to accept a move down. As with many decisions in life, the attractiveness of a demotion often depends upon the nature of the alternatives. In recent cuts of technical personnel, companies such as General Electric and Chrysler first tried to place as many employees as possible in lower-level jobs rather than terminate them. Those who were moved down rather than out were viewed as being quite fortunate.

4 As the economy settles into a period of slower growth, expectations of rapid advancement may diminish and the upward-mobility norm may weaken. There is already evidence that the American success ethic is moving away from advancement and money as success symbols, toward self-fulfillment. As Daniel Yankelovich put it:

> Since World War II most Americans have shaped their ideas of success around money, occupational status, possessions, and the social mobility of their children. Now, ideas about success are beginning to revolve around various forms of self-fulfillment. If the key motif of the past was "keeping up with the Joneses," today it is, "I have my own life to live, let Jones shift for himself."

As part of this quest for personal self-fulfillment (which does not necessarily have to occur on the job), people may be more likely to take a lower-level job that gives them more autonomy or challenge or simply more freedom to pursue fulfillment off the job.

Other organizations are using downward transfers to open up management training and mobility options that otherwise would not exist. One large Canadian oil company has been experimenting with downward transfers at senior executive levels. This company has learned certain principles that increase the success of downward transfers. First, the people who are chosen to be moved down should be people who are known (by themselves and other employees) to be outstanding performers. This helps dissociate downward movement from failure (and, it is to be hoped, may even associate it with success). Over time, if enough obviously competent people are moved down, the norm of promotion-as-a-sign-of-success may be replaced with movement-as-a-sign-of-success. People to be moved down should be informed well in advance and told that they may be moved back to their present levels later.

Why are outstanding performers moved down? First, because even if a person is performing successfully at his or her job, there are still many equally promising people at the next level down, waiting for a higher-level challenge. Moving one person down temporarily gives many more people a good opportunity for development. The obviously successful person would be more secure and more effective in a downward move than would a less outstanding performer. Second, there may be "hot spots" at a lower level in the organization that call for the temporary trouble-shooting services of a successful higher-level person. Perhaps a tough marketing problem needs to be solved or maybe a department needs reorganizing. A key executive could come in on a one-year assignment, clean things up, and then move back to his previous level or to a new "hot spot."

A second principle is that important ground rules must be established: (1) No one will suffer a cut in pay as a result of a downward move, and (2) no one moved down will be terminated (to make it clear that the next move after moving down isn't out the door). People moved down thus received a sort of "tenure" that gave them more security than most other employees.

What are some of the preliminary results of the downward-transfer system in this firm? The most obvious is that intraorganizational mobility and flexibility have increased. More young people can move up into high-responsibility positions faster than before. They can also move back down and into other functional areas more easily.

What about the effects on the people moved down? According to the personnel director, the first few people (as one might anticipate) had mixed emotions about it. After several months, however, they began to appreciate the freedom from higher-level responsibilities and pressures. They appreciated having a bit more time to spend with their families, getting to know their grandchildren, and so on. They also enjoyed the stimulation of working with younger managers—learning new ideas and techniques from them and transmitting wisdom and experience to them.

An unintended consequence of these downward transfers has been an improvement in two-way communication, especially in the upward direction.

Corporate tenure

Some of the career-management policies we have just discussed, such as cross-functional transfers and downward moves, are often difficult to implement because of the threats they may pose to the person's security in the organization. One way to increase employees' sense of security, and at the same time to establish tougher performance standards and feedback, is through a system of corporate tenure.

Such a novel system has been used in a medium-sized Pennsylvania manufacturing firm. The president of this firm, Robert Seidel, took a look at how various types of organizations develop personnel. He decided that universities, for all their problems, did have one promising feature: the tenure system. The tenure system forces the university to take a good hard look at a person's performance and to give him or her straight feedback: "up or out."

Seidel modified the tenure system in this way. When a new employee is hired, he or she is put on a short-term probation period, a customary procedure in many organizations. At the end of the period, the employee's immediate superior and a personnel expert carefully appraise the person's performance. If it has been satisfactory, the employee is encouraged to stay on.

At this point, however, a novel twist occurs. The two evaluators make a second judgment: If there were to be an economic downturn and we had to make a 20 percent staff cut, would this person be in the 20 percent we would terminate? The answer to this question, which is fed back to the employee, gives him a realistic idea of where he stands with the company. People who are not in this 20 percent marginal group are thus granted a form of organizational tenure. Knowing that their jobs are secure, they feel freer to assume the risks of interdepartmental transfer, promotion, or demotion. Interestingly, this tenure does not result in "slacking off," perhaps because of clear standards of high performance in the organization.

What about the effect on the people in the 20 percent group? Often they elect to remain in the organization. In some cases, the feedback results in improved performance. One major advantage of this tenure system is that it forces the organization to appraise new employees all the time, not just on a "crash" basis when a personnel cut is necessary.

The need for internal mobility

The common theme in all these methods of providing for better career development in a slower growth economy is increased intraorganizational mobility. If job changes are not going to be facilitated so much by the entrance or departure of people or by the opening up of new positions, we will have to find new ways to move people around within the organization.

We know from the work of Paul Lawrence and Jay Lorsch and others that organizations have to become more flexible if they are to adapt to changes and uncertainty in the external environment. The methods we have been discussing (downward transfers, cross-functional moves, and so on) are all specific ways in which the organization can increase its own flexibility and that of its human resources.

Executives are rethinking their norms about what kind of movement is appropriate. Both employees and the organization have to plan career moves more carefully and work harder at career development, because the economy is no longer doing the job for us. In an ironic twist, a slow growth economy is giving (or forcing upon) individuals and organizations more control over the way careers unfold.

WHAT IS NOT BEING DONE ABOUT CAREER DEVELOPMENT?

So much for the good news; now let's see where less progress is being made.

Integrating career development and manpower planning

Work on organizational careers has a schizophrenic aspect. On the one hand, there are attempts to facilitate the careers of individual employees through career counseling, goal setting, and so forth (the micro approach). At the other extreme, manpower planners chart the moves of large numbers of people through various positions in the organization—identifying future staffing gaps, "fast tracks," and the like (the macro approach). But these two types of career planning are rarely integrated.

Most organizations, in fact, use only one of these approaches—an unfortunate practice no matter which one they choose. The company that focuses on individuals, for example, may well do a good job of developing people—but if overall corporate manpower needs are ignored, these individuals may be "all developed with no place to go" or find themselves being routed into dead-end jobs.

On the other hand, the organization that develops corporate manpower plans without adequately developing and training people to move through various positions (or to move through a different sequence of positions) is not really managing and planning careers, but merely monitoring them. Even in the organization that is doing both micro and macro career planning, most of the potential of each approach is lost if (as is often the case) the micro and macro people don't talk to each other.

It seems almost trite to suggest that the micro and macro facets of career management be integrated because it seems so straightforward and reasonable. One wonders why this integration does not occur more often. One reason is that organizations large enough to need systematic career management generally have career counseling and manpower planning in different departments. Practitioners in each area often come out of different professional disciplines—counselors from psychology, and manpower planners from economic or systems analysis. And it is difficult to integrate the two—to undertake sound manpower forecasts and then to translate them into specific training and development activities.

Dealing with second-generation EEO problems

Many organizations are now into what we might call Phase II of affirmative action. The main need in Phase I, which concerned recruitment and selection, was to get more women and minority employees to enter managerial and professional positions. Now that more women and minorities *are* entering these positions, other problems arise—such as the need for training and development, meeting new needs of new kinds of employees, and coping with the reactions of white male employees.

The problem of providing organizational support A subtle pattern seems to be evolving, in which some executives subvert EEO goals while apparently implementing them. The equation for this process is "Equal opportunity + low support = discrimination." If a woman or minority employee is hired for a position traditionally occupied by white males, the new person will probably need some technical training as well as informal advice, coaching, and support. In fact, most of us need—and receive—all kinds of informal help and support in any new job. However, when female or minority employees are placed in a nontraditional position (that is, given equal employment opportunity), they are often socially isolated from peers and senior colleagues who could give them words of wisdom, feedback, prodding, encouragement, "Dutch uncle" talks, and the like; these new employees are simply left alone to do their job—and frequently to fail. One young woman, for example, was hired by a high-prestige (and high-pressure) university despite the concern some people felt about her lack of experience and confidence in dealing with the demanding students she would encounter. A senior faculty member assured the others that he would take her "under his wing" and help her cope with her environment. So she was hired—the first women in her department—and all eyes were on her. And the senior professor left for a sabbatical as soon as she arrived! No one else was willing to act as a substitute sponsor in his absence. Without support or counsel, she floundered in the classroom. She spent so much time working on her teaching that she didn't spend much time on research—and no one "bugged" her to do any publishing. Now the reaction of her colleagues is, "Well, we tried giving a woman a chance; I guess we'd better not make *that* mistake again." Thus with equal opportunity and low support, low initial expectations for the person's success can create a vicious self-fulfilling prophecy.

The problem of meeting the needs of the white male Because of the slow economy, promotions are harder to come by these days—and those that *are* available are often used to advance women and minority employees. Consequently, the white male often feels frustrated and demotivated. It is no consolation to him to say that this reverse discrimination is a temporary corrective measure to make up for past generations of discrimination in favor of white males. After all, he wasn't responsible for what happened earlier, so why should he suffer now?

The group being hurt most is white males of average competence. Outstanding performers will always have corresponding career opportunities. And poor performers are likely always to have problems—but right now, EEO activity is giving them a handy scapegoat. It is the average white male who is most likely to lose out in competition with women and minorities who show equal performance and qualifications.

Most companies seem aware of this problem, but see little they can do about it. They often handle the issue by cloaking promotion data in great secrecy—perhaps in the hope that if white males aren't told they're not getting anywhere, maybe they won't notice it! The irony here is that in many companies white males tend to overestimate their relative disadvantage. More open information would probably show that white males are moving faster than their perceptions would suggest.

One way to deal with this issue is to be sure that white males receive at least as much career counseling and assistance in career planning as do women and minorities, because the former group may need to plan their career moves more carefully. The white male may have a greater need for occupational information inside and outside the company than do other, higher-priority groups. In fact, many companies started career-planning programs for women and minorities only and then opened them up to all employees. In these organizations, white males have more career-planing services now available than they ever would have had without EEO pressures.

Another strategy—a high-risk, but high-potential one—would be to hold career workshops in which male and female employees, black and white, meet to discuss their feelings about career opportunities and explore methods of aiding their career development. Such group sessions could meet employees' need for: (1) ventilating feelings, (2) being counseled, (3) getting career information, (4) doing some self-assessment, and (5) solving career problems.

Managing dual careers

As more women embark upon full-time work careers, more dual-career families come into existence. When both husband and wife have full-time careers, their personal career flexibility decreases (if they want to live together), so career planning becomes more difficult and necessary. It is, of course, more difficult to transfer a dual-career employee to a different city or, if the spouse is transferred by his or her firm, to attempt to make a similar move for the partner who works for you. You may find yourself losing good people because of a spouse's career. Alternatively, you might find it difficult to attract someone whose spouse could not find good career opportunities in your organization's geographical area.

The best way for organizations to deal with dual careers is not clear. Many executives do not yet see the problem as an important one. The first step, therefore, is to demonstrate to managers the ways in which dual careers can affect their organization. Our preliminary research indicates that the main problem caused by dual careers comes in making personnel transfers. Recruitment and hiring do not seem to be so strongly affected, although again managers may just be less aware of the dual-career people they lose in the hiring process than of the ones they hire and can't transfer.

Companies seem to be dealing with the transfer problem by adopting a more flexible attitude toward people who turn down transfers. An employee is now informally granted more transfer refusals without prejudice to future promotions than in the past. There also seems to be more effort to find developmental moves within the same geographic location. This is another reason why cross functional moves may become more common.

Another corporate response to dual careers is an increasing awareness that the organization has some stake in the spouse's career, even if the spouse works elsewhere. Thus various supportive services, mainly informal, are being extended to unemployed spouses (for example, help in setting up job interviews with other organizations.) Nepotism rules are also being relaxed, making it easier for husband and wife to work for the same organization or even in the same department. (The emerging norm in many organizations is that spouses can work in the same department as long as one is not supervising the other.) Flexible workhours are helpful, too.

Some organizations are finding that attracting dual-career people requires dual recruiting, or helping to find a job for the spouse as well as the primary candidate. This may require cooperative, interorganizational recruiting. Dealing with another organization's personnel executives, over whom you have no control, can be a real test of managerial and persuasive skills. The fact is, however, that the spouse's career opportunities have become a bargaining point in recruiting and retaining talented dual-career employees. This issue is just beginning to show up with younger, more junior people. In time, these will become key people and then the problem will be critical. The executive who responds that this is the couple's problem, not the organization's, will lose many good employees. The issue, we feel, is a real organizational "time bomb."

GENERAL PRINCIPLES OF EFFECTIVE CAREER PLANNING

So far, we've examined what novel ideas are being tried and what isn't being done. Let's conclude with a few general guidelines about what *should* be done in developing employee careers.

Utilize the career-growth cycle

First, let's consider just how career growth occurs. This process, shown in Figure 1, is triggered by a job that provides challenging, stretching goals. The clearer and more challenging the goals, the more effort the person will exert—and the more effort exerted, the more likely it is that good performance will result. If the person does a good job and receives positive feedback, he or she will feel successful (psychologically successful). Feelings of success increase a person's feelings of confidence, self-worth, or self-esteem. This internal gratification leads the person to become more involved in work, which in turn leads to the setting of future stretching goals. Let us consider more specifically how a company might use this growth cycle.

Plan and utilize the job itself

Since the career-growth cycle is triggered by challenging work goals, the person's job should be made as challenging as possible (as we explained earlier). Too many companies see career development only as something done by "those people in personnel." Each job should represent a challenge, and the sequence of jobs should be planned to provide a systematic and continuing growth of career skills.

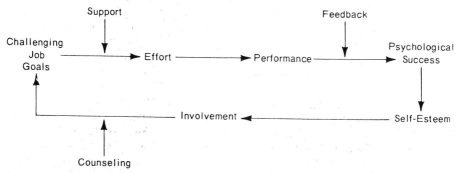

Fig. 1 The career-growth cycle.

Goal setting In general, people tend not to set work goals for themselves. But when they do, the results can be dramatic. This doesn't mean that you need a formal MBO system—just mutual agreement between you, your boss, and your subordinate on a few specific objectives over the next few months that will help the employee focus his or her efforts.

Frequent performance review and feedback Although most organizations have formal policies regarding performance appraisals, few performance appraisals are actually handled properly for the benefit of employees. People need feedback to help assess how well they have performed and where changes should be made. Such feedback can be given informally, on a continuing basis, instead of in a stressful, formal, once-a-year ordeal. It is also easier to provide feedback if specific goals have been set; then you can talk not only about how well activities were carried out, but also about whether certain ones were carried out at all.

Counseling and support from the boss When building the conditions for career success into the job, don't forget the boss. As a source of support (in translating goals into action) and counseling and planning (for translating involvement into future goals), supervisors can be far more influential than any personnel or career specialist. The supervisor is also the best person to provide goal-setting stimulation and performance feedback.

Train and reward supervisors for career-planning skills

If the supervisor is to be expected to provide support, feedback, and counseling, don't think this will happen easily. One reason supervisors don't do more along these lines now is that they don't feel comfortable doing it. And they feel uncomfortable for a number of reasons. One is that they often lack the necessary skills. A second reason is that they often experience role conflict between being a "boss" and being a "helper." A two- or three-day training program would be an enormous aid for supervisors, enabling them to learn both how to conduct good performance appraisals and how to be good informal agents of career planning. This approach to career planning is already being taken in one of the major auto manufacturers, with good results.

Tying employee development specifically into the supervisor's own performance appraisal is another good way to reward these activities. This is a simple idea, but it is rarely practiced. General Electric has been successful in including managers' affirmative action progress in their performance appraisals. The result has been a great increase in EEO attainments. A large Canadian computer company requires each manager to pick and develop a successor before the manager will be considered for promotion. This is a very clear and powerful way of linking the career development of subordinates to the career progress of the manager.

Personnel specialists as monitors Tying career development into the everyday work environment of supervisors frees personnel specialists to act in an indirect, support role (which is what a staff function is intended to be, anyway). Personnel people can work in two ways: (1) They can train the supervisors in the career-developing skills just discussed, and (2) they can monitor the process to make sure that periodic goal setting, feedback, and career planning are discussed. The following application of these ideas gives more details.

An illustrative example: AT&T Several of these principles are illustrated in career programs being used at AT&T. Joel Moses, a personnel specialist, cites one early identification program—the Initial Management Development Program—for non-college employees being considered for management positions. The employees first go through a one-day assessment program. Then they are given feedback by a trained person (either in personnel or in the person's own department), who then continues to function as the employee's *career counselor.* Explicit career plans are made. Then the person and the boss jointly set work targets to help achieve the career plan. Although most of the planning is done within the employee's department, the personnel specialist functions as monitor of the process. The third-party career counselor is useful because of the high turnover in superior-subordinate relationships.

Another program is a successor to the Initial Management Development Program, but is more "user oriented" than IMDP. The stress is on *boss training* in the areas of job design, joint target setting, and appraisal skills. At the end of the first year of employment, the person goes through a two-day assessment program. Following this is a meeting with the person's boss, a member of the assessment center, and a personnel coordinator. One of three decisions is made: Terminate, don't promote, or prepare for middle management. A feedback meeting is held with the employee to discuss the results of the assessment process. Then in the second year a career plan is drawn up—entailing a target job, the training needed, interim assignments, and a time frame. The three parties review this plan and the progress made every six months.

The following principles are reflected in these AT&T programs:

1 Emphasize the development of high-potential people. Don't try to change people who lack management potential.

2 Set specific development objectives. Identify specific job experiences and skills the person needs (for example, "ability to supervise a central office PBX group.")

3 Train the supervisor to provide the day-to-day job experiences (for example, challenging goals and feedback) that facilitate career development.

4 Give personnel experts the responsibility for structuring and monitoring the development *process,* but reserve for the employee and the supervisor the responsibility for its actual content.

CONCLUSION

The more we use the job itself and the superior-subordinate relationship for career development and call upon the personnel department for outside resources and process monitors, the better use we are making of the respective resources of each.

We hope that the new process of career development will not be accepted or implemented without careful thought and planning, since it could become just another management fad. Rather, career development, the enhancement of human talent, should be viewed as a management function that has always been performed in effective organizations—yet one that can benefit from being conceptualized and practiced in new ways.

SELECTED BIBLIOGRAPHY

A comprehensive source on career theory, factors in career success, organizational career-management practices, and self-management of careers is Douglas T. Hall's *Careers in Organizations* (Goodyear Publishing Company, 1976). For the more technical readers, a test of the model of career development in this paper and a description of the careers of priests are found in Douglas T. Hall and Benjamin Schneider's *Organizational Climate and Careers: The Work Lives of Priests* (Seminar [Academic] Press, 1973). A good discussion of the impact of the first job and the first boss is found in J. Sterling Livingston's "Pygmalion in Management," (*Harvard Business Review*, July–August, 1969, pp. 81–89). A thorough and highly readable report of how individual differences and early job experiences affect employee career development is found in Douglas W. Bray, Richard J. Campbell, and Donald L. Grant's *Formative Years in Business: A Long-Term Study of Managerial Lives* (John Wiley & Sons, Inc., 1974). For a comprehensive review of the research on obsolescence and midcareer development, see H. G. Kaufman's *Obsolescence and Professional Career Development* (AMACOM, A division of American Management Associations, 1974). Several perspectives on women's careers are found in Francine E. Gordon and Myra Strober's *Bringing Women into Management* (McGraw-Hill, Inc., 1975). And finally, an excellent, entertaining, and professional source book for self-directed career planning is Richard N. Bolles's *What Color Is Your Parachute? A Practical Manual for Job Hunters and Career Changers* (Ten Speed Press, 1974).

FOR DISCUSSION AND REVIEW

1 What solutions are offered for the turnover problem?
2 Explain job pathing and cross-functional moves. How can they improve career-development effectiveness?
3 What are the challenges advanced against the norm of upward mobility?
4 Discuss the notion of corporate tenure.
5 How can career development and manpower planning be integrated? What benefits might result from such an integration?
6 Explain "second-generation" EEO problems.
7 Discuss, in your own words, the logic behind the career-growth cycle (Fig. 1).

D. EVALUATION OF TRAINING AND DEVELOPMENT PROGRAMS

J. L. Goldstein

Evaluation Procedures

Rational decisions related to the selection, adoption, support, and worth of the various training activities require some basis for determining that the instructional program was responsible for whatever changes occurred. Instructional analysts should be able to respond to the following questions:

1 Does an examination of the various criteria indicate that a change has occurred?
2 Can the changes be attributed to the instructional program?
3 Is it likely that similar changes will occur for new participants in the same program?

These questions could be asked about measures at each criterion level (for example, reaction, learning, behavior, results). Thus, evaluations of training programs are not likely to produce dichotomous answers. However, training analysts who expect results to lead to a value or no-value judgment are unrealistically imposing a simplistic structure and are raising false expectations among the recipients and sponsors of training research.

The unique objectives and constraints of each instructional setting make attempts to generalize results to other programs extremely hazardous. Kirkpatrick (1959) expressed this view by suggesting ". . . that one training director cannot borrow evaluation results from another; he can, however, borrow evaluation techniques" (p. 3). Before discussing particular methodologies for training evaluation, it is important to recognize that there are many different viewpoints about the desirability of evaluation, the approach to evaluation, and the effects of evaluation. The following sections discuss the most prominent of these viewpoints.

VIEWS OF THE EVALUATION PROCESS

Negativists, positivists, and frustrates

One continuum of thought revolves around the necessity for evaluation. As expressed by Randall (1960), negativists are those individuals who feel that evaluation of training is either impossible or unnecessary—that the value of formal instructional programs cannot be demonstrated by quantitative analysis. They feel that learning in an instructional setting is irrelevant and that improved performance in the transfer setting will be obvious without evaluation techniques. On the other end of the continuum are the positivists, who believe that scientific evaluation of training is the only worthwhile approach. This group suggests that instructional analysts should not waste time and money on anything other than a controlled study. In the center of these two groups are the frustrates, who recognize that training programs must be evaluated but are concerned with the methodology necessary to perform the evaluation. This group recognizes that all programs will be evaluated, either formally or informally; thus, it is concerned with the quality of the evaluation rather than with the decision whether to evaluate or not.

Each group's generalizations have a degree of validity. This text supports the view that the evaluation process is difficult but that the potential worth of evaluation remains undetermined because few evaluation studies are conducted. The negativist's viewpoint treats evaluation of programs in extremes—the program is either good or bad. Instead, training programs should be considered dynamic entities that slowly accomplish their purpose in meeting predesigned objectives. Without systematic evaluation, there is no feedback to provide the information necessary to improve programs or quality information to make decisions. It is also difficult to accept the negativist's view that trainee improvements in the transfer setting will be obvious. A consideration of the difficulties associated with criterion contamination alone makes it clear that casual observations are not likely to provide much more than the observer's biased opinion. The positivists, on the other hand, would not permit a study except under completely controlled conditions. This view, if carried to an extreme, could result in research only in academic laboratories where systematic control of the environment can be maintained. While the data collected in these settings are important, the approach could have the undesired effect of reducing our understanding of instructional programs in real settings. The most reasonable approach is offered by the frustrates (the appropriate category for those participating in training research today). It is important to use the most systematic procedures available that fit the particular setting being investigated, to control as many of the extraneous variables as possible, and to recognize the limitations of the design being utilized. Thus, the better experimental procedures control more variables, permitting a greater degree of confidence in specifying program effects. While the constraints of the environment may make a perfect evaluation impossible, an awareness of the important factors in experimental design makes it possible to avoid a useless evaluation. The job of the training analyst is to choose the most rigorous design possible and to be aware of its limitations. These limitations should be taken into account in data interpretation and in reports to program sponsors.

TYPES OF EVALUATION

There are also varying opinions about the most appropriate type of evaluation. One dimension, discussed in this section, includes formative and summative evaluation. Another dimension, discussed in the next section, includes formal instructional research, action research, and casual research.

Formative and summative evaluation

As originally conceived by Scriven (1967), formative evaluation is utilized to determine if the program is operating as originally planned or if improvements are necessary before the program is implemented. The major concern of summative evaluation is the evaluation of the final product with the major emphasis being program appraisal. Thus, formative evaluation stresses tryout and revision processes, primarily using process criteria, while summative evaluation uses outcome criteria to appraise the instructional program. However, process criteria (such as daily logs of activities) are also important in summative evaluation, because they supply the information necessary to interpret the data. Of course, both formative and summative evaluations can lead to feedback and program improvements. Design changes based on summative evaluations are determined by the degree to which program objectives are achieved. Improvements based on formative evaluations are more related to how closely the program is operating to the original design. The formative evaluation should be completed and judged adequate before summative evaluations are begun. Many research problems result from one-shot evaluation studies that attempt to combine formative and summative evaluations. Thus, the program is often appraised as if it is a completed product when it has not been implemented as originally designed.

A false concern with formative evaluations is that methodological difficulties might be caused by the continual changes adopted from collected data. But that constant modification is exactly the purpose of the formative period, and experimental design considerations should not prevent the necessary changes. Once the formative evaluation is completed, experimental design provides the foundation for the summative evaluation. On the other hand, satisfactory formative data indicating that the program is operating as designed do not mean that summative evaluations are unnecessary, just as the satisfaction of the personnel responsible for the implementation of the program does not mean that the program is meeting the stated objectives.

Formal instructional research, action research, and casual research

Borg (1963) developed an interesting comparison of these three types of research in educational settings. Table 5.1 shows that most of the categories are appropriate for all types of instructional settings. Since the remainder of this chapter will consider the methodological factors of these types of research (for example, sampling and design), this discussion will concentrate on more general considerations.

Practical, statistical, and scientific significance Analysts sometimes overemphasize the importance of statistically significant changes. It is quite possible to achieve statistically significant changes so small that they have virtually no meaning to the organization's objectives. On the other hand, the achievement of practical significant changes assumes that the differences are indeed reliable and will recur when the next instructional group is exposed to the treatment. Interacting with both ideas is the concept of scientific significance—that is, the establishment of meaningful results that permit generalizations about training procedures beyond the immediate setting being investigated. As Campbell, Dunnette, Lawler, and Weick (1970) suggest for managerial training, "Once the effects of such a program are mapped out for different kinds of trainees and for different types of criterion problems under various organizational situations, the general body of knowledge concerning management training has been enriched" (p. 284). If the instructional program is well designed, it should contribute to the solution of organizational goals, as well as add to the body of instructional knowledge.

METHODOLOGICAL CONSIDERATIONS

Each research design has different assets and liabilities in controlling extraneous factors that might threaten the evaluator's ability to determine: (1) if a real change has occurred, (2) whether the change is attributable to the instructional program, and (3) whether the change is likely to occur again with a new sample of subjects. Specific research designs will be discussed in a later section, but several general design concepts, including control groups and pre/post-testing, are mentioned here as background for the presentation of the sources of error that can affect the validity of the experimental design.

Pre /post-testing

The first question is whether the participants, after exposure to the instructional program, change their performance in a significant way. A design to answer this question would use a pretest administered before the instructional program begins and a post-test given after exposure to the instructional program. The timing of the post-test for the evaluation of an instructional program is not easily specified. A post-test at the conclusion of the training program provides a measure of the changes that have occurred during instruction, but it does not give any indication of later transfer performance. Thus, other measures should be employed after the participant has been in the transfer situation for a reasonable time period. Comparisons can then be made between (1) the pretest and the first post-test, (2) the pretest and the second post-test, and (3) the first and second post-tests. For convenience, this section will refer only to pre- and post-tests, but it is important to remember that one post-test immediately after training will ordinarily not suffice. An additional factor in the analysis of pre- and post-test scores is how scores on the pretest affect the degree of success on the post-test. One possibility is that the participant who initially scored highest on the pretest will perform best on the post-test. In order to examine this effect, some researchers (Mayo & DuBois, 1963) have suggested that the pretest scores should be partialed out of the post-test.

The variables measured in the pre- and post-tests must be associated with the objectives of the training program. The expected changes associated with the instructional program should be specified so that statistically reliable differences between the pre- and post-tests can confirm the degree to which the objectives have been achieved. This text does not attempt to treat the statistical considerations in instructional evaluation analyses except to warn the reader that statistical expertise is necessary to properly evaluate programs.

Control groups

The specification of changes indicated by pre- and postmeasurement is only one consideration. It must be determined that these changes occurred because of the instructional treatment. To eliminate the possibility of other explanations for the changes between the pre- and post-test, a control group is used (treated like the experimental group on all variables that might contribute to pre/post differences except for the actual instructional program). With control procedures, it is possible to specify whether the changes in the experimental group were due to the instructional treatment or to other factors, like the passage of time, maturation factors, or events in the outside world. The particular kinds of errors that can occur will be specified in the next section, but, as an example of the necessity for control groups, we can consider the placebo effect. In medical research, the placebo is an inert substance administered to the control group so that the subject cannot distinguish whether he is a member of the experimental or the control group. This allows the researcher to separate the effects of the actual drug from the reactions induced by the subject's expectations and suggestibility. In instructional research, similar cautions must be taken to separate the background effects sometimes employed in the experimental setting and the actual treatment. It is possible that treatment effects in an experimental group in which videotape feedback is being investigated are caused by the presence of recording equipment and numerous observers (Isaac & Michael, 1971). Thus, the control group should be presented with similar attention. In medical and psychological research, there is concern about experimenters who unknowingly interact with subjects and shape their behavior, through subtle cues, toward the predicted results. While control groups do not provide a solution for this latter problem, researchers should be aware of these potential dangers.

Before discussing specific research designs, it is necessary to consider those factors that contribute sources of error. D. T. Campbell and J. C. Stanley have

Table 5.1

Differences Among Formal Instructional Research Action Research, and the Causal Approach to Problem Solving in Education

AREA	FORMAL EDUCATIONAL RESEARCH	ACTION RESEARCH	CASUAL OR "COMMON SENSE" APPROACH
1. Goals	To obtain knowledge that will be generalizable to a broad population and to develop and test instructional theories.	To obtain knowledge that can be applied directly to the local classroom situation and to give the participating teachers in-service training.	To make changes in the current procedure that appear likely to improve the situation.
2. Sampling	Research worker attempts to obtain a random or otherwise unbiased sample of the population being studied but is usually not completely successful.	Pupils available in the class of the teacher or teachers doing the research are used as subjects.	Some casual observations of pupil behavior may be made by the teacher after the change decided upon has been in effect for a while.
3. Experimental design	Design is carefully planned in detail prior to start of the study and adhered to as closely as possible. Major attention is given to maintaining comparable conditions and reducing error bias. Control of extraneous variables is important.	Procedures are planned in general terms prior to start of study. Changes are made during the study if they seem likely to improve the teaching situation. Little attention is paid to control of the experimental conditions or reduction of error. Because participating teachers are ego-involved in the research situation, bias is usually present.	If classroom testing of the decision is attempted, procedures are planned only in the most general terms. No attempt is made to establish common definitions or procedures among participating teachers.

4. Measurement	An effort is made to obtain the most valid measures available. A thorough evaluation of available measures and a trial of these measures usually precede their use in the research.	Less rigorous evaluation of measures than in scientific research. Participants often lack training in the use and evaluation of educational measures but can do satisfactory job with help of a consultant.	Usually no evaluation is made except for the casual observations of the teachers participating. The teacher's opinion as to whether the new procedure is an improvement or not depends almost entirely on whether the teacher approves the change.
5. Analysis of data	Complex analysis often called for. Inasmuch as generalizability of results is a goal, statistical significance is usually emphasized.	Simple analysis procedures usually are sufficient. Practical significance rather than statistical significance is emphasized. Subjective opinion of participating teachers is often weighted heavily.	Subjective opinion of the participants is usually the only procedure used. No attempt made at objective analysis.
6. Application of results	Results are generalizable, but many useful findings are not applied in educational practice. Differences in training and experience between research workers and teachers generate a serious communication problem.	Findings are applied immediately to the classes of participating teachers and often lead to permanent improvement. Application of results beyond the participating teachers is usually slight.	Decisions reached are applied immediately in classes of participating teachers. Even if the decision leads to improvement, it is often changed later because no evidence is available to support its continuance. This approach leads to educational fads and "change for the sake of change."

Adapted from Borg, W. R. *Educational Research.* Copyright © 1963, 1971 by David McKay Co. Inc. Reprinted by permission of the publisher.

organized and specified these threats to experimental design, and, for the most part, their labels and organization are utilized.

INTERNAL AND EXTERNAL VALIDITY

Internal validity asks the basic question "Did the treatment make a difference in this particular situation?" Unless internal validity has been established, it is not possible to interpret the effects of any experiment, training or otherwise. External validity refers to the generalizability or representativeness of the data. The evaluator is concerned with generalizability of his results to other populations, settings, and treatment variables. External validity is always a matter of inference and thus can never be specified with complete confidence. However, the designs that control the most threats to internal and external validity are, of course, the most useful.

Threats to internal validity

These threats are variables other than the instructional program itself that can affect its results. The solution to this difficulty is to control these variables so that they may be cast aside as competing explanations for the experimental effect. Threats to internal validity include the following.

History. History refers to the specific events, other than the experimental treatment, occurring between the first and second measurements that could provide alternative explanations for results. When tests are given on different days, as is almost always the case in instructional programs, events occurring between the testing periods can contaminate the effects. For instance, an instructional program designed to produce positive attitudes toward safe practices in coal mines may produce significant differences that have no relationship to the material presented in the instructional program because a coal-mine disaster occurred between the pre- and post-test.

Maturation. Maturation includes all biological or psychological effects that systematically vary with the passage of time, independent of specific events like history. Participants become older, fatigued, or more or less interested in the program between the time of the pre-test and the time of the post-test. Thus, performance can change for reasons unrelated to the instructional material.

Testing. This variable refers to the influence of the pretest on the scores of the post-test. This is an especially serious problem for instructional programs in which the pretest can sensitize the participant to search for material or to ask friends for information that provides correct answers on the post-test. Thus, improved performance would occur simply by taking the pre- and post-tests, without any intervening instructional program.

Instrumentation. This threat to validity results from changes in the instruments that might result in differences between pre- and post-test scores. For example, fluctuations in mechanical instruments or changes in grading standards can lead to differences, regardless of the instructional program. Since rating scales are commonly employed as a criterion in training research, it is important to be sensitive to differences related to changes in the rater (for example, additional expertise in the second rating, bias, or carelessness) that can cause error effects.

Statistical regression. Participants for instructional research are often chosen on the basis of extreme scores. Thus, students with extremely low and extremely high intelligence-test scores may be chosen for participation in a course using programed instruction. In these cases, a phenomenon known as statistical regression often occurs. On the second testing, the scores for both groups regress toward the middle of the distribution. Thus, students with extremely high scores would tend toward lower scores, and those with extremely low scores would tend toward higher scores. This regression occurs because tests are not perfect measures; there will always be some change in scores from the first to the second testing simply because of measurement error. Since the first scores are at the extreme ends, the variability must move toward the center (the mean of the entire group). Students with extremely high scores might have had unusually good luck the day of the first testing, or students with extremely low scores may have been upset or careless that day. On the second administration, however, each group is likely to regress toward the mean.

Differential selection of participants. This effect stems from biases in choosing comparison groups. If volunteers are used in the instruction group and randomly chosen participants are used in the control group, differences could occur between the two groups simply because each was different before the program began. This variable is best controlled by random selection of all participants, with appropriate numbers of participants (as determined by statistical considerations) for each group. Random selection is a particular problem in educational settings where one class is chosen as the control group and another class as the experimental group. Establishing experimental and control groups by placing individuals with matched characteristics (for example, intelligence, age, sex) in each group is still not the best alternative. Often, the critical parameters that should be used to match the participants are not known, and thus selection biases can again affect the design. One alternative is a combination of matching and randomization in which participants are matched on important parameters; then, one member of each pair is assigned randomly to the treatment or control group.

Experimental mortality. This variable refers to the differential loss of participants from the treatment or control group. In a control group of volunteers, those persons who scored poorly on the pretest may drop out because they are discouraged. Thus, the group in the experimental program may appear to score higher than the control group, because the low-scoring performers have dropped out.

Interactions. Many of the above factors—for example, selection and maturation—can interact to produce threats to internal validity. When younger students are compared with older students over a period of a year, there are differences in initial selection and differences in maturation changes that could occur at varying rates for each of the different groups.

Threats to external validity

External validity refers to the generalizability of the study to other groups and situations. Internal validity is a prerequisite for external validity, since the results of the study must be valid for the group being examined before there can be concern over the validity for other groups. The representativeness of the investigation determines the degree of generalizability. For example, when the data are initially collected in a low socioeconomic setting, it is difficult to claim that the instructional program will work equally well for a high socioeconomic area. Campbell and Stanley list the following threats to external validity.

Reactive effect of pretesting. The effects of pretests often lead to increased sensitivity to the instructional procedure. Thus, the participant's responses to the training program might be different from the responses of individuals who are exposed to an established program without the pretest; the pretested participant might pay attention to certain material in the training program only because he knows it is covered in test items.

Interaction of selection and experimental treatment. The characteristics of the group selected for experimental treatment determine the generalizability of the findings to other participants. The characteristics of employees from one division of the firm may result in the treatment's being more or less effective for them, as compared to employees from another division with different characteristics. Similarly, characteristics of school students, like socioeconomic status or intelligence level, may make them more or less receptive to particular instructional programs.

Reactive effects of experimental settings. The procedures employed in the experimental setting may limit the generalizability of the study. Observers and experimental equipment often make the participants aware of their participation in an experiment, which can lead to changes in behavior that cannot be generalized to those individuals who will participate in the instructional treatment when it is non-experimental. The Hawthorne studies have become the standard illustration for the "I'm a guinea pig" effect. This research shows that a group of employees continued to increase production regardless of the changes in working conditions designed to produce both increases and decreases in production. Interpreters believe that the experimental conditions resulted in the workers' behaving differently. Explanations for the Hawthorne effect include: novelty; awareness of being a participant in an experiment; changes in the environment due to observers, recording conditions, and social interaction; and daily feedback on production figures (Isaac & Michael, 1971). Since the factors that affect the treatment group will not be present in future training sessions, the performance obtained is not representative of that of future participants.

Multiple-treatment interference. The effects of previous treatments are not erasable; therefore, threats to external validity occur whenever there is an attempt to establish the effects of a single treatment from studies that actually examined multiple treatments. Thus, trainees exposed to role playing, films, and lectures may perform best during the lectures, but that does not mean they would perform in a similar manner if they were exposed to lectures all day long without the other techniques.

EXPERIMENTAL DESIGN

This section presents some of the many designs that examine the effects of experimental treatments. The previous sections on internal and external validity discussed some of the factors that make it difficult to determine whether the treatment produced the hypothesized results. As we shall see, these threats are differentially controlled by the various designs. Given a particular setting, the researcher should employ the design that has the greatest degree of control over threats to validity. Certainly, it is possible to avoid choosing a useless design. In many cases, the main difficulty has been the failure to plan for evaluation before the program was implemented. In these instances, the utilization of a few procedures—for example, pre/post-testing and control groups—could dramatically improve the quality of information.

For convenience in presenting the experimental designs, T_1 will represent the pretest, T_2 the post-test, X the treatment or instructional program, and R the random selection of subjects. Campbell and Stanley (1963) have organized a detailed examination of the variables that should be considered when choosing a research design. The designs in this text, organized into several different categories, provide examples of the numerous approaches available. The first category includes pre-experimental designs that do not have control procedures and are valueless in analyzing cause-and-effect relationships. Experimental designs, the second category, have varying degrees of power that permit some control of threats to validity. The third category includes quasi-experimental designs that are useful in many social-science settings where investigators lack the opportunity to exert full control over the environment.

Pre-experimental designs

1. The one-shot case study:

In this method, commonly called the case-study approach, the subjects are exposed to the instructional treatment (without a pretest) and then are tested once. This design has a total absence of control, and all threats to internal validity are present. Thus, there is no scientific value to this approach. The only bases for comparisons are intuitions and impressions. As Campbell and Stanley have observed, these studies often involve a tedious collection of specific detailed data that cannot substitute for a more rigorous design. The only purpose that this design can serve is to collect preliminary information for a more thorough investigation.

2. The one-group pretest/post-test design:

When this design is employed, the participants are given a pretest, presented with the instructional program, and then given a post-test. This design is widely utilized in the examination of instructional settings, because it provides a measure of comparison between the same group of subjects before and after treatment. Unfortunately, without a control group, it is difficult to establish whether the experimental treatment is the prime factor determining any differences that occur between the testing periods. Thus, the many threats to internal validity, including changes in history, maturation, testing effects, changes in instrumentation, and statistical regression, are not controlled. This design does, however, control biases due to subject mortality.

Research example of pre-experimental designs

Golembiewski and Carrigan (1970) carried out a training program that utilized a pre/post design without a control group in one of a series of investigations designed to change the style of a sales unit in a business organization. They had a series of goals, including: the integration of a new management team, an increase in congruence between the behaviors required by the organization and those preferred by the men, and a greater congruence of individual needs and organizational demands. The training program consisted of a laboratory approach using sensitivity training to encourage the exploration of the participant's feelings and reactions to the organization. The program also included confrontations in which management of various levels were given an opportunity to discuss their ideas and feelings. The instrument used to measure pre- and postexperimental changes was Likert's profile of organizational characteristics, which includes items related to leadership, character of motivational forces, communication, interaction influence, decision making, goal setting, and control.

After statistical analyses, the authors concluded that the learning design had the intended effect in terms of the measured attitudes. Golembiewski and Carrigan indicated that they had included all the managers in the treatment and so did not have a control group. Thus, their design did not permit them to be certain that the effects were a result of the training program rather than of random factors or the passage of time. This design uncertainty is expressed by Becker (1970) in an article entitled "The Parable of the Pill":

> There once was a land in which wisdom was revered. Thus there was great excitement in the land when one of its inhabitants announced that he had invented a pill which made people wiser. His claim was based on an experiment he conducted. The report of the experiment explained (1) that the experimenter secured a volunteer; (2) the volunteer was first given an IQ test; (3) then he swallowed a pill which he was told would make him more intelligent; (4) finally he was given another IQ test. The score on the second IQ test was higher than on the first, so the report concluded that the pill increased wisdom.
>
> Alas, there were two skeptics in the land. One secured a volunteer; gave him an IQ test; waited an appropriate length of time; then gave him another IQ test. The volunteer's score on the second test exceeded that of the first. Skeptic One reported his experiment and concluded that taking the first test was an experience for the subject and that the time between the tests allowed the subject to assimilate and adjust to that experience so that when he encountered the situation again he responded more efficiently. Time alone, the skeptic argued, was sufficient to produce the increase in test score. The skeptic also pointed out that time alone could have produced the change in test score reported in the experiment on the Wisdom Pill.
>
> Skeptic Two conducted a different experiment. He held the opinion that most people were to some extent suggestible or gullible and that they readily would accept a suggestion that they possessed a desired attribute. He further believed that people who accept such a suggestion might even behave in a way such as to make it appear, for a time at least, that they indeed did possess the suggested ability. Therefore, the skeptic secured a volunteer; gave him an IQ test; had him ingest a pill composed of inert ingredients; told him the pill would increase his intelligence; then gave him another IQ test. Skeptic Two dutifully reported his subject achieved a higher score on the second test and, based on his hypothesis, explained how the disparity arose. He also pointed out that the increase in test score in the Wisdom Pill experiment could have been due to the taking of the pill and expectations associated with taking the pill rather than to the ingredients in the pill.
>
> The inventor of the wisdom pill drafted a reply to the two skeptics. He wrote that, although he did not employ a control group or a placebo group, he is confident that the pill's ingredients caused the observed change because that change is consistent with the theory from which he deduced the formula for his pill [p. 94].[1]

The point in the parable is that Skeptic One, Skeptic Two, or the inventor of the pill may be right. There is no way of being certain, given the present design, what was responsible for the effect.

Essentially, pre-experimental designs do not provide good information about the impact of the treatment. They should be used only to collect preliminary data. The next group of designs shows how easily many of the pre-experimental designs

---

[1]   From Becker, S. W. The parable of the pill. *Administrative Science Quarterly*, 1970, 15, 94–96. Reprinted by permission of *Administrative Science Quarterly* and the author.

can be improved. Design 1 can be strengthened by adding a pretest, and both Design 1 and Design 2 can be improved by adding a control group. Even where the environment makes a control group impractical, these designs can be improved by using the time-series approach (described in the section on quasi-experimental designs).

Experimental designs

3. Pretest/post-test control-group design:

Experimental Group (R)	T_1	X	T_2
Control Group (R)	T_1		T_2

In this design, the subjects are chosen at random from the population and assigned randomly to the experimental group or control group. Each group is given a pre- and post-test, but only the experimental group is exposed to the instructional treatment. If there is more than one instructional treatment, it is possible to add additional experimental groups.

This design represents a considerable improvement over Designs 1 and 2, because many of the threats to internal validity are controlled. The differential selection of subjects is controlled by the random selection. Variables like history, maturation, and pretesting should affect the experimental group and the control group equally. Statistical regression based on extreme scores (if subjects are chosen that way) is not eliminated but should be equal for the two groups because of the random selection procedures. However, any effects not part of the instructional procedure that are due to differential treatment of subjects in the control and experimental groups must still be controlled by the experimenter. This design is affected by external threats to validity, which are not as easily specified as the threats to internal validity. The design does not control the effects of pretesting; thus, T_1 could have sensitized the participants to the experimental treatment in a way that makes generalizations to future participants difficult. Generalizations would also be hampered because subjects in the experiment might be different from those who will participate at later times and because the guinea-pig effect could lead to differences between the experimental and control groups. This latter concern is dependent on the ingenuity of the experimenter in reducing the differences between groups by treating the control group in the same manner as the experimental group (except for the specific instructional treatment).

The difficulties associated with external validity should not freeze the researcher into inactivity. While threats to internal validity are reasonably well handled by experimental designs, generalizations, which are the core of external validity, are always precarious. As Campbell and Stanley point out, experimenters try to generalize by scientifically guessing at laws and by trying out generalizations in other specific cases. Slowly, and somewhat painfully, they gain knowledge about factors that affect generalizations. (For example, there is now ample evidence that pretesting does sensitize and affect participants.) As shown in the following design, a control for pretest sensitization is relatively easy to achieve by adding a group to Design 3 that is exposed to the treatment without first being presented with the pretest.

4. Solomon four-group design:

Group

1 (R)	T_1	X	T_2
2 (R)	T_1		T_2
3 (R)		X	T_2
4 (R)			T_2

The Solomon four-group design represents the first specific procedure designed to consider external-validity factors. This design adds two groups that are not pretested. If the participants are randomly assigned to the four groups, this design makes it possible to compare the effects of pretesting. (Group 4 provides a control for pretesting without the instructional treatment.) It also permits the evaluator to determine the effects of some internal-validity factors. For example, a comparison of the post-test performance for Group 4, which was not exposed to pretesting or instructional treatments, to the pretest scores for Groups 1 and 2 permits the analysis of the combined effects of maturation and history.

Research example of experimental designs

Goodacre (1955) reported on an evaluative study of a supervisory training program at B. F. Goodrich Company that fits into the classification of experimental designs. The program consisted of conferences, lectures, and discussions for different supervisory and managerial personnel on topics related to the understanding of human behavior, decision making, employee selection, employee progress, and job evaluation. The experimental design was developed in conjunction with the program and built into the instructional procedure. The 800 participants were randomly placed into two groups—an experimental group and a control group. As Goodacre notes, random selection was necessry to assure that the groups would be comparable on variables like age, length of service, job level, and intelligence. The control group did not participate in the training program, but, in all other regards, it was treated similarly to the experimental group. Various criterion measures, including attitude scales, achievement tests, and ratings by immediate supervisors, were administered both before and after training.

As reported by J. P. Campbell et al. (1970), the control group did not show any significant changes, but the experimental group improved on the achievement tests, self-confidence ratings, and post-training performance measures. This is one of the few studies that not only used a rigorous design but also attempted to measure performance on the job and in the training program. Goodacre and Campbell et al. note that one problem with the performance ratings was that the raters knew who participated in the training program. Yet, even with that difficulty, the experimental design permitted the control of many threats to internal validity that plague pre-experimental design. However, it did not control for the external-validity threats of pretesting sensitization.

Quasi-experimental designs

5. The time-series design:

T_1 T_2 T_3 T_4 X T_5 T_6 T_7 T_8	

This design is similar to Design 1, except that a series of measurements are taken before and after the instructional treatment. This particular approach illustrates the possibilities of utilizing quasi-experimental designs in situations in which it is not possible to gain the full control required by experimental designs. An examination of the internal-validity threats shows that this design provides more control than Design 1. If there are no appreciable changes from pretests 1 to 4, it is unlikely that any effects will occur due to maturation, testing, or regression. The major internal-validity difficulty with this design is the history variable; that is, events that may happen between T_4 and T_5 (such as environmental changes and historical occurrences) are not controlled by this procedure.

The use of the time-series design does not control most of the external-validity threats. Thus, it is necessary to be sensitive to any relationships between the treatment and particular subject groups (like volunteers) that might make results difficult to generalize to other groups, and it is also necessary to be aware that subjects might be sensitized to particular aspects of the instructional program through the use of pretests.

6. The nonequivalent control-group design:

| Experimental Group | T_1 | X | T_2 |
| Control Group | T_1 | | T_2 |

The nonequivalent control-group design is the same as Design 3, except that the participants are not assigned to the groups at random. (The choice of the group to receive the instructional treatment is made randomly.) This design is often used in educational settings where there are naturally assembled groups, such as classes. If there is no alternative, this design is well worth using and is certainly preferable to designs that do not include control groups (such as Design 2). The more similar the two groups and their scores on the pretest, the more effective the control becomes in accounting for extraneous influences—for instance, internal-validity factors like history, pretesting, maturation, and instrumentation. However, the investigator must be especially careful, because this design is vulnerable to interactions between selection factors and maturation, history, and testing. Since the participants were not chosen randomly, there is always the possibility that critical differences exist that were not revealed by the pretests. For example, some studies use volunteers who might react differently to the treatment because of motivational factors. Thus, the investigator must be sensitive to potential sources of differences between the groups. The dangers of instrumentation changes and of differential treatment of each group (unrelated to the treatment) remain a concern for this design as well as for Design 3.

Although the external-validity issues are similar to those for Design 3, the nonequivalent control-group design does have some advantages in the control of the reactive effects of experimental settings. The utilization of intact groups makes it easier to design the experiment as part of the normal routine, thus reducing some of the problems associated with the guinea-pig effect. Since this design is not as disruptive, it is also possible, in some settings (for example, educational systems), to have a larger subject population, thus increasing generalizability.

Research example of quasi-experimental designs

A study by Canter (1951) illustrates a quasi-experimental design employing pre/post measures with nonequivalent control groups. The purpose of this investigation was to train supervisory personnel in human relations—that is, to establish facts and principles so that supervisors could become more competent in their knowledge and understanding of human behavior. The criteria consisted of a test battery including measures of supervisory behavior, social judgment, and logical reasoning.

The experimental group contained supervisors from one department, and the control group contained members from two other departments. Since the participants were not randomly chosen, Canter checked variables like age, sex, mental alertness, and years of service. While there were no statistical differences due to considerable variability in the scores, the author indicated that differences in number of years of service and mental alertness were discernible. The results of the study indicated that changes in performance favored the trained group.

While this design controls history and maturation factors reasonably well, there are problems related to selection interactions and factors like history and testing. The participants in this program worked under different supervisors and in different psychological and physical environments. The effects of these selection factors are unknown, but of special concern is the fact that the department heads for these participants did observe certain aspects of the training.

Summary

Campbell and Stanley have summarized threats to validity for various designs (see Table 5.2). They warn us about using the summary table without a full understanding of the various designs and threats to validity. While it is often best to use regularly employed personnel in operating the training program, the design of the program and the statistical analyses require adept professionals. Experts working closely with the regular staff will create the most productive program, design, and analyses.

A FINAL WORD

In summary, it is important to note that the literature abounds with studies of designs that do not justify the conclusions reached by their authors. Sadly, the majority of research utilizes pre-experimental designs (pre/post, no control; or post, no control). To add to the difficulties, most of this research employs criteria reflecting training performance (reactions and learning), with little attention to criteria that may be available at a later time in the transfer situation. The studies sometimes reflect a lack of sophistication, but, in most instances, the evaluators appear fully knowledgeable about the inadequacies of their design and even comment about the uncontrolled factors before going on to justify their conclusions. It is difficult to interpret data from training and educational settings because of the many possible contaminants. In many instances, the researchers simply could not impose strong experimental designs (such as Design 4). However, many of the quasi-experimental designs could have been utilized with little extra effort. The difficult process of properly evaluating our instructional programs must be undertaken. Dunnette and Campbell (1968) summarize the important minimum requirements for evaluation.

What needs to be done?

The *scientific* standards necessary for properly evaluating training experiences are few in number and disarmingly simple, but ... they are almost never put into practice.

First, measures of trainees' status should be obtained *before* and *after* the training experience. Ideally, the measures should sample, as broadly as possible, trainee *behaviors* relevant to the organization's problems and/or to the

Table 5.2

Sources of Invalidity for Designs 1 through 6

	SOURCES OF INVALIDITY											
	INTERNAL								EXTERNAL			
	HISTORY	MATURATION	TESTING	INSTRUMENTATION	REGRESSION	SELECTION	MORTALITY	INTERACTION OF SELECTION AND MATURATION, ETC.	INTERACTION OF TESTING AND X	INTERACTION OF SELECTION AND X	REACTIVE ARRANGEMENTS	MULTIPLE-X INTERFERENCE
Pre-experimental designs:												
1. One-shot case study X T₂	−	−				−	−				−	
2. One-group pretest/ post-test design T₁ X T₂	−	−	−	−	?	+	+	−	−	−	?	
True Experimental Designs:												
3. Pretest/post-test control- group design R T₁ X T₂ R T₁ T₂	+	+	+	+	+	+	+	+	−	?	?	
4. Solomon four-group design R T₁ X T₂ R T₁ T₂ R X T₂ R T₂	+	+	+	+	+	+	+	+	+	?	?	
Quasi-Experimental Designs:												
5. Time series T₁ T₂ T₃ T₄ X T₅ T₆ T₇ T₈	−	+	+	?	+	+	+	+	−	?	?	
6. Nonequivalent control- group design T₁ X T₂ T₁ T₂	+	+	+	+	?	+	+	−	−	?	?	

Note: A minus indicates a definite weakness, a plus indicates that the factor is controlled, a question mark indicates a possible source of concern, and a blank indicates that the factor is not relevant.

Adapted from Campbell, D. T., & Stanley, J. C. *Experimental and Quasi-Experimental Designs for Research.* Chicago: Rand McNally, 1963. © 1963 by the American Educational Research Association, Washington, D.C. Used by permission.

aims of the training procedures, but attitudinal, perceptual, and other self-report measures may also prove useful. Second, measured changes shown by the trainees between pre- and post-training periods should be compared with changes, if any, occurring in a so-called control group of similar, but untrained, persons. Using control groups is the only way to assure that changes observed in the experimental (or trainee) groups are actually the result of training procedures instead of possible artifactual effects—such as the mere passage of time, poor reliability of measures, Hawthorne effects, or other spurious components. Finally, a third standard necessary for most training evaluation studies stems from the possibility of interaction between the evaluation measures and the behavior of the trainees during the program. For example, if trainees are asked beforehand to answer questions about their supervisory "styles", they may be alerted to look for the "correct answers" during training in order to answer the same questions "more appropriately" (i.e., more in line with the desires of the trainer) when they are asked again after their training. One way of estimating the degree of interaction between such measures and the training content is to provide a quasi-control group which takes part in the training program *without* first completing the measures. Then, comparisons between the two trained groups (experimental and quasi-control) on the after-measures may give estimates of the relative amounts of change actually due to training or due simply to having been alerted by prior exposure to the measures.

Unfortunately, these three rather simple standards for learning what training accomplishes are actually very difficult to meet, and they have been applied only rarely . . . [p. 8].[2]

The importance of the improvements that can be realized by rejecting pre-experimental designs and by considering the three factors stressed by Dunnette and Campbell—that is, pre- and post-tests, control groups, and a control for pretest sensitization—should be emphasized. In most instances, the inclusion of these procedures requires some planning, but it is well worth the effort in terms of the quality of information. Even in those cases in which it is not possible to implement all the procedures, a degree of forethought can provide dividends. Thus, in the situations in which a control group is not possible, a time-series design is preferable to a one-group pretest/post-test design. Thoughtful considerations can often provide solutions when the environment appears to dictate otherwise. For example, Rubin (1967) managed to obtain a control group for a sensitivity-training procedure while still providing the treatment for all participants. This was accomplished by having a selected number of trainees complete a pretest by mail several weeks before the treatment commenced. This group then completed the questionnaires again shortly before the treatment began for all participants. These pre- and post-test scores without an intervening treatment provided a control group that was later compared to pre- and post-test scores separated by the treatment condition.

REFERENCES

Becker, S. W. The parable of the pill. *Administrative Science Quarterly,* 1970, **15,** 94–96.

Borg, W. R. *Educational Research.* New York: David McKay, 1963, 1971.

Campbell, D. T., & Stanley, J. C. *Experimental and quasi-experimental designs for research.* Chicago: Rand McNally, 1963.

Campbell, J. P., Dunnette, M. D., Lawler, E. E. III, & Weick, K. E., Jr. *Managerial behavior, performance, and effectiveness.* New York: McGraw-Hill, 1970.

Canter, R. R., Jr. A human relations training program. *Journal of Applied Psychology,* 1951, **35,** 38–45.

Dunnette, M. D., & Campbell, J. P. Laboratory education: Impact on people and organizations. *Industrial Relations,* 1968, 8, 1–27, 41–44.

Golembiewski, R. T., & Carrigan, S. B. Planned change in organization style based on the laboratory approach. *Administrative Science Quarterly,* 1970, 15, 79–93.

Goodacre, D. M. Experimental evaluation of training. *Journal of Personnel Administration and Industrial Relations,* 1955, 2, 143–149.

Issac, S., & Michael, W. B. *Handbook in research and evaluation.* San Diego: Knapp, 1971.

---

[2] From Dunnette, M. D., & Campbell, J. P. Laboratory education: Impact on people and organizations. *Industrial Relations,* 1968, 8, 1–45. Copyright 1968 by the Regents of the University of California, Berkeley. Reprinted by permission.

Kirkpatrick, D. L. Techniques for evaluating training programs. *Journal of the American Society of Training Directors,* 1959, **13**, 3–9, 21–26; 1960, **14**, 13–18, 28–32.

Mayo, G. D., & DuBois, P. H. Measurement of gain in leadership training. *Educational and Psychological Measurement,* 1963, **23**, 23–31.

Randall, L. K. Evaluation: A training dilemma. *Journal of the American Society of Training Directors,* 1960, **14**, 29–35.

Rubin, I. Increased self-acceptance: A means of reducing racial prejudice. *Journal of Personality and Social Psychology,* 1967, **5**, 233–239.

Scriven, M. The methodology of evaluation. In *Perspectives of curriculum evaluation.* American Educational Research Association Monograph, No. 1. Chicago: Rand McNally, 1967.

FOR DISCUSSION AND REVIEW

1 Distinguish between negative, positive, and "frustrate" views of the evaluation process; between formative and summative evaluation.

2 Action research models would evaluate training differently than would formal education research. Explain the differences in these approaches.

3 Define internal and external validity. Review the "threats" to each.

4 What point relative to evaluating training programs was made in "The Parable of the Pill"?

5 What are the "costs" associated with using an experimental versus a quasi-experimental design to evaluate training programs?

INTERVIEW WITH WILLIAM G. DYER

William G. Dyer is Professor in the Organizational Behavior Department at Brigham Young University. He is also a private consultant to such companies as Exxon Oil, General Foods, Honeywell, Standard Oil of Indiana, and Lawrence Livermore Laboratories. Dr. Dyer is the author of several books on organizational and interpersonal change. He has B.A. and M.A. degrees from Brigham Young University and a Ph.D. from the University of Wisconsin.

Q What would be an organization's responsibility for training and development? What is the individual's responsibility? Is this a fifty-fifty proposition?

A Seems to me that there's fairly good evidence that the most effective training is done as a management responsibility. Where managers have worked under good role models, where they have had good coaching, where they have had a good mentor-mentee relationship, they have learned more about management in that process. I think it is an organization's responsibility to make sure that new managers are placed under good manager-tutors, that they have a good learning experience and good role models to watch. The organization then has responsibility to see if there are gaps in the experience base and to provide some kind of new learning experience, such as job rotation, training programs, whatever, that would help fill in those gaps. I think there's a fairly strong responsibility for the organization to monitor this development process. I also think that the individual does need to be responsible for his or her own career planning, own reading, and own kind of program for learning and developing in key areas. If the organization does not have a system or program that rewards, encourages and supports learning and growth, it is difficult for the individual to continue individual development alone. I see it as a joint activity, probably with some more long-range emphasis placed on the organization, if the organization wants to prepare people for careers in its system.

Q Where do organizations typically fall down in their training programs—at the assessment, design, or evaluation phase? What are the reasons for this?

A I would say that one of the big problems in most training is the feeling that training is separate from ongoing management. Managers are sent away to get training and do not see training as organic to a management position. Training should be seen as something that managers provide their subordinates, an integral process in the whole management system. When we rely on others outside the management process to do training, it is something that is done *to* people. This, I feel, is always less effective than training that is seen as a continuing process, a natural component of one's work. I think training people sometimes are at fault, because, in order to protect their field and their jobs, they sometimes latch on to the training area and want to keep it as something separate. This, I think, is a mistake. Training people ought to be working out ways to help managers conduct their own training rather than to do it for them. I also think that when people are sent away to training programs, they run into problems when they come back, because their new learnings are not supported by the formal or informal systems. People are suspicious of them and the evidence (starting early in the Fleishman studies) indicates that the training effects get washed out very quickly when the training is not rewarded and supported inside the organization.

Q Organization Development (O.D.) seems to have lost some of the magic or certainly the visibility it had in the late sixties and early seventies. Do you agree? What major factors have influenced the development of O.D. during recent years? Where is it headed?

A I think that O.D. is probably not as much of a buzz word or fad as it was earlier. The solid contributions of organization development have now been incorporated more into general management processes and more common acceptable labels are now being used. We are now talking about organizational effectiveness, organizational diagnosis, organizational improvement, rather than O.D. These terms are more acceptable to managers. Some of the practices associated with O.D., like T-groups and sensitivity training, have dropped out to a large degree and certain other procedures are much more acceptable and are continuing, like team building, interteam building, organizational diagnosis, survey research, management by objectives, job analysis, job enrichment, and pay and compensation improvements. All of these things now are seen as part of organizational improvement. Managers accept all of this more easily and with much less use of buzz words. I think that O.D. is now moving in some areas with better research and better organizational analyses. We have better theories about organizations as systems. I think O.D. is moving more into open systems analysis and open system planning and into helping managers and organizations deal with the interface with the wider environment. In a reverse direction, I think that O.D. is now moving back away from group processes and team building into more individual processes—more career assessment, career planning, assessment centers, focusing on helping people look at where they are and where they're going in their organizational lives.

Q You have initiated, managed, or supported some very innovative, successful programs. Can you please describe some of these? What environment prevailed that facilitated the success of these programs? What advice could you offer today's training and development professionals regarding gaining and maintaining the power in an organization that allows them to experiment with different types of training?

A Whenever I have been able to work in an organization where a training and development program has been successful, it's been because somebody with influence or power has had a strong "hurt" or felt need. Whenever we've had people who have just been "interested" or who think it might be a "good idea" to try something, but don't feel any compelling need, then there's no disequilibrium in the system. When that condition occurs, people tend not to maintain any continuity or thrust in their efforts to change. The important thing is to identify those things that are real problems, that are of real concern, and then build programs that address themselves directly to those kinds of needs, and not get trapped into doing something that people do not really want or feel is needed. I've been working with an oil company where one concern of the employee-relations department has been to get their personnel people involved more in training and organization development. Employee-relations personnel are not experienced in these areas and usually deal in more traditional personnel functions, such as compensation, benefits, industrial relations, and labor relations. Through a powerful corporate-headquarters development group, a program was established to invite managers and personnel people together to learn what organization development is about, to plan a development program around one of their own problems, and then to implement it and critique the whole process. This is one way to get personnel people involved in a whole new area, and do it in concert with managers. This seems to have value in terms of expanding the thrust and function of personnel people. I've also been working with a major foods organization where they have had some strong felt need at the upper levels of management to assess and improve current management practices. A program was devised to gather data on management performance, share the data with managers, and have them plan specific programs for their own improvement. This organization was also willing to experiment with some new sociotechnical systems; that is, they tried designing plants in a new way, using autonomous work teams, creating a whole new sociotechnical environment which has had some interesting payoffs. You have to have managers who feel a need and are willing to take some risk and some internal people (both personnel and training people) and managers who are willing to experiment and to work with new ways of functioning.

The way training and development people maintain or gain power in an organization is to have a strong theory base that they can articulate and a strong understanding of the research in the field. They also need some ability to explain the theory behind training and development and confidence that they can stand up and represent that position well and not just collapse when managers raise the tough questions. When people in training and development do not have a theory base, or don't know the research, they lack confidence and tend to agree to measures that may not really be effective. They also need to be able to confront managers and participate in some hard-headed negotiations about what really is needed to make a difference. If training and development people just go along with the decisions of others, this will, over the long haul, weaken them and their power and influence.

Q Career management, particularly relating to women and minorities, is becoming a dominant theme in recent training and development literature. In our discussion about the responsibilities for development, the emphasis seems to have been on planning for both the organization and the individual, yet so many successful people we talked to indicate that their careers just happened. Did yours? Do the complexities presented by specialized technology, increased job competition, and more highly qualified job seekers preclude the ad hoc career today?

A I don't believe that successful careers just happen or that their development is completely ad hoc. Still, I do think that, in almost anyone's career, there are certain unplanned, unforeseen kinds of opportunities that emerge. Thus, if people are trained and prepared, they are able to take advantage of these events. I don't think anybody can anticipate particular growth opportunities, new markets, or new positions opening up. Instead, somebody retires or dies, making an opportunity available. That is always going to be the case. But it is the person who is prepared—who has developed his or her skills and competencies—who will be able to take advantage of those opportunities. This kind of emergent opportunity was true in my career—things happened that I didn't completely plan, and I think that still occurs. It is crucial to spend enough time developing the appropriate background and skills to be able to take advantage of opportunities when they arise. I don't think anybody can so thoroughly plan out a career that he or she can know exactly what is going to happen five, ten, or twenty years into the future. We encourage planning, but everyone should be prepared to take advantage of emergent opportunities.

Q What advice would you give an aspirant to a successful managerial career? What characteristics should he or she develop? Is the specialist or the generalist likely to be more successful on the job?

A I almost always work with organizations as an outside consultant in a staff capacity, so I have to talk about a managerial career as an observer rather than as a direct participant. My observations about people who are really effective managers are that they all seem to be very bright, they have good minds, they are very quick in analyzing and assessing situations, and they are able to think creatively and quickly. They need to have a high energy level and must be willing to invest a tremendous amount of time and energy into their work. In other words, they must be willing to work long and hard. I think they are usually risk takers; that is, they are willing to take risks, but risks that are intelligent, based on data and insight. They are generally capable of working effectively with others, they don't alienate people, and they are able to build effective working units or teams. I also find that effective managers are able to use power. They don't back away from tough issues and tough decisions and they are able to use power with a certain degree of grace so that they don't alienate people along the way. Also, they have an ability to gather data, to identify problems—not just solve problems, but *identify* those problems—and then get the best resources together to work on them. They seem to have good cognitive insight—they can see what is going on in the larger picture and thus effectively plan for the future.

I see the same thing that Katz pointed out in a *Harvard Business Review* article: there is a different skill-mix requirement for managers at different levels. As people move up to higher levels, I think they need a different skill mix. At higher levels they need more conceptual or cognitive skills—that is, an ability to plan, to think, and to organize—whereas at the lower levels they deal much more with specific technical problems. At the higher levels people work more as generalists and less as specialists.

Q In the articles preceding this discussion, much emphasis is placed on assessing training needs. How would the assessment process differ when training for improvement of current performance versus training the employee for a future job?

A When trying to improve current performance, it is critical that management training be based on clear, accurate data about how managers are currently performing. Too often training programs are not based on any notion about where the manager really needs to improve. The good training programs for improving current performance are based on data concerning what the manager is actually doing. There is a difference between training to improve current performance and training in order to meet the requirements of a future job. In the future a person may be required to do more planning or organizing and delegating than he or she is currently doing. Therefore, as you prepare for the future, you would train in different kinds of skill areas. In designing and conducting a training program, it is important to know whether you are trying to improve current performance or train for the future. Thus, in order to make your training relevant, it is important to do a good job of assessing the training need before a program is designed.

Q What are the trade-offs between training and selection? We know it's cheaper to put resources into training for entry-level jobs and perhaps use fairly unsophisticated selection procedures, because the jobs aren't very demanding and in many cases a large number of people could qualify minimally and then be trained after hiring. However, when we choose a vice-president, we do not anticipate much training to be required. We put our resources into selection instead. Please comment.

A That statement is generally true. In entry-level management jobs, the skill-mix requirement is heavily weighted at the technical level, and people generally enter with technical competency. Thus, it is easier for them to deal with the technical aspects of the job while they are training to increase management skills that they don't currently have. At the lower levels, managers need to be exposed to a good manager from whom they can begin to learn by the role-model and the coaching-mentor process. It's much tougher to find mentors at the higher levels of management. Who, for example, is going to be the mentor for a new chief executive officer? At that level, you really need to select well, because there aren't available the kinds of built-in learning opportunities that a mentor/mentee relationship offers. You can't keep top-level managers in limbo while you train them. You assume that they already have the qualifications to begin to function there. I think selection is more important at the top level, although there may be some specific functions that new managers still may need to learn. For instance, they may be moving into new operations and may need to learn something about the requirements of the new systems. Or they may be involved in long-range planning and, if that was not one of their previous functions, they may need more training in that area. Even at the higher levels, new managers are going to require some training, depending on the requirements of the position.

Q Where is the training and development process going? What will be its functions in the future? What techniques are likely to become more popular? What will a training program of the 1980s and 1990s look like? What type of people will staff it? How will colleges and universities supplement the organization's training program?

A Some of the issues that will surround training in the next decade are these: Will we train in terms of contingency or situational theory, or in terms of universal theory? That is, are there some universal characteristics of good management, regardless of the situation, or is management determined by the situation? In the past, we have assumed the universal position and we have held that all managers need to learn how to delegate, how to motivate others, how to communicate, how to make decisions, and how to solve problems. As a result, most training programs were based on universal characteristics. Contingency theory and research, however, indicate that managers manage in specific situations, around specific problems and demands, and that one of the big problems in training is that if we train generally, these general traits don't apply to the specific situation. So, training is going to have to blend contingency theory with universals or general characteristics. Such programs are just emerging and good training people are going to design in both directions.

We are also going to have to do more training internally; that is, have team training, training of people together. There will be more training of different levels of management together, so that managers at one level will be trained with their bosses. There will be more emphasis on internal training organic to the position. Although the evidence about the effectiveness of training performed away from the organization is not very good, it probably will continue. In many companies, as long as profits are fairly good, training is regarded as a reward and people are sent to California or Florida or some other nice place as a reward for performance, and the manager may not even be expected to come back and improve. In the future, however, there will be much more emphasis on the assessment of training. Training people are going to have to be better trained in assessment and evaluation techniques. They will probably have to have stronger backgrounds in research and statistics. Managers are going to require that training programs demonstrate their effectiveness and produce some hard data as evidence. People who go into training are going to need better training in theory and design, so that they really will be innovative and creative, have good theory about learning, and be able then to assess and evaluate their programs. Training people need more observation, diagnostic, and process skills to enable them to do more on-the-job consulting as a way of conducting training. They will be watching managers, working with them one-on-one, or working with ongoing working units and teams. Training people will be doing more work improving things internal to the organization.

Colleges and universities will probably continue to have training centers and training programs, partly as a "seeding," getting managers prepared to do things internally, or as a way of exposing them to new ideas. The intensive management-development programs—advanced management programs where people go for longer periods of time—will still be a way for companies to give people a kind of quick MBA, exposing them to the general areas of management.

Q What challenges lie ahead for those in this field?

A The argument for training is so compelling that organizations will continue to consider training to be an area of interest and concern. The argument for training is that nobody is perfect, everybody can improve, nobody has reached his or her maximum level of effectiveness, and people can learn to improve their effectiveness. It is very difficult to disprove that argument. Any organization that wants to have a competitive advantage is going to find that training can make a crucial difference. If we can get good training programs that make sense, and if it can be shown that these programs actually improve performance, managers are going to buy these programs. But training people must be able to understand clearly the theory of training, show that it does make a difference, and assess and evaluate programs. If they can do this, training is going to be an important factor in almost any organization. But the burden is going to be on training people to present their case clearly and to demonstrate that training really does improve bottom-line figures, profits, or whatever the organization really is concerned about.

Maintaining and Improving Commitment, Performance, and Productivity

INTRODUCTION

Section Six focuses on the maintenance and improvement of performance and productivity in an organization. While performance improvement is the responsibility of each organization member, broad, formal programs to improve performance are typically implemented by those in personnel. Today, an enormous amount of attention is given in our society to quality of work life and productivity. Personnel practitioners differ as to the importance of these issues and the best strategies to alleviate problems in these areas. Section Six provides information useful in sorting out this controversy.

Parts A and B of Section Six deal with the use of intrinsic and extrinsic rewards. Locke's lead article presents an argument for eliminating government involvement in quality-of-life issues. Hackman et al. explain an important new strategy for redesigning jobs to add more variety, challenge, feedback, and other intrinsic rewards. A description of the classic failure in job redesign, the Non-Linear Systems story, is also documented here. This case study makes fascinating reading, given the conceptual pieces that precede it.

Extrinsic rewards are primarily offered through wage, salary, bonus, and benefit programs in an organization. Nash and Carroll and Belcher review the entire wage and salary process and present excellent guidelines for job evaluation, implementation of wage structures, and the use of money to motivate performance. Henderson reviews the laws affecting such programs and Lawler discusses the considerable consequences that may result if workers are not satisfied with their pay. Beatty and Schneier compare three strategies for motivating workers, two of which—MBO and job enrichment—were discussed in previous readings. They recommend a technique that is becoming popular and increasingly visible in organizations, but, like other techniques, is controversial. Behavior modification, a learning theory translated to on-the-job behavior, is explained in the Beatty and Schneier piece.

Finally, absenteeism, the four-day week, and occupational health and safety are discussed in Part C. All three issues concern the utilization of human resources and the three articles presented summarize current thinking on each.

A. THE USE OF INTRINSIC REWARDS: JOB SATISFACTION AND JOB ENRICHMENT

Edwin A. Locke

The Case Against Legislating the Quality of Work Life

In a recent article in this journal,* Edward E. Lawler proposed that companies be required to provide data on the "quality of work life" in their annual reports. He argued that this could be measured by means of "behavioral outcomes" such as employee turnover, absenteeism, alcoholism, drug addiction and mental illness. To insure that these indices or the conditions which allegedly give rise to them do not deviate from "acceptable" levels, Lawler suggested that companies which exceed such levels could be taxed or fined proportionately by the government. The justification offered for these proposals was simply his belief that without legislation, "work life will not improve for many people."

This writer disagrees strongly with Lawler's proposals and will demonstrate that they are based on wrong premises and faulty logic.

First, an implicit premise of Lawler's position is that employees have a "right" to a satisfying job. Consider what this would actually mean. Job satisfaction results (with certain qualifications) when an employee gets what he wants from his job. Thus, if an employee has a "right" to job satisfaction, it means that other people must be forced to provide him with the kind of job he wants. This means that he has the "right," in effect, to enslave others. But what about the rights of these others, i.e., the people who must provide these jobs. What if they do not *want* to (or cannot) provide for all the wants of their employees? Why do those who want jobs, but cannot provide their own, have rights, while those with the knowledge and ability to create them have none? This is not only enslavement but the enslavement of the competent *because* they are competent.

Clearly there is a contradiction implied in the premise that there is a "right" to job satisfaction. Since there can be no right to violate a right, there can be no "right" to a satisfying job. Every person has the right to *pursue* his or her own happiness, but does not have the right to force others to provide it, either on the job or off.

Second, Lawler's proposals assume that companies are the cause of the "behavioral outcomes" which he wants to eliminate, e.g., alcohol and drug addiction, mental illness, turnover.

There is not a single study in the literature which shows job dissatisfaction per se to be a cause of alcohol or drug addiction or mental illness. It is well known that these conditions involve profound cognitive disturbances (e.g., value conflicts, improper methods of mental functioning) which have nothing to do with the job the person holds (except to make the employee less effective). Furthermore, an employee accepts and retains his job by choice. No one forces him to accept a given job or to keep it, once accepted, forever. If an employee feels that his job is boring, frus-

From *The Personnel Administrator* 21, no. 4 (May 1976): 19–21. Reprinted by permission of the American Society for Personnel Administration, Berea, Ohio.

*"Should the quality of work life be legislated?", January 1976.

trating, or stifling, or that the costs outweigh the benefits, he is free to quit and look for a better job.

It is true that many jobs are boring and repetitive, but these jobs are often highly paid (e.g., automobile assembly lines) which is why the employees chose them in the first place. Those who find them unbearable, despite the money, typically quit. Employees who choose to remain permanently on such jobs usually do so for one of two reasons: either they are not capable of anything more complex and therefore are not overly dissatisfied, or they are not willing to use their minds to learn more advanced skills and therefore have no right to expect a better job or to force others to provide one. (Some people may also get "trapped" in such jobs through miscalculation or poor planning, but even this does not give these people the right to force others to pay for their errors.)

Behavioral outcomes such as turnover and absenteeism may be caused partly by company policies (pay, type of work, supervision, etc.) but only partly. Turnover, especially, is influenced by numerous other factors, including: the state of the economy, technological developments in the industry, the nature of the local work force, the industry wage scale, government wage and unemployment policies, changes in demographic patterns, events in the employees' personal lives and the values and attitudes the employees bring with them to the job. Thus, holding the company solely responsible for turnover (not to mention alcoholism and mental illness) is grossly unjust.

Furthermore, turnover is not necessarily unhealthy. It provides an escape valve for individuals who are not happy in a given company and allows them to look for a better situation elsewhere. The company also benefits by getting rid of disgruntled employees. Turnover is sometimes highest for the best (most able, most healthy, most ambitious) employees, because their high aspirations and great self-confidence make them difficult to satisfy.

If low turnover and absenteeism are to be taken as indicative of job satisfaction, then the slave labor camps of Soviet Russia (which also have low rates of alcoholism and drug abuse) should be taken as the epitome of a good environment. It is true that slave labor camps undermine mental health, but the fact that four out of Lawler's five criteria of job satisfaction are favorable to such an environment demonstrates the inadequacy of these criteria divorced from a wider context (e.g., what causes these outcomes, why, etc.?).

Thirdly, Lawler's analogy between legislation regarding the work environment and antipollution legislation is invalid. Rational pollution laws differ in two fundamental respects from Lawler's proposed legislation concerning jobs. For one, rational pollution laws are designed to prohibit the *initiation* of force (in the form of pollutants) by one person against another. Such laws are valid because the victim is harmed against his will. Since no voluntary trade is involved, the victim's rights are violated. Secondly, rational pollution laws are *objective;* they prohibit an individual from taking actions which result in provable physical harm to other persons or their property based on objective standards. (Admittedly, all existing pollution laws are not rational by these criteria.)

In contrast, Lawler's proposals for legislation regarding the quality of work life are not designed to prohibit the initiation of force by a company against an employee. As noted above, a company can only offer an individual a job; it cannot force him to accept one. Rather than protecting the employee's rights, Lawler's proposals would violate those of company owners by denying their right to design jobs according to their own judgment. Further, Lawler provides no objective standards for defining a "healthy" work situation. In fact, he provides no standards at all except for certain arbitrarily chosen "behavioral outcomes" (e.g., alcoholism) which, for the reasons stated above, are totally inappropriate.

My fourth comment concerns Lawler's conclusions. After discussing at great length the need for government legislation to force improvements in the quality of work life, and the various alternative methods that could be used for measuring it, he suddenly acknowledges that behavioral outcome measures are not yet adequately developed to serve as a basis for fining or regulating companies. He then argues that companies nevertheless should be forced to provide this information in their annual reports, the most important benefit being that it would "focus the attention of managers on the way the human resources in the organization are being managed."

If it is in a manager's self-interest to develop and report such data, one wonders why Lawler does not believe they will do it voluntarily. But then Lawler again switches focus and asserts (without evidence) that this information is needed by stockholders to evaluate companies.

At this point, the real motive for the proposed legislation emerges. Since corporate officers cannot be "trusted" to provide stockholders with accurate information on the quality of work life, "people trained in behavioral science would be needed to audit the human system, just as accountants audit the financial system." In the last analysis, Lawler's proposals seem to be nothing less than a technique for *enhancing the status and importance of social scientists through legislation* (i.e., force). Does this advocacy of force imply that Lawler believes social scientists cannot *persuade* businessmen of their importance? If so, could one reason be that they have not yet made a good case for themselves?

For all the reasons given above, I find Dr. Lawler's proposals dangerous and illadvised. Job satisfaction and mental health are clearly desirable goals, but they cannot and should not be legislated. Health and happiness can only be achieved if an individual uses his mind properly. But no one can force a man to think; he must do it by choice. The proper role of government in this process is indirect; by protecting individuals from the initiation of force and fraud by others, it leaves each person free to think, to act on his judgment and to enjoy the benefits of his actions. Dr. Lawler, however, advocates that the government reverse its proper role and initiate force against its own citizens. These arbitrary and capricious proposals pose a threat not only to the financial integrity of the corporations which produce our wealth, but to the individual liberty of all citizens.

FOR DISCUSSION AND REVIEW

1 Briefly summarize the author's argument against legislating the quality of work life.
2 What responsibilities should an organization have to provide quality of working life?
3 What arguments would you propose in response to the author's argument?

J. Richard Hackman,
Greg Oldham, Robert Janson,
Kenneth Purdy

A New Strategy for Job Enrichment

Practitioners of job enrichment have been living through a time of excitement, even euphoria. Their craft has moved from the psychology and management journals to the front page and the Sunday supplement. Job enrichment, which began with the pioneering work of Herzberg and his associates, originally was intended as a means to increase the motivation and satisfaction of people at work—and to improve productivity in the bargain.[1-5] Now it is being acclaimed in the popular press as a cure for problems ranging from inflation to drug abuse.

Much current writing about job enrichment is enthusiastic, sometimes even messianic, about what it can accomplish. But the hard questions of exactly what should be done to improve jobs, and how, tend to be glossed over. Lately, because the harder questions have not been dealt with adequately, critical winds have begun to blow. Job enrichment has been described as yet another "management fad," as "nothing new," even as a fraud. And reports of job-enrichment failures are beginning to appear in management and psychology journals.

This article attempts to redress the excesses that have characterized some of the recent writings about job enrichment. As the technique increases in popularity as a management tool, top managers inevitably will find themselves making decisions about its use. The intent of this paper is to help both managers and behavioral scientists become better able to make those decisions on a solid basis of fact and data.

Succinctly stated, we present here a new strategy for going about the redesign of work. The strategy is based on three years of collaborative work and cross-fertilization among the authors—two of whom are academic researchers and two of whom are active practitioners in job enrichment. Our approach is new, but it has been tested in many organizations. It draws on the contributions of both management practice and psychological theory, but it is firmly in the middle ground between them. It builds on and complements previous work by Herzberg and others, but provides for the first time a set of tools for *diagnosing* existing jobs—and a map for translating the diagnostic results into specific action steps for change.

What we have, then, is the following:

1 A theory that specifies when people will get personally "turned on" to their work. The theory shows what kinds of jobs are most likely to generate excitement and commitment about work, and what kinds of employees it works best for.

2 A set of action steps for job enrichment based on the theory, which prescribe in concrete terms what to do to make jobs more motivating for the people who do them.

© 1975 by the Regents of the University of California. Reprinted from *California Management Review* 17, no. 4: 57–71 by permission of the Regents.

Acknowledgements: The authors acknowledge with great appreciation the editorial assistance of John Hickey in the preparation of this paper, and the help of Kenneth Brousseau, Daniel Feldman, and Linda Frank in collecting the data that are summarized here. The research activities reported were supported in part by the Organizational Effectiveness Research Program of the Office of Naval Research, and the Manpower Administration of the U.S. Department of Labor, both through contracts to Yale University.

3 Evidence that the theory holds water and that it can be used to bring about measurable—and sometimes dramatic—improvements in employee work behavior, in job satisfaction, and in the financial performance of the organizational unit involved.

THE THEORY BEHIND THE STRATEGY

What makes people get turned on to their work?

For workers who are really prospering in their jobs, work is likely to be a lot like play. Consider, for example, a golfer at a driving range, practicing to get rid of a hook. His activity is *meaningful* to him; he has chosen to do it because he gets a "kick" from testing his skills by playing the game. He knows that he alone is *responsible* for what happens when he hits the ball. And he has *knowledge of the results* within a few seconds.

Behavioral scientists have found that the three "psychological states" experienced by the golfer in the above example also are critical in determining a person's motivation and satisfaction on the job.

- *Experienced meaningfulness:* The individual must perceive his work as worthwhile or important by some system of values he accepts.

- *Experienced responsibility:* He must believe that he personally is accountable for the outcomes of his efforts.

- *Knowledge of results:* He must be able to determine, on some fairly regular basis, whether or not the outcomes of his work are satisfactory.

When these three conditions are present, a person tends to feel very good about himself when he performs well. And those good feelings will prompt him to try to continue to do well—so he can continue to earn the positive feelings in the future. That is what is meant by "internal motivation"—being turned on to one's work because of the positive internal feelings that are generated by doing well, rather than being dependent on external factors (such as incentive pay or compliments from the boss) for the motivation to work effectively.

What if one of the three psychological states is missing? Motivation drops markedly. Suppose, for example, that our golfer has settled in at the driving range to practice for a couple of hours. Suddenly a fog drifts in over the range. He can no longer see if the ball starts to tail off to the left a hundred yards out. The satisfaction he got from hitting straight down the middle—and the motivation to try to correct something whenever he didn't—are both gone. If the fog stays, it's likely that he soon will be packing up his clubs.

The relationship between the three psychological states and on-the-job outcomes is illustrated in Figure 1. When all three are high, then internal work motivation, job satisfaction, and work quality are high, and absenteeism and turnover are low.

What job characteristics make it happen?

Recent research has identified five "core" characteristics of jobs that elicit the psychological states described above.[6-8] These five core job dimensions provide the key to objectively measuring jobs and to changing them so that they have high potential for motivating people who do them.

Toward meaningful work Three of the five core dimensions contribute to a job's meaningfulness for the worker:

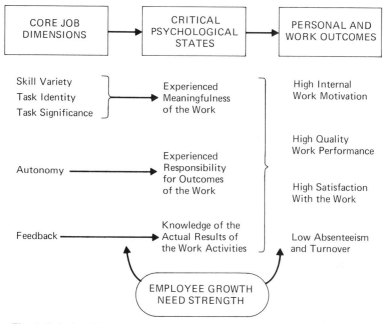

Fig. 1 Relationships among core job dimensions, critical psychological states, and on-the-job outcomes.

1 *Skill variety*—the degree to which a job requires the worker to perform activities that challenge his skills and abilities. When even a single skill is involved, there is at least a seed of potential meaningfulness. When several are involved, the job has the potential of appealing to more of the whole person, and also of avoiding the monotony of performing the same task repeatedly, no matter how much skill it may require.

2 *Task identity*—the degree to which the job requires completion of a "whole" and identifiable piece of work—doing a job from beginning to end with a visible outcome. For example, it is clearly more meaningful to an employee to build complete toasters than to attach electrical cord after electrical cord, especially if he never sees a completed toaster. (Note that the whole job, in this example, probably would involve greater skill variety as well as task identity.)

3 *Task significance*—the degree to which the job has a substantial and perceivable impact on the lives of other people, whether in the immediate organization or the world at large. The worker who tightens nuts on aircraft brake assemblies is more likely to perceive his work as significant than the worker who fills small boxes with paper clips—even though the skill levels involved may be comparable.

Each of these three job dimensions represents an important route to experienced meaningfulness. If the job is high in all three, the worker is quite likely to experience his job as very meaningful. It is not necessary, however, for a job to be very high in all three dimensions. If the job is low in any one of them, there will be a drop in overall experienced meaningfulness. But even when two dimensions are low the worker may find the job meaningful if the third is high enough.

Toward personal responsibility A fourth core dimension leads a worker to experience increased responsibility in his job. This is *autonomy,* the degree to which the job gives the worker freedom, independence, and discretion in scheduling work and determining how he will carry it out. People in highly autonomous jobs know that they are personally responsible for successes and failures. To the extent that their autonomy is high, then, how the work goes will be felt to depend more on the individual's own efforts and initiatives—rather than on detailed instructions from the boss or from a manual of job procedures.

Toward knowledge of results The fifth and last core dimension is *feedback*. This is the degree to which a worker, in carrying out the work activities required by the job, gets information about the effectiveness of his efforts. Feedback is most powerful when it comes directly from the work itself—for example, when a worker has the responsibility for gauging and otherwise checking a component he has just finished, and learns in the process that he has lowered his reject rate by meeting specifications more consistently.

The overall "motivating potential" of a job Figure 1 shows how the five core dimensions combine to affect the psychological states that are critical in determining whether or not an employee will be internally motivated to work effectively. Indeed, when using an instrument to be described later, it is possible to compute a "motivating potential score" (MPS) for any job. The MPS provides a single summary index of the degree to which the objective characteristics of the job will prompt high internal work motivation. Following the theory outlined above, a job high in motivating potential must be high in at least one (and hopefully more) of the three dimensions that lead to experienced meaningfulness and high in both autonomy and feedback as well. The MPS provides a quantitative index of the degree to which this is in fact the case (see Appendix for detailed formula). As will be seen later, the MPS can be very useful in diagnosing jobs and in assessing the effectiveness of job-enrichment activities.

Does the theory work for everybody?

Unfortunately not. Not everyone is able to become internally motivated in his work, even when the motivating potential of a job is very high indeed.

Research has shown that the *psychological needs* of people are very important in determining who can (and who cannot) become internally motivated at work. Some people have strong needs for personal accomplishment, for learning and developing themselves beyond where they are now, for being stimulated and challenged, and so on. These people are high in "growth-need strength."

Figure 2 shows diagrammatically the proposition that individual growth needs have the power to moderate the relationship between the characteristics of jobs and work outcomes. Many workers with high growth needs will turn on eagerly when they have jobs that are high in the core dimensions. Workers whose growth needs are not so strong may respond less eagerly—or, at first, even balk at being "pushed" or "stretched" too far.

Psychologists who emphasize human potential argue that everyone has within him at least a spark of the need to grow and develop personally. Steadily accumulating evidence shows, however, that unless that spark is pretty strong, chances are it will get snuffed out by one's experiences in typical organizations. So, a person who has worked for twenty years in stultifying jobs may find it difficult or impossible to become internally motivated overnight when given the opportunity.

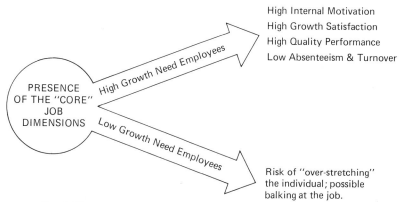

Fig. 2 The moderating effect of employee growth-need strength.

We should be cautious, however, about creating rigid categories of people based on their measured growth-need strength at any particular time. It is true that we can predict from these measures who is likely to become internally motivated on a job and who will be less willing or able to do so. But what we do not know yet is whether or not the growth-need "spark" can be rekindled for those individuals who have had their growth needs dampened by years of growth-depressing experience in their organizations.

Since it is often the organization that is responsible for currently low levels of growth desires, we believe that the organization also should provide the individual with the chance to reverse that trend whenever possible, even if that means putting a person in a job where he may be "stretched" more than he wants to be. He can always move back later to the old job—and in the meantime the embers of his growth needs just might burst back into flame, to his surprise and pleasure, and for the good of the organization.

FROM THEORY TO PRACTICE: A TECHNOLOGY FOR JOB ENRICHMENT

When job enrichment fails, it often fails because of inadequate *diagnosis* of the target job and employees' reactions to it. Often, for example, job enrichment is assumed by management to be a solution to "people problems" on the job and is implemented even though there has been no diagnostic activity to indicate that the root of the problem is in fact how the work is designed. At other times, some diagnosis is made—but it provides no concrete guidance about what specific aspects of the job require change. In either case, the success of job enrichment may wind up depending more on the quality of the intuition of the change agent—or his luck—than on a solid base of data about the people and the work.

In the paragraphs to follow, we outline a new technology for use in job enrichment which explicitly addresses the diagnostic as well as the action components of the change process. The technology has two parts: (1) a set of diagnostic tools that are useful in evaluating jobs and people's reactions to them prior to change—and in pinpointing exactly what aspects of specific jobs are most critical to a successful change attempt; and (2) a set of "implementing concepts" that provide concrete guidance for action steps in job enrichment. The implementing concepts are tied directly to the diagnostic tools; the output of the diagnostic activity specifies which action steps are likely to have the most impact in a particular situation.

The diagnostic tools

Central to the diagnostic procedure we propose is a package of instruments to be used by employees, supervisors, and outside observers in assessing the target job and employees' reactions to it.[9] These instruments gauge the following:

1 The objective characteristics of the jobs themselves, including both an overall indication of the "motivating potential" of the job as it exists (that is, the MPS score) and the score of the job on each of the five core dimensions described previously. Because knowing the strengths and weaknesses of the job is critical to any work-redesign effort, assessments of the job are made by supervisors and outside observers as well as the employees themselves—and the final assessment of a job uses data from all three sources.

2 The current levels of motivation, satisfaction, and work performance of employees on the job. In addition to satisfaction with the work itself, measures are taken of how people feel about other aspects of the work setting, such as pay, supervision, and relationships with co-workers.

3 The level of growth-need strength of the employees. As indicated earlier, employees who have strong growth needs are more likely to be more responsive to job enrichment than employees with weak growth needs. Therefore, it is important to know at the outset just what kinds of satisfactions the people who do the job are (and are not) motivated to obtain from their work. This will make it possible to identify which persons are best to start changes with, and which may need help in adapting to the newly enriched job.

What, then, might be the actual steps one would take in carrying out a job diagnosis using these tools? Although the approach to any particular diagnosis depends upon the specifics of the particular work situation involved, the sequence of questions listed below is fairly typical.

Step 1. Are motivation and satisfaction central to the problem? Sometimes organizations undertake job enrichment to improve the work motivation and satisfaction of employees when in fact the real problem with work performance lies elsewhere—for example, in a poorly designed production system, in an error-prone computer, and so on. The first step is to examine the scores of employees on the motivation and satisfaction portions of the diagnostic instrument. (The questionnaire taken by employees is called the Job Diagnostic Survey and will be referred to hereafter as the JDS.) If motivation and satisfaction are problematic, the change agent would continue to Step 2; if not, he would look to other aspects of the work situation to identify the real problem.

Step 2. Is the job low in motivating potential? To answer this question, one would examine the motivating potential score of the target job and compare it to the MPS's of other jobs to determine whether or not *the job itself* is a probable cause of the motivational problems documented in Step 1. If the job turns out to be low on the MPS, one would continue to Step 3; if it scores high, attention should be given to other possible reasons for the motivational difficulties (such as the pay system, the nature of supervision, and so on).

Step 3. What specific aspects of the job are causing the difficulty? This step involves examining the job on each of the five core dimensions to pinpoint the specific strengths and weaknesses of the job as it is currently structured. It is useful at this stage to construct a "profile" of the target job, to make visually apparent where im-

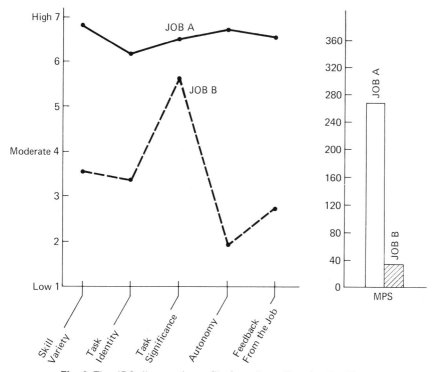

Fig. 3 The JDS diagnostic profile for a "good" and a "bad" job.

provements need to be made. An illustrative profile for two jobs (one "good" job and one job needing improvement) is shown in Figure 3.

Job A is an engineering maintenance job and is high on all of the core dimensions; the MPS of this job is a very high 260. (MPS scores can range from 1 to about 350; an "average" score would be about 125.) Job enrichment would not be recommended for this job; if employees working on the job were unproductive and unhappy, the reasons are likely to have little to do with the nature or design of the work itself.

Job B, on the other hand, has many problems. This job involves the routine and repetitive processing of checks in the "back room" of a bank. The MPS is 30, which is quite low—and indeed, would be even lower if it were not for the moderately high task significance of the job. (Task significance is moderately high because the people are handling large amounts of other people's money, and therefore the quality of their efforts potentially has important consequences for their unseen clients.) The job provides the individuals with very little direct feedback about how effectively they are doing it; the employees have little autonomy in how they go about doing the job; and the job is moderately low in both skill variety and task identity.

For Job B, then, there is plenty of room for improvement—and many avenues to examine in planning job changes. For still other jobs, the avenues for change often turn out to be considerably more specific: for example, feedback and autonomy may be reasonably high, but one or more of the core dimensions that contribute to the experienced meaningfulness of the job (skill variety, task identity, and task significance) may be low. In such a case, attention would turn to ways to increase the standing of the job on these latter three dimensions.

Step 4. How "ready" are the employees for change? Once it has been documented that there is need for improvement in the job—and the particularly troublesome aspects of the job have been identified—then it is time to begin to think about the specific action steps which will be taken to enrich the job. An important factor in such planning is the level of growth needs of the employees, since employees high on growth needs usually respond more readily to job enrichment than do employees with little need for growth. The JDS provides a direct measure of the growth-need strength of the employees. This measure can be very helpful in planning how to introduce the changes to the people (for instance, cautiously versus dramatically), and in deciding who should be among the first group of employees to have their jobs changed.

In actual use of the diagnostic package, additional information is generated which supplements and expands the basic diagnostic questions outlined above. The point of the above discussion is merely to indicate the kinds of questions which we believe to be most important in diagnosing a job prior to changing it. We now turn to how the diagnostic conclusions are translated into specific job changes.

The implementing concepts

Five "implementing concepts" for job enrichment are identified and discussed below.[10] Each one is a specific action step aimed at improving both the quality of the working experience for the individual and his work productivity. They are: (1) forming natural work units; (2) combining tasks; (3) establishing client relationships; (4) vertical loading; (5) opening feedback channels.

The links between the implementing concepts and the core dimensions are shown in Figure 4—which illustrates our theory of job enrichment, ranging from the concrete action steps through the core dimensions and the psychological states to the actual personal and work outcomes.

After completing the diagnosis of a job, a change agent would know which of the core dimensions were most in need of remedial attention. He could then turn to Figure 4 and select those implementing concepts that specifically deal with the

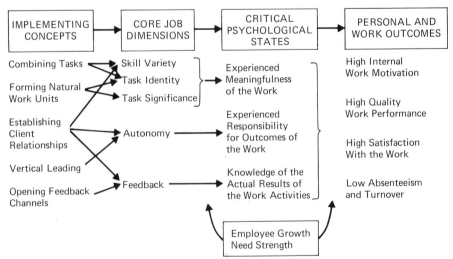

Fig. 4 The full model: how use of the implementing concepts can lead to positive outcomes.

most troublesome parts of the existing job. How this would take place in practice will be seen below.

Forming natural work units The notion of distributing work in some logical way may seem to be an obvious part of the design of any job. In many cases, however, the logic is one imposed by just about any consideration except jobholder satisfaction and motivation. Such considerations include technological dictates, level of worker training or experience, "efficiency" as defined by industrial engineering, and current workload. In many cases the cluster of tasks a worker faces during a typical day or week is natural to anyone *but* the worker.

For example, suppose that a typing pool (consisting of one supervisor and ten typists) handles all work for one division of a company. Jobs are delivered in rough draft or dictated form to the supervisor, who distributes them as evenly as possible among the typists. In such circumstances the individual letters, reports, and other tasks performed by a given typist in one day or week are randomly assigned. There is no basis for identifying with the work or the person or department for whom it is performed, or for placing any personal value upon it.

The principle underlying natural units of work, by contrast, is "ownership"—a worker's sense of continuing responsibility for an identifiable body of work. Two steps are involved in creating natural work units. The first is to identify the basic work items. In the typing pool, for example, the items might be "pages to be typed." The second step is to group the items in natural categories. For example, each typist might be assigned continuing responsibility for all jobs requested by one or several specific departments. The assignments should be made, of course, in such a way that workloads are about equal in long run. (For example, one typist might end up with all the work from one busy department, while another handles jobs from several smaller units.)

At this point we can begin to see specifically how the job-design principles relate to the core dimensions (cf. Figure 4). The ownership fostered by natural units of work can make the difference between a feeling that work is meaningful and rewarding and the feeling that it is irrelevant and boring. As the diagram shows, natural units of work are directly related to two of the core dimensions: task identity and task significance.

A typist whose work is assigned naturally rather than randomly—say, by departments—has a much greater chance of performing a whole job to completion. Instead of typing one section of a large report, the individual is likely to type the whole thing, with knowledge of exactly what the product of the work is (task identity). Furthermore, over time the typist will develop a growing sense of how the work affects coworkers in the department serviced (task significance).

Combining tasks The very existence of a pool made up entirely of persons whose sole function is typing reflects a fractionalization of jobs that has been a basic precept of "scientific management." Most obvious in assembly-line work, fractionalization has been applied to nonmanufacturing jobs as well. It is typically justified by efficiency, which is usually defined in terms of either low costs or some time-and-motion type of criteria.

It is hard to find fault with measuring efficiency ultimately in terms of cost-effectiveness. In doing so, however, a manager should be sure to consider *all* the costs involved. It is possible, for example, for highly fractionalized jobs to meet all the time-and-motion criteria of efficiency, but if the resulting job is so unrewarding that performing it day after day leads to high turnover, absenteeism, drugs and alcohol, and strikes, then productivity is really lower (and costs higher) than data on efficiency might indicate.

The principle of combining tasks, then, suggests that whenever possible existing and fractionalized tasks should be put together to form new and larger modules of work. At the Medfield, Massachusetts plant of Corning Glass Works the assembly of a laboratory hot plate has been redesigned along the lines suggested here. Each hot plate now is assembled from start to finish by one operator, instead of going through several separate operations that are performed by different people.

Some tasks, if combined into a meaningfully large module of work, would be more than an individual could do by himself. In such cases, it is often useful to consider assigning the new, larger task to a small *team* of workers—who are given great autonomy for its completion. At the Racine, Wisconsin plant of Emerson Electric, the assembly process for trash disposal appliances was restructured this way. Instead of a sequence of moving the appliance from station to station, the assembly now is done from start to finish by one team. Such teams include both men and women to permit switching off the heavier and more delicate aspects of the work. The team responsible is identified on the appliance. In case of customer complaints, the team often drafts the reply.

As a job-design principle, task combination, like natural units of work, expands the task identity of the job. For example, the hot-plate assembler can see and identify with a finished product ready for shipment, rather than a nearly invisible junction of solder. Moreover, the more tasks that are combined into a single worker's job, the greater the variety of skills he must call on in performing the job. So task combination also leads directly to greater skill variety—the third core dimension that contributes to the overall experienced meaningfulness of the work.

Establishing client relationships One consequence of fractionalization is that the typical worker has little or no contact with (or even awareness of) the ultimate user of his product or service. By encouraging and enabling employees to establish direct relationships with the clients of their work, improvements often can be realized simultaneously on three of the core dimensions. Feedback increases, because of additional opportunities for the individual to receive praise or criticism of his work outputs directly. Skill variety often increases, because of the necessity to develop and exercise one's interpersonal skills in maintaining the client relationship. And autonomy can increase because the individual often is given personal responsibility for deciding how to manage his relationships with the clients of his work.

Creating client relationships is a three-step process. First, the client must be identified. Second, the most direct contact possible between the worker and the client must be established. Third, criteria must be set up by which the client can judge the quality of the product or service he receives. And whenever possible, the client should have a means of relaying his judgments directly back to the worker.

The contact between worker and client should be as great as possible and as frequent as necessary. Face-to-face contact is highly desirable, at least occasionally. Where that is impossible or impractical, telephone and mail can suffice. In any case, it is important that the performance criteria by which the worker will be rated by the client must be mutually understood and agreed upon.

Vertical loading Typically the split between the "doing" of a job and the "planning" and "controlling" of the work has evolved along with horizontal fractionalization. Its rationale, once again, has been "efficiency through specialization." And once again, the excess of specialization that has emerged has resulted in unexpected but significant costs in motivation, morale, and work quality. In vertical loading, the intent is to partially close the gap between the doing and the controlling parts of the job—and thereby reap some important motivational advantages.

Of all the job-design principles, vertical loading may be the single most crucial one. In some cases, where it has been impossible to implement any other changes, vertical loading alone has had significant motivational effects.

When a job is vertically loaded, responsibilities and controls that formerly were reserved for higher levels of management are added to the job. There are many ways to accomplish this:

• Return to the job holder greater discretion in setting schedules, deciding on work methods, checking on quality, and advising or helping to train less experienced workers.

• Grant additional authority. The objective should be to advance workers from a position of no authority or highly restricted authority to positions of reviewed, and eventually, near-total authority for his own work.

• Time management. The job holder should have the greatest possible freedom to decide when to start and stop work, when to break, and how to assign priorities.

• Troubleshooting and crisis decisions. Workers should be encouraged to seek problem solutions on their own, rather than calling immediately for the supervisor.

• Financial controls. Some degree of knowledge and control over budgets and other financial aspects of a job can often be highly motivating. However, access to this information frequently tends to be restricted. Workers can benefit from knowing something about the costs of their jobs, the potential effect upon profit, and various financial and budgetary alternatives.

When a job is vertically loaded it will inevitably increase in *autonomy*. And as shown in Figure 4, this increase in objective personal control over the work will also lead to an increased feeling of personal responsibility for the work, and ultimately to higher internal work motivation.

Opening feedback channels In virtually all jobs there are ways to open channels of feedback to individuals or teams to help them learn whether their performance is improving, deteriorating, or remaining at a constant level. While there are numerous channels through which information about performance can be provided, it generally is better for a worker to learn about his performance *directly as he does his job*—rather than from management on an occasional basis.

Job-provided feedback usually is more immediate and private than supervisor-supplied feedback, and it increases the worker's feelings of personal control over his work in the bargain. Moreover, it avoids many of the potentially disruptive interpersonal problems that can develop when the only way a worker has to find out how he is doing is through direct messages or subtle cues from the boss.

Exactly what should be done to open channels for job-provided feedback will vary from job to job and organization to organization. Yet in many cases the changes involve simply removing existing blocks that isolate the worker from naturally occurring data about performance—rather than generating entirely new feedback mechanisms. For example:

• Establishing direct client relationships often removes blocks between the worker and natural external sources of data about his work.

• Quality-control efforts in many organizations often eliminate a natural source of feedback. The quality check on a product or service is done by persons other than those responsible for the work. Feedback to the workers—if there is any—is belated and diluted. It often fosters a tendency to think of quality as "someone else's concern." By placing quality control close to the worker (perhaps even in his own hands), the quantity and quality of data about performance available to him can dramatically increase.

• Tradition and established procedure in many organizations dictate that records about performance be kept by a supervisor and transmitted up (not down) in the organizational hierarchy. Sometimes supervisors even check the work and correct any errors themselves. The worker who made the error never knows it occurred—and is denied the very information that could enhance both his internal work motivation and the technical adequacy of his performance. In many cases it is possible to provide standard summaries of performance records directly to the worker (as well as to his superior), thereby giving him personally and regularly the data he needs to improve his performance.

• Computers and other automated operations sometimes can be used to provide the individual with data now blocked from him. Many clerical operations, for example, are now performed on computer consoles. These consoles often can be programmed to provide the clerk with immediate feedback in the form of a CRT display or a printout indicating that an error has been made. Some systems even have been programmed to provide the operator with a positive feedback message when a period of error-free performance has been sustained.

Many organizations simply have not recognized the importance of feedback as a motivator. Data on quality and other aspects of performance are viewed as being of interest only to management. Worse still, the *standards* for acceptable performance often are kept from workers as well. As a result, workers who would be interested in following the daily or weekly ups and downs of their performance, and in trying accordingly to improve, are deprived of the very guidelines they need to do so. They are like the golfer we mentioned earlier, whose efforts to correct his hook are stopped dead by fog over the driving range.

THE STRATEGY IN ACTION: HOW WELL DOES IT WORK?

So far we have examined a basic theory of how people get turned on to their work; a set of core dimensions of jobs that create the conditions for such internal work motivation to develop on the job; and a set of five implementing concepts that are the action steps recommended to boost a job on the core dimensions and thereby increase employee motivation, satisfaction, and productivity.

The remaining question is straightforward and important: *Does it work?* In reality, that question is twofold. First, does the theory itself hold water, or are we barking up the wrong conceptual tree? And second, does the change strategy really lead to measurable differences when it is applied in an actual organizational setting?

This section summarizes the findings we have generated to date on these questions.

Is the job-enrichment theory correct?

In general, the answer seems to be yes. The JDS instrument has been taken by more than 1,000 employees working on about 100 diverse jobs in more than a dozen organizations over the last two years. These data have been analyzed to test the basic motivational theory—and especially the impact of the core job dimensions on worker motivation, satisfaction, and behavior on the job. An illustrative overview of some of the findings is given below.[8]

1 People who work on jobs high on the core dimensions are more motivated and satisfied than are people who work on jobs that score low on the dimensions. Employees with jobs high on the core dimensions (MPS scores greater than 240) were compared to those who held unmotivating jobs (MPS scores less than 40). As shown in Figure 5, employees with high MPS jobs were higher on (a) the three psychological states, (b) internal work motivation, (c) general satisfaction, and (d) "growth" satisfaction.

2 Figure 6 shows that the same is true for measures of actual behavior at work—absenteeism and performance effectiveness—although less strongly so for the performance measure.

3 Responses to jobs high in motivating potential are more positive for people who have strong growth needs than for people with weak needs for growth. In Figure 7 the linear relationship between the motivating potential of a job and employees' level of internal work motivation is shown, separately for people with high versus low growth needs as measured by the JDS. While both groups of employees show increases in internal motivation as MPS increases, the *rate* of increase is significantly greater for the group of employees who have strong needs of growth.

How does the change strategy work in practice?
The results summarized above suggest that both the theory and the diagnostic instrument work when used with real people in real organizations. In this section, we summarize a job-enrichment project conducted at The Travelers Insurance Companies, which illustrates how the change procedures themselves work in practice.

The Travelers project was designed with two purposes in mind. One was to achieve improvements in morale, productivity, and other indicators of employee well-being. The other was to test the general effectiveness of the strategy for job enrichment we have summarized in this article.

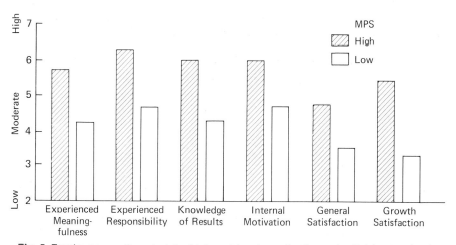

Fig. 5 Employee reactions to jobs high and low in motivating potential for two banks and a steel firm.

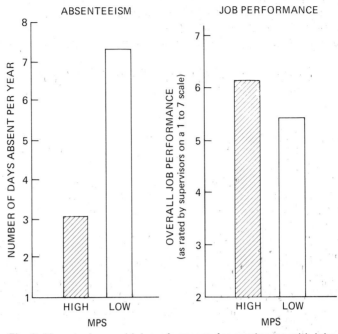

Fig. 6 Absenteeism and job performance for employees with jobs high and low in motivating potential.

Fig. 7 Relationship between the motivating potential of a job and the internal work motivation of employees. (Shown separately for employees with strong versus weak growth-need strength.)

The work group chosen was a keypunching operation. The group's function was to transfer information from printed or written documents onto punched cards for computer input. The work group consisted of ninety-eight keypunch operators and verifiers (both in the same job classification), plus seven assignment clerks. All reported to a supervisor who, in turn, reported to the assistant manager and manager of the data-input division.

The size of individual punching orders varied considerably, from a few cards to as many as 2,500. Some work came to the work group with a specified delivery date, while other orders were to be given routine service on a predetermined schedule.

Assignment clerks received the jobs from the user departments. After reviewing the work for obvious errors, omissions, and legibility problems, the assignment clerk parceled out the work in batches expected to take about one hour. If the clerk found the work not suitable for punching it went to the supervisor, who either returned the work to the user department or cleared up problems by phone. When work went to operators for punching, it was with the instruction, "Punch only what you see. Don't correct errors, no matter how obvious they look."

Because of the high cost of computer time, keypunched work was 100 percent verified—a task that consumed nearly as many man-hours as the punching itself. Then the cards went to the supervisor, who screened the jobs for due dates before sending them to the computer. Errors detected in verification were assigned to various operators at random to be corrected.

The computer output from the cards was sent to the originating department, accompanied by a printout of errors. Eventually the printout went back to the supervisor for final correction.

A great many phenomena indicated that the problems being experienced in the work group might be the result of poor motivation. As the only person performing supervisory functions of any kind, the supervisor spent most of his time responding to crisis situations, which recurred continually. He also had to deal almost daily with employees' salary grievances or other complaints. Employees frequently showed apathy or outright hostility toward their jobs.

Rates of work output, by accepted work-measurement standards, were inadequate. Error rates were high. Due dates and schedules frequently were missed. Absenteeism was higher than average, especially before and after weekends and holidays.

The single, rather unusual exception was turnover. It was lower than the companywide average for similar jobs. The company has attributed this fact to a poor job market in the base period just before the project began, and to an older, relatively more settled work force—made up, incidentally, entirely of women.

The diagnosis

Using some of the tools and techniques we have outlined, a consulting team from the Management Services Department and from Roy W. Walters & Associates concluded that the keypunch-operator's job exhibited the following serious weaknesses in terms of the core dimensions.

- Skill variety: there was none. Only a single skill was involved—the ability to punch adequately the data on the batch of documents.

- Task identity: virtually nonexistent. Batches were assembled to provide an even workload, but not whole identifiable jobs.

- Task significance: not apparent. The keypunching operation was a necessary step in providing service to the company's customers. The individual operator was isolated by an assignment clerk and a supervisor from any knowledge of what the operation meant to the using department, let alone its meaning to the ultimate customer.

• Autonomy: none. The operators had no freedom to arrange their daily tasks to meet schedules, to resolve problems with the using department, or even to correct, in punching, information that was obviously wrong.

• Feedback: none. Once a batch was out of the operator's hands, she had no assured chance of seeing evidence of its quality or inadequacy.

Design of the experimental trial

Since the diagnosis indicated that the motivating potential of the job was extremely low, it was decided to attempt to improve the motivation and productivity of the work group through job enrichment. Moreover, it was possible to design an experimental test of the effects of the changes to be introduced: the results of changes made in the target work group were to be compared with trends in a control work group of similar size and demographic make-up. Since the control group was located more than a mile away, there appeared to be little risk of communication between members of the two groups.

A base period was defined before the start of the experimental trial period, and appropriate data were gathered on the productivity, absenteeism, and work attitudes of members of both groups. Data also were available on turnover; but since turnover was already below average in the target group, prospective changes in this measure were deemed insignificant.

An educational session was conducted with supervisors, at which they were given the theory and implementing concepts and actually helped to design the job changes themselves. Out of this session came an active plan consisting of about twenty-five change items that would significantly affect the design of the target jobs.

The implementing concepts and the changes

Because the job as it existed was rather uniformly low on the core job dimensions, all five of the implementing concepts were used in enriching it.

• Natural units of work. The random batch assignment of work was replaced by assigning to each operator continuing responsibility for certain accounts—either particular departments or particular recurring jobs. Any work for those accounts now always goes to the same operator.

• Task combination. Some planning and controlling functions were combined with the central task of keypunching. In this case, however, these additions can be more suitably discussed under the remaining three implementing concepts.

• Client relationships. Each operator was given several channels of direct contact with clients. The operators, not their assignment clerks, now inspect their documents for correctness and legibility. When problems arise, the operator, not the supervisor, takes them up with the client.

• Feedback. In addition to feedback from client contact, the operators were provided with a number of additional sources of data about their performance. The computer department now returns incorrect cards to the operators who punched them, and operators correct their own errors. Each operator also keeps her own file of copies of her errors. These can be reviewed to determine trends in error frequency and types of errors. Each operator receives weekly a computer printout of her errors and productivity, which is sent to her directly, rather than given to her by the supervisor.

• Vertical loading. Besides consulting directly with clients about work questions, operators now have the authority to correct obvious coding errors on their own. Operators may set their own schedules and plan their daily work, as long as they meet schedules. Some competent operators have been given the option of not verifying their work and making their own program changes.

Results of the trial

The results were dramatic. The number of operators declined from ninety-eight to sixty. This occurred partly through attrition and partly through transfer to other departments. Some of the operators were promoted to higher-paying jobs in departments whose cards they had been handling—something that had never occurred before. Some details of the results are given below.

• Quantity of work. The control group, with no job changes made, showed an increase in productivity of 8.1 percent during the trial period. The experimental group showed an increase of 39.6 percent.

• Error rates. To assess work quality, error rates were recorded for about forty operators in the experimental group. All were experienced, and all had been in their jobs before the job-enrichment program began. For two months before the study, these operators had a collective error rate of 1.53 percent. For two months toward the end of the study, the collective error rate was 0.99 percent. By the end of the study the number of operators with poor performance had dropped from 11.1 percent to 5.5 percent.

• Absenteeism. The experimental group registered a 24.1 percent decline in absences. The control group, by contrast, showed a 29 percent *increase*.

• Attitudes toward the job. An attitude survey given at the start of the project showed that the two groups scored about average, and nearly identically, in nine different areas of work satisfaction. At the end of the project the survey was was repeated. The control group showed an insignificant 0.5 percent improvement, while the experimental group's overall satisfaction score rose 16.5 percent.

• Selective elimination of controls. Demonstrated improvements in operator proficiency permitted them to work with fewer controls. Travelers estimates that the reduction of controls had the same effect as adding seven operators—a saving even beyond the effects of improved productivity and lowered absenteeism.

• Role of the supervisor. One of the most significant findings in the Travelers experiment was the effect of the changes on the supervisor's job, and thus on the rest of the organization. The operators took on many responsibilities that had been reserved at least to the unit leaders and sometimes to the supervisor. The unit leaders, in turn, assumed some of the day-to-day supervisory functions that had plagued the supervisor. Instead of spending his days supervising the behavior of subordinates and dealing with crises, he was able to devote time to developing feedback systems, setting up work modules and spearheading the enrichment effort—in other words, managing. It should be noted, however, that helping supervisors change their own work activities when their subordinates' jobs have been enriched is itself a challenging task. And if appropriate attention and help are not given to supervisors in such cases, they rapidly can become disaffected—and a job-enrichment "backlash" can result.[11]

Summary

By applying work-measurement standards to the changes wrought by job enrichment—attitude and quality, absenteeism, and selective administration of controls—Travelers was able to estimate the total dollar impact of the project. Actual savings in salaries and machine rental charges during the first year totaled $64,305. Potential savings by further application of the changes were put at $91,937 annually. Thus, by almost any measure used—from the work attitudes of individual employees to dollar savings for the company as a whole—The Travelers test of the job-enrichment strategy proved a success.

CONCLUSIONS

In this article we have presented a new strategy for the redesign of work in general and for job enrichment in particular. The approach has four main characteristics:

1 It is grounded in a basic psychological theory of what motivates people in their work.

2 It emphasizes that planning for job changes should be done on the basis of *data* about the jobs and the people who do them—and a set of diagnostic instruments is provided to collect such data.

3 It provides a set of specific implementing concepts to guide actual job changes, as well as a set of theory-based rules for selecting *which* action steps are likely to be most beneficial in a given situation.

4 The strategy is buttressed by a set of findings showing that the theory holds water, that the diagnostic procedures are practical and informative, and that the implementing concepts can lead to changes that are beneficial both to organizations and to the people who work in them.

We believe that job enrichment is moving beyond the stage where it can be considered "yet another management fad." Instead, it represents a potentially powerful strategy for change that can help organizations achieve their goals for higher quality work—and at the same time further the equally legitimate needs of contemporary employees for a more meaningful work experience. Yet there are pressing questions about job enrichment and its use that remain to be answered.

Prominent among these is the question of employee participation in planning and implementing work redesign. The diagnostic tools and implementing concepts we have presented are neither designed nor intended for use only by management. Rather, our belief is that the effectiveness of job enrichment is likely to be enhanced when the tasks of diagnosing and changing jobs are undertaken *collaboratively* by management and by the employees whose work will be affected.

Moreover, the effects of work redesign on the broader organization remain generally uncharted. Evidence now is accumulating that when jobs are changed, turbulence can appear in the surrounding organization—for example, in supervisory-subordinate relationships, in pay and benefit plans, and so on. Such turbulence can be viewed by management either as a problem with job enrichment, or as an opportunity for further and broader organizational development by teams of managers and employees. To the degree that management takes the latter view, we believe, the oft-espoused goal of achieving basic organizational change through the redesign of work may come increasingly within reach.

The diagnostic tools and implementing concepts we have presented are useful in deciding on and designing basic changes in the jobs themselves. They do not address the broader issues of who plans the changes, how they are carried out, and how they are followed up. The way these broader questions are dealt with, we believe, may determine whether job enrichment will grow up—or whether it will die an early and unfortunate death, like so many other fledgling behavioral-science approaches to organizational change.

Appendix: For the algebraically inclined, the Motivating Potential Score is computed as follows

$$MPS = \left[\frac{\text{Skill Variety} + \text{Task Identity} + \text{Task Significance}}{3} \right]$$

$$\text{X Autonomy} \quad \text{X Feedback}$$

It should be noted that in some cases the MPS score can be *too* high for positive job satisfaction and effective performance—in effect overstimulating the person who holds the job. This paper focuses on jobs which are toward the low end of the scale—and which potentially can be improved through job enrichment.

REFERENCES

1 F. Herzberg, B. Mausner and B. Snyderman, *The Motivation to Work* (New York: John Wiley & Sons, 1959).
2 F. Herzberg, *Work and the Nature of Man* (Cleveland: World, 1966).
3 F. Herzberg, "One More Time: How Do You Motivate Employees?" *Harvard Business Review* (1968), pp. 53-62.
4 W. J. Paul, Jr.; K. B. Robertson and F. Herzberg, "Job Enrichment Pays Off," *Harvard Business Review* (1969), pp. 61-78.
5 R. N. Ford, *Motivation Through the Work Itself* (New York: American Management Association, 1969).
6 A. N. Turner and P. R. Lawrence, *Industrial Jobs and the Worker* (Cambridge, Mass.: Harvard Graduate School of Business Administration, 1965).
7 J. R. Hackman and E. E. Lawler, "Employee Reactions to Job Characteristics," *Journal of Applied Psychology Monograph* (1971), pp. 259-286.
8 J. R. Hackman and G. R. Oldham, *Motivation Through the Design of Work: Test of a Theory*, Technical Report No. 6, Department of Administrative Sciences, Yale University, 1974.
9 J. R. Hackman and G. R. Oldham, "Development of the Job Diagnostic Survey," *Journal of Applied Psychology* (1975), pp. 159-170.
10 R. W. Walters and Associates, *Job Enrichment for Results* (Reading, Mass.: Addison-Wesley, 1975).
11 E. E. Lawler III; J. R. Hackman, and S. Kaufman, "Effects of Job Redesign: A Field Experiment," *Journal of Applied Social Psychology* (1973), pp. 49-62.

FOR DISCUSSION AND REVIEW

1 Review the theory behind this job-enrichment strategy. Why is employee need strength important?
2 Define skill variety, task identity, and task significance.
3 Why is feedback an important determinant of performance?
4 What does the MPS measure?

5 Review the authors' diagnostic procedure. Review their implementing concepts.
6 Would this strategy be appropriate for all jobs? For all persons?
7 Explain vertical job loading.
8 How representative of other organizations is the authors' case study. What problems might be encountered if the strategy were implemented in the military?

Erwin L. Malone

Non-Linear Systems, Inc.: An Experiment in Participative Management that Failed

Non-Linear Systems, Inc., located in Del Mar, California, principally manufactures a complete line of digital electrical measuring instruments, ranging in price from $500 to over $20,000 per unit, which are also tailored to specific requirements of such customers as U.S. governmental agencies, universities, and through subcontractors, utilities, petroleum, chemical, textile, and other industries. The company grew from an initial five employees in 1952 to a high of 340 (75 percent of them male) in the 1960s; it now employs one-third that number. Dun and Bradstreet rated the company as a $6 million enterprise. For years NLS was the leader in an industry where it and six competitors took 95 percent of the available business and some 50 others shared the remaining 5 percent.

The company had been in business for 8 years and was firmly established in its field before the experiment in "participative management" was initiated in 1960–61. There never had been unionization in any department of the company. The experiment was completely voluntary on the part of the company. It was set up by a liberal-minded president whose early life observations of the critical impact of working policies and conditions on his parents, himself, and others generated an insatiable interest in methods to better human relations in industry and develop each individual's potential to the full. The experiment was instituted after years of deliberation and long conferences with professional scientists and industrialists who professed similar interests and after many months of discussion with employees and with their full consent.

ELEMENTS OF THE PARTICIPATIVE MANAGEMENT EXPERIMENT

The general theory of the Non-Linear Systems experiment drew on the writings of behavioral scientists and included the following points:

•   Work is as natural as play or rest, and if made a source of satisfaction, it will be performed willingly and voluntarily.

•   In the service of objectives to which he is committed, man requires little or no external direction or control. He will exercise self-direction and self-control. The degree of his self-control will depend upon the degree to which he is committed to these objectives.

Condensed from "The Non-Linear Systems Experiment in Participative Management," *The Journal of Business of The University of Chicago* (January 1975), © 1975 by the University of Chicago, 5801 Ellis Avenue, Chicago, Ill. 60637.

• Commitment to objectives is a function of rewards associated with their achievement, these rewards being those which go to satisfy man's physiological, psychological, safety, social, ego, and self-actualization needs.

• Many humans not only are ready to accept responsibility, they seek to shoulder it. Avoidance of responsibility, lack of ambition, and emphasis on security are not inherent human characteristics.

• The powers of imagination, ingenuity, and creativity are more widely distributed throughout the population than most executives admit. They simply await the proper time, place, stimulus, and atmosphere of receptivity to pour forth.

• Under the conditions of modern industrial life, man's intellectual potentialities are only partially realized.

These beliefs were translated into specific objectives and then into changes in the structure and procedures of the firm as follows:

Wages. To eliminate the punishment-reward psychology of hourly wages, toward the end of 1960 all hourly rated employees (who were already being paid higher-than-average area wages of $1.90 an hour, or $76 a week) were advanced $0.60 an hour and placed on a straight salary of $100 a week. Thereafter no deductions were made for arriving late, for leaving early, for cleanup or washup time in any amount, or for fatigue or coffee breaks taken at the employee's convenience. No records were kept of these or of any other work absences.

Not long after the new salary scale was put into effect, older employees requested the president of NLS to start new employees at the rate of $85 a week instead of at the $100 a week rate and that salary scale was adopted, with the increase to $100 a week coming after a probationary period of flexible length.

Organization. Prior to the experiment, NLS operated with a traditional "vertical" organization. In the experiment, although the corporate-level structure remained the same, the organization structure shown on charts distributed throughout the plant was vastly different. In the new setup there were three "zones." Zone 1: trustee management. This consisted of the four members of the board of directors and had the responsibility to determine the basic policies and the basic course of the business. Zone 2: general management. This was an eight-member Executive Council consisting of seven members chosen by the president, plus the president himself. The council was to establish operating policies; plan, coordinate, and control the business as a whole; and appraise results. The Executive Council was to operate as a unit, never directing or controlling. Decisions were to be advisory, by mutual consent of the members present at any meeting. Zone 3: departmental management. At this level were the 30 department units, also called project teams. Each consisted of three to 12 employees, including the department manager. They were to "manage the business of their departments for the objectives defined and authorized by the Executive Council." Department managers were responsible for day-to-day methods, operations, and procedures in their units.

Executive Council meetings were held daily for a period, then weekly. Managers of project and production teams met daily or as needed. Managers of other departments met irregularly.

Production setup. Prior to the time of change, two assembly lines produced two basic models of digital voltmeters. These assembly lines were discontinued in 1960–61. They were replaced by departmental units of three to 12 people, each in a separate room, each headed by a manager, each responsible for creating completed instruments from parts brought to it from the stockroom. Each group assembled, calibrated, inspected, packed its instruments, usually making five to 10 instruments at a time. Each group worked at its own pace, making its own decisions as to whether each man would make a complete instrument from start to finish or whether the group would operate on an assembly-line basis with each person contributing certain operations to the line. Each group worked out its own internal problems of tardiness, absences, jealousies, breaks, and grievances; only in rare instances did such problems reach the Executive Council. Groups made their own rules of procedure. If they kept any records, it was because they chose to do so. Records were not required.

The manager of a group was well qualified from his previous work experience to lead the group, but he was not a "boss" or a disciplinarian. Since the members of his group had the authority to do about what they wished, when, as, and how they wished, his job was one of consultation, direction, and advice at this lowest level. The group (unit) managers reported to the Executive Council as a whole, not to any individual member.

Indoctrination programs. At the start of the experiment, every effort was made to acquaint each member of the organization, individually, with the new policy of the company and to inform one department after another of the potential benefits as the details of operation were described.

Training procedures. Each new employee was informed as to the company's policies and operations and received on-the-job training of some length. Thereafter, any employee, male or female, could have almost any type of job training he or she desired, inside or outside the plant, paid for in full by the company upon its completion.

Time clocks. Time clocks were eliminated from all departments of the plant.

Record keeping. So far as production and personnel records were concerned, NLS became a company that operated essentially on a "put nothing in writing" basis.

Accounting. The Accounting Department as a unit was eliminated. Accountants were dispersed to purchasing, shipping, and personnel where separate books were kept, balances being reported to the treasurer at intervals.

Inspection. The Inspection Department, as such, was eliminated. Each separate production unit was made responsible for the quality of its work, the members of each unit deciding how and when the inspection, or inspections, would be made on the product the unit made.

TERMINATION OF THE EXPERIMENT

For 5 years those who visited the plant at Del Mar to witness firsthand this pioneering test of a new theory, came, saw, and departed unaware of any serious defects in the firm's operations. Yet early in 1965, NLS introduced modifications so extensive and extreme as to signify the end of the experiment in participative management. These included the following: "Line" organization procedures were reestablished at the top levels; direct supervision was provided; specific duties and responsibilities were assigned; standards of performance and quality were reestablished; authority was delegated commensurate with responsibility; records were reinstituted and maintained; remuneration was related to effort; and factory department units were accorded a large measure of autonomy to schedule work within their units in the fashion they wished. In this respect the department units function reasonably closely to the manner in which they operated during the years of the experiment. The state of the firm at that point was as follows: Sales volume was not measuring up to expectations, and for the actual volume of sales, administrative and sales costs were heavy; organization restlessness had been developing at management levels; productivity as a whole remained unchanged; employee layoffs began in 1963, and other layoffs occurred in 1964 and 1965; competition in the industry was multiplying; the sales force resisted efforts to decrease sales costs; and the company was finding itself becoming progressively less profitable the longer it continued with participative management. The question was arising: How long would the company be able to afford the luxury of pursuing a theory of operation that bid fair to bring about its demise?

WHY DID THE EXPERIMENT FAIL?

Business conditions. It has been said that the firm made overoptimistic predictions of sales, leading to excessive increases in sales, advertising, development, engineering, and in other outlays. Thus when the error was realized (in 1965) the firm was forced to jettison all but the most essential programs and tighten cost controls in every possible way. Actually, in the period from 1953 to 1960 the company had experienced a phenomenal rate of growth, with sales doubling year after year. It cannot be said, now or then, that such a trend would not have continued.

Sales volume did increase each year from 1960 to 1963, but the rate of increase diminished. Late in 1963 and again in 1965 sales dropped sharply. At these times orthodox management would have reduced plant employment in line with the incoming order rate, but such an action would have been in conflict with the goals of job and personal security. Layoffs were not given the degree of serious consideration that was warranted until long after the problem of diminishing sales first arose, although the costs of retaining this manpower reserve were tremendous and were depleting the firm's treasury. Even when layoffs did occur, the higher-salaried engineering and research personnel were shifted to lower-rated production jobs without the usual downward salary adjustment, in the belief that this would keep them available when improved conditions warranted their services.

Organization and autonomy. The form of organization adopted under the experiment in participative management left many former administrators restless and frustrated because they no longer had specific operating responsibilities. Members of the Executive Council were practically immobilized as "sideline consultants."

When department managers went to the Executive Council for advice perhaps only one, or, at the most, two council members had the proficiency in the specific matters to be able to advise. When these men were not available, others could not make decisions that would be meaningful. So either the department managers made up their own minds or frustration developed as the problems remained unsolved. And many of these managers had need of the guidance and training they normally would have received had they worked directly under individually responsible supervisors. Under participative management they were chiefly on their own. And no matter how well experienced, young men in subordinate positions appear to want some measure of authoritative direction—someone else to help shoulder some of their problems.

Wages, production, and productivity. After the end of the experiment, a number of NLS executives told the author that the wage increase from $76 to $100 per week was a substantial burden on the company. Yet, during the experiment, reports such as these were common in the press: "Productivity in man-hours per instrument has steadily improved. Today it is 30 percent better than at any period in the company's history." But President Kay and the members of the Executive Council who were interviewed in July 1965 were in complete agreement with the statement that "on some items there may have been a productivity increase, but on other items there may have been a productivity decrease. In the plant as a whole, there probably was no change in productivity."

Quite a different matter is that of increased production (the output of the factory in any given time). In 1963 the output from the factory was in the neighborhood of 30 percent more than it was in 1960. But the number of employees rose from 240 to 340, an increase of 42 percent over the same period.

Layoffs. At least one outside consultant to NLS has told the author that, if the company had possessed greater financial resources, standard instruments could have been stocked in a warehouse during periods when sales were low and employee layoffs avoided. Though the principle of inventory buildup during slack periods would supplement the participative management theory, it hardly can apply at NLS where a total of perhaps ten instruments would have comprised a maximum salable inventory. Working capital was sufficient for NLS's needs; it was not due to lack of working capital that no appreciable inventory of instruments was carried.

Sales-force behavior and competition. Over the period of the experiment (and since), there was an increase in the number and vigor of competitors. To increase a company's sales in such a market, the company must provide something extra in the way of design, operation, adaptability, quality, service, or delivery. Beginning in 1960 NLS anticipated this and was quite successful in retaining its leadership with a major share of the market. During 1960, 19 sales offices were opened throughout the country, staffed by salaried salesmen. Each district office was given a flat yearly sum to cover salaries, expenses for travel and entertainment, the purchase of new cars every 2 years, and office expenses. Each district office ran its own affairs, had its own bank account, paid its own bills, and sent the paid receipts to the home office. Sales reports and salesmen's expense books were not required. Sales increased, but unfortunately the increased sales volume was not commensurate with the increased sales costs. In 1964 an attempt was made to lower sales costs by requesting each sales district to service its own customers rather than have servicemen sent out from the home office. A number of salesmen—some competent to service and others not—refused to service instruments, although the practice was not unusual in the industry. In 1965, after the experiment's end, salaried salesmen were replaced by commission sales agents.

Product quality. The quality of work was acceptable. Yet, because no company records were kept from 1960 to 1965, there is no statistical basis for published reports like these: "Improvements in quality steadily reduced the number of complaints from the field. Though the business doubled in the four years after the assembly lines were dismantled, the number of complaints diminished by over 70 percent during that time."

Job satisfaction. Employee satisfaction with a job at NLS depended on the employee's position. For shop workers NLS was a good place to work, and there was always a long list of applicants waiting to be hired. Employees brought in their relatives: 18 percent were related in 1965. Absenteeism was 2.8 percent in 1960 and 2.5 percent in 1965, and labor turnover was 4–5 percent in both years, about normal for manufacturing plants in the Del Mar area. Morale was high and grievances were few. Department managers experienced a drop in morale during the course of the experiment. Early in the experiment, these technically skilled employees had often remained working at the plant long after quitting time. Toward the end they departed promptly after putting in an 8-hour day, and their offices were deserted on Saturdays, Sundays, and holidays as never before. Despite "ideal" working conditions and high salaries, 13 of the 30 department managers who were with the company in 1962 were not with NLS in 1965. For the seven executives who made up the Executive Council, the experiment seems to have been highly unsatisfactory. The Executive Council did not prove to be effective in working out, or even in raising policy differences, and the seven subordinate executives felt that participative management had restricted rather than widened their horizons. They made constant, rather unsuccessful, attempts to define specific duties for their individual members.

Creativity. There is no evidence of an unusual development of human potential. During the 5 years of the experiment, many men were helped by the training and instruction they received, and many enlarged their work skills. But only two gave indications of greatness, and in 5 years any plant with 300 or more employees should expect to find two men of well-above-average caliber.

Profitability. When NLS initiated participative management in 1960, it looked forward to increasing the prosperity and well-being of everyone concerned. No thought may have been given to raising profits above the 1959–60 level reached prior to the experiment, but it hardly could have been expected that profits, which had increased yearly from 1953 to 1960, would begin in 1961 to spiral downward until the losses sustained compelled abandonment of the experiment in 1965. A behavioral scientist who had been employed on the NLS experiment since its inception has commented: "I think we know now that human relations don't have a lot to do with profit and productivity."

AFTERMATH: WHAT DID THE EXPERIMENT SHOW?

In 1965 NLS retreated to relatively conventional management methods. The results are described by a long-time director with considerable business experience: "both management and factory workers appear not dissatisfied with these changes. The company probably avoided bankruptcy by abandoning the experiment and returning to orthodox methods of management; it is now operating with a small profit and expanding into other, but related, fields." Beyond this, the question remains of what the NLS experiment shows about the validity of the human relations and participative management approaches. The following conclusions are offered as being reasonably supported by the evidence:

1 The removal of the high-level NLS executives from their individual responsibilities for planning, directing, and controlling specific areas of operations was not successful.

2 For the lower levels of management, where productivity and job satisfaction dropped as a result of the experiment, these department managers wanted and needed more direction than the Executive Council was able to give, either collectively or as individuals.

3 At the level of the shop floor, job satisfactions increased, but there was no marked welling up of energy and creativity, much less a productivity improvement sufficient to overcome the loss of productivity at the executive levels, and none should be expected.

4 Over all, the sort of thorough-going adoption of human relations theories tried at NLS may be possible only while a firm enjoys an unusually profitable, protected market and has owners who are willing to accept unusually high frustrations and negligible or negative future returns. Smaller, more limited applications of a vastly modified participative management-human relations approach may continue to be considered in frameworks that retain effective supervision and rewards. But in a competitive market a company must receive from its employees enough in return to

offset the extra costs of higher wages, additional benefits, lower work standards, better work conditions, and less efficient operations. If it does not, it soon will cease to exist.

FOR DISCUSSION AND REVIEW

1 Why did Non-Linear Systems engage in the experiment?
2 Explain the nature of the experiment and its conceptual base. What changed in the organization?
3 Why was the experiment ended? Why did it fail? Do you feel these results are generalizable to other organizations and therefore argue against participation? Why or why not?
4 What are the implications of this experiment?

B. THE USE OF EXTRINSIC REWARDS: WAGE AND SALARY ADMINISTRATION

A. N. Nash

S. J. Carroll, Jr.

Installation of a Job-Evaluation Program

Development and installation of a job-evaluation program must be performed in a series of identifiable steps if success is to be achieved. These include preliminary planning, getting accurate job descriptions, determining the criteria against which jobs will be compared, selecting an evaluation or decision system, applying the system by actually evaluating jobs, and implementing the results.

PRELIMINARY PLANNING

Several issues must be resolved before the evaluation process is undertaken. The need for job evaluation must be established. Others in the organization must be convinced of the need for evaluation, and for cooperation. Decisions must be made about who should carry out the evaluation, and the jobs to be studied must be identified.

Identifying the need

If minimizing employee dissatisfaction is accepted as the principal objective of job evaluation, then evidences of dissatisfaction related to the wage structure would demonstrate a need. If a less sophisticated decision system is doing the job, it might be legitimately concluded that there is no need to invest additional resources. Of course, job evaluation could be used as a preventive measure as an organization begins to grow. Conceivably, it might have more beneficial results if adopted before major hassles develop over the wage structure rather than after friction has reached an advanced stage.

Evidence of dissatisfaction is often found when turnover, absenteeism, work stoppages, arguments and fights, exit interviews, and attitude surveys are examined. The trouble with some of these indicators, such as turnover and absenteeism, is that they may be caused by factors that have nothing to do with the wage structure. Thus, greater reliance should be placed on attitude survey results, exit interviews, and just plain griping by employees. If management is spending an excessive amount of time on wage-structure decisions, this could be considered evidence of need for job evaluation. However, this factor is unlikely to be more important than evidence of employee discontent. Usually, the more griping and discontent there is, the greater is the need for management to be concerned. Thus, the two considerations are not entirely independent. Future projections of organizational expansion with the usual increase in the number of different jobs would also be relevant to identifying need. Even if existing circumstances and jobs provide only marginal evidence of need, the addition of future jobs could tip the balance in favor of adopting job evaluation.

Before the final decision is made to undertake job evaluation, the expected benefits should be compared to the cost. Recent evidence on the cost of job evaluation does not appear to exist. An early survey indicates that initial costs (for just administrative consulting time) of installing job evaluation might be about 5 percent of payroll (Briggs, 1951). Additional start-up costs include expenses arising out of the practice of *red circling* (delaying downward adjustments) existing rates that are too high and immediately raising out-of-line rates that are found to be too low. The delay in adjusting red-circled rates downward is usually required to get employees to accept the job-evaluation system. Costs associated with this aspect appear to range from less than 1 percent of first-year annual payroll to over 2 percent. Lytle's study (1954) suggests that, after these initial costs are incurred, the cost of keeping the program going often does not exceed one percent of the payroll.

Getting cooperation

If the personnel department has done a good job of identifying evidence of need and estimates of cost, it should not be too difficult to convince top management and the employees of the desirability of job evaluation. Top management should be persuaded that they can eliminate many of the headaches of trying to make the decisions themselves. They could be using their time more effectively if they were not being harassed with these decisions, they could still hold onto the purse strings through their control of the wage-level decision, and, with a relatively small additional investment, the decisions could be made in a much more systematic and defensible manner. It should be possible to convince employees of the value of job evaluation by pointing out that the decision will no longer be made exclusively by management, that it will be made more carefully than it has been in the past, that job evaluation will provide a mechanism for considering the gripes they've been expressing, and that no present employee's wage will be adversely affected by this approach.

Choosing the evaluators

If minimizing employee dissatisfaction and maximizing their acceptance of the wage-structure decision is the primary goal of job evaluation, the use of a committee composed of at least some employee representatives would be desirable. Determining how many members to include involves a trade-off between good representation of employees on the various types of jobs and the problems that occur when a committee gets too large and it takes forever to make a decision that often is suboptimal because of compromises.

   If the issue of whether to have a committee or single rater is considered from a measurement standpoint, evidence on the test-retest reliability of five-man committee judgments versus individual judgments shows a marked superiority for the five-man, pooled judgment (Lawshe & Wilson, 1947; Scott, 1963; Christal, Madden, & Harding, 1960). However, the evidence does not consistently suggest that more than five are needed. Studies by Lawshe and Wilson and by Scott indicate clearly that a reliability of approximately .94 was attained when five-member committees were used. The Air Force study indicates that it took 20 evaluators to attain a reliability of .93 while five only achieved a reliability of about .80. Unfortunately, Madden and Harding indicate their data may underestimate the true reliabilities because of methodological problems. Also, the use of a long 15-factor system could contribute to the lower correlations, because there is evidence that shorter systems seem to be more reliable. Thus it seems probable that for most systems in most situations, five evaluators should be enough. One way of accommodating conflicting considerations is to use a revolving membership, so that employees are included on the committee only for evaluation of jobs in which they are most interested. This is feasible if jobs included in the evaluation are broken down into relatively homogeneous groups commonly referred to as *job series* and a wage structure is developed for each series. Studies reported by Christal, Madden, and Harding support this practice. They found that *job familiarity* of raters had a modest, statistically significant impact when specific factors and jobs were evaluated (Harding & Madden, 1960; Christal & Madden, 1960; Madden, 1960; Madden, 1962). Those jobs with which the evaluator was most familiar tended to get a higher rating. Homogeneous clusters of jobs rated by those familiar with and interested in them should control for this biasing effect. Job series will be discussed in the next section.

Committee members should be reasonably intelligent, rational employees who are widely respected by at least a particular subgroup of employees. Whether to include a union leader on the committee if the organization is unionized has already been discussed to some extent. Management would find it desirable to obtain union acceptance of job evaluation as the decision system and to have one or more union representatives on the committee to enhance acceptance and communication of decisions. However, a union is a political organization operating in a business environment. Thus, the union would probably be better off accepting job evaluation as an initial decision technique, reserving the right to appeal decisions through grievance or bargaining channels. The role of union leaders would be to champion the gripes of any disgruntled job group, blaming management if relations aren't too good. Such grievances would be presented initially to the job-evaluation committee for consideration. And if satisfaction is not achieved, grievances would be appealed through the most attractive channels. This enables the union to tacitly approve of job evaluation, reserving the right to take up the cudgel if one or more of its members is wronged, while not getting itself responsibly involved in initial decisions.

The research evidence that exists appears to support this view. Several studies show that the majority of plans in unionized organizations are not jointly administered (Baker & True, 1947; Bureau of National Affairs, 1957; Badenhoop & Jareel, 1956; Slichter, Healy, & Livernash, 1960). In fact, some unions have explicitly indicated that they accepted job evaluation but did not want joint responsibility in administering it.

Finally, should representatives of management or personnel, or both, be included on the committee? The presence of a personnel specialist can be justified on the grounds that he may have developed more of an impartial image than line managers and should be able to assist as an expert in job evaluation. One desirable arrangement would be to have personnel department representatives serve in an *ex officio* capacity, so that their technical knowledge could be used at the committee's pleasure without dominating its decisions.

Management would, of course, have every right to expect to serve on any committee evaluating its jobs, and managerial job evaluation is increasing in popularity (Rosensteel, 1957). However, it is probably best not to have managerial representatives involved in committee evaluation of nonmanagerial jobs, especially if their presence is unlikely to change the results substantially, as in the study reported by Chambliss (1950). Lawler and Hackman (1969) report evidence suggesting that operative employees may be less likely than management to assign high pay rates to jobs. Research shows good reliability (consistency) between trained job evaluators, and one study indicates that inexperienced evaluators reach as high a level of inter/rater agreement as do experienced evaluators (Hay, 1946; Chesler, 1948; Lawshe & Farbro, 1949; Ash, 1948; Hazel, 1966; Lawshe & Wilson, 1947; Scott, 1963). Thus, there is little support for an assumption that the typical interested employee would not handle himself well on such a committee.

JOB DESCRIPTIONS

All jobs need to be placed into their proper niche in the wage structure with some decision approach. Thus, virtually all jobs need to be evaluated, and, as mentioned previously, even managerial and professional jobs are frequently included in job evaluation (Dinsmore, 1964). Research and experience indicate, however, that it is best to split jobs into homogeneous job clusters or job series—for example, production, office-clerical, and managerial-technical—and to evaluate each series separately. A system with four separate series has been recommended for the federal government's vast array of jobs by its job-evaluation study committee (United States Civil Service Commission, 1972). The use of job clusters facilitates construction and use of a decision system tailored to the characteristics of the particular jobs in the series. Thus, physical demand, working conditions, and hazards might be important criteria for production jobs, while for the other series such factors would have virtually no applicability. A series approach should improve the reliability of the evaluators' judgments. However, if the series approach is adopted, it is still necessary ultimately to decide the worth of each series relative to the others. Figure 5.2 illustrates the problem and how it might be resolved. The experience of an organization that reverted to a single, universal system is discussed by Schuster (1966).

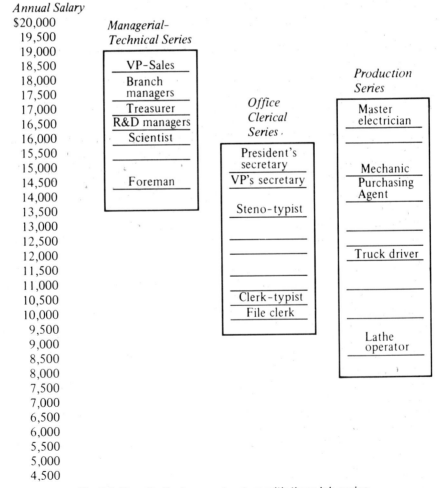

Fig. 5.2 Hypothetical wage structure with three-job series.

After the evaluation committee has been designated and planning has been completed, written descriptions of each job to be evaluated must be made available to the committee members so that they do not have to rely on memory or incomplete knowledge. The evaluation process contains so many other opportunities for error that it is important that disagreement over the duties and responsibilities of jobs not be an additional one. A recent review of research studies on job analysis found conflicting evidence on the reliability and validity of job-analysis results, depending on who did the analysis and the methods used in collecting job information (Prien & Ronan, 1971). Thus, it is important in a job-analysis program to make sure that all parties affected have a chance to look over the resulting job descriptions and agree they are reasonably accurate.

In many situations it may be that job descriptions have already been developed in the organization, since job descriptions have many uses in personnel administration other than just as an aid for job evaluation. Job descriptions provide a basis for manpower planning, defining human characteristics needed in job applicants if they are to have a good chance of succeeding on a job, identifying training needs and content of training programs, and facilitating the employee-appraisal process by identifying desirable behaviors of job incumbents. Because job analysis is used in so many ways, it is often considered to be the cornerstone of personnel administration. Survey evidence indicates that the need to facilitate job evaluation has been the most frequent impetus for job-analysis programs (Jones and DeCoths, 1969). A job description replica is presented in Figure 5.3.

Although there is considerable variability in practice, most job descriptions are organized into three distinct sections. The first is the *identification* section, which includes the job title, alternate titles, job code numbers including any that might be in the *Dictionary of Occupational Titles,* date of the analysis, location of the job both organizationally and physically, number of positions, and the name of the job analyst who collected the information and wrote the description. All of this information is designed to eliminate confusion about what job is being described and to enable the resolution of any questions that arise.

The second section of the job description, *work performed,* describes in detail the tasks and responsibilities of the job. This section is usually organized on a chronological or functional basis, depending on the nature of the job. The chronological approach is considered preferable when possible, because it demonstrates the sequence of the tasks and shows how they are interrelated. If the job does not have a cyclical or sequential character, the functional approach is used. The functional approach lists the most important and frequently performed aspects of the job first and then occasional functions.

The final section is often called the *human requirements* section and provides information about the worker characteristics required to perform the duties and tasks listed in the previous part of the description. The definition of these requirements is quite judgmental as contrasted with the factual nature of information included in the work-performed section. Because it is desirable to separate fact from opinion, these latter two sections of the job description should be separated. Usually the human requirements are inferred from the described duties. Unless verified through some sort of empirical process or study, these requirements should be regarded as tentative.

A great deal of emphasis has recently been placed on the need to realistically and thoroughly identify the psychological and social demands of each job (Dunnette, 1967). These features are usually difficult to identify and describe, but current stress on enlarging and enriching jobs alludes to the growing importance of

Identification

Incinerator Stoker	2-Male	552	April 1962
Job Title	Number Employed	Job Code	Date of Analysis

Water Department—Sewage Treatment Division	Nash
Location in Organization	Analyst

Work performed (daily duties):

Summary: Ignites, regulates, stokes, cleans, and generally tends the furnace used in burning refuse of the city collected by city refuse trucks.

1. *Shakes ashes into pit:* At the beginning of each 4-hour burning cycle, worker shakes ashes accumulated during previous 4-hour cycle into ash pit by manually oscillating grates back and forth with 75-pound cast iron grate crank. Lifts crank from floor, attaches crank to protruding grate ends (14 grates), and turns each grate 5 to 10 times. (40 to 60 minutes each day)
2. *Charges (fills) furnace:* Determines the rate at which furnace is to be filled with refuse by evaluating combustibility (moisture content, density, etc.) of refuse. Fills firebox by pulling 2 overhead metal handles dangling from chains that open overhead trapdoors, thus allowing refuse to fall into firebox. Does this every 5 to 10 minutes depending on speed with which refuse is burning. Signals overhead craneman (who fills bins above the overhead doors) when to stand clear of bins, fill certain hoppers, or come to the stoking floor. (30 minutes)
3. *Stokes furnace:* Determines when and how to stoke (stir) by checking pyrometer (temperature gauge) to keep temperature between 1600° and 1800° and by adjusting decisions to character of furnace. Stokes fire by lifting each of 7 (12 feet long, 25-pound) iron stokers leaning against furnace side, rams stokers through each of 7 (4-foot space between) open vents in furnace doors, and pushes and pulls stoker in the burning refuse. (One of the two positions is cramped and stoker must walk over 4 moving protruding cone machines.) (3 hours per day)
4. *Operates mechanical aids to control fire:*
   a. Weighs refuse by observing scale (9.6 tons burned on the average each hour).
   b. Determines when mechanical cones (4), which stir and agitate burning refuse, should run and starts and stops them by pushing button.

Fig. 5.3 Job description.

these job attributes. Such considerations ought to be included in any attempt to evaluate different jobs. For example, Ingham's study (1970) of large and small organizations indicates that employees consciously select either large or small firms depending on what is important to them—a socially and psychologically rewarding experience in a small organization, or a more deprived experience in a large organization, with higher wages as an offsetting consideration.

A commonly used derivative of a job description is the job specification. This is usually a one-page condensation of a job description in which much of the work-performed section is eliminated and a one-paragraph summary is substituted.

A frequent but questionable practice is the use of job specifications as the basis for job evaluation, either as a substitute or supplement for job descriptions. In some cases job specs are constructed in job-evaluation language (in the same terminology as is used in defining decision criteria) so that the committee can easily relate them to their decisions. A study by Chesler (1948) on the reliability of different job-evaluation systems suggests that "keying the job descriptions to the language of the standard job evaluation manual was probably the main reason extremely high reliabilities were obtained." If the job description (or specification) says "job

    c. Determines when and how fast variable speed, forced draft air fans should be turned on and engages them by pushing a mechanical lever (light pressure required). (10 to 15 minutes)

5. *Occasional daily duties:*
    a. Cleans up floor under open vents with broom and shovel, and throws dirt and fallen refuse back into furnace through open vent.
    b. One to 5 times a day, refuse located in bins over trapdoors located on top of furnace catches fire, and stoker goes up and helps overhead craneman put it out with a shovel.
    c. Stoker occasionally assists laborer in loading ashes into rail cars by unlocking hinge, pulling trapdoor back, and letting ashes fall into car. (30 minutes)

Human requirements (specifications):

1. *Education:* No formal requirements. Ability to follow simple verbal instructions.
2. *Experience:* Needs a good record of being capable of doing manual work in order to obtain the job, and about 2 months general orientation and familiarization with the furnace and related equipment to perform the job adequately.
3. *Supervision received:* Qualified worker on this job receives instructions daily and at more frequent intervals as needed. Half of time these workers have no supervisors present. Work is repetitive and once learned doesn't need continuous close supervision. Overhead craneman fills in as acting supervisor when regular supervisor is absent. However, he is not within visual proximity of stokers while operating crane.
4. *Errors:*
    a. Failure to control temperature properly could damage refractories worth several thousand dollars. Pyrometer makes this unlikely and errors are easy to detect before serious damage results.
    b. Failure to do a good job of stoking will result in only partial burning of refuse and hence greater volume of ashes to be disposed of.
5. *Contact with others:* Casual contact with maintenance crews during day shift. Also refuse truck crews occasionally enter building when unloading refuse.
6. *Confidential information:* None
7. *Working conditions:* Dirty, hot (120° to 140°) in summer and cold (unheated) in winter, danger from exploding objects in furnace which may throw burning ash out vents in furnace doors, noisy, danger of tripping over rotating cone machines, danger of banging fingers, smoky (got so smoky when refuse on top of overhead doors caught fire that the analyst had to go outside for air), toxic and nauseous fumes.

---

requires a high school education," and one of the gradations of the education scale of the manual is "12 years of schooling required," it is little wonder that sober judges can reliably rate the educational requirements of such a job.

    This use of job specs is a debatable practice. Usually the human requirements section from which the job specification is derived has been written by an organization job analyst. Thus, to a large degree, it is his judgment that goes into the evaluation, rather than that of the committee. The argument favoring the use of job specifications is that it makes the committee's job much easier. Because the job analyst is more familiar than the committee with each job he has analyzed and written up, he is in a better position to make these judgments. However, his biases and individual peculiarities are built into his judgments, and it is argued here that the committee ought to start out with only the job facts (work performed) and take it from there. Often, not only are the job analyst's biases built into his judgments, but traditional requirements that have existed for years are perpetuated by his judgments. For example, job specs commonly require higher educational attainment than the job really requires. Perhaps the main reason for this is that education is associated with status and present employees like to associate with high-status people, even though jobs do not require it. Also, job-analysis information customarily relies on information provided by employees holding the jobs being analyzed, and invariably such employees tend to "blow up" their jobs and job requirements. The job analyst is supposed to be able to compensate for and detect such tendencies, but it probably would be better to not depend on his ability to do this. The principal objective of job evaluation is the minimization of employee dissatisfaction. If the job specs are not used, the final decision will be less vulnerable to criticism than if they are, because no one can argue that the judgments of a job analyst—who is paid by the firm—were influential in the job-worth decisions.

As an alternative it is advocated that only the identification and work-performed sections of job descriptions should be provided to the committee, but that the job analyst should sit in on committee discussions as an ex officio personnel advisor and answer any questions from committee members. This arrangement enables him to be of assistance to the committee without dominating its decisions—as he might if his judgments, as reflected in the human-requirements section, were incorporated in the job description as the known requirements of the job. As long ago as 1936, Balderston, in a discussion of the need for a description of the work being done on a job as a prerequisite to setting job rates, suggested that "a job definition or description [is needed] rather than a specification such as would help in hiring."

REFERENCES

Ash, P. The reliability of job evaluation rankings. *Journal of Applied Psychology,* 1948, **32,** 313–20.

Badenhoop, L. E., & Jareel, A. N. Wages and related practices in the machinery industries. *Monthly Labor Review,* 1956, **8,** 908–916.

Baker, H., & True, J. *The operation of job evaluation plans.* Princeton, N.J.: Princeton University, Industrial Relations Section, 1947.

Balderston, C. C. Wage setting research. *Personnel Journal,* 1936–7, **15,** 222.

Briggs, H. S. Cost of installing a job evaluation plan. *Management Record,* 1951, **12,** 422–423.

Bureau of National Affairs. *Job evaluation.* Survey #40 of BNA's Personnel Policies Forum, Washington, D.C., 1957, 1–14.

Chambliss, L. A. Our employees evaluate their own jobs. *Personnel Journal,* 1950, **29,** 141–142.

Chesler, D. J. Reliability and comparability of different job evaluation systems. *Journal of Applied Psychology,* 1948, **32,** 465–475.

Chesler, D. J. Reliability of abbreviated job evaluation scales. *Journal of Applied Psychology,* 1948, **32,** 622–628.

Christal, R. E., & Madden, J. M. Effect of degree of familiarity in job evaluation. *USAF Personnel Laboratory,* Wright Air Development Division, Air Research and Development Command, Lackland AFB, Texas, WADD-TN-60-257, Oct. 1960, 1–8.

Christal, R. E., Madden, J. M., & Harding F. D. Reliability of job evaluation ratings as a function of number of raters and length of job description. *USAF Personnel Laboratory,* Wright Air Development Division, Air Research & Development Command, Lackland AFB, Texas, WADD-TN-60, 1960, 1–8.

Dunnette, M. D. *Personnel selection and placement.* Belmont, Calif.: Wadsworth, 1967.

Harding, F., Madden, J., & Colson. Analysis of some aspects of the air force position evaluation system. *USAF Personnel Laboratory*, July, 1960.

Hay, E. N. Training the evaluation committee in factor comparison job evaluation. *Personnel*, 1946, **23**, 46-56.

Hazel, J. T. Reliability of job ratings as a function of time spent on evaluation. *Journal of Industrial Psychology*, 1966, **4**, 16-19.

Ingham, G. K. *Size of industrial organization and worker behavior.* London: Cambridge University Press, 1970.

Jones, J., & DeCoths, T. Job analysis: National survey findings. *Personnel Journal*, 1969, **48**, 805.

Lawler, E. E., & Hackman, J. R. The impact of employee participation in the development of pay incentive systems: A field experiment. *Journal of Applied Psychology*, 1969, **53**, 467-71.

Lawshe, C. H., & Farbro, P. C. Studies in job evaluation: VIII. The reliability of an abbreviated job evaluation system. *Journal of Applied Psychology*, 1949, **33**, 158-66.

Lawshe, C. H., Jr., & Wilson, R. F. Studies in job evaluation: VI. The reliability of two point rating systems. *Journal of Applied Psychology*, 1947, **31**, 355-365.

Lytle, C. W. *Job evaluation methods.* New York: Ronald Press, 1954, 34-35.

Madden, J. M. Familiarity effects in evaluative judgments. *USAF Personnel Laboratory*, Wright Air Development Division, Air Research and Development Command, Lackland AFB, WADD-TN-60-261, November 1960, 1-6.

Madden, J. M. The effect of varying the degree of rater familiarity in job evaluation. *Personnel Administration*, 1962, **25**, 42-46.

Prien, E. P., & Ronan, W. W. Job analysis: A review of research findings. *Personnel Psychology*, 1971, **24**, 271-296.

Rosensteel, D. H. Supervisory compensation—An interim report. *Personnel*, 1957, **33**, 356.

Schuster, J. R. Job evaluation at Xerox: A single scale replaces four. *Personnel*, 1966, **43**, 15-19.

Scott, W. E., Jr. The reliability and validity of a six factor job evaluation system. Doctoral Dissertation, Purdue University, 1963.

Slichter, S. H., Healy, J. J., & Livernash, E. R. The impact of collective bargaining on management. Washington, D.C.: The Brookings Institution, 1960, Chapters 19-20.

U. S. Civil Service Commission. Job evaluation pay review task force to the U.S. civil service commission. *Findings and recommendations*, January, 1972, **1**, 168.

FOR DISCUSSION AND REVIEW

1 What factors should be considered in determining the wage-structure decision? What alternative solutions are available?

2 Review the major steps in the job-evaluation implementation process. What can be done to make the process less subjective?

David W. Belcher

Wage and Salary Administration

1.0 WHAT IS WAGE AND SALARY ADMINISTRATION?

Wage and salary administration (or compensation administration, as the field is often called) is the process of managing pay. At the most basic level, this means solving (and where possible, preventing) pay problems of organizations. At another level, this means building and operating policies and programs so that both organizations and employees see a gain from their mutual relationship. This, in turn, means that wage and salary administration is concerned with building the terms of trade so that most employees will want to continue the relationship and that organizations and employees will want to meet some of the other's goals.

1.1 What is wage and salary administration trying to do?

Because all organizations have limited resources, wage and salary administration's major goal is to get the maximum possible returns for the resources spent. More specific goals are to: (1) get and keep the numbers and types of employees needed by the organization, (2) get and keep the quality of employees the organization can afford, (3) give employees consistent signals from all types of pay and of what the organization expects from the types of pay, (4) motivate extra performance from some employee groups, (5) get employee acceptance of the fairness of what they get and what they give in return, (6) control compensation to insure that the organization gets maximum returns from its limited means.

Meeting these objectives is complicated by the growing numbers of different jobs and employee groups in organizations. Different employee groups expect different things from employment and expect to provide different things as their part of the bargain. Likewise, the growing number of kinds of compensation makes the task of keeping signals straight a tough one. Equally troublesome is the fact of steadily rising incomes and expectations, so that all solutions are temporary.

All of these objectives are important, and it is pointless to suggest that one is more important than another. But the goal of employee acceptance of equity deserves special mention. Although equity or "fairness" has always been used in discussing pay, it has only recently been recognized that equity is in the eyes of the beholder. When organizations are trying to get, keep, and motivate employees, it is equity as seen by employees, not by employers, that gets results. While the employer may be able to influence the employee's perception of equity, that influence is limited. Further, the employee in determining equity considers not only what he gets but what he gives; he decides what things to include in both sides.[1] The em-

---

Reprinted by permission from *Staffing Policies and Strategies*, Volume 1 of the *ASPA Handbook of Personnel and Industrial Relations* (Yoder and Heneman, eds.), copyright © 1974 by The Bureau of National Affairs, Inc., Washington, D.C. 20037.

[1]   Adams, J. S., Inequity in Social Exchange, in L. Berkowitz (ed.), *Advances in Experimental Social Psychology*, Vol. 2 (New York: Academic Press, 1965), pp. 267–299; Lawler, E. E., Equity Theory as a Predictor of Productivity and Work Quality, *Psychological Bulletin*, 1968, *70*, 596–610; Pritchard, R. D., Equity Theory: A Review and Critique, *Organization Behavior and Human Performance*, 1969, *4*, 176–211; Goodman, P. S., and Friedman, A, An Examination of Adams' Theory of Inequity, *Administrative Science Quarterly*, 1971, *16*, 271–288.

ployer, in contrast, typically sees equity as what other employers pay and has not thought very much about what things he gets in return.[2]

1.2 What are common pay problems of organizations?

Most pay problems are questions of equity that imply a comparison between what is and what should be. Examples are: the worker who sees others in the organization doing the same work but getting more pay; the worker who sees himself doing more difficult or more important work and wants more pay; the trainee who expects automatic increases every six months as he acquires experience; the engineer who expects yearly pay increases in accord with his growing experience in his field; the supervisor who expects to be paid more than his subordinates; the manager who observes that his counterparts in other organizations are paid more; the union that demands that its members be paid the same rate that other organizations in the industry are paying; the union that demands that its members get increased pay because the cost of living has increased; the manager who wants part of his pay in a form that will leave him more after income taxes.

Every manager and compensation administrator could easily add to this list of pay problems. But what is common to all of them is that they imply comparisons—between how much pay is received and how much of what is paid for and/or between the individual's present situation and some benchmark. This suggests that if people and organizations can agree on what is being compared and with what, pay problems are on their way to solution.

Pay relationships within the organization are probably the primary concern of most employees. Employees compare their pay with fellow employees, but in deciding what is fair they compare not only what they get but what they give for it. Different employee groups compare different things, and members of separate employee groups are unlikely to make comparisons with members of other employee groups unless they are in frequent contact with each other.

Employees also compare their pay with that of employees seen as comparable in other organizations. But employee groups differ greatly in the extent to which they make outside comparisons, and they decide which comparisons are proper. While employees and unions can influence these comparisons, their influence is limited by the fact that comparisons are hard to change and probably impossible to change back again.

Because pay comparisons are actually "what I get to what I give compared to what he gets to what he gives," making comparisons outside the organization is difficult. Also, for most employee groups, relative difficulty or importance of jobs is an important part of the comparison. Employee groups that emphasize comparisons outside the organization assign less importance to level of work and more to other factors.

Obtaining high performance on jobs is considered by most organizations to be the primary pay problem. Actually, there are many ways of getting high performance from employees that do not involve pay. Further, there is no solid evidence that merely providing higher pay brings better performance.[3] As discussed in Section 5.0 of this Chapter, attempting to obtain employee performance by rewarding outstanding performers may be possible only with certain employee groups and may involve difficulties for organizations even with these groups.

---

[2]   Lawler, E. E., III, *Pay and Organizational Effectiveness: A Psychological View* (New York: McGraw-Hill Book Co., 1971), p. 12.

[3]   *Ibid.,* p. 133.

Because people act on the basis of what they see and believe, many pay problems come down to the need for building and operating pay policies, programs, and practices so that employees can know how the organization is trying to define the terms of employment. Even more important is the communication of these policies, programs, and practices, so that employees can see and believe what the organization is trying to do. The best communication media, of course, are the decisions of managers on pay questions. Words are useful, but action speaks much louder. Pay intentions and actions must not only be fair and give consistent signals of what the organization is trying to do, but employees must believe that they are fair and receive and accept the signals.

2.0 WHAT IS PAY?

Pay is what employees get as a result of employment. To most people it is a three-letter word for money. But money from employment comes in a number of forms—in cash or checks, in various kinds of benefits, and sometimes in the form of goods and services that have a money value. What about nonfinancial rewards such as a challenging job, a good boss, congenial associates, and pleasant working conditions? Most people agree that these things may be good reasons for working for an organization and may even be partial substitutes for money, but they do not consider them to be pay. Are they?

. . .

4.0 WHAT SHOULD ORGANIZATIONS PAY FOR?

The logical answer to this question is, of course, that organizations should pay for what they need—presumably a form of human behavior called work. But the definition of work has proved elusive and becomes more so with each passing year. Is the organization that hires highly decorative receptionists paying for work? Is the organization that employs a scientist whose work is his life paying for work? Is the organization that pays a premium for M.B.A.s or for five years of experience paying for work?

Economists get rid of the problem by stating that organizations employ labor units which vary with skill level and other qualifications. Variations in the efficiency with which organizations use labor units are handled by stating that what an organization really pays is labor cost per unit of output.

But organizations cannot escape answering the question of what they pay for because they hire real people who get real pay. Further, these people learn what the organization wants from what they see is actually rewarded in organizations. Thus, while organizations have assumed along with economists that they were hiring unspecified labor services, the people hired have learned what organization pay systems have taught them. Organizations, aware that the major advantage of hiring people is their innate flexibility, cannot be blamed for accepting the economists' view of employment. But neither can employees be blamed for learning what the organization actually pays for.

Organization pay systems have taught employees that organizations pay for jobs. But jobs are usually distinguished for pay purposes by comparing what the job requires in skill, effort, acceptance of responsibility, and willingness to work under certain conditions. Since these sound like personal qualities to employees and when organizations do sometimes pay for personal qualities (pretty secretaries, age, extra experience), it is not difficult for employees to believe that the organization pays for personal traits whether needed or not rather than for jobs. Organization pay systems usually tell employees that pay raises are based upon merit, but the employees often learn that the factor most highly correlated with size of raise is seniority or changes in the cost of living. Benefits going to all employees or geared to length of service teach employees that these rewards are pay for belonging to the organization.

Wage incentive plans are designed to teach employees that pay is for output rather than time. In practice, however, they teach that extra pay comes from increased effort alone. Indeed, if output depends upon cooperation or versatility (which are not rewarded in individual wage incentive plans), employees may resent making contributions for which they are not paid. Where management incentive plans pay off on variables over which managers have no control, they teach that pay is not based upon performance.

Actually, organizations should try and are trying to pay for (1) the job the person holds, (2) extra performance on that job, and (3) membership in the organization. In order to get this across to employees, most organizations have to think more than they have about what they expect from employees and to convey their expectations to employees. Paying for the job means paying for work as defined by the job. When personal traits are required to do the job, paying for the job is also paying for the required personal qualities. When personal traits are not required by the job, paying for them involves paying for the person's membership in the organization. When individuals are permitted to design their own jobs, they may be expected to do so in ways that require their particular qualifications. However, organizations that pay for personal traits not required by the job the person is holding are paying for membership rather than the job.

Organizations must learn and teach their employees that it is legitimate to pay for membership in organizations. Organizations meet their goals because they get and keep members. They have shown that they are intuitively aware of this by providing benefits, which because they are paid to everyone, are membership rewards. Pay for seniority and for personal qualifications adjudged to be needed but not fully used are likewise legitimate membership rewards.

Paying for extra performance is more difficult both for organizations to do and to teach employees that they are doing so. First, it is necessary to recognize that getting performance does not depend upon paying for extra performance. It is quite possible to obtain the desired performance by designing the organization and the jobs so that holding the job achieves it. Performance standards and management by objectives represent this approach. Second, some employees and some employee groups have such job and organization commitment that they make contributions at every opportunity and reward themselves (largely with intrinsic rewards—those they pay themselves) for them. The task for the organization with these individuals and groups is to remove barriers to performance.

Paying for extra performance in organizations requires that these conditions be met: (1) the individuals must want more pay, (2) they must believe that their efforts will result in better performance, and (3) they must believe that better performance will lead to more pay.[10] The first condition only requires the comment that people differ in their desire for more pay. Moreover, the law of diminishing returns exists. The second condition, however, requires not only that employees be properly selected and trained but that they accept the organization's definition and measurements of performance. This in turn requires that the performance be within employees' control.

The third condition is the most difficult for organizations to meet. Providing more pay on any basis other than performance weakens the pay-performance rela-

---

[10]   Chapter 6 in Lawler, *Pay and Organizational Effectiveness (see note 2).*

tionship. Also, employees must be able to see that the best peformers always get the most pay. This probably requires eliminating the pay secrecy that exists in most organizations.[11]

These conditions are hard to meet in most organizations. Although logically an organization should decide on rational grounds whether it can meet the conditions, the belief that people should be paid for performance may be too strong for logic to prevail. It may also be that people so want to believe that their pay is based upon their performance that performance pay plans will work when people want more pay and believe their efforts result in good performance. But it should be recognized that the belief that better performance results in more pay is fragile. People learn from what organizations do, not from what they say.

5.0 CAN PAY MOTIVATE PERFORMANCE OR ONLY MEMBERSHIP?

Although this question has just been answered, it arises so often from advocates of the job-enrichment movement and others that it requires some attention. Herzberg, for example, states that money cannot motivate performance because it is a hygiene factor rather than a motivator.[12] McClelland believes that money only motivates performance of those low in achievement motivation.[13] Others have pointed out that pay is not closely related to performance in organizations.[14] This last point is the telling one. When organizations do not closely relate performance and pay, there is no good reason why pay should motivate performance.

In fairness it must be said that motivating performance through pay is very difficult for organizations. Meeting the conditions specified in the previous section for paying for performance is not only difficult, it may conflict with paying for jobs and membership in the organization. When people do not want to be paid for extra performance or do not believe that organizations can measure or appraise their performance accurately, they may be motivated to leave by performance-based pay plans. When employees want more money but see that they must lose other equally valued rewards (pleasant social relationships or their feelings of fairness or security, for example) as a result of better performance, they may not only find the extra money but also the organization less attractive

. . .

7.1 What are the methods and techniques?

The typical compensation program consists of a number of plans, methods or techniques, and policies or ground rules. Most of the techniques are involved with paying for jobs—job analysis, job evaluation, job grading, job pricing. A number of plans purport to pay for performance—incentive plans, merit pay plans, special merit award plans. Although most compensation programs admit to only one plan that pays for membership in the organization (benefit programs), in reality many include a number of other plans that do so—general increases, automatic increase

[11]   *Ibid.*, p. 174.

[12]   Herzberg, F., One More Time: How Do You Motivate Employees? *Harvard Business Review*, 1968, *46* (No. 1), 53–62.

[13]   McClelland, D. C., Money as a Motivator: Some Research Insights, *Management Review*, 1968, *57* (No. 2), 23–28.

[14]   Haire, M., Ghiselli, E. E., and Gordon, M. E., *A Psychological Study of Pay* (Monograph No. 636; *Journal of Applied Psychology*, 1967, *51* (No. 4), pp. 1–24; Brenner, M. H., and Lockwood, H. C., Salary as a Predictor of Salary: A 20-Year Study, *Journal of Applied Psychology*, 1965, *49* (No. 4), 295–298; Evans, W. A., Pay for Performance: Fact or Fable?, *Personnel Journal*, September 1970, *49*, 726–731; Patten, T. H., Merit Increases and the Facts of Organizational Life, *Management of Personnel Quarterly*, Summer 1968, *1*, 30–38.

plans, maturity curves, pay planning programs, profit sharing. In addition, compensation programs include a number of control techniques—budgets, ratios. Pay levels, pay relationships, and pay increases are also partially programmed by policies and ground rules. Most programs include provisions for communicating the pay program, but organizations are not known for their openness in this area.

What are purposes of the techniques? Each of these techniques has a purpose which hopefully is known by managers at all levels, but is less likely to be known or understood by employees. The following tabulation briefly outlines the purpose of the plans and techniques.

Technique	*Purpose*
Job analysis	To obtain information about jobs. (Job information is required for job evaluation, job and organization design, recruitment, selection, training, and supervision.)
Job evaluation	To distinguish between jobs and arrange them in a hierarchy.
Job grading	To group jobs to ease pay administration.
Job pricing	To set prices on jobs or paygrades. (Job pricing often makes use of wage or salary surveys and is often done in collective bargaining.)
Incentive plans	To pay for output rather than time. (In practice, individual plans pay for extra effort while group and plantwide incentive plans pay for cooperation more than for effort.)
Merit pay plans	To pay for superior performance. (In practice, performance is unspecified and unreliably appraised. Often, under such plans, seniority correlates more highly with pay than does performance.)
Special performance awards	To pay for superior performance. (Usually *not* part of regular pay but one-shot rewards for outstanding performance.)
Benefits	To pay for membership in the organization. (The benefit program typically includes (1) provisions for economic security, (2) payments for time not worked, (3) extra payments for time worked, (4) nonproduction awards and bonuses. Some organizations include various employee services. Benefits may vary by occupational group, often by seniority, but *not* by performance.)
General increases	To pay for membership. (Pay increases going to all employees to compensate for changes in living costs, general economic conditions, or labor markets.)
Automatic increase plans	To pay for membership. (Pay increases tied to seniority. Although they may be partially based

Technique	*Purpose*
	upon merit, the tie to performance is so tenuous that employees do not believe it is.)
Maturity curves	To pay for membership. (Paying professional employees for additional years of experience. Although assumed to include performance, actually seniority and potential performance are rewarded.)
Pay planning programs	To pay for membership. (Planning pay increases in advance with due regard to internal and external pay relationship and potential performance. In such plans pay for performance is so attenuated as to be invisible to employees.)
Profit sharing	To pay for membership. (Because only the top two or three people in an organization can trace the relationship between their performance and profits, profit sharing is a reward for belonging to a profit-sharing organization.)
Controls	To insure consistent application of the compensation program and to control costs.
Communication	To create employee beliefs that they get fair pay and inform employees of appropriate behavior. (In practice, because of pay secrecy policies, neither purpose is well met. Action speaks louder than words.)
Policies and ground rules	To guide pay decisions of managers. (Because pay decisions are made at several levels in organizations of any appreciable size, consistent decisions require policies.)

8.0 DIFFERENT PROGRAMS FOR DIFFERENT EMPLOYEE GROUPS?

Most organizations have what is essentially one pay program for all employee groups with some minor variations in techniques for different groups. There have been a number of reasons for this approach. One is the tendency for organizations to look at cost and quantity of labor services rather than what they get in return. Another is the mistaken belief that equity demands it. A third, perhaps, is the fear that unions will demand what is given to the more favored groups.

Actually, organizations have been moving toward more differentiation of pay programs for different employee groups within one common program. All organizations, for example, differentiate between exempt and nonexempt employees. Most large organizations have somewhat different pay programs for production employees, clerical employees, salesmen, professional employees, and managers within a common framework. Some organizations make finer distinctions. In many organizations, pay programs for salesmen, professionals, and managers fit uncomfortably (if at all) within the common pay program.

The future will undoubtedly see more real differences in pay programs for different employee groups. As organizations learn to accept employee definitions of pay fairness and to design pay packages to get the kinds of behavior they want from employees, they will be managing many more different kinds of pay programs.

All employee groups will be paid for membership in the organization, although the form of pay will differ by employee groups and perhaps by individuals within groups. Certain groups (professionals and managers, for example) will be paid for membership rather than the jobs they presently hold. Most employee groups will continue to be paid for the jobs they hold, but as at present with craftsmen, some groups will be paid for what they can do (pay for membership) rather than what they are doing at present. Pay for performance may well be confined to fewer employee groups, but within these groups organizations will be more careful in defining needed performance and showing employees the relationship between their performance and their pay.

. . .

11.0 HOW DO ORGANIZATIONS PAY FOR JOBS?

As mentioned previously, all organizations, except for the small minority with personal rate systems, pay for jobs. This is done by differentiating jobs and paying individuals for the jobs they hold. In formal compensation programs, differentiating jobs and determining pay for jobs are usually done in two steps—job evaluation and job pricing.

11.1 Job evaluation

Job evaluation is the process of comparing jobs in order to determine their position in a hierarchy. It may be formal or informal. Informal job evaluation occurs whenever jobs are compared within organizations. Any collective bargaining agreement makes use of at least informal job evaluation,[18] including those involving unions officially opposed to formal job-evaluation programs (UAW, Packinghouse Workers, and some others). These situations typically either establish labor grades and establish rates for them or compare individual jobs and bargain rates for each. Also, organizations using "job slotting" for jobs of professional personnel are using at least informal job evaluation.

Formal job evaluation has been defined as an attempt to determine and compare the demands which the normal performance of particular jobs makes on normal workers without taking account of the individual abilities or performance of the workers concerned.[19] It involves the comparison of jobs by the use of formal or systematic procedures in order to determine the relative position of one job to another in a hierarchy. The real object of investigation and comparison is the content of the job, not individuals who hold the jobs.

The job-evaluation process consists of a number of steps. The first, known as job analysis, is a study of jobs in the organization. The second is determining the factor(s) that place one job at a higher level in the job hierarchy than another. The third involves developing or choosing a system for appraisal of the jobs according to the factors selected. The fourth step is using the system to evaluate the jobs resulting in a job hierarchy.

When the job hierarchy or structure has been established, it is priced out to arrive at a wage structure. It is useful to separate the internal wage structure and job evaluation conceptually, however, because job evaluation may be only one of the factors in wage determination. Unions, for example, may insist on bargaining the

---

[18]   Gomberg, W., A Collective Bargaining Approach to Job Evaluation, *Labor and Nation*, November–December 1946, *2*, 52.
[19]   *Job Evaluation* (Studies and Reports, New Series, No. 56; Geneva: International Labour Organization, 1960).

wage structure. Organizations may find that labor market considerations force a compromise between job structure and wage structure.[20]

The development of job evaluation can be traced to civil service classification systems and the early use of job analysis in selection and time study. Thus its origins go back to the 19th century. The first point system was developed in 1925.[21] Today it is employed as a standard compensation practice throughout the world. Although it is more prevalent in the United States than elsewhere, its use is expanding in other countries. In the U.S., job evaluation is found in organizations employing about two thirds of the employed labor force.[22] Larger organizations are somewhat more likely to use job evaluation than small ones, but job-evaluation plans are found even in very small organizations. In Great Britain, slightly over half of large organizations use job evaluation; but although its use is growing in smaller organizations only about 30 percent use job evaluation. Sweden has a number of industrywide job-evaluation plans covering about 20 percent of blue-collar workers, and the use of job evaluation there is growing. West Germany has a number of industrywide and regional job-evaluation plans. Holland has had a nationwide job-evaluation plan for blue-collar workers since 1948. Russia has a system that classifies individuals, assigns them to occupations, and determines wages by occupation and industry—a job-evaluation/employee-classification system.[23]

Responsibility for job evaluation is assigned to one or more committees, a department, or a consultant. Not infrequently all three are used at various stages. Committees have the advantage of securing support and collaboration of management and employees. Members must be selected carefully for analytical ability, fairness, and commitment to the project, because the actual work of job evaluation is usually done in committee. Broad representation on committees is desirable as an aid in communication, but committees of five are optimum size for effective work. A common solution is to rotate supervisors and employees as members. Although organizations may fear employee participation out of concern that employees are motivated to get the highest pay rate they can for their own job, there is evidence that employees are less prone to overpay for jobs than managers.[24] Some organizations confine committee membership to employees, and some consultants suggest an equal number of management and employee representatives.[25] In joint installations, of course, union members are regular members of committees.

Consultants are sometimes used in job evaluation installations, but apparently less frequently than in the past.[26] Successful consultants are careful to see that or-

---

[20]　For an excellent discussion of the factors affecting internal wage structure, see Chapter 5, Hildebrand, G. H., External Influences and the Determination of the Internal Wage Structure. in J. L. Meij (ed), *Internal Wage Structure* (Amsterdam: North-Holland Publishing Company, 1963).

[21]　Lott, M. R., *Wage Scales and Job Evaluation* (New York: Ronald Press Company, 1926).

[22]　Stone, C. H., and Yoder, D., *Job Analysis*, 1970 (Long Beach, Calif.: California State College, 1970), pp. 18–19.

[23]　Information on European practice is from an excellent British study, *Job Evaluation* (National Board for Prices and Incomes (NBPI), Report No. 83 and Supplement; London: Her Majesty's Stationery Office, September 1968).

[24]　Lawler, E. E., and Hackman, J. R., The Impact of Employee Participation in the Development of Pay Incentive Plans: A Field Experiment, *Journal of Applied Psychology*, 1969, *53*, 467–471.

[25]　Chambliss, L. A., Our Employees Evaluate Their Own Jobs, *Personnel Journal*, 1950, *28*, 141–142; Computer-Assisted Job Evaluation, *The Executive* (Wellington, New Zealand), March 1, 1970, pp. 15–16.

[26]　Mann, K. O., Characteristics of Job Evaluation Programs, *Personnel Administration*, 1965, *28*, 45–57.

ganization members are deeply involved in installation and are able to operate the plan when the consultant leaves. Consultants are most likely to be employed where no present organization member possesses the necessary expertise. They are more likely to be employed when a complex rather than a simple plan is to be installed. Some consultants are brought in at the insistence of unions in joint installations. Consultants are often brought in to insure objectivity in the evaluation of management jobs.

Some organizations assign job-evaluation installation as well as operation to a compensation unit. Those who do so are focusing on the technical nature of the task and the difficulty of getting managers at any level to devote the time the program requires. Unfortunately, this approach loses the communication and education advantages of the committee approach that may be impossible to achieve in any other way.

Union participation in job-evaluation installation ranges from full participation to indifference. One survey found that four out of five unionized firms involved the union during installation in some way, and 48 percent of union contracts have job-evaluation provisions.[27] Some job-evaluation plans have been installed and maintained as a joint venture. The best known is the plan in the basic steel industry.[28] Less well known is the plan in the West Coast paper industry. Even in joint installations, union participation varies. Joint union-management job evaluation would seem to assure union interest and understanding and some help in explaining the plan to employees. Joint plans tend to be more successful than unilateral plans. Perhaps most unions prefer to review the findings after management has completed installation. That review may vary from use of the grievance procedure if a union member objects to his rate to bargaining changes in the job hierarchy. Many job-evaluation installations are made solely by the employer, sometimes because the employer insists and sometimes because the union refuses to participate or to even acknowledge the existence of the plan.

Official union position in the United States on job evaluation, with a few exceptions such as the steelworkers, has been one of opposition, chiefly on the grounds that it limits collective bargaining. However, this position is not well correlated with practice. Unions typically accept the idea of a job hierarchy and favor job rates rather than personal rates. As they train more members in job-evaluation techniques and as more employers accept the idea that wage determination is a separate matter from job evaluation, more unions may be expected to attempt to secure the advantages of a rational job hierarchy and job rates through participation in job evaluation. One of the fallouts of job evaluation is an increase in information available to the negotiators.[29]

Success of job evaluation is usually gauged by employee, union, and organization satisfaction with it. Surveys report organization satisfaction of about 90 percent, with unionized organizations reporting higher satisfaction than nonunion organizations.[30] Employee acceptance is the primary criterion of organizations in

[27] *Personnel Management—Policies and Practices* (New York: Prentice-Hall, 1966), Section 15, 107.

[28] Stieber, J., *The Steel Industry Wage Structure* (Cambridge, Mass.: Harvard University Press, 1959).

[29] *Job Evaluation*, NBPI Report No. 83, p. 16 (see note 23); Corina, J., *Forms of Wage and Salary Payment for High Productivity* (Paris: Organization for Economic Cooperation and Development, 1970), p. 84.

[30] Patton, J. A., *Job Evaluation in Practice: Some Survey Findings* (Management Report No. 54; New York: American Management Association, 1961), pp. 73–77; *Job Evaluation*, NBPI Report No. 83 Supplement, p. 7 (see note 23).

determining the success of job evaluation. Both increasing use of employees on job-evaluation committees and the elaborate communications programs of organizations installing job-evaluation plans suggest organization concern with employee understanding and acceptance. Obviously, the more simple the job-evaluation plan the easier it is to explain.

Job evaluation involves two types of costs: (1) the costs of determining the job hierarchy, and (2) effects on payroll. The former consists of the time spent on the project by organization members and perhaps the fee of a consultant. This cost varies greatly with type of plan, peculiarities of company organization, level of jobs being evaluated, size and make-up of committees, and extent of union participation. An early estimate of $65 to $100 per job[31] may be a bit high but more recent data cite from two to four hours of time for evaluating each job in factory, office, and technical classifications, and the cost of evaluating the job of first-line supervisor at $65.[32] Joint union-management job evaluation takes longer, as does the evaluation of managerial and professional jobs. Payroll effects also vary greatly. The range from published reports has been from published reports has been from zerod upward, with a recent report stating that 3 to 6 percent is typical for white-collar employees.[33]

The meaning of both types of figures is difficult to interpret because of the variables affecting them: One survey found that more than half of surveyed organizations reported that job evaluation had saved money, and another 30 percent reported that other gains more than compensated for the expense.[34]

. . .

11.12 Job-evaluation factors

Job comparison requires that jobs be compared on some basis. Even ranking requires an answer to the question: "On what?" The "what" consists of one or more factors.

An important point about job-evaluation factors is that they tell employees what places a job at a higher level in the hierarchy. When it is realized that the measure of success of job evaluation is acceptance, the communication aspect of job-evaluation factors becomes even more important.

It is also apparent that organizations expect quite different behavior from different employee groups and that employee groups expect to provide different behaviors and attributes. This would suggest that job-evaluation factors used to compare the jobs of different employee groups should be quite different. There is also an economic and pragmatic reason for different factors for different job clusters or families. Wages of jobs in different job clusters do not always move together and in equal amounts. Job-content comparisons are stronger within narrow job clusters, somewhat weaker among broader clusters or functional groups, and weakest between broad clusters.[49]

---

[31]   Lytle, C. W., *Job Evaluation Methods* (2d ed.; New York: Ronald Press Co., 1954), pp. 34–35.

[32]   *Personnel Management—Policies and Practices,* Section 15 (see note 27); Zollitsch, H. G., and Langsner, A., *Wage and Salary Administration* (2d ed.; Cincinnati: South-Western Publishing Co., 1970), pp. 161–162.

[33]   Briggs, H. S., Cost of Installing a Job Evaluation Plan, *Management Record,* 1951, *13,* 429–433; Kress, A. L., Job Evaluation for White-Collar Workers in Private Sector Employment in the United States, *International Labor Review,* 1969, *100,* 341–357.

[34]   *Personnel Management—Policies and Practices* (see note 27).

[49]   Livernash, E. R., The Internal Wage Structure, in George W. Taylor and Frank C. Pierson (eds.), *New Concepts in Wage Determination* (New York: McGraw-Hill Book Co., 1957), 148–153.

Most large organizations do employ different job-evaluation factors and separate job-evaluation plans for at least broad functional groups. At least production, clerical, sales, and managerial jobs are evaluated separately.

In spite of the communication aspect of job-evaluation factors, apparently very little study has been done on the process of determining them. Perhaps the major reason for this is the wide use of readymade plans designed by employer associations and consultants. In the most widely used of these plans factors were chosen by a group of 25 experienced managers.[50] Although it is quite possible to find out what factors employees use to compare jobs, there is little evidence that organizations have done so, except perhaps in some union-management plans. But even in these cases, consultants are more likely to be employed.

Although lists of factors used in job-evaluation plans are long, they may almost universally be reduced to skill, effort, responsibility, and willingness to work under certain working conditions. The major differences between plans are in the weighting of factors rather than in the factors themselves.

It has been shown that different job-evaluation plans yield very similar results and that a limited number of factors yields results that are very similar to those from many factors.[51] But if job-evaluation factors tell employees what organizations pay for on jobs and successful job-evaluation plans are those that are accepted, both plans with more than a few factors and employee participation in choosing factors are suggested.

Some of the newer approaches to job analysis may, however, result in factors that can be used universally in comparing jobs. The PAQ developed by McCormick is one example. Another is the data-people-things classifications at present used by the U.S. Department of Labor. It is significant that these are the factors that sociologists have found to determine the functional importance of occupations.[52] In addition, the relationship between the data-people-things hierarchies and Jaques' time span of discretion has been noted.[53] If this factor does indeed cover all aspects of work and is accepted as doing so, one-factor job evaluation would be possible. But, although there has been a limited amount of experimentation with using time span of discretion as one of the factors in job-evaluation and a few single-factor job-evaluation plans have appeared,[54] most plans use a number of factors.

11.13 Job-evaluation methods

Job-evaluation methods are means of comparing jobs. The basic methods are ranking, classification, factor comparison, and point rating. The ranking and factor-comparison methods compare jobs to other jobs in terms of one or more factors. The classification and point methods compare jobs to one or more rating scales developed to measure one or more factors. The ranking and classification methods

[50]   Fisher, V., What's Right with Job Evaluation? *Industrial Management,* April 1961, *3,* 21-27

[51]   Studies by Lawshe and Associates at Purdue, published in *Journal of Applied Psychology.* Cf. 1944, *28,* 189-198; 1945, *29,* 413-419; 1946, *30,* 117-128, 310-319, 426-434; 1947, *31,* 355-365; 1948, *32,* 118-129; 1949, *33,* 158-166.

[52]   Hall, R. H., *Occupations and the Social Structure* (Englewood Cliffs, N. J.: Prentice-Hall, 1969).

[53]   Fine, S. A., *The 1965 Third Edition of the Dictionary of Occupational Titles—Content, Contrasts, and Critique* (Kalamazoo, Mich.: Upjohn Institute for Employment Research, 1968).

[54]   Goldenberg. S. J., Significant Difference: A Method of Job Evaluation, *Canadian Personnel and Industrial Relations Journal,* 1968, *15,* 19-23; Charles, A. W., Installing Single-Factor Job Evaluation, *Compensation Review,* 1971, *3,* 9-21.

are often called nonquantitative methods because the end result is a job structure in which each job has a position but not a numerical value. The so-called quantitative methods (factor comparison and point) result in numerical values for jobs and thus a finer differentiation within job structures.

The ranking and classification methods, which tend to be used in smaller organizations, appear to be the least used methods both in this country and abroad.[55] But there may be a trend toward the use of less complex plans stemming from (1) the fact that they yield results almost identical with more complicated methods, and (2) growing awareness that employee understanding and acceptance is more easily obtained with less complex plans. A recent survey of manufacturers in Arizona found the classification and ranking methods more widely used than either the point or the factor-comparison system. Even the larger organizations (200 to 2500 employees), although more likely to use the complex methods than medium or small organizations, made more use of the nonquantitative methods.[56]

As its title implies, the job-ranking method ranks the jobs from highest to lowest. After analyzing the jobs and choosing one or more factors on which to rank, raters are asked to rank the jobs. Although with simple ranking only a small number of jobs can be ranked, with the paired-comparison method (comparing jobs two at a time) this limitation disappears. Averaging the ranks assigned by several independent raters yields a composite ranking of jobs.

In the past the ranking method was often used without job analysis and with instructions to rank the "whole job" without further instructions. This not only necessitated raters with wide knowledge of the organization's jobs, it probably also insured that all raters were using different factors to compare jobs. Often, moreover, jobs were ranked by departments and a committee was assigned to dovetail departmental rankings.

When jobs are analyzed and one or more factors used for ranking jobs, the ranking method is adaptable to any size of organization. Families or clusters of jobs, or all jobs in the organization can be ranked. With the aid of computers, the paired-comparison method can handle any number of raters, jobs, and factors.

When only one factor is employed to rank jobs, or more than one factor bearing equal weights, the procedure is appropriately called a ranking method. But when factors are assigned different weights the procedure more appropriately might be called a factor-comparison method. One consultant assembles a committee of workers and management and has each member rank the jobs on overall importance using paired comparisons. After each rater has ranked the jobs three times, the results are fed into a computer which produces a rank-order list of jobs.[57] If desired, a more complex method is produced by having the raters rank the jobs on overall importance and a set of other factors. The results are fed into the computer along with market rates to produce factor weights.

The job-classification method involves defining a number of classes or grades of jobs and fitting jobs into the classes provided. A major advantage of the method is that most organizations and employees tend to classify jobs. In fact, many organizations, after completing job evaluation by another method, classify jobs into grades to aid in pay administration. These organizations may in fact have a job-

[55]   Mann, pp. 45–47 (see note 26); *Evaluation*, NBPI Report No. 83 Supplement, p. 8 (see note 23).
[56]   Flippo, E. B., Ashley, K., Finefrock, T., Jackson, D., and Olmstead, M. L., Personnel Practices in Arizona Manufacturing Companies: Development and Compensation, *Arizona Review*, November 1972, *21*, 8–13.
[57]   Computer-Assisted Job Evaluation (see note 25).

classification method in that they only refer to the original job evaluation plan when agreement on job placement cannot be made without it. Another advantage is its flexibility as evidenced by its successful use by the largest organization in the world (the U.S. Government) for a long period of years. In fact, it is the primary job-evaluation method at most levels of government in the U.S. and has been able to classify successfully millions of kinds and levels of jobs.

Disadvantages of the classification method are (1) the difficulty of writing grade descriptions and (2) the judgment required in applying them. Because the grading method considers the job as a whole, the factors used are unweighted and unscored, which often means that a little of one factor may be balanced by much of another. Thus, terms which express the amount of factors in jobs in the grade are depended upon to distinguish one grade from another.

After jobs have been analyzed and separated by type, and factors to distinguish jobs have been selected, descriptions of the class or grade are written. One statement may be written to describe a grade or a series of grading rules that place jobs in different grades. A committee is usually assigned the task of writing grade descriptions or grading rules. Usually, the grade descriptions of the two extreme grades are written first, then the next two extremes, and so on. If the committee assigned the task of writing grade descriptions is also assigned the task of classifying jobs, it may classify jobs as soon as the first two grade descriptions are written or complete all the grade descriptions before classifying jobs. Organizations developing their own classification systems usually find it wise to separate jobs by type and to determine factors, write grade descriptions, and classify jobs for each job cluster or family separately. Different job families usually require different numbers of grades.

In view of the heavy use of readymade point systems, it is surprising that organizations do not make more use of the classification plans readily available from the various governmental units in this country. It is even more surprising, when it is remembered that using these plans is free, while proprietary point plans usually cost the fees of a consultant.

The factor-comparison method compares jobs to each other by making judgments concerning which jobs contain more of certain factors than others. It is a refinement of the ranking method because jobs are compared directly in both. Although only 5 to 10 percent of job-evaluation plans are factor-comparison plans, the idea of comparing jobs to each other as well as to a scale is used in many combination plans.

Perhaps the major advantage claimed for the factor-comparison method is that it provides a custom-built installation in each organization. But the complexity of the method makes it difficult to explain to employees as well as making installation time-consuming and costly.

Actually, the factor-comparison method is not one method but a number of them all based upon job-to-job comparison. The basic method involves (after analyzing jobs): (1) ranking key jobs on five "universal" factors, (2) weighting the factors by dividing the wage paid each key job among the five factors, (3) developing a job comparison scale from key jobs on which vertical judgments (step 1) and horizontal judgments (step 2) agree.[58] Key jobs are defined as those bearing correct wage rates. The job-comparison scale is completed by comparing other jobs to key jobs factor by factor and placing them on the scale.

---

[58]   Benge, E. J., Burk, S. L. K., and Hay, E. N., *Manual of Job Evaluation* (New York: Harper and Brothers, 1941).

Several variations of the basic method have been offered[59] to meet situations where jobs with correct pay cannot be found and to facilitate job-evaluation for specific job clusters including the percent method;[60] what is called a job profile; and the guide-chart profile method, designed for management jobs.[61] Other modifications of the factor-comparison method involving other factors and multiple comparisons for management jobs have been developed.

One of the most interesting modifications of factor comparison is the well-known steel industry plan. The steps followed in developing the plan were those of the basic method with two exceptions: factors were selected and defined by the parties; weights for factors (and degrees of factors) were developed statistically by correlating job rankings on the factors and the existing wage rates of key jobs.[62] After the factor and degree weights were obtained, they were described in narrative form in a job evaluation manual which was used to evaluate jobs as it is in a point system. Thus the plan is a combination factor-comparison/point system.

The point method of job evaluation involves developing a rating scale for each of a number of factors, using the scales to evaluate jobs, and summing the scores attained on the separate scales to arrive at a point score for the job. Obviously, the validity of the method depends upon the factors chosen and the ratings scales constructed.

The primary advantages of the point method are the stability of the scales and the fact that accuracy and consistency tend to increase with rater familiarity with them. In addition, the factors and degrees used in the plan tell employees rather explicitly how job attains its place in the hierarchy. The major disadvantages of point plans are the difficulty of developing them and their complexity.

The difficulties involved in developing a point plan undoubtedly account for the heavy use of readymade plans. In large part, the greater usage of point plans over other types of plans is due to the availability of a number of readymade plans.

Point plans are usually developed for job families (factory jobs, clerical jobs, management jobs). After analyzing the jobs under study, developing a point plan involves: choosing and defining factors, defining degrees, and assigning values to factors and degrees. The final task is writing up a job-evaluation manual which consists of the scales developed to evaluate jobs.

The most widely used point plans have been promoted by employer associations, but many consultants have developed their own plans. Some large organizations have developed their own plans. Among point plans developed for particular job families there is a rather remarkable similarity of factors and a good deal of similarity in weights.

Although logically success of job evaluation should depend upon organizations' developing their own plans based upon factors which apply to their jobs, readymade plans apparently have sufficient flexibility to work. One survey of U.S. companies

---

[59]   Hay, E. N., Four Methods of Establishing Factor Scales in Factor Comparison Job Evaluation, in *The AMA Handbook of Wage and Salary Administration* (New York: American Management Association, 1950), pp. 56–65.

[60]   Turner, W. D., The Per Cent Method of Job Evaluation, *Personnel*, 1948, *24*, 476–492; Hay, E. N., Creating Factor Comparison Key Scales by the Per Cent Method, *Journal of Applied Psychology*, 1948, *32*, 456–464.

[61]   Hay, E. N., and Purves, D., The Profile Method of High-Level Job Evaluation, *Personnel*, 1951, *28*, (No. 2), 162–170; Hay, E. N., and Purves, D., A New Method of Job Evaluation: The Guide Chart-Profile Method, *Personnel*, 1954, *31*, 72–80; Hay, E. N., Setting Salary Standards for Executive Jobs, *Personnel*, 1958, *34*, 63–72.

[62]   Edwards, P. M., Statistical Methods in Job Evaluation, *Advanced Management*, 1968, *33*, 158–163.

found that 93 percent of those using a readymade plan considered it to be success-ful.[63] The British survey cited previously found that 90 percent of plans installed with the aid of consultants were rated as successful compared to 89 percent of plans where consultants were not used. Many, perhaps most, consultants have their own readymade plans.

Although most job-evaluation plans typify one of these four methods or some combination of them, some others are in use. One is Jaques' method of distinguish-ing jobs in terms of time span of discretion (the longest time an employee is permit-ted to exercise discretion without review of his actions by his superior). Jaques insists that his approach is job measurement rather than job evaluation. He holds that employees are intuitively aware of the level of their work and fair pay for it and that time span of discretion and thus job level can be measured.

Unfortunately, even with Jaques' detailed instructions,[64] measuring time spans has proved difficult. Some studies have shown that time span can be measured and that its results correlate with job evaluation on professional and managerial jobs but less so on manual jobs.[65] Another study found that time span is not correlated with either job level or individual ability.[66] Another problem with the time-span ap-proach has been with limiting job comparisons to one factor. Employees appear to believe that several factors are required to explain differences between jobs. Thus, some job-evaluation plans incorporate time span as one of the factors. Although time-span measurement has had limited use, if it is defined as the decision-making aspect of jobs, at least two job-evaluation plans are based upon such a single fac-tor.[67]

Another, called the guideline method of job evaluation, does not use factors at all but relies almost entirely on the labor market to determine relative job position in the hierarchy. In this method, a survey of market rates is made for a larger number of jobs (often, 50 percent of an organization's jobs). The market rates are compared to a schedule of pay grades constructed on the basis of 5-percent inter-vals. This schedule includes a minimum rate, a midpoint, and a maximum rate for each grade. The range width varies from 30 percent in the lower grades to 60 per-cent in the higher ones. The job-evaluation process consists of matching market rates to the closest midpoint in the schedule. Adjustments of one or two grades may be made to accommodate internal relationships. When surveyed jobs have been placed into grades, the remaining jobs are positioned by ranking them against sur-vey jobs. All jobs in the organization are evaluated at one time and final ordering in-cludes all of the organization's jobs. The method, developed by Smyth and Murphy Associates, has reportedly been tested in a number or organizations.[68]

Both economic theory and organization practice suggest that large organiza-tions with a number of job clusters can accommodate the market and internal rela-tionships best by administering separate pay structures for the separate job clus-ters. While apparently the guideline method can reconcile the different economic

[63]   Job Evaluation Comes of Age, *Personnel,* 1960, *37,* 4-5.
[64]   Jaques, E., *Equitable Payment* (see note 8); Jaques, E., *Time-Span Handbook* (Lon-don: Heinemann, 1964).
[65]   Atchison, T., and French, W., Pay Systems for Scientists and Engineers, *Industrial Relations,* 1967, *7,* 44-56; *Job Evaluation,* NBPI Report No. 83, p. 7 (see note 23).
[66]   Goodman, P. S., An Empirical Examination of Elliot Jaques' Concept of Time-Span, *Human Relations,* 1967, *20,* 155-170.
[67]   Goldenberg (see note 54); Charles (see note 54).
[68]   Pasquale, A. M., *A New Dimension to Job Evaluation* (Management Bulletin No. 128; New York: American Management Association, 1969).

forces operating on different job clusters, it does so by placing more reliance on wage and salary surveys than is usually given and perhaps more than they deserve. More important, the method tells employees no more about what places a job at a higher level than does collective bargaining.

Still another approach to job evaluation is the use of a statistical technique called cluster analysis to determine job relationships. From cluster analysis, job relationships emerge that can be used to classify jobs. Factors are specified by the job clusters that result or from those that serve to create job relationships. Although clustering techniques are still under development, a number of studies have shown their applicability to job evaluation using different kinds of factors.[69]

Some other experimental approaches to job evaluation have employed the Guttman technique of scale analysis[70] (a method of determining if the scale is measuring only one variable) and the semantic differential technique[71] (a method of measuring meaning).

. . .

12.0 HOW DO ORGANIZATIONS PAY FOR PERFORMANCE?

Organizations employing rate ranges, incentive plans, and special performance awards assume that they are paying for superior performance. Almost all organizations have wage or salary ranges for a considerable proportion of their employees, and they typically insist that movement through these ranges is based upon merit. Most organizations have incentive plans that apply to some employee groups. Pay ranges apply to many production employees and almost all clerical, professional, and managerial employees. Incentive plans apply to many production employees, a large proportion of salesmen and managers, a smaller proportion of clerical workers and professional employees. Most employee groups are paid under either ranges or incentive plans. Managers, however, typically are paid under both arrangments.

The existence of rate ranges and incentive plans does not assure that employees are paid for performance. As noted, not only are the requirements for using pay to reward performance difficult to meet, but also organizations have not been diligent in meeting them. Few organizations have been careful in specifying what performance the organization wants; few employees know what performance is rewarded. Where organizations have specified what performance is wanted (as in incentive plans), they often leave out other kinds of performance that employees know their organizations need but do not pay for. Nor have organizations been careful to distinguish performance that can be made by the employee from changes over which the employee has no control.

This section discusses payment arrangements that are assumed to reward performance, emphasizing conditions under which they can reward performance rather than membership in the organization.

---

[69]   Thorndike, R. L., Who Belongs in the Family?, *Psychometrika*, December 1953, *18*, 267–276; Orr, D. B., A New Method for Clustering Jobs, *Journal of Applied Psychology*, 1960, *44*, 44–49; Dunnette, M. D., and Kirchner, W. D., A Checklist for Differentiating Different Kinds of Sales Jobs, *Personnel Psychology*, 1959, *12*, 421–429; Hemphill, J. K., Job Desciptions for Executives, *Harvard Business Review*, 1959, *37*, 63–68; Reeb, M., How People See Jobs: A Multidimensional Analysis, *Occupational Psychology*, 1959, *33*, 1–17.
[70]   Patten, T. H., Jr., Evaluating Managerial Positions by Evalograms, *Personnel Administration*, 1966, *29*, 17–26.
[71]   Triandis, H. C., Comparative Factorial Analysis of Job Semantic Structures of Managers and Workers, *Journal of Applied Psychology*, 1967, *51*, 297–302.

12.1 True performance ranges

Very few true performance ranges exist. The evidence shows that pay is not closely related to performance in many organizations that claim to have merit ranges.[94]

Most employees in the United States work under rate ranges. The majority of office workers in all sections of the country and the majority of plant workers in many areas do so as well.[95] Single-rate programs are unusual for office workers, but there is evidence that single-rate programs for plant workers are growing.[96] Organizations usually justify rate ranges on the grounds of individual differences in employee performance. There is no question but that large differences in employee productivity exist—differences in production between the best and worst employee of up to five or six times have been noted.[97] But not all jobs permit significant differences in performance. Other conscious or unconscious purposes of rate ranges are: (1) to recognize differences in employee qualifications (usually measured by experience), (2) to meet employee expectations of wage increases, (3) to reduce wage costs in collective bargaining (a union demand for an automatic range may be less costly than a general increase).[98] Still another is industry practice.[99] Obviously, only the first of the purposes for rate ranges opens the possibility of paying for performance.

There is evidence that the concept of a rate range is changing.[100] The original idea of a rate range was that the average qualified employee should receive the job rate (the rate that would be assigned under a flat rate system); poorer performers should receive lower rates; and only superior performers should receive more than the job rate. In some practice, the average employee expects to reach the maximum of the range if his performance is merely satisfactory, and many organizations are meeting these expectations. Obviously, under the latter definition a rate range has limited scope in paying for performance. Sixty percent of the schedules covering clerical, professional, and administrative employees in large organizations regard the midpoint of the range as the market value of the job. It is likely that schedules for managers and professionals have a higher proportion and that ranges where the job rate is the top of the range are most prevalent for plant workers.[101]

In establishing rate ranges, range spread reflects the purpose emphasized by the organization. Within-grade ranges typically vary from 10 to 25 percent for hourly jobs, from 25 to 35 percent for office jobs, and from 30 to 100 percent for

---

[94]   Lawler, E. E., and Porter, L. W., Predicting Managers' Pay and Their Satisfaction with Their Pay, *Personnel Psychology*, 1966, *19*, 363–373; Svetlik, B., Prien, E., and Barrett, G., Relationships between Job Difficulty, Employee's Attitude toward His Job, and Supervisory Ratings of the Employee's Effectiveness, *Journal of Applied Psychology, 1964*, *48*, 320–324; Haire, Ghiselli, and Gordon (see note 14); Brenner and Lockwood (see note 14); Slichter, S. H., Healy, J. J., and Livernash, E. R., *The Impact of Collective Bargaining on Management* (Washington: Brookings Institution, 1960), pp. 602–606.

[95]   U.S. Department of Labor, *Area Wage Surveys, Selected Metropolitan Areas*, 1968–69 (Bulletin No. 1625–90; Washington: U.S. Government Printing Office, 1970), pp. 68–69.

[96]   Cox, J. H., Time and Incentive Pay Practices in Urban Areas, *Monthly Labor Review*, 1971, *94*, 53–56.

[97]   Richardson, M. W., Forced-Choice Performance Records, *Personnel*, 1949, *26*, 207; Douty, H. M., Some Aspects of Wage Statistics and Wage Theory, in Industrial Relations Research Association, *Proceedings of the Eleventh Annual Meeting* (Madison, Wis., 1958), p. 201.

[98]   Fogel, W., Wage Administration and Job Rate Ranges, *California Management Review*, 1965, *7*, 77–84.

[99]   U.S. Department of Labor, *Salary Structure Characteristics in Large Firms*.

[100]   Slichter *et al.*, p. 604 (see note 94).

[101]   U.S. Department of Labor, *Salary Structure Characteristics in Large Firms*.

management jobs. The progression presumably follows the opportunity for differential performance on jobs. But it is also influenced by range definition (see above), industry or area practice, and promotion policy and practice for separate employee groups. Separate pay schedules for clerical employees have an average spread of 30 percent in large organizations; combined professional and administrative schedules, 37 to 47 percent; and combined clerical, professional, and administrative schedules, 35 to 45 percent.[102] Range spread is also affected by the size of pay increase required to be noticeable to employees. . . .

12.2 Special performance awards

Perhaps the best way to insure that pay is tied to performance and that the relationship is seen by employees is to pay for performance separately. Although such special performance awards have long been advocated[109] and a few organizations have them, just how many is unknown. An especially interesting recent suggestion[110] is to divide pay into three parts. One part, pay for the job, would be the same for everyone assigned to the job. A second part would be different for employees of different length of service and perhaps for other personal qualifications. The third part of pay would be for performance in the previous period which could be zero or low for poor performers and high for superior performers. This third portion of pay, based entirely on the individual's performance would vary over time.

12.3 Incentive plans[111]

Incentive plans assume that performance can be measured and thus increased pay can be tied to increased performance. In this they differ from merit ranges in which it is assumed that performance can only be evaluated or appraised. Performance measurement requires determining the kind(s) of performance to be measured, the units of measurement, and a standard against which actual performance is to be compared, as well as standardizing the conditions of work.

Although most people probably think of incentive plans in connection with factory jobs, they are used for almost all kinds of work. Their major application has been to production jobs. But they are also applied to maintenance and repair work, materials handling, inspection, stockroom work, janitorial work, warehousing, shipping, office work, transportation, hospital work, and even construction work. One of the major applications of incentive plans is in sales work where about 80 percent of organizations use them.[112] Top management jobs are almost universally paid partially on the basis of an incentive plan. Middle management, supervisors, and professionals are paid partially on incentive in some organizations. . . .

13.0 HOW DO ORGANIZATIONS PAY FOR MEMBERSHIP?

A large proportion of employee compensation is not designed to compensate for the specific job to which an employee is assigned or for his performance but for his membership in the organization. Pay for membership indicates that organizations

---

[102]   Ibid.

[109]   Constello, T. W., and Zalkind, S. S., Merit Raise or Merit Bonus: A Psychological Approach, *Personnel Administrator*, 1962, *25*, 10–17: Scanlon, B. K., Is Money Still the Motivation?, *The Personnel Administrator*, 1970, *15*, 8–12.

[110]   Lawler, *Pay and Organizational Effectiveness*, p. 167 (see note 2).

[111]   See Chapter 6.3 for details concerning incentive plans and Chapter 4.5 on employee evaluation.

[112]   Dauner, J. R., Salesmen's Compensation: Have We Kept Pace?, *Akron Business and Economic Review*, Summer 1972, *3*, 33–37.

are aware that they are not purchasing labor service alone but sufficient organization attachment on the part of employees to enable the organization to accomplish its goals.

Organizations vary in the proportion of total compensation they pay for membership. Organizations that see the need to secure a long-term commitment from most members in order to permit the organization to achieve its goals would be expected to have more membership rewards than organizations that regard employment as temporary. Those employee groups with the strongest commitment to the organization have always received membership rewards. As employee groups are asked to or wish to extend their commitment to the organization, they demand membership rewards, and organizations provide them.

The forms of compensation discussed in this section are those that pay for membership in the organization rather than for the job or performance. The process of paying for membership need not be conscious on the part of either organizations or their members. Some of the membership rewards discussed in this section may be considered performance or even job rewards by some employee groups and by some organizations. It is the author's view that they are membership rewards and that both organizations and their members would gain by realizing it.

13.1 General increases
Most organizations in inflationary periods are faced with the necessity of providing general increases to adjust for increases in living costs and to keep up with changing labor markets. Such increases, however, do not reward employees for the job they hold or for performance on that job. They represent "equity" adjustments for employees whose continuing membership in the organization is sought.

13.2 Automatic ranges
Organizations with automatic ranges in which individual pay increases are based upon length of service are paying for membership measured by seniority. Those with so-called merit ranges in which pay changes of individuals are keyed to experience, considerations of intra- or inter-department consistency, or a feeling that employees expect regular increases are likewise paying for membership in the organization.

13.3 Maturity curves
A good example of a membership reward that may be seen by employees or even organizations as a performance reward is the maturity curve or career curve.[130] Although maturity curves vary pay by appraisal of performance, the major explanatory variable is years since degree. An additional unit of age or seniority is assumed to represent additional contributions regardless of the performance level.

Actually, maturity curves represent a measurement of membership in the field rather than the organization. Although the individual may be employed by a single employer for a long period of time, he sees his development in his field as a contribution that should be recognized by the employer. The employer is expected to pay for this membership in the field. It is up to the organization to use the contributions that membership implies.

---

[130]   Smith, R. A., Achieving Flexibility in Compensation Administration, *Compensation Review*, 1970, *2*, 6-14; Foster, K. E., Accounting for Management Pay Differentials, *Industrial Relations*, 1969, *9*, 80-87.

13.4 Pay planning

A common program in large organizations to insure that pay-increase decisions are consistent within and between departments and reflect organization and market realities is called pay planning.[131] Managers plan pay increases for subordinates at one point in time using information and sometimes help from a staff department. While pay planning programs may meet the constraints faced by large organizations and may include performance as one of numerous inputs, planning increases in advance represents paying for continued membership in the organization.

13.5 Profit sharing

Another membership reward, perceived as a performance reward by some organizations, is profit sharing. Although early discussions of profit sharing emphasized increased efficiency and lower costs as goals and results of profit sharing,[132] more recent reports are less likely to do so.[133] There is some evidence that employee attitudes toward organizations improve with profit sharing and that employees are more likely to have a feeling of partnership with management. But employees do not believe that an individual can link his own work to profit results or that profit sharing eliminates freeloaders.[134]

Profits are influenced by so many variables that it is very difficult for an individual to believe that his profit share is related to his performance. In small organizations with cash plans and continuous communication efforts, it may be possible to maintain employee beliefs in the performance-reward relationship, but such beliefs are vulnerable to any occurrence that reduces profits while the individual maintains his performance. Larger organizations with cash plans are less likely to be able to foster these beliefs. Deferred plans involve the additional hurdle that payment is not immediate but often delayed for years. But profit sharing does encourage continued membership, at least for some groups of employees, by instilling a sense of partnership with management and promising more rewards when profits permit them.

13.6 Compensation security plans

Perhaps the most clearcut membership reward is a compensation security plan in which the organization signals its desire for continued employee membership in the organization by providing a guarantee of employment or income. A similar symbol is salaried status for all employees.[135] While salaried status is symbolic only (in that salaried as well as hourly employees are laid off in adverse economic conditions), compensation security plans provide for some employment or income security. Only a few organizations have placed all employees on salary, but some large industrial unions have demanded salary status for members. Organizations having such plans report few absenteeism problems. But the fact that giving increased status to one employee group results in a decrease in relative status for others on salary may account for employer resistance.

---

[131]   Sibson, pp. 103–109 (see note 17).

[132]   Baird, D., Profit-Sharing Doubles Production, *Mill and Factory*, 1953, *52*, 133–136; Lincoln, J. F., Incentive Management (Cleveland: Lincoln Electric Company, 1957).

[133]   Metzger, B. L., and Colletti, J. A., *Does Profit Sharing Pay?* (Evanston, Ill.: Profit Sharing Research Foundation, 1971).

[134]   Best, R. D., Profit Sharing and Motivation for Productivity, in *A Symposium of Profit Sharing and Productivity Motivation* (Madison, Wis.: Center for Productivity Motivation, University of Wisconsin, 1961).

[135]   Kaponya, P. G., Salaries for All Workers, *Harvard Business Review*, 1962, *40*, 49–57; Weeks, D. A., Salaries for Blue Collar Workers. *The Conference Board Record.* 1965, *2*, 15.

Although there are more compensation security plans than salary-for-all plans, they, too, are limited. Plans guaranteeing wages or employment are limited[136] by the contingent liability assumed by employers, the tendency of all decisions to affect the guarantee, and the hesitation of unions to give up previously won gains in order to provide flexibility in work assignment. Plans providing income security meet most of these problems by using insurance principles to limit the employer's liability, but although they have been adjudged successful, they have not spread beyond a few large industries.[137]

13.7 Fringe benefits

The hodgepodge of economic rewards lumped under the terms "fringe benefits," "wage supplements," "nonwage benefits," "social wages," "supplementary employee remuneration," "supplementary compensation," and "indirect payment practices" all represent rewards for membership in the organization rather than for the job or for performance (see Chapters 6.6 and 6.7 of this Handbook). In addition to lack of agreement on what to call them, there is lack of agreement on what is or is not to be included in them, the purposes they are to serve, responsibility for programs, the costs and values of their various elements, the units in which the costs and values are to be measured, and the criteria that decisions are to meet. As a result, decisions about benefits are more complex than those concerned with wages and salaries.

An example of the controversy over what to include is found in the different definitions used by the U.S. Chamber of Commerce and the U.S. Bureau of Labor Statistics, both of which have been surveying benefits for over 20 years.[138] While both include social insurance, private welfare plans, and paid leaves, BLS includes premium pay while the Chamber of Commerce does not, and the Chamber of Commerce includes paid company time off the job and certain employee services while BLS does not. The National Industrial Conference Board includes as fringe benefits those that fall into the following categories: (1) extra payments for time worked, (2) payments for time not worked, (3) payments for employee security, and (4) payments for employee services. One analysis of employer and union purposes in installing fringe benefits and services concludes that penalty payments, paid leave, and protections from economic hazards are not compensation but obligations of employers for the social welfare of employees assumed by employers as a condition of employment.[139]

Whatever is to be included, the benefit package is an important part of total compensation. Since 1964, BLS has defined total compensation as all payments to workers subject to income tax withholding and all payments made by the employer to government agencies, insurance companies, or trustees for insurance and wel-

---

[136]   *Personnel Practices in Factory and Office: Manufacturing* (Studies in Personnel Policy, No. 194; New York: National Industrial Conference Board, 1964), p. 113.
[137]   U.S. Department of Labor, *Supplementary Unemployment Benefit Plans and Wage-Employment Guarantees* (Bulletin No. 1425-3; Washington: U.S. Government Printing Office, June 1965), p. 4; Becker, J., *Guaranteed Income for the Unemployed* (Baltimore: Johns Hopkins Press, 1968); Beier, E. H., Financing Supplementary Unemployment Benefit Plans, *Monthly Labor Review*, 1969, *92*, 31–35; Schaffer, B. K., Experience with Supplementary Unemployment Benefits: A Case Study of the Atlantic Steel Company, *Industrial and Labor Relations Review*, 1968, *22*, 85–94.
[138]   Fox, H., *Comparing the Costs of Fringe Benefits*, The Conference Board Record, 1967, 4, 29–35.
[139]   Allen, D., Fringe Benefits: Wages or Social Obligation? (Ithaca, N.Y.: Cornell University, 1964).

fare.[140] Note that this definition includes (1) extra payments for time worked, (2) payments for time not worked, and (3) payments for employee security. Employee services are not included largely on the grounds that their costs are not readily identifiable.

The definition of compensation offered in Section 2.0 of this Chapter was that it consists of those items recognized by employees. Thus fringe benefits are those rewards for membership in the organization seen as part of compensation by employees.

. . .

15.0 HOW DO YOU PUT IT ALL TOGETHER?

Discussion of compensation controls indicates that some parts of compensation are controlled by several different parts of the organization and some by none. It also shows that organizations have not designed the controls well to get the kinds of employee behavior they need. Nor are the controls designed to obtain different behavior from different employee groups. Most organizations have a number of widely varying employee groups and are adding more—more professionals, more women, more members of minority groups. The compensation that some of these groups expect and the behavior that they expect to be paid for (and that the organization expects) differ greatly from other groups.

Different rewards for different groups call for coordination of compensation decisions. When responsibility for different rewards is assigned to separate organization units and some rewards are no one's responsibility, employees receive contradictory signals. The logical solution for organizations is to assign the development of reward packages to one organization unit. Reward packages should be based upon the characteristics of the work force of the organization.

Coordination of rewards into an integrated whole is essential if the organization is to gain maximum value from compensation. This means that job and organization design and other nonfinancial rewards must be coordinated with economic rewards. It is equally important that compensation be integrated with the behavior desired from each employee group. Thus the organization must determine what it wants from each employee group and how it can best distribute its resources to obtain it. For some groups in highly programmed work the organization may expect only that the individual maintain his membership and meet the minimum standards of his job in return for specified economic rewards. For other groups, the organization needs extra performance and commitment and this requires that the employee see a connection between his performance above the minimum and additional pay.

Organizations obviously differ—in size, technology, organization climate, organization structure, and so forth. Some may want to and perhaps have to merely exchange money for employee time. But most organizations must develop and manage a number of different reward packages designed to get the behavior the organization needs from each group. Proper use of organization resources demands that each group receive consistent signals of required behavior from all kinds of pay.[158]

---

[140]　Bauman, A., *Measuring Employee Compensation in U.S. Industry*, Monthly Labor Reveiw, 1970, 93, 17-24.

[158]　Managerial concerns about both policy and practice in the area of wage and salary administration inevitably involve many other areas of personnel and labor relations management. Managers must consider, for example, changes in legislation and public policy, especially those concerned with equal employment opportunities and civil rights; changing needs and expectations of work force members; the reliability and validity of tests, interviews, and personnel appraisals; and the propriety and adequacy of statistical analysis used in development of a useful and dependable data base for planning and policy formulation, control, and audit.

FOR DISCUSSION AND REVIEW

1 What are common pay problems in organizations?
2 Can pay motivate performance?
3 Review the job-evaluation methods covered in the article.
4 How do organizations pay for performance versus for membership?
5 Should pay rates be open or secret in an organization? Why?

R. I. Henderson

Laws Affecting Compensation Administration

1890—The Sherman Antitrust Act

This legislation was enacted to protect trade and commerce against unlawful restraints and monopolies. It declared that any person or groups who monopolized, or attempted to monopolize, or conspired with any other person or persons to monopolize any part of the trade or commerce among several states to be guilty of a misdemeanor. The important effect of this law with regard to compensation is that certain actions of unions were considered to be acting in restraint of trade and thus were monopolies; however, nowadays most union concerted action is not considered to violate the act.

1914—The Clayton Act

This act supplemented the existing legislation against restraint of trade. It was hailed by Samuel Gompers, president of the American Federation of Labor, as the "Industrial Magna Charta" as it specifically defined the labor of human beings as not a commodity or article of commerce and thus, to a degree, freed labor unions from the antitrust statutes of the Sherman Act. In reality, it did not improve the legal status of union operations, and in a way it increased employers' abilities to obtain injunctions against certain union actions.

1931—The Davis-Bacon Act

This act provided for the Secretary of Labor to set rates of wages for laborers and mechanics employed by private contractors and subcontractors working for the federal government. Amendments to the act provided for employee benefits and required contractors or subcontractors to make necessary payments for these benefits.

1932—The Norris-LaGuardia Act

This act defined and limited the jurisdiction of federal courts involved in issuing restraining orders or temporary or permanent injunctions in cases growing out of labor disputes. Its main input was to recognize the legitimate interest of a union and its members beyond direct employment relations, thus legalizing peaceful picketing, secondary boycotts, and other union "self-help" activities. It also specifically declared the "Yellow Dog" contracts in which employers required from their workers nonunion membership or activity as a precondition of employment to be unenforceable.

Reprinted by permission from R. I. Henderson, *Compensation Management*, Appendix IV (Reston, Va.: Reston Publishing Co., 1976).

1933—The Wagner-Peyser Act

This act provided for the establishment of the state employment service system. The federal government provided 50 percent of the funding for state-operated employment systems meeting prescribed minimum standards of personnel and operating procedures.

1935—The Social Security Act of 1935

This act established the Federal Old-Age, Survivors, Disability, and Health Insurance System as well as the federal-state unemployment compensation system. This act and its amendments now cover most wage earners in nonagricultural industries, many farm workers, and self-employed people. The system is financed by equal employer and employee contributions which amount to 5.85 percent of the employee's earnings up to a maximum of $15,300 per year. Self-employed persons pay out of their own pockets 7.9 percent of net income in excess of $400 up to the $14,100 maximum. Amendments also provide for medicaid and medicare programs.

1935—The National Labor Relations Act of 1935 (better known as the Wagner Act)

This act created the National Labor Relations Board (NLRB). It empowered the "Board" to oversee employer practices and to insure employees the right of self-organization, to bargain collectively through representatives of their own choosing, and to engage in concerted activities for the purpose of collective bargaining or other mutual aid or protection. It specifically listed practices in which employers were forbidden to engage. It greatly increased the power of unions and led to the rapid rise of successful unionization activities in American industries.

1936—The Walsh-Healey Public Contracts Act

This act sets basic labor standards for employees working on government contracts calling for the manufacture or furnishing of materials, supplies, articles, or equipment in an amount exceeding $10,000. This law contains minimum wage, maximum hours, and safety and health provisions. It requires that time and a half be paid for work over 8 hours a day and 40 hours a week.

1938—The Fair-Labor Standards Act (FLSA)

This act and its amendments contain minimum wage, maximum hours, overtime pay, equal pay, record keeping, and child labor provisions for the majority of American workers. It also specifically defines those groups of employees who are exempt from its requirements (exempt employees). It states that overtime pay must be at a rate of not less than one and one-half times for all hours worked over 40 in a workweek. The minimum hourly wage beginning January 1, 1976 is $2.30 per hour for the majority of those covered by the act. Farm workers on large farms will have the $2.30 per hour rate effective May 1, 1978.

1947—The Portal-to-Portal Act

This act provides that under certain conditions employees begin drawing pay from the moment they enter company property until the time they leave it. The intention of this act was to compensate employees who had to spend a considerable amount of time getting to their work stations after entering company property.

1947—The Labor-Management Relation Act
(better known as the Taft-Hartley Act)

This amendment to the Wagner Act principally related to extending government intervention into labor relations. It recognized the right to refrain from or engage in concerted union activities, thus outlawing closed-shop agreements, although it did permit union shops except where prohibited by state laws. The "right to work" laws of a number of states resulted from this act. It also defined certain union unfair labor practices as well as further definitions of employer rights. Further, it established the Federal Mediation and Conciliation Services (FMCS) as an independent government agency.

1959—The Labor-Management Reporting and Disclosure
Act of 1959 (better known as the Landrum-Griffin Act)

This act was intended to protect the rights of union members and was considered to be "the Bill of Rights" of members of labor organizations. In order to enhance these rights, the act declared as essential that labor organizations and their officials adhere to the highest standards of responsibilities and ethical conduct in administering the affairs of their organizations, particularly as these affected labor-management relations. It defined in specific terms these ethical standards and procedures for guaranteeing the safeguard of the rights of union members.

1963—The Equal Pay Act (EPA)

This act stated that employees of one sex may not be paid wages at a rate lower than that paid employees of the opposite sex doing work requiring equal skill, effort, and responsibility and performed under similar working conditions.

1964—The Civil Rights Act

This act contains Titles I through Title VII. Title VII specifically relates to the broad field of employment. *Title VII* is known as the *Equal Employment Opportunity Act of 1964*, as amended. It established the Equal Employment Opportunity Commission. It makes it an unlawful employment practice for an employer to discriminate against any individual with respect to hiring, compensation, terms, conditions, or privileges of employment because of race, color, religion, sex, or national origin. It prohibits limiting, segregating, or classifying employees in any way that would deprive them from employment opportunities, including initial hiring, promotions, layoffs, or terminations. Figure IV-1 describes the major equal employment opportunity laws, regulations, and guidelines.

1967—The Age Discrimination in Employment Act of 1967

This act promotes the employment of the older worker based on ability rather than age; prohibits arbitrary age discrimination in employment; and helps employers and employees find ways to meet problems arising from the impact of age on employment. It protects individuals 40 to 65 years old from age discrimination.

1972—Equal Employment Opportunity Act of 1972

This act empowered the Equal Employment Opportunity *Commission* to prevent any person from engaging in any unlawful employment practice as described in Title VII of the Civil Rights Act of 1964. It also empowered the Commission to investigate unlawful employment practices on the part of state government, governmental agencies, and political subdivisions.

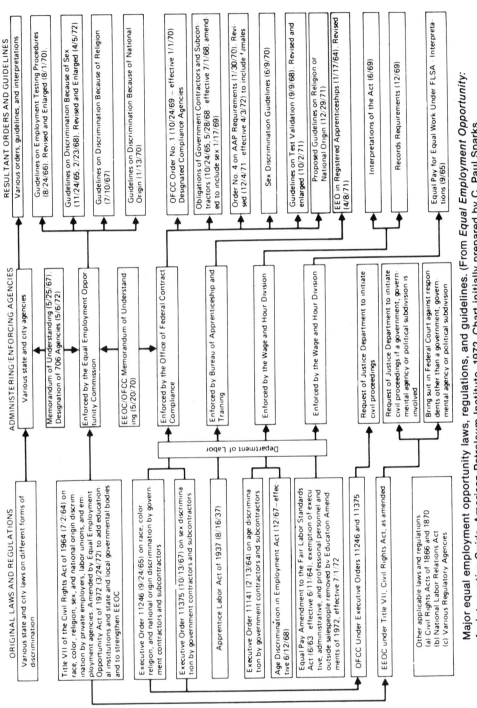

Major equal employment opportunity laws, regulations, and guidelines. (From *Equal Employment Opportunity: An Interpretive Guide,* American Petroleum Institute, 1972. Chart initially prepared by C. Paul Sparks, Humble Oil and Refining Company, Houston, Texas.)

1974—Employee Retirement Income Security Act of 1974 (ERISA)

This act, in effect, renegotiated every pension contract in the country. It provides for the creation of government-run, employer-financed corporations that will protect employees against a failing pension plan. In addition, it sets regulations regarding vesting rights (equity accorded an employee under a pension plan should his employment be terminated before retirement), portability rights (the transfer of an employee's vested benefits from one organization to another), and fiduciary standards to prevent dishonesty in the funding of pension plans. The Social Security Administration will maintain records of individuals entitled to pension plans.

FOR DISCUSSION AND REVIEW

1 Review each of the laws described in the article.
2 Tell how each law might affect an organization's wage and salary system.

E. E. Lawler

The Consequences of Pay Dissatisfaction

In the literature, pay dissatisfaction is said to be responsible for everything from poor job performance to strikes. Figure 13.1 shows some of the most frequently mentioned consequences of pay dissatisfaction. Despite the fact that pay satisfaction is often credited with the power to influence a large number of factors, there is no theory or view of why dissatisfaction with pay should affect all these variables. There are some mini-theories that try to explain why it affects one or two (Brayfield & Crockett, 1955), but most researchers have simply not tried to explain the relationships they have reported. It is likely that pay dissatisfaction affects such things as job performance and job satisfaction for somewhat different reasons. Because of this, we must—at least partially—work at the mini-theory level and deal separately with some of the variables shown in Figure 13.1.

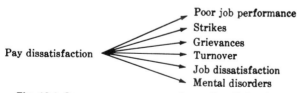

Fig. 13.1 Some consequences of pay dissatisfaction.

It is not necessary, however, to state a separate theory of why pay dissatisfaction influences turnover, absenteeism, strikes, etc. There are some common elements here, and we must try to recognize them. There are common elements in that many of these consequences of pay dissatisfaction are influenced by the same feel-

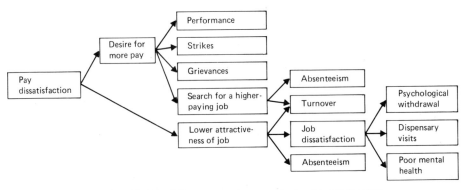

Fig. 13.2 Model of the consequences of pay dissatisfaction.

ings or reactions that people have when they are dissatisfied with their pay. Many of the behaviors shown in Figure 13.1 are behavioral outcroppings of the same kind of employee feelings, feelings that are influenced or affected by feelings of pay dissatisfaction. Figure 13.2, which is a Model of the Consequences of Pay Dissatisfaction, illustrates this point; it shows that two important kinds of feelings people have about their job are influenced by pay dissatisfaction. First, it shows that people's desire for money increases as pay dissatisfaction increases (Alderfer, 1969). Second it shows that the attractiveness of the job decreases as pay dissatisfaction increases. This simply reflects the fact that when a person says that he is dissatisfied with his pay, he is also saying that he regards the pay rewards associated with holding his job as too low. People are not attracted to jobs that have low rewards attached to them (Graen, 1969).

The model shows that it is the impact of pay dissatisfaction on the attractiveness of the job and on the person's desire for more money that relates pay dissatisfaction to such behaviors as absenteeism and turnover. Feelings of dissatisfaction, because of their impact on people's desire for money, lead to those behaviors which are likely to result in more money—joining a union, searching for a new job, performing better, presenting grievances, and striking. Because feelings of pay dissatisfaction lower the attractiveness of a job they lead to turnover, absenteeism, and job dissatisfaction. Thus, the model agrees with the frequently stated view that pay dissatisfaction is related to a number of variables (Herzberg, Mausner, Peterson, & Capwell, 1957). The model also argues that there are common underlying reasons that cause these various factors to be related to pay dissatisfaction. This approach is different from the usual approach, which treats the relationship between pay dissatisfaction and each of the variables separately (Brayfield & Crockett, 1955) and does not examine the reasons for the relationships. The model clearly points out the reason these diverse variables are related to pay dissatisfaction: that is, they are partially or wholly influenced by one or both of the important feelings or reactions that result when people are dissatisfied with their pay.

TURNOVER

The model shows that pay dissatisfaction can be a determinant of turnover. The emphasis here is on voluntary turnover, since the expectation is that pay dissatisfaction can affect only the employee's decision to change jobs, and this is what is reflected in voluntary turnover figures. Pay dissatisfaction should not be related to employer-initiated terminations. Chapter 11 focused on the decision to stay in the same job versus taking another job. It emphasized that a person will be motivated to accept another job and to quit his present one when he perceives that the valence of the outcomes associated with taking the new job are more positive than those associated with holding his present job. Since pay is one of the positively valued outcomes that a person gets for holding a job, and since the valence of pay generally increases with the amount, it follows that the higher the pay, the higher the valence of the job. Thus, other things equal, people will gravitate toward higher-paying jobs. It follows from this that turnover should be associated with pay dissatisfaction and job dissatisfaction. As has been stressed, when a person says he is dissatisfied with his pay he is also saying that he wants more money and that holding his job does not lead to highly valued pay outcomes (Graen, 1969). A person who says he is satisfied with his pay, on the other hand, is saying that holding his job does lead to highly valued pay outcomes. Clearly, the person who perceives that his job leads to highly valued rewards is more likely to hold onto his job than one who perceives that his job does not lead to such rewards. The former is less likely to search for other jobs and to see other jobs as more attractive than his present one.

It is not realistic, however, to predict that pay dissatisfaction should be perfectly correlated with turnover. First, pay is just one of the rewards that influences the attractiveness of a job. A person may be dissatisfied with his pay but satisfied with other job aspects, and because of this, he may feel that his present job is more desirable than any alternative one. He may also remain on his job even though he is dissatisfied with the pay if he feels that there is a low probability of obtaining a better-paying job. This would seem to be a particularly important influence in times of high unemployment. Thus, in such periods one might expect pay dissatisfaction to be quite unrelated to turnover; even though a person has a low-paying job, the probability of his finding a better one is low, and he therefore would not quit his present job. Note, too, that pay-desires satisfaction may influence turnover. A person may quit a job even though he is satisfied with his pay if he feels that his career pay objectives cannot be satisfied on it, but can be satisfied elsewhere. In summary, the thinking outlined so far suggests that turnover should bear a strong, but far from perfect, relationship to pay dissatisfaction and that the relationship should be strongest in periods of full employment.

Data from two studies generally support the view that people who are dissatisfied with their pay will be more likely to think about leaving their present job than people who are satisfied with their pay. Penner (1966) reports that employees dissatisfied with their pay were twice as likely to consider changing jobs as those who were satisfied. Similar data have been reported by Haire (unpublished) on the basis of a study of M.I.T. Sloan fellows.

There is also evidence that employees who are dissatisfied with their pay are not only more likely to think about leaving their jobs, but are actually more likely to leave in greater numbers than satisfied workers. As might be expected, many studies have shown that total job satisfaction is related to turnover (for reviews of this literature see Brayfield & Crockett, 1955; Herzberg, Mausner, Peterson, & Capwell, 1957; Schuh, 1967 and Vroom, 1964). In general the studies have found that pay dissatisfaction is a good predictor of turnover but that it is not as good a predictor as total job satisfaction. Hulin (1966) found a good relationship between overall satisfaction and turnover among female clerks, but little relationship between pay dissatisfaction and turnover. Hulin points out that this finding may be due to the fact that the female employees studied had low economic needs. This follows from the view presented in Chapter 10, which stressed that pay will not influence turnover unless it is important. Wickert (1951) has also represented data which show that pay dissatisfaction is not necessarily the best predictor of turnover. Hulin (1968) has recently reported a follow-up study on his original sample of clerks. It shows that when pay satisfaction increased among the employees, turnover dropped substantially. This, of course, provides evidence that pay satisfaction has the power to influence turnover even when pay is relatively unimportant. It is also in agreement with the point that turnover and pay dissatisfaction should be strongly related during periods of full employment, since the data were collected when employment was high. Some data collected by Weitz and Nucklos (1953) are in agreement with those reported by Hulin. They show that 83 percent of the employees who reported that their pay was adequate were still with the company at the end of a year, while only 67 percent of those who reported it was too low were still with the company. Thus, although the data are skimpy, they generally support the view that under most conditions pay dissatisfaction leads to turnover among employees to whom pay is important.

Three studies have presented data that indirectly support the view that pay dissatisfaction will be more strongly related to turnover in times of full employment than in times of unemployment. Behrend (1953) found evidence that in periods of unemployment very little voluntary turnover takes place. Similar data have been reported by Brissenden and Frankel (1922) and by Woytinsky (1942). This evidence does not, of course, provide direct support for the view that pay dissatisfaction and turnover will be more strongly related under conditions of full employment. In order to test this directly, one would need to compare the correlation of pay dissatisfaction and turnover during a period of full employment with the correlation of the two in a period of high unemployment, and this has not been done. The data suggest, however, that the correlation may be higher under full employment, since they support part of the reasoning that led to this view. The data show that a "reality" factor influences turnover decisions and that, because of this, in times of unemployment people are likely to hold onto their jobs even though they are dissatisfied with them. This condition undoubtedly comes about because no viable alternatives are available during periods of unemployment. Thus, in times of high unemployment, it is unlikely that pay dissatisfaction would bear a strong positive relationship to turnover. On the other hand, in the full-employment situation where a number of people are changing jobs, pay dissatisfaction has been shown to be positively related to turnover by several studies.

In summary, the data generally support the view that pay dissatisfaction is related to turnover; they clearly indicate, however, that the two are not always highly related. The relationship seems to be strongly affected by general employment conditions, by the person's satisfaction with other aspects of his job, and by the importance the individual attaches to pay.

ABSENTEEISM

The model in Figure 13.2 shows that absenteeism may be affected by pay dissatisfaction. It is not necessarily true, however, that a strong relationship should be expected, as a brief look at why they might be expected to be related should explain. The discussion of the job-attendance decision emphasized that the decision is based upon a comparison of the valence of the outcomes associated with going to work and the valence of those associated with not going. A number of the outcomes involved here are not monetary, and for this reason pay factors can never predict absenteeism perfectly. People might decide to go to work to see their friends, regardless of the financial outcomes. But even where pay dissatisfaction comes into play, it is a rather indirect influence. As the model shows, it influences the attractiveness of the job, which, in turn, is one factor that influences absenteeism. Job attractiveness can influence absenteeism because in many organizations high absenteeism can lead to loss of job. Where this is true, it would stand to reason that people will go to work regularly to protect the job they hold if and only if the job is attractive to them. Thus, high job attractiveness should lead to low absenteeism where absenteeism means loss of job.

Pay dissatisfaction should also be related to absenteeism if a person will lose his pay for not showing up for work. The more dissatisfied the person is with his pay, the less he tends to value the amount he will lose by not showing up. Because of this attitude, the person who is dissatisfied with his pay will be less likely to show up than the one who is satisfied. Thus, low pay satisfaction can be a cause of absenteeism when absenteeism means loss of money. When absenteeism does not mean loss of pay or loss of job then the previously stated reasons to expect pay dissatisfaction to be related to absenteeism do not appear to hold.

The model shows that searching for a new job might also lead to high absenteeism. This reflects the fact that employees are sometimes absent from their job in order to look for a new job. Since looking for a new job is often motivated by pay dissatisfaction, it follows that pay dissatisfaction can potentially cause absenteeism even when absenteeism is not likely to cause loss of pay or job. This factor is likely to operate only when other possible jobs are available. Equity theory would also predict that pay dissatisfaction would lead to absenteeism. According to equity theory, underpayment should lead employees to try to reduce their inputs, and certainly one way to do this is to be absent. In short there are a number of different reasons for predicting that pay dissatisfaction will lead to high absenteeism, but most of them apply only under certain conditions. Thus, although in most situations it might be expected that pay dissatisfaction and absenteeism will be related, the reason for the relationship will vary, depending on such factors as whether or not absenteeism is perceived to result in loss of pay or loss of job and whether or not alternative jobs are available locally.

One of the difficulties in doing research on absenteeism is that absenteeism is not a unitary trait. A simple measure of how many days a person is absent from work reflects absences due to a number of causes. People can be absent because of sickness and injury and because they simply have decided not to make the effort to come to work. There is no reason to believe that pay dissatisfaction can strongly influence absences that are due to many kinds of sickness or disability. It is possible, however, that it can influence absences that are due to certain kinds of mental and psychosomatic illnesses. What is needed, of course, is a measure of absenteeism that reflects a person's tendency to go to work when is physically able. On this measure, the record of a person who loses thirty days a year because of actual sickness should look different from that of a person who loses thirty days a year because he is not motivated to go to work. Unfortunately, there is no direct way to establish why a person missed work on a given day. Metzner and Mann (1953) have suggested that data on frequency of absence best reflect how motivated the person is to go to work. A measure of total days absent seems to be more heavily weighted by illness-caused absence. Illness tends to lead to long periods of absence. A record of many one- or two-day absences, on the other hand, usually reflects lack of motivation to appear for work. Thus, number of separate absence periods probably is a better measure of a person's motivation, although it is far from a perfect measure.

Despite the difficulties of measuring absenteeism, several studies have reported significant relationships between overall job satisfaction and absenteeism. Kerr, Koppelmeir, and Sullivan (1951) have reported a relationship of −.44 between absenteeism and job satisfaction, and Fleishman, Harris, and Burtt (1955) have reported a correlation of −.25 between morale and absence rates. Two studies have looked specifically at the relationship between absenteeism rate and pay dissatisfaction. Metzner and Mann (1953) report that only 43 percent of white-collar workers who were absent four or more times in six months were satisfied with their pay while 69 percent of those who were absent once or not at all were satisfied. Van Zelst and Kerr (1953) report that pay satisfaction correlates −.17 with number of days absent. This is a low correlation, but not surprising in light of the fact that this study used number of days absent as its measure of absenteeism. As was pointed out, this measure is not very sensitive to the kind of absenteeism that is expected to occur because of pay dissatisfaction. Overall, there is not a great deal of evidence to support the view that absenteeism can result from pay dissatisfaction; but what data there are, are consistent with this view. Clearly, research is needed to determine how different factors affect the relationship between absenteeism and pay dissatisfaction.

PERFORMANCE

In the last twenty years, the relationship between job satisfaction and job performance has been given much research attention. It is beyond the scope of this book to treat in detail the history of this research (see Porter & Lawler, 1968a). It is appropriate, however, to point out that initially the researchers expected that job satisfaction should be related to job performance, because of the strong influence of job satisfaction on job performance (Brayfield & Crockett, 1955). The evidence has not supported this view. Most studies have found only weak relationships between job satisfaction and performance. Vroom (1964) reports a median correlation of .14 between the two. As he points out, some researchers have reported strong positive relationships, while others have reported strong negative relationships. Lawler and Porter (1967b) have stressed that job satisfaction, rather than being a cause of performance, may be caused by performance. They point out that good performance often leads to high rewards, which, in turn, lead to high satisfaction and thus they predict that job satisfaction should be related to performance only where rewards are related to performance. Lawler and Porter (1967b) present some data to support their prediction, and they are in agreement with the view that satisfaction is sometimes strongly related to performance but at other times not.

The model in Figure 13.2 suggests that pay dissatisfaction possibly can affect job performance. Pay dissatisfaction leads to a stronger desire for more pay, which can lead to a strong motivation to perform. This of course will happen only where good performance is seen to lead to higher pay. According to this line of reasoning, it is possible to predict that pay dissatisfaction should lead to better performance when workers feel that pay is based upon performance. To the extent that this tendency operates, it should lead to a negative relationship between pay satisfaction and performance. It is also possible that pay dissatisfaction and a desire for more money may lead to lower productivity. Whyte (1955) has pointed out that workers on piece rates sometimes restrict their production in an effort to induce management to raise the rates. Thus, rather than producing more in order to earn more, they produce less—at least on a short-term basis. Still, it is important to note that they are motivated to produce less by a desire to earn more.

These are not the only tendencies that are likely to influence the relationship between pay satisfaction and performance. Pay satisfaction is influenced by the amount of money a person receives and by the amount he feels he should receive. Where good performers actually receive more pay than poor performers, there should be a tendency for pay satisfaction to be positively related to performance because of the ability of good performance to lead to higher pay and the ability of higher pay to lead to greater pay satisfaction. In this situation there should be a positive relationship between pay satisfaction and performance.

Overall, it appears that there is one tendency that could lead to a negative correlation between pay satisfaction and performance (pay dissatisfaction → desire for pay) and another that could lead to a positive correlation (performance → pay → pay satisfaction). Given these conflicting tendencies, it is no wonder that there has often been confusion about the relationship between pay satisfaction and job performance. If these two tendencies are of equal strength, then one would expect a zero relationship between pay satisfaction and performance. One would also expect a zero relationship between pay satisfaction and performance where pay is not related to performance, since for either of these tendencies to come into play, pay must be related to performance. Depending upon which of the tendencies is stronger, one would expect a different kind of relationship to exist between pay and performance. If the pay dissatisfaction-causes-performance tendency is stronger, then performance should be negatively related to pay satisfaction, but if the performance-leads-to-pay tendency is stronger, then pay satisfaction should be positively related to performance.

There are some good reasons to believe that the performance-leads-to-pay tendency will be stronger in most situations and that, because of this, pay satisfaction typically will be positively related to performance. Desire for pay is only one of many factors that influence performance, and pay satisfaction is only one of several factors that influence desire for pay. Thus, the causal link from pay satisfaction to performance is inevitably a very weak one and for this reason would rarely be expected to create a strong tendency for pay satisfaction to affect performance. On the other hand, the causal link from performance to pay can be quite strong, as can the link from pay to pay satisfaction. Thus, it is possible that performance can fairly strongly influence pay satisfaction. According to this line of reasoning it would be expected that where pay is based upon performance, pay satisfaction should be positively related to performance. Where pay is not based upon performance, however, pay satisfaction and performance should not be related. Where pay is negatively related to performance, then pay satisfaction should be negatively related to performance. Finally, it should be noted that pay satisfaction might be negatively related to performance where pay is not related to performance, but where people feel they can obtain more pay by performing well. This situation is unlikely to exist, but if it did, a negative relationship should exist because of the tendency of people who are dissatisfied with their pay to work harder in order to earn more money. The performance-leads-to-pay tendency would not be operating in this case and thus there would not be the offsetting tendency that might lead the higher performers to be more satisfied with their pay.

Two studies have specifically focused on the relationship between pay satisfaction and performance under conditions of pay based upon performance and under conditions of pay not based upon performance. These studies are, of course, just what is needed to test the view that performance will be positively related to pay satisfaction where pay is based upon performance, but not related where pay is not based on performance. In the more interesting of these studies Schneider and Olson (1970) found a correlation of .25 between performance and pay satisfaction in a merit pay hospital, but a 0 correlation between them in a hospital where pay was based upon seniority. Porter and Lawler (1968a) have reported somewhat similar data, showing that, for a group of managers whose pay was not based upon performance, no relationship existed between pay satisfaction and performance. For a group whose pay was performance-based, however, they found a positive relationship. This evidence suggests that the stronger causal tendency is that of performance causing pay satisfaction, rather than pay satisfaction causing performance, since a positive relationship would be expected from the view that performance causes pay satisfaction. It also supports the view that pay satisfaction will be related to performance only when pay is based upon performance. . . .

JOB SATISFACTION

Figure 13.2 shows that pay dissatisfaction tends to decrease the attractiveness of a job and, as a result, tends to lead to high job dissatisfaction. When a person says he is dissatisfied with his pay, he is saying that one aspect of his job (his pay) is not attractive to him or, in other words, not what he feels it should be. Since a person's feeling of job satisfaction is influenced directly by his feeling with respect to the adequacy of the important elements of the job, it follows that a person who is dissatisfied with his pay is likely to be less satisfied with his job than is a person who is satisfied with his pay. Pay satisfaction, however, should not be expected to bear a very close relationship to overall job satisfaction. It is only one of a number of important influences on how satisfied a person will be with his job. In order to predict job satisfaction well, one must know how satisfied a person is in all the areas of the job that are important to him (Schaffer, 1953). Knowing how satisfied a person is with his pay provides one clue about how satisfied he is with his job. In some instances, it may turn out to be a surprisingly good predictor of job satisfaction. One of the reasons is that the degrees of satisfaction which employees express concerning different aspects of their jobs often are correlated moderately well (Vroom, 1964). Thus, when a person says he is dissatisfied with his pay, he is also likely to be dissatisfied with other aspects of his job, and therefore to express high overall job dissatisfaction.

Studies have tried to determine the impact of pay satisfaction on job satisfaction by asking employees what influences their job satisfaction. Typically employees have reported that pay satisfaction influences job satisfaction. In one of the earlier studies of this type, Walker and Guest (1952) found that of 180 workers interviewed, 126 gave "good pay" as an important reason for liking their jobs. In another early study of this type, Evans and Laseau (1950) found that 41 percent of the employees at G.M. reported that wages were an important determinant of job satisfaction.

More recently a number of studies of this type have been done, almost all of them designed to test Herzberg's two-factor theory of job satisfaction. It is beyond the scope of this book to review all this research, but it is important to note a few of the points which are relevant to pay satisfaction. Based upon their initial study, Herzberg et al. (1959) classified pay as a dissatisfier, that is, as a factor which contributes to or affects only dissatisfaction. According to this view, feelings of pay satisfaction cannot lead to feelings of job satisfaction, but feelings of pay dissatisfaction can lead to feelings of job dissatisfaction. The data from that study, however, supported the view that pay can operate both as a dissatisfier and as a satisfier. That is, the data showed that when people are satisfied with their pay they feel good about their job, but when they are dissatisfied with their pay they feel dissatisfied with their job. At least fifty studies have tested Herzberg's theory since 1959, and they have consistently tended to replicate the finding of the original study as far as pay is concerned. Pay is mentioned as a factor that can cause dissatisfaction and as a factor that can cause satisfaction (House & Wigdor, 1967). This would seem to provide strong support for the view that pay satisfaction/dissatisfaction can and does influence job satisfaction/dissatisfaction. This evidence is particularly important since it provides some support for the view expressed in the model—that it is pay satisfaction that influences job satisfaction rather than the reverse.

A second approach to studying the relationship between job satisfaction and pay satisfaction involves simply correlating the two factors. According to our model, the expectation would be that they should bear a moderate positive relationship to each other. Data from a number of studies are in agreement with this view. Wernimont (1964) has reported a correlation of .19 between pay satisfaction and job satisfaction. Hulin and Smith (1967) have reported correlations of .32 and .30 between pay satisfaction and job satisfaction for male and female office workers. Of particular interest in this study is the finding that feelings of pay satisfaction correlated with subjects' statements about both their feeling of job satisfaction and their feeling of job dissatisfaction. This is important since it supports the view that people's feelings of satisfaction with their pay influence their feelings of both job satisfaction and job dissatisfaction. Thus, it appears that at least for pay it does not make sense to speak of job satisfaction and job dissatisfaction as on two separate continuums à la Herzberg. Pay satisfaction seems to affect employees' feelings of job satisfaction and job dissatisfaction as if a continuum stretching from satisfied to dissatisfied existed.

Armstrong (1968) has reported correlations of .18 and .37 between pay satisfaction and job satisfaction. Hinrichs (1968) reports that pay satisfaction correlates between .28 and .43 with job satisfaction for five groups of employees. Thus, it seems that pay satisfaction typically correlates around .30 with job satisfaction. This is not a high correlation, but it is in line with the view that pay satisfaction is just one of a number of variables which influence job satisfaction. Overall, a large amount of evidence has been reviewed which supports the view that pay satisfaction is an important influence on job satisfaction. When employees are satisfied with their pay, this contributes to their feeling of job satisfaction, and when they are dissatisfied, this contributes to their feelings of dissatisfaction.

PAY AND JOB SATISFACTION

A number of studies have shown that the amount of pay a person receives for holding his job correlates with his job satisfaction. This, of course, should be expected from the relationship found between pay satisfaction and job satisfaction. Amount of pay influences pay satisfaction, and pay satisfaction influences job satisfaction. It does not follow, however, that amount of pay should be very highly correlated with pay satisfaction. . . . Amount of pay is only one of a number of influences on pay satisfaction, and as has been stressed, pay satisfaction is only one of the factors which influence job satisfaction.

Typical of the actual relationships found between pay rates and job satisfaction is that reported by Smith and Kendall (1963). Within the plants they studied, they found a mean correlation of .25 between wage rate and job satisfaction. Studies which report positive correlations between satisfaction and income have been done on college graduates (Barnett, Handelsman, Stewart, & Super, 1952; Miller, 1941; Thompson, 1939), on British factory workers (Marriott & Denerley, 1955), and on a national sample of American workers (Centers & Cantril, 1946). Stockford and Kunze (1950) report that workers who begin a new job with wages that are low compared with their previous wages have more negative attitudes toward the employer and are more likely to quit. This finding fits with the view that the impact of pay rate on satisfaction is influenced by both actual pay level and by wage history. In this study, as would be expected, attitudes were more closely related to relative wage rate than to absolute wage rate. When all the evidence is considered together, a rather strong case can be made to support the view that wage rates bear a moderate relationship to job satisfaction.

UNION MEMBERSHIP, STRIKES, AND GRIEVANCES

Joining a union, filing grievances, and going on strike are behaviors which employees can use to obtain more money. The model shows that employees who want more money are particularly prone to engage in these activities. Since pay dissatisfaction causes an increased desire for more money, it follows that pay dissatisfaction should lead to more strikes and grievances. There is quite a bit of evidence to support the view that pay dissatisfaction and the resultant desire for more pay are an important influence on union membership, strikes, and grievance behavior. Stagner (1956) reports data which show that employees see unions as organizations that can help them to obtain higher wages and that employees join unions in order to obtain higher wages. Related to these points is a study by Smith (1962). His data show that employees who are dissatisfied with their jobs feel more positive toward unions than do satisfied employees. Thus, it appears that when employees are dissatisfied with their jobs and want more pay, they feel more positive toward unions and are likely to join them because of the perceived ability of unions to obtain more money for most employees.

A study by James (1951) shows a direct relationship between pay satisfaction and strike behavior. He compared a group of striking workers with a comparable control group of workers who were not striking. The strikers showed much higher levels of pay dissatisfaction than did the controls. Unfortunately, James had no measure of the workers' attitudes before the strike. It would be helpful to know if the level of pay dissatisfaction could predict the occurrence of strikes. Still, the data do provide some support for the view that pay dissatisfaction can lead to strikes, and there is a great deal of evidence that pay dissatisfaction is an important influence on employees' willingness to strike. Basically, the research evidence suggests that dissatisfaction with wages, hours, and fringe benefits is given by unions as the principal cause for 70 to 80 percent of all strikes. The evidence also suggests that strike frequency in a country is closely related to some economic indicators. One relationship shows that as unemployment goes up, strikes tend to be less frequent. This undoubtedly reflects the fact that people are more satisfied with their own job when they see many other people out of work, and it probably reflects the riskiness of a strike in periods of economic downturn. Strike frequency is not perfectly related to economic conditions, however.

It is all too easy to overemphasize the role that economic issues play in causing strikes because such issues are easy to identify and talk about. The evidence is clear that they are just one of a number of causes of strikes. They may be the most important, but this remains to be shown. All that is clear at this point is that they are important and that they are the most frequently talked about reason for going on strike. One difficulty encountered in doing research on this topic is that it is socially acceptable to talk about striking for more money, but it is not so easy to talk of striking for more interesting work. Thus, about all that can be concluded is that, as shown in the model, strikes are motivated by economic conditions.

Practically the same points that were made in discussing strikes can be made in discussing grievances. Grievances do frequently seem to be filed as a result of pay dissatisfaction, and a large number of them are specifically concerned with economic issues, particularly where wage incentive plans are in effect (Whyte, 1955).

But like strikes, grievances are often caused by other kinds of dissatisfaction. They can be an effective way of harassing management and venting employee hostility over other issues. Grievances over economic issues like strikes are a socially acceptable way to express these kinds of dissatisfaction. Because of this situation, we must be careful not to overinterpret the role of pay dissatisfaction in producing grievances.

In summary, the evidence quite clearly shows that, as suggested by the model, pay dissatisfaction can lead employees to join unions, go on strike, and file grievances. In general, the link between these behaviors and pay dissatisfaction seems to be stronger than the link between pay dissatisfaction and such behaviors as absenteeism and performance. Overall, it is clear that pay dissatisfaction can be quite costly to organizations. It erodes people's commitment to their jobs and leads to absenteeism, turnover, and other important but not always fully appreciated causes of low productivity, poor performance, and high costs.

THE EFFECTS OF OVERPAYMENT

It was stressed . . . that perceived overpayment produces quite a different reaction in people from perceived underpayment. Overpayment produces feelings of guilt, discomfort, and anxiety which, as equity theory stresses, people try to reduce. There are a number of ways in which this can be done. . . . Four of the most important ways [are described below].

Unfortunately, very little research has been done on how people reduce feelings of inequity due to overpayment, although some research has been done on the effects of overpayment on productivity and quality. There has also been relatively little research on why people choose different modes of inequity reduction.

Altering outcomes

The evidence [presented earlier] suggested . . . that people will reduce their outcomes when they are paid on a piece rate by restricting their productivity. There is little research to prove it, but it seems that people may also decrease their outcomes by reducing the perceived value or amount of some of the nonmonetary outcomes of their job. They may, for example, come to feel that a task is boring and uninteresting and thereby reduce the intrinsic outcomes of the job. Changing their cognition of the outcomes is probably the preferred way of reducing feelings of overpayment for most people, at least it is probably preferable to decreasing pay outcomes. The latter is obviously financially expensive, whereas changing cognitions about task interest and value involves relatively little cost.

Altering inputs

[The evidence] suggests that when subjects are overpaid they may increase their inputs in order to reduce their feeling of inequity, although . . . it is not clear that this actually leads them to work harder. There is evidence that it may lead them to increase their perceptions of their inputs. Thus, in one study (Lawler, Koplin, Young, & Fadem, 1968), it was found that overpaid subjects reported higher qualifications than equitably paid subjects, despite the fact that the former were initially made to feel overpaid by being told that they had low job qualifications. It is hardly surprising that people are more inclined to increase their perception of their inputs than to increase their actual inputs. Clearly, the former is much easier and less costly. People can also increase their perceived inputs by increasing their perception of the difficulty of the job they are doing. Again, changing this perception is much easier than actually working harder. Unfortunately, very little attention has been given to the effects of overpayment on employees' perceptions of their own inputs. Most of the research has tried to measure the behavioral consequences of overpayment. This is too bad, since it is quite possible that in actual work situations employees change their perception of their inputs rather than their behavior when confronted with feelings of overpayment. Thus, the strongest impact of overpayment may be on perceptions rather than on job behavior directly.

Changing comparison other

People may reduce feelings of overpayment by changing their comparison other. Although this subject has received little research attention, Patchen (1961) has established that comparisons are important and that subjects who make certain kinds of comparisons feel inequity while others do not. Patchen also found that very few people chose comparison others who had less favorable input-outcome balances than themselves. It would seem to follow that by changing the comparison other from someone who has a balance similar to or better than himself, a person could reduce his feelings of overpayment. This may be a common method of reducing feelings of overpayment, since it is certainly easy to do and, according to equity theory, should be very effective.

Other's inputs and outcomes

Overpayment inequity may be reduced by changing one's perception of the input-outcome balance of the comparison other. Specifically, this might involve upgrading other's outcomes or downgrading his inputs. Lawler (in press) has presented a great deal of evidence to show that subjects often do distort the pay outcomes of others. What is more, other's pay outcomes are usually distorted upward, and the more they are distorted upward, the less likely is the person who is distorting them to feel overpaid. This provides at least some evidence that distorting other people's outcomes is a viable way to reduce one's feelings of being overpaid, and it suggests that people use it to reduce feelings of inequity due to overpayment. It is also possible to downgrade the inputs of others in order to reduce or prevent a feeling of overpayment. Adams (1965) has presented some evidence that this does in fact happen, but other supporting evidence is very sparse. It would seem to be a relatively frequent approach to reducing feelings of overpayment, since it can be done at a relatively low cost and does not require a serious realignment of one's self-image or perceptual system.

PREFERRED METHODS OF REDUCING FEELINGS OF INEQUITY DUE TO OVERPAYMENT

Adams (1965) has presented some propositions that attempt to predict which inequity reduction approach people will choose. He suggests, as has been stressed here, that certain types of cognitive changes may be the most frequently chosen. As a general rule it seems that people will avoid choosing an inequity reduction approach that:

1 Will result in their losing positively valued outcomes (e.g., money)
2 Will have negatively valued consequences for them (e.g., getting tired from working hard for extra productivity or quality)
3 Will involve a major change in their self-image or concept.

Thus, the preferred methods of reducing feelings of inequity due to overpayment will be (roughly in order of preference):

1 Changing comparison other (unless it is long established and related to a person's self-concept)

2 Changing the perception of comparison person's inputs and/or outcomes
3 Raising the perception of own inputs (unless low inputs are central to self-image)
4 Reducing the perceived value of own outcomes.

These four relatively preferred approaches involve cognitive changes. Actually altering one's inputs and outcomes clearly would rank very low in such a list. This suggests that more support for equity theory might be found in studies that examine cognitive changes than has been found in the studies that have looked for behavioral changes. Many of the latter studies may have missed important cognitive changes that were going on.

Given the large number of ways of reducing feelings of overpayment and the ease with which many of them can be employed, it is hardly surprising that most researchers have reported that very few employees actually feel overpaid (Lawler, 1965a). Still, the effect of overpayment is of interest, particularly on a theoretical level, since by studying how people reduce feelings of overpayment, one can learn something about how people deal with uncomfortable feelings, such as guilt. Clearly, the whole topic of why people choose different approaches to reducing inequity is open to research.

Overall, the evidence shows that both underpayment and overpayment affect pay satisfaction. The effects of underpayment have been researched more extensively, and they also seem to be more relevant for organizations, since they include such things as absenteeism, turnover, and strikes—which have a direct impact on organizational effectiveness. Overpayment on the other hand seems to be dealt with on a cognitive level. It is possible for employees to deal with underpayment on a cognitive level. They could for example change their comparison other or increase their perception of their inputs but there is little evidence to suggest that they do deal with their feelings of perceived underpayment this way. Feelings of underpay seem to be effectively dealt with only by an increase in pay and probably because of this they are much more stable and long lasting than are feelings of overpayment.

REFERENCES

Adams, J. S. Injustices in social exchange. In L. Berkowitz (Ed), *Advances in Experimental Social Psychology*. Vol. 2. New York: Academic, 1965, 267–299.

Alderfer, C. P. An empirical test of a new theory of human needs. *Organizational Behavior and Human Performances*, 1969, 4, 142–175.

Armstrong, T. B. Occupational level as an indicator of "satisfactiers" and "dissatisfiers": A test of the Herzberg et al. theory. Paper presented at I.B.M. Personnel Research Conference, August 1968.

Barnett, G. J., Handelman, I., Stewart, L. H., & Super, D. E. The occupational level scale as a measure of drive. *Psychological Mongraphs*, 1952, 66, No. 10 (Whole No. 342).

Behrend, H. Absence and labour turnover in a changing economic climate. *Occupational Psychology*, 1953, 27, 69–79.

Brayfield, A. H., & Crockett, W. H. Employee attitudes and employee performance. *Psychological Bulletin*, 1955, 52, 396–424.

Brissenden, P. F., & Frankel, E. *Labor Turnover in Industry*. New York: Macmillan, 1922.

Centers, R., & Cantril, H. Income satisfaction and income aspiration. *Journal of Abnormal and Social Psychology*, 1946, 41, 64–69.

Evans E. E., & Laseau, LaV. N. My job contest. *Personnel Psychology*. Monograph No. 1, 1950.

Fleishman, E. A., Harris, E. F., & Burtt, H. E. *Leadership and Supervision in Industry.* Columbus: Ohio State University, Bureau of Educational Research, 1955.

Graen, G. Instrumentality theory of work motivation: some experimental results and suggested modifications. Journal of industrial supervisors. *Personnel Psychology*, 1962, 15, 303–314.

Haire, M. Questionnaire on pay. Unpublished paper. Cambridge, Mass.: M.I.T.

Herberz, F., Mausner, B., Peterson, R. O., & Capwell, D. F. *Job Attitudes: Review of Research and Opinion.* Pittsburgh: Psychological Service of Pittsburgh, 1957.

House, R. J., & Wigdor, L. A. Herzberg's dual-factor theory of job satisfaction and motivation: a review of the evidence and a criticism. *Personnel Psychology*, 1967, 20, 369–390.

Hulin, C. L. Job satisfaction and turnover in a female clerical population. *Journal of Applied Psychology*, 1966, 50, 280–285.

Hulin, C. L. Effects of changes in job-satisfaction levels on employee turnover. *Journal of Applied Psychology*, 1968, 52, 122–126.

Hulin, C. L., & Smith, P. A. An empirical investigation of two implications of the two-factor theory of job satisfaction. *Journal of Applied Psychology*, 1967, 51, 396–402.

James, J. An experimental study of tensions in work behavior. *University of California Publications in Culture and Society*, 1951, 2, (4) 203–242.

Jerr, W. A., Koppelmeir, G., & Sullivan, J. J. Absenteeism, turnover and morale in a metal fabrication factory. *Occupational Psychology*, 1951, 25, 50–55.

Lawler, E. E. Manager's perceptions of their subordinates' pay and of their superiors' pay. *Personnel Psychology*, 1965, 18, 413–422(a).

Lawler, E. E. Secrecy and the need to know. In R. House, M. Dunnette, & H. Tosi (Eds.), *Readings in Managerial Motivation and Compensation,* in press.

Lawler, E. E., Koplin, C. A., Young, T. F., & Fadem, J. A. Inequity reduction over time in an induced overpayment situation. *Organizational Behavior and Human Performance*, 1968, 3, 253–268.

Lawler, E. E., & Porter, L. W. The effect of performance on job satisfaction. *Industrial Relations*, 1967, 7, 20–28.(b)

Marriott, R., & Denerley, R. A. A method of interviewing used in studies of workers' attitudes: II. Validity of the method and discussion of the results. *Occupational Psychology*, 1955, 29, 69–81.

Metzner, H., & Mann, F. Employee attitudes and absences. *Personnel Psychology*, 1953, 6, 467–485.

Miller, D. C. Economic factors in the morale of college trained adults. *American Journal of Sociology*, 1941, 47, 139–156.

Patchen, M. *The Choice of Wage Comparisons.* Englewood Cliffs, N. J.: Prentice-Hall, 1961.

Penner, D. D. A study of the causes and consequences of salary satisfaction. Crotonville, N. Y.: General Electric Behavioral Research Service (mimeo), 1966.

Porter, L. W., & Lawler, E. E. *Managerial Attitudes and Performance.* Homewood, Ill.: Irwin-Dorsey, 1968. (a)

Schaffer, R. H. Job satisfaction as related to need satisfaction in work. *Psychological Monographs*, 1953, 67, (14), Whole No. 364.

Schneider, B., & Olson, L. K. Effort as a correlate of an organizational reward system and individual values. *Personnel Psychology,* 1970, 23, 313-326.

Schuh, A. J. The predictability of employee tenure: A review of the literature. *Personnel Psychology,* 1967, 20, 133-152.

Smith, K. H. Psychological inquiry into attitudes of industrial draftsmen toward unionism. Ph.D. dissertation, Wayne University, 1962.

Smith, P. C., & Kendall, L. M. Cornell Studies of job satisfaction: VI. Implications for the future. Unpublished manuscript, Cornell University, 1963.

Stager, R. *Psychology of Industrial Conflict.* New York: Wiley, 1956.

Stockford, L. O., & Kunze, K. R. Psychology and the pay check. *Personnel,* 1950, 27, 129-143.

Thompson, W. A. Eleven years after graduation. *Occupations,* 1939, 17, 709-714.

Van Zelst, R. H., & Kerr, W. A. Workers' attitudes toward merit rating. *Personnel Psychology,* 1953, 6, 159-172.

Vroom, V. H. *Work and Motivation.* New York: Wiley, 1964.

Walker, C. R., & Guest, R. H. *The Man on the Assembly Line.* Cambridge, Mass.: Harvard, 1952.

Weitz, J., & Nucklos, R. C. The validity of direct and indirect questions. Ph.D. dissertation, University of Minnesota, 1964.

Whyte, W. F. (Ed.) *Money and Motivation: An Analysis of Incentives in Industry.* New York: Harper, 1955.

Wickert, F. R. Turnover, and employees' feelings of ego-involvement in the day-to-day operations of a company. *Personnel Psychology,* 1951, 4, 185-197.

Woytinsky, W. S. *Three Aspects of Labor Dynamics.* Washington, D. C.: Social Science Research Council, 1942.

FOR DISCUSSION AND REVIEW

1 Review the negative consequences of pay dissatisfaction.
2 What is the relationship between job satisfaction and pay satisfaction?
3 Explain the way underpayment and overpayment perceptions might influence performance.
4 How is pay dissatisfaction related to strikes and grievances?

Richard W. Beatty
Craig Eric Schneier

A Case for Positive Reinforcement

Many managers can easily differentiate between their good and poor employees and appreciate the consequences of poor performance in terms of an organization's profit, productivity, and competitive advantage. The causes of poor performance have been examined frequently, and solutions have been offered in the form of improved techniques for selecting better employees, training programs to teach

From *Business Horizons,* April 1975, pp. 57-66. Copyright © 1975 by the Foundation for the School of Business at Indiana University. Reprinted by permission.

needed skills, and motivational schemes designed to increase the quantity and quality of performance on the job.

Managers, however, are involved only indirectly with selection and training problems; these matters are usually the primary responsibility of psychologists, personnel technicians, and other experts. Essentially, selection is a problem of picking the person to fit the job. Such a person possesses the knowledge, skills, and abilities needed to perform well, or can be trained if required. Industrial psychology and personnel administration have made some important advances in the areas of selection and training to aid managers. But the manager is usually left with ineffective employees, often described as having motivation problems, after the "experts" have departed. The major assumption underlying this type of performance problem is that the employee has the abilities and skills to perform well, but lacks the willingness to do so.

In attempting to solve motivation problems, two well-publicized performance improvement remedies have been proposed, each with a large and zealous following. These two approaches are job enrichment (JE) and management by objectives (MBO). Both have strengths and weaknesses, and each is applicable to different aspects of the motivation problem. However, these remedies are not the only ones available. The explicit systematic use of positive reinforcement (PR) is another approach, one with great potential for improving performance at work.

The major assumptions, advantages, and disadvantages of each of these three methods will be discussed and a case made for the use of PR as an alternative method for resolving motivation problems. PR can be used compatibly with JE and MBO.

JOB ENRICHMENT

JE is a motivational technique, familiar to most managers, which emphasizes the need for challenging and interesting work. It suggests that jobs be redesigned so that intrinsic satisfaction is derived from doing the job. In its best applications, JE leads to a "vertically" enhanced job by adding functions from other organizational levels, making the job contain more variety and challenge, and offer autonomy and pride to the employee. The essence of JE is thus to change the content of jobs and make the work more challenging and meaningful.

JE makes several assumptions about people which are frequently accepted as universal truths and which need to be made more explicit. First, JE assumes that when intrinsic satisfaction is offered, extrinsic rewards (those from outside the immediate job) become secondary in importance. Second, JE assumes that extrinsic rewards (for example, pay and working conditions), if effective at all, are only effective as motivators in the short run. Third, JE assumes that people require self-actualization on the job and look to jobs rather than off-the-job activities as their primary sources of satisfaction and self-actualization.

If we accept these assumptions concerning the reasons for the lack of motivation which leads to good performance, JE would seem to be an appropriate remedy for monotonous, routine jobs; for jobs with large accident, turnover, and absenteeism rates; or for organizations in which employees feel alienated or powerless. There are problems, however. JE cannot be successfully applied to all jobs. For example, many management jobs have been enriched with autonomy and responsibility, yet performance is lacking. There are also obvious problems in the implementation of JE; employees may want more and more say in policy formation, causing management to feel threatened with loss of power and control. Finally, for employees who want off-the-job satisfaction or are primarily concerned with work as a means to an end (for example, a bigger bag of groceries, a mortgage payment, or a new car), JE may simply not be appropriate.

In short, JE operates on the major premise that satisfaction, gained through self-actualization and challenge on the job, leads to high performance. But the existence of a direct causal sequence from satisfaction to performance has been doubted for some time. C. N. Greene, among others, has suggested that a reverse relationship (performance — satisfaction) may be more accurate.[1] That is, performance may be the cause—not the result—of satisfaction at work. The situations for which JE is applicable, its assumptions about motivation, and its motivational consequences are summarized in the accompanying table.

MANAGEMENT BY OBJECTIVES

The second remedy often proposed for motivation problems, MBO, is concerned with job performance, not job satisfaction. In MBO, employees help determine performance goals and are evaluated on the degree to which they attain these goals. Employees are made aware of what is expected of them and judged according to the "results." They are left free, within limits, to choose their own means of attaining their objectives. MBO usually proceeds through the following phases: goal setting, action planning, implementation, and review and evaluation. Many variants of the process are currently in vogue, however.

MBO, like JE, is founded on a set of implicit motivational assumptions. The MBO approach assumes that high performance can be achieved when employees know the specified goals, participate in the goal-setting process, and know the results. All of these are assumed to lead to increased employee motivation. With MBO, the cause of poor performance rests with ill-defined goals of the job, rather than job content, as in JE.

MBO would thus be appropriate where job results are not well understood and performance standards are ambiguous; where criteria for appraisal are inadequate or covertly subjective; where control problems are significant; where role conflict and/or role ambiguity exists; and where communication between superior and subordinates is poor. In such situations, MBO, because it develops explicit goals for which individuals and organizations are held accountable, could improve performance.

However, as in the case of JE, the assumptions on which MBO are based may not be universally applicable. Even if objectives are clearly identified and communicated, effective performance may not result. Employees may feel that the objectives are those of management and are determined irrespective of their needs. Further, there may be instances when the results have been produced by circumstances beyond the employee's control (for example, budget cuts and market deficiencies), despite considerable effort and desired job behavior. Thus, the relationship between job behavior and job performance may not be so direct as is often assumed in MBO. When employees see that behavior does not lead to desired results, perhaps because of factors beyond their control, they may quit trying.

The goal-setting process in MBO may also lead to an overemphasis on quantifiable results at the expense of collaboration and teamwork. MBO can cause suboptimization when one division or department attempts to maximize its objectives at the expense of other divisions' goals, and can cause minimally acceptable results to become organizational norms by the establishment of minimum outputs.

---

[1]   Charles N. Greene, "The Satisfaction–Performance Controversy," *Business Horizons* (October 1972), pp. 31–41.

Job Enrichment, Management by Objectives, and Positive Reinforcement: Compatible Solutions to the Motivation Problem

PROBLEM DIAGNOSIS	MOTIVATIONAL ASSUMPTIONS	JOB-TYPE APPLICABILITY	TIME FRAME FOR DISTRIBUTION OF REWARDS	MOTIVATIONAL CONSEQUENCES/IMPLICATIONS	
				POSITIVE	NEGATIVE
		JOB ENRICHMENT			
Jobs are extremely monotonous, segmented and routine. Apathy, absenteeism, and turnover are excessive.	JE assumes that intrinsic rewards from job content (for example, challenge and autonomy) are the keys to long-run motivation because people want to satisfy higher level needs on the job.	JE is the best for lower level jobs because these are typically routine and repetitive.	JE assumes that workers receive intrinsic satisfaction upon completion of a challenging job.	Jobs are more interesting and challenging; thus people are motivated to improve quality and to lower absenteeism and turnover.	Employees may feel that they have more to say about their jobs than they really do or than management intended. Some employees may not want challenging jobs, but simply a chance to earn money in order to satisfy their needs off the job.
		MANAGEMENT BY OBJECTIVES			
Jobs are ill-defined, and performance criteria are ambiguous and subjective. Employees feel they do not know where they stand and what is required of them.	MBO assumes that people will work to attain objectives to which they are committed. This commitment is attained by allowing employees to participate in goal setting.	MBO is difficult to apply to higher level jobs because these often have the most ambiguous objectives or standards.	MBO formally dispenses feedback in the appraisal interview. Informally, feedback can be dispensed by supervisors at anytime.	MBO can reduce ambiguity related to one's job, promote communication between superiors and subordinates, and allow effort to be directed to organizational goals.	By emphasizing results rather than behavior, MBO can ignore such factors as discretion and judgment and can overquantify job objectives. Employees may feel that their

POSITIVE REINFORCEMENT

Behavioral objectives are not specified or are ambiguous. There is heavy reliance on punishment and threat, and little provision for rewarding employees.

PR assumes that desired behavior must be positively reinforced in order to sustain it, that variable schedules of reinforcement are powerful for controlling behavior, and that punishment has some negative side-effects that deter its effectiveness.

PR can be applied to all jobs because it does not involve job content. Instead, it involves the relationship between job behavior and its consequences.

PR allows dispensed reinforcement to be of any one of several schedules (for example, continuous, fixed, or variable).

Performance can be improved if desired behavior is specified and linked to valued consequences. The use of punishment at work often leads to escape and avoidance behaviors rather than to an increase in desired behavior.

The same behavior can receive both positive and negative reactions from different groups, thus putting employees in a conflict situation. Identifying desired behavior is time consuming and costly; it requires detailed observation by supervisors, who are often already overburdened.

participation in goal setting is not authentic. They may be defensive and anxious about their evaluations and try to cover up their mistakes to make their performance look good.

Furthermore, organizations can be overburdened with the paperwork often required by MBO systems.

Finally, although good MBO programs stress continual feedback, perhaps the greatest deficiency in the implementation of MBO is failure to provide immediate feedback from management to employees. Often feedback comes only at prescribed intervals, such as the six- and twelve-month formal performance review sessions, and thus is often not received by employees immediately after performing a job. This is in direct contrast with what we know about the timing of effective feedback.

The improbability of universal application of MBO is due both to its primary focus on job results, while often ignoring job behavior, such as effort, and the practical problems often associated with its implementation. MBO is thus not a complete remedy to the problem of poor performance, although there are situations in which it is certainly applicable (see table).

An analysis of the motivational assumptions of JE and MBO shows that each may be effective in some instances, but neither is a panacea. Both approaches see the root of the problem as being in the nature of jobs—job content in the case of JE and job objectives in the case of MBO. Although JE and MBO can be effective remedies to performance problems, they are often seen as the only remedies, and thus they may be overused and applied indiscriminately, irrespective of the cause of poor performance. Another solution, Positive Reinforcement (PR) can offset the major weaknesses of both JE and MBO.

POSITIVE REINFORCEMENT

The emphasis in a PR program is placed on the desired job behavior that leads to job outcomes or results, rather than results alone; on providing direct links between job behavior and rewards; and on the use of positive reinforcement, rather than punishment or the threat of punishment.

At the base of the PR approach is the relationship between behavior and its consequences. Consequences can be viewed as outcomes in an individual's environment related to the demonstration of certain behaviors which may be thought of as positive and desirable (for example, praise from a supervisor) or negative and undesirable (for example, a disciplinary lecture). In both cases, the frequency of behavior may be increased as the result of these consequences. If the consequence does, in fact, increase the occurrence of the behavior it is called a reinforcer. For example, praise—a positive reinforcer—when dispensed after the employee arrives at work on time may increase the occurrence of punctuality. A negative reinforcer—a disciplinary lecture—dispensed after tardy arrival may also increase the occurrence of punctuality. However, increases in the occurrences of desired behavior through the use of an aversive stimulus are effective only if the person substitutes the desired behavior for the undesired behavior in order to avoid the aversive stimulus. (This may not necessarily be the case, as will be discussed later.)

Therefore, reinforcers (positive and negative) can be effective in controlling desired job behavior if they are closely linked to the performance they are meant to control. When reinforcement does not immediately follow the desired behavior, it loses much of its effectiveness because an employee fails to associate the contingent relationship between the cause (for example, desired job behavior) and the effect (for example, reward).

If we can specify behavior in the work setting that leads to effective performance, identify reinforcers that control behavior, and dispense positive reinforcement upon evidence of the desired behavior, we can improve performance.

Obviously, this procedure is already practiced; organizations do offer positive reinforcement for desired performance. However, the process is usually done poorly and unsystematically, with lengthy time lags and indirect ambiguous relationships between behavior and consequences. Further, negative reinforcement and punishment, rather than positive reinforcement, may be relied upon too heavily. These practices violate the major concepts of the PR model. Before expanding this point, a few more concepts of the PR model need to be introduced.

Schedules of reinforcement

The idea of schedules or frequency of reinforcement is also critical to the PR approach. Reinforcement can be dispensed on a "continuous" schedule, in which every appropriate behavior is reinforced, as in piece rate and commission pay plans, or on a "variable" schedule, in which only a proportion or ratio of desired behaviors is reinforced. Reinforcement can also be dispensed at fixed intervals of time, as when employees receive a weekly or biweekly salary, or where wages are computed on the basis of an interval of time (for example, hourly).

In fact, few work settings use variable or intermittent schedules in which they vary the scheduling of positive reinforcement for effective performance. For example, it is possible to reward an employee after five successful demonstrations of a specific job behavior, then after ten demonstrations, and so on. The number of behaviors required for reinforcement under this schedule may vary from one to ten, but will average around five per reward.

An example of the power of this variable ratio schedule is the slot machine. Reinforcement in the form of winning is not dispensed each time nor on a regular basis, but on a random or intermittent basis. Therefore, the player is highly motivated to continue playing; the next play may be a winner.

Continuous and variable schedules may differ in their effect upon desired behavior. When a reinforcer is withdrawn from a person accustomed to a continuous schedule, the person soon stops demonstrating the desired behavior, but if the reinforcer is removed from a person accustomed to a variable schedule he may continue to demonstrate desired behavior over a long period of time. Thus, the variable schedule is a more efficient and powerful tool in that fewer reinforcers tend to prolong the demonstration of desired behaviors.

Punishment

Unlike reinforcement, punishment influences behavior by presenting a negative stimulus or withdrawing a positive stimulus in order to reduce the frequency of undesirable behavior. The relationship between punishment and negative reinforcement is often confused; they differ in that punishment is designed to remove behavior from a repertoire while negative reinforcement generates behavior.

The punctuality example may help show how these two ideas are related. As stated earlier, negative reinforcement increases the frequency of an alternative behavior as a person seeks to avoid an aversive stimulus. But punishment decreases the frequency of behavior. In negative reinforcement, an aversive stimulus (a disciplinary lecture) that follows a behavior (arriving late to work) may increase the frequency of a desired behavior (punctuality) as this behavior removes the aversive stimulus. This occurs if punctuality is the next response in the employee's behavior repertoire when certain behavior is removed.

However, increased absenteeism may be the behavior strengthened by the negative reinforcement of tardiness. For example, if a person finds himself arising late in the morning and unable to get to work on time, he may decide to take the whole day off to avoid the disciplinary lecture. But the disciplinary lecture, when known to follow late arrival for work, is punitive if it decreases the frequency of future tardiness.

Decreasing the frequency of an undesirable behavior may not lead to the increase of a desired behavior or strengthen any specific alternative behavior. For example, to avoid the punishment associated with tardiness, an employee may resort to a series of undesired behaviors, such as increased absenteeism, lying about illness, or having other employees clock him in. These behaviors avoid punishment, but are damaging to the organization. They are, however, readily observed in organizations relying too heavily on punishment.

Because punishment often suppresses undesired behavior and does not necessarily replace undesirable behaviors with desirable ones, desirable behaviors must simultaneously be positively reinforced; otherwise, proper responses may not be learned. For example, a child brings home an unsatisfactory report card and the parent commands the child, "Never bring home a report card like that again!" To escape punishment, the child may learn not to bring the report card home or to duplicate the parent's signature on the card. What the child has not learned is how to improve his or her grades through hard work, because such behavior has not been rewarded by the parent. In addition, the child may also learn to dislike the parent, because the parent is a punishing agent, just as an employee may learn to dislike a punishing supervisor, and resort to absenteeism, turnover, or cover-up of mistakes to escape punishment.

The PR model in organizations

Perhaps the best-known example of the PR model is Emery Air Freight's experience under the direction of Edward Feeney, in which feedback is given to employees to show how actual performance differs from the employee's own perceptions and from company standards. This feedback is very important; it requires employees to change their behavior in the desired direction to receive positive reinforcement (often in the form of praise) and recognize when they are surpassing previous performance levels.

Emery's annual savings from the use of PR in one program alone (the use of containers for shipments) has been reported to be $650,000.[2] This system does not attempt to make jobs intrinsically rewarding (as JE does) or rely on mutual goal setting to help further structure job goals (as MBO does). Instead, the system concentrates upon immediate feedback on actual job behavior and uses positive reinforcement in the form of praise.

Lesser known examples of the success of the PR model include training programs where positive reinforcement is used systematically to hasten learning; an organization which gives cash bonuses for perfect attendance; a hardware store which uses a lottery to reward those with exemplary attendance records; and a manufacturing organization in which attendance is significantly improved by the use of variable schedules to dispense rewards. In another example, Michigan Bell Telephone experimented with PR and reported that the absenteeism of 1,000 operators was cut almost in half when schedules were changed to permit immediate reinforcement.

---

[2]   For reports of Feeney's efforts, see "At Emery Air Freight: Positive Reinforcement Boosts Performance," *Organizational Dynamics* (Winter 1973), pp. 41–50, and "Performance Audit, Feedback, and Positive Reinforcement," *Training and Development Journal* (November 1972), pp. 8–13.

CRITICISMS OF JE AND MBO

The PR approach is also critical of traditional methods of rewarding performance in organization. Ambiguous relationships too often exist between performance and rewards because they fail to specify the behavior necessary in order to receive rewards. In fact, in many job situations rewards are offered not for performing well or even adequately, but for not performing poorly, with no provisions for rewarding excellent performance.

Further, we are guilty of neglecting what we know about the importance of immediate feedback. Techniques like MBO can help identify excellent performance, but the evaluation process in MBO is typically held some time after performance; therefore, the effect of the reward given for that performance is considerably lessened. For example, in a recent discussion of the use of money to motivate managers, Sidney R. Wilson noted an inconsistency: "Rarely is there an identifiable relationship between changes in compensation (salary, bonus, or stock) and personal performance. Even if there were, the reward comes so long after the performance that it could not possibly have any incentive value."[3]

Further, because rewards are often not contingent upon desired behaviors, employees do not know precisely why they received a reward. Perhaps more important, they do not know specifically what must be done in order to receive awards. Thus, we often not only fail to build a direct relationship between desired behavior and reward and fail to reward immediately after the observation of desired behavior, but also we may be actually reinforcing poor performance. This is because many rewards appear to be available to employees regardless of performance level. If we pay an employee every week and offer little or no reinforcement during that period, we are actually reinforcing both desired and undesired behaviors.

Management by exception or punishment?

In addition to the ineffective use of rewards through systems such as MBO, the technique known as management by exception can be seen as a means of negative reinforcement or as punishment. If management by exception is used, employees know that only when something goes wrong will they be contacted by a supervisor. They may be docked in pay or called into the superior's office or somehow be confronted. Therefore, they may not be working for rewards, but may be merely trying to avoid punishment.

This approach may be satisfactory in accomplishing desired behavior if the desired behavior is the next in the person's response hierarchy. If not, as previously noted, desired behavior may not be forthcoming and unfortunate side-effects such as avoidance and dislike of the punishing manager may occur.

Motivational assumptions of PR

Like other remedies for improving performance, PR is based on certain assumptions about motivation. PR assumes that at least some people derive job satisfaction through extrinsic rewards rather than through the work itself. Such persons may find intrinsic satisfaction in off-the-job activities which are permitted by jobs which provide extrinsic, tangible rewards such as money.

Further, the assumption made in JE that employees' higher level needs can be properly diagnosed by managers so that they can then design jobs to fulfill these needs is not necessary in the PR system; it relies on general extrinsic reinforcers

---

[3]   Sidney R. Wilson, "Motivating Managers With Money," *Business Horizons* (April 1972), pp. 15–24.

such as pay, which can subsequently be exchanged by employees to meet their needs as they perceive them. The implications of PR's motivational assumptions are noted in the figure.

The carrot and the stick

Many charge that PR is a manipulative scheme—a device to control employee behavior via the carrot and stick (reward-punishment) philosophy of management. There are several responses to this criticism. One is that organizations presently attempt to control behavior by offering rewards and punishment for performance, but are doing an ineffective job. This is due to the lack of systematic planning and, as shown, to overemphasis on the use of the stick. PR can alleviate the harmful effects of punishment by concentrating on positive reinforcement.

PR also specifies an individual's job objectives in behavioral terms so that employees know precisely what is expected of them. This approach is more in the interest of employees than seducing them with human relations training or with shallow attempts to permit participation in either the design of jobs or performance evaluations, while actually requiring unwavering conformity to management standards and goals.

Problems and PR

There are practical problems with PR, which must be resolved through careful planning and experimentation, as well as philosophical issues which can evoke controversy and emotion from participants. One practical issue is the specification of desired behavior. Identification of behavioral objectives is often easy for many routine and/or entry-level jobs; however, managerial jobs may be unprogrammed and entail many different responsibilities. A behavioral analysis of managerial positions is a difficult yet necessary prerequisite to the implementation of PR.

Even if we specifically identify desired behaviors, these behaviors may simultaneously be rewarded by management and punished by work groups or families. For example, high output may attract praise from supervisors and scorn from co-workers, who see it as leading to higher output quotas. Hard work and long hours may be positively reinforced by the organization but resented by one's family. Further, a PR program may require that a supervisor observe subordinate behavior more frequently in order to dispense PR. Such additional demands may be resented.

Philosophical issues can also hinder the effectiveness of a PR program. As was noted, many believe that PR is tantamount to the manipulation and control of people by reward and punishment, and images of white rats in Skinner's experiments come to mind. As Walter Nord has stated, this view is in direct contradiction to the image many people would prefer to have of themselves: "Modern Americans, especially of the managerial class, prefer to think of themselves and others as being self-actualizing creatures operating at the top of Maslow's need hierarchy, rather than as animals being controlled and even manipulated by their environment."[4]

Of course, these charges have been addressed by proponents of PR. Practical problems can be alleviated as we study jobs, especially managerial jobs, in behavioral terms. This necessitates, of course, detailed observation, identification, and analysis of what people do at work, which should produce categorizations of work activities and their frequencies. Proponents of PR would also argue that we are controlling work behavior now, but that by relying so heavily on punishment

---

[4]   Walter Nord, "Beyond the Teaching Machine: The Neglected Area of Operant Conditioning in the Theory and Practice of Management," *Organizational Behavior and Human Performance* (November 1969), pp. 375–401.

and negative reinforcement, we are not doing it effectively. PR may not lead to the resentment and emotional stress which often accompany punishment.

Of course, the practical problems, as well as the reservations many have about the implications of PR, can be overcome principally by experimenting in actual organizational settings and by citing the persuasive evidence of successful implementations which continue to appear in the literature.

THE COMPATIBILITY OF PR

A most advantageous aspect of the PR system is its compatibility with the other remedies for performance problems, JE and MBO, as well as with present personnel practices. PR offers organizations a way to more objectively and immediately reward performance at all levels and in all jobs, to facilitate specification of desired performance levels, and to deemphasize punishment and its harmful effects.

Intrinsic motivation (for example, JE) is not universally applicable, nor is it sufficient to sustain performance. External rewards still control performance to a large extent. Structuring jobs, providing feedback, and allowing for participation in goal setting are likewise not sufficient as they are not applicable to all employees and jobs. Therefore, it is suggested that all three possible solutions to performance problems be explored. Obviously, in many cases more than one solution may be necessary.

Further, a diagnosis of the task, the people, and the structure of organizations should precede attempts to apply a technique to motivational problems, whether it be JE, MBO, or PR. The interdependency of these variables is vital because they can form a situation which can limit the applicability of any one technology to improve performance. In his discussion of JE, John Morse supports this point: "Job enrichment is a design mechanism that either fits or does not fit the task and technology to which it is being applied. It is also a design mechanism and technique that either fits or does not fit the personality of the individuals whose jobs are being enriched."[5]

This statement is equally applicable to MBO and PR. It suggests that the effective application of a specific technique to alleviate the motivation problem hinges upon the congruence of existing variables in the organization with the assumptions that a particular technique makes about the problem. As can be seen from the table, each of the three techniques results from somewhat different diagnoses of the motivation problem. Each has a certain range of job-type applicability, time frame, and positive and negative consequences for the organization and its employees. There are at least three ways to deal with motivation problems; all three should be considered and perhaps used in combination.

SUMMARY

Poor employee performance is perhaps the most pervasive problem in organizations today. We have attributed poor performance to two general causes. The first, which can be called the deficiency problem, occurs when employees do not possess the necessary abilities, skills, or attributes. This problem can be alleviated by selection strategies and training programs.

There may still exist a problem of poor performance, however, even when the employees possess the proper abilities, skills, and attributes. We have termed this a motivational problem, the second cause of poor performance. We have argued that

---

[5]   John Morse, "A Contingency Look at Job Design," *California Management Review* (Fall 1973), pp. 67–75.

it is perhaps the more serious problem in organizations. Two well-publicized remedies have been offered—JE and MBO—but these, and their many variants, have been effective only to a limited degree.

A third solution to the problem of improving job performance through a motivation technique is available. This solution is PR, which focuses on actual behavior rather than on measures of effectiveness by emphasizing positive rewards rather than punishment and by systematically recognizing the power of immediate feedback and different reinforcement schedules. An analysis of PR often reveals the current ineffective and illogical use of rewards presently offered in organizations.

We have offered a contingency approach to the motivation problem. The contingency concept implies that there is only one best way to solve organization problems, but that there may be several equally effective programs. The contingency or situational approach necessitates a thorough diagnosis of the organization's setting in order to identify the problems that exist and to identify techniques which are effective for these specific problems.

When a manager diagnoses poor performance as a motivation problem rather than a deficiency problem, the following steps should be taken:

• The manager should assess the job for its ability to offer challenging work to employees. If more intrinsic motivation is thought to be necessary, he can look into JE as a partial solution.

• The manager should assess the objectives of the job to determine whether or not they have been communicated to the worker, have been defined specifically, and whether the worker has received feedback about his results relative to these goals. If there are deficiencies here, MBO may be investigated as a partial solution.

• The manager should assess the extrinsic rewards offered to the worker in a job. Are they of sufficient quantity and types to improve performance? Are they offered soon after proper performance? Are they contingent upon evidence of performance? Are rewards substituted for threat of punishment or punishment to control behavior? To the extent that these questions are unsatisfactorily answered, PR as a partial solution to the motivation problem needs to be investigated.

• It is time that managers recognize the power of rewards and punishment for controlling work behavior and performance in organizations. They should systematically and explicitly examine the unintended consequences of their inadequate use of contingencies of reinforcement, their overemphasis on threat and punishment, and their ineffective use of rewards and schedules of reinforcement in the work setting.

FOR DISCUSSION AND REVIEW

1 Explain the motivational assumptions behind job enrichment; MBO; and PR.
2 For what types of jobs would JE and MBO seem most applicable?
3 Define the following: positive reinforcement; negative reinforcement; punishment; schedules of reinforcement.
4 Review the arguments against behavior modification and respond to them.
5 What is management by punishment?

C. WITHDRAWAL FROM WORK, HOURS OF WORK, AND SAFETY

Lyman W. Porter

Richard M. Steers

Organizational, Work, and Personnel Factors in Employee Turnover and Absenteeism[1]

To those concerned with studying the behavior of individuals in organizational settings, employee turnover and absenteeism represent both interesting and important phenomena. They are relatively clear-cut acts of behavior that have potentially critical consequences both for the person and for the organization. It is probably for this reason that turnover and absenteeism have been investigated in a relatively large number of studies to date and are likely to remain a key focus of personnel research by psychologists. It is the purpose of this article to provide a review that (a) comprehensively covers the most recent research on the topic; (b) relates the research findings in a systematic fashion to the organizational and working environment; and (c) attempts to provide a basic conceptual framework for viewing the findings. Attention is focused on only those studies that include data believed to represent avoidable turnover or absenteeism. It must be recognized, however, that accurately distinguishing between avoidable and unavoidable turnover and absenteeism is not always an easy task.

In the past, there have been some four reviews of the literature dealing with turnover and absenteeism. Three of these (Brayfield & Crockett, 1955; Herzberg, Mausner, Peterson, & Capwell, 1957; Vroom, 1964) are now somewhat dated in relation to all of the research carried out during the past decade or so, and the fourth (Schuh, 1967) represents a highly specialized review of only a portion of the available literature. Before proceeding to our own analysis of the recent literature, it will be helpful to summarize briefly what was uncovered by these previous reviews.

Brayfield and Crockett (1955) and Herzberg et al. (1957) both found evidence of a strong relationship between employee dissatisfaction and withdrawal behavior (i.e., both turnover and absenteeism). Brayfield and Crockett went further, however, to point out major methodological weaknesses in a number of the studies, such as the failure to obtain independent measures and the use of weak or ambiguous measurement techniques. In fact, such flaws were so prevalent that they questioned whether methodological changes alone would substantially alter the magnitude or direction of many of the obtained relationships. In general, then, Brayfield and Crockett pointed as much to a need for increased rigor in research techniques as toward the acceptance or rejection of an attitude-withdrawal relationship.

Several years later, Vroom (1964) again reviewed the literature pertaining to job satisfaction and withdrawal. The results of his analysis generally reinforced the earlier conclusions. Vroom reported that the studies he reviewed showed a consistent negative relationship between job satisfaction and the propensity to leave. In

From *Psychological Bulletin* 80, no. 2 (1973): 151–176. Copyright © 1973 by the American Psychological Association. Reprinted by permission.

[1] This research was supported by a grant from the Office of Naval Research, Contract No. N00014-69-A-0200-9001, NR 151-315. The authors wish to express their appreciation to Richard T. Mowday, Eugene F. Stone, Joseph E. Champoux, and William J. Crampon for their valuable comments on an earlier draft.

addition, he found a somewhat less consistent negative relationship between job satisfaction and absenteeism. Vroom interpreted the findings concerning job satisfaction and withdrawal as being consistent with an expectancy/valence theory of motivation; namely, workers who are highly attracted to their jobs are presumed to be subject to motivational forces to remain in them, with such forces manifesting themselves in increased tenure and higher rates of attendance.

Schuh's (1967) review focused primarily on studies of the prediction of turnover by the means of personality and vocational inventories and biographical information. From his review, he concluded that there was not a consistent relationship between turnover and scores on intelligence, aptitude, and personality tests. On the other hand, some evidence was found that vocational interest inventories and scaled biographical information blanks could be used to fairly accurately predict turnover. Moreover, a very small number of older studies pertaining to job satisfaction were cited in the review, and these too seemed predictive of turnover.

Taken as a whole, these reviews and their conclusions point to the importance of job satisfaction as a central factor in withdrawal. In the review that follows, we attempt to build on the previous ones by citing the rather extensive recent literature (over 60 studies) that for the most part has not been previously covered. First, recent studies concerning the role of *overall* job satisfaction in withdrawal are reviewed. Next, and more specifically, the literature is categorized according to (a) organization-wide factors, (b) immediate work environment factors, (c) job content factors, and (d) personal factors. These seem to us to be meaningful groupings in terms of the variety of possible "internal factors" (i.e., variables related to an individual's interaction with the work situation) that could be involved in withdrawal behavior. Omitted from the present analysis is the obviously crucial set of "external" factors pertaining to such things as economic conditions, the availability of specific job opportunities, and various unavoidable causes of withdrawal (e.g., pregnancy, illness, etc.).

Throughout this review we are particularly concerned with the potential role that "met expectations" may have on withdrawal behavior. The concept of met expectations may be viewed as the discrepancy between what a person encounters on this job in the way of positive and negative experiences and what he expected to encounter. Thus, since different employees can have quite different expectations with respect to payoffs or rewards in a given organizational or work situation, it would not be anticipated that a given variable (e.g., high pay, unfriendly work colleagues, etc.) would have a uniform impact on withdrawal decisions. We would predict, however, that when an individual's expectations—whatever they are—are not substantially met, his propensity to withdraw would increase. We will return to the possible role of met expectations following our review of the various segments of the recent literature pertaining to withdrawal.

JOB SATISFACTION AND WITHDRAWAL

Subsequent to the publication of the earlier reviews, a number of new investigations have appeared concerning the relationship of overall job satisfaction to turnover and absenteeism. These findings are briefly summarized here in order to determine how they relate to the earlier findings as previously reviewed.

In two related predictive studies of particular merit, Hulin investigated the impact of job satisfaction on turnover among female clerical workers. Using the Job Descriptive Index as a measure of job attitudes, Hulin's (1966) first study matched each subject who subsequently left the company over a 12-month period with two "stayers" along several demographic dimensions. Significant differences were found between the stayer and leaver groups on mean satisfaction scores. Hulin concluded that at least in this sample, subsequent leavers *as a group* could be accurately distinguished from stayers based on a knowledge of the workers' degree of job satisfaction up to 12 months prior to the act of termination.

These findings raised the question as to the possibility of reducing this turnover by increasing a worker's degree of satisfaction on the job. Toward this end, the company instituted new policies in the areas of salary administration and promotional opportunities. Approximately 1–1½ years after these changes, Hulin (1968) again administered the Job Descriptive Index to a sample similar to the previous one. Subsequent leavers were matched with two stayers each, and again it was found that termination decisions were significantly related to the degree of worker satisfaction. Equally important was the finding that satisfaction scores with four of the five Job Descriptive Index scales rose significantly between the first and second studies. Simultaneously, the department's turnover rate between these two periods dropped from 30% during the first study period to 12% during the second.

Other important studies have yielded essentially the same results among life insurance agents (Weitz & Nuckols, 1955), male and female office workers (Mikes & Hulin, 1968), retail store employees (Taylor & Weiss, 1969a, 1969b), and female operatives (Wild, 1970).

Taking a somewhat different approach to the topic, Katzell (1968) and Dunnette, Arvey, and Banas[4] investigated the role of employee expectations at the time of hire as they related to later job experiences and turnover. In both studies, no significant differences were found to exist at the time of entry between the expectation levels of those who remained and those who later decided to leave. However, as time went on, significant differences did emerge; those who remained generally felt their original expectations were essentially met on the job, while those who left felt their expectations had not been met.

Also relevant to the role of met expectations in the participation decision are the field experiments of Weitz (1956), Youngberg (1963), and Macedonia (1969). These studies (described in greater detail below) found that where individuals were provided with a realistic picture of the job environment—including its difficulties—prior to employment, such subjects apparently adjusted their job expectations to more realistic levels. These new levels were then apparently more easily met by the work environment, resulting in reduced turnover.

Many studies, therefore, point to the importance of job satisfaction as a predictor of turnover. However, it appears that expressed intentions concerning future participation may be an even better predictor. In a large scale investigation of managerial personnel, Kraut[5] consistently found significant correlations between expressed intent to stay and subsequent employee participation. Such findings were far stronger than relationships between expressed satisfaction and continued participation. And, in a study of turnover among Air Force pilots. Atchison and Lefferts (1972) found that the frequency with which individuals thought about leaving their job was significantly related to rate termination. Based on these preliminary findings, an argument can be made that an expressed intention to leave may represent the next logical step after experienced dissatisfaction in the withdrawal process.

---

[4]   M. D. Dunnette, R. Arvey, & P. Banas. Why do they leave? Unpublished manuscript, 1969.

[5]   A. I. Kraut. The prediction of turnover by employee attitudes. Unpublished manuscript, 1970.

While considerable investigation has been carried out since the previous reviews concerning the relation of job satisfaction to turnover, only two studies have been found considering such satisfaction as it relates to absenteeism. Talacchi (1960), using the Science Research Associates' Employee Inventory, found a significant inverse relation between job satisfaction and absenteeism among office workers. He did not, however, find such a relation concerning turnover. And Waters and Roach (1971), using the Job Descriptive Index with clerical workers, found significant inverse relations between job satisfaction and both turnover and absenteeism.

In summary, the recent evidence concerning the impact of job satisfaction on withdrawal (especially on turnover) is generally consistent with the findings as reviewed by Brayfield and Crockett (1955), Herzberg et al. (1957), and Vroom (1964). (These new findings are summarized in Table 1.) It appears, however, that the major asset of these more recent findings is not simply their confirming nature but rather their increased methodological rigor over those studies reviewed previously. Most of the earlier studies contained several design weaknesses (see, e.g., the discussion by Brayfield & Crockett) which the more recent studies have overcome to a significant degree. For example, 12 of the 15 new studies reviewed here were predictive in nature. In addition, several of the research instruments used in the more recent studies (e.g., the Job Descriptive Index) appear to be more rigorously designed in terms of validity, reliability, and norms. Thus, these newer studies go a long way in the direction of providing increased confidence in the importance of job satisfaction as a force in the decision to participate.

SPECIFIC FACTORS RELATED TO WITHDRAWAL

While consideration of the role of overall job satisfaction in the decision to participate is important, it tells us little about the roots of such satisfaction. Knowing that an employee is dissatisfied and about to leave does not help us understand *why* he is dissatisfied, nor does it help us determine what must be changed in an effort to retain him. For the answer to these critical questions, it is necessary to look more closely at the various factors of the work situation as they potentially relate to the propensity to withdraw. We begin our discussion with those factors that are generally organization-wide in their impact on employees and move toward those factors that are more unique to each individual.

Organization-wide factors

Organization-wide factors for purposes of this discussion can be defined as those variables affecting the individual that are primarily determined by persons or events external to the immediate work group. Under this rubric would fall such factors as pay and promotion policies and organization size. The relation of these two organization-wide variables to withdrawal is discussed separately.

Pay and promotion Pay and promotion are considered jointly here because of the frequently related nature of the two variables and because of the similarity of findings between these two variables and withdrawal. It should be kept in mind, however, that the two are not synonymous; while promotion usually carries with it some increase in salary, the reverse certainly does not hold. There is no lack of empirical investigations into the relationships between pay and promotion and withdrawal, nor is there much disagreement over the conclusion that low pay and lack of promotional opportunities can represent a primary stated cause for withdrawal (Conference Board, 1972; Friedlander & Walton, 1964; Hulin, 1968; Know-

Table 1

Studies of Relation of Job Satisfaction to Turnover and Absenteeism

INVESTIGATOR(S)	POPULATION	n^a	TYPE OF WITH-DRAWAL STUDIED	RELATION TO WITHDRAWAL
Weitz & Nuckols (1955)	Insurance agents	990	Turnover	Negative
Weitz (1956)	Insurance agents	474	Turnover	Negative
Talacchi (1960)	Departmental workers	NA	Turnover	Zero
Youngberg (1963)	Insurance salesmen	NA	Absenteeism	Negative
Hulin (1966)	Female clerical workers	129	Turnover	Negative
Hulin (1968)	Female clerical workers	298	Turnover	Negative
Katzell (1968)	Student nurses	1852	Turnover	Negative
Mikes & Hulin (1968)	Office workers	660	Turnover	Negative
Dunnette et al. (see Footnote 4)	Lower level managers	1020	Turnover	Negative
Macedonia (1969)	Military academy cadets	1160	Turnover	Negative
Taylor & Weiss (1969a 1969b)	Retail store employees	475	Turnover	Negative
Kraut (see Footnote 5)[b]	Computer salesmen	Varied	Turnover	Negative
Wild (1970)	Female manual workers	236	Turnover	Negative
Waters & Roach (1971)	Female clerical workers	160	Turnover	Negative
			Absenteeism	Negative
Atchison & Lefferts (1972)[b]	Air Force pilots	52	Turnover	Negative

Note. NA=not available.

[a] Sample sizes reported here and on the following tables reflect the actual number of subjects used in the data analysis from which the reported results were derived.

[b] Both Kraut, and Atchison and Lefferts found that an expressed intention to leave represented an even more accurate predictor of turnover than job satisfaction.

les, 1964; Patchen, 1960; Ronan, 1967; Saleh, Lee, & Prien, 1965). The remaining analytic question is *how* pay and promotion affect withdrawal.

One answer to this question may be found in expectancy/valence theory (Porter & Lawler, 1968; Vroom, 1964). Using such an approach, it appears that at least two factors could account for the effect of compensation on withdrawal: (a) the perceived equity of rewards compared to expended effort; and (b) the expectation that continued participation will result in more positively valent outcomes than any alternative behavior. A significant amount of research exists to support the first part of such a theory (i.e., the necessity of perceived equitable rewards), while no research to date has been found that tested the role of *anticipated* rewards on withdrawal.

One of the earliest studies of the perceived equity of compensation was carried out by Patchen (1960) among oil refinery workers. The results of this study demonstrated that it was the perceived fairness of pay and promotion rather than simply their amount or rapidity that was the primary cause of absenteeism. Moreover, Knowles (1964) found that failure on the part of factory workers to attain their "expected wage" was a better predictor of propensity to resign than was the amount of the wage itself. Additional, though less conclusive, evidence of this phenomenon can be found in Bassett (1967).

Studies by Hulin (1968) among clerical workers and by Kraut (see Footnote 5) among computer salesmen also arrived at similar conclusions. Both studies found satisfaction with pay and promotion to be negatively associated with turnover. And Dunnette et al. (see Footnote 4) found turnover among managers to be inversely related to met expectations concerning rate of promotion. However, they found met expectations with pay to be unrelated to turnover. Finally, Telly, French, and Scott (1971) found that perceived inequity concerning both pay and promotion among hourly production workers was not significantly related to turnover. They explained this finding, however, by noting that the jobs were unionized and afforded little opportunity for compensation to be associated with individual effort.

Company incentive programs aimed at reducing absenteeism and turnover can also be subsumed under the compensation factor. Two related experimental field studies have recently appeared which investigated the impact of such programs—and the degree of participation in their design—on absenteeism. In the first experiment, three autonomous work groups independently developed their own incentive plans to reward good attendance (Lawler & Hackman, 1969). These plans were then imposed on other work groups by the company. Two additional groups served as control groups and received no treatment. A significant increase in attendance resulted only in those three groups who formulated their own plans. In a follow-up study 1 year later incentives were discontinued in two of the three original participative groups (Scheflen, Lawler, & Hackman, 1971). It was found that attendance dropped below pretreatment levels in these two groups, while attendance remained high in the third group. Apparently, the removal by higher management of a plan mutually agreed to among the workers served to destroy the norm of good attendance established by the group.

These two studies clearly point to the fact that attention by management solely to the mechanical aspects of a pay plan may be insufficient to insure the success of the plan. Employee participation in the design and implementation of such a plan may indeed have a greater impact on its success than the mechanics of the plan itself by increasing the perceived equity of the program, which, in turn, could lead to reduced tendencies toward withdrawal.

The existing evidence, then, tends to indicate that when an employee withdraws from the organization because he failed to receive a certain level of pay or a promotion, he does not do so only because of a perceived need or desire for the extra income or higher position. In addition, the perceived *inequity* of the action—that is, the failure of such action to meet his expectations—apparently often has significant impact on his decision. The employee can therefore be seen as maintaining his investment of time and effort in many cases only so long as he receives what *he* considers a fair return on that investment.

Organizational size Only one study has been uncovered that empirically related organizational size (as distinct from subunit size) to withdrawal. Ingham (1970), in a study of eight British firms of varying size, found size of the organization to be highly related to absenteeism but weakly related to turnover. To explain such findings, he advanced the argument that employees were attracted to either large or small organizations for different reasons. Workers in the larger plants (which paid higher wages) were viewed as being more sensitive to the economic aspects of their employment and less concerned with noneconomic factors. Employees of smaller plants, on the other hand, appeared to be setting lower acceptable wage levels and, simultaneously, demanding significantly higher noneconomic rewards (which were apparently more abundant in the small organizations). Since the differing expectations of the two groups were met in similar degrees by their respective environments, turnover rates for the two groups could be expected to be similar.

On the other hand, Ingham argues that absenteeism is a function of the degree of employee identification with the organization. Following this approach, workers in large and small firms would have roughly the same rate of turnover because their differing expectations would be respectively met, but the greater degree of impersonality brought on by the increased bureaucratization of the larger firms would reduce the employee's identification with that type of firm. The result would be increased absenteeism in the larger organizations. Unfortunately, sufficient evidence is not presented in Ingham's own study to demonstrate the validity of such a hypothesis. Thus, while the theoretical explanation goes far in contributing thought-provoking insights into the withdrawal process, much more empirical work is necessary before confidence in the hypothesis as a predictive device could be achieved.

The results of this study, along with the other investigations relating organizational environment factors to withdrawal, are summarized in Table 2.

Summary Pay and promotional considerations often appear to represent significant factors in the termination decision. While several of the recent studies reviewed above simply confirmed such a conclusion, other studies investigated the reasons behind such a relationship. These studies fairly consistently pointed out the importance of perceived equity and met expectations as important forces in such a decision. The size of the pay raise or the rate of promotion, while important in and of themselves, are, in addition, weighed by an employee in the light of his expectations, given his level of self-perceived contribution. The resulting determination of his degree of satisfaction or dissatisfaction then apparently inputs into his decision to remain or to search for preferable job alternatives.

The results of one study indicated that turnover rates appear to be fairly constant among organizations of varying sizes, while absenteeism is significantly higher in larger firms than in smaller ones. Some theoretical considerations were offered to explain this variance but were not effectively substantiated by empirical data.

Table 2

Studies of Relations between Organization-Wide Factors and Turnover and Absenteeism

FACTOR	POPULATION	n	TYPE OF WITHDRAWAL STUDIED	RELATION TO WITHDRAWAL
Satisfaction with pay and promotion				
Patchen (1960)	Oil refinery workers	487	Absenteeism	Negative
Friedlander & Walton (1964)	Scientists and engineers	82	Turnover	Negative
Knowles (1964)	Factory workers	56	Turnover	Negative
Saleh et al. (1965)	Nurses	263	Turnover	Negative
Bassett (1967)[a]	Engineers	200	Turnover	Negative
Ronan (1967)	Administrative & professional personnel	91	Turnover	Negative
Hulin (1968)	Female clerical workers	298	Turnover	Negative
			Turnover (pay)	Zero
Dunnette et al. (see Footnote 4)	Lower level managers	1020	Turnover (promotion)	Negative
Kraut (see Footnote 5)	Computer salesmen	Varied	Turnover	Negative
Telly et al. (1971)	Factory workers	900	Turnover	Zero[b]
Conference Board (1972)	Salesmen; management trainees	Varied	Turnover	Negative
Participation in compensation plan design				
Lawler & Hackman (1969)	Custodians	83	Absenteeism	Negative
Scheflen et al. (1971)	Custodians	NA	Absenteeism	Negative
Organization size				
	Factory workers	8 units	Turnover	Zero
Ingham (1970)			Absenteeism	Positive

Note: NA=not available.

[a]Bassett posited such a relationship but did not specifically test for it.

[b]This relation was explained by the nature of the union contract, which standardized pay and promotion procedures based essentially on seniority.

Immediate work environment factors

A second set of factors instrumental in the decision to withdraw centers around the immediate work situation in which the employee finds himself. In previous reviews, Brayfield and Crockett (1955) found that negative employee attitudes toward their job context (especially at the lower levels) were significantly related to absenteeism and, to a lesser extent, to turnover. And Herzberg et al. (1957) found that such factors as the nature of the social work group were of particular importance in the decision to participate.

Since these reviews were published, significant research has been carried out which tends to supplement existing knowledge concerning the importance of immediate work environment factors in withdrawal. Factors to be considered here include (a) supervisory style, (b) work unit size, and (c) the nature of peer group interaction.

Supervisory style Since the importance of supervisory style on employee behavior was first brought into focus by the Michigan and Ohio State leadership studies (Katz, Maccoby, Gurin, & Floor, 1951; Katz, Maccoby, & Morse 1950; Stogdill & Coons, 1957), research on this subject has continued to grow. Several recent studies address themselves specifically to the relationship between the nature of supervision and turnover and absenteeism.

Fleishman and Harris (1962) studied the impact of supervisory consideration and of initiating structure on turnover among production workers. Using the Supervisory Behavior Description Questionnaire (Fleishman, 1957a), they found that turnover (and grievances) were highest for those work groups whose foremen were rated low in consideration, regardless of the degree of structuring behavior shown. However, this relationship was found to be curvilinear, not linear. Critical levels appeared beyond which increased consideration or decreased structure had not effect on turnover rates.

Some reinforcement for these findings came in later study by Skinner (1969). Also using the Supervisory Behavior Description Questionnaire, as well as the Leadership Opinion Questionnaire (Fleishman, 1957b, 1968), she found a similar curvilinear relationship between consideration and turnover among a sample of factory workers. Up to a point, higher supervisory consideration was associated with lower turnover; beyond this point, little relation was detected between the two factors.

The centrality of supervisory consideration as a factor in turnover has also been demonstrated by Saleh et al. (1965) in their survey of recently terminated hospital nurses. Using an ex post facto study design, they found lack of consideration to be the second most cited reason for termination (after job content). Also, in a study of male hourly production workers who quit within the first year of employeement, Ley (1966) found a highly significant correlation ($r=.76$) between turnover and authoritarian ratings of employees' foremen.

In a more rigorous, predictive study among clerical workers, Hulin (1968) found significant differences between stayers and leavers with respect to satisfaction with supervisory relations. Taylor and Weiss (1969a, 1969b), however, took issue with Hulin in their study of retail store employees. In their sample, they found no significant relationship between turnover and satisfaction with the nature of supervision.

Finally, in an effort to test the applicability of Adams' theory of inequity to turnover, Telly et al. (1971) surveyed a large sample of hourly production workers drawn at random from shops rated either high or low in turnover (based on *previous* turnover rates). It was found that high-turnover groups perceived significantly greater inequity with respect to the treatment they received from both supervisors and leadmen. Telly et al. speculated that when an employee perceives inequitable treatment, he may feel frustrated and will not contribute his best efforts toward the primary goals of the organization; if this perceived inequity becomes excessive, he will actually separate himself from the organization.

Several investigations have looked at more specific facets of supervisory behavior as they relate to withdrawal. One previously reviewed study of particular merit, carried out by Ross and Zander (1957), investigated the effects of recognition and feedbacks on turnover. The researchers measured the strength of certain needs as well as the perceived extent to which the needs were met at work. The results showed that no significant differences existed between those who remained and those who later terminated concerning their perceived need strength for recognition and feedback on their jobs. However, significant differences were found to exist between the two groups as to the perceived extent to which these needs were actually met. It was concluded that receiving sufficient recognition and feedback to meet expectations represented a significant factor in the employee's decision to participate.

Similar findings have been shown in a more recent study of turnover among engineers (General Electric Company, 1964a). This investigation involved matching a small sample of highly rated engineers who voluntarily quit with a corresponding sample of remaining engineers who reported to the same managers. Attitudinal measures were taken prior to termination. Two important findings came out of this study: (a) Those who left had much less favorable attitudes with respect to the amount of feedback they received from their supervisor to improve their present or future performance and (b) major disagreements existed between those who left and their supervisors over job goals. According to these findings, the supervisors should be able to exert at least some influence over the decision to leave through improved mutual understanding with the worker as to job requirements and methods for performance improvement. Such a conclusion is reinforced by a similar study in the same company (General Electric Company, 1964b). Although this latter investigation did not study turnover, it did find that when a company-sponsored work-planning-and-review program was used in work groups and departments, improvements in attitudes resulted in exactly the same two areas cited above a reasons for terminating.

Finally, one study has been found which attempted to relate the amount of managerial experience to turnover. In an investigation of white-collar personnel in a large manufacturing company, Bassett (1967) found that turnover was substantially higher among employees whose supervisors had less than 5 years of managerial experience. While the methodology is not particularly rigorous here, Bassett has raised an important issue that appears particularly relevant to turnover among newly hired employees. Future investigations may find that managerial experience must be considered by a company in determining where to place new employees if turnover among such personnel is to be reduced.

Work unit size The literature concerning the relationship between the size of the work group and withdrawal was reviewed several years ago (Porter & Lawler, 1965), but the major points are summarized briefly here since they are directly relevant to the overall picture of the withdrawal process.

Four studies were reviewed by Porter and Lawler that investigated the relationship between unit size and turnover but only among blue-collar workers. Three of the four studies found that turnover was greater in large units than in small ones (Indik & Seashore, 1961; Kerr, Koppelmeier, & Sullivan, 1951; Mandell, 1956), while the fourth found no such relationship (Argyle, Gardner, & Cioffi, 1958).

Twelve studies were also reviewed by Porter and Lawler dealing with the impact of unit size on absenteeism. In 10 of the 12 studies, a positive linear relationship was found between increased absenteeism and increases in unit size (Acton Society Trust, 1953; Baumgartel & Sobol, 1959; Hewitt & Parfitt, 1953; Indik & Seashore, 1961; Kerr et al., 1951; Metzner & Mann, 1953; Revans, 1958). However, such results were only found among blue-collar workers. The only study that investigated both blue- and white-collar workers' absences found no relationship between unit size and absenteeism among white-collar employees (Metzner & Mann, 1953). The final study reviewed was carried out by Argyle et al. (1958), who found a curvilinear relationship between unit size and absenteeism. The lowest absence rates were found to occur in the middle-sized groups.

No new studies relating work unit size to withdrawal have been found that were published since the 1965 review. A clear tendency emerges from that analysis for greater withdrawal rates to be associated with larger work groups among blue-collar workers. However, no such relationship has yet been conclusively demonstrated among white-collar workers. A possible explanation for the trend in findings among blue-collar employees could be that increases in unit size result in increased dissatisfaction with the available intrinsic rewards (cf. Porter & Lawler, 1965). For example, increases in size could result in lower group cohesiveness, higher task specialization, and poorer communications. Such results could make it more difficult to fulfill one's expectations, resulting in increased dissatisfaction that would lead to increased tendencies to withdraw. We would expect such an explanation to be more applicable to blue-collar than to white-collar employees since, on the whole, white-collar employees have more autonomy in their jobs and are usually in a better position to discover alternate avenues to intrinsic rewards.

Peer group interaction One of the most potent forces in the socialization process within an organization is the interactive dynamics between the individual and his peers. Such interaction can provide support and reinforcement necessary for adjustment and attachment to the work environment. Conversely, failure to secure such support may result in alienation from the workplace. Because of the potential importance of such a factor, it should prove useful to investigate the relation of peer group interaction to the employee's decision to remain with or leave his employing organization.

In a study of turnover among management trainees, Evan (1963) found that avoidable terminations were significantly lower when a trainee was assigned to a department with two or more other trainees than when he was assigned to a department either alone or with only one other trainee. Evan speculated from these findings that a new employee (trainee) who has substantive support of other new employees will be better able to contend with the stresses and ambiguities created by a new job than he would without such support.

The importance of co-worker support in retention has also been pointed out by Farris (1971). In a predictive study among scientists and engineers, he found that both perceived-low inclusion in the organization and perceived-low group cohesiveness were somewhat effective predictors of employee turnover. And, Telly et al. (1971), in their study of production workers, found that perceived equity of the social aspects of their jobs was significantly and inversely related to turnover. Apparently, the workers were more inclined to stay when their expectations in their relations with co-workers were substantially met. Findings of a similar nature have also been demonstrated by Hulin (1968) among clerical workers.

Waters and Roach (1971) studied both forms of withdrawal among female clerical workers using the Job Descriptive Index and found that, while co-worker satisfaction was significantly and inversely related to absenteeism, it was unrelated to turnover. Here, using the same instrument as Hulin on presumably similar populations, quite different results were obtained concerning turnover. Similarly, Taylor and Weiss (1969a, 1969b) also found satisfaction with co-worker relations was unrelated to turnover in their sample of retail store employees. Thus, while the majority of investigations showed a strong positive relationship between satisfaction with co-worker relations and propensity to remain, these findings do not go unchallenged. It appears that, once again, satisfaction with a particular factor does not have equivalent degrees of impact on all types of employee groups with respect to the decision to participate.

Summary These findings, summarized in Table 3, provide a relatively clear picture of the relation of at least three immediate work environment factors to an employee's decision to participate or withdraw. Several studies have pointed to the importance of supervisory style as a major factor in turnover. Apparently, when one's expectations concerning what the nature of supervision should be like remain substantially unmet, his propensity to leave increases. No studies, however, have been found relating supervisory style to absenteeism. This neglect of absenteeism studies is rather surprising considering the widely accepted notion of the centrality of the supervisor as a factor in such withdrawal.

The size of the working unit has been shown to be related to both turnover and absenteeism among blue-collar workers; however, insufficient evidence is available to draw conclusions concerning such influence on managerial or clerical personnel.

Finally, most of the research in the area of co-worker satisfaction demonstrates the potential importance of such satisfaction in retention. Such findings, however, are not universal. A possible explanation for the divergent findings is that some people have a lower need for affiliation than others and may place less importance on satisfactory co-worker relations. Alternatively, it is possible that some organizational settings provide for a greater degree of peer group interaction, thereby increasing the probability that one's level of expectations would be met in this area. In either event, co-worker dissatisfaction cannot be overlooked as a possible cause of attrition.

Job content factors

It has long been thought that the duties and activities required for the successful performance of an individual's particular job can have a significant impact on his decision to remain with and participate in the employing organization. Such job requirements are presumed to represent for the individual either a vehicle for personal fulfillment and satisfaction or a continual source of frustration, internal conflict, and dissatisfaction. In recent years, several new investigations have appeared which provide added clarity to the role of such job-related factors in the withdrawal process. Four such factors will be discussed here: (a) the overall reaction to job content, (b) task repetitiveness, (c) job autonomy and responsibility, and (d) role clarity.

Overall reaction to job content We are concerned in this section primarily with studies concentrating on the general level of satisfaction with the assigned tasks. Investigations of such specific facets of work as job autonomy or task repetitiveness will be dealt with in later subsections.

Dunnette et al. (see Footnote 4), in their retrospective study of young managers, found that both those who later left and those who remained recalled being highly optimistic concerning the nature of their work at the time of entry into the organization. The level of expectations of both groups was essentially the same. The first job assignment, however, brought disappointment and dissatisfaction to both groups. But while the failure of the first job assignments to meet individual expectations existed for both groups initially, significant differences arose with later assignments. The employees who subsequently remained with the organization perceived themselves as moving into jobs more closely aligned with their expectations, while those who eventually left moved into jobs which were perceived as increasing the disparity between individual expectations and the realities of the job. Thus, again, failure to meet one's expectations appears to be a major contributing variable in the decision to withdraw.

Similar findings concerning the impact of the job itself on the participation decision have been demonstrated elsewhere without the use of retrospective techniques. Significant relations between turnover and dissatisfaction with the nature of work have been found among female clerical workers (Waters & Roach, 1971), female manual workers (Wild, 1970), male production workers (Telly et al., 1971), computer salesmen (see Footnote 5), and student nurses (Saleh et al., 1965). One study, however, among female clerical workers failed to find such a relationship (Hulin, 1968). Dissatisfaction with work has also been shown to be significantly related to increased absenteeism among female clerks (Waters & Roach, 1971). Finally, and more specifically, turnover has been found to be inversely related to the perceived opportunity to fully utilize one's abilities on the job (Taylor & Weiss, 1969a, 1969b) and to the perceived importance of the work performed (Katzell, 1968; Taylor & Weiss, 1969a, 1969b).

Now let us turn to an analysis of two important and more specific aspects of the nature of work.

Task repetitiveness The required technology of a job often imposes severe constraints on personal actions and activities at work. Pressures for increased production or efficiency may result in increased fractionation or routinization of certain jobs. This repetitiveness of task may then contribute, along with other factors, to increased job stress. While efficiency or reduced operating costs may be the goal of such actions as the routinization of job technology, such a goal may at times have the unintended consequence of *increasing* costs through increases in absenteeism and turnover. Several studies point to such a possibility.

Guest (1955), in a follow-up study of the classic investigations by Walker and Guest (1952), interviewed 18 workers who quit their assembly line jobs after 12 to 15 years on the job. Despite the small number in the sample, a definite trend emerged in which the stress resulting from the routine and fractionated nature of the required job technology was seen as the primary factor prompting termination from the organization. Some support for Guest's conclusion was offered by Wild (1970) and Lefkowitz and Katz (1969), both of whom found similar results among recently terminated factory workers. However, no control groups were used in any of these studies, so it is not possible to ascertain whether those who remained had equally negative feelings toward their jobs. This lack of adequate controls was overcome in the predictive study by Taylor and Weiss (1969a, 1969b) among retail store employees. Here it was found that variety of work was significantly and negatively related to turnover.

A somewhat different conclusion was arrived at by Kilbridge (1961), who found no clear relationship between employee turnover and the repetitive nature of the job in two manufacturing firms. However, absenteeism was found to be somewhat

Table 3

Studies of Relations between Immediate Work Environment Factors and Turnover and Absenteeism

FACTOR	POPULATION	n	TYPE OF WITH-DRAWAL STUDIED	RELATION TO WITHDRAWAL
Satisfaction with supervisory relations				
Fleishman & Harris (1962)	Production workers	NA[a]	Turnover	Negative (curvilinear)
Saleh et al. (1965)	Nurses	263	Turnover	Negative
Ley (1966)	Production workers	100	Turnover	Negative
Hulin (1968)	Female clerical workers	298	Turnover	Negative
Skinner (1969)	Production workers	85	Turnover	Negative (curvilinear)
Taylor & Weiss (1969a, 1969b)	Retail store employees	475	Turnover	Zero
Telly et al. (1971)	Production workers	900	Turnover	Negative
Receipt of recognition and feedback				
Ross & Zander (1957)	Female skilled workers	507	Turnover	Negative
General Electric Company (1964a)	Engineers	36	Turnover	Negative
Supervisory experience				
Bassett (1967)	Technicians and engineers	200	Turnover	Negative
Work unit size				
Kerr et al. (1951)	Production workers	894	{ Turnover, Absenteeism	Positive, Positive
Acton Society Trust (1953)	Factory workers	91	Absenteeism	Positive

Study	Sample	n	Measure	Result
Hewitt & Parfitt (1953)	Factory workers	179	Absenteeism	Positive
Metzner & Mann (1953)	Blue-collar workers	251	Absenteeism	Positive
Mandell (1956)	White-collar workers	375	Absenteeism	Zero
	Clerical workers	320	Turnover	Positive
Argyle et al. (1958)	Production departments	86	{ Turnover / Absenteeism	Zero / Positive (curvilinear)
Revans (1958)	Factory workers	Varied	Absenteeism	Positive
Baumgartel & Sobol (1959)	Blue- and white-collar workers	3900	Absenteeism	Positive
Indik & Seashore (1961)	Factory workers	NA	{ Turnover / Absenteeism	Positive / Positive
Satisfactory peer group interactions				
Evan (1963)[b]	Management trainees	300	Turnover	Negative
Hulin (1968)	Female clerical workers	298	Turnover	Negative
Taylor & Weiss, (1969a, 1969b)	Retail store employees	475	Turnover	Zero
Farris (1971)	Scientists and engineers	395	Turnover	Negative
Telly et al. (1971)	Production workers	900	Turnover	Negative
Waters & Roach (1971)	Clerical workers	160	Turnover	Zero
			Absenteeism	Negative

Note: NA=not available.

[a] A total of 56 foremen plus approximately 3 subordinates of each foreman took part in the study: specific n not reported.

[b] Inference based on study results.

higher on the more repetitive jobs. On the basis of these results, Kilbridge advanced the notion that attempting to explain withdrawal in terms of the repetitiveness of the job represents too simple an explanation for a complex relationship. He argued that such job conditions as group pressures and opportunities to earn incentive pay seem to have a greater influence than task repetitivenuess on withdrawal. Such an argument is in accord with the position advanced by Hulin and Blood (1968) that merely enlarging or enriching jobs will not necessarily result in reduced alienation and withdrawal from work.

Job autonomy and responsibility In addition to his findings concerning the relationship between job stress and turnover, Guest (1955; also Walker & Guest, 1952) also found turnover to be related to a perceived lack of autonomy over one's work. Since this finding, several other studies have appeared which attempted to clarify this relationship.

Ross and Zander (1957), for example, found that both stayers and leavers entered the organization with similar levels of expectations concerning the degree of autonomy that would be present on the job. However, while those who later left reported being given significantly less autonomy than they expected, those who remained generally reported that the amount of job autonomy allowed met their expectations. Similarly, Turner and Lawrence (1965) found a direct relationship between the amount of autonomy and responsibility allowed on a job and attendance.

Building on the work of Turner and Lawrence and others, Hackman and Lawler (1971) studied the impact of several job dimensions on absenteeism. The primary independent variables used in this study were (a) strength of desire for the satisfaction of higher order needs (e.g., feelings of accomplishment, personal growth, etc.) and (b) description of jobs on four core dimensions (variety, autonomy, feedback, and task identity). It was found that absenteeism was significantly and inversely related to both autonomy and task identity but not to variety or feedback. In addition, strong support was shown for the potential moderating effect of higher order need strengths on absenteeism. Employees who strongly sought satisfaction of higher order needs demonstrated lower absence rates when working on jobs rated high on the four job dimensions; no such relation was found for subjects rated low on such need strengths. Apparently, where the job provides a means by which the employees desirous of higher order need satisfaction can work towards the satisfaction of such needs, their resulting satisfaction with the job can be manifested through increased attendance.

Finally, two additional predictive studies among clerical workers and retail store emloyees have shown significant positive relationships between satisfaction with one's perceived level of responsibility and autonomy and propensity to remain (Taylor & Weiss, 1969a, 1969b; Waters & Roach, 1971.

Role clarity Kahn, Wolfe, Quinn, Snoek, and Rosenthal (1964) have suggested three conditions which can lead to role ambiguity: (a) rapid organizational change, (b) organizational complexity, and (c) managerial philosophies concerning communications. When such ambiguity remains for prolonged periods of time, a feeling of futility and general job dissatisfaction may result which, according to this model, can often lead to withdrawal, psychologically if not physically. Based on this thinking, it appears useful to assess the available research as it applies to the relationship between the clarity or ambiguity of one's organizational role and withdrawal. All of the data deal with turnover so no conclusions can be reached concerning absenteeism.

In an early investigation, Weitz (1956) tested the hypothesis that job applicants who were provided with a clear picture of their jobs prior to employment would be more likely to remain with the organization than those who did not receive this information. Using a well-controlled field experimental design, he mailed each new job applicant in the experimental group a booklet describing in detail the job tasks and functions; applicants in the control group received no such booklet. Results of the study clearly demonstrated that prior knowledge and understanding of the role requirements on a job were a significant factor in continued participation among those applicants who joined the organization. Using variations of Weitz' field experimental design, both Youngberg (1963) and Macedonia (1969) arrived at similar conclusions. In addition, Youngberg found that increased realism of job expectations was also significantly related to later satisfaction on that job.

In a questionnaire survey of staff nurses, Lyons (1971) found that perceived role clarity was negatively related to voluntary turnover, propensity to leave, and job tension and positively related to work satisfaction. While the correlations were nonsignificant for nurses classified as low on a need-for-clarity index, such correlations were significantly higher for nurses with a high need for clarity. Lyons concluded from these findings that certain individuals have a higher tolerance for ambiguity in their job and that such persons are little affected by unclear roles. On the other hand, individuals less tolerant of role ambiguity tend to quit at a higher rate if their roles are left relatively unspecified.

All four of these studies represent excellent research in terms of methodology. While more research is deemed desirable here, the investigations, when taken together, are clear in their results. Prior information concerning the nature of the job can lead to more realistic expectations on the part of many new employees as to what type of job environment they are entering. Such prior knowledge can allow the job applicant to know what is to be expected of him if he joins as well as what types of rewards are possible in exchange for his participation. Thus, we would expect some individuals to conclude *prior* to employment that the rewards offered by the organization did not justify the effort and to decide not to join in the first place. Those who did accept employment with such prior knowledge, on the other hand, would have a more accurate picture of the required efforts and possible rewards, resulting in a greater degree of congruence between individual role and reward expectations and later job experiences. Since rewards would be perceived here as being far more equitable with the employee's adjusted (and presumably more realistic) expectations, turnover due to unmet expectations should tend to diminish.

Summary In general, turnover has been found to be positively related to dissatisfaction with the content of the job among both blue- and white-collar workers. Insufficient evidence is available, however, to draw any such conclusions concerning absenteeism, but initial investigations point to a similar relationship. More specifically, the available data tend to indicate that both absenteeism and turnover are positively associated with task repetitiveness, although such a conclusion may represent an oversimplification of the nature of the relationship (see, e.g., Hulin & Blood, 1968). Finally, a strong positive relation has been found consistently between both forms of withdrawal and a perceived lack of sufficient job autonomy or responsibility.

The degree of role clarity on the part of the individual can apparently affect turnover in two ways. First, an accurate picture of the actual tasks required by the organization can function to select out, prior to employment, those who do not feel

Table 4

Studies of Relations between Job Content Factors and Turnover and Absenteeism

FACTOR	POPULATION	n	TYPE OF WITH-DRAWAL STUDIED	RELATION TO WITHDRAWAL
Satisfaction with job content				
Saleh et al. (1965)	Nurses	263	Turnover	Negative
Hulin (1968)	Clerical workers	298	Turnover	Zero
Katzell (1968)	Students nurses	1852	Turnover	Negative
Dunnette et al. (see Footnote 4)	Lower-level managers	1020	Turnover	Negative
Taylor & Weiss (1969a, 1969b)	Retail store employees	475	Turnover	Negative
Kraut (see Footnote 5)	Computer salesmen	Varied	Turnover	Negative
Wild (1970)	Female manual workers	236	Turnover	Negative
Telly et al. (1971)	Production workers	900	Turnover	Negative
				Negative
Waters & Roach (1971)	Clerical workers	160	Absenteeism	Negative
Task repetitiveness				
Guest (1955)	Automobile assembly line workers	18	Turnover	Positive
		568	Turnover	Zero

Study	Sample	N	Measure	Relationship
Kilbridge (1961)	Production workers	331	Absenteeism	Positive
Lefkowitz & Katz (1969)	Factory workers	80	Turnover	Positive
Taylor & Weiss (1969a, 1969b)	Retail store employees	475	Turnover	Positive
Wild (1970)	Female manual workers	236	Turnover	Positive
Job autonomy and responsibility.				
Guest (1955)	Automobile assembly line workers	18	Turnover	Negative
Ross & Zander (1957)	Female skilled workers	507	Turnover	Negative
Turner & Lawrence (1965)	Blue-collar workers	403	Absenteeism	Negative
Taylor & Weiss (1969a, 1969b)	Retail store employees	475	Turnover	Negative
Hackman & Lawler (1971)	Telephone operators and clerks	208	Absenteeism	Negative
Waters & Roach (1971)	Clerical workers	160	Turnover	Negative
Role clarity				
Weitz (1956)	Insurance salesmen	474	Turnover	Negative
Youngberg (1963)	Insurance salesmen	NA	Turnover	Negative
Macedonia (1969)	Military academy cadets	1260	Turnover	Negative
Lyons (1971)	Nurses	156	Turnover	Negative

Note: NA = not available.

the rewards offered justify doing such tasks. And, secondly, accurate role perceptions can serve to adjust the expectations of those already employed to more realistic levels as to what is expected of them in terms of performance. The resulting increased congruence between expectations and actual experience apparently can serve to increase satisfaction and continued participation. No conclusions can be drawn concerning the effect of role clarity on absenteeism due to a lack of investigations on the subject.

The results of those studies relating to job content are summarized in Table 4.

Personal factors

Factors unique to the individual also appear to have a significant impact on the problems of turnover and absenteeism. Such factors include (a) age, (b) tenure with the organization, (c) similarity of job with vocational interest, (d) personality characteristics, and (e) family considerations. While often overlooked by investigators, the inclusion of such items are central to developing a comprehensive model explaining the dynamics of work participation.

Age Existing empirical evidence generally agrees that there is a strong negative relationship between increased age and turnover (Bassett, 1967; Farris, 1971; Fleishman & Berniger, 1960; Ley, 1966; Minor, 1958; Robinson, 1972; Stone & Athelstan, 1969). One study, however, found such a relationship in women but not in men (Shott, Albright, & Glennon, 1963). Also, this relationship was found to be reversed in another study for employees during training periods, but after 6 months on the job, the typical pattern emerged (Downs, 1967).

While turnover generally appears to be inversely associated with age, absenteeism may well be directly related to it, although such relationships are probably weak. De la Mare and Sergean (1961) and Cooper and Payne (1965) both found age among blue-collar workers to be positively related not only to the frequency of absences but also their duration. However, Naylor and Vincent (1959) found absenteeism among female clerical workers to be unrelated to age.

Length of service Closely associated with age is tenure with an organization and, not surprisingly, many corresponding results emerge. In a study of turnover among factory workers, Knowles (1964) found that length of service on an employee's *previous* job was a highly accurate predictor of the likelihood of his remaining on his present job. Moreover, Shott et al. (1963) found that clerical workers who had long tenure with their present employer also worked at least 10 months for their previous employer. Similar findings have been demonstrated by Fleishman and Berniger (1960) and by Robinson (1972). Such findings reinforce the traditional "job hopper" phenomenon so common in the personnel manager's repertoire of evaluative employment tools.

The implications of increased tenure for absenteeism are somewhat less clear since the available data are not consistent. Hill and Trist (1955), in a longitudinal study, found little variation in absenteeism rates among workers with differing amounts of tenure. Baumgartel and Sobol (1959), on the other hand, found a negative relationship between increased tenure and absenteeism among male blue-collar workers, but they also found a positive relationship between such tenure and absenteeism among female blue-collar workers and among white-collar employees of both sexes. Surely more investigation is warranted here to clarify such apparently contradictory findings.

Similarity of job with vocational interest While empirically sound interest inventories have existed for some time, there is a definite paucity of recent research relating such inventories to turnover and absenteeism (Schuh, 1967). Only three relatively recent studies using interest inventories to predict turnover have been found. No studies have been found concerning absenteeism.

Boyd (1961) and Ferguson (1958) both investigated the predictive value of the Strong Vocational Interest Blank for indicating potential turnover among white-collar workers. Boyd, studying engineers, found that those employees who remained longer on the job scored higher on those factors of the Strong Vocational Interest Blank that would typically indicate an interest in engineering (e.g., mechanical-technical interests). Similarly, Ferguson concluded from his investigation of insurance salesmen that those expressing high interest in selling terminated much less frequently than those not possessing such interest, particularly if they were somewhat successful on the job.

A third example of the implications for tenure of congruence between interests and job is provided by Mayeske (1964). Using the Kuder Preference Record in a study of 125 foresters, he found that turnover was significantly and inversely related to preference ratings for outdoor activities.

Personality characteristics Other personal factors, in addition to vocational interests, also appear to have a direct impact on turnover and absenteeism. In an exploratory study of the relation of various personality traits to turnover among engineers, Meyer and Cuomo (1962) found that those who left typically manifested higher degrees of achievement orientation, aggression, independence, self-confidence, and sociability than those who stayed. Stayers, on the other hand, were seen by interviewers as possessing more emotional stability, maturity, sincerity, stronger job identification, and more moderate achievement orientations. Farris (1971) also found high achievement orientation to be a predictor of turnover among technical and scientific personnel.

Manifest anxiety has been found to be significantly related to absenteeism among industrial workers (Sinha, 1963) and to turnover among workers on hazardous jobs (Hakkinen & Toivainen, 1960). This latter study also found turnover to be inversely related to emotional stability. Finally, turnover has been shown to be related to high degrees of sociability, ascendance, and neuroticism among foremen (MacKinney & Wolins, 1960) and to high authoritarianism ratings among mental hospital ward attendants (Cleland & Peck, 1959).

From the limited evidence available, a tendency appears to emerge for those employees who leave the organization to manifest characteristics near polar positions at either end of various personality trait continua. For example, those who are fairly unstable emotionally or exhibit high anxiety tend to withdraw. Similarly, employees demonstrating a very high degree of independence, self-confidence, and aggressiveness, as well as those with very high career aspirations, also appear to leave more often. It can be hypothesized from these limited findings that organizations tend to retain as more permanent employees those clustering nearer the center of such continua.

Family size and responsibilities Research on the impact of family considerations on withdrawal have centered around two related variables: (a) family size and (b) family responsibilities.

Naylor and Vincent (1959) and Stone and Athelstan (1969), studying absenteeism and turnover, respectively, among female samples found that increases in family size were related to increased tendencies to withdraw. On the other hand, Knowles (1964) found increased family size to be inversely related to turnover among male factory workers. This differential impact of size on male and female turnover can easily be explained by the nature of traditional role differentiation in the past. Whether such trends continue in the face of the current reevaluation of role divisions between men and women remains to be demonstrated.

Closely related to family size are the needs and requirements placed on an individual as a result of being responsible for a family. Guest (1955) found that some turnover among male factory workers resulted from pressure exerted by their spouses, who feared the physical and emotional strains of the job would break up what they considered a normal family life. Similarly, Saleh et al. (1965) found that a full 30% of their sample of recently terminated nurses cited "family reasons" as their primary reason for resignation. Finally, evidence has been found in three studies that older women (whose children are either grown or require less attention) consistently demonstrated lower termination rates than their younger counterparts (Fleishman & Berniger, 1960; Minor, 1958; Robinson, 1972).

Summary The findings concerning personal factors in withdrawal are summarized in Table 5. Age is strongly and negatively related to turnover, while being somewhat positively (though weakly) related to absenteeism. Similarly, increased tenure appears to be strongly related to propensity to remain. One possible explanation here may be that increases in tenure result in increases in personal investment on the part of the employee in the organization (i.e., after a while, he may not be able to "afford" to quit). No solid conclusions can be drawn concerning the impact of tenure on absenteeism, however, due to conflicting results.

From limited studies, turnover appears to be related positively to the similarity between job requirements and vocational interests. No studies were found that related such interests to absenteeism, however. Predicting turnover or absenteeism from interest inventories (assuming they are properly validated) represents an important possibility for organizations because such data can be collected *prior* to employment. Such an advantage does not exist for most predictors of withdrawal.

The majority of studies investigating the relationship between personality traits and withdrawal center around turnover so no conclusions can be drawn about their relation to absenteeism. Apparently, the possession of more extreme personality traits may lead to an increased tendency to leave the organization. While further investigation is definitely in order here, a tendency exists for employees manifesting very high degrees of anxiety, emotional instability, aggression, independence, self-confidence, and ambition to leave the organization at a higher rate than employees possessing such traits in a more moderate degree. The implications of such a phenomenon, if borne out by further research, need also to be investigated for their effects on organizational efficiency and effectiveness. That is, if such a pattern really exists, research is needed as to the desirability for the organization of accepting a higher turnover rate in exchange for possible resulting increases in performance from such mobile employees. No research has been found that demonstrates that low-turnover employees (those possessing more moderate personality traits) are in fact better performers. Thus, reduced turnover may be an undesirable goal if it is bought at the price of reduced work-force effectiveness.

Finally, family size and family responsibilities were generally found to be positively related to turnover and absenteeism among women, while their impact on men appears to be mixed.

SUMMARY AND DISCUSSION

The foregoing review clearly shows that a multiplicity of organizational, work, and personal factors can be associated with the decision to withdraw. It is possible, however, to summarize briefly those factors for which sufficient evidence exists to draw meaningful conclusions concerning their relation to withdrawal.

In general, very strong evidence has been found in support of the contention that *over-all* job satisfaction represents an important force in the individual's participation decision. In addition, based on preliminary evidence, such satisfaction also appears to have a significant impact on absenteeism. These trends have been demonstrated among a diversity of work group populations and in organizations of various types and sizes. Moreover, the methodologies upon which these findings are based are generally of a fairly rigorous nature.

However, as noted earlier, it is not sufficient for our understanding of the withdrawal process to simply point to such a relationship. It is important to consider what constitutes job satisfaction. Under the conceptualization presented here, job satisfaction is viewed as the sum total of an individual's met expectations on the job. The more an individual's expectations are met on the job, the greater his satisfaction. Viewing withdrawal within this framework points to the necessity of focusing on the various factors that make up the employee's expectation set.

We have proposed four general categories, or "levels" in the organization, in which factors can be found that affect withdrawal. Sufficient evidence exists to conclude that important influences on turnover can be found in each of these categories. That is, some of the more central variables related to turnover are organization-wide in their derivation (e.g., pay and promotion policies), while others are to be found in the immediate work group (e.g., unit size, supervision, and co-worker relations). Still others are to be found in the content of the job (e.g., nature of job requirements) and, finally, some are centered around the person himself (e.g., age and tenure). Thus, based on these findings, the major roots of turnover appear to be fairly widespread throughout the various facets of organizational structure, as they interact with particular types of individuals.

On a more tentative level, initial findings indicate that role clarity and the receipt of recognition and feedback are also inversely related to turnover. However, not all of the possible factors reviewed here have been found to be clearly or consistently related to termination. For example, conflicting data exist concerning the influence of task repetitiveness and of family size on such withdrawal.

Much less can be concluded about the impact of these factors on absenteeism due to a general lack of available information. Sufficient evidence does exist, however, to conclude with some degree of confidence that increased unit size is strongly and directly related to absenteeism. In addition, tentative evidence suggests that opportunities for participation in decision making and increased job autonomy are inversely related to such behavior.

One further point warrants emphasis here concerning the turnover studies reviewed above. To a large extent, there is an underlying assumption, often inferred but sometimes stated, that the reduction of all turnover is a desirable goal. Such an assumption may be questioned on several grounds. First, from the individual's point of view, leaving an unrewarding job may result in the procurement of a more satisfying one. Second, from the organization's standpoint, some of those who leave may be quite ineffective performers, and their departure would open positions for (hopefully) better performers. The important point here is that a clear distinction should be made in future research efforts between effective and ineffective leavers.

Table 5

Studies of Relations between Personal Factors and Turnover and Absenteeism

FACTOR	POPULATION	n	TYPE OF WITH-DRAWAL STUDIED	RELATION TO WITHDRAWAL
Age				
Minor (1958)	Female clerical workers	440	Turnover	Negative
Naylor & Vincent (1959)	Female clerical workers	220	Absenteeism	Zero
Fleishman & Berniger (1960)	Female clerical workers	205	Turnover	Negative
de la Mare & Sergean (1961)	Industrial workers	140	Absenteeism	Positive
Shott et al. (1963)	Male office workers	561	Turnover	Zero
Cooper & Payne (1965)	Female office workers	392	Turnover	Negative
Ley (1966)	Construction workers		Absenteeism	Positive
Bassett (1967)	Factory workers	100	Turnover	Negative
	Technicians and engineers	200	Turnover	Negative
Downs (1967)	Public service organiza-tion trainees	1736	Turnover	Positive
	Public service organiza-tion employees (after training)		Turnover	Negative
Stone & Athelstan (1969)	Clerical workers	453	Turnover	Negative
Farris (1971)	Scientists and engineers	395	Turnover	Negative
Robinson (1972)	Female clerical workers	200	Turnover	Negative
Tenure				
Hill & Trist (1955)	Factory workers	289	Absenteeism	Zero
	Male blue-collar workers		Absenteeism	Negative
Baumgartel & Sobol (1959)	Female blue-collar, male and female white-collar workers	3900	Absenteeism	Positive

Reference	Worker group	N	Criterion	Relationship
Fleishman & Berniger (1960)	Female clerical workers	205	Turnover	Negative
Shott et al. (1963)	Male and female office workers	561	Turnover	Negative
Knowles (1964)	Factory workers	56	Turnover	Negative
Robinson (1972)	Female clerical workers	200	Turnover	Negative
Congruence of job with vocational interests				
Ferguson (1958)	Insurance salesmen	520	Turnover	Negative
Boyd (1961)	Engineers	326	Turnover	Negative
Mayeske (1964)	Foresters	125	Turnover	Negative
"Extreme" personality characteristics*				
Cleland & Peck (1959)	Ward attendants	54	Turnover	Positive
Hakkinen & Toivainen (1960)	Miners	135	Turnover	Positive
MacKinney & Wolins (1960)	Male production foremen	175	Turnover	Positive
Meyer & Cuomo (1962)	Engineers	1360	Turnover	Positive
Sinha (1963)	Industrial workers	110	Absenteeism	Positive
Farris (1971)	Technical personnel	395	Turnover	Positive
Family size				
Naylor & Vincent (1959)	Female clerical workers	220	Absenteeism	Positive
Knowles (1964)	Male factory workers	56	Turnover	Negative
Stone & Athelstan (1969)	Female physical therapists	453	Turnover	Positive
Family responsibilities				
Guest (1955)	Male auto assembly line workers	18	Turnover	Positive
Minor (1958)	Female clerical workers	440	Turnover	Positive
Fleishman & Berniger (1960)	Female clerical workers	205	Turnover	Positive
Saleh et al. (1965)	Nurses	263	Turnover	Positive
Robinson (1972)	Female clerical workers	200	Turnover	Positive

*See text for more detailed description.

The loss of an effective employee may cost far more than the loss of an ineffective one, and the costs of efforts to retain the latter may well exceed the benefits. Third, given the present state of technological flux, turnover may in some ways be considered a necessary evil. It may be necessary to simply accept certain levels of turnover as the price for rapid change and increased efficiency.

Methodological considerations

Before discussing the implications of the findings covered in this review, some attention should be paid to the methodologies employed in these studies. While methodological problems with particular studies have been discussed in the body of the review where appropriate, some general issues warrant emphasis here.

A major weakness of many of the studies is the failure to design the investigations in a predictive fashion. For example, all four of the studies reviewed here concerning task repetitiveness collected the majority of their data (including attitudinal measures) *after* termination. Under such circumstances, it is difficult to ascertain which factor is the true dependent variable; indeed, it is quite probable that the act of withdrawal significantly altered the attitudinal predisposition under study.

Moreover, many studies failed to provide for adequate control groups in their study designs. Thus, for example, a finding that most terminees characterized their jobs as being high in stress may lose meaning if it is simultaneously found that those who remained also perceived high stress. The matching of stayers with leavers along several demographic dimensions, as has been done by Ross and Zander (1957) and Hulin (1966, 1968), reduce such potential spuriousness of results. Similarly, it should prove useful if future studies made greater use of cross-validational and cross-organizational designs for both turnover and absenteeism. If we are to use the knowledge we have gained or will gain in any meaningful way, it is important to have some idea of its generalizability across work environments.

With a few notable exceptions, the "limited alternative" questionnaire technique has been used almost exclusively in the attitudinal research on withdrawal. The singular use of such a procedure, while advantageous for statistical and analytical purposes, may have the effect of omitting from consideration important areas relevant to an individual's withdrawal decision. In this regard, it appears a useful strategy would be the increased use of supplemental data collection techniques (e.g., open-ended interviews) in concert with the questionnaires. Such a procedure would have the advantage of providing greater explanatory power and increased insight into the potential range of factors associated with withdrawal.

Since the earlier reviews by Brayfield and Crockett (1955) and Herzberg et al. (1957), some advancements have been made in the literature in the areas of increased validation and reliability of the instruments employed. Good examples of such instruments for use in turnover and absenteeism studies are the Job Descriptive Index and the Minnesota Satisfaction Questionnaire. However, further efforts are necessary in the area to provide a broader array of validated instruments to gain increased comprehension of the phenomena. Similarly, better measures of turnover and absenteeism are also needed to differentiate more accurately avoidable from unavoidable reasons.

In addition, the majority of the studies reported here collected attitudinal measures at one point in time and compared these measures to withdrawal rates. Such procedures fail to take into account changes in attitudes as they may or may not affect the withdrawal decision. Furthermore, such studies do not provide an adequate basis for drawing conclusions concerning directions of causality. More attention should also be paid in the future to designing investigations which include researcher interventions designed to alter expectancies and to comparing the effects of such interventions to potential differences in rates of withdrawal. A useful lead has been taken here by Lawler and Hackman (1969; also, Scheflen et al., 1971), where variables in the work situation were experimentally manipulated and changes in attendance rates over time were systematically compared against control groups. Future research should therefore make better use of the longitudinal and field experimental designs (including adequate controls) to isolate more precisely the study variables for purposes of analysis.

Met expectations and turnover

The preceding review of turnover and absenteeism studies highlights the fact that there is an abundance of findings concerning the former and a relative paucity of findings concerning the latter. Because of this difference and because of the potential danger of undue generalizations from a joint treatment of the topics, the role of met expectations on turnover *only* are discussed here. A later section will consider the problem of absenteeism.

The major turnover findings of this review, when taken together, point to the centrality of the concept of met expectations in the withdrawal decision. Under such a conceptualization, each individual is seen as bringing to the employment situation his own unique set of expectations for his job. It is likely, based on the results presented here, that most employees place a fairly high valence on the attainment of their expectations in certain areas, such as pay, promotion, supervisory relations, and peer group interactions. In addition, however, each individual appears to place varying importance on a host of other potential "rewards" available from his job. For some, the most important factor may be challenging work, while for others it may be the status attached to one's job; for some, it may be both. Whatever the composition of the individual's expectation set, it is important that *those* factors be substantially met if the employee is to feel it is worthwhile to remain with the organization. Doubling the salary of a man who is genuinely disinterested in money may have little effect in ensuring his continued participation. While this set of expectations may be modified over time in response to past rewards, available alternatives, and other factors, it is toward the present or anticipated satisfaction of this fairly unique set of expectations that we must direct our attention if we are to understand the termination decision.

In general, then, the decision to participate or withdraw may be looked upon as a process of balancing received or potential rewards with desired expectations. Such an explanation, however, raises questions as to what the organization can do if it wants to reduce such turnover. Based on the literature, several seemingly contradictory approaches result. In an effort to clarify these apparent contradictions, we will discuss in detail the findings of six of the more important studies as they apply to the problem at hand.

Ross and Zander (1957), Katzell (1968), and Dunnette et al. (see Footnote 4) found that the mean levels of *initial* expectations of those who remained and those who later decided to leave were essentially the same. Thus, while individuals may vary considerably in terms of their own expectation set, no significant differences were found between stayers and leavers as a group at the time of entry into the organization. However, those who later left reported significantly lower levels of met expectations as time went on. Since the original expectations were similar, the significant differences between the two groups in the degree to which such expectations were actually met could have resulted from the existence of differential reward levels. Those who left may have failed, in general, to meet their expectation on the job and sought satisfaction elsewhere. Following this approach, turnover could presumably be reduced somewhat through an increase in the reward levels so they would be more congruent with the more stationary expectation levels.

Weitz (1956), Youngberg (1963), and Macedonia (1969), on the other hand, altered the experimental groups' initial expectations, resulting in distinct differences between the stayers' and leavers' mean levels of expectation at the time of entry into the organization. Those who later decided to remain presumably had more realistic levels upon entry. A unitary reward system can be inferred from these findings, suggesting that one key to the reduction of turnover would be to clarify expectations among entering personnel so as to bring them into closer alignment with the available rewards.

While the first set of findings here appears to be in conflict with the second set, closer analysis demonstrates that it is quite possible to achieve a viable synthesis. It appears from these investigations that both expectation levels and reward levels are variable within certain limits. Such possible fluctuations are depicted in the hypothetical example shown in Figure 1. Following this example, we can first apply the results of Ross and Zander, Katzell, and Dunnette et al. where both stayers and leavers entered the organization with similar mean expectation levels, represented in Figure 1 by the column labeled E_1. As a result of differential reward levels, represented in Figure 1 by R_1, R_2, and R_3, some employees would tend to perceive that rewards met or exceeded expectations (in the case of R_1), resulting in increased satisfaction and an increased propensity to participate. Other employees, however, would perceive rewards to be below their expectations (in the case of R_2 and R_3), resulting in decreased satisfaction and an increased propensity to leave.

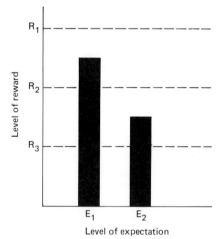

Fig. 1 Hypothetical example of expectations × rewards interaction as they relate to decision to withdraw.

Next, we can apply the model to the findings of Weitz (1956), Youngberg (1963), and Macedonia (1969). Here, the mean expectation level of those who later left remained unchanged (represented by E_1), while the mean level of those who stayed was generally adjusted downward (to E_2) by increasing the employees' knowledge about the nature of the job. Thus, even with the impact of differential reward levels, it can be seen that, on the whole, a greater number of those who stayed would be more likely to experience met expectations than those who later left. The stayers, with more realistic expectation levels, would have a greater number of potential reward levels (R_1 and R_2) lying above their expectation levels than would the leavers (R_1 *only*), thereby increasing the chances of meeting or exceeding their expectations on the job.

The use of such a model points to at least three actions that the organization might attempt in its effort to reduce turnover. First, attempts can be made to enrich the total amount of potentially available rewards. This action should serve to increase the probability that reward expectations will be met. Such a procedure may have limited applicability, of course, due to structural and financial constraints on the organization. Various feasible approaches do exist, however, for improving rewards in such areas as supervisory and co-worker interactions, recognition and feedback on performance, and fairness (if not increases) in compensation policies. Second, organizations may consider the installation of cafeteria-style compensation plans (Lawler, 1971) to allow the employee a greater selection of rewards toward which to work. Such increased selection should serve in part to increase the likelihood that more of his expectations can be met on the job. Third, and perhaps most important, the organization can attempt to increase the present or potential employee's accuracy and realism of expectations through increased communications concerning the nature of the job and the probable potential payoffs for effective performance. Where the employee fully understands what is expected of him and what the organization offers in return, the likelihood of his forming unrealistic expectations should decrease, resulting in increased possibilities that his expectations are actually met.

The clarification for the employee of both expectations and potential rewards, then, should have the effect of generally increasing the degree to which such expectations are met. Where these expectations have been essentially satisfied and where the employee has no reason to believe they will not continue to be satisfied in the future, we would expect an increase in the propensity to remain and participate in the activities of the organization. Where the individual's expectations by and large remain unsatisfied and where alternative forms of employment exist which promise greater satisfaction, we would expect an increased tendency to leave.

Met expectations and absenteeism

The organization's tendency not to accept even minimal turnover appears often to be matched by a somewhat unconcerned attitude toward absenteeism. Perhaps this is due, in part, to an inability in many cases to distinguish accurately between avoidable and unavoidable absenteeism for purposes of measurement. It may be, however, that the costs to the organization due to poor attendance may be far greater than the costs of turnover. The studies reviewed here indicate that those employees in which the organization has the least investment (young, low-tenured employees) have the greatest incidences of turnover, while those employees who are older and more mature (and in whom the organization typically has greater investment) apparently have increased incidences of absenteeism. If this is the case, a redirection of effort may be in order away from the study of turnover and toward a better understanding of the more temporary forms of withdrawal. Too often in the past, absenteeism has been considered simply an analogue of turnover, and it has been assumed, without sufficient evidence, that the two shared identical roots.

Several important dimensions exist along which absenteeism as a form of withdrawal can be distinguished from turnover: (a) The negative consequences for the individual that are associated with absenteeism are usually much less than those associated with turnover. For example, with the prevalence of company sick leave policies, an employee can miss work (up to a point) without salary loss. (b) Absenteeism is more likely to be a spontaneous and relatively easy decision, while the act of termination can be assumed to be more carefully considered over time in most cases. (c) Absenteeism may sometimes represent a substitute type of behavior for turnover, particularly where alternative employment is unavailable. In this sense, absenteeism may allow for temporary avoidance of an unrewarding situation without the loss of the benefits of employment; turnover, on the other hand, represents a complete severance of the individual from such benefits.

In view of some of these differences, it is important to compare the two types of withdrawal as they simultaneously relate to specific factors in the work environment. March and Simon (1958) hypothesize that no differences exist between absenteeism and turnover insofar as the factors inducing such forms of behaviors are concerned. However, the evidence as reviewed above does not entirely support such a position (e.g., Kilbridge, 1961; Waters & Roach, 1971). In fact, of the 22 tested relationships in the studies reviewed here where data were available on both turnover and absenteeism among the same samples, only 6 found significant relations in the same direction between the factors under study and *both* types of withdrawal. The remainder found certain factors significantly related to one form of withdrawal but not the other. Such findings suggest that some important differences may exist between the causes of turnover and those of absenteeism.

Whether a model similar to that proposed for turnover (Figure 1) also applies in a somewhat modified version to absenteeism remains to be demonstrated. Even so, one can speculate that such a model is applicable but that different thresholds exist for the two forms of withdrawal. That is, it is possible that the failure by and large to meet one's expectations on the job would lead to increased tendencies both to terminate and to go absent. However, a far greater disparity between such expectations and rewards may be necessary for an individual to decide to quit than to simply decide not to come to work on a particular day.

Future directions for research

Based on this review, several fairly obvious voids exist in our knowledge of turnover and absenteeism which require further study. To begin with, much more emphasis should be placed in the future on the psychology of the withdrawal *process*. While correlational studies abound (particularly with respect to turnover) which relate various factors to withdrawal, our understanding of the manner in which the actual decision is made is far from complete.

Second, a major focus should be placed on differential expectation levels at the time of entry into the organization and the extent to which these expectations are met or altered over the course of employment. This strongly suggests the need for as much attention to expectations as to reactions to the work situation.

Third, some attention should be directed toward the study of differentially valued employees in relation to withdrawal. Organization investments (e.g., compensation, additional training, experience) in employees can vary considerably across hierarchical levels and functions. Similarly, some employees are rated higher by the organization in terms of performance and potential. Little is known about the relation of these factors to withdrawal. It is possible that the more valued employees quit or exhibit high rates of absenteeism for quite different reasons than those who are less valued.

Fourth, more investigation is necessary which simultaneously studies both turnover and absenteeism among the same samples as they are affected by various factors in the organizational situation. Such designs would increase our knowledge not only of the potentially different roots of each type of withdrawal but also of possible interactive effects between the two.

Finally, future research should include more emphasis on determining the effects of specific organizational interventions on turnover and absenteeism. The increased use of longitudinal designs and well-controlled field experiments would significantly increase the confidence we could place in the presumed impact of significant variables on withdrawal.

REFERENCES

Acton Society Trust. *Size and morale.* London: Author, 1953.

Argyle, M., Gardner, G., & Cioffi, I. Supervisory methods related to productivity, absenteeism and labor turnover. *Human Relations,* 1958, **11,** 23-40.

Atchison, T. J., & Lefferts, E. A. The prediction of turnover using Herzberg's job satisfaction technique. *Personnel Psychology,* 1972, **25,** 53-64.

Bassett, G. A. *A study of factors associated with turnover of exempt personnel.* Crotonville, N.Y.: Behavioral Research Service, General Electric Company, 1967.

Baumgartel, H., & Sobol, R. Background and organizational factors in absenteeism. *Personnel Psychology,* 1959, **12,** 431-443.

Boyd, J. B. Interests of engineers related to turnover, selection, and management. *Journal of Applied Psychology,* 1961, **45,** 143-149.

Brayfield, A. H., & Crockett, W. H. Employee attitudes and employee performance. *Psychological Bulletin,* 1955, **52,** 396-424.

Cleland, C. C., & Peck, R. F. Psychological determinants of tenure in institutional personnel. *American Journal of Mental Deficiency,* 1959, **64,** 876-888.

Conference Board. *Salesmen's turnover in early employment.* New York: Author, 1972.

Cooper, R., & Payne, R. Age and absence: A longitudinal study in three firms. *Occupational Psychology,* 1965, **39,** 31-43.

De La Mare, G., & Sergean, R. Two methods of studying changes in absence with age. *Occupational Psychology,* 1961, **35,** 245-252.

Downs, S. Labour turnover in two public service organizations. *Occupational Psychology,* 1967, **41,** 137-142.

Evan, W. M. Peer-group interaction and organizational socialization: A study of employee turnover. *American Sociological Review,* 1963, **28,** 436-440.

Farris, G. F. A predictive study of turnover. *Personnel Psychology,* 1971, **24,** 311-328.

Ferguson, L. W. Life insurance interest, ability and termination of employment. *Personnel Psychology,* 1958, **11,** 189-193.

Fleishman, E. A. A leader behavior description for industry. In R. M. Stogdill & A. E. Coons (Eds.), *Leader behavior: Its description and measurement.* (Ohio Studies in Personnel; Research Monograph No. 88) Columbus: Ohio State University, Bureau of Business Research, 1957. (a)

Fleishman, E. A. The Leadership Opinion Questionnaire. In R. M. Stogdill & A. E. Coons (Eds.), *Leader behavior: Its description and measurement.* (Ohio Studies in Personnel; Research Monograph No. 88) Columbus: Ohio State University, Bureau of Business Research, 1957. (b)

Fleishman, E. A. *Revised Manual for Leadership Opinion Questionnaire.* Chicago: Science Research Associates, 1968.

Fleishman, E. A., & Berniger, J. One way to reduce office turnover. *Personnel,* 1960, **37,** 63-69.

Fleishman, E. A., & Harris, E. F. Patterns of leadership behavior related to employee grievances and turnover. *Personnel Psychology,* 1962, **15,** 43-56.

Friedlander, F., & Walton, E. Positive and negative motivations toward work. *Administrative Science Quarterly,* 1964, **9,** 194-207.

General Electric Company, Behavioral Research Service. *Attitudes associated with turnover of highly regarded employees.* Crotonville, N.Y.: Author, 1964. (a)

General Electric Company, Behavioral Research Service. *A comparison of work planning program with the annual performance appraisal interview approach.* Crotonville, N.Y.: Author, 1964. (b)

Guest, R. H. A neglected factor in labour turnover. *Occupational Psychology,* 1955, **29,** 217-231.

Hackman, J. R., & Lawler, E. E., III. Employee reactions to job characteristics. *Journal of Applied Psychology,* 1971, **55,** 259-286.

Hakkinen, S., & Toivainen, Y. Psychological factors causing labour turnover among underground workers. *Occupational Psychology,* 1960, **34,** 15-30.

Herzberg, F., Mausner, B., Peterson, R. O., & Capwell, D. F. *Job attitudes: Review of research and opinion.* Pittsburgh: Psychological Service of Pittsburgh, 1957.

Hewitt, D., & Parfitt, J. A note on working morale and size of group. *Occupational Psychology,* 1953, **27,** 38-42.

Hill, J. M., & Trist, E. L. Changes in accidents and other absences with length of service. *Human Relations,* 1955, **8,** 121-152.

Hulin, C. L. Job satisfaction and turnover in a female clerical population. *Journal of Applied Psychology,* 1966, **50,** 280-285.

Hulin, C. L. Effects of changes in job-satisfaction levels on employee turnover. *Journal of Applied Psychology,* 1968, **52,** 122-126.

Hulin, C. L., & Blood, M. R. Job enlargement, individual differences, and worker responses. *Psychological Bulletin,* 1968, **69,** 41-55.

Indik, B., & Seashore, S. *Effects of organization size on member attitudes and behavior.* Ann Arbor: University of Michigan, Survey Research Center of the Institute for Social Research, 1961.

Ingham, G. *Size of industrial organization and worker behaviour.* Cambridge: Cambridge University Press, 1970.

Kahn, R., Wolfe, D., Quinn, R., Snoek, J., & Rosenthal, R. *Organizational stress: Studies in role conflict and ambiguity.* New York: Wiley, 1964.

Katz, D., Maccoby, E., Gurin, G., & Floor, L. *Productivity, supervision and morale among railroad workers.* Ann Arbor: University of Michigan, Survey Research Center, 1951.

Katz, D., Maccoby, N., & Morse, N. *Productivity, supervision and morale in an office situation.* Ann Arbor: University of Michigan, Institute for Social Research, 1950.

Katzell, M. E. Expectations and dropouts in schools of nursing. *Journal of Applied Psychology,* 1968, **52,** 154-157.

Kerr, W., Koppelmeier, G., & Sullivan, J. Absenteeism, turnover and morale in a metals fabrication factory. *Occupational Psychology,* 1951, **25,** 50-55.

Kilbridge, M. Turnover, absence, and transfer rates as indicators of employee dissatisfaction with repetitive work. *Industrial and Labor Relations Review,* 1961, **15,** 21-32.

Knowles, M. C. Personal and job factors affecting labour turnover. *Personnel Practice Bulletin,* 1964, **20,** 25-37.

Lawler, E. E., III. *Pay and organizational effectiveness: A psychological view.* New York: McGraw-Hill, 1971.

Lawler, E. E., III, & Hackman, J. R. Impact of employee participation in the development of pay incentive plans: A field experiment. *Journal of Applied Psychology,* 1969, **53,** 467-471.

Lefkowitz, J., & Katz, M. Validity of exit interviews. *Personnel Psychology,* 1969, **22,** 445-455.

Ley, R. Labour turnover as a function of worker differences, work environment, and authoritarianism of foremen. *Journal of Applied Psychology,* 1966, **50,** 497-500.

Lyons, T. Role clarity, need for clarity, satisfaction, tension and withdrawal. *Organizational Behavior and Human Performance,* 1971, **6,** 99-110.

Macedonia, R. M. Expectation-press and survival. Unpublished doctoral dissertation, Graduate School of Public Administration, New York University, June 1969.

MacKinney, A. C., & Wolins, L. Validity information exchange. *Personnel Psychology,* 1960, **13,** 443-447.

Mandell, M. *Recruiting and selecting office employees.* New York: American Management Association, 1956.

March, J. G., & Simon, H. A. *Organizations.* New York: Wiley, 1958.

Mayeske, G. W. The validity of Kuder Preference Record scores in predicting forester turnover and advancement. *Personnel Psychology,* 1964, **17,** 207-210.

Metzner, H., & Mann, F. Employee attitudes and absences. *Personnel Psychology,* 1953, **6,** 467-485.

Meyer, H., & Cuomo, S. *Who leaves? A study of background characteristics of engineers associated with turnover.* Crotonville, N.Y.: General Electric Company, Behavioral Science Research, 1962.

Mikes, P. S., & Hulin, C. Use of importance as a weighting component of job satisfaction. *Journal of Applied Psychology,* 1968, **52,** 394-398.

Minor, F. J. The prediction of turnover of clerical employees. *Personnel Psychology,* 1958, **11,** 393-402.

Naylor, J. E. & Vincent, N. L. Predicting female absenteeism. *Personnel Psychology,* 1959, **12,** 81-84.

Patchen, M. Absence and employee feelings about fair treatment. *Personnel Psychology,* 1960, **13,** 349-360.

Porter, L. W., & Lawler, E. E., III. Properties of organization structure in relation to job attitudes and job behavior. *Psychological Bulletin,* 1965, **64,** 23-51.

Porter, L. W., & Lawler, E. E., III. *Managerial attitudes and performance.* Homewood, Ill.: Irwin, 1968.

Revans, R. Human relations, management and size. In E. M. Huge-Jones (Ed.), *Human relations and modern management.* Amsterdam: North-Holland Publishing, 1958.

Robinson, D. D. Prediction of clerical turnover in banks by means of a weighted application blank. *Journal of Applied Psychology,* 1972, **56,** 282.

Ronan, W. W. A study of some concepts concerning labour turnover. *Occupational Psychology*, 1967, **41**, 193–202.

Ross, I. C., & Zander, A. Need satisfaction and employee turnover. *Personnel Psychology*, 1957, **10**, 327–338.

Saleh, S. D., Lee, R. J., & Prien, E. P. Why nurses leave their jobs—An analysis of female turnover. *Personnel Administration*, 1965, 28, 25–28.

Scheflen, K. C., Lawler, E. E., III, & Hackman, J. R. Long-term impact of employee participation in the development of pay incentive plans: A field experiment revisited. *Journal of Applied Psychology*, 1971, **55**, 182–186.

Schuh, A. The predictability of employee tenure: A review of the literature. *Personnel Psychology*, 1967, **20**, 133–152.

Shott, G. L., Albright, L. E., & Glennon, J. R. Predicting turnover in an automated office situation. *Personnel Psychology*, 1963, **16**, 213–219.

Sinha, A. K. P. Manifest anxiety affecting industrial absenteeism. *Psychological Reports*, 1963, **13**, 258.

Skinner, E. Relationships between leadership behavior patterns and organizational situational variables. *Personnel Psychology*, 1969, **22**, 489–494.

Stogdill, R., & Coons, A. (Eds.) *Leader behavior: Its description and measurement.* Columbus: Ohio State University, Bureau of Business Research, 1957.

Stone, T. H., & Athelstan, G. T. The SVIB for women and demographic variables in the prediction of occupational tenure. *Journal of Applied Psychology*, 1969, **53**, 408–412.

Talacchi, S. Organization size, individual attitudes and behavior: An empirical study. *Administrative Science Quarterly*, 1960, **5**, 398–420.

Taylor, K., & Weiss, D. Prediction of individual job termination from measured job satisfaction and biographical data. (Research Report No. 30) Minneapolis: University of Minnesota, Work Adjustment Project, October 1969. (a)

Taylor, K., & Weiss, D. Prediction of individual job turnover from measured job satisfaction. (Research Report No. 22) Minneapolis: University of Minnesota, Work Adjustment Project, May 1969. (b)

Telly, C. S., French, W. L., & Scott, W. G. The relationship of inequity to turnover among hourly workers. *Administrative Science Quarterly*, 1971, **16**, 164–172.

Turner, A. N., & Lawrence, P. R. *Industrial jobs and the worker: An investigation of response to task attributes.* Boston: Harvard University Press, Division of Research, 1965.

Vroom, V. *Work and motivation.* New York: Wiley, 1964.

Walker, C. R., & Guest, R. H. *The man on the assembly line.* Cambridge: Harvard University Press, 1952.

Walters, L. K., & Roach, D. Relationships between job attitudes and two forms of withdrawal from the work situation. *Journal of Applied Psychology*, 1971, 55, 92–94.

Weitz, J. Job expectancy and survival. *Journal of Applied Psychology*, 1956, **40**, 245–247.

Weitz, J., & Nuckols, R. C. Job satisfaction and job survival. *Journal of Applied Psychology*, 1955, **39**, 294–300.

Wild, R. Job needs, job satisfaction, and job behavior of women manual workers. *Journal of Applied Psychology*, 1970, **54**, 157–162.

Youngberg, C. F. An experimental study of "job satisfaction" and turnover in relation to job expectancies and self expectations. Unpublished doctoral dissertation, New York University, 1963.

FOR DISCUSSION AND REVIEW

1 What is the authors' definition of withdrawal? Why would its study be important for the personnel professional charged with the task of improving productivity?
2 How is job satisfaction related to withdrawal? How are unmet expectations related to withdrawal?
3 Critique, overall, the research reviewed. What deficiencies do the authors point out?
4 What four classes of factors have been found to relate to withdrawal?
5 Discuss whether organization-wide and job-environment factors, as opposed to personal factors, are better explanations for withdrawal.

B. J. Hodge

Richard D. Tellier

Employee Reactions to the Four-Day Week

The four-day work week has been one of the more widely debated topics in business in recent years. On one hand, it has been heralded as a momentous social innovation that provides the employee with a choice in the manner in which he earns his "daily bread."[1] On the other hand, it has been decried as just another management tactic to undermine the advances that have been achieved by labor in the areas of hours of work per day and per week. Most likely, the truth lies somewhere between these extremes.

A NEED FOR RESEARCH

Ever since the late 1960s, a growing number of firms has been converting to the four-day work week.[2] Thus, it has become increasingly important for the businessman to have available results from the research designed to resolve the unanswered organizational and psychological issues surrounding the reduced work week. Several studies—most notably that by Wheeler and associates[3]—have extensively examined the impact of the four-day week on the performance of the firm. The general conclusion has been that productivity and profits typically increase after the reduced work week is implemented. However, some companies have experienced significant problems with the four-day week (one commonly mentioned problem is that of interfacing with the five-day world) and a few have had to return to the five-day week.

While the effect of the reduced work week on the organization's operations has been widely studied, employee reactions to the four-day week have not been extensively examined.[4] To quote Hellriegel:

> There is no scarcity of alleged advantages or disadvantages to the 4–40 plan. The writing on the subject has been highly impressionistic, emphasizing the perceptions of individuals, managers, union leaders, or journalists of what they see to be the present or future effects of conversion. While some hard data are

From *California Management Review* 18, no. 1 (Fall 1975). Reprinted by permission.

available from a few firms on turnover, absenteeism, and productivity, systematic studies which readily can be used as guidelines for other firms have not been conducted.[5]

In order to at least partially fill this void, the authors recently conducted a nationwide study of employees who are presently working a four-day week. The fundamental purpose of this study was to determine how employees react to the reduced work week. This was done by measuring resultant changes (if any) in their satisfaction with their jobs. Additionally, the research was designed to ascertain the primary effects of the four-day week that give rise to these changes in employee job satisfaction.

BACKGROUND

Favorable employee reaction has often been cited as one major reason for the success of the four-day week. The factors mentioned that contribute to this employee satisfaction typically relate to both on-the-job and off-the-job facets of human behavior and range from increased satisfaction with the work itself to satisfaction with more and better-arranged leisure time.

With regard to on-the-job aspects of employee job satisfaction, reductions in absenteeism, tardiness, and turnover are frequently presented as indices of increased employee satisfaction. Kanter[6] notes that one industrial firm attributes its very survival to the recruitment benefits gained from the four-day week and quotes employees as saying that their work had actually become more enjoyable as a result of the shorter week.

With regard to off-the-job facets of employee job satisfaction, Steele and Poor[7] found that the most frequent comment made by employees on a four-day week is that their jobs provide more and better-arranged leisure time. The longer weekend enables the employee to make better use of the time he spends away from work; this results in an increased liking of both the job and the company.

But analyses of the impact of the reduced work week on employees have by no means been entirely favorable. Among the undesirable effects of the four-day week on employee satisfaction with the job that are commonly cited are increased worker fatigue, scheduling problems with others who are on the five-day week (such as a working spouse), the increased financial cost of missing a day of work without a bona fide excuse, and an increased work load on the first day back at the job. Additionally, some writers have argued that the reduced work week is detrimental to the employee in that it gives him an extra day of leisure, which may only result in increased boredom. It has been noted that for many workers the time spent away from the job constitutes a "horrible vacuum of inactivity."[8] Thus, the four-day week for these employees would be an undesirable phenomenon.

With this debate concerning the advantages and disadvantages of the shorter work week as background, a nationwide study of four-day employees was undertaken to determine their reactions to the reduced work week and the primary reasons for those reactions. Three basic questions were addressed by this research:

1 In general, does an employee's satisfaction with his job change as a result of the four-day week?

2 Is the extent of this change (if any) in the employee's satisfaction with his job a function of either employee or organizational demographic characteristics?

3 What are the primary effects of the four-day week which contribute to this change (if any) in the employee's satisfaction with his job?

METHOD

Seiler's behavioral systems model of the organization[9] was used as the basis for the research. This model describes a dynamic sequence of causal relationships between altered inputs (such as changes in job satisfaction). Based on these causal relationships, five hypotheses were formuated that were designed to provide insight to the answers to the questions posed above. Stated in the null form, these hypotheses are:

1 For all employees in general, no change in job satisfaction occurs as a result of the transition to the four-day week.

2 For employees within a specific employee organizational demographic grouping (see Table 1 for groupings), no change in job satisfaction occurs as a result of the transition to the four-day week.

3 For employees within a specific organizational demographic grouping (see Table 2), no change in job satisfaction occurs as a result of the transition to the four-day week.

4 For each employee demographic characteristic, there is no difference between employee groupings with regard to the extent of the change (if any) in job satisfaction that occurs as a result of the transition to the four-day week.

5 For each organizational demographic characteristic, there is no difference between employee groupings with regard to the extent of the change (if any) in job satisfaction that occurs as a result of the transition to the four-day week.

Each of the alternative hypotheses was nondirectional, thus allowing for both increases and decreases in job satisfaction possibly occurring as a result of the four-day week.

The questionnaire used in the study was comprised of a fact sheet, a "Job Satisfaction Index" scale, and two open questions regarding employee "likes" and "dislikes" of the four-day week. The face sheet provided pertinent demographic data about the respondent, such as his sex, age, marital status, and so forth. The Job Satisfaction Index scale was a slightly modified version of Brayfield and Rothe's Index of Job Satisfaction scale[10] and was used to provide an indication of the extent (if any) to which the respondent's satisfaction with his job had changed as a result of the four-day week. Typical scale items were: "As a result of the four-day week, I am more inclined to consider my job as being rather unpleasant," and "As a result of the four-day week, I am more enthusiastic about my work." The possible responses for each item ranged from "strongly agree" to "strongly disagree." The adjusted split-half reliability coefficient for the modified scale ($r = 0.89$) was slightly higher than that originally reported by Brayfield and Rothe ($r = 0.87$). The Thurstone scaling procedure used to develop the eighteen items of the scale resulted in nine favorable and nine unfavorable statements, balanced with respect to intensity.[11] Hence, the central (null) score over all items implied "no change in job satisfaction," while low and high scores reflected decreases and increases. The two open questions of the study were: "What are some of the things you like about the change to the four-day work week?" and "What are some of the things you dislike about the change to the four-day work week?" The hypotheses were tested using standard parametric statistical methods, and the two open questions were content analyzed[12] with regard to substance and frequency of responses.

The study data were gathered through a stratified random sampling procedure designed to include a wide variety of both employees and organizations with respect to demographic characteristics. Copies of the questionnaire were sent to 371 employees of twelve four-day companies throughout the United States. The elapsed time since having made the conversion to the reduced work week ranged from twelve to thirty-nine months, with a median of nineteen months. Only employees who had been in their present jobs at least three months prior to the change in the work week were included in the study. Of the 274 questionnaires returned, 223 were usable.

RESULTS

As noted previously, the study was designed to address three basic questions regarding employee reactions to the reduced work week. The findings of the research are described in terms of how they relate to each of these questions.

Question 1. In general, does an employee's satisfaction with his job change as a result of the four-day work week? Tables 1 and 2 summarize the results of the forty-eight hypothesis tests conducted in response to the first question. In each of these analyses, the mean change-in-job-satisfaction score for the respondents in the specific demographic grouping being investigated was tested against a null value of no change. Positively signed test statistics imply an increase in job satisfaction, while negative test statistic values imply a decrease.

Basically, no matter how the employees were classified (whether by sex, age, or any other of the demographic classifications examined by the study), the conclusion was reached that employees are substantially more satisfied with their jobs as a result of the conversion to the four-day week. In only one case was this conclusion doubtful, and then only because of a very small sample size (only three of the respondents had an annual salary of $20,000 or above). No demographic characteristic, either for the employee or for the organization, could be identified that resulted in the worker's being less satisfied (or, even at a minimum, just as satisfied) with his job as a result of the conversion to the reduced work week.

Question 2. Is the extent of this increase in the employee's satisfaction with his job a function of either employee or organizational demographic characteristics? Table 3 summarizes the results of the twelve hypothesis tests conducted in response to the second question of the study. In each of these tests, one-way analysis of variance was used to test the mean change-in-job-satisfaction scores for the several demographic groupings within each classification for equality. Significant test statistics imply that one or more means are not equal to the others, while nonsignificant test statistics imply that all means are equal.

For eleven of the twelve employee and organizational demographics investigated by the research, the conclusion was reached that the extent of increase in job satisfaction experienced by the employee is not a function of his own or his organization's particular demographic characteristics (for instance, both male and female workers experience comparable increases in job satisfaction). In the remaining instance the results of the ANOVA were significant. For the employee demographic of time in present job, there was evidence that the worker who had been in the same job for a prolonged period of time was even more satisfied with the reduced work week than were other employees. However, a comparable chi-square test for independence between time-in-present-job and change-in-job-satisfaction gave the opposite result, that is, acceptance of the null hypothesis of independence ($p < 0.10$).

Table 1
Changes in Employee Job Satisfaction Resulting
from the Four-Day Week, by Employee Demographics

GROUPING	NUMBER[1]	t^2
All employees	223	15.562*
By sex		
Male	138	11.580*
Female	83	10.188*
By age		
Under 25	33	5.389*
25–34	81	9.346*
35–44	46	6.368*
45–54	34	9.255*
55 and over	23	4.228*
By marital status		
Unmarried; no dependents	35	4.810*
Unmarried; with dependents	16	4.554*
Married; no dependents	60	9.033*
Married; with dependents	112	11.074*
By education		
No/some high school	37	7.204*
High school diploma	111	11.928*
Some college	43	3.871*
Undergraduate work	19	6.296*
Graduate work	11	4.624*
By annual salary		
Under $5,000	14	2.947**
$5,000–9,999	156	12.847*
$10,000–14,999	36	6.151*
$15,000–19,999	11	6.343*
$20,000 and over	3	1.996
By time in present job		
Under 5 years	109	10.761*
5–9 years	68	8.318*
10–14 years	30	4.138*
15 years or more	15	13.633*
By time in all jobs		
Under 5 years	25	4.579*
5–9 years	56	8.729*
10–14 years	37	7.189*
15–19 years	31	4.058*
20 years or more	72	9.120*
By job type		
Blue-collar	118	10.224*
White-collar	92	11.823*

[1]May not total 223 in some instances because of nonresponses.
[2]Test statistic for change-in-job-satisfaction mean value with a null value of no change.
*$p < 0.01$
**$p < 0.05$

Table 2
Changes in Employee Job Satisfaction Resulting
from the Four-Day Week, by Organizational Demographics

GROUPING	NUMBER	t^1
By geographical location		
Northeast	23	7.582*
South	120	8.925*
North central	39	7.250*
West	41	11.781*
By number of four-day employees		
25 or fewer	53	6.060*
26–100	55	5.563*
101–250	66	14.539*
Over 250	49	7.548*
By industry class		
Manufacturing	77	11.301*
Wholesale/retail	20	3.772*
Finance/insurance	38	6.594*
Services	51	6.093*
Government	37	6.025*
By labor force type		
Unionized	60	10.000*
Nonunionized	163	12.346*

[1]Test statistic for change-in-job-satisfaction mean value with a null value of no change.
*$p < 0.01$

Table 3
Differences between Employee in Extent of Increase
in Job Satisfaction Resulting from the Four-Day Week

DEMOGRAPHIC	F^1 (d.f.)
By employee demographics	
Sex	0.285 (1,219)
Age	1.484 (4,212)
Marital status	0.879 (3,219)
Education	1.391 (4,216)
Annual salary	0.174 (4,215)
Time in present job	3.669 (3,218)*
Time in all jobs	0.863 (4,216)
By organizational demographics	
Geographical location	1.148 (3,219)
Number of four-day employees	2.507 (3,219)
Industry class	0.696 (4,218)
Labor force type	0.874 (1,221)

[1]Test statistic for equality of change-in-job-satisfaction means for all demographic groupings with a particular classification.
*$p < 0.05$

Table 4
Primary Effects of the Four-Day Week on Employees

EFFECT	NUMBER OF TIMES MENTIONED	t^1
Favorable		
More leisure time (longer weekend)	186	2.695*
More time for personal business	58	2.630*
More time for family	39	2.769*
More time for housework	25	2.185**
Facilitates work accomplishment	22	0.927
Reduced commuting time/costs/problems	13	1.168
More time for travel	12	0.965
More time for hobbies	11	1.317
Increased overtime opportunities	8	-0.021
Increased moonlighting opportunities	4	-1.013
Unfavorable		
General dislike of longer workday	85	-6.508*
Conflict with 5-day schedules	26	-1.841
Increased fatigue at work	18	-2.625*
Detracts from work accomplishment	14	-2.189**
Conflict with holidays	8	0.006
Increased cost of unexcused absence	4	-0.982

[1]Test statistic for difference of change-in-job-satisfaction means between those who cited a particular effect and those who did not (d. f.=221).
*$p < 0.01$; **$p < 0.05$

Question 3. What are the primary effects of the four-day work week which contribute to this increase in the employee's satisfaction with his job? Table 4 summarizes the results of the content analysis and statistical tests performed on the responses to the two open questions of the study. From these questions, 533 responses regarding sixteen categories of "likes" and "dislikes" of the four-day week were obtained. Of these 533 comments, 378 were favorable toward the reduced work week while the remaining 155 were unfavorable. By far, the most common positive effect of the four-day week was the more (and better-arranged) leisure time afforded by the longer weekend—186 of 223 respondents cited this as a desirable aspect of the conversion. The most common negative effect cited by the respondents was the often-mentioned general dislike of the longer workday. (However, it should be noted that eighty-six respondents stated that they had no dislike whatsoever with regard to the four-day week).

For each of the sixteen effects obtained by the content analysis, a difference-of-means test was performed to determine whether change-in-job-satisfaction means were equal for both those who cited a particular effect and those who did not. Positively signed test statistics imply a greater mean for those who cited, while negative test statistic values imply a greater mean for those who did not cite. The results of these tests indicate that (at a minimum) leisure time, personal business, family life, housework, length of workday, fatigue, and work accomplishment are the primary factors which are affected by the four-day week. As would be expected, the four favorable effects are positively related to job satisfaction, while the three unfavorable effects are negatively related. Overall, it appears that employees are favorably affected by the reduced work week for the reasons noted in Table 4, and that this generally favorable reaction gives rise to the substantial and pervasive increase in satisfaction with the job that is demonstrated in Tables 1, 2, and 3.

CONCLUSIONS

The four-day week has become increasingly popular in recent years. Consequently, more and more businessmen are contemplating a conversion to the reduced work week. While the impact of the four-day work week on the operations of the organization has been studied in some depth (and found to be, in most instances, a positive one), the effect of the reduced work week on employees had not been extensively investigated.

Accordingly, a nationwide study of employee reactions to the four-day week was undertaken. Based on data gathered from a wide variety of employees and organizations, it was concluded that, for the numerous reasons noted, employees on the whole react favorably to the reduced work week. This generally favorable reaction is reflected by a substantial and virtually universal increase in employee satisfaction with the job, the extent of which is not (at least in most cases) a function of either employee or organizational demographics. Hence, it would appear to be to the businessman's benefit to seriously evaluate the possibility of a conversion to the reduced work week. Not to do so could be a serious mistake.

REFERENCES

1 P. E. Samuelson, "Foreword," in R. Poor, ed., *4 Days, 40 Hours* (Cambridge, Mass.: Bursk and Poor Publishing, 1970), p. 7.
2 D. Hellriegel, "The Four-Day Workweek: A Review and Assessment," *MSU Business Topics* (Spring 1972), p. 40.
3 K. E. Wheeler, R. Gurman, and D. Tarnowieski, *The Four-Day Week* (New York: American Management Association, Inc., 1972).
4 A pioneering study in this area, but limited with respect to employee and organizational demographics, is that conducted by Steele and Poor in 1970; see J. L. Steele and R. Poor, "Work and Leisure: The Reactions of People at 4-Day Firms," in Poor, op. cit., pp. 105–122.
5 Hellriegel, op. cit., p. 43.
6 L. E. Kanter, "An Industrial Pioneer Rescued by the 4-Day Week," in Poor, op.cit., pp. 39–46.
7 Steele and Poor, op. cit., p. 111.
8 J. A. Wilson, "The Meaning of the 4-Day Week: Retreat from Work or Assent to Leisure?", *Pittsburgh Business Review* (March–April 1972), p. 3.
9 J. A. Seiler, *Systems Analysis in Organizational Behavior* (Homewood, Ill.: Irwin, 1967), p. 33.
10 A. H. Brayfield and H. F. Rothe, "An Index of Job Satisfaction," *Journal of Applied Psychology* (October 1959), pp. 307–311.
11 Ibid.
12 F. N. Kerlinger, *Foundations of Behavioral Research* (New York: Holt, Rinehart and Winston, 1964), pp. 544–553.

FOR DISCUSSION AND REVIEW

1 Why is the four-day work week controversial?
2 Describe the type of study which was conducted—its sample, its method, and its results.
3 For what types of organizations and jobs would the four-day week seem most appropriate? Why?

Fred K. Foulkes

Learning to Live with OSHA

After nearly three years of experience with the Occupational Safety and Health
Act, better known simply as OSHA, more and more businessmen are raising questions about the problems associated with the act and the way it is being implemented. One business executive underscored the view held by many OSHA critics
when he said, "The act wasn't needed, it is being implemented too rapidly and with
a hard hand, and the cost of compliance is so high that it threatens our corporation's competitive positions."

Employee rights under OSHA regulations

Signed into law on December 29, 1970, the Occupational Safety and Health Act provides five important rights for the employee (or his or her representative):

1 The employee who believes that a violation of a job safety or health standard
exists which threatens physical harm, or that an imminent danger exists, may request an inspection by sending a signed written notice to the Department of Labor.
(His or her name is not revealed to the employer when the employee requests anonymity.) Under the provisions of the act, the employee may not be discharged or discriminated against for filing such a complaint.

2 When the Department of Labor inspector arrives, customarily unannounced, an
employee representative may accompany the compliance officer on his or her visit
for the purpose of aiding the inspection. This is the so-called "walk-around right."
(An employee representative usually exists only in the unionized workplace. In nonunion workplaces, normally there is no employee representative on the walk-
around, but the compliance officer does question employees as he sees fit.)

3 If the employer is cited by OSHA and protests either the fine or the abatement
period, the employee is entitled to participate in the hearing and to object to the
period of time fixed in the citation for abatement of the violation.

4 With respect to exposure to toxic materials or other physically harmful agents,
the employee may observe the company's monitoring processes. If the substance is
defined as toxic and covered by an OSHA standard, the employee is entitled to
information about his or her exposure period.

5 The employee's authorized representative (rather than the employee) may request that the Secretary of HEW determine "whether any substance normally
found in the place of employment has potentially toxic effects in such concentra-
tions as used or found." If HEW makes this finding, the Secretary of Labor may
institute a rule-making procedure to set a safe exposure level for that substance.

But along with its critics, OSHA has its supporters among employers, union
leaders, and public interest groups. One corporate officer, whose company has established an in-plant training and self-inspection program, says, "We have cut our
lost-time per million man-hours by 50%." And the manager of another but smaller

---

Reprinted by permission from *Harvard Business Review*, November–December 1975,
pp. 57–67. Copyright © 1975 by the President and Fellows of Harvard College; all rights
reserved.

company, which reduced its workmen's compensation cost by 25% in a one-year period, boasts, "We're making OSHA pay."

In my study of business's experience with OSHA, I have yet to hear a single word of criticism about the act's stated purpose "to assure so far as possible every working man and woman in the nation safe and healthful working conditions and to preserve our human resources." Rather, the criticisms I have heard about OSHA focus mainly on the confusion and complexity of the act's interpretation and implementation.

Like any other relatively new federal legislation of such scope, OSHA poses significant problems for those it affects—in this case, businessmen. Both large and small business establishments face difficulties, especially relating to OSHA's sometimes confusing or arbitrary standards, its impact on management-labor relations, and the cost of compliance.

This brings me to the purpose of this article—namely, (a) to discuss these major problem areas, the implications of which are not always so obvious, and (b) to suggest ways in which business management can effectively respond to OSHA's regulations. Although OSHA's most visible impact to date has been in the area of occupational safety, its most significant effect over time will be in health. The reason is that industrial hygiene and occupational medicine are taking on increasing importance and will demand top management's most careful attention and involvement. Consider, for example, these statistics:

- The National Safety Council estimates that more than 14,000 employees are killed and 2.2 million suffer disabling injuries each year as a result of accidents on the job.
- The President's first report on OSHA estimates that there may be at least 100,000 deaths and 390,000 new cases of disabling diseases each year caused by exposure to such substances as asbestos, lead, silica, carbon monoxide, and cotton dust.

Before turning our attention to the problem areas and their implications, however, let me first present a brief historical overview of the Occupational Safety and Health Act.

FOCUS AND LOCUS

In the United States, it seems, major federal legislation regarding management-labor relations occurs every 12 years—the Wagner Act of 1935, The Taft-Hartley Act of 1947, and the Landrum-Griffin Act of 1959. History will record, I believe, that 1971—the year in which the Williams-Steiger Act (OSHA) became effective—was no exception.

Today, OSHA covers some 57 million employees in more than 4.6 million business establishments throughout the country that are engaged in interstate commerce. Only public employees—that is, those serving federal, state, and municipal governments—and private employees, such as miners, who are covered by other safety and health acts, are excluded from the OSHA provisions. (For a summary of basic employee rights under OSHA, see the ruled insert on the preceding page.)

Located in the Department of Labor and with a budget of nearly $70 million, the Occupational Safety and Health Administration is responsible for setting and enforcing standards, encouraging the individual states to develop their own safety and health programs, and establishing certain record-keeping requirements.

Established simultaneously with OSHA, the National Institute for Occupational Safety and Health (NIOSH) is located in the Health, Education, and Welfare Department and has a budget of nearly $30 million. NIOSH conducts research and recommends criteria to OSHA on health standards, undertakes education and training programs, and performs work in the area of safety engineering.

The three-member Occupational Safety and Health Review Commission, much like the National Labor Relations Board although procedurally different, handles the appeals of employers on violations and penalties.

The act provides that the individual states may resume responsibility for employee safety and health if they submit acceptable plans. But their plans have to be "at least as effective" as the federal plan and, once approved, they are federally monitored. As of July 1973, 11 states have had their plans approved, and 4 other states are awaiting legislation.

Trivial and important matters

Business's experience with OSHA during the nearly three years since the act was signed into law on December 29, 1970 reveals that there have been any number of examples, both trivial and important, of what I call "start-up problems."

For example, one of the provisions of the act requires separate bathrooms for male and female employees. As a result, according to one well-circulated story, a Mom-and-Pop store had to install a second bathroom (a ruling subsequently overturned). In addition, early in the act's administration, there was a ban on round toilet seats (split seats were required), a ban on providing ice water to employees (a legacy from the time when ice came from rivers), and a requirement for a hook inside the bathroom.

There is also a case on record of a $50 fine imposed on an Illinois company for failure to display the Labor Department's safety poster. But, as it turned out, OSHA was delinquent, since it had failed to provide the sign to begin with. The company appealed the fine and the OSHA commission later rescinded the penalty.

These and other similarly trivial matters, which for the most part are unrelated to occupational safety and health, resulted, the critics argue, from the too rapid and haphazard collection and publication of the original OSHA standards.

However, there are also stories that are not amusing at all. One reported to me is about a plant manager who insisted that he could tell how long a man had worked in the plant simply by looking at the results of the employee's hearing tests. There was marked deterioration in hearing ability over time; and the company, with an average decibel reading in excess of 115, was doing very little to get the noise level down to the OSHA standard of 90. The manager had in fact told the OSHA inspector that "hundreds of hours of engineering effort are being devoted to the problem," a statement he privately admitted later was "a bold-face lie."

Specificity of standards There are problems relating to the OSHA standards, which have been communicated in a poorly organized way. For example, the sections of the act are indexed, but the index is not coded to page numbers; and some of the standards are unclear or imprecise or too rigidly enforced.

The act states, for instance, that "in the absence of an infirmary, clinic, or hospital in near proximity to the workplace which is used for the treatment of all injured employees, a person or persons shall be adequately trained to render first aid."

The employer may rightly wonder how the phrase "in near proximity" is to be interpreted. And yet, is this something the Labor Department can or should make more precise? In the construction industry, the phrase has been interpreted to mean 15 minutes, but a man can bleed to death in 3 minutes. Sometimes, it is better to leave language imprecise, for every establishment would benefit if its employees had some Red Cross Training.

Conversely, some standards may be too precise or too rigidly enforced. For example, rest rooms are supposed to be located no more than 200 feet from an employee's workplace and not more than one flight of stairs away for every female employee. Surely, the intent of the original standard was not to compel the employer to construct another rest room if the present one was, say, 215 feet away. In mid-1973 OSHA changed this requirement, eliminating the arbitrary 200-foot specification.

There are two types of OSHA standards: the so-called "horizontal" regulations that apply to all industries and relate to fire extinguishers, exits, electrical groundings, and machine guards; and the "vertical" provisions that apply to particular industry groups such as maritime or construction.

The OSHA regulations call for minimum safety and health precautions. For the most part, they are consensus standards, being derived from previous legislation or from such organizations as the National Fire Protection Association and the American National Standards Institute (ANSI). The fact that they are consensus standards poses a problem, however. Standards such as those of ANSI were meant to be guidelines or bench marks with which the employer could compare his company's performance. They were not designed with the idea in mind that they would someday turn up as legislative minimums to which the employer must conform.

As one manager I interviewed said, "These were voluntary standards developed by industry groups, with some industries more involved than others and with uneven support from companies; now they've come back to haunt us as law." But time, experience, and the decisions of the OSHA Review Commission are clearing up most of the problems relating to the standards. In fact, OSHA now issues a monthly publication, "Job Safety and Health." And the National Safety Council has produced a detailed set of guides to the standards, as well as several volumes of self-evaluation work sheets.

Violations and citations

OSHA experience has shown that certain violations are prevalent in particular industries. In the construction industry, for instance, the chief violations are in scaffolding, electrical installations, and failure to shore up trenches. In lumber and other wood-products industries, violations are mostly a matter of inadequate guards on machinery such as saw blades, and failure to provide handrails and fire extinguishers.

Despite the fact that the great majority of all OSHA citations are of a nonserious nature, only about 25% of the business establishments inspected get a clean bill of health, and this has been a relatively constant percentage during the short life of the act. (The phrase "clean bill of health" is somewhat misleading because most of the inspectors seem more safety- than health-oriented.)

One could argue that business management apparently considers the citations fair, since 95% of the employers cited for alleged violations do not contest the citation, the penalty, or the time prescribed for elimination or abatement of the hazard. These are two reasons, however, why this figure and line of argument could be misleading.

First, the fines to date have generally been low, and the cost in both time and money of appealing would probably exceed the amount of the fine. Some businessmen have, however, appealed on principle, and with respect to the abatement periods as well as the amounts of the fines. I know one chief executive who appealed just to give his company lawyers some experience in dealing with OSHA.

Second, the review commission in a few instances has actually increased the amounts of the fines after reexamining some cases. In one particular case, an employer who had appealed a $650 fine was ordered to pay $1,000.

Of all the cases appealed to the OSHA Review Commission, less than half of them were subsequently modified, with the majority of the latter being decided in the employer's favor.

MAJOR PROBLEM AREAS

Cognizant top managers recognize that OSHA is having, and will continue to have, a significant impact on both the contract negotiation and contract administration aspects of the labor-relations process, particularly as more and more employees become familiar with their rights under the act. OSHA also gives added clout to the historical interest of unions in safety and health. We have already seen movement in this direction with the establishment of safety offices by several international unions, as well as the issuance of safety and health bulletins by the Industrial Union Department of the AFL-CIO and by the International Association of Machinists.

All too often in the past, unions and managements have approached health problems by establishing special benefits for affected workers rather than by working to improve on-the-job conditions; but there are signs that union demands are changing. The establishment of union safety offices is a good indication that future concerns will be increasingly directed toward upgrading working conditions.

Consider these recent negotiation demands of the Oil, Chemical, and Atomic Workers International Union, AFL-CIO, which resulted in a four-month strike against Shell Oil:

- health and safety committees in plants, with workers being paid by the company for time devoted to meetings;

- management contributions equivalent to two cents per hour for health and safety research;

- periodic surveys by qualified union-approved industrial health consultants to determine if any hazards exist in work areas, with full disclosure to employees of the results;

- union access to all company information on the morbidity and mortality records of employees;

- compensation for employees' time devoted to plant-site inspections and health-committee meetings.

If the union obtains and makes use of the data gleaned from personal health records, employee death rates, illnesses, and physical examinations, we can expect that there will be demands for changes in refinery procedures as well as in benefits.

Union demands have also been made which guarantee that their rank and file will not be penalized for refusing to perform work under clearly hazardous conditions. Unions feel that the individual employee, with the backing of a specially trained union committeeman, should be a cojudge with management of what constitutes a clearly hazardous condition.

Spill-over effects

Although joint safety committees predate OSHA, this legislation will undoubtedly lead to the creation of more such committees in the future. Labor Department literature actually encourages the formation of safety and health committees, and there is much evidence to suggest that they can be helpful. After all, the employee is the one who sees unsafe methods and hazardous conditions, who can suggest improved methods and help to obtain cooperation in implementing them, and who has a vested interest in doing so.

For the most part, however, this is not the case in the health area. Often the employee (and the employer too) simply does not know the long-term negative effects of the health hazards to which he or she is exposed.

OSHA also has a spill-over effect in the area of contract administration that sometimes tends to disrupt production. Many employers believe that most accidents are caused by employee carelessness (indeed, the National Safety Council estimates that 75% to 80% of industrial accidents are caused by persons who lack "safety consciousness"). Nevertheless, the OSHA Review Commission has affirmed the legal position that employees cannot receive citations.

Rather, OSHA holds employers responsible for seeing to it that their employees wear safety equipment (e.g., glasses, ear muffs or plugs—interim measures permitted until noise is reduced to specified levels—protective helmets, and so forth). Moreover, the employers are subject to fines for unsafe practices even if there is no accident.

Obviously, this means not only that employers must engage in more safety training for their supervisors and employees, but also that they must be prepared to discipline employees for noncompliance with safety work rules. And, unless the union leaders are willing to back the company, this will lead to more grievances.

These days, however, many grievances are being filed by employees who have refused to work in unsafe conditions and who have then been subjected to management discipline. In general, one can conclude (assuming the lessons of the past are a guide to the future) that, if the grievance goes all the way to arbitration, the arbitrator will rule it is proper for an employee to refuse to work in unsafe surroundings. The exceptions to this rule are those unsafe conditions in which (a) the employee could have corrected the situation, (b) the job necessarily involved hazardous work, or the alleged hazard was not extremely unusual, or (c) the employer had previously determined that the work in question was not in fact dangerous.[1]

Another aspect of this issue concerns the right of a group of employees to refuse to work in protest of allegedly hazardous working conditions. It is debatable—depending on what is arbitrable under the terms of the contract—whether such action is a protected activity, not subject to the usual no-strike contract clause.

Although their apprehensions may be exaggerated, some employers fear that OSHA is having a negative impact on management-labor relations in still other ways. A copy of any citation—whether the situation is immediately corrected or subsequently appealed to the review commission—must be posted at or near where the violation occurred, thereby hurting the employer's reputation not only with his own employees but possibly in the community as well. If a condition is found to exist which could reasonably be expected to cause immediate death or serious injury, OSHA can go to the nearest U.S. district court and ask that the operation be closed down until the violation is corrected. The OSHA inspector is also supposed to immediately inform all employees in the affected area that such a condition exists—a wise practice but one that hardly encourages or promotes employer-employee goodwill.

---

[1]   *Labor Relations Expediter* (Washington, The Bureau of National Affairs, Inc.), p. 223, LRX-45.

OSHA has also brought about increased examination and questioning of management's manning decisions and equipment selection. For example, a union could claim that the size of a particular crew is unsafe or that a piece of equipment fails to provide a safe workplace. While such allegations were sometimes made prior to OSHA, they will probably become even more common in the future. In any case, it is clear that OSHA's effect on management-labor relations is significant.

Small-business headaches

The Occupational Safety and Health Act poses significant problems for small business establishments. Exemption from the law's coverage, proposed in several pending congressional bills, would perhaps eliminate these headaches for small businesses, but it would not be an action in the public interest. While it has been appropriate to ease the record-keeping requirements for business establishments with fewer than 8 employees, there are several reasons why it would be poor national policy to exempt companies with fewer than 15 to 25 employees (the cut-off figures cited in some of the House and Senate bills).

First, 30% of the nation's work force are in businesses that have fewer than 25 employees, and the statistics seem to indicate that small businesses have the highest injury rates. If the purpose of the act is to reduce the number of occupational deaths, injuries, and illnesses, the employees of small businesses should be no more vulnerable than the employees of larger companies.

Second, if a small electrical subcontractor, for instance, were exempt, his "unsafe" practices could cause undue risks for all the workers on a large construction project.

Third, if small business were exempt, larger companies could be put at a competitive disadvantage, since it costs money to comply with OSHA. For example, the small contractor who saves money by not shoring up his trenches would have an unfair bidding advantage over the larger contractor.

Although exemption from OSHA's coverage is not the answer, some adjustments will have to be made for small business. I shall briefly discuss such possibilities later in this article.

ORGANIZATIONAL RESPONSE

Except for the uniformity of the record-keeping requirements, there has been an uneven response to the provisions of the act. There are three reasons for this not surprising occurrence:

1 Some standards are so unclear that many businessmen are genuinely confused as to what is required. Sometimes, they are confused even when the standards are clear.

2 Unless the businessman is in one of the five target industries (roofing and sheet metal; meat and meat products; lumber and wood products; manufacturers of mobile homes, campers, and snowmobiles; and stevedoring) in which the injury and illness rate is high relative to the national average, he can figure that the probability of an inspection is quite low. OSHA has only 600 inspectors with which to cover more than 4.6 million business establishments, or fewer than the government assigns to the mining industry alone. (Mine workers are not covered by OSHA but come under a special law administered by the Interior Department's Bureau of Mines.)

3 Even if the business establishment is inspected and violations are found, the penalties associated with being cited are not very high. For example, when a stu-

dent fatality led to an OSHA inspection of a large Eastern engineering school, the inspectors found 1,650 instances of 66 different types of violations (e.g., broken step-ladders; poor housekeeping; unguarded vacuum pumps, fans, and high-voltage areas; and aisles blocked by bicycles chained to posts). OSHA cited and assessed the university slightly less than $1,800 in fines, or about a dollar for each violation.

In my experience, I have found that large companies usually know what is expected of them, what is technologically feasible, and approximately what it will cost to bring their plants into compliance. (I should also add here that, in some large companies, because of management's much earlier focus on coping with safety and health problems, OSHA is having very little impact.) Without the benefit of a safety department and staff, most small companies—particularly in certain industries—are less clear about what is expected of them and about the costs involved.

In some large companies, the safety directors privately refer to OSHA's initials as "Our Savior Has Arrived"; their reference, of course, is to the fact that top management is now paying more attention to their views than ever before. Unless top management demands competence and lends its weight to the views of the in-house expert—whether the issue is affirmative action, pollution control, or safety and health—usually little happens, especially when significant sums of money may be involved.

In one large company, the safety director said, "There are many critical things which need to be done, but I can't get managers to spend the money. I need a big OSHA fine to wake up management and make my job easier."

In another large company, a corporate OSHA committee—made up of representatives from industrial relations, legal services, and the insurance staff—was formed; but the committee's function was strictly advisory. Consequently, some managers implemented the committee's recommendations and others did not. This points up the dual need for top management support and for the broadening of the committee's membership to include line managers.

Another condition in this same company also served to greatly diminish the importance of OSHA. During a governmental inspection in response to an employee complaint, the inspector failed to note certain violations that the company managers themselves were aware of.

The government can cite and penalize, the employee can complain and monitor, the union can demand and negotiate, the safety directors can advise and recommend—but those with the leverage to do the most are the employers themselves. Voluntary compliance by employers is really the only way the act will achieve its objectives.

In-house support

Once companies become aware of their responsibilities, they must organize to get the job done. A large chemical company recently appointed not only a corporate vice president for safety but also a corporate vice president for health, with both officers reporting to the president. Making two separate appointments is most appropriate in the chemical industry, which is particularly sensitive to health issues. And health—as opposed to safety— is being given growing attention as more is learned about toxic substances and as additional standards in the health area are issued. In announcing these appointments, the company's president said:

> "We have always attached great importance to the safety and health of our employees, and the company has received many awards for excellent safety records. In this connection, I would like to emphasize that we are sympathetic with the aims of recent legislation embodied in the Occupational Safety and

Health Act. It is our intention to not only comply fully with this act but offer to go further than the law requires in continuing to comply, as we have in the past, with the dictates of human conscience.

"In view of the complexity of the law and the growing scope of our operations, I believe the time has come to designate corporate administration for safety and health protection, thereby assisting the staff-and-line organization in all divisions of our company."

To give added force to its commitment to safety and health, top management must take safety and health into account in supervisory evaluations. As in other areas, goals and objectives need to be set. However, emphasis on goals can be carried too far or can be subverted, as in the case of one company that put a lot of emphasis on reducing lost-time accidents. When the president was pointing with pride to the success of this program, he was embarrassed to learn that there had been a corresponding increase in the number of non-lost-time accidents per million employee hours.

Another important way top management can emphasize safety and health is to ensure that these matters are covered by employee and supervisory training programs. This would be in addition to the training which the act mandates, such as that required in forklift truck driving and respirator wearing. Carelessness and job boredom account for too many accidents in the factory and in the office. Therefore, employees should be involved in analyzing the reasons for accidents and in developing essential work practices to minimize such on-the-job hazards. It goes without saying that the first-line supervisor is a key person in the process.

Outside assistance

Many employers would like to ask an OSHA inspector to visit the plant for a dry-run inspection. But the law discourages employers from making such a request because, if an inspector comes, by law he is obligated to do a full inspection, cite, and fine. In lieu of a dry-run inspection, however, there are several things the employer who wants to get into compliance with the act can do.

For one, the employer can request technical consulting aid from, and have his questions answered by, an OSHA regional office. Some employers are fearful that such inquiries will trigger an inspection; but if the employer is worried, he need not give his name when he telephones.

For another, the employer can request a free health-hazard evaluation by NIOSH. However, because of companies' fears of future inspections, NIOSH has received only a few requests, mainly from employees. Employers should not be so wary, however, since NIOSH will not contact OSHA on its results unless its survey reveals an "imminent danger" situation.

Also, OSHA puts on one-week courses on voluntary compliance for employers at its training institute near Chicago's O'Hare airport. Recently, the institute contracted for $3 million worth of training from National Safety Council chapters.

The employer can also turn to sources other than OSHA and NIOSH for outside help. One that should not be overlooked is the company's workmen's compensation insurance carrier. Insurance companies have active loss-prevention specialists who can offer advice with respect to in-plant health facilities, noise levels, machine guarding, and so forth. While these specialists cannot guarantee that compliance with their advice will ensure the passing of a subsequent OSHA inspection, whatever corrective steps the company takes will undoubtedly impress an inspector as well as hopefully reduce injuries and illnesses.

Insurance companies have a strong incentive for offering such an advice-giving service, in addition to the obvious one of getting an edge on competition. If we assume, for example, that the corrective steps recommended by the insurer lower the accident rate, the result is a reduction in what the insurance company pays out but not its premium income—at least, not for a year with large companies. And in the case of small companies, present methods of setting workmen's compensation insurance rates do not include rate reductions for outstanding safety records.

The employer should recognize, however, that insurance companies carry out inspections using their own standards, not those of OSHA. This means that an insurer's requirements might exceed OSHA's in some areas but not even cover some of the act's requirements in others. The most glaring example of this discrepancy is in the occupational health field. The workmen's compensation laws of most states do not cover many of the occupational diseases; therefore, they are few guidelines from the insurance industry.

Nevertheless, the insurance company is a good place to start; but the employer should recognize that even a clean bill of health from his insurance carrier does not guarantee the same from OSHA. And, of course, the insurance company has no liability if, after one of its inspections, the employer subsequently receives a citation because of an OSHA inspection.

Besides OSHA, NIOSH, and his insurance carrier, the employer has available still other sources of help. Useful information can be obtained from equipment manufacturers, other employers (especially those who have had an inspection), trade associations, and so forth. In addition, the local fire department may be willing to make fire protection suggestions.

OSHA inspector Even though the odds are that a company will not be inspected, it is wise for any employer to prepare for the possible arrival of an OSHA inspector. Since every employer is but one employee complaint away from a full inspection, someone in the company should be designated to greet and guide a compliance officer on his tour. If an inspector arrives in response to an employee complaint, the employer should ask for a copy of the complaint, if one is not furnished.

The employer, on the other hand, should have at his disposal the company's records with respect to injury-producing accidents. The employer should also have the answer to certain typical questions which are likely to be asked (e.g., is there a person trained in first aid available on each shift?).

During and after the OSHA inspection, the employer should feel free to ask the inspector for suggestions on possible ways to correct certain safety violations. The inspector is an excellent source of information, and the employer would be wise to take advantage of his knowledge while he is on site.

At the conclusion of the inspection, the employer should obtain a general review of the hazards that were found, and should also ask the compliance officer if any hazards were noted which would be in violation of a not-yet effective OSHA standard. By the middle of 1974, for example, all mechanical power presses must conform with strict new guarding requirements. Since the inspector notes potential (as well as actual) violations on his report, the employer should make himself aware of such information, for a reinspection is likely once new standards become effective.

Costs and benefits

In purchasing new equipment and in building new plants, it is important to make sure that OSHA standards are met. Because the act has no grandfather clause, the costs of changing existing or ordering new equipment for old plants will be substantial. With regard to costs, McGraw-Hill's first annual survey of U.S. investment in employee safety and health revealed that in 1973 U.S. industry had planned to spend $3.1 billion on equipment for employee safety and health, a 26% rise over 1972. And the survey revealed that higher amounts will be spent in the future.

However, other than some continuing costs brought on by OSHA associated with record-keeping, maintenance, and inspections, expenditures made to comply with OSHA regulations are one-time costs. Also, under Phase IV for Tier I companies the cost of meeting new federal employee safety and health standards, in the same category as product safety costs, are considered allowable costs and, as such, may be used as justification to the Cost of Living Council for price increases.

Tier 2 and Tier 3 companies, which can institute price increases without going to the council, can also use these costs as justifications should any questions be asked. Of course, the ability to raise prices depends as well on market conditions.

On the other side of the ledger, a safe and more healthful working environment should result in a decrease in lost wages, reduced insurance costs, lower medical expenses, and higher productivity.

The costs of compliance are now part of a new ball game, and those than cannot adapt may run into real trouble. For example, in Philadelphia the cost of workmen's compensation for longshoremen is about $25 per $100 of wages; but, in Newport News, the bill is just $9 per $100 of wages. Increasingly, therefore, maritime companies are having their ships unloaded in Virginia as opposed to Philadelphia.

Simpler things to do

It is also imperative that those in safety and industrial hygiene be listened to with new top-management understanding, sympathy, and support. Because safety and health have taken on new importance, so should the roles of safety and health personnel. And those roles need to be defined better so that more coordination takes place among safety, medical, industrial relations, manufacturing, and so forth.

Naturally, the company management should be alert to new standards (subscriptions to *Job Safety and Health* and the *Federal Register* are a must). The employer has the right to challenge OSHA standards. The Secretary of Labor consults with an advisory group on the issues raised by employers, publishes proposed changes in the *Federal Register,* and invites interested parties to make their views known at a hearing. Similarly, top management should keep up with the OSHA Review Commission decisions, as one would keep up with decisions handed down by the National Labor Relations Board, Equal Employment Opportunity Commission, and Environmental Protection Agency.

On an operational and day-to-day level, a company should always ask for the credentials of anyone who purports to be an OSHA inspector and contact the OSHA area office to corroborate his identity.

(There have been several reported instances throughout the country in which bogus inspectors—industrial spies and those trying to shake down managements—have tried to gain access to plants under false pretenses.)

CONCLUSION

Most of my recommendations in this article on "learning to live with OSHA" make sense mainly for the large company. For the smaller company, the ability to live with OSHA may be aided by future legislation. Some House and Senate bills contain attractive proposals which would allow OSHA to consult and counsel smaller companies, without being required to do an inspection. Such consultation would help smaller companies with one of their most urgent problems—namely, knowing what they need to do to comply.

Small Business Administration loans should continue to be available, and OSHA safety and health courses and materials might also be developed particularly for small companies in certain industries. Small companies are obviously going to have to band together, rely on trade associations, employ qualified specialists, and seek the help of their insurance carriers. The trade associations, instead of arguing for exemption, should make suggestions to help solve the practical problems that the act causes for small business.

Small business and its representatives also ought to support the recommendations made in the recent report of the National Commission on State Workmen's Compensation Laws concerning experience rating for small organizations. Currently, the small company has no strong economic incentive to encourage safety, for those with outstanding safety records in their insurance class do not receive corresponding reductions in their insurance rates.

FOR DISCUSSION AND REVIEW

1 What was the objective of OSHA?
2 Summarize the rights employees have under OSHA regulations.
3 What have been the major criticisms of OSHA operations?
4 What are the major problem areas in organizational environments with regard to OSHA regulations? What industries seem to have the most trouble complying?
5 What specific problems does OSHA present to small businesses?
6 In general, what has been the organizational response to OSHA?

INTERVIEW WITH GEORGE H. KUPER

Mr. Kuper was nominated by the President and confirmed by the Senate as Executive Director of the National Center for Productivity and Quality of Working Life in May of 1976. He has been actively engaged in the formulation and implementation of national productivity growth policy since 1972. With the former National Commission on Productivity, he served first as Director of Public Sector Programs and subsequently as Acting Executive Director. Before joining the federal government, Mr. Kuper held management positions in both the public and private sectors.

As an entrepreneur and consultant, Mr. Kuper has been the founding principal in three corporations and a director of five additional companies. He has specialized in manpower planning, financial systems, and productivity improvement efforts for small companies and local governments. Mr. Kuper received an undergraduate degree from Johns Hopkins University and graduate degrees from both the London School of Economics and Political Science and Harvard University School of Business Administration.

Q Could you explain when and how the National Center for Productivity and Quality of Working Life was developed, and what type of work it does?

A The National Center was created as an independent agency by the 94th Congress through Public Law 94–136 (the National Productivity and Quality of Working Life Act of 1975), which was signed by the President on November 28, 1975.

The Center's purpose is to establish a national policy for "encouraging productivity growth consistent with the needs of the economy, the natural environment, and the needs, rights, and best interests of management, the work force, and consumers." Its enabling legislation also calls for a concerted action on the part of the federal government to address the productivity needs of our society.

The legislation establishing a program to develop a policy on the nation's productivity growth grew out of five years' experience with trying to better understand our country's position and its ability to improve productivity over the long term. The Center is successor to the National Commission of Productivity which was originally established by Presidential order in August 1970 and which received legislative authority in the summer of 1971. This effort to build a national consensus behind a productivity policy was interrupted by other economic issues which overshadowed the productivity discussions; consequently, the productivity commission lapsed temporarily, then was recreated in June 1974 under a one-year authorization as the National Commission on Productivity and Work Quality. The Commission was then replaced by the Center.

The National Center is governed by a Board of Directors composed of leading representatives of business, labor, government, consumers, academics, and other prominent people appointed by the President with the approval of the Senate. By design it is a small organization with a limited budget, and it draws on the broad experience of the members of the Board for direction in establishing and pursuing the seven primary objectives, which are listed below together with a summary of the Center's past and current activities:

1 *Encourage labor-management cooperation to enhance productivity and improve the quality of working life.* Through conferences, seminars, and publications, and in cooperation with state universities and other privately funded organizations, the Center is providing technical assistance and encouragement in the formation of labor-management committees in local plants, throughout entire industries, and on a community-wide basis. These committees, working outside of the collective bargaining process, are finding solutions to work-related problems.

2 *Document and recommend policies to satisfy the nation's capital investment needs from a productivity standpoint.* Through a committee of its Board of Directors the Center has been making an in-depth study of the availability of capital funds. It is also assessing the potential for a greater contribution of educational institutions to productivity in manufacturing, and is working on the development of a program to increase the availability of new technology to small- and medium-size firms.

3 *Without compromising legislative intent, identify and recommend changes in government regulations which will improve productivity growth.* Research is being carried out with Center funding to measure the impact of government regulations on productivity. A massive study of the steel industry, for example, will develop a methodology for use by every industry, and will also provide those who write legislation with guidelines on how national goals can be met without adversely affecting productivity.

4 *Develop and recommend more effective approaches to improving productivity in the public sector.* Individual public officials and various organizations working with governmental units, with Center assistance, are establishing procedures for improving the quality of services and improving the quality of working life of public employees.

5 *Improve the review, coordination, and integration of productivity enhancement efforts of other federal agencies.* A report on a study of productivity in the federal government will be released in FY 1978. The Center has also established liaison with all other government agencies to coordinate federal support of private-sector productivity efforts, and also coordinate activities to improve productivity within the federal government itself. For example, the Center is providing technical assistance to the Air Force in the formation of labor-management committees among the civilian employees at all Air Logistics Command Centers.

6 *Stimulate and support task forces which have been formed to conduct programs for industrywide productivity improvement.* Task forces have been formed in a number of industries, including railroads, food distribution, construction, and airlines. Once established, some of these task forces have evolved into formal long-term arrangements under the general guidance of the professional or trade association representing that industry.

7 *Encourage the development of better techniques to measure productivity, and develop among the general public a better understanding of the importance of productivity to the general welfare.* A task force composed of a number of leading economists has been established to improve productivity measurements. In the area of public information the Center has published more than 40 studies, reports, and self-help manuals on techniques for improving productivity and the quality of working life. These are distributed to industry, labor, and academic leaders through an audience control system which directs material only to those people who have previously expressed a specific interest in a given area of productivity.

The need for a national focus on issues affecting productivity growth has been gaining acceptance as the understanding of productivity's role in increasing our standard of living and the serious threat to continued high rates of productivity improvement increases. But there are often important differences of opinion as to how to achieve the objective of greater productivity improvement. The Center is an organization through which different sectors of the economy can work toward reconciling those differences. People who have worked with the Center in the past feel that it has demonstrated a unique potential for developing a consensus and universal support for productivity improvement.

Nevertheless, the cooperative spirit which the Center has nurtured to date by its very nature is fragile and requires constant attention and respect for the individual needs of all interested parties. Appropriate with its consensus-building role, the Center does not assume responsibility for individual organizations to improve productivity; rather, it seeks to identify external barriers to those individual efforts and aid in the removal of those barriers.

Q   We hear so much about both productivity and quality of working life. Could you define those concepts for us? The latter seems especially vague.

A   When we talk about productivity in our society we are using a term that encompasses the efforts of all of us to improve the efficiency and effectiveness with which we consume all of our resources in the delivery of goods and services. In these broad terms, productivity might be defined as the relationship between the volume of goods and services produced and the physical inputs used in their production. Productivity, therefore, can be measured in terms of the ratio of output to the input of a number of different factors—labor, capital, energy, materials, or some combination of these.

What is important to realize is that, although we generally measure productivity as output per unit of labor input, or how much labor time is associated with the volume of output, the concept does not imply that the work force has the sole responsibility for productivity improvement. In a highly technological society all of the other factors, such as the education and skill of the work force, technological innovation, capital and capacity utilization, scale of production, flow of materials, quality of management, and the state of labor relations must be taken into consideration.

All of these factors vary considerably in relative importance from company to company, from industry to industry, and from sector to sector of our society. When trying to improve productivity, none can be ignored, yet the relative balance of each may be different.

In an effort to pull these issues together for a better understanding of what has to be done in order to solve our productivity growth problems, the former Commission observed in its policy statement that the most crucial factors could be conveniently grouped under three broad headings: first, human resources—that is, the level of health, education, skills, ingenuity, and dedication of all people involved in the production of goods and services, and the extent to which we continue to maintain and improve this productive capability; second, technology and capital investment—that is, the process through which productivity-enhancing innovations are conceived, developed, financed, and diffused throughout the economy in both the private and public sectors; third, government's participation—that is, the process through which government regulates and affects the actions of individuals and organizations in the interest of the community, and the extent to which this process affects the ability of the economic system to foster continued productivity improvements.

Although the focus of this book and these questions is primarily on the human-resources side of the equation, it is important to bear in mind that some combination of these factors must be considered if we are to achieve our productivity expectations.

The fact that the title of the Center includes "quality of working life" is significant. It does not imply that the traditional approaches to productivity growth employed in the past by American industry (i.e., capital investment, technology, training, education, etc.) have diminished in importance, but rather that the human-resources aspect of the solution has become more apparent as we attempt to relate the benefits of productivity improvement more directly to those responsible for achieving it. The improvement of the quality of working life is not the sole route to productivity, nor is it the only way to improve the standard of living that we have come to expect in our society; but it is a critical part of a very complicated equation.

I feel that the term "quality of working life" has evolved in response to what is sometimes referred to as the malaise of American workers, whose higher level of education and greater expectations for a better life have encouraged demands for improvements in the workplace environment. Over the years we evolved a highly interdependent economic system which does not appear to allow the individual much control of life at work, and the worker increasingly had little feel for the relationship between the work performed and the product produced. Importantly, the skills and talents of individuals to improve the method by which the product or service was produced were lost.

There have been many attempts to define, in simple terms, what we mean by "quality of working life." Indeed, the lack of consistent definition reflects the difficulty of addressing the problem. Professors Herrick and Maccoby and others have used the terms "security, equity, individuation, and democracy" to describe quality of working life, putting it in terms of individual needs. Similarly, management has come to describe quality of working life in terms of organizational needs as they apply to specific settings.

Q   What role do you feel the Center has in improving the quality of working life in the United States?

A   I hope my response to the previous question is evidence that the quality of working life is an essential ingredient for improving productivity. We feel at the Center that labor-management cooperation for improving productivity and quality of working life is essential. It must be understood, however, that there are major institutions on which we rely for our economic performance which must be respected if we are to bring about that cooperation, not the least of which is the collective bargaining process itself.

We have devoted a large portion of our resources to encouraging joint labor-management efforts. In this work we have found it helpful to picture labor relations simplistically as something of a continuum on which a range of conditions might be present. At the lower end we see management and labor in a perpetual state of crisis, evidenced by high grievance rates and work stoppages. Next up the continuum is mutual respect maintained through the adversary process. Higher still are cooperative efforts for specific purposes, as in the steel industry and the retail food industry where joint approaches have been taken to address mutually recognized problems. At the very upper end of the spectrum, where a high degree of mutual trust and confidence has been established, labor and management have expanded the scope of cooperative efforts. These are concerned with enlarging the decision-making role of the worker in the production process, and giving workers a say in work structuring, job content, supervision, plant layout, and other working conditions that are covered by the broad term "quality of working life."

It should be clear, I think, that although we waffle a bit on the definitions, those of us who are concerned with the direction of our economic society are in agreement on some of the things that must be done in order to improve both productivity and the quality of working life.

Q Has industry, on the whole, been receptive to your programs?

A The first response to this question is straightforward: we are too new and too small to have had a major impact on industry as a whole. More accurately we might answer that, in some cases, we have worked together with labor and management in specific industries, and have established a level of confidence that allows acceptance of what we have to say.

We have, of course, had our failures as well as our successes. One interesting aspect of this whole business is that it is always easier to rely on someone else to achieve productivity improvement, and I think some of our sponsors have had erroneous expectations that we would shoulder the burdens that rightfully belong to the managers of resources. However, I sense a growing recognition among industry leaders that productivity problems within an industry transcend the traditional organizational boundaries, and they require a significant amount of attention from a number of different organizational units. With some success the National Center has drawn on management and labor leaders from individual industries (including state and local governments) to form a productivity agenda that the whole industry can pursue with its own resources. We have found that the credibility of issues jointly established in this way adds to the probability of real improvement. This also opens up the opportunity for a useful partnership with government in which government assistance is rendered in an area of real need as determined by the industry itself.

There is always a question in a nonauthoritarian society such as ours as to whether we will have the patience to stick to this new operating methodology long enough to demonstrate its value. These efforts represent significant shifts in operating style and entail certain risks; they are not short term—their benefits accrue only in the long term.

Q In the articles in this book that precede your comments, various approaches to improving productivity and quality of working life are described. Do you see any single techniques as being especially effective? Do others have untapped potential?

A This book has concentrated exclusively on the human-resources side of productivity improvement. There are many techniques available, most of which have been eloquently covered. It is important to bear in mind, however, that whatever technique is applied must be appropriate to the level of mutual respect that must be honored. For instance, a major job-redesign program would be totally unsuitable for a company which has had a recent history of labor strife.

One of the risks associated with the exclusive concentration on the human-resources aspects of the problem of productivity and quality of working life is that expectations might be created that are very difficult to fulfill. For instance, the development of technology and the application of capital may be essential to significant improvement in the quality of working life. Therefore, productivity improvement programs which include these factors are the ones which, I believe, have the greatest probability of success.

As I mentioned earlier, we place heavy emphasis on labor-management cooperation to bring about changes in certain problem areas, and it has been our experience that the use of incentives to reward the participants in proportion to the improvements have been successful. One caveat to observe, however, is that whenever incentive plans are introduced one must be careful that the behavior being encouraged is that which is best for the organization's health and future.

Also, whatever plan is adopted requires constant and consistent attention from management, and its success depends to a large extent on managerial ability. This point was brought home to us by work conducted for us by Professor Richard Johnson of the Stanford Business School who studied corporative managerial styles in the United States and Japan. He took a large sample of matched pairs of American and Japanese companies and industries which produce similar products in the United States and Japan. Comparisons were made between Japanese-owned-and-operated companies in the United States and American-owned-and-operated companies in the United States; and American-owned-and-operated companies in Japan and Japanese-owned-and-operated companies in Japan. The findings, unfortunately, were inconclusive. In fact, it would appear that American managers operating plants in Japan outperform Japanese managers in Japan; in more or less the same ratio the Japanese-managed plants in America outperformed American-managed plants in America. We therefore conclude that the management style and techniques are not as important as the *attention paid to the nature and demands of the work force,* which is characteristic of a foreign manager working with people of a different culture.

Q Obviously the issues of productivity and quality of working life are complex and multifaceted. What suggestions would you offer to the personnel specialist who has responsibility for improving both in his or her organization? Where could he or she begin? Of what importance is top management's commitment?

A In my discussions with personnel managers, industrial-relations directors, and other professionals in large institutions, I have found a great contrast in the degree of their understanding of individual needs within an organization. I have found that managers and chief executive officers of small companies are more aware of what is needed for productivity growth, self-fulfillment, and other issues of quality of working life. It may be asking too much of the personnel manager to place less concern on the personnel management function, as such, and more emphasis on the needs and expectations of the people being managed. Such emphasis can come only from the top management level, and there is no doubt in my mind that the commitment of the chief executive officer is absolutely essential if the personnel function is to operate in any way other than as a buffer between the CEO and the work force.

Personnel functions, in my experience, are primarily designed to help the individual employee understand how she or he can advance within the context of the organization. What I am suggesting, perhaps, is that the focus should be shifted so that the employee can see how he or she can advance within a self-defined context as well.

By way of illustration: one of the country's most innovative public administrators, Mr. William Donaldson, once observed that some of his city employees rushed home as soon as possible from their jobs to pursue hobbies of great intricacy and determination. His reaction was to pull together a team of people who like to invent things in their spare time. That team now wanders from one city department to another, inventing things that improve not only the department's delivery of services but also the jobs associated with that service function.

Q Are productivity and quality-of-working-life problems for blue-collar workers only? Are these problems confined to the assembly line? Are there productivity problems in such professional occupations as law, medicine, engineering, and management? If so, what different approaches should be applied to these jobs as opposed to blue-collar positions? What special problems do these professions pose for productivity improvement?

A The productivity and quality of working life of an organization are the responsibility of the manager, but, in addition, the manager generally has total responsibility for his or her own productivity and job satisfaction as well. Everyone of us has known that we might have done a job better or more efficiently at one time or another. The difference in this respect is that the blue-collar worker relies on an institution to remind him that he might have done better, whereas the manager or professional most likely must rely on less immediate and direct signals.

The frustrations of our working life, however, including an understanding of the context in which we labor, apply equally to white-collar and blue-collar workers. A chief executive of a multimillion-dollar American firm confided to me that after he had advanced beyond the stage of personal involvement in a drawing or engineering plan, he took less pleasure in the rewards from his job because they came largely as a result of the direct efforts of others. The manager's remoteness from the production process as well as the end product may be as debilitating to the manager as it is to the organization. Our knowledge of how to deal with this issue would indicate a ripe area for investigation and experimentation.

Q Could you please comment on the future of the quality-of-working-life issue in this country? Is its importance and visibility likely to increase? What part do you see individuals, personnel departments, governments, and unions playing regarding this problem in the future?

A Our economic society is blessed with institutions that have been able to modify themselves in response to many different demands. The mobilization of our industrial machine behind our World War II efforts is but one example of this ability to respond. I am particularly encouraged by the directions we are now taking in the area of quality of working life. These differ so markedly from those being followed in Europe, which have come primarily as a result of legislative fiat. In this country we have equally impressive demonstrations that progess has resulted from voluntary action, jointly endorsed by management and labor. There is no doubt in my mind that we will achieve significant developments in the organization of work in our society over the next decade. What is significant is that it will be done voluntarily.

Personnel Administration and Human-Resource Management in the Contemporary Environment

---

INTRODUCTION

Section Seven examines how the external environment impacts personnel administration today. Parts A and B focus separately on the two primary external factors now affecting the operation of personnel programs: EEO issues and the unions.

In Section Four, we discussed EEO legislation and its impact on selection; the present set of readings rounds out our examination of the impact of EEO on personnel. First, O'Leary reviews the reasons why, in the past, women have failed to reach the job status of men. Schwartz and Waetjen relate interesting ideas concerning very overt barriers to women in male-dominated organizations.

Next, two articles discuss recent EEO legislation and the problems it presents when affirmative action programs (AAP) are attempted. Disagreements and conflicts plague the implementation of laws, guidelines, and orders and the court cases required to sort them out are slow in coming. As noted in Section Four, the emerging nature of EEO and AAP practices, mandated by ever-changing legislation, often puts personnel professionals in a difficult position regarding compliance. While sound personnel practices are perhaps the best assurance for compliance, the most recent literature must always be consulted.

Unions offer both constraints and opportunities to those in personnel. Salpukas reviews some new roles for unions today brought about by increased concern for quality of life at work, while Bowers explains the practical implications of legislated arbitration in the public sector.

Like EEO law, union influence pervades all personnel programs previously discussed in this book. Today, the effective personnel administrator has not only the specialized training and knowledge to implement effective personnel programs, but also the philosophy and personality needed to be effective in a rapidly changing, increasingly complex environment. The challenges—as well as the opportunities—this environment offers to those in personnel are enormous.

A. EQUAL EMPLOYMENT OPPORTUNITY (EEO) AND AFFIRMATIVE ACTION

Virginia E. O'Leary

Some Attitudinal Barriers to Occupational Aspirations in Women[1]

One of the critical problems confronting business and industry as they attempt to comply with current legislative efforts to equalize the distribution of men and women within the organizational hierarchy centers around the question of how to motivate the woman worker to aspire to ascendency into positions of higher status and responsibility. The following is a review of the literature focusing on those psychological factors which may interact to inhibit the woman worker from engaging in the kinds of achievement-directed behavior necessary to ensure her promotion into managerial ranks.

Some of these factors, such as societal sex role stereotypes, attitudes toward women in management, attitudes toward female competence, and the prevalence of the "male managerial" model, are external to the woman herself but may create barriers to her job-related aspirations. Internal factors which may serve to inhibit the expression of upward occupational aspirations include fear of failure, low self-esteem, role conflict, fear of success, as well as the perceived consequences of occupational advancement and the incentive value associated with such expectations. These last two variables, expected consequences and their incentive values, are regarded by Atkinson and Feather (1966) as crucial determinants of the nature and degree of achievement-related behaviors. If the anticipated consequences of a particular behavioral response (i.e., promotion) have negative valence, such responses may be inhibited.

MALE PROMOTERS' ATTITUDES TOWARD WOMEN IN MANAGEMENT

To the extent that promotional decisions on women are made by men in positions of authority, one obvious barrier to successful occupational advancement for women lies in the attitudes of their promoters toward women in management. A classic study of male attitudes toward women executives was conducted by the *Harvard Business Review* (Bowman, Wortney, & Greyser, 1965). Male executives rated their attitudes toward female executives in the mildly favorable to mildly unfavorable range (48% of a comparable sample of female executives rated their attitudes in the strongly favorable category). While the males sampled felt that women in management had no appreciable negative effects on efficiency and production, one third of those sampled felt that females in managerial positions had a "bad" effect on employee morale. Fifty-one percent of the male respondents felt women were temperamentally unfit for management. Eighty-one percent did not agree that men feel comfortable with a female boss. Only 27% indicated that they would feel comfortable working for a woman. Similar results were obtained by Gilmer (1961).

These findings reflect the norm in American culture that women should not

From *Psychological Bulletin*, 81, no. 11: 809–826. Copyright © 1974 by the American Psychological Association, Inc. Reprinted by permission.

[1]   The author is grateful to Charlene E. Depner for her invaluable assistance in the preparation of this article and to David W. Shantz for his careful reading and critical review of earlier versions of the manuscript.

have authority over men of equivalent age and social class. Other prevalent male attitudes which may be anticipated to adversely affect promotional decisions on women include (a) women are given preferential treatment and premature advancement due to the influence of "pressure groups"; (b) the employment of women jeopardizes the institution of the family; (c) the presence of women in the job setting makes social interactions difficult; (d) women are less able to cope with crises than men; and (e) women require inordinate amounts of sick leave—due to menstruation and pregnancy (Loring & Wells, 1972; Lynch, 1973).

Recent research by Bass, Krusell, and Alexander (1971) looking at how managers perceive women and their relationship to work revealed several factors that influenced their ability to accept women on an equal basis with men in the work situation. The factor that male managers felt most strongly about was deference, for example, norms defining the interaction between men and women. It did not appear that women were perceived as less capable than men, but rather, the managers indicated that other men and women would prefer having male supervisors and that they themselves would be uncomfortable with a woman supervisor. The other factor that influenced managers in their negative perception of women at work was women's perceived lack of dependability, as a function of women's "biological" and "personal" characteristics. Further, classification of the data in terms of the managers' level of interaction with women (none, subordinate, peer, superior) indicated that men who did not work with women had more positive regard for women than men who did and the least favorable attitudes toward working women were expressed by male managers in superior positions to women. Bass et al. (1971) suggested that so long as men judge women from positions of superiority, women may continue to be viewed in an unfavorable light. Indeed, research on black–white contact indicates that contact between equals most facilitates positive attitudes (Allport, 1958).

Katz[2] suggested that the attitudes of women toward successful women are more favorable than those of men toward successful women. However, while men report punitive and unaccepting attitudes toward successful women, these attitudes are subject to influence in the environment in which success occurs. If female success is depicted as occurring in an environment in which female participation is as frequent as male participation, males tend to react favorably to this success; when success is associated with "deviant" female stereotypic sex role inappropriate behavior, males react punitively. The success of the woman is not so much the issue as is the deviant nature of her actions. These findings suggest that the attitudes of male managers toward women in management may be influenced by the actual number of women having attained high-level positions within a particular organization.

Rosen and Jerdee (1973) examined the way sex role stereotypes—perceptions and expectations of what is appropriate behavior for males and females—influence evaluations of male and female supervisory behavior. Undergraduate students and bank supervisors were asked to read one of six versions of a supervisory problem (with either a male or a female supervisor and with eight male, female, or mixed subordinates) and to evaluate the effectiveness of four supervisory styles. The results indicated that the evaluations of the efficacy of certain supervisory styles were subject to the influence of sex of supervisor and subordinate.

---

[2]   M. L. Katz. Female motive to avoid success: A psychological barrier or a response to deviancy? Unpublished manuscript. Princeton, New Jersey, Educational Testing Service, 1973.

A reward style was rated as more effective for male supervisors, while a friendly dependent style was rated as more effective for supervisors of either sex when used with subordinates of the opposite sex. On the other hand, evaluations of threat and helping styles did not differ for male and female supervisors. It should be noted that the similarity of ratings made by subjects of both sexes provides evidence that men and women share common perceptions concerning sex role appropriate behavior for individuals in supervisory positions. The pervasiveness of such firmly entrenched expectations may inhibit the flexibility with which women in managerial positions adapt their supervisory styles to maximize effective performance.

Unfortunately, there has been little systematic research into the nature of the qualifications expected of female applicants for administrative positions. A recent study by Cecil, Paul, and Olins (1973) attempted to identify the qualities perceived to be important for male and female applicants for the same job. Results indicated that standard variables frequently used to evaluate job applicants are perceived to be of different importance depending on whether the applicant is a male or a female. Personality–appearance and skills–education were perceived to be more important in evaluating the female applicant, while motivation–ability and interpersonal relations were weighted more heavily in evaluating the male. Despite the fact that the instructions were worded identically, the female was apparently perceived as more of a typical clerical employee than the male.

Such attitudes reflect the tendency of those making promotional decisions to evaluate potential managers in accordance with a fundamentally "male" managerial model.

THE MALE MANAGERIAL MODEL

American society values success and the model upon which the definition of success is based as essentially a male sex role appropriate one. For example, it is the male, not the female, sex role stereotype which coincides with the managerial model. McGregor (1967) wrote,

> The model of the successful manager in our culture is a masculine one. The good manager is aggressive, competitive, firm and just. He is not feminine, he is not soft and yielding or dependent or intuitive in the womanly sense. The very expression of emotion is widely viewed as a feminine weakness that would interfere with effective business processes [p. 23].

In describing the managerial model, Loring and Wells (1972) observed,

> Men are supposed to be tough, concerned for the dollar, practical and objective enough to face the facts and act accordingly. Even if someone gets hurt in the process, a man is supposed to be strong enough to do what has to be done. Such strength, toughness, and total responsibility, even occasional, necessary violence are attributed to men as "natural." . . . He is expected to repress those aspects of himself which are associated with the feminine in our culture [p. 92].

Women do not fit into the "executive mold." Bowman (1964) quoted one junior executive,

> I would like to recommend people for promotion on merit alone, but I am justifiably afraid that my own judgment will be called into question if I recommend anyone who deviates too markedly from the kind of person I see getting ahead in my company [p. 189].

Women, evidently, "deviate too markedly," as Bowman's research revealed that factors of race, sex, and national origin appear to be more important deterrents to promotion than the candidate's dishonest, self-seeking, or authoritarian tendencies.

One explanation for the widespread acceptance of the validity of the male managerial model lies in the prevalence of myths regarding the nature of women's job commitment and their competence.

MYTHS REGARDING COMPETENCE AND COMMITMENT

Persistent myths concerning the sincerity of the commitment on the part of the female worker continue to influence promoters' perceptions of her and to have a detrimental effect on her chances for advancement. Crowley, Levitin, and Quinn (1973) tested the validity of several commonly held beliefs regarding women workers on a large, nationwide sample.

Crowley et al. (1973) found no support for the notion that women work only for "pin money." Fully 40% of their female sample were economically independent. One third of the female sample were the sole wage earners in their households. Yet the myth persists, and male workers continue to be regarded as better candidates for promotion on the basis of economic need.

Also unfounded was the belief that women are more concerned with the socioemotional aspects of their jobs. Like the males sampled, women regard the concern and competence of their supervisor as more important to the job than the opportunity to make friends. Still, management expresses the fear that women supervisors would allow emotional factors to supersede objective judgment.

Crowley and her colleagues found no factual basis for several prevalent assumptions regarding the motivations and aspirations of female workers. Such notions include (a) women would not work if economic reasons did not force them into the labor market; (b) women are more content than men with an intellectually undemanding job; (c) women are less concerned than men that their work be self-actualizing; and (d) women are less concerned with "getting ahead." Empirical data contradict each of these myths.

These findings lend support to the contention that the aspirations and motivations of workers of each sex are more similar than societal stereotypes would lead us to believe. Yet women workers continue to be plagued by myths and half myths which, to the extent they are accepted by those involved in making promotional decisions, may adversely affect their opportunities for advancement.

Another commonly held belief in our society is that women are less competent than men. Goldberg (1968) asked college students to rate professional articles on value, persuasiveness, profundity, writing style, and competence. Identical papers received higher ratings from subjects of both sexes when they were attributed to male authors. Bem and Bem (1970) replicated these findings. In the absence of authoritative opinion, male artistic endeavors were judged superior to those attributed to a female (Pheterson, Kiesler, & Goldberg, 1971). Highly competent male applicants for a study abroad were judged superior to females of equally high merit (Deaux & Taynor, 1973). On tasks perceived as male appropriate by the rater, a good performance by a male was attributed to skill, while the same performance by the female was seen to be the result of chance (Deaux & Enswiller, 1973). In the same study, good performance on the part of the male was attributed to general intelligence. Independent of the task, males were rated as more skillful than females. Both sexes, then, attribute internal causality to successful performance by males. In a recent study by Taynor and Deaux (1973), a woman's performance was considered more deserving of a reward than a man's when the performance was somewhat out of role and when that performance was declared admirable by an authoritative source. Similarly, Pheterson et al. (1971) found that for a woman's artistic competence to be evaluated more favorably than that of a man, the painter had to be described as carrying on a full-time job as well as pursuing a creative avocation (a better-than-average accomplishment), and some indication of outside recognition for the demonstration of competence was necessary. It appears, therefore, that in order for a highly competent female to gain recognition for her accomplishments, these accomplishments must be regarded as demonstrably exceptional (out of role or within a context requiring unusual drive and dedication) and their worth supported by the positive evaluation of an authoritative source.

Feather (1969) demonstrated that regardless of original expectation of success, females tended to rely more often on variable external attributions, that is, luck, than males, following both success and failure on a task. It thus appears that not only do observers differentially evaluate male and female performances, but males and females themselves differ in self-evaluation.

The findings cited above may be regarded as evidence for the existence of a societal bias against the recognition of female competence. This bias may stem from the belief that females are not endowed with the masculine attributes which make success more likely.

A recent study by Spence and Helmrich (1972) lends support to such an interpretation. Male and female students were shown one of four videotaped versions of a female stimulus person being interviewed. The stimulus person portrayed either a competent or incompetent individual who was either feminine or masculine in her interests. The attributes of competency and masculinity of interests combined in such a way to make the masculine-competent female more rather than less attractive, regardless of the sex of raters or their expressed attitudes toward women. Apparently, if a female stimulus is portrayed as possessing highly valued male attributes (competence) and correspondingly appropriate masculine interests, subjects of both sexes are willing to acknowledge their shared preference for individuals possessing those societal traits valued most highly. The origins of this problem may lie in convincing men and women that such valued traits are not by definition possessed exclusively by men. While the prevalence of the myth that women are less competent than men may be rendered ineffective in laboratory situations, the prevalence of such attitudes in the general society may continue to interfere with the ability to accurately predict and assess females' job performance.

Insofar as promoters perceive the characteristics of women workers as discrepant from the predominately "masculine" criteria inherent in the male managerial model to which they adhere, it is reasonable to anticipate that such attitudes may constitute barriers to higher occupational attainment for women.

Thus far, the discussion has focused on empirical findings directly relevant to expressed attitudes toward women in management. It is plausible to assume that such attitudes reflect societally held sex role stereotypes.

SOCIETAL SEX ROLE STEREOTYPES

Society assigns particular characteristics to males and females for the purpose of enhancing performance in traditional sex roles. The stereotypic images of the achieving male and nurturant female become a powerful force in the socialization of children as they grow into adulthood. Norms governing the approved masculine or feminine image are clearly defined and consensually endorsed (Fernberger, 1948; Lunnenborg, 1970; McKee & Sherriffs, 1959; Seward, 1946; Sherriffs & McKee, 1957; Steinman & Fox, 1966). Broverman, Vogel, Broverman, Clarkson, and Rosenkrantz (1972) reported a high degree of agreement regarding the differing characteristics of males and females in a large sample comprised of subjects of both sexes, various ages, religious affiliations, educational levels, and marital statuses.

An analysis of those characteristics most commonly ascribed to each sex reveal that attributes valued highly in men reflect a "competency" cluster including such items as objectivity, skill in business, and decision-making ability. Female-valued traits comprise a "warmth-expressiveness" cluster antithetical to the male profile. That is, the ideal female does not possess male-valued traits. Similarly, McKee and Sherriffs (1957) found that components of the masculine image generated by their subjects included (a) rational competence and ability and (b) vigor, action, and effectiveness, while the female stereotype consisted of (a) social skills and graces and (b) warmth and emotional support. Further, subjects of both sexes agree that male-valued traits are more socially desirable than female-valued traits (Rosenkrantz, Vogel, Bee, Broverman, & Broverman, 1968).

Indeed, the ascription of greater desirability to the male has been repeatedly demonstrated. Smith (1939) asked children 8–15 years old to vote on which sex possessed the most socially desirable traits. As age increased both boys and girls evinced a progressively higher opinion of males and lower opinion of females. It thus appears that girls as they grow up learn to value boys more and themselves less (Prather, 1971). Similar results have been reported by Mendelsohn and Dobie.[3] Fernberger (1948) reported that college students cast male rather than female story characters in situations demanding intelligence and "all around superiority." Sherriffs and Jarret (1953) report that their subjects demonstrated a "systematic preference" for males. The prevalence of consensually endorsed negative valuation of female traits may result in women holding a negative opinion of their worth relative to that of men (Broverman, Broverman, Clarkson, Rosenkrantz, & Vogel, 1970).

However, the question of the extent to which sex role stereotypes influence the self-conceptions of men and women cannot be resolved on the basis of empirical evidence to date. While the sex difference literature does suggest a high degree of correspondence between male and female self-conceptions and their concepts of ideal same and opposite sex stereotypic profiles (McKee & Sherriffs, 1959; Rosenkrantz et al., 1968; Steinman & Fox, 1966), it is difficult to assess the relationship between self-concept and differentially valued sex role stereotypes. As Constantinople (1973) pointed out, the majority of measures used to differentiate males from females with regard to dimensions of masculinity–femininity, sex role adoption, sex role preference, and sex role identity are based on the assumption that masculinity and femininity represent a single bipolar dimension. The usual procedure for obtaining male versus female self and opposite sex–other profiles involves asking subjects to respond to trait and adjective checklists, characterizing males, females, and self. While the sequence of response to these differential instructions is typically counterbalanced, the very fact that all operations are performed on the same set of scales may artificially elicit bipolar characterizations, artifactually anchored. Thus, caution must be exercised in interpreting the results of sex differences in response to both self and sex role stereotypic profiles generated in this fashion. Further, it appears reasonable to anticipate that the presentation of differential instructional sets used to elicit stereotypic profiles, for example, "typical male" and "typical female" versus "ideal male" and "ideal female," may have different psychological

---

[3]   R. Mendelsohn and S. Dobie. Women's self conception: A block to career development. Unpublished manuscript. Lafayette Clinic, Department of Mental Health, Detroit, Michigan, 1970.

meaning within the sex role stereotypic framework. Comparative studies utilizing differential instructional sets are presently not available.

Although the manner in which sex role stereotypes with their associated values influence the self-concepts of individuals has not been empirically documented, it is clear that the prevalence of such consensually endorsed stereotypes, attributions of competence, and commitment will substantially affect women's self-perceptions and influence behavioral responses based on these perceptions. The findings presented in the foregoing sections indicate that female respondents share men's bias against the recognition of competence in women, generate the same sex role stereotypic profiles as their male counterparts, and endorse the ascription of more positively valued traits to men. Consistent with the evidence indicating a readiness on the part of women to subscribe to stereotypic sex role definitions are data suggesting that women's self-esteem scores are lower than those of men. Such relatively negative self-concepts may reasonably be anticipated to constitute a formidable barrier to the achievement striving of women.

SELF-CONCEPT

In general, girls have a more negative self-image than boys (Putnam & Hansen, 1972) and girls from lower socioeconomic backgrounds are even less certain about their self-worth than girls from middle-class backgrounds (Tiedt, 1972).

Bennett and Cohen (1959) reported that women see themselves as "nervous," "anxious," "uncertain," "hasty," "timid," "stupid," and "domestic." McClelland (1965) observed that women are perceived as the opposite of men. Both sexes describe men as "large," "strong," "hard," and "heavy." Having established the male profile, subjects then characterize women antithetically, that is, "small," "weak," "soft," and "light." Apparently, the possibility that characteristics might be shared by both sexes was not entertained by respondents of either sex.

Women have traditionally been reared to want to fill the role in which society casts them. They are trained to model themselves after the accepted image. According to Bardwick (1971) the origins of ego style in the female lie in an empathetic, intuitive, person-oriented style of perception and in the central role that the motive to affiliate plays in the development of self-esteem among women (Douvan & Adelson, 1966; Hoffman, 1972). For women, affiliation is seen as achievement and an affirmation of the self. The subjective quality of feminine ego functions is praised and valued in the warm mother–child and husband–wife relation which have traditionally characterized the feminine role. However, as the culture at large values vocational achievement and rewards ego styles more likely to result in vocational success, the female may perceive her very personality qualities as second rate.

Korman (1970) hypothesized that all other things being equal, individuals will engage in and find satisfying those behavioral roles which will maximize their sense of cognitive consistency. To the extent that their self-concept concerning the job or task situation requires effective performance in order to result in consistent cognition, they will be motivated to engage in effective performance. Further, to the extent that an individual has self-cognition of himself as a competent, need-satisfying individual, he will choose and find most satisfying those situations which are in balance with these self-perceptions. According to Korman's formulation, one of the most important factors determining task performance of a given individual is relevant to socially influenced self-esteem. To the extent that a woman's self-esteem incorporates traditionally feminine stereotypic notions, it is plausible to anticipate that she will be hesitant to engage in behaviors requiring characteristics societally typified as male sex role appropriate.

Hollander (1972) found a negative relationship between the demonstration of academic achievement and social self-esteem scores for females but not for males. Females with A averages in high school had significantly lower self-esteem scores than females with C averages; the reverse was true for males. Hollander's interpretation of these findings suggests the existence of a positive relationship between self-esteem and exhibition of sex role appropriate behavior.

Results reported by Gordon and Hall (1974) indicate that the best predictor of a woman's happiness and satisfaction is her self-image. Interestingly, the more potent, supportive, and unemotional a woman feels (predominately masculine characteristics) the more satisfied and happy she reports herself to be. The inconsistency evidenced in these findings suggests that the incorporation of masculine traits into women's self-descriptions may differentially affect their overall estimation of self-worth. Those characteristics more closely tied to sex role inappropriate behavior may depress positive self-evaluations, while those associated with masculine traits may enhance such evaluations. Further research on the relative impact of counter-stereotypic self-definitions along these dimensions is necessary to clarify the relationship between the ascription of more valued masculine characteristics and women's self-concepts.

Campbell's (1971) work with the Strong Vocational Interest Blank revealed that women working in such traditionally masculine fields as mathematics and chemistry fail to select the more "flamboyant" items (e.g., "be a professional dancer," "thrilling and dangerous activities," etc.) endorsed by women in occupational roles (e.g., airline stewardesses, fashion models, and entertainers) which require more stereotypically feminine attributes such as poise, charm, and physical beauty. One explanation for these findings lies in the notion that the adoption of male-valued traits (i.e., rational, analytic orientation) may preclude the development and/or expression of traits highly valued in the female.

The relative impact of societal sex role stereotypes on women's self-conceptions is difficult to evaluate. However, if as Bardwick (1971) suggested, the value one places on the self determines the level of self-esteem and the lower a person's self-esteem the greater the anxiety and the greater the tendency to assume a societally prescribed role, it is plausible to suggest that women, whose self-esteem is lower than their male counterparts', may be hesitant to engage in behaviors requiring the assumption of highly valued male sex role appropriate traits. Regardless of whether this negative conception of feminine value is internalized in the self-concept of a given women or simply a reflection of what she considers to be the females' sex role appropriate stance as reflected by societal stereotypes, it may be anticipated to effect the achievement-directed behavior of that woman.

Women are caught in a double bind, unable to optimally fulfill the role requirements for the more socially desirable achieving individual and those for the ideal woman simultaneously. The women who seeks employment in a traditionally masculine position is faced with a dilemma. Society views the ideal woman as an expressive individual lacking in the masculine attributes of logic and drive. If she feels that because she is not a man she is not endowed with the competency characteristics ascribed to men, she may suffer from lack of confidence concerning her ability to do the job well. If, on the other hand, she feels that she has the potential to manifest masculine traits, she may feel that allowing such characteristics to surface might be detrimental to her femininity, rendering her "less of a woman."

To the extent that a woman perceived herself as possessing both the masculine attributes associated with probable successful competitive achievement and interests in marriage and family considered appropriately feminine, she might experience role conflict. If the conflict between competing goals was sufficiently strong, the existence or mere anticipation of such a dilemma might result in the suppression of achievement striving.

ROLE CONFLICT

As the majority of female participants in the labor force are married women, much current discussion has focused on how women should or do perform in both career and family roles. Traditional research on role theory has dealt with the nature of role conflict, its antecedents and consequences, rather than adaptations to such conflicts. Kahn, Wolfe, Quinn, Snock, and Rosenthal (1964) demonstrated the impact of personal, interpersonal, and organizational factors on role conflict, in turn, on such factors as satisfaction and tension. Sales (1969) has further shown that role conflict may contribute to somatic illness. Little attention has focused, however, on coping strategies for dealing with such conflicts and the relationship of such strategies to such resulting factors as satisfaction and tension.

Hall (1972) offered a model of role conflict coping behavior based upon three levels in the role process. Following Levinson (1959), role is not defined as a unitary concept but rather as a process involving three components to a person in a given social position: (a) structurally given demands, (b) personal role conception, and (c) role behavior. On the basis of both one's perception of these demands and one's own personality, a person formulates a definition of what demands it is necessary to meet, and hence, how to behave.

According to Hall (1972) the numerous subidentities of women often present a clear example of chronic role conflict, defined by Kahn et al. (1964) as mutually competing demands by role senders (people who communicate role expectations). Hall sees the major role problem a woman faces as the result of conflicts arising from multiple roles, rather than from conflicting expectations within a particular role. Further, the conflicts between roles are often a function of role overload and time conflicts, rather than a function of intrinsic role incompatibility. Women, because they often must bear primary responsibility for the home and children, are more likely than men to face the competing demands of their role senders simultaneously.

Given the three levels of the role processes described by Levinson, Hall (1972) developed a model of role conflict coping behaviors which intervene in the role process at each level. Type I coping, structural role redefinition, involves altering external, structurally imposed expectations relative to a person's position. Type II coping is a personal role redefinition, changing one's expectations and one's own behavior in a given position rather than attempting to change the environment. Type III coping through reactive role behavior involves attempts to meet all of the role demands experienced.

Through a pilot sample and a subsequent survey of college educated women, Hall (1972) identified 16 behavioral strategies which may be classified under these three general types. The relationship between coping style and satisfaction was explored with data from the two samples. Type I coping was positively related to satisfaction, while Type III coping was negatively related to satisfaction. Type III coping includes behaviors such as planning, scheduling, organizing better, and working harder. Kroeker (1963) suggested that these strategies of dealing with conflict may reflect defensive rather than coping behavior. The fact that the impact of Type III coping strategies is strongest on women employed part-time and who report the fewest number of roles lends credence to the defensive interpretation. Objectively, part-time work probably entails less conflict than full-time work, and having one or two roles involves less conflict than having three or four or more roles. Women working part-time who perform fewer roles probably expect themselves to be able to handle conflict successfully. However, if they adopt defensive behavioral strategies, they may feel less adequate than women who cope actively with a greater number of conflicts.

Hall[4] examined role pressures, coping behaviors, self-image, satisfaction, and happiness of married women as a function of age, life stage, and number of life roles. He found the married woman's stage in life was strongly related to her experiences of role conflict and pressure, while age was not. As life stage was measured in terms of ages and number of children in the family, the results indicate that children are a major influence on a married woman's perceived role pressures. For example, her satisfaction with the way she manages her role drops steadily through the Full House Plateau when all the children are in school (Lopata, 1966) and then rises again when the children begin to leave home. As the woman's number of roles increases, she experiences more conflict, feels more time pressure, and uses more Type II coping (personal role redefinition). It is possible that during this stage in her life cycle the focus of organizational concern should not be on how to motivate her to achieve occupationally but rather on how to help her to cope with her role conflicts, thereby removing obstacles to effective performance.

Hall and Gordon (1973) reported that among married women, employed or not, home pressures are the most important contributors to experienced role conflict, (low) satisfaction, and (low) happiness. Apparently, home-related activities are of prime concern to married women, regardless of their personal orientation (career versus traditional). The conflicts experienced by women were strongly related to their perception of what men expect to see in women (Gordon & Hall, 1974). Conflicts involving nonhome roles were strongly associated with the women's perceptions of the average man's image of a feminine woman. Further, the greatest influence on the woman's self-related conflicts was again her view of the male stereotype of femininity. This appears to support the popular argument that men control women not only through overt power and discriminatory behavior but also through the impact they have on women's attitudes and internal conflicts.

Komarovsky (1973) sampled attitudes of college men toward changing sex role expectations for women. The majority of men sampled felt that women should have the opportunity to pursue careers at all levels and expressed higher esteem for working women than for housewives. Yet, most men were adamant in their expressed preference for "traditional wives" whose major concerns centered around the needs of husband and family. Apparently, ideological positions may be expected to assume a secondary place in the face of daily living in the eyes of even the most "enlightened" man. It is not surprising that women are sensitive to the attitudes of their significant males.

It has been demonstrated that working wives express conflict over desire to work and concern about working. They weigh the benefits of working against concern for the well being of their children and the nature of the marital relationship (Nye & Hoffman, 1963; Siegel & Haas, 1963). The literature relevant to career development among women suggests that the availability of support from a "significant" male may play a role in determining both the occupational aspirations and performance of women (Hawley, 1971; Lynch, 1973). It is thus plausible to assume that the absence of such support may strengthen the perception of role conflict and inhibit the ascendance of women already in the labor force into positions requiring greater responsibilities and time commitments.

---

[4] D. T. Hall. Role and identity processes in the lives of married women. Unpublished manuscript. York University, Administrative Behavior Research Program, 1972.

Berger and Luckmann (1967) presented a theory of role development in which they suggested that roles develop from habituated human activity (those actions repeated frequently and cast into a pattern). The specification of what types of acts are to be performed by what type of actors is termed typification. Research indicates that women engaged in occupations presently typified as male sex role appropriate suffer from role conflict (Holstrom, 1972; Poloma, 1972; Rapaport & Rapaport, 1972). Berger and Luckmann's theory would predict a reduction in role conflict once women's participation in nontraditional female roles is typified.

However, American society has designated the role of breadwinner and status-giver to the male, while the female's role revolves around homemaking tasks. In analyzing the responses of 54 dual-professional couples, Poloma and Garland (1971) found that the assumption of a professional role by the wife did not mean a dramatic change in family roles. Their data yielded no indication that either men or women desired an equal sharing of both masculine and feminine role tasks in the family. While society may be approaching the day when the average married woman holds some kind of job, it does not appear likely that any dramatic increase in the prestige of the feminine role or any reversal of male–female roles in the family will result. Blood and Wolfe (1960) have shown certain differences in division of labor in families where the wife is employed outside the home, but they found no indication that the overall "relative balance" had been upset. It thus appears likely that American working women will continue to be subject to the pressures stemming from role conflicts inherent in their dual responsibilities, and these pressures may constitute another barrier to their ascendency into higher level occupational positions.

One factor which may heighten the salience of concern over role conflict among women is the lack of available female role models successfully combining marriage and family with occupational achievement.

LACK OF NONTRADITIONAL ROLE MODELS

Almquist and Angrist (1971) suggest that career aspirations of college women are explicable within a combined role-model-reference group framework. Kemper (1968), utilizing the reference group concept to explain achievement motivation, alluded to the function of the role model as a comparison group (or individual) which demonstrates for the individual how something is done in the technical sense. The essential quality of the role model is that he (or she) possesses skills and displays techniques which the actor lacks (or thinks she lacks) and from which, by observation and comparison with his or her own performance, the actor can learn. Hence, in order for achievement to occur, the actor needs a role model to emulate. The role model does not motivate, influence, reward, or persuade the actor; the model merely provides a technical explanation of how the role is to be performed.

Women who aspire to a career do not substitute the work role for the more traditional wife-mother-homemaker one but choose an additional role (Turner, 1964). In order to realistically aspire to, and perform successfully in, occupational roles requiring high levels of achievement-directed behavior, women require role models who illustrate how to combine marriage and career satisfactorily.

A number of studies have examined the influence of mother's occupational choice and role satisfaction on the work orientation (traditional versus nontraditional) of their daughters (Almquist & Angrist, 1971; Astin, 1968; Siegel & Curtis, 1963; Tangri, 1972; White, 1967). In general the findings indicate that working mothers, women who serve as role models successfully combining family and career and expressing satisfaction with their lifestyle, have daughters who are similarly oriented (Baruch, 1967). These girls apparently learned a favorable definition of the working mother role.

Further, research suggested that college women for whom careers are salient were more likely to indicate professors and persons in the occupation as the most important source of influence on their occupational choice. Similar results were obtained by Tangri (1972). Noncareer salient women were more likely to name family members or friends, but very often felt that no one had influenced their choice (Almqist & Angrist, 1971; Simpson & Simpson, 1963).

Almquist and Angrist (1971) suggested that faculty role models may provide psychological incentives to select a particular occupation. These incentives include rewards for academic performance or work activity in which the model aids the neophyte in developing a self-concept as a person capable of operating effectively in a given occupation. Unfortunately, comparable research examining the influence of role models on the career aspirations of women in industrial settings is not available. However, the literature is replete with suggestions concerning the importance of providing female role models to aid in the acculturation of women into nontraditional occupational roles (Brenner, 1972; Buchanan, 1969; Greenfield, 1972; Loring & Wells, 1972; Tiedt, 1972). To defy societal role expectations requires a strong personality, particularly since few females have the opportunity to observe models of women who are intelligent, attractive, and respected in their careers.

A study conducted by Joesting and Joesting (1972) suggested that qualified female role models may enhance the self-image of women students. Male and female students were asked to rate the value of being a woman. Half of the students were enrolled in a class taught by a qualified male instructor, half by a qualified female instructor. Ten percent of all male subjects and 26% of the women subjects in the class taught by a male instructor thought there was nothing good about being a women. Only 5% of the women enrolled in the class taught by the female instructor thought there was nothing good about being a woman.

Shein (1972) suggested that if a woman's self-image incorporates the feminine role aspects she may be less likely to acquire those job characteristics or engage in those behaviors associated with the masculine managerial position, since such characteristics and behaviors are inconsistent with her self-image, unless viable role models are available to her who represent the integration of "the best of both worlds." It should be noted that mere imitation of the male managerial style by a female cannot necessarily be expected to result in a viable model to be emulated by other women. The absence of female role models functioning successfully in a masculine sex role appropriate position may be considered a barrier to the occupational aspirations and achievement directed behaviors of women in the labor force.

One final set of factors which may serve to inhibit the achievement strivings of women in organizational settings is related to women's expectations regarding the probability that the effort involved in such striving will be positively reinforced.

ACHIEVEMENT MOTIVATION

The literature on achievement motivation has assumed that the motive to achieve is one of the major determinants of anyone's striving for success. While a theoretically consistent body of data exists which allows the prediction of achievement behavior as a function of achievement motive, it is applicable only to men. Investigations of women's need to achieve have produced puzzling and ambiguous results (Angelini, 1958; Field, 1953; French & Lesser, 1964; Lesser, Krawitz, & Packard, 1963; Veroff, Wilcox, & Atkinson, 1953). The projective measures of achievement motivation typically employed are not correlated with achievement effort or with academic and intellectual performance for females (Entwisle, 1972). Unlike men, women do not respond uniformly to a single achievement context cue—the masculine competitive model (French & Lesser, 1964). Neither do women show an increase in thematic apperception need for achievement imagery when exposed to experimental conditions of achievement motivation arousal stressing the appeal to competence and mastery (Alper & Greenberger, 1967; McClelland, Atkinson, Clark, & Lowell, 1953; Veroff et al., 1953). In fact, under certain conditions women exhibit a decrement in expressed achievement motivation after arousal manipulations (French & Lesser, 1964).

It has been acknowledged that the conventional job setting is only one situation in which achievement motivation may be manifested. Heckhausen (1967) maintained that achievement motivation may be operating in "all activities in which a standard of excellence is thought to apply." Rosen (1956) suggested that achievement motivation can be, and frequently is, expressed through nonvocational behavior. However, the most commonly used method of assessing achievement motivation is a projective technique subject to the vagaries of a scoring system developed on male data collected in response to male competitive cues.

Numerous investigators have questioned the predictive validity of the concept of need achievement (Klinger, 1966; Smith, 1968; Solomon, 1968) and have pointed to the difficulties involved in obtaining replicable results in studies employing the traditional fantasy-based measures of achievement motivation (Entwisle, 1972; Katz, 1967; Weinstein, 1969). Entwisle (1972) suggests that the lack of predictive validity in studies utilizing fantasy measures of need achievement stems from the low reliability of the measure (.30 to .40). Conceptually, the notion of motive to achieve has, for most psychologists engaged in the study of human behavior, an intuitive appeal. Further empirical validation of the construct is necessary to present an empirically valid and reliable case for the viability of the construct as an appropriate theoretical explanation for a given class of phenomena Low reliability of the traditional measures may help explain the failure to find relationships between achievement motives and achievement behavior among women.

Achievement goals emphasized in various roles differ. Females' achievement orientations are likely to be manifested in situations which represent societally defined sex role appropriate behavior. For women, important areas of achievement are social skill and interpersonal relations. Indeed, women set high attainment values and standards of performance in female sex role appropriate tasks (Battle, 1965, 1966; Stein, 1971; Stein, Pohly, & Mueller, 1971). Further these values and standards predict women's task performance (Battle, 1965; Crandall, Katkovsky, & Preston, 1962; Stein et al., 1971). Finally, arousal treatments stressing social skill have been demonstrated to result in increased achievement imagery among women (Field, 1953; French & Lesser, 1964). Thus, it appears women subscribe to many different goals as a function of their sex role orientation (traditional versus nontraditional). It is plausible to suggest that each woman chooses achievement contexts in which she can strive for the goals she values most highly. If, as Stein and Bailey (1973) suggest, social skills are a central area of achievement concern for many females, scoring systems applied to imagery expressing affiliative concerns may reflect achievement rather than affiliative imagery among female subjects.

A number of studies concerned with sex differences in achievement motivation in children indicate no significant difference in achievement efforts between boys and girls (Crandall et al., 1962; Crandall & Robson, 1960). However, data from the same studies indicate that girls lack confidence in their work and look for help and approval from adults more than do boys. It may be that the origins of the achievement efforts exhibited by boys and girls lie in evocation of different types of achievement motivation.

Veroff (1969) distinguished between two types of achievement motivation: autonomous achievement motivation which stems from internalized personal standards and social comparison achievement motivation which is activated in response to standards of excellence established by others. Due to differences in child-rearing practices and socialization, males develop stronger autonomous achievement motivation, while females become more receptive to external cues on standards for appropriate achievement-directed behavior. The female, lacking the firm internal foundations of autonomous motivation, becomes highly sensitive to social feedback. In fact, several researchers (V. C. Crandall, 1964; V. J. Crandall, 1963; Garai & Scheinfield, 1968) have suggested that achievement behavior in girls is not motivated by mastery strivings, as with boys, but by affiliative motives.

It has been suggested that females have greater affiliative needs than do males (Hoffman, 1972; Oetzel, 1966; Walberg, 1969), and thus one may expect that conflict between affiliation and achievement will occur more frequently among women. If a women receives, or even anticipates, negative feedback concerning achievement-directed behavior, she may curtail her achievement strivings, particularly if the sources of such feedback are those upon whom she relies for the satisfaction of her affiliative needs.

Atkinson (1964) and McClelland (1958) described the motive to achieve as a motive to be competent in a situation where there are standards of excellence. The expectancy-value theory of motivation (Atkinson & Feather, 1966) suggests that achievement-directed behavior is the result of the multiplicative interaction of three covert variables. These are (a) the strength of the motive to achieve, (b) the expectancy of the consequences of success in a specific situation, and (c) the value of such consequences. The person with a high achievement motive may be characterized as one who has developed an internal standard of excellence, is independent and persistent, undertakes realistic tasks, performs well academically, and has clearly understood goals. This model yields accurate predictions of the direction, magnitude, and persistence of achievement behaviors only for males. The expectancies for, and incentive values of, achievement-related success differ for males and females.

FEAR OF FAILURE

Fear of failure may also be a factor in women's apparent reluctance to aspire to higher level positions. Fear of failure results in an approach–avoidance conflict in response to achievement goal attainment. According to Atkinson (1957) the motive to avoid failure is considered a disposition to avoid failure and/or a capacity for experiencing shame and humiliation as a consequence of failure. Tendencies to avoid failure combat those to approach success and result in characteristic patterns of achievement goal selection.

The genesis of fear of failure may be rooted in the socialization process. As the male grows to maturity he must develop appropriate coping mechanisms for dealing with failure. The female, not expected to compete in the marketplace, may lack such crucial training. Thus, it is not surprising that Kagan and Moss (1962) found a significant correlation between fear of failure in childhood and adulthood among female but not male subjects.

High-fear-of-failure individuals are more likely to select cautiously low or unrealistically high career goals (Mahone, 1960). They are less likely to select career goals best suited to their abilities. However, although unrealistically high goals may be selected, the level of aspiration is lower for high-fear-of-success individuals (Burnstein, 1963; Littig, 1963; Rim, 1963). High-fear-of-failure individuals manifest greater withdrawal tendencies and, as Heckhausen (1967) stated, are content with the simpler occupations if it means avoiding the uncertainties and exertions of a more demanding career. If, as the literature suggests, women generally suffer from lack of confidence and self-esteem, it is plausible to suggest that they may be more vulnerable to failure fears, and this may in turn affect their selection of achievement goal contexts.

MOTIVE TO AVOID SUCCESS

Horner (1972) regarded the motive to avoid success as the mediating factor in achievement context choice. According to her formulation, success in a traditionally masculine context may have a negative valence for women. Such success is linked with fear of social rejection and doubts about one's femininity and normality. Thus, Horner (1970) characterized the successful woman as one who feels "anxious, guilty, unfeminine and selfish." Maccoby (1963) made a similar observation, suggesting that the professional woman "pays the price in anxiety" for diverging from the conventional female role. In both formulations, femininity and success in traditionally male achievement contexts are regarded as conflicting, if not mutually exclusive, goals. Horner (1970) wrote

> As a whole, society has been unable to reconcile personal ambitions, accomplishment and success with femininity. The more successful or independent a woman becomes, the more afraid society is that she has lost her femininity and therefore, must be a failure as a wife and mother [p. 55].

The perception of achievement and affiliation as mutually exclusive goals may result in the suppression of achievement-directed behavior. Indeed, Baruch (1966) demonstrated a decline in achievement motivation among women during the twenties and early thirties when the affiliative concerns of marriage and child rearing were most salient.

Horner (1972) demonstrated the existence of a motive to avoid success among able college women. Females high in the motive to avoid success were found to perform less well in a mixed-sex competitive situation than in a noncompetitive situation, while the reverse held for women low in the motive to avoid success. Further, the findings of Schwenn[5] indicated that women scoring low in the motive to avoid success exhibit a greater degree of willingness to report high grades to a male friend than did high-scoring women. She also found that women high in the motive to avoid success changed their career aspirations toward a more traditionally feminine direction during their college years more often than women low in the motive to avoid success.

According to Horner's (1972) formulation, male-oriented performance situations should arouse the motive to avoid success more than female-oriented performance situations because success at male-oriented activities may imply "behavior unbecoming to a lady" and may arouse the anticipation of negative social consequences. Success at female-oriented activities, on the other hand, is less likely to arouse the expectation of negative consequences, either social or self-esteem, since the negative incentive value of success should be greater for performance tasks which are generally considered masculine than for those which are generally considered feminine.

---

[5]   M. Schwenn. Arousal of the motive to avoid success. Unpublished junior honors thesis, Harvard University, 1970.

It is interesting to note that several studies examining the personality characteristics of female PhDs (presumably low in the motive to avoid success) have failed to reveal qualities indicative of neuroticism and anxiety to an extent greater than that found in more traditionally oriented female populations (Bachtold & Werner, 1971; O'Leary & Braun, 1972).

Further, choice of a traditionally masculine role does not necessarily spawn fear of social rejection on the part of achieving women. In a study by Hawley (1972) women reported that the "significant men in their lives" had a model of femininity not unlike the one they themselves adhered to. Since nontraditionally oriented women view significant men as endorsing their life-style, it would be difficult to characterize such women as fearful of social rejection or as questioning their normality.

The findings of Makowsky[6] lend support to the predictions derived from Horner's (1972) theory. Women scoring high in the motive to avoid success performed optimally on a task labeled "feminine" and in competition with other women, while women scoring low in the motive to avoid success performed optimally on a task labeled "masculine" in competition with men. Each group then, realized achievement goals which corresponded to their value orientation. Further, women low in the motive to avoid success did not indicate that they felt "unsexed" by their choice of achievement context. The fact that women low in the motive to avoid success performed less well on tasks labeled "feminine" may be due to the fact that the attribution of a task as female sex role appropriate does not constitute arousal conditions sufficient to elicit the motive to achieve in subjects low in the motive to avoid success. In response to a questionnaire, both groups agreed on the importance of femininity, and in fact, the low scorers on motive to avoid success rated themselves as significantly more feminine than the high scorers.

The efficacy of fantasy-based measures of the motive to avoid success is subject to the same criticisms as attempts to utilize projective techniques to assess the motive to achieve. Concern has been expressed by a number of investigators regarding the reliability of Horner's (1972) scoring system, the ambiguity surrounding the concept of fear of success and uncertainty regarding variables captured in the fear-of-success measure, as well as the difficulty in obtaining correlations between assessed motives to avoid success and the suppression of achievement-directed behavior (Tresemer, 1973). At present it may be premature to speculate about the prevalence and stability of Horner's (1972) construct. More reliable and precise scoring procedures are necessary, and research is needed to isolate those responses most strongly associated with the inhibition of achievement. Until these questions are resolved, the validity of the fear-of-success construct will remain open to question. However, on the assumption that the theoretical concept of motive to avoid success may prove viable, it is reasonable to suggest that the evocation of such a negative action tendency may constitute a barrier to achievement-directed behavior among women.

CONCLUSION

The foregoing discussion has attempted to identify those psychological factors which may interact to inhibit the expression of achievement-directed behavior in women, thereby constituting barriers to the ascendance of female participants in the labor force into managerial ranks.

---

[6] V. P. Makowksy. Fear of success, sex role orientation of the task, and competitive conditions as variables affecting performance in achievement oriented situations. Unpublished manuscript, St. Lawrence University, 1972.

The empirical findings represented in many of the studies reviewed do not provide data adequate to assess the validity of many of the hypotheses suggested. The literature relevant to attitudinal barriers to occupational aspirations in women is insufficient in breadth and scope to bridge a number of obvious inferential gaps. Too often college students comprised the subject samples, limiting the generalizability of the results; where attitudes were surveyed no data bearing on behavioral measures were collected. This is not as much a comment on the inadequacy of research design employed as on the present state of the art relevant to this topic. The purpose of the present review is to pull together available evidence from a number of diverse investigations, many of which were not conceived as related to questions concerning occupational aspirations in women, in an attempt to provide a suggestive framework for future research of a more applied nature.

It is hoped that the findings reported will have implications for those involved in the implementation of programs aimed at motivating women to aspire to managerial positions. Attempts to empirically specify the relative impact of each of the factors identified as potential obstacles to occupational aspirations among women are needed. Future investigations in this area should focus on problems as diverse as modifying existing societal attitudes, providing environmental support for dealing with pressures which may arise from the reality of role conflicts, and a redefinition of the exclusively male managerial model. The development of new assessment procedures may be required to ensure the objective evaluation of women's potential managerial abilities, and new training programs may be required to ease the acculturation of women into nontraditional roles (Bray, 1971; Kay, 1972).

As industry turns its attention toward the identification of women with managerial potential and begins to provide new training opportunities for these women, careful evaluation will be required of new programs in order to determine which of those factors identified in the present article as constituting possible barriers to achievement-directed behavior in women are of predictive importance and what kinds of training procedures may be utilized effectively to diminish their impact on the occupational aspirations of women.

REFERENCES

Allport, G. W. *The nature of prejudice.* New York: Doubleday, 1958.

Alper, T. G., & Greenberger, E. Relationship of picture structure to achievement motivation in college women. *Journal of Personality and Social Psychology,* 1967, **7**, 362–371.

Almquist, E. M., & Angrist, S. S. Role model influences on college women's career aspirations. In A. Theodore (Ed.), *The professional woman.* Cambridge, Mass.: Schenkman, 1971.

Angelini, A. L. Um novo metodo para aviar a motivacao [A new method of evaluating human motivation]. In J. W. Atkinson (Ed.), *Motives in fantasy, action, and society.* Princeton, N. J.: Van Nostrand, 1958.

Astin, H. S. Career development of girls during high school years. *Journal of Counseling Psychology,* 1968, **15**, 536–540.

Atkinson, J. W. Motivational determinants of risk taking behavior. *Psychological Review,* 1957, **64**, 359–372.

Atkinson, J. W. *An introduction to motivation.* Princeton: Van Nostrand, 1964.

Atkinson, J. W., & Feather, N. T. *A theory of achievement motivation.* New York: Wiley, 1966.

Bachtold, L. M., & Werner, E. E. Personality profiles of women psychologists. *Developmental Psychology,* 1971, **5**, 273–278.

Bardwick, J. M. *Psychology of women: A study of biocultural conflicts.* New York: Harper & Row, 1971.

Baruch, R. The interpretation and resumption of women's careers. (Harvard Studies in Career Development Report 50) Cambridge, Mass.: Center for Research in Careers, 1966.

Baruch, R. The achievement motive in women: Implications for career development. *Journal of Personality and Social Psychology,* 1967, 5, 260-267.

Bass, B. M., Krusell, J., & Alexander, R. H. Male manager's attitudes toward working women. *American Behavioral Scientist,* 1971, 15, 77-83.

Battle, E. S. Motivational determinants of academic task persistence. *Journal of Personality and Social Psychology,* 1965, 2, 209-218.

Battle, E. S. Motivational determinants of academic competence. *Journal of Personality and Social Psychology,* 1966, 4, 634-642.

Bem, S. L., & Bem, D. J. Case study of a nonconscious ideology: Training the woman to know her place. In D. J. Bem (Ed.), *Beliefs, attitudes and human affairs.* Belmont, Calif.: Brooks/Cole, 1970.

Bennett, E. M., & Cohen, L. R. Men and women: Personality patterns and contrasts. *Genetic Psychology Monographs,* 1959, 59, 101-155.

Berger, P. L., & Luckmann, T. *The social construction of reality.* New York: Doubleday, 1967.

Blood, R., & Wolfe, D. M. *Husbands and wives: The dynamics of married living.* New York: Macmillan, 1960.

Bowman, G. What helps or harms promotability. *Harvard Business Review,* 1964, 42, 6-26, 184-196.

Bowman, G., Wortney, B. N., & Greyser, S. H. Are women executives people? *Harvard Business Review,* 1965, 43, 14-28; 164-178.

Bray, D. The assessment center opportunities for women. *Personnel,* 1971, 48, 30-34.

Brenner, M. Management development for women. *Personnel Journal,* 1972, 51, 65-69.

Broverman, I. K., Broverman, D. M., Clarkson, F. E., Rosenkrantz, P., & Vogel, S. R. Sex role stereotypes and clinical judgments of mental health. *Journal of Consulting Psychology,* 1970, 34, 1-7.

Broverman, I. K., Vogel, R. S., Broverman, D. M., Clarkson, F. E., & Rosenkrantz, P. S. Sex-role stereotypes: A current appraisal. *Journal of Social Issues,* 1972, 28, 59-78.

Buchanan, E. Women in management. *Personnel Administration,* 1969, 32, 21-26.

Burnstein, E. Fear of failure, achievement motivation, and aspiring to prestigeful occupations. *Journal of Abnormal and Social Psychology,* 1963, 67, 189-193.

Campbell, D. P. The clash between beautiful women and science. In A. Theodore (Ed.), *The professional woman.* Cambridge, Mass.: Schenkman, 1971.

Cecil, E. H., Paul, R. J., & Olins, R. A. Perceived importance of selected variables used to evaluate male and female job applicants. *Personnel Psychology,* 1973, 26, 397-404.

Constantinople, A. Masculinity-femininity: An exception to a famous dictum. *Psychological Bulletin,* 1973, 80, 389-407.

Crandall, V. C. Achievement behavior in young children. *Young Children,* 1964, 20, 77-90.

Crandall, V. J. Achievement. In H. W. Stevenson (Ed.), *Child Psychology: The 62nd Yearbook of the National Society for the Study of Education.* Part 1. Chicago: University of Chicago Press, 1963.

Crandall, V. J., Katkovsky, W., & Preston, A. Motivational and ability determinants of young children's intellectual achievement behaviors. *Child Development*, 1962, **33**, 643–661.

Crandall, V. J., & Robson, S. Children's repetition choices in an intellectual achievement situation following success and failure. *Journal of Genetic Psychology*, 1960, **97**, 161–168.

Crowley, J. E., Levitin, T. E., & Quinn, R. P. Seven deadly half truths about women. *Psychology Today*, March 1973, pp. 94–96.

Deaux, K., & Enswiller, T. Explanations of successful performance on sex-linked tasks: What's skill for the male is luck for the female. *Journal of Personality and Social Psychology*, 1973, **29**, 80–85.

Deaux, K., & Taynor, J. Evaluation of male and female ability: Bias works two ways. *Psychological Reports*, 1973, **32**, 261–262.

Douvan, E., & Adelson, J. *The adolescent experience.* New York: Wiley, 1966.

Entwisle, D. To dispel fantasies about fantasy-based measures of achievement motivation. *Psychological Bulletin*, 1972, **77**, 377–391.

Feather, N. T. Attribution of responsibility and valence of success and failure in relation to initial confidence and task performance. *Journal of Personality and Social Psychology*, 1969, **13**, 129–144.

Fernberger, S. W. Persistence of stereotypes concerning sex differences. *Journal of Abnormal and Social Psychology*, 1948, **43**, 97–101.

Field, W. F. The effects on thematic apperception of certain experimentally aroused needs. In D. McClelland, J. W. Atkinson, R. A. Clark, & E. L. Lowell (Eds.), *The achievement motive.* New York: Appleton-Century-Crofts, 1953.

French, E. G., & Lesser, G. S. Some characteristics of the achievement motive in women. *Journal of Abnormal and Social Psychology*, 1964, **68**, 119–128.

Garai, J. E., & Scheinfield, H. Sex differences in mental and behavioral traits. *Genetic Psychology Monographs*, 1968, **77**, 169–299.

Gilmer, B. *Industrial psychology.* New York: McGraw-Hill, 1961.

Goldberg, P. H. Are women prejudiced against women? *Transaction*, 1968, **5**, 28–30.

Gordon, F. E., & Hall, D. T. Self-image and stereotypes of femininity: Their relationship to women's role conflicts and coping. *Journal of Applied Psychology*, 1974, **59**, 241–243.

Greenfield, L. B. Women in engineering education. *Contemporary Education*, 1972, **43**, 224–226.

Hall, D. T. A model for coping with role conflict: The role behavior of college educated women. *Administrative Science Quarterly*, 1972, **17**, 471–486.

Hall, D. T., & Gordon, F. E. The career choices of married women: Effects on conflict, role behavior, and satisfaction. *Journal of Applied Psychology*, 1973, **58**, 42–48.

Hawley, P. What women think men think. *Journal of Counseling Psychology*, 1971, **3**, 193–199.

Hawley, P. Perceptions of male models of femininity related to career choice. *Journal of Counseling Psychology*, 1972, **19**, 308–313.

Heckhausen, H. *The anatomy of achievement motivation.* New York: Academic Press, 1967.

Hoffman, L. W. Early childhood experiences and women's achievement motives. *Journal of Social Issues*, 1972, **28**, 129–156.

Hollander, J. Sex differences in sources of social self-esteem. *Journal of Consulting and Clinical Psychology,* 1972, **38**, 343-347.

Holstrom, L. L. *The two-career family.* Cambridge, Mass.: Schenkman, 1972.

Horner, M. S. Femininity and successful achievement: A basic inconsistency. In J. M. Bardwick, E. Douvan, M. S. Horner, & D. Gutmann (Eds.), *Feminine personality and conflict.* Belmont, Calif.: Brooks/Cole, 1970.

Horner, M. S. Toward an understanding of achievement related conflicts in women. *Journal of Social Issues,* 1972, **28**, 157-176.

Joesting, J., & Joesting, R. Sex differences in group belongingness as influenced by instructor's sex. *Psychological Reports,* 1972, **31**, 717-718.

Kagan, J., & Moss, H. *Birth to maturity.* New York: Wiley, 1962.

Kahn, R. L., Wolfe, D. M., Quinn, R., Snock, J. D., & Rosenthal, R. H. *Organizational stress.* New York: Wiley, 1964.

Katz, I. The socialization of academic motivation in minority group children. In D. Levine (Ed.), *Nebraska Symposium on Motivation* (Vol. 15). Lincoln: University of Nebraska Press, 1967.

Kay, J. M. A positive approach to women in management. *Personnel Journal,* 1972, **51**, 38-41.

Kemper, T. Reference groups, socialization and achievement. *American Sociological Review,* 1968, **33**, 31-45.

Klinger, E. Fantasy need achievement. *Psychological Bulletin,* 1966, **66**, 291-306.

Komarovsky, M. Cultural contradictions and sex roles: The masculine case. *American Journal of Sociology,* 1973, **78**, 873-884.

Korman, H. K. Toward a hypothesis of work behavior. *Journal of Applied Psychology,* 1970, **54**, 31-41.

Kroeker, T. Coping and defensive function of the ego. In R. W. White (Ed.), *A study of lives.* New York: Atherton Press, 1963.

Lesser, G. S., Krawitz, R., & Packard, R. Experimental arousal of achievement motivation in adolescent girls. *Journal of Abnormal and Social Psychology,* 1963, **66**, 59-66.

Levinson, D. Role, personality and social structure in organizational settings. *Journal of Abnormal and Social Psychology,* 1959, **58**, 170-180.

Littig, L. W. Effect of anxiety on real and ideal vocational aspiration among grammar school boys. *Nature,* 1963, **199**, 1214-1215.

Lopata, H. Z. The life cycle of the social role of the housewife. *Sociology and Social Research,* 1966, **51**, 5-22.

Loring, R., & Wells, T. *Breakthrough: Women in management.* New York: Van Nostrand Reinhold, 1972.

Lunnenborg, P. W. Stereotypic aspects in masculinity-femininity measurement. *Journal of Consulting and Clinical Psychology,* 1970, **34**, 113-118.

Lynch E. M. *The executive suite: Feminine style.* New York: AMACOM, 1973.

Maccoby, E. E. Woman's intellect. In S. M. Farber & R. L. Wilson (Eds.), *The potential of women.* New York: McGraw-Hill, 1963.

Mahone, C. H. Fear of failure and unrealistic vocational aspiration. *Journal of Abnormal and Social Psychology,* 1960, **60**, 253-261.

McClelland, D. C. Risk-taking and children with high and low need for achievement. In J. W. Atkinson (Ed.), *Motives in fantasy: Action and society.* Princeton: Van Nostrand, 1958.

McClelland, D. C. Toward a theory of motive acquisition. *American Psychologist,* 1965, **20**, 321-333.

McClelland, D. C., Atkinson, J. W., Clark, R. H., & Lowell, E. L. *The achievement motive.* New York: Appleton-Century-Crofts, 1953.

McGregor, D. *The professional manager.* New York: McGraw-Hill, 1967.

McKee, J. P., & Sherriffs, A. C. The differential evaluation of males and females. *Journal of Personality,* 1957, 25, 356-371.

McKee, J. P., & Sherriffs, A. C. Men's and women's beliefs, ideals, and self concepts. *American Journal of Sociology,* 1959, 65, 356-363.

Nye, F. T., & Hoffman, L. *The employed mother in America.* Chicago: Rand McNally, 1963.

Oetzel, R. M. Annotated bibliography and classified summary of research in sex differences. In E. E. Maccoby (Ed.), *The development of sex differences.* Stanford, Calif.: Stanford University Press, 1966.

O'Leary, V. E., & Braun, J. S. Antecedents and correlates of academic careerism in women. *Proceedings of the 80th Annual Convention of the American Psychological Association,* 1972, 7, 277. (Summary)

Pheterson, G. I., Kiesler, S. B., & Goldberg, P. A. Evaluation of the performance of women as a function of their sex, achievement, and personal history. *Journal of Personality and Social Psychology,* 1971, 19, 114-118.

Poloma, M. M. Role conflict and the married professional woman. In C. Safilios-Rothschild (Ed.), *Towards a sociology of women.* Lexington, Mass.: Xerox College Publishing, 1972.

Poloma, M. M., & Garland, T. N. The myth of the egalitarian family: Familial roles and the professionally employed wife. In A. Theodore (Ed.), *The professional woman.* Cambridge, Mass.: Schenkman, 1971.

Prather, J. Why can't women be more like men: A summary of the sociopsychological factors hindering women's advancement in the professions. *American Behavioral Scientist,* 1971, 15, 39-47.

Putnam, B., & Hansen, J. C. Relationship of self-concept and feminine role concept to vocational maturity in young women. *Journal of Counseling Psychology,* 1972, 19, 436-440.

Rapaport, R., & Rapaport, R. N. The dual-career family: A variant pattern and social change. In C. Safilios-Rothschild (Ed.), *Towards a sociology of women.* Lexington, Mass.: Xerox College Publishing, 1972.

Rim, Y. Risk-taking and need for achievement. *Actua Psychology,* 1963, 21, 108-115.

Rosen, B. C. The achievement syndrome. *American Sociological Review,* 1956, 21, 203-211.

Rosen, B., & Jerdee, T. H. The influence of sex-role stereotypes on evaluations of male and female supervisory behavior. *Journal of Applied Psychology,* 1973, 57, 44-48.

Rosenkrantz, P. S., Vogel, S. R., Bee, H., Broverman, I. K., & Broverman, D. M. Sex-role stereotypes and self concepts in college students. *Journal of Consulting and Clinical Psychology,* 1968, 32, 287-295.

Sales, S. M. Organizational role as a risk factor in coronary disease. *Administrative Science Quarterly,* 1969, 14, 325-336.

Seward, G. H. *Sex and the social order.* New York: McGraw-Hill, 1946.

Shein, V. Fair employment of women through personnel research. *Personnel Journal,* 1972, 51, 330-335.

Sherriffs, A. C., & Jarret, R. F. Sex differences in attitudes about sex differences. *Journal of Psychology,* 1953, 35, 161-168.

Sherriffs, A. C., & McKee, J. P. Qualitative aspects of beliefs about men and women. *Journal of Personality*, 1957, **25**, 451–464.

Siegel, A. E., & Curtis, E. H. Familial correlates of orientation toward future employment among college women. *Journal of Educational Psychology*, 1963, **44**, 33–37.

Siegel, A. E., & Haas, M. B. The working mother: A review of research. *Child Development*, 1963, **34**, 513–542.

Simpson, R. L., & Simpson, I. Occupational choice among career-oriented college women. *Marriage and Family Living*, 1963, **33**, 377–383.

Smith, M. Competence and socialization. In J. A. Clausen (Ed.), *Socialization and society*. Boston: Little, Brown, 1968.

Smith, S. Age and sex differences in children's opinions concerning sex differences. *Journal of Genetic Psychology*, 1939, **54**, 17–25.

Solomon, D. Psychosocial deprivation and achievement dispositions. In *Perspective on human deprivation*. Bethesda, Md.: National Institute of Child Health and Human Development, 1968.

Spence, J. T., & Helmrich, R. Who likes competent women: Sex-role congruence of interests, and subject's attitudes toward women as determinants of interpersonal attraction. *Journal of Applied Social Psychology*, 1972, **2**, 197–213.

Stein, A. H. The effects of sex role standards for achievement and sex role preference on three determinants of achievement motivation. *Developmental Psychology*, 1971, **4**, 219–231.

Stein, A. H., & Bailey, M. M. The socialization of achievement orientation in females. *Psychological Bulletin*, 1973, **80**, 345–366.

Stein, A. H., Pohly, S. R., & Mueller, E. The influence of masculine, feminine and neutral tasks on children's achievement behavior, expectancies of success and attainment values. *Child Development*, 1971, **42**, 195–207.

Steinman, H., & Fox, D. J. Male-female perceptions of the female role in the United States. *Journal of Psychology*, 1966, **64**, 265–276.

Tangri, S. S. Determinants of occupational role innovation among college women. *Journal of Social Issues*, 1972, **28**, 177–199.

Taynor, J., & Deaux, K. When women are more deserving than men: Equity, attribution, and perceived sex differences. *Journal of Personality and Social Psychology*, 1973, **28**, 360–367.

Tiedt, S. M. Realistic counseling for high school girls. *The School Counselor*, 1972, **19**, 354–356.

Tresemer, D. Fear of success: Popular but unproven. In C. Travis (Ed.), *The female experience*. Delmar, Calif.: CRM, 1973.

Turner, R. H. Some aspects of women's ambition. *American Journal of Sociology*, 1964, **70**, 271–285.

Veroff, J. Social comparison and the development of achievement motivation. In C. P. Smith (Ed.), *Achievement related motives in children*. New York: Russell Sage, 1969.

Veroff, J., Wilcox, S., & Atkinson, J. W. The achievement motive in high school and college age women. *Journal of Abnormal and Social Psychology*, 1953, **48**, 108–119.

Walberg, H. J. Physics, femininity, and creativity. *Developmental Psychology*, 1969, **1**, 47–54.

White, K. Social background variables related to career commitment of women teachers. *Personnel and Guidance Journal*, 1967, **45**, 48–52.

Weinstein, M. S. Achievement motivation and risk preference. *Journal of Personality and Social Psychology*, 1969, **13**, 153–172.

FOR DISCUSSION AND REVIEW

1 Review male promoters' attitudes toward women in management.
2 How might the myths the author discusses affect the success of women in management?
3 What role conflicts are felt by women in managerial positions? What is the conclusion drawn from research on women's achievement estimation?
4 The author notes that certain factors prevent women from behaving in ways that would facilitate their rise in an organization. How might these barriers be overcome? Are women's attitudes part of the problem? Why?

Eleanor Brantley Schwartz

Walter B. Waetjen

Improving the Self-Concept of Women Managers

Many newly appointed female managers find making the management team is one thing; playing first-string is something else. Needed, in addition to ability and qualifications, is a strong "sense of self." Supervisors of women managers have found many of them less confident, more conservative, and less risk-taking than their male counterparts. Competent women bring to management many invaluable qualities—but to be or to become an equal, they must feel equal. Moreover, nothing is so unequal as when equals are treated unequally.

What difference does it make for us to know what a person believes oneself to be? If our orientation is slanted strongly, and almost exclusively, to production of goods or services, then the answer is that it doesn't make much difference. But if the orientation gives dual consideration to production of materials and to personal development of those involved in production, the answer is that it's crucially important to know what persons believe about their capabilities, strengths, deficiencies and weaknesses. Also, for managers to know a person's self-concept enables them better to understand a person *and* to predict his or her behavior.

THE SELF-CONCEPT

One of the most recent explanations of human behavior is self-concept; i.e., what one sees and believes about oneself. Little application of self-concept theory has been made to managerial behavior, especially that of women managers. Although much research has now been done on female executives in a business environment, and some comparative research exists on male and female leadership, there is little empirical research on the female manager's *self-concept* as it relates to her *managerial* behavior. Practically no attention has been given to understanding how the self-concept of the female manager is affected by the professional environment within which she operates. For instance, how does she perceive her managerial role? To what extent does her self-concept hamper her managerial effectiveness? What is the congruence between her self-concept and management role expectations? These

---

Reprinted by permission from *The Business Quarterly*, Winter 1976, pp. 20–27.

questions must be answered, in addition to others such as: Can her managerial behavior be legitimately understood outside the self-concept that directs and supports this behavior? How can management, and particularly the supervisor of a woman manager, help her develop a more positive self-concept and motivation to succeed?

Women are recent additions to the managerial ranks, and this recency does not permit assumptions about similarity of self-concepts of male and female managers. Thus, the broad purposes of this article are to identify certain aspects of the female's self-concept as it relates to management (e.g., self-concept as a selector of management experience, role of significant others in development of self-concept) and to discuss how these aspects hold promise to supervisors of female managers for understanding, predicting, and changing their self-concept.

MAINTAINING AND ENHANCING THE SELF-CONCEPT

Out of a welter of research in the fifties, self-concept came to be regarded as a complex, but organized, dynamic system of beliefs one holds about what kind of person one is; that is, conclusions about one's typical ways of handling typical life situations. The self-concept is the center of an individual's personal universe since all experiences are perceived, interpreted, and understood from this personal framework. Motivation, in this context, may be viewed as a product of one's constant striving to maintain and enhance the self-concept.

It seems that there is not an innate concept of self. Initially, self-concept arises as a result of appraisals from others. We observe, compare, listen to and internalize these reflected appraisals. As others (parents, friends, spouse, siblings; or later as an adult in the organizational environment, superiors, peers, subordinates) evaluate our behavior and communicate that evaluation to us so do we come to perceive ourselves. Once we believe we are a certain kind of person with particular traits, abilities, and aversions, we strive to maintain or to justify these beliefs.

One's gender is a powerful determinant of self-concept and motivation. Beliefs about appropriate behavior for each sex are firmly imbedded in society's institutions. The male role has incorporated achievement-oriented, autonomous, aggressive, and "masterful" types of behavior and attitudes. Boys come to see themselves as strong, powerful, dominant, competitive, and aggressive.[1] In contrast, the female roles have been focused on supportive, dependent, affiliated and passive types of behavior and attitudes.[2]

Although these divergent self-concepts result more from socialization than from biological fact,[3] both sexes have emphasized "male" traits for successful executive managerial behavior. Men and women tend to use masculine attributes to describe effective managers, and they equate masculinity with superiority.

Thus, management, traditionally viewed as a "masculine" occupation, has been perceived to require traits more commonly ascribed to men: leadership ability, self-confidence, aggressiveness, desire for responsibility, emotional stability, and analytical thinking.[4] But women have demonstrated the ability to be effective executives and managers. One validation of this view is derived from a study[5] in which employers who had women working for them rated their experience with women managers. Ninety-five % of the respondents described their experience with women managers as excellent, very good, or good. Seeing oneself primarily in a supportive role to the male, however, has inhibited career aggressiveness in most females. The general tendency has been to defer to the male.

Deference was learned early by females when the process of socialization was having its intended impact. This hesitancy can be likened to the high school prom, with all the females waiting to be chosen or invited to dance. Such "waiting-to-be-asked" behavior may continue on into their careers making women reticent to seek recognition. How do men perceive this behavior? Simply that women are not interested in careers.

Males and females will change their self-concepts as sex roles change. New beliefs are emerging slowly about family, the man-woman relationship, and career aspirations and behavior. Despite the early cultural conditioning that makes women uncomfortable about appearing aggressive or making demands in their own interest, they are beginning to sense the need for role expansion. Females more than males are significantly more favorable toward women expanding their role opportunities.[6] It has also been found that women are more favorable than men toward role expansion for women in business.[7]

MANAGERIAL BEHAVIOR AND SELF-CONCEPT

We develop a conception of ourselves as managers, just as we do with regard to other roles. Our thesis is that managerial motivation is affected by one's self-concept. We are generally well informed about intellectual factors that affect success or failure, but most of us are not equally knowledgeable about nonintellectual factors, such as self-concept. Yet, the more positive our self-concept, the greater our chance for succeeding. Our self-concept also determines how we meet failure or tolerate ambiguity. The person who can tolerate failure generally has a great sustaining reserve of success, and, therefore, is a person who has a healthy self-concept. Toleration of ambiguity—necessary to managerial survival—is achieved by one who sees himself as open to different and often conflicting points of view and alternatives in decision making.

Description of one's self-concept is complicated by the fact that it can never be observed directly since it is an inferred psychological structure. We can only note its manifestations; for instance, if women's self-concept embodies the feminine sex-role stereotype, their job aspirations and job behavior are correspondingly influenced. Although competence and intelligence can be found equally among women and men, the "masculine" managerial model prevents some women from seeking an executive career since ". . . 'masculine' managerial behaviors would be inconsistent with their feminine self-image."[8] On the other hand, when women perceive the management process "as creating opportunities, releasing potential, removing obstacles, encouraging growth, providing guidance, they can then see themselves as managers."[9] But the management structure of most organizations (and, therefore, allocation of power) is based on male values and prerogatives, which has created role conflict within many women—i.e., uncertainties about their abilities, personal role, and success as a manager. For example, to be considered a competent manager, women must assume masculine characteristics. To be "feminine" and successful "as a woman," however, women must adopt traditional sex-role appropriate behavior. This role conflict has suppressed achievement striving and upward movement in the corporate structure. Though they resist the myths about what is feminine, many women still are sensitive to charges they are not. As a result, few women have sought traditionally "male" positions, even though the number of educated women is at an all time high, because they have lacked ". . . motivation rather than ability."[10]

Social pressures have convinced most women they were unfeminine, selfish, or deviant if they pursued a management career. Rather than a motive to success,[11] women's achievement goals may be lessened more by fear of sex-role inappropriateness. This may also explain why most women in middle and upper managerial positions tend to be in or have entered through staff rather than line positions.[12] As concluded in one study, ". . . women have felt constrained to begin in areas of specialization for which they could claim special insight or ability."[13] Cut off from male support, women have sought specialist positions where they work as individuals and often become highly proficient in an esoteric job. Thus, they shine under a sunlamp. While this may be temporarily enhancing to her self-concept, and does in fact remove a woman from threat to self-concept, it does little to prepare her for the managerial role.

SIGNIFICANT OTHERS AND MANAGERIAL BEHAVIOR

In most companies, the female manager has received little organizational or peer reinforcement. Organizational concern and career-development decisions have favored the male.

What the female manager's potential ultimately amounts to depends largely on top management's success in creating a leadership environment that brings out this potential. The power of significant others at all company levels and of the masculine structure of the organization upon the female's self-concept and managerial behavior, however, has been largely ignored by top management. To function as an effective part of the management team, the female manager must have equal worth with the male members of the management team. Management must recognize that as much difference exists between female managers and nonmanagers as between male managers and nonmanagers. More generalizations are based on traits traditionally attributed to women than to objective empirical observations of women managers.[14]

Although there is not convincing evidence that "one sex is brighter or more creative than the other, or that there are innate differences in cognitive functioning,"[15] most significant others—superiors, peers, subordinates—have believed women different from men in ways that affect managerial performance. They have been perceived to have different skills, habits and motivations that make them undesirable leaders. The idea that neither men nor women like to work for women and that they have lower career aspirations than men, less commitment to work, more concern with friendships than with the work itself, and make poorer leaders because they are not assertive—or if they are assertive, they are too dictatorial and bitchy—is prevalent in literature on women executives.

Without the needed acceptance and reinforcement, females have felt inferior and inadequate as managers. Some women have been unsure how far they can assert themselves without "putting off" superiors, subordinates, and peers; others have been unsure how removed they should be from men; and still others have been apprehensive as to the extent they should adapt to "male" norms or compete on "male" terms.

While women managers may be accepted intellectually as a colleague, covert actions and attitudes can thwart her job effectiveness. For example, if she is thought of more as a woman than as a competent manager, then there may be a lack of backing and authority from higher management. In turn, this could undercut support from subordinates and, concomitantly, her confidence and motivation. Supervisors and colleagues, instead of accepting her and helping her adjust to her new role, may stand aloof, watching critically, expressing doubt she can do the job and, in general, expecting her to fail. The message communicated by significant others is "We know women don't usually make good managers, so we really don't expect you to succeed."

If women are to succeed as managers, top management must alleviate negative influences within the corporate structure that erode the female's self-concept as a manager. Emotional and professional support from top management, in general, and particularly from their immediate supervisors, lowers role conflict and increases the female's professional self-esteem.

IMPLICATIONS FOR MANAGEMENT

The critic would be quick to say that we would turn an executive or manager into a psychotherapist—whole or half-baked. Not so. Yet it is true that the effective manager is one who can accomplish corporate objectives by drawing on the resources of subordinates. Supervising individuals and coordinating work in one area with that of counterparts in other areas is a major part of the manager's job. To do this well a manager must ask for and give support to supervisors, colleagues, and subordinates. For many complex reasons, women, who are not seen as having the same aspirations as their male colleagues, and do not share male behaviors, have found it difficult to be part of a management team. That difficulty could stem in large measure from problems inherent in the self-concept system.

The thrust of this article is that women, in order to be successful managers, must have a self-concept that enables them to be comfortable in and successful with the range of situations, expectations, and roles that are part of the total managerial responsibility. But if the self-concept embodies even vestiges of gender and sex role stereotypes then there are problems not only for the woman manager, but also for the persons with whom she works. The business world operates on perceptions and behaviors that reflect conventional male and female upbringing. Breaking through these sex conventions and stereotypes requires effort and a willingness to be open-minded.[16] Avowals to be tolerant are not enough. Just telling the female manager she is capable is not enough. When job expectations are at sharp variance with the female manager's self-concept, she can feel threatened. And being threatened, the ensuing defensive behavior may not be at all useful in terms of solving the problem. It may even be regarded by the manager's superior as innate inadequacy or willful neglect of duty. Thus, women in developing a sense of self as a manager may experience some identity crisis, anxiety, and resentment—all of which are debilitating in terms of getting the job done.

STRATEGIES FOR IMPROVING THE WORK ENVIRONMENT

There are techniques to help the female manager build a more positive self-concept. The techniques we present relate directly to improving the self-concept of the female manager, and to altering the work environment. While a neat distinction between these two approaches has been postulated, the separation is more easily achieved in writing than in actual practice.

Necessity for role definition The ultimate corporate put-down is to have an impressive title, a plush office, two secretaries and not know what one is to do. With the current pressure to employ women into managerial positions, there is a real danger of employing such persons without having a clear-cut job description with delineated responsibilities, accountability, and resources necessary to get the job done. When a person does not have a definition of job responsibilities, it is a certainty that the "three c's" will be realized—confusion, conflict, and competition. Everyone will be confused about what the new woman manager is to do, including the woman manager herself! Conflict will occur simply because in trying to do *something*, the new manager will inadvertently encroach on the job responsibilities and professional turf of subordinates, peers, and superiors. None of them will take to this encroachment kindly. In fact, some males will see it as a confirmation of their long-standing belief that women don't want to share responsibility, rather, they want to usurp it. Unproductive competition will occur as a by-product of the confusion and conflict.

To ensure productivity of the individual and for the corporation, women managers must be assimilated into the structure of the business rather than setting them apart. This requires that her place in the hierarchy of the company be clarified so that male peers treat her as an equal. Should this not be done, the female manager, in short time, will gravitate to a position where she becomes highly proficient in a narrow field that bears only peripheral relationship to the rest of the enterprise.

Eliminating institutionalized roadblocks Broaching the subject of discrimination evokes responses like the following, "Our company makes it a policy not to discriminate, etc., etc." True, that may be company policy, but what about institutionalized discrimination? These are the behaviors that are below the level of awareness, that we do not think about before doing them, that come as "second nature," and that seem so right simply because we've been doing them for so long.

The forms of institutionalized discriminatory behavior are manifold. In opening a meeting, for example, the words "Good morning, gentlemen . . . (hesitation) . . . and lady" makes the woman feel that she is an outsider when a simple "good morning" would suffice. Examples of other seemingly small and inconsequential behaviors make people feel as though they are set apart and that they do not belong to the organizations which employ them: female managers frequently are not invited to meetings to which their male predecessors were invited; they tend not to be included in the informal discussions that take place in the office setting; they often are not included in the routing of inter-office memoranda; and, they may be spoken to in condescending terms. Threat and degradation of the female's self-concept is the aftermath of these institutionalized behaviors. The paradox is that some institutionalized behaviors may be perceived by males directly opposite to the way females see them. That is, the male sees them as reflecting acceptance of females, whereas the females see these behaviors as setting them apart and excluding them.

While it is true that we live in a world whose imperfections may outlive all of us, it is equally true that we can remove many of these imperfections if we focus attention upon them. Women managers cannot be treated as outsiders without serious consequences regarding their productivity and that of their support staff. If their leader has no influence, then it follows that their department and they have no influence, so, "why go all out?" Treating women differently undermines their influence, which undermines their work, which undermines their self-concept, thereby serving to the disadvantage of all concerned. The point is, the corporation employs managers, not "women" managers or "male" managers.

STRATEGIES FOR IMPROVING SELF-CONCEPT

Recognizing that women managers want to succeed, want to be part of the management team, and that they are apprehensive about their new role, the woman manager's superior has at hand a number of techniques that may be employed. At the heart of the suggestions is the recognition that self-concept can change, albeit it takes time. More than that, it takes concerted and calm effort.

People inform us of their self-concept in a host of ways but two things are of special significance to managers who want to understand their subordinates. First, is to *listen for self-referential statements*. These statements often begin with the words, "I can (can't)," "I like (don't like)," "I think (don't think)," "I believe (don't believe)," etc. The list is endless. By listening carefully over a period of time, the manager will become sensitive to recurring self-references or to those made with emphasis. Even if guesses about one's subordinates' self-concepts are rudimentary, they are better than nothing at all and far better than hunches, biases or prejudice—particularly at a time when women are entering the managerial world.

Second, the self-concept is a selector of experience. Behavior is consistent with the way we see and believe ourselves to be. Thus, we get an insight into the second way a manager has to learn about the self-concepts of subordinates: What employees enjoy doing, volunteer to do, or devote much time to is, in fact, a behavior statement or self-concept and can be discerned by observation. Conversely, the avoidance behavior of employees tells us what they dislike doing or what makes them feel inadequate.

We do not advocate that people be given work assignments only in terms of what they say they like or don't like, or what their behavior suggests they would choose to work on or to avoid. But by knowing something about a person's self-concept and, therefore, his behavioral choices, the manager is better able to assign work that is nonthreatening, better prepared as to how to present work assignments to subordinates, and can play a positive role in helping individuals to develop a stronger and more positive self-concept.

Presuming that the woman manager's superior has, in fact, listened carefully to her self-referential statements and observed her behavioral choices, it is now possible for non-threatening and realistic work objectives to be established. These work objectives need not be strictly in line with those ways in which an individual perceives herself, but it is important to realize that if they are to be different, they can be only *slightly* different than the prevailing self-concept. There can be and should be minor dissonance. When there is minor discrepancy between the self-concept and the work objectives, mild anxiety occurs which serves as a motivating factor. Research reveals that while high anxiety is debilitating, low anxiety is tolerable to the individual, causing him or her to do something about resolving the discrepancy. What the individual does, of course, is to apply oneself to the managerial tasks and objectives. Ideally, these objectives are established in consultation between the woman manager and her superior. The clearer and more specific the work objectives, the more specific and goal-directed the behavior of the woman manager.

As work proceeds toward achieving these objectives, the superior emphasizes the positive aspects of performance. This can be done by using factual, non-evaluative language. This: "You resolved Jones' grievance without having it go to arbitration," rather than, "You handled that Jones grievance beautifully." The former emphasizes what the woman manager *did*, while the latter emphasizes what the superior *thinks* and how he evaluates it. A strong and positive self-concept is built on the former. A dependency relationship, and even apprehension, is built on the latter. Factual expression of success provides the "stuff" on which a realistic self-concept is built—and all self-concepts should be realistic. Only after the success of one's performance has been reflected to the woman manager should the negative aspects of performance be transmitted. Again, this is done in a factual and non-evaluative manner. Evaluation is unnecessary if the work objective has been delineated in specific terms, for the woman manager can compare the factual statement with the work objective and make the evaluation herself. Such a self-evaluation carries considerably less threat to the self-concept than if it is done by the superior, who after all, is a significant other in the psychological life of the woman manager. This is not coddling or pampering; it is a means by which a strong, realistic self-concept may be enhanced. These procedures are usually reversed, in that we tell individuals what they have not done well, and then as an after-thought (or never) we tell what has been done well. Curiously, the reason for doing this is that we want to help people do better the next time, and we can only do better, so the thinking goes, if we correct mistakes. In correcting those mistakes, we feed people all negatives and then hope that they will emerge with positive self-concepts. How paradoxical! How much managerial talent has been lost because of good intentions we can only speculate.

Whether we like it or not, all people, including women managers, bring their self-concepts to work. One's self-concept is not left on the doorstep of the corporate offices each morning. We have emphasized the role of women managers because they are a class of people newly arrived in the managerial structure. Their role models are few and far between, and, therefore, they cannot be expected to fit into a totally new managerial role, corporate environment, and working relationship without some assistance, although we do not by any means advocate making it easier for them than for anyone else. The suggestions we have made for understanding and improving self-concept are applicable to males and females alike. We would not suggest they not be used with males, but we do believe there are strong and compelling reasons for these techniques to be used with women managers.

NOTES

1 Eleanor E. Maccoby and Carol N. Jacklin, *The Psychology of Sex Differences*, Stanford, California, Standford University Press, 1974, p. 349.
2 Lisa Gray-Shellberg, and others, "Resolution of Career Conflicts: The Double Standard in Action," (Paper presented at the 80th Annual Convention of the American Psychological Association, September 1972), p. 3.
3 See Jean D. Grambs and Walter B. Waetjen, *Sex: Does It Make A Difference?*, North Scituate, Massachusetts, Duxbury Press, 1975; Margaret Mead, *Male and Female: A Study of the Sexes in a Changing World*, New York, N.Y., Dell Publishing Company, Inc., 1971.
4 See Ben Rosen and Thomas H. Jerdee, "Sex Stereotyping in the Executive Suite," *Harvard Business Review*, March–April, 1974, pp. 45–58; "The Influence of Sex-Role Stereotypes on Evaluations of Male and Female Supervisory Behavior," *Journal of Applied Psychology*, 1973, pp. 44–48.
5 Eleanor Brantley Schwartz, *The Sex Barrier in Business*, Georgia State University, 1971.
6 Janet T. Spence and Robert Helmreich, "The Attitudes Toward the Rights and Roles of Women in Contemporary Society," *Selected Documents in Psychology*, Journal Supplement Abstract to the American Psychological Association, 1972.
7 Lawrence H. Peters, James R. Terborg, and Janet Taynor, "Women as Managers Scale (WAMS): A Measure in Management Positions," Abstracted in the Journal Supplement Abstract Service, *Catalog of Selected Documents in Psychology*, 1974.
8 Virginia E. Schein, "Think Manager—Think Male, The Changing Face of Management: Women as a Managerial Resource," *Atlanta Economic Review*, March–April, 1976, pp. 21–24.
9 Mildred E. Buzenburg, "Training and Development of Women Executives: A Model," *Collegiate News and Views*, Fall, 1975, p. 21.
10 L. R. Hoffman and N. F. Maier, "Social Factors Influencing Problem Solv-

ing in Women," *Journal of Personality and Social Psychology*, Volume 4, October, 1966, pp. 382–390.

11 Matina S. Horner, "Women's Will to Fail," *Psychology Today*, Volume 3, November, 1960, pp. 36–38.

12 David Tresemer, "Fear of Success Popular, But Unproven," *Psychology Today*, March, 1974, p. 84.

13 W. Lloyd Warner, et. al., "Women Executives in the Federal Government," *Public Personnel Review*, Volume 23, October, 1962, pp. 227–234.

14 Sidney I. Lirtzman and Mahmoud A. Wabba, "A Managerial Myth: Differences in Coalitional Behavior of Men and Women in Organizations," *Proceedings of the 32nd Annual Meeting of The Academy of Management*, 1973, p. 178.

15 Op. cit., Grambs and Waetjen, p. 171.

16 Gene Marine, *A Male Guide to Women's Liberation*, (Holt, Rinehart, and Winston), 1972.

FOR DISCUSSION AND REVIEW

1 Explain the notion of self-concept. What importance does it have for understanding women managers' behavior?

2 What has been the result, according to the authors, of the conditioning of most women in regard to self-concept?

3 What techniques do the authors suggest for improving the work environment in order to build self-image?

The New OFCCP Guidelines: What Happened?

On November 23, 1976, the United States Departments of Justice and Labor and the United States Civil Service Commission issued the Federal Executive Agency Guidelines on Employee Selection Procedures. The issuance of these guidelines was the culmination of a four-year development process which included extensive participation on the part of the American Society for Personnel Administration and other representatives of the professional and business community.

The guideline development effort also was marked by controversy which grew out of the position of the NAACP Legal Defense Fund and other civil rights groups that the new guidelines, in the form they were taking, would erode or eliminate many of the standards set by the Equal Employment Opportunity Commission Guidelines issued in 1970, and would wipe out many of the victories won in the courts on such standards.

In a sense, too, the effort was marked by failure. Even though new and more professionally acceptable guidelines were issued, the government's original intent was to develop and promulgate a uniform federal position on what employers must do to demonstrate the validity/job relatedness of their selection procedures. Since the EEOC ultimately refused to endorse the new guidelines and chose instead to reissue its 1970 document on November 24, 1976, the effort at uniformity fell short.

Reprinted by permission from *The Personnel Administrator* 22, no. 2 (February 1977): 30–34.

Throughout this process, ASPA has been represented by Mr. Frank W. Erwin. Mr. Erwin, president of Richardson, Bellows, Henry & Company, Inc., a nationally-known personnel research firm, has had extensive and long experience in validation research and its requirements and also serves on such bodies as the advisory panel currently examining the decline in college board test scores. He combines this experience with an outstanding record of government service and an intimate understanding of its machinery.

Mr. Erwin, if you were called upon to characterize the four-year federal effort to develop new guidelines on employee selection procedures, how would you describe it?

Given the present state of affairs, two competing sets of federal requirements on the same subject with those being regulated left in the middle, to describe the guideline effort as extraordinary is something of an understatement.

Nevertheless, I would say first that the effort and its results are highly encouraging. An attempt *was* made by the government to bring about uniform standards and we *do* have new guidelines which are more realistic and more reflective of professional standards.

It also should be noted that while the 1970 guidelines were issued and republished without provision for comment, with the new guidelines, professionals, users and civil rights organization representatives were given full and equal opportunity to comment throughout the development process and many such comments were adopted before the final version was published.

At the same time, however, and even with opportunity for comment, the guideline and regulation development process generally has an arbitrary nature about it which is a source of concern. The federal agency staff which prepares such documents usually has strong ideas on the subject along with substantial power to pursue what is "thought" to be right rather than what is "actually" right. They also have considerable latitude to highlight the comments which serve their purpose and give less weight to those comments which do not serve their purpose. In short, those to be affected by guidelines and/or regulations and who comment on them do not have a full measure of neutral treatment in terms of how those comments impact on the final products.

Finally, and in the fullest negative sense of this particular effort, the bizarre nonuniform outcome serves as an example of what can happen when mismanagement and abuse of authority is permitted to run unchecked. The Equal Employment Opportunity Commission's refusal to describe in specific terms its problems with the new draft, its refusal after September 1975 to engage in meaningful discussion with the other agencies, and its petulant republication of its 1970 guidelines as if nothing had been changed since then should not have been tolerated.

As we indicated at the outset, ASPA was extensively involved in the guideline development process. Could you give us some background on how that came about?

To understand that you should first know that ASPA's involvement is a part, albeit a major part, of a much larger effort to bring reason back into civil rights enforcement. By way of some history and explanation, the 1970 EEOC Guidelines, even though issued without provision for comment, came at a time when those to be affected were still lulled into complacence by the word "guidelines." There also had been very little enforcement experience under the Act and the Supreme Court's *Griggs* v. *Duke Power* decision was still some seven months away.

By 1973, however, the situation had changed drastically. EEOC and Office of Federal Contract Compliance Enforcement activities were well underway and were disturbingly punitive and unreasonable in nature, with overly zealous and untrained investigators and compliance officers being permitted extraordinary latitude.

At the same time, it was increasingly clear that EEOC and the courts were tending to use the 1970 guidelines not as guidelines but as a rigid checklist against which demonstrations of job relatedness were to be judged and technical standards were being rewritten in court decision footnotes.

With this background, the fact that new guidelines were being prepared by the Equal Employment Opportunity Coordinating Council (EEOCC) became a matter of serious concern. As a consequence and after a series of meetings among various private and public organizations and associations, an Ad Hoc Industry Group was created which ASPA chose to join. The title of the group was really a misnomer, because it left an initial impression that the problem being addressed was the usual one of industry objecting to regulation. It actually was not the real nature of the group or the problem. As it was structured those who represented the group's positions to the federal agencies were outstanding psychologists in the industrial field and what was being represented generally were practical expressions of professional standards which the 1970 guidelines and the early drafts of the new guidelines did not adequately reflect. The comments of the American Psychological Association and the Industrial and Organizational Psychology Division of that association confirmed that the biggest disagreements were largely on professional grounds. In summary, the objective of requiring job relatedness showings for procedures having an adverse impact was never in question. What was being debated was the proper interpretation of professional methodology and standards for undertaking such showings.

What happens now that new guidelines are in print?

Even though there are new guidelines, the process is far from over. A communication link must be established with the new administration's choices for the pertinent agency positions. The two guidelines problem is still to be resolved. How the new guidelines are followed by compliance personnel is also a matter for concern. Finally the issuing agencies already have published 39 questions and answers designed to provide further detail and guidance on the new guidelines. These will require comment.

Are the questions and answers helpful?

No, they are not. In fact, they contain serious technical deficiencies and in their present form create new requirements which take away a great deal of what caused ASPA, The American Psychological Association, Division 14 of that association, IPMA and the Ad Hoc Group to support issuance of the new guidelines. That support is now being severely strained but I'm hopeful that changes can be made so as to avoid its withdrawal. It's clear that the question and answer process must include provision for comment before publication in the *Federal Register*. These first 39 questions and answers did not include that provision and suffer because of it.

What we have been discussing thus far are the "policy" implications of the new guidelines and the republished guidelines. What about the practical implications? Until change is made at the policy level, how do those being regulated try to comply with two sets of requirements on the same subject?

As much as I wish it were so, there is no way to answer that question with absolute certainty. Until the differences are resolved in the Executive Branch or in the Courts, I think that the safest course to follow is to analyze both sets of guidelines on a section-by-section basis and follow the more stringent requirement in each section wherever possible. Since EEOC does not provide reporting guidance, validation research reports should follow the requirements of the documentation section of the new guidelines. The new guidelines also can serve to provide interpretive guidance to follow where EEOC requirements are vague or nonexistent. I think that employers who adopt this strategy usually will find their job relatedness demonstrations to be in compliance with the new guideline requirements and at least part of the EEOC guideline requirements.

On a broader scale than the guidelines, there is a great deal of concern about what the Carter Administration or the Congress will do to change the federal civil rights enforcement structure generally. Do you have any thoughts on that?

It's impossible not to have thoughts on that subject. First, there are certain to be oversight hearings in the Congress on the performance of EEOC and OFCCP. The General Accounting Office has been spending considerable time in this area. Several reports already have been issued and several more are yet to come. Second, there are several "super EEO agency" bills circulating in the Congress and I'm sure that somewhere within the Executive Branch there is study being given to some kind of similar reorganization.

Quite apart from that, I am concerned that the civil rights movement in this country may lose ground in the years to come and that the philosophy and mismanagement of the federal civil rights effort may be the major cause of that loss. From the beginning, the approach of EEOC, OFCCP and other involved agencies has been heavily punitive. The powers granted have tended to be abused and there has been little differentiation in the use of those powers between those who are trying to comply and those who are not. Combined with interagency and interoffice conflicts, the absence of sound investigation and evidence procedures and due process, and the sham of so called "conciliation" efforts, the Federal Government's philosophy is substantially eroding the good faith efforts being made by the many organizations trying sincerely to meet equal employment opportunity objectives.

In short, we have made great strides since 1965 in the elimination of employment discrimination in this country and the punitive approach probably was necessary to get it started and it's still required with some recalcitrants. In 1977, however, the point generally has been made. The equal employment commitment is now a major thread in the fabric of our society. If the tone of the federal effort is permitted to shift from the punitive to the positive and if investigators are trained and the positive philosophy enforced, then more time will begin to be spent on development of jobs rather than development of defenses and we will make even greater strides in the years to come. Without such a change in philosophy *and* people, even cease and desist powers and double the budget will fail. The issues will be resolved in the courts in cases involving organizations with much better facts than what the courts have seen thus far. The net result can only be a major and tragically unnecessary setback to objectives which most of us share.

FOR DISCUSSION AND REVIEW

1 As of 1977, what two sets of guidelines had been published? How will this lack of uniformity impact organizations trying to comply?
2 What are the major differences in the two sets of guidelines? Which seem more lenient; more quantitative?
3 What does the author recommend organizations do in order to comply with the guidelines now?

Lewis J. Ringler

EEO Agreements and Consent Decrees May Be Booby-traps!

Many of the employers who voluntarily entered into conciliation or consent agreements with the Equal Employment Opportunity Commission or joined in consent decrees fashioned by Federal Courts to obtain relief from alleged illegal discriminatory employment practices are discovering that they may have booby-traps on their hands.

In retrospect, these employers, in their attempts to solve or settle significant equal employment opportunity problems, may have been lured into a state of false security. Recent Federal Court decisions have held such agreements and decrees may not be pleaded as a complete affirmative defense against legal actions brought as the result of implementing the terms of these agreements.[1]

Early in the 1970s many employers elected to solve their equal employment opportunity problems by voluntarily entering into conciliation agreements with the Equal Employment Opportunity Commission or with national organizations representing minorities. Others voluntarily consented or were forced as a result of adverse court decisions to become parties to consent decrees under the jurisdiction of Federal Courts.

The American Telephone and Telegraph Company and its Bell System affiliates was one of the first giant employers to enter into a broad consent agreement. This employer did not admit to, nor did the Federal Government require it to admit to, any act of discrimination. However, American Telephone and Telegraph agreed to enter into this consent agreement only after the Equal Employment Opportunity Commission vigorously opposed its application for a rate increase. Parties to this agreement were the Equal Employment Opportunity Commission, the U.S. Department of Labor and other Federal enforcement agencies. The agreement was filed with a Federal District Court. The first five year cost of this settlement, which was consummated in 1973, has been estimated to be in excess of seventy-five million.

Employers such as Anaconda Aluminum, Virginia Electric Power, Lorillard, Household Finance, Wheaton Glass, Sardis Luggage, Libby Owens Ford, Braniff Airways and Western Electric, after litigating alleged unlawful employment practices, were forced to become parties in conjunction with the Federal Government to consent decrees. The financial penalties imposed by the terms of these decrees amount to an estimated aggregate of $59.2 million.

The Bank of California voluntarily entered into a consent agreement with representatives of the National Organization for Women (NOW), the National Association for the Advancement of Colored People (NAACP) and other national minority interest groups. This agreement, which was filed with a Federal District Court, later became the model for similar agreements entered into by many other large California banks.

In 1974 all the companies representing the steel industry except one were forced to enter into a consent decree by a Federal Court.[2] During this same period many of the trucking companies which comprise the trucking industry were also forced to join with Federal District Courts in consent decrees.[3] The unusual feature of those agreements involved the incorporation of the employment functions

Reprinted by permission from *The Personnel Administrator* 22, no. 2 (February 1977): 16–21.

involving non-management employees covered by the industry-wide collective bargaining agreements in the consent decrees negotiated for each industry. The national unions representing these employees were: United Steelworkers of America (steel industry) and the International Brotherhood of Teamsters, Chauffeurs, and Warehousemen. Helpers of America (trucking industry) joined as parties-in-interest.

Many employers favored the conciliation agreement or consent decree approach because of the assumption these agreements bought from the courts the assurance that issues resolved at the time of initial negotiation would bar the relitigation of the same issues should they arise in a future action brought under Title VII or other appropriate legislation.

However, at this point in time, other employers began to question the wisdom of entering into conciliation agreements or consent decrees. They realized after reviewing a number of Supreme Court and Federal Court decisions that they had been lured into a sense of false security. The court decisions vividly pinpointed the legal pitfalls encountered when a conciliation agreement or consent decree is entered as an affirmative defense against an alleged unlawful employment practice previously litigated by the Federal Government against an employer and resolved by terms of the agreement. Some of the startling decisions reached by the courts in these cases are summarized as follows:

1 *Daniel McAleer* vs. *American Telephone and Telegraph Company*, U.S. District Court, District of Columbia, Civil Action No. 75–2049 (June 9, 1976). American Telephone and Telegraph Company has been in the process of implementing the provisions of the consent decree discussed above. Its affirmative action section establishes goals and time-tables to improve the employment situation for non-management women and minorities previously under-utilized within the company's employment population.

Prior to joining the consent agreement, the union contract's standards for promotion of non-management employees called for the selection of the best qualified employee and where more than one candidate of equal qualities was under consideration, length of service was the deciding factor. The terms of the consent agreement forced the company to ignore more qualified, longer service, non-minority candidates who qualified for a promotion and forced the selection of a lesser qualified minority or female candidate. The Communication Workers of America, which represents the non-management employees, was not a party to the consent agreement although it was invited to join.

The company promoted a female employee, passing over a more qualified, more senior white male who was entitled to the promotion under the provisions of the union contract. The white male filed a Sex Discrimination Action under the Civil Rights Act of 1964 against the company seeking both the promotion and damages. The Communication Workers of America joined claiming the action taken by the company interfered with its ability to represent its members and secure their employment rights under the union contract. The company pleaded the court approved consent agreement as a defense to all claims set forth in the charge.

The Federal District Court in its decision issued on June 6, 1976 held as follows:

a) The consent decree was a final judgment of a Federal Court and therefore was not subject to review or modification by another Federal Court.

b) The male employee who was passed over was not entitled to the promotion since the female was protected by the terms of the consent agreement.

c) The male employee had a legal course of action under the "Civil Rights Act of 1964, Title VII", since he was a victim of discrimination. He was to be compensated

EEO BACKGROUND

In order to understand how the paradoxical situation described in this article developed, it is necessary to follow the relatively short but volatile evolutionary stages through which equal employment opportunity legislation and its enforcement has passed. Initially the protection of employees from discriminatory employment practices fell within the jurisdiction of the individual States. However, during the period of widespread unrest which took place during the 1960s, the forces of social justice were strong enough to force the shifting of this protection from the state to national level.

The Congress of the United States became very active during this period in the enacting of equal employment opportunity legislation beginning with the passage of the Equal Pay Act of 1963. This Act was quickly followed by the Civil Rights Act of 1964, Title VII as amended; Federal Age Discrimination in Employment Act of 1967; Equal Employment Opportunity Act of 1972; Vocational Rehabilitation Act of 1973 and Vietnam Era Veterans Readjustment Act of 1974.

In addition, Executive Order 11246, issued in 1965 by President Johnson, and subsequent amendments require contractors wishing to perform services for or sell goods to the Federal Government[1] to develop and implement affirmative action programs designed to eliminate discriminatory employment practices in their operations. These problems are enforced through a continual monitoring system established by several Federal Compliance Agencies.

With the passage of the Civil Rights Act of 1964, Title VII, equal employment opportunity became the law of the land. This Act made the elimination of employment discrimination based on race, color, religion, sex or national origin in all industries affecting interstate commerce an avowed objective of the Federal Government.

During the lengthy debates which preceded the enactment of this legislation many employers as well as members of Congress expressed fear that the equal employment opportunity provisions of the Act would mandate the hiring of minorities by companies on the basis of quotas at the expense of non-minorities. To allay the concern that each employer would be forced to immediately hire a sufficient number of minorities to bring the ratio of minorities on the payroll in conformity to the percentage of minorities to whites in the community where the employers' places of businesses were located, Section 702(j) was placed in the Act. The purpose of this Section was to clarify that the equal em-

---

[1] An employer doing at least $50,000 worth of business with the government and having at least 50 employees is required to develop and implement separate written affirmative action plans—one for women and racial minorities, one for handicapped persons and disabled veterans and veterans of the Vietnam Era.—OFCCP, Equal Employment Opportunity Duties of Government Contractors, 41 CFR (60-1.40; 60-741.5 and 60-250.4)

---

for damages resulting from the company's action in trying to correct its past wrongful conduct which consisted of discriminating against females and minorities.

d) The union was free to pursue a charge of an unfair labor practice for breach of contract against the company. However, this Court did not have jurisdiction to adjudicate an unfair labor practice action as this came within the jurisdiction of the National Labor Relations Board.

e) The company was not permitted to plead the consent agreement as an affirmative defense against the claim set forth in the unlawful employment practice charge. The Court said "where a Court order is necessary to force a company to correct past wrongful conduct, the consent agreement cannot be pleaded as a defense from liability arising from the act."

ployment opportunity provisions did not require preferential treatment be given to any individual or group even where the composition of an employer's work-force is not in balance with the percentage of the minority population found in the employer's service area.

After the passage of the Civil Rights Act of 1964, Title VII, the courts soon became overloaded with cases alleging employment discrimination against employers. However, before the courts could order relief it was mandatory a determination be made that the Civil Rights Act gave them the power to impose relief without violating Section 702(j) of the Act.

The Supreme Court of the United States solved this problem in 1965[2] when it held Federal Courts not only had the power but the duty to render decrees which would eliminate the discriminatory effects of the past as well as bar discrimination in the future.

Soon after the above decision was announced, the lower courts construed this delegation of power as authorizing them through voluntary or Court-ordered decrees to force employers to establish and fully implement affirmative action programs in those situations where it was necessary to cure the ill effects of past discrimination. The Courts also recognized that this obligation should be imposed with extreme caution and discretion as well as ensure the remedial programs ordered be uniform in nature and exist only as long as necessary to effectuate the purpose of the Civil Rights Act.

The courts most frequently exercised their authority to fashion affirmative relief through the use of voluntary and consent decrees in cases where the employment practices of employers were found to be neutral on their face and did not intend to discriminate, but in practice, had the effect of perpetuating past discrimination.[3]

The determination by the Supreme Court that courts had the power to order employers to take affirmative action to end past discrimination; the swift enforcement of these powers by the lower courts; and the aggressiveness of the Equal Employment Opportunity Commission (the enforcement arm established by the Civil Rights Act) in using its sweeping investigative powers to initiate class suits discrimination actions against carefully chosen large employers, put each employer subject to this legislation on notice that it would have to quickly decide on a course of action to meet the challenges inherent in this legislation.

---

[2] Louisiana vs. United States, 380 U.S. 145 (1965)
[3] Local 53 of the International Association of Heat and Frost Insulators and Asbestos Workers vs. Vogler, 407 F 2d, 1047 (1967); United States vs. Local 189, United Paper Makers and Paper Workers, Eastern District Court of Louisiana (1968) 282 F. Supp. 39, 45; Quarles vs. Phillip Morris, Inc., Eastern District Court of Virginia (1968) 279 F. Supp. 505, 516 and United States vs. United Brotherhood of Carpenters and Joinders of America, Local 169, 457 F 2d, 210 (7th Circuit) 1972.

---

2 *EEOC* vs. *Kimberly-Clark Corp.*, U.S. District Court, Western District of Tennessee, Western Division, No. C-73-42 (March 27, 1974).

Kimberly-Clark laid off 10 female employees at its Memphis Plant over a period of several months during 1965 and 1966. Those employees filed a sex discrimination action in the above-captioned court in 1966. Soon afterwards, they also filed a class action suit covering the same issues with the EEOC against both the company and the Paper Mill Workers Union. After a full hearing, the Court dismissed the action on its merits after a consent decree was consummated as a full and final settlement to all claims.

The Equal Employment Opportunity Commission filed an action on behalf of the same employees in the same court on June 15, 1973, covering the layoffs in

1965 and 1966 but adding an additional charge. The company refused to restore their seniority rights for the period of time they were laid off. As a defense to this action, the company pleaded the consent decree which resolved the issues set forth in the later action except for the seniority question.

The Court held the EEOC could not relitigate the terms of the initial settlement entered into with the court but could assert the rights of the individuals with regard to their seniority rights on the basis the company had not carried out its obligations under the terms of the 1967 consent decree.

3 *Cox* vs. *Allied Chemical Corp.,* U.S. Court of Appeals, Fifth Circuit, No. 75-2109 (Sept. 15, 1976).

The employer signed a conciliation agreement with the Equal Employment Opportunity Commission which changed the application of seniority for purposes of promotion, transfer and layoffs. Formerly seniority was applied on a departmental basis and when an employee transferred to another department, seniority did not carry over from the former department. Under the EEOC agreement transferred black employees received credit for prior seniority for all purposes except layoffs. In the case of layoffs they received credit only for the time spent in their assigned department at the time of layoff. Two black employees who were parties to the consent agreement and subsequently transferred were laid off. They were not credited with their total service with the employer since under the EEOC agreement seniority for layoff purposes reverted to a departmental basis. The two employees, along with a white employee, filed a discrimination action against the employer charging the application of the seniority system in the case of layoffs violated the Civil Rights Act of 1964, as amended.

The Court held the employees who signed the initial EEOC conciliation agreement waiving certain rights to court actions could still intervene in a subsequent racial discrimination suit brought against their employer. The mere fact that employees signed a waiver did not establish that they knowingly and voluntarily relinquished their rights under Title VII of the Civil Rights Act of 1964, as amended. The employer could not plead the signed conciliation agreement as a defense to this action.

4 *United States of America* vs. *International Brotherhood of Electrical Workers,* U.S. District Court, Eastern District of Louisiana, Civil Action No. 71-1779 (Aug. 6, 1976).

The International Brotherhood of Electrical Workers, Local 130 and the Regional Chapter of the National Electrical Contractor Association and the New Orleans Electrical Joint Apprenticeship and Training Committee entered into a consent decree with the Federal Court enjoining them from discriminating against blacks in apprenticeship programs.

In 1975 the EEOC, representing the Federal Government, filed an action against a number of electrical contractors who had signed a collective bargaining agreement with the union but were not signatories to the consent decree. The basis of the action was that the contractors discriminated against blacks who were furnished by the union for the respective apprenticeship programs and therefore violated the terms of the consent decree. The question involved was whether there was privity of contract as to the consent decree even though the contractors did not sign the decree and in some cases had no knowledge it even existed.

The Court held it is well established a party cannot be bound by a consent agreement to which it was not a party and consequently cannot be held in contempt for the performance of the discriminatory acts prohibited by the decree.

Since the Equal Employment Opportunity Commission is legally bound to conciliate alleged unlawful employment practices and the courts still use the consent decree to enforce equal employment opportunity legislation violations, employers will be forced to settle a number of the discrimination actions filed against them in this manner. However, the prudent employers will take advantage of the recent court decisions to substantially reduce the hazards when negotiating the terms of such an agreement. The attorney charged with drafting such an agreement should be sure its terms reflect some or all of the following items:

1 Withdrawal of all pending charges.

2 Final and complete resolution of all issues.

3 Adequate settlement within the framework of the facts to cover all parties who might bring future actions.

4 Limit the amount of monitoring activities to be conducted by the EEOC.

5 Provide notice for all class members permitting them to comment on settlement and electing not to be bound by its terms—agreement to be cancelled if a certain percentage of class members elect not to be bound.

6 Provide that signers release past, present and future claims under Title VII and other appropriate equal employment opportunity legislation.

7 Limit attorney fees of charging parties.

8 Ensure all appropriate parties, such as labor unions, are made parties-in-interest.

A number of employers have decided the time has arrived for them to take affirmative action through the judicial process and other means to defend themselves against the unreasonable actions of the Equal Employment Opportunity Commission as well as those selected members of society who are protected by the Equal Employment Opportunity legislation. An example of the counter-attack now taking place involves Shippers Dispatch, Inc. of South Bend, Indiana, a trucking industry member who joined in a partial consent decree ordered by the U.S. District Court, Washington, D.C. on March 20, 1974. This employer is currently facing a tremendous financial liability as the result of carrying out the terms of this consent decree.

For many years the trucking industry has recognized and appreciated the substantial potential liability exposure assumed by over-the-road truck drivers. These drivers normally operate 10-speed tractor-trailers weighing up to 72,000 pounds over thousands of national, state and local highways throughout the United States during all hours of the day and night, in close proximity to thousands of passenger cars operated by members of the public.

Trucking firms, in recognition of their duty to provide safety to the public and the possible financial disaster facing them should a driver become involved in a catastrophic accident, established extremely high skill and related requirements for all individuals who desire to qualify for an over-the-road driver job.

Shippers Dispatch, in fulfilling the minority employment goals established by the terms of the consent decree for over-the-road-driver job classification, was forced to reduce its prior applicant evaluation standards and select drivers from the available minority labor pools who were under qualified for this job.

An applicant who was evaluated by the substantially lower employment standards was employed for one of the over-the-road driver vacancies. Subsequently this driver was involved in an accident with a passenger automobile which resulted in the death of the driver and severe injuries to two of the passengers. The truck driver was cited for reckless operation and failure to drive on the right-hand side of the road. The living occupants of the passenger car filed a $2.4 million lawsuit for damages against Shippers Dispatch, Inc.

In an attempt to force the Federal Government to assume at least a share of the financial liability to the private parties involved in this tragedy, Shippers Dispatch filed suit in Federal Court seeking indemnification from the United States of America.[4] This lawsuit is based on the premise that Shippers Dispatch was compelled to employ the less qualified minority truck driver because of a Federal Court order and therefore the Federal Government is financially liable to the injured parties. This case is currently on appeal before the U.S. Sixth Circuit Court of Appeals in Cincinnati, Ohio.

The Shippers Dispatch case represents what can happen when the Federal Government becomes involved in the management of a company's employment function. The consent decree forces the company to employ a fixed percentage of less qualified minorities by a certain date without regard to the affect of this action on cost, production quality or potential financial liability. After observing the current plight of Shippers Dispatch resulting from its "good faith" efforts to comply with the Federal Government's mandate, the American people should be concerned as to the catastrophic situations that may develop when and if the Federal Government forces the airline companies to employ less qualified individuals for airplane pilot positions.

The most promising defense available to employers in their struggle against the equal employment opportunity monster is to go on the offense, individually and/or collectively. They must use every possible means available to put pressure on all Federal Government agencies involved in the enactment, implementation and enforcement of discrimination laws. Suggested actions to be taken are:

1 Total resistance to the EEOC when it becomes involved;

2 Fighting all EEOC actions through the courts using every legal means to gain favorable decisions;

3 Use all publication and mass media communication techniques to ensure the public is made aware of the legislative reforms needed to eliminate the "reverse discrimination" programs being forced upon the non-minority segment of the population;

4 Apply continuing pressure on members of Congress until they enact the reforms necessary in this legislation whereby employers will not be forced to continue defending against alleged unlawful employment practices arising from implementing the terms of conciliation agreements and consent decrees forced upon them by the Federal Government.

By going on the offense, employers are putting everyone on notice they are not against the elimination of discrimination at the workplace or on-the-job, but want to reinstate a fundamental legal concept which has been the foundation of our democratic way of life—once an agreement such as a consent decree is reached through the judicial process its terms are to be honored by all parties to it, including the Federal Government.

REFERENCES

1 *Cox* vs. *Allied Chemical Corp., U.S. Court of Appeals, Fifth Circuit No. 75 2109 (Sept. 15, 1976); Williamson* vs. *Bethlehem Steel Corp., 468 F2d 1201 (2 Cir. 1972); EEOC* vs. *Kimberly Clark Corp., 511 F2d 1352 (6 Cir. 1975)*

2 *United States of America* vs. *United States Steel Corp., U.S. District Court, Northern District of Alabama, Southern Division (May 2, 1973)*

3 *United States of America vs. Trucking Employers, Inc., U.S. District Court, District Court of Columbia, Civil Action No. 74-453 (March 20, 1974); Chathy vs. Johnson Motor Lines, Inc., U.S. District Court, Western District Court of North Carolina, Charlotte Division No. 72-262 (Dec. 20, 1974); Rodriguez vs. East Texas Motor Freight, U.S. Court of Appeals, Fifth Circuit No. 73-2801 (Nov. 25, 1974)*

4 *Shippers Dispatch, Inc. vs. United States of America, U.S. District Court, Northern District of Ohio, Eastern Division, Case No. C75-1084 (Oct. 28, 1976). This case was filled by Reminger & Reminger Co., L.P.A., Cleveland, Ohio on behalf of its client, Shippers Dispatch, Inc.*

FOR DISCUSSION AND REVIEW

1 In what sense are EEO agreements and consent decrees "booby-traps"?

2 Discuss the merits of the AT&T and Kimberly-Clark Corporation cases from the point of view of consent decrees and agreements.

3 What does the author recommend consent decrees contain?

Robert H. Flast

Taking the Guesswork Out of Affirmative Action Planning

There is a growing interest in flow models of employee mobility, which summarize the movements of employees between occupational groups within an organization during a fixed time period *(Figure 1)*.

Such models have been used in manpower planning and, most recently, in affirmative action planning.[1] The purpose of this article is to present a new use of flow models as a forecasting technique in affirmative action planning.

One component of affirmative action planning is the specification of time limited distribution goals for women and minorities. Such goal setting results in numerical targets showing the numbers of women and minorities planned for each occupational group in the organization at a specific point in the future. The achievement of these goals by the organization's management is accomplished, or not, through the formulation of goal oriented hiring and promotion policies.

A company's hiring and promotion policies have a direct and obvious impact on the likelihood of the company meeting its affirmative action goals. The problem then arises as to how to identify or assess those policies which, if implemented, could potentially best meet the goals of the affirmative action plan.

Hiring policies can include consideration of recruitment techniques, employment sources, external labor market factors, and screening techniques. However, for the purpose of this article, a hiring policy is defined as the net result of all of these factors or, in other words, the actual distribution of employees hired in the various occupational groups during a specified time interval.

Reprinted by permission from *Personnel Journal* 56, no. 2 (February 1977): 68–71. Copyright © February 1977 by *Personnel Journal*.

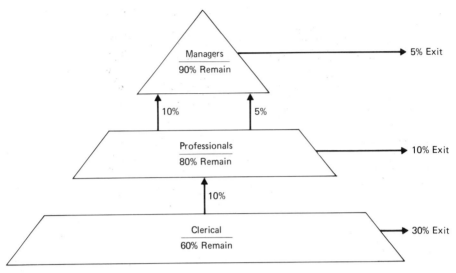

Fig. 1 Year to year flow between groups.

Similarly, promotion policies can include consideration of internal development activities and labor market factors, turnover, internal screening and placement techniques, and performance appraisal and compensation programs. However, here a promotion policy is defined as the net result of all of these factors, or the observed movements of employees between occupational groups within the organization during a specified time interval.

The flow models developed to date have been used to forecast the expected distribution of employees in occupational groups, given specified starting or current distributions, hiring policies, and promotion policies. Any or all of these factors can be varied and the results can be recorded and compared with the results from previous combinations of factors.

While such forecasts may be useful in decision making, they can only reveal the relative effectiveness of various combinations of hiring and promotion policies. They cannot, for example, highlight hiring policies which will meet the desired affirmative action goals at a minimum cost, given the specified starting distributions and promotion policies. Therefore, they cannot be used to identify combinations of policies which are optimal solutions to the achievement of affirmative action goals.

In the material which follows, the basic flow model described above is used to develop a more useful forecasting and planning technique for affirmative action managers. This technique, in contrast to the flow models, can be used to identify precise combinations of hiring and promotion policies which are likely to result in the attainment of the company's affirmative action goals.

SAMPLE COMPANY PROFILE

To illustrate the application of this new technique and to contrast it with the flow model technique, the following hypothetical consulting company was created. This organization consists of two occupational levels or groups, professionals and managers. Over the years they have observed that their female employees move through and out of the organization, from year to year, as shown by the statistics in Table 1.

Table 1
Flow Model of Female Employees

GROUP BEGINNING THE YEAR AS:	PERCENT ENDING THE YEAR AS:			
	PROFESSIONALS	MANAGERS	TERMINATIONS	TOTAL
Professionals	60%	10%	30%	100%
Managers	5%	80%	15%	100%

Sixty percent of the female professionals and 80% of the female managers end each year in the same occupational group as they began the year. However, this does not imply that the same individual professionals and managers remain in their groups year after year. Similarly, 10% of the professionals are promoted to managers each year and 5% of the managers are demoted to professionals. Finally, 30% of the professionals and 15% of the managers leave the organization each year. Table 1, then, summarizes the results of the organization's promotion and development policies.

The current and planned occupational distributions for women are shown in Table 2. The planned distribution is the two year goal which the organization has set as part of its affirmative action plan.

Table 2
Occupational Distributions

GROUP	CURRENT NUMBER	TWO YEAR GOAL
Professionals	80	80
Managers	20	40
Total	100	120

Given the information in Tables 1 and 2, the company would like to determine the *minimum* yearly hiring distribution of women which will most likely result in the goals being met. As will be shown in the next section, the flow model approach cannot provide a solution to this problem.

FLOW MODEL SOLUTIONS

The flow model approach consists of systematically testing various hiring distributions until a satisfactory solution, which meets the goals, is found. The first hiring distributions usually tested are the current year's planned distribution, if one exists, and the average yearly distribution over the past several years. These distributions for female employees are shown in Table 3. The planned distribution is twice as large as the average historical distribution because the company believes it will have to hire more aggressively than it has in the past in order to meet its goals.

Table 3
Hiring Distributions

GROUP	PLANNED HIRES	AVERAGE HIRES
Professionals	20	10
Managers	5	2
Total	25	12

To determine whether the planned hiring distribution will meet the company's goals, the flow model approach proceeds as follows:

1 Of the 80 current professionals, 60% will remain professionals at the end of the first year, or 48. Of the 20 current managers, 5% will be demoted to professionals during the first year, or one. Twenty additional professionals will be hired, yielding 69 professionals at the end of the first year.

2 Of the 20 current managers, 80% will remain managers at the end of the first year, or 16. Of the 80 current professionals, 10% will be promoted to managers during the first year, or eight. Five additional managers will be hired, yielding 29 managers at the end of the first year.

Sixty-nine professionals and 29 managers begin the cycle again during the second year. The flow model approach is repeated to find the resulting distribution at the end of year two:

1 Of the 69 professionals at the start of the second year, 60% will remain professionals at the end of the second year, or 41.40. Of the 29 managers at the start of the year, 5% will be demoted to professionals during the second year, or 1.45. Twenty additional professionals will be hired, yielding 62.85 or 63 professionals at the end of the second year.

2 Of the 29 managers at the start of the second year, 80% will remain managers at the end of the second year, or 23.20. Of the 69 professionals at the start of the year, 10% will be promoted to managers during the second year, or 6.90. Five additional managers will be hired, yielding 35.10 or 36 managers at the end of the second year.

Therefore, using the company's planned hiring distribution of 20 professionals and five managers each year, the company will most likely fail to meet its two year affirmative action goals by 17 professionals (80–63) and four managers (40–36). Any hiring distribution such as the average hiring distribution, which is less than the planned distribution tested so far, will result in the company's failing to meet its goals by more than the shortages found using the planned distribution.

At this point the company would try another hiring distribution such as twice the planned distribution, or 40 professionals and 10 managers each year. Using the flow model approach this distribution would yield 95.10 or 96 professionals at 46.10 or 47 managers at the end of two years, or 16 professionals and seven managers over the goals. While this hiring distribution meets the goals, it is not the minimum hiring distribution sought by the company. Using the flow model approach, the company will have to pursue, in this trial and error fashion, the desired minimum hiring distribution.

If the company had set three or more year goals, the flow model approach described above would be repeated as many times as necessary to project the expected distributions. The only assumptions required by this approach are that the company maintains a constant hiring distribution, which is subject to its control, and that the flow model percentages remain constant over the years being projected, which can be influenced, but probably not controlled, by the company.

The major weakness of the flow model approach described above, is that it cannot provide a direct solution to the company's problem of determining the minimum yearly hiring distribution for women which will most likely result in the company's goals being met. Using the same information as the flow model approach, the optimizing approach presented in the next section can provide the direct solution desired by the company.

THE OPTIMAL SOLUTION

If we let P and M stand for the minimum numbers of professionals and managers that have to be hired each year to satisfy the goals, we can compute each year's distribution of professionals and managers in terms of P and M, using the same logic as the flow model approach:

1 Of the 80 current professionals, 60% will remain professionals at the end of the first year, or 48. Of the 20 current managers, 5% will be demoted to professionals during the first year, or one. P additional professionals will be hired, yielding 49 plus P professionals at the end of the first year (49 + P).

2 Of the 20 current managers, 80% will remain managers at the end of the first year, or 16. Of the 80 current professionals, 10% will be promoted to managers during the first year, or eight. M additional managers will be hired, yielding 24 plus M managers at the end of the first year (24 + M).

Therefore, 49 plus P professionals and 24 plus M managers begin the cycle again during the second year:

1 Of the 49 + P professionals at the start of the second year, 60% will remain professionals at the end of the second year, or .60(49 + P) = 29.40 + .60P. Of the .24 + M managers at the start of the year, 5% will be demoted to professionals during the second year, or .05(24 + M) = 1.20 + .05M. P additional professionals will be hired, yielding (29.40 + .60P) + (1.20 + .05M) + P = (30.60 + 1.60P + .05M) professionals at the end of the second year, based on the annual hiring distribution of P and M professionals and managers.

2 Of the 24 + M managers at the start of the second year, 80% will remain managers at the end of the year, or .80(24 + M) = 19.20 + .80M. Of the 49 + P professionals at the start of the year, 10% will be promoted to managers during the second year, or .10(49 + P) = 4.90 + .10P. M additional managers will be hired, yielding (19.20 + .80M) + (4.90 + .10P) + M = (24.10 + .10P + 1.80M) managers at the end of the second year.

So far we have simply created a general algebraic expression for the flow model approach. If we replace P and M, in the equations derived above, with any values, such as the planned hiring distribution, P = 20 and M = 5, then the equations will yield the second year distributions found earlier, 62.85 or 63 professionals and 35.10 or 36 managers.

However, our objective is to find positive values for P and M which will satisfy our two year goals of 80 professionals and 40 managers. Therefore, we want the (30.60 + 1.60P + .05M) professionals at the end of the second year to be at least equal to 80. Similarly, we want the (24.10 + .10P + 1.80M) managers at the end of the second year to be at least equal to 40. Finally we want the amounts by which we exceed our goals to be as small as possible. If we let E stand for the greater of the two excesses, then we can solve this problem using linear programming as follows:

$$\text{Minimize: E}$$
$$\text{Subject to: } 0 \le (30.60 + 1.60P + 0.05M) - 80 \quad E$$
$$0 \le (24.10 + 0.10P + 1.80M) - 40 \quad E$$
$$0 \le P, M$$

Solving this linear program yields a minimum E, equal to zero, when P = 30.65 and M = 7.13.

Therefore, the company need only hire 31 professionals and eight managers each year in order to meet its affirmative action goals in two years.

If the company had set three or more year goals, the flow model approach would be used to obtain algebraic expressions in P and M for the desired year, and a linear program would be created using the goals for that year, in order to solve for P and M, as in the two year case demonstrated above. The assumptions made concerning the constant hiring distribution and flow model percentages are the same as those made in the flow model approach.

GENERAL SOLUTION

The optimal approach presented above for two occupational groups can be extended to any number of groups if we introduce vectors and matrices to express the approach. If we let d_0 represent the starting distribution vector, which was (80,20) in our example, F represent the flow model percentage matrix, which was $\begin{pmatrix} .60 & .10 \\ .05 & .80 \end{pmatrix}$ in our example, then the distribution after one year or d_1 will be equal to: $d_1 = d_0F + h$. Similarly the distribution after two, three or more years will be equal to: $d_2 = d_1F + h$ after the second year; $d_3 = d_2F + h$ after the third year; and $d_n = d_{n-1}F + h$ after the nth year.

Since each year's distribution can be expressed as a function of the previous year's distribution, any distribution can ultimately be expressed in terms of d_0, F, h and n:

$$d_n = d_0F^n + h\,(F^0 + F^1 + F^2 + \ldots + F^{n-1})$$

where F^0 is the identity matrix 1. This algebraic expression is equivalent to the flow model approach in predicting any year's distribution, when the starting and hiring distributions (d_0 and h) and the flow model percentages (F) are known.

However, in the optimal approach developed above we stated that h was not known and that our goals for year n were known. If we let the vector g_n represent our goals for year n, (80,40) in our sample problem, and E represent the greater amount by which we exceed any of these goals for a given h, we can solve for the minimum hiring distribution by using linear programming as follows:

Minimize: E
Subject to: $(0, 0, \ldots 0) \le d_n - g_n$ $(E, E, \ldots E)$
$(0, 0, \ldots 0) \le h$

Since d_n contains the vector h, the solution to this linear program yields a value for h which minimizes E, for any g_n, d_0 and F.

Finally, in addition to identifying the minimum hiring distribution for the problem stated above, the linear programming solution can include additional constraints, if they are required or if their potential impact is of interest. For example, ceilings may be imposed on the yearly hiring rates for certain groups due to the limited availability of training facilities, or to the strict enforcement of promotion from within policies.

SUMMARY

The optimizing approach presented above provides a simple and direct solution for the affirmative action manager who would like to determine the minimum yearly hiring distribution for women, or for any group, which will most likely result in the achievement of the company's affirmative action goals for that group. In contrast, the flow model approach provides only a trial and error technique which yields solutions that either fail to meet or may exceed the goals by unnecessary and perhaps costly amounts. In addition, the optimizing approach is simple to derive, program and apply.

The affirmative action manager can use this approach as a general planning and problem solving tool. In addition to answering the questions posed in this article, the technique can be used to explore the impact on a calculated minimum hiring policy of planned or observed changes in the promotion and development policies of the company.

Finally, the use of this forecasting technique enables companies to quantify their affirmative action programs in terms of dynamic hiring and promotion policies. Government compliance agencies can then adopt more realistic and meaningful measures of progress in their review procedures of affirmative action programs.

REFERENCES

1 N. C. Churchill, J. K. Shank, "Affirmative and Guilt-Edged Goals," *HBR*, March–April 1976, p. 111, and "An Application of Markov Chains for Affirmative Action Planning," an unpublished Master's thesis by R. Forst, Cornell University, 1976.

FOR DISCUSSION AND REVIEW

1 What does the author mean by the term "flow model"? How can a flow model be used to assess adverse impact?
2 How is an "optimal" solution reached in the flow model? What criteria are used to determine if the solution is optimal?
3 What information must be supplied in order to use the procedure explained in the article?

B. THE UNION

Agis Salpukas

Unions: A New Role?

"My people don't talk to behaviorists."

"It is a case of middle-class outsiders looking down at the poor workers again."

"A lot of academics are writing about it. Their goal is to create a lot of jobs for professionals who have not done any real work in their lives."

These are some of the milder comments from union leaders discussing the issue of job discontent. With some exceptions the prevalent mood within the labor movement is one of cynicism, suspicion, and impatience.

Leaders do believe that major changes have to be made at the workplace; that workers' expectations are rising; that there are new frontiers for collective bargaining.

But most object to the way the issue of work has been portrayed by the press, by researchers, and by experts. They are skeptical about its depth, and most believe it will not soon result in rank and file pressure on them to make demands at the bargaining table. They are unimpressed by outsiders writing about it. What do they know about what workers really feel and want?

"What do they expect a worker to say if he's asked, 'Would you like to have your job more interesting?'" one leader of the Steelworkers posed.

Many are also outraged by what they believe is a by-product of the writing and studies—that workers are portrayed as subhuman because they put in eight or ten hours a day on jobs that are stupid and dirty. "Sure work is dull and monotonous," Leonard Woodcock, head of the United Automobile Workers (UAW) union, told delegates at a conference of production workers in Atlanta, in February of 1973. "But if it's useful, the people who do it are entitled to be honored and not degraded, which is what's going on in this day and time."

Such a view seems defensive and a misinterpretation of the motives of researchers and writers who really argue the opposite: that workers are creative, intelligent people who want to think, to have responsibility and challenge in their work, but are frustrated by the way jobs are now set up.

Union leaders often lash out, however, because they are concerned about raising worker expectations when there are few answers on the horizon. Sure it is good to experiment in a highly controlled situation in a small plant, but what will happen when you try to apply the same methods to large industries? What will happen to productivity? Will the changes be lasting? Can American industry undergo these changes and remain competitive with the rest of the world?

Ben Fischer, director of contract administration for the Steelworkers union, said, "These sociologists and behaviorists are out to destroy the economic system and don't have any idea what will take its place."

Many union leaders are also suspicious of experimentation begun by management to change and enrich jobs. Why should management suddenly reverse its long

Agis Salpukas, "Unions: A New Role?" in *The Worker and the Job: Coping with Change,* Jerome M. Rosow, ed., © 1974, pp. 99–117. Reprinted by permission of Prentice-Hall, Inc., Englewood Cliffs, New Jersey.

tradition of increasing efficiency by cutting manpower? Some of the experiments give them good cause for alarm—responsibility and work are often added without a change in wages—and begin to look like the old "speedup."

Some of the early efforts to deal with job discontent often reinforced their cynicism. In the late 1960s some auto plants tried to bribe workers to come in on Fridays and Mondays, when absenteeism ran up to 10 percent, by offering green stamps and glasses to those with good attendance records. Some companies, eager to get aboard the humanization of work bandwagon, sometimes passed off as job enrichment innovations that would have been implemented even if they had never heard of the concept. General Motors in announcing the opening of a new line to build motor homes stressed that teams of men would perform the work. What was not mentioned was that most motor home assembly lines use teams of workers since that is the most efficient way to set up jobs due to the slowness of the line. Several months later, when demand went up and line speed had to be increased, the team concept was abandoned since it did not lend itself to the new production schedule.

There is also a threat to the role of unions themselves inherent in management experiments to change work. At the General Foods plant in Topeka, Kansas, where workers rotate into and learn every major job at the plant, several approaches by union organizers have been rebuffed. Since they have easy access to top management, are consulted on major decisions and get pay increases based on the amount they learn, most workers feel that there is no need for a union. Although the experiment is in a plant employing a small, highly select group of 60 workers, the implications for unions cannot be ignored. Humanizing jobs poses a challenge to unions—at the very least it will lead to a redefinition of their role. It is not surprising, therefore, that union leaders are wary.

Thomas R. Brooks, a labor historian, summed up these feelings in an October, 1972, article in the *Federationist,* the official magazine of the AFL-CIO:

> The impetus for time and motion studies is pretty much the same as that behind job enrichment of participatory management. Substituting the sociologist's questionnaire for the stopwatch is likely to be no gain for the workers. While the workers have a stake in productivity, it is not always identical with that of management. Job enrichment programs have cut jobs just as effectively as automation or engineer's stopwatches. And the rewards of productivity are not always equitably shared.

HISTORY

Turn of the century

Labor's stance is explained to a large degree by the way the labor movement evolved in the United States. When the theories of scientific management of Frederick Taylor were being widely applied in industry at the turn of the century and when Henry Ford and James Couzens were building the first assembly line in Highland Park from 1912 to 1914 the trade union movement was small. Its organization was built on skilled workers. The American Federation of Labor craft unions often excluded the industrial workers who were multiplying as fast as the new technology and theories of Ford and Taylor were spreading in American industry in the 1920s. Trade union membership numbered about 4 million during that period when wages were rising, jobs plentiful. The only real challenge to the emerging industrial system came from the Wobblies or Industrial Workers of the World who fought many sporadic battles but never developed a unified movement or concerted strategy.

Their hope for one big general strike that would bring about fundamental change in the economic system remained a dream.

Most business leaders had the same freedom from union interference as Mr. Ford and his driving, brilliant engineers. Even though the workers were unorganized they resisted Mr. Ford at first. He divided the jobs of mechanics and tradesmen into 37 tasks which were eventually transferred onto a moving line. Some men could turn out seven thousand parts in a nine-hour day. The skilled workers, however, left in droves. Just as Mr. Ford had perfected the assembly line at the end of 1913, he faced a major labor crisis. The turnover of the labor force for that year was 380 percent and to keep a force of 100 men, he had to hire 963.

He solved the crisis through what has often been considered as a humanitarian gesture but was really a desperate attempt to keep the lines going. On January 5, 1914, he announced a five-dollars-a-day pay, almost double the prevailing wage rates. Thousands of new workers flocked to the gates of Highland Park. This new work force traded skills for money and human pace for assembly-line speed. They also submitted their private lives to the paternal discipline of what Keith Sward in *The Legend of Henry Ford* calls the "Ford Sociology Department." The initial resistance of workers to the discipline of the new industrial system was unorganized and easily defeated by management.

Unions in the 1930s

By the time the trade union movement began to organize industrial workers on a large scale in the 1930s, the system of work fragmentation, time and study methods, and a hierarchical management which left few initiatives to workers had become firmly entrenched. The early drives by the Congress of Industrial Organizations (CIO), which was founded in 1935, did not challenge the existing system—it was difficult enough to gain recognition and to prevent management from destroying the embryo unions. Although the union movement had the friendly administration of Franklin D. Roosevelt in the White House and had legally won the right to organize and bargain collectively through the National Labor Relations Act of 1935, they still had to win recognition largely through their own efforts.

The most important struggle of that era, the sit-down strike by the auto workers in Flint in 1936 and 1937, clearly shows the priorities at that time. Faced with a hostile police force and local government and management, the union had little energy left even to deal with such basic issues as wages and hours. Before the Flint strike average annual earnings of auto workers were $1,200 to $1,300 and there was little job security. Workers were often selected by foremen on the basis of how quickly they jumped to their commands. Even though the fledgling unions had immediate, pressing needs to fill, they nevertheless made important inroads into management's authority in the plants. In the agreement with General Motors, the skeleton of the present grievance procedure was initiated. It gave the workers a means to deal with what they considered arbitrary treatment. Many local strikes also succeeded in putting limits on the work pace. Shortly after the sit-down strike a UAW worker in Fisher Body plant 1 wrote, "The inhuman speed is no more. We now have a choice and have slowed the speed of the line. And are now treated as human beings, and not as part of the machinery" (Sidney Fine, *Sit-down*, 1969).

Union and management prerogatives

By the end of World War II the union movement had grown to 16 million workers. Most major industries had accepted it as a permanent force in the economic system. Collective bargaining had also become the recognized method by which unions and businesses would work out their differences.

There was great concern on the part of management on just how far unions would press. Provisions of the National Labor Relations Act stated merely that employers were required to bargain "in respect to rate of pay, wages, hours of employment, or other conditions of employment." President Harry S. Truman called a conference of top industry and union leaders to see if they could set specific limits on what could be brought to the bargaining table. They could not reach an agreement. The statement of the labor leaders at the end of the conference held in 1945 gives an insight into the role that they had carved out for their movement.

The union leaders showed sympathy for management's concern that

> in the past few years efforts have been made by certain unions to extend the scope of collective bargaining to include other matters and operating problems involving the function of management to direct the operation of business. The functions and responsibilities of management must be preserved if business and industry is to be efficient, progressive, and to provide more good jobs.

It was a basic acceptance of the free enterprise system and management's right to run the industries.

At the same time the labor members of the committee refused to spell out areas that would be off limits for bargaining. "It would be extremely unwise to build a fence around the rights and responsibilities of management on the one hand, the unions on the other," they wrote. "The experience of many years shows that with the growth of mutual understanding, the responsibilities of one of the parties today may well become the joint responsibility of both parties tomorrow." Most unions have maintained that position up to the present—there are no areas that are taboo in collective bargaining.

Priorities after the war

Although free to do so in theory, unions have not made any major thrust to gain management's prerogatives either in running the plants or in how to set up the work. After World War II, the trade unions concentrated on forcing industry to recognize new areas that could be bargained on. When the UAW brought pensions to the bargaining table in the 1949 negotiations, there was a bitter attack on the union for entering an area that management considered its own. Since then unions have pushed into many new areas including health insurance, adequate protection against layoffs, and compensation for disability. In other advanced countries protection was often obtained through government programs. In the United States, where unions did not spawn a labor party, protection for workers when they became ill, were laid off, or retired had to be squeezed out of employers. The unions have never been able to let up the pressure to keep up with the costs in these benefit areas. Walter Reuther and Charles E. Wilson, head of General Motors, also worked out a system for wage increases which committed the union to seek to improve productivity and to support rapid technological change. In the 1948 contract, General Motors gave the union cost-of-living protection—pay would be adjusted to keep up with inflation—and wage increases were tied to gains in productivity.

This system became the pattern for many other unions. Their leaders welcomed rapid technological advance since it could produce a bigger pie from which to cut their slice. In 1955, Reuther speaking on behalf of the CIO told the Joint Congressional Committee on the Economic Report:

> First of all, we fully realize that the potential benefits of automation are great, if properly handled. If only a fraction of what technologists promise for the future is true, within a very few years automation can and should make possible a four-day week, longer vacation periods, opportunities for earlier retirement, as well as vast increases in our material standards of living.

At the same time automation can bring freedom from the monotonous drudgery of many jobs in which a worker today is no more than a servant of the machine. It can free workers from routine, repetitious tasks which the new machines can be taught to do and can give the workers who toil at those tasks the opportunity of developing higher skills.

Most unions remained passive as their industries were transformed through new technology which often had a big effect on the nature of the work. From the cornucopia of automation came many of the things Reuther spoke about. In the General Motors plant in Lordstown, Ohio, for example, 104 cars an hour roll off the line compared to 55 cars an hour at the average plant. Many of the jobs have been made physically easier. But it has retained the drudgery and has even reduced the skills further. Higher production and speed have been obtained by breaking the jobs down further in the classical Taylor method.

There were also immediate pressures which kept the unions out of dealing with the effects of what Reuther aptly called the "silent revolution" of technology. During the 1950s the intense competition between the free world and the Communist countries made many leaders in the trade union movement concerned that the predominance of the United States was threatened.

Resistance to demands from management for greater efficiency was also difficult considering the inroads that foreign producers had made into the American economy. Trips to Japan have often had a sobering effect on union leaders. Douglas Fraser, the head of UAW's Chrysler Department, on a tour of the Japanese auto industry in 1972 found absenteeism unheard of in many plants and rates of work speed that would not be tolerated in the United States.

Struggles over efficiency

Throughout this period many industries put the pressure on the unions to change work rules and standards which management felt impeded productivity. Perhaps the longest and most bitter of these struggles has been the battle between UAW's General Motors Department and General Motors Assembly Division. The division has been on a continuous drive to improve efficiency and has been willing to go through strikes to achieve its goals. In 1972, there were bitter strikes at the Lordstown plant in which the company lost $150 million in sales. The longest strike in General Motors history, lasting 172 days, was in its Norwood, Ohio, plant and cost the company about $100 million.

The strike at Lordstown in which 8,000 workers from UAW local 1112 closed the plant from March 3 to March 24 in 1972 received nationwide coverage. A mythology has since grown around the strike which in its most radical form contains the following misconceptions: that the strike was caused by a new, "freaked out" generation of workers who because of boredom and stupidity in the jobs revolted against their own union leadership. Talk of the "Lordstown syndrome" symbolizing a worker revolt against present jobs has become common at conferences and seminars.

Such mythology has only driven a further wedge between academics and union leaders who must patiently explain the complex set of issues that caused the Lordstown strike. Both the union and management, disturbed by widespread misinterpretation of the strike, have issued position papers explaining the causes.

Reduced to its simplest terms the struggle was over an old issue—speedup. Ever since the first production line came into existence, there has been continual strife over work rate—unions seeking to set clear standards that would define what is expected of a worker in a job; management seeking to keep a free enough hand so that the standards do not become blocks to new technology and efficiency.

GM approach Under General Motors the struggle has assumed a new dimension and sophistication. A whole separate management division made up of tough specialists in assembly-line operations, called General Motors Assembly Division, has been given the task of making plants more efficient. Since 1965, General Motors Assembly Division has undergone rapid expansion, and in 1973 it supervised eighteen plants employing 91,000 workers or about 75 percent of General Motors production.

Each plant that General Motors Assembly Division has taken over underwent the following pattern of consolidation. The separate Fisher Body plant and assembly plant were merged into one unit. This led to duplicate jobs and the new management team cut manpower. Also, most jobs in the plant were reevaluated and cuts made in every department. The result was that workers often were made to take on additional tasks to make up for cuts. Workers resisted, arguing that this violated existing work standards, and they often refused to perform the new tasks. The company then invoked its right to discipline workers by barring them from the plant for days or weeks without pay. The bitterness increased and workers often resorted to acts of sabotage such as breaking windshields, breaking off rear view mirrors, and slashing upholstery.

Management's explanation for the resistance was that it was caused by the political struggle within locals. Since one full union shop committee was eliminated in the consolidations, union leaders vying to be elected to the new committee fed the unrest to establish a reputation of militancy among the workers. During the struggle at Lordstown, management conceded, however, that cuts were made beyond mere duplication of jobs and that internal union politics, while a factor, was not the main cause of the strike. The intent in each of the consolidations, eight of which resulted in strikes, was to push each local union as far as possible to see how much manpower reduction would be tolerated. At the end of each strike, most locals claimed they had preserved their former manpower levels and the best terms of their old agreements.

The struggle with General Motors Assembly Division over work standards does not end with the settlement of the strikes. For the division has combined the principles of scientific management with the computer and can get an instant reading of the efficiency of each plant down to individual departments. The plants are also ranked according to the productivity. The ranking results in constant pressure on the bottom half of the plants to improve efficiency. Since ranking is never-ending there is no final goal and the pressure is never-ending. To Mr. Joseph E. Godfrey, the general manager of General Motors Assembly Division, the constant pressure is not a disturbing fact but a construction to be proud of—the ultimate competitive system. The position of General Motors Assembly Division, he said, is that it has the right to reorganize jobs any way it wants in order to make them more efficient. "If within reason and without endangering their health," he explained, "we can occupy a man for 60 minutes, we've got that right."

The thrust and philosophy of General Motors Assembly Division is of great significance to the issue of job discontent. The division represents one of the most far-reaching and concerted efforts to apply the methods evolved under Frederick Taylor in our economy. Its goal is to find the best and most efficient way through "scientific analysis" and then have the worker comply. Local contracts, customs, workers' attitudes cannot stand in the way; they must be made to conform.

General Motors Assembly Division has achieved a good part of its goals in the plants it has taken over. After bitter strikes, production returned to normal and years later some plants have developed good relations between management and the local union. But what about worker attitude?

Workers' response Charles Tyler, the president of UAW Local 93, recalled that when General Motors Assembly Division took over his plant in 1968 about 1,200 people out of a work force of 4,000 were eliminated. The union members decided not to strike because of the high unemployment at that time. "The people were left bitter," he said. "Frankly it doesn't bother me when I can put something over on management. They hurt so many people it doesn't bother my conscience. That's the view of most workers here."

At Lordstown many workers said in interviews that the atmosphere in the plant had been changed after General Motors Assembly Division took over. "Just a year ago they gave out these awards for quality work," one worker said pointing to a set of newly minted coins on the mantelpiece. "Then this new outfit comes in and says we're not working hard enough. They cut manpower so that you can't do the job right. How can they talk about quality when that's their attitude?"

As Leonard Woodcock put it in a speech before the UAW collective bargaining convention held in Detroit in spring, 1973: "The first big step in humanizing the workplace is for the employers and their representatives to accept their employees, our members, as human beings."

Underneath the immediate issues in the struggle between the UAW and General Motors Assembly Division is a larger one—that the authority that management has in the plants is increasingly being challenged by workers. That greater efficiency is not a sacred principle that should sweep over the personalities and aspirations of workers. That the contradiction between values of a democratic society where the leaders and laws are subject to the check of citizens and the authoritarianism of the workplace is becoming less tolerable to workers. As UAW Vice President Irving Bluestone has frequently pointed out:

> The workplace is probably the most authoritarian environment in which the adult finds himself. Its rigidity and denial of freedom lead people to live a double life; at home they enjoy substantially the autonomy and self-fullfillment of free citizens; at work they are subject to constant regimentation, supervison and control by others.

CHALLENGE BY RANK AND FILE

Workers are increasingly raising issues that challenge this dichotomy; there are demands that the present method of discipline in which workers can be punished and then can appeal the action through a long drawn-out grievance procedure should be changed. This system contradicts the basic concept that a man is innocent until proven guilty; that workers have a say about working overtime and should not be disciplined if they refuse because of some prior personal commitment; and that they should have some means of immediate appeal to an impartial official in matters of health and safety.

These aspirations came dramatically to the fore at a meeting called by the leadership of the Steelworkers union in 1970 which brought together a small group of young steelworkers and local union leaders from all over the country. Meeting with I. W. Abel, the president of the union, and other top leaders in small informal groups they were asked: Why the wildcats? Why don't you go to the shop stewards with complaints? Why the conflict with foremen? Why are so many young workers leaving only after a short time in the mills? The young workers were shown a slick, multiple-image film which quickly took them through the history of their union—a proud story of continuous betterment of wages, fringes, and time off.

What the young workers stressed at the end of the meeting, however, was that while they were grateful for the economic gains they felt largely powerless in their daily dealings with management in the plants. When it was too hot or there were fumes, complaints usually brought promises but little action. If there were unsafe conditions why were they not corrected immediately? What's the use of filing a grievance if you have to wait up to a year for a decision? they asked.

Since the meeting, the union and the companies have worked out an agreement where the grievance procedure has been speeded up and made more responsive. First-line supervisors and foremen must now make a greater effort at resolving complaints at the plant-floor level. The basic change has been in the attitude of the foremen, who can no longer dismiss a worker's gripe by saying, "If you don't like it, file a grievance."

Collective bargaining and noneconomic issues

Often, however, the response by the union leadership is not so immediate. There are a number of reasons why issues related to job discontent and greater worker rights on the plant level have not become primary demands pressed by top union leaders at the major nationwide negotiations. Nat Goldfinger, the head of the AFL-CIO research department, gave a succinct summary of what has motivated unions in the past 25 to 30 years. "Unions," he said, "have been aiming their major guns on the big issues where there is an immediate payoff and immediate pressure from the rank and file. That means wages, hours, fringes, pensions, holidays, more time off."

Recurring major and minor recessions in the economy have not enabled unions to get too far away from bread and butter issues. In such times it is difficult to consider how machines and plants are affecting workers—the priority is to get the factories to produce again. The inflation following these periods again makes economic issues predominate as unions seek to catch up with the rising cost of living in their contracts.

The process by which unions arrive at their bargaining goals and the nature of collective bargaining itself makes it difficult for noneconomic issues to reach top-level negotiations. Every union's bargaining demands are formulated basically through a process which takes thousands of resolutions from union locals and eventually boils them down to a smaller, more manageable list of demands. The thrust of this process is to find those demands that have the most widespread support and to eliminate those that may be unique to a particular plant or area. Obviously, economic matters—higher wages, better pensions, better health insurance—have the most universal appeal. They are also easily translated into specific demands since the costs can be figured and the company can determine how much it is willing to give up. The costs of the agreement can also be planned ahead, a crucial factor for management.

Noneconomic goals do not have the same universality or predictability. Even such a basic issue as voluntary overtime, which has emerged within the UAW, can cause division among workers at a plant—some favoring the idea, others concerned that if enough workers decide not to work they would deprive those who do want to put in overtime. Management also cannot predict the cost: How many workers will volunteer? How much extra plant capacity will be needed to make up the lack of volunteers? What will the cost be of losing the flexibility to meet short, peak demand without overtime? Can the issue be turned against management by workers refusing to work overtime to cut off production and to put on pressure to achieve some other demand?

Due to these factors, management has traditionally been much tougher on noneconomic issues. Management argues that such demands impinge on the sacred area of management prerogatives and are therefore not negotiable.

A candid explanation of this process was given by George Morris, Jr., director of labor relations at General Motors, in a speech before the Conference Board in June, 1971. He argued that the Nixon administration's wage and price controls had put management at a serious disadvantage in collective bargaining. The effect of controls, he said, was to encourage unions to seek demands in noneconomic areas while taking away management's main weapon in dealing with these issues—its hold over the purse strings. What Mr. Morris was describing was the very essence of collective bargaining—that to get one item you may have to trade off another. Management's strategy was to make concessions on money items to prevent gains in noneconomic areas. In the 1970 negotiations he brought out that through this trade-off strategy,

> without controls and through tough collective bargaining, we prevented any erosion of the right to subcontract work which is so necessary to our business, to introduce new technology, to schedule overtime and to maintain efficiency and discipline, all of which matters, among many others, were the subject of serious union demands.

The evolution of nationwide industry bargaining, where union and management meet once every three years to work out a new contract, has tended to defer dealing with the everyday frustration that workers experience in the plants. Local bargaining units do not have the power, even with strike action, to make a breakthrough on such a major issue as voluntary overtime on the local level. Nevertheless, certain issues such as health and safety, which in the past were dealt with mostly on the local plant level, pushed their way into the national bargaining table in the early 1970s. Even before the passage of the Occupational Health and Safety Act in 1970 many workers in heavy industry had become concerned about noise and pollution in their work environment. They often resorted to wildcat strikes to correct conditions.

Since the passage of the act, federal, management, and union educational campaigns have further increased worker awareness. Within the UAW, for example, some workers regard the right to strike over health and safety and the setting up of an independent plant official to deal immediately with unsafe conditions as a more important demand than an increase in wages. The ability to trade off noneconomic issues with a good economic package has therefore become more limited.

Rank and file attitudes and job discontent

So far, however, discontent with the work itself has not emerged as an issue that brings such immediate pressure from the rank and file. In interviews during the early seventies with many workers who had an intense dislike for their jobs and working conditions, I found few who thought of working through their unions to bring about changes. Usually they saw the solution up to themselves. They hoped to escape from the plant through more education or by saving up to start their own business, or by piling up seniority to land one of the more desirable jobs.

Thousands do leave every year as shown by the high turnover in many industries. The high turnover is a major reason unions feel little pressure for changing the work—the most dissatisfied leave rather than fight.

Those who do stay and fight often find themselves isolated from their fellow workers and the union. A 24-year-old worker who helps assemble gasoline tanks in a plant in Buffalo explained: "The guys will fight on wage issues, but when it comes to taking on a foreman for the way he treats you—in that kind of thing nobody sticks together. I'm not crying. You can make your own fight."

When one does make his own fight he is often disciplined and becomes involved with the grievance procedure. This procedure has emerged as an important alternative for a worker who wants to redress a wrong in the plant. But he often approaches a shop steward who has many other immediate problems to deal with and may discourage a worker from going through the process, which may take up to a year to resolve if the complaint is serious. Also, while the grievance procedure is beneficial in keeping off the bargaining table many problems unique to an individual worker, it can also serve as a safety valve and keep problems out of negotiations that should become part of collective bargaining.

Rank and file attitudes are also a factor. Some workers are suspicious of change—a feeling that the plant may not be the best place but at least the rules are known. Lee Jones, a committee man at the Ford Stamping plant in Buffalo represented by Local 897, recalled that when he worked in the plant in the 1950s he had tried to get his department to rotate jobs.

> I got the guys to go along with me and we approached the foreman. We want to rotate, we told him. Most of the time we were told no. We'd pretend we were using our tools, goof around, slow down. Then we'd come back and say, "It's monotonous. Why don't you let us rotate, change off during the day? We'll feel better, be more awake, and we'll go beyond our quota." So some times for a while he'd let us rotate. But I tell you, guys with my attitude were definitely in the minority. Most guys want to get that better job and hold on. If you try to impose something on the guys they didn't ask for, often you'll just have chaos.

He said that even making a simple change without getting a good idea of the sentiment of the members can leave union leaders out on a limb. His local, he recalled, had won an agreement from management to have vacations split so some of the younger men with less seniority could get a week off in the summer to be with their children who were out of school. "The older guys just raised hell, and the clause was dropped from the agreement," he said.

Differences between older workers, who usually have the seniority and better jobs, and the younger workers can be a major obstacle to change.

During a tour of a Chrysler plant which had a program to enrich jobs, I asked an older worker whether he wanted his job changed. He had been in the plant since 1935, had one of the more skilled jobs, and was due to retire in several years. He was responsible for adjusting and balancing the front wheels. "I've got it down. I really wouldn't want anyone fooling with it," he answered.

The issue of job discontent also has surfaced only rarely at the conventions and meetings held by unions to form their bargaining goals. An exception was the February 1973 conference of production workers of the UAW in Atlanta where union leaders asked the delegates to focus on noneconomic issues. Numerous speakers advocated improvements in health and safety in the plants, the right to refuse overtime, and the reform of the way discipline was meted out. Many examples were given of workers bringing up these issues right on the plant floor.

Only one speaker brought up the issue of the work itself. Charles Gifford, president of Local 999, addressed the conference near the end and asked Mr. Woodcock: "You can't build a union based on economics only. We have to deal with the boring, repetitive jobs in production. How can you continue to restore the dignity of work if you just talk about economics?"

SOLUTIONS

Up to 1973 most union leaders sought the solution in more free time, a shorter work week, more break time and holidays, and earlier retirement. In an interview with

Mike Wallace in 1960, Mr. Reuther said that the way to satisfy a worker's inner needs was through greater leisure where he could find satisfaction for his creative urges. The Steelworkers union won a major breakthrough in 1963 in this direction when 250,000 of their production workers became eligible for a 13 week vacation every five years. The UAW, when the issue of working conditions became pressing in the early 1960s, won 24 minutes relief time from General Motors in 1961 and in the next contract the time was increased to 46 minutes per shift.

1973 UAW negotiations

A significant breakthrough came in the 1973 UAW negotiations, where noneconomic issues dominated the bargaining. That was the first nationwide bargaining where working conditions overshadowed wage demands. For a decade rank and file and local union leaders had been unhappy over mandatory overtime, health and safety, and the slow grievance procedure in the plants.

During the negotiations, at the height of the heat wave in July and August, three inner-city plants with a mostly black work force staged wildcat strikes. The walkouts were sparked by small radical groups of workers who succeeded in getting the support of many workers who walked off job areas where temperatures were above 100 degrees. The UAW revived the "flying squads" of the 1930s to isolate the radical leaders and persuade the rank and file to return to work. During the 1930s these squads had been used to protect UAW pickets from goon squads hired by the auto companies to break strikes.

Also, in an unprecedented step the UAW suspended national bargaining so top union leaders could tour the Chrysler plants. They found conditions in some of the older plants deplorable. Throughout the rest of the bargaining UAW leaders resisted Chrysler efforts to turn them away from the noneconomic issues. In the past, company negotiators had often succeeded in getting the union to retreat from such demands by sweetening the wage and benefit package.

None of the gains in the new contract matched what local leaders and workers had expected, but they were important chinks through which the UAW can win further concessions. On overtime, the UAW failed to achieve its goal of making it totally voluntary but a worker can be asked to work only one extra hour a day. Workers can also insist on taking every third Saturday off with no forced overtime on Sunday. However, to qualify for such limited overtime a worker must have a perfect attendance record for the previous week—an important gain for Chrysler management which in the 1970 negotiations reported to the UAW leaders that increasing absenteeism was seriously disrupting production. Chrysler also won the concession to schedule mandatory overtime during model start-time and guarantees that its key plants would also get special consideration.

On health and safety local union leaders had sought the right to strike over uncorrected safety violations and to keep a full-time representative on duty who could shut down a work area that he found to be hazardous. This they failed to win. The agreement provides, however, for weekly inspections of plants for safety and cleanliness and allows the UAW's International Safety Committee to respond immediately to disputes that reach an impasse.

The union did not win the principle that a worker cannot be disciplined until he has gone through the grievance procedure. This has been an emotional issue in which workers want to gain a right similar to that recognized in procedures before the courts—that a person is innocent until proven guilty.

Chrysler also gave the union a letter in which it pledged to include the UAW in the company's attempts to improve jobs. The UAW can bring in outside consultants or have the company look into experiments in the field of humanizing jobs if union leaders believe that promising attempts are being overlooked. The letter of intent is unique to collective bargaining and could lead the UAW into greater efforts to change assembly-line work.

There has been some shift, however, within the union movement toward the view that changes may eventually be needed in the work itself. The UAW meeting for the production workers in the 1973 negotiations was the first of its kind in the union's history, and the leaders called the conference solely to get a sense of what was bothering the workers in the noneconomic areas.

Increasing turnover and absenteeism are beginning to worry not only management but union leaders as well. It affects their bargaining and union strength. In return for the gains they make in the contract, they have the responsibility of guaranteeing to the company that the members will live up to the agreement. When a union's ability to maintain the discipline of its own workers is jeopardized, its power is weakened in the eyes of management.

Beginnings of union involvement

The Communication Workers Union, for example, has kept an eye on the efforts of Robert N. Ford at American Telegraph and Telephone to enrich jobs, but has not become a part of the effort itself. John Morgan, assistant to the union president, has kept close watch on the efforts to see what effects they have on the existing contracts. But the union has no plans to become involved. "Our people," Mr. Morgan explained," "tend to feel that our primary job is to look after wages and hours which are tangible. When you get into job enrichment it is hard to define and to get agreement as to what it means."

The American Federation of State, County and Municipal Employees of the AFL-CIO, one of the fastest-growing unions in the country, has gone further. Aided by federal funds, the union has embarked on a career development program. Workers doing the lowest jobs in hospitals, such as mopping floors, changing sheets and emptying bedpans, have been upgraded and given some of the responsibilities of practical nurses. "We got them involved in delivering health care," Jerry Wurf, the president of the union, said. "Instead of being people who felt they were always in the way, they now feel needed. There's been a big jump in morale." He continued:

> The trouble with unions, is that they are still trying for that five or ten cents an hour. That's a carryover from the Depression. We've got to concentrate more on a worker's overall satisfaction, with what he does in the world. American labor leadership doesn't have an understanding for that yet and they don't have the guts to quarrel with the old goals. They often wait for the hysteria of the workers to think of wider horizons.

Yet most unions leaders hold the view as expressed by William Winpisinger, a vice president of the Machinists union, who in an article in the *Federationist* in 1972 wrote: "If you want to enrich the job, enrich the paycheck. The better the wage, the greater the job satisfaction. There is no better cure for the Blue Collar Blues."

This simple maxim has been contradicted daily by the behavior of the rank and file. Increasing absenteeism, turnover, local strikes, limits on overtime, challenges to foremen, demand for early retirement, all indicate that workers have been willing to risk economic gains to improve their lot.

There is a story told around Detroit in which a union leader asked a worker on the line why he was absent on Fridays and only worked four days a week. "Because I can't make enough money by working only three days," he shot back.

The satisfaction of a big paycheck, while still important, no longer makes up for unsatisfying work under bad conditions. With a work force that spends more time in school and enters jobs with more education and higher expectations, the demands for improvements in the noneconomic areas should continue to grow.

The present system arriving at bargaining goals and the process of collective bargaining itself, however, have not adequately responded to these trends. Unions and management have not evolved adequate methods to deal with these issues. The meeting of young steelworkers in 1970 was held in secret and its results not publicized. Just the fact that there was a need for the meeting brought out that the regular union machinery, such as union conventions, were not adequate in getting a sense of what was agitating rank and file members.

It is not so much a matter of reforming the procedure as a change in attitude of union leaders that is important. The danger in being cynical and suspicious is that unions may be left standing by the wayside while management begins to experiment with changing jobs and searching for new incentives. It would be unfortunate if the trade union movement did not have influence over the attempts. A good hard-nosed interest by unions into the research would serve as a check on manipulative and phony solutions, such as giving green stamps or free glasses to workers who have a good attendance record.

It is also doubtful that extensive, meaningful changes can take place without unions being willing to use their main weapon—the strike threat. Leonard Woodcock told the bargaining convention in 1973 that you can only have confrontation in collective bargaining, "if you have in sight a solution to the problem which has produced the confrontation. And as matters stand, we do not have, no one has, the ready answers to the question of how best the work can be done in a humane way."

Yet, given the thrust of management, which is still toward greater work fragmentation and adaptation of the worker to the plant, one must ask how seriously management will pursue the solutions without prodding from the labor movement. Also, the long-range answers to increased job satisfaction may mean no improvement or even a decline in productivity. Clearly those solutions will only be applied if union leaders begin to think that the overall satisfaction of their members is as worthwhile as enriching the paycheck.

FOR DISCUSSION AND REVIEW

1   Trace the historical development of unions' reaction to work design and noneconomic issues.
2   Explain the basic issues in the Lordstown case. What were the UAW and the GM responses?
3   Discuss collective bargaining over noneconomic issues. Is this a new role for unions?
4   What are the author's forecasts for the future?

Mollie H. Bowers

Legislated Arbitration: Legality, Enforceability, and Face-saving

DEFINITION AND SCOPE

Legislated arbitration is a type of binding interest arbitration which can be defined as follows:

1 The procedure is applied to a specific set of negotiations in the public sector.
2 Resort to arbitration is *required* by law as the final step in dispute settlement.
3 A decision is made by the arbitrator or panel on the issues in dispute between the parties.
4 The award issued by the arbitrator or panel is final and *bilaterally binding*.

A deliberate effort has been made to avoid using the term "compulsory arbitration" because the term has been indiscriminantly applied to as widely different systems as those existing in Australia, Pennsylvania, Michigan, and Canada. Furthermore, laws pertaining to arbitration are not "compelled" upon specific interest groups to any greater extent than is legislation regarding civil rights, taxes, traffic regulations, and so forth. Legislated arbitration, therefore, is a *legislated* method for determining working conditions as are all other laws enacted by Congress and by the state legislatures to determine conditions which affect the lives of people.[1]

Sixteen U.S. jurisdictions currently have statutes providing legislated arbitration as the final step in dispute settlement for police and/or fire fighters. These jurisdictions are: Rhode Island; Pennsylvania; Michigan; Wyoming; South Dakota; Wisconsin; Alaska; Washington (state); Denver, Colorado; Vallejo and San Francisco, California; New York City (all public employees); Minnesota; Texas; and Massachusetts.

LEGALITY

The impact of legislated arbitration on collective bargaining and its effectiveness in settling labor disputes are the paramount considerations. Less significant, but nonetheless influential in policy making, have been legal arguments against the procedure. The concept of legislated arbitration has been impugned as an abdication of representative government and an unconstitutional delegation of legislative authority to a private person to set government wages and working conditions.

Based on these arguments, there has been a long standing effort by the courts to curtail the use of any form of interest arbitration in the public sector. One of the earliest cases concerned the attempt by an Illinois highway commissioner and the owner of condemned property to resolve a dispute over a fair price through arbitration. The use of arbitration was challenged, however, and in the ensuing case the court ruled that

> Where the law imposes a personal duty upon an officer in relation to a matter of public interest, he can not delegate it to others and therefore, such officers can not submit such matters to arbitration.[2]

From *Public Personnel Management*, July-August 1974, pp. 270–278, © 1974. Reprinted by permission of the International Personnel Management Association, 1313 E. 60th St., Chicago, Illinois 60637.

More recent precedent setting cases involved the cities of Baltimore[3] and Cleveland.[4] In both instances, decisions against arbitration were based on the reasoning that government authority is public property and therefore may not be delegated to others.[5] This type of thinking was representative of the judicial disposition toward interest arbitration of public sector disputes even into the 1960s.

The first major decision supporting arbitration was *Norwalk Teachers' Association* v. *Board of Education* in 1951.[6] As a result of this case, an *ad hoc*, bipartite agreement to arbitrate a narrow range of issues was deemed legitimate. Other decisions followed which incorporated the more tolerant approach toward public sector interest arbitration as set forth in the Norwalk case.

The initial victory for a law sanctioning interest arbitration on the spectrum of contract issues came in 1954.[7] This case was initiated to contest the legality of several sections of the Minnesota Charitable Hospitals Act of 1947.[8] A portion of that 1954 decision contained the significant ruling that arbitrable issues encompassed almost everything except union security.

Nevertheless, laws providing legislated arbitration for police and/or fire fighters have been subjected to separate tests of constitutionality. In 1969, a strong legal challenge to the Pennsylvania law was launched in *Harney* v. *Russo*[9] over the questions of criteria for decision making and the one-man, one-vote principle. In an ingenious decision, the court held that the obvious legislative policy to protect the public from strikes by police and firemen, public employees who hold critical positions, was a sufficient standard to guide arbitrators in executing the legislative will. The court further elaborated:

> To require a more explicit statement of legislative policy in a statute calling for labor arbitration would be sheer folly. The great advantage of arbitration is, after all, to deal with each case on its own merits in order to arrive at a compromise which is fair to both parties.

In these rulings, the Pennsylvania court has denied the validity of accepted opinions regarding the necessity of criteria. Rather, it has advocated the radical (perhaps innovative) position that consideration of the merits of the case is of paramount importance with sufficient constraint being provided by the context of the bargaining relationship between the parties.

The court also determined that the one-man, one-vote principle was inapplicable to legislated arbitration because the functions of an arbitration panel cannot be considered legislative in nature. It reasoned that even though an arbitration panel could affect public spending, this is not sufficient cause to define its functions as "legislative," and therefore subject to the one-man, one-vote principle.

The constitutionality of the Pennsylvania law was also questioned in a second case involving the City of Washington.[10] The issues were the right of appeal and the scope of arbitrability. On the question of appeals, the court rendered a strict interpretation of the law that "No appeal therefrom shall be allowed in any court." This decision is, however, qualified by the over-riding right of the courts to review the work of any adjudicatory body to determine whether it has exceeded its legal authority. In essence, the scope of arbitrability was limited to the consideration of legitimate terms and conditions of employment. According to the court, although the public employer may not hide behind self-imposed legal restrictions, an arbitration award may only require the employer to do that which he could do voluntarily.

Legislated arbitration for fire fighters has been tested in the Wyoming Supreme Court.[11] The court unequivocally resolved the nondelegation issue in its statement that the statute conferred upon arbitrators the right to execute the law and not to make the law.[12] Also at stake was the question of home rule. The court held municipalities are creatures of the state and that, therefore, the legislature can authorize the manner of determining the pay and working conditions of municipal employees.

The legality of arbitration for Rhode Island fire fighters was contested on the grounds that the law did not include adequate criteria and that it was an improper delegation of authority.[13] With respect to criteria, the court ruled that the statute already contained criteria "sufficient to meet the constitutional requirements that the delegated powers be confined by reasonable norms and standards." To resolve the issue of nondelegation, the court distinctively defined the role of arbitrators as that of ". . . public officers or agents of the legislature when they were carrying out their arbitration duties under the statute."

In Michigan, legislated arbitration for police and fire fighters has withstood two bouts in the circuit courts. Both cases grew out of noncompliance suits brought by fire fighter and police organizations against the City of Dearborn. Similarly, in both cases, the city raised the broader question of constitutionality as its chief defense. In the first case, the defendant charged violation of home rule, illegal delegation, usurpation of the power to tax, and denial of due process.[14] None of these contentions was upheld by the court.

The judgment on home rule was based on the principle of preemption. Article IV, Section 40 of the Michigan constitution reserves the power to enact laws for the resolution of public employee disputes for the state legislature. A curt reply was issued in response to the charge of illegal delegation stating that "The law is clear that where the standards are sufficient, there is no unlawful or improper delegation of legislative authority." The court acted with similar dispatch on the remaining two issues. It ruled that there was nothing in the law or the award that either imposed a tax or diminished Dearborn's taxing authority and that the statute prescribed careful procedures and constraints as well as judicial review. Consequently, there was no merit to Dearborn's contentions to the contrary.

The issues in the second case were nearly the same except that the question of criteria replaced due process.[15] Both courts used similar reasoning in upholding legislated arbitration. On the matter of criteria, the court in this case simply recognized the existence of detailed and comprehensive standards embodied in the statute.

The record, however, is not one of perfect acceptability. In 1973, a circuit court in South Dakota declared the binding arbitration provision of the Firemen's and Policemen's Arbitration Act to be unconstitutional in the case of *City of Sioux Falls* v. *Sioux Falls Firefighters Local 813, et al.*[16] According to Judge George W. Wuest, his decision was based upon a constitutional interpretation of improper delegation which appeared in *Erie Firefighters Local No. 293* v. *Arthur Gardner.*[17] The outcome in both these cases was a result of the fact that the power to fix salaries and other forms of compensation was delegated to municipalities by the state constitution. The judge also stated that this question of improper delegation could be resolved by a change in the state constitution (similar to the one which paved the way for Pennsylvania's Act 111) which is, in fact, underway.

Only the shallows of this case can be plumbed at this early date. The Sioux Falls case does not appear to have been initiated as a strategic maneuver to bring to light the inconsistency between the act and the state constitution before revision was completed. Rather, the city seems to have been seeking the short-run objective of forestalling arbitration proceedings which portended to be favorable to the fire fighters. At this writing the Sioux Falls case has been appealed to the South Dakota Supreme Court where, the indications are, the lower court decision is likely to be reversed.

The annals of these cases contain a valuable commentary on the meaning and significance of the struggle to establish the legality and acceptability of legislated arbitration in public sector labor relations. In large measure, they seem to support J. Joseph Loewenberg's theory that legal action is chiefly an important means of sublimating destructive dissatisfaction and of clarifying obligations under an unfamiliar procedure.[18]

Particularly from the standpoint of constitutionality, it is apparent that the magnitude of legal obstacles to legislated arbitration for police and fire fighters has been exaggerated by numerous people. Especially in the last decade, legal opposition to legislated arbitration has been eased as part of the broader effort to revise public sector labor relations policy. Arvid Anderson has described this process in more pragmatic terms, stating that the courts will find new answers to overcome traditional obstacles, if the public wants legislated arbitration as a means of resolving public employee disputes.[19]

There is also substantial evidence that even the so-called doctrine of improper delegation is based on fragile legal theory. David Shenton has asserted that "the doctrine of nondelegation is entirely judge made and its history is, therefore, riddled with inconsistencies and contradictions."[20] To support his opinion, Shenton researched the U.S. Constitution and found no restraints on the delegation of authority that would necessarily undermine the legality of legislated arbitration. He also cites as evidence Kenneth Davis' findings that the Supreme Court has invalidated only three laws (New Deal cases decided in 1935-36) as being unlawful delegations of legislative power.[21] Although further pursuit of these arguments is not within the scope of this paper, delving into the doctrine of nondelegation would provide a rewarding and provocative research project for scholars of constitutional or administrative law.

ENFORCEABILITY

Next to its allegedly "chilling effect" upon collective bargaining, the strongest practical argument against legislated arbitration has been that it will not work. Legislated arbitration may not be able to eliminate the specter of illegal strikes or the use of other pressure tactics by police and fire fighters endeavoring to circumvent an award they consider unacceptable. Furthermore, arbitration awards are not self-enforcing.[22] One or both parties can express its dissatisfaction by rejecting the legal obligation to be bound by the award. The problem of noncompliance can also arise because management representatives are dependent upon the action taken by municipal decision-making bodies for funds to implement an award. These potential difficulties have led numerous critics to the erroneous conclusion that, in terms of dispute settlement, there is no practical advantage to supplanting existing fact-finding procedures with legislated arbitration.

In support of legislated arbitration, it must be kept in mind that no procedure yet devised has achieved total compliance. The legal obligation binding labor and management to an arbitration award is an expressive and instrumental deterrent to noncompliance. The propensity of one or both parties to reject an award is influenced by their regard for the rule of law. In U.S. society, law and order has been given a high priority, creating strong psychological and public pressure to conform to established rules and regulations. Additionally, the courts have a legal basis for enforcing an arbitration award which does not exist with other types of dispute settlement procedures. Consequently, noncompliance may not necessarily provide relief from a repugnant award.

Additionally, if strike controls can work at all, legislated arbitration has the advantage of having been largely conceived by employee groups such as police and fire fighters. If these employees undermine arbitration, they will only be forcing themselves into the untenable position of having to choose between a potential decline in bargaining power or an illegal job action to achieve their employment objectives. Moreover, in spite of their opposition to arbitration, many public managers are reluctant to abandon the procedure and to confront the practical and political problems which can be associated with a strike in a public service as well as its potential impact on a settlement.

Legislated arbitration is not, however, a panacea. There is no guarantee that all collective bargaining impasses will be peacefully and satisfactorily resolved. To be meaningful any evaluation must proceed from a consideration of the anticipated extent of noncompliance and the foreseeable degree of difficulty in the enforcement of awards.

At this early stage of experience, there is tangible and persuasive evidence that legislated arbitration is working well itself and in comparison with other dispute settlement techniques. Noncompliance is not a prevalent phenomenon. According to available records, Michigan is the only jurisdiction which has had any strikes in the public safety services since legislated arbitration was enacted.

There are also strong indications that defiance is not the typical manifestation of dissatisfaction with an award.[23] Loewenberg has made the observation that "More frequently, . . . dissatisfaction has been made known through publicity and legal action." Publicity, according to Loewenberg, usually takes the form of:

> Letters to the press, the administrative agency in charge of designating arbitrators, or the neutral arbitrators themselves . . . indicating the grounds of the displeasure and demanding some kind of explanation or rectification.[24]

This tactic is significant because of its cathartic effect upon disgruntled parties and its ability to be pursued without disrupting work schedules.

Legal action has thus far had its greatest appeal to municipalities as a potential means of preventing implementation of an award. A variety of tests have been used including constitutionality, the validity of the award, and even suits against the impartial arbitrator.[25] Despite the potential implications of a legal challenge, however, the impact has been primarily psychological rather than practical. Undoubtedly, however, the testing process will continue until the parties become accustomed to legislated arbitration and questions about specific aspects of the procedure have been resolved.[26]

Legal proceedings to enforce an award have been initiated in both Michigan and Pennsylvania. Thus far, the courts have been successful in achieving compliance in every case.

It is highly unlikely that the imposition of penalties can enhance enforcement of arbitration awards. There has already been ample and dramatic demonstration, under the Taylor Law, for example, that penalties are not necessarily appropriate or effective in curbing defiance by employee organizations in a strike situation.

There is always the possibility that an award will be rejected, although legislated arbitration probably justifies greater optimism than any other procedure in its potential to achieve peaceful and satisfactory impasse resolution. Effective techniques have not been perfected, however, to cope with noncompliance should it occur. The only unqualified conclusion that can be made with respect to enforceability is that it has not yet become a problem.

FACE-SAVING

Emphasis has thus far been placed on the conventional role of legislated arbitration when the public employer and the employee organization are antagonists. There are other variations which can occur under a system of legislated arbitration, the most pertinent to this study being the face-saving aspect of resort to arbitration. In this situation, even though one or both parties are unwilling to accept any available settlement in negotiations, the parties may not really be at odds with each other. Labor and management may even share common goals such as improving the quality and enhancing the efficiency of public services. Problems of political support from their respective constituents and/or the existence of a common adversary in the legislature or budgetary authority can cause the parties to prefer arbitration as a means of legitimating the terms on which they are tacitly in agreement.[27] Since the impartial arbitrator is usually blamed for the outcome, he is frequently referred to as a 'scapegoat.'

The face-saving function of arbitration has aroused considerable concern among labor relations experts. Strong opposition to face-saving has been voiced by Morris Sackman, who has equated the function with the "prostitution of legislated arbitration." According to Sackman, the legitimate purpose of legislated arbitration is to provide a final resolution where the *negotiating parties* are unable to reach a settlement and not where there is a disagreement between the top labor or management leadership and their respective constituents and decision-making bodies.[28] In his opinion,

> Either party has the right to expect constituent ratification of an agreement once the top leadership has given its approval. . . . Public sector collective bargaining is immature as long as the legislature is permitted to escape by voting down a negotiated agreement. It reveals three major, perhaps critical, deficiencies in the collective bargaining experience: (1) a misunderstanding of the role and function of ratification on the management side; (2) a failure to force the public to confront the impact of collective bargaining—that it is costly; and (3) a failure, therefore, to hold public managers fully accountable for the quality of the settlement.
>
> . . . Substituting arbitration for confrontation in this situation delays, and may even prevent, the emergence of workable bargaining relationships.

Others hold a more moderate position. Their concern is that resort to legislated arbitration might become the rule, rather than an exceptional solution to a particular type of impasse, thereby supplanting collective bargaining.[29] These are serious considerations and should neither be ignored nor treated lightly. It is imperative, therefore, to gain a better understanding of the face-saving function.

On the theoretical level, one author has pointed out that even ". . . the strike threat does not itself serve to generate a contact zone in the face-saving case if third party intervention is available."[30] Being both a "strike-like" procedure and a form of third party intervention legislated arbitration is, therefore, self-limiting. He cautions that harsh criticism of the procedure is not necessarily appropriate because ". . . the arbitration threat is not failing to discharge a function which would have been discharged by the strike threat."

Several labor relations experts interviewed by this author were candid in acknowledging instances where the strike had been used as a face-saving device in private sector labor relations. Nevertheless, collective bargaining has still managed to thrive in this sector. It is reasonable to propose, therefore, that it is not the mere availability of face-saving that is potentially dangerous to collective bargaining but rather the existence of external forces which continuously generate the need to resort to arbitration to legitimate an agreement.

The problems of legislated arbitration are at least as much socioeconomic as procedural. The financial crisis of the cities and taxpayer revolts in reaction to soaring inflation pose a significant threat to the vitality of public employee collective bargaining. Regardless of the essentiality of the service, the political risks of granting even a justifiable wage increase can be enormous for the public employer. Contract rejection, once thought to be primarily a union tactic, has become a weapon used against both the public employer and the employee organization by legislative and budgetary authorities. Concurrently, union leaders are having difficulty selling restraint to their members after years of subsidizing taxpayers by virtue of substandard wages.

These conditions are serious in themselves. They are also symptomatic of a deeper malady which has afflicted the American mentality as a consequence of the traditional favoritism shown to private enterprise. Public employees have rising wage and benefit expectations and the index of municipal spending has soared largely as a consequence of attempts to meet these demands. These are, however, only the preliminaries. John Kenneth Galbraith, in *The Affluent Society* (1958), boldly exposed the dispositions which have shaped American attitudes toward the public services:

> In the general view it is privately produced production that is important, and that nearly alone. This adds to the national well-being. . . . Public services, by comparison, are an incubus. They are necessary . . . But they are a burden . . . At best public services are a necessary evil; at worst they are a malign tendency against which an alert community must exercise eternal vigilance.

Galbraith goes on to explain that "Such attitudes have led to some interesting contradictions" noting, in particular, that "We set great store by the increase in private wealth but regret the added outlays for the police force by which it is protected." In consequence, "Although [public services] may be defended, their volume and quality are almost never a source of pride."

Actually, this information should not be a startling revelation to many citizens. Galbraith wrote *The Affluent Society* over a decade and a half ago and his theme has become so well known that it was recently reiterated in a *Time* magazine article, "Empty Pockets on a Trillion Dollars a Year" (March 13, 1972).

The penchant of Americans for privitism has placed public employees and even their employers on a collision course with the public. According to the *Time* article, a significant factor contributing to this potentially disastrous situation has been ". . . a persistent refusal by Americans to tax themselves heavily enough to pay for public services." Admittedly, progress has been made since the Great Depression when Chicago teachers' salaries were withheld and scrip was issued to be redeemed once large corporations paid their municipal taxes.[31] Where the level of taxation is concerned, however, there is substantial evidence that Americans are guilty of protesting too much as these figures from the *Time* article indicate:

> Though almost every American feels oppressed by taxes, the U.S. is in fact one of the most lightly taxed of all industrial nations. Total U.S. tax collections equal only 31% of the country's gross national product v. 33% in Germany, 37% in Canada, 41% in Sweden, and 43% in Britain.

The growth of public services to keep pace with demand has been retarded by archaic and redundant tax policies. Taxes have been kept low in some areas despite inescapable needs and the fruits of economic growth have been frequently distributed in the form of income and/or property tax cuts rather than expanded public services.

Prevailing attitudes and tax policies have been an obstacle to the establishment of viable bargaining relationships in public employment. They have retarded stabilization by fostering, if not forcing, contract rejection. Especially when the decision involves larger municipal appropriations, the political repercussions of making a decision—any decision—have often encouraged escape through arbitration. Neither improving the design of an arbitration system nor scrapping the procedure entirely are remedies for these conditions.

CONCLUSION

The legality of legislated arbitration may continue to be challenged to express defiance or to clarify the terms of a newly promulgated statute. For all practical purposes, however, the sting seems to have been taken out of these challenges. The courts are reversing their historical opposition to legislated arbitration and now have begun to support use of this procedure especially in disputes involving public safety employees. Concomitantly, research has shown that the so-called doctrine of improper delegation lacks a firm foundation in jurisprudence.

There has been a high rate of voluntary compliance with arbitration awards. Where one of the parties has been recalcitrant, moreover, enforcement has been achieved successfully through the courts. The viability of this record, however, still remains to be tested. Two factors which are likely to have an especially strong impact on enforceability are the use of various systems of final offer selection and the emergence of a trend toward a more balanced distribution between labor and management of the outcome of arbitration awards. Furthermore, the Montreal Police Strike has demonstrated dramatically that impartial arbitrators can be more instrumental in precipitating non-compliance with an award than the parties to a dispute.[32]

The exploitation of legislated arbitration as a face-saving device by either party is likely to continue indefinitely. There are indications, however, that public attitudes and policies are being reoriented toward placing a high priority on expenditures for public services. Large sums of money have recently been committed to cleaning up the environment while interest in law and order has provided police with leverage to obtain substantial supplemental funds from various public and private agencies (e.g. Law Enforcement Assistance Administration, the Safe Streets Act, and the Police Foundation). These funds have made it easier for many municipalities to meet the costs of personnel and equipment for their police departments. Similar benefits, however, have not yet been afforded to other public agencies such as the fire service. Fire chiefs across the country, therefore, have begun to protest what they consider to be discrimination by launching campaigns in the media and in Congress to attract public attention to the plight of "the forgotten service."[33]

NOTes

1 Robert G. Howlett, "Impasse Resolution and Strikes," *California Public Employee Relations,* Series No. 12 (Berkeley: University of California, March 1972), p. 25.

2 *Mann v. Richardson,* 22 111., 481 (1873).

3 *Mugford, et al. v. Mayor and City Council of Baltimore,* Cir. Ct. No. 2 of Baltimore, April 13, 1944, 8 LC 62 137.

4 *City of Cleveland v. Division 268, Amalgamated Association of Street, Electric Railway and Motor Coach Employees of America,* 30 0.0. 395 (1945).

5   Mugford, et al., *op. cit.*
6   *Norwalk Teachers' Association* v. *Board of Education,* 83 A. 2d 482, 20 LC
    66, 543 (1951).
7   *Fairview Hospital Association* v. *Public Building Service and Hospital
    Employees Union Local 113,* 241 Minn. 523. 64 N.W. 2d 16, 25 LC 68 285
    (1954).
8   Minnesota Charitable Hospitals Act, Chapter 179.35-139.39, Minnesota
    Statutes of 1961.
9   *Harney* v. *Russo,* 435 Pa. 183, 255 A. 2d 560 (1969).
10 *City of Washington, Pennsylvania* v. *Police Department,* 436 Pa. 168, 259 A. 2d
    560 (1969).
11 *State of Wyoming on the Relation of Fire Fighters Local No. 946, IAFF,
    et al.* v. *City of Laramie, Wyoming, et al.,* 437 P. 2d 295, 304 (1968).
12 This ruling was based on the reasoning of the Pennsylvania supreme court in
    an earlier case involving the *Erie Firefighters Local No. 293* v. *Arthur
    Gardner,* 406 Pa. 395, 178 A. 2d 691, 695 (1961). The Pennsylvania court
    stated, "If the delegation of power is to make the law, which involves a dis-
    cretion of what the law shall be, then the power is nondelegable. If the con-
    ferred authority is the power or discretion to execute the law already deter-
    mined and circumscribed, then the delegation is unobjectionable."
13 *City of Warwick* v. *Warwick Regular Firemen's Association, S.E.,* 256 A. 2d
    206 (1969).
14 *Dearborn Fire Fighters Union, Local 412, IAFF* v. *City of Dearborn,* (Civil
    Action No. 171-115).
15 *Police Officers' Association of Dearborn* v. *City of Dearborn,* (Civil Action
    No. 180 06).
16 *City of Sioux Falls* v. *Sioux Falls Firefighters Local 813 et al.,* Cir. Ct.
    Fourth Judicial Circuit, memorandum opinion, November 5, 1973.
17 "Binding Impasse Arbitration Provisions of S.D. Police-Firemen's Arbitra-
    tion Act Held Unlawful," *Government Employee Relations Report,* No. 535,
    December 31, 1973, p. B-5. Erie Firefighters, *op. cit.*
18 J. Joseph Loewenberg, "Compulsory Binding Arbitration in the Public
    Sector." A paper prepared for the International Symposium on Public
    Employment Labor Relations, New York City, May 4, 1971, pp. 32–33.
19 Arvid Anderson, "Compulsory Arbitration Under State Statutes," *Pro-
    ceedings,* New York University 22nd. Annual Conference on Labor, 1970,
    p. 269.
20 David G. Shenton, "Compulsory Arbitration in the Public Service," *Labor
    Law Journal,* Vol. 17, No. 3 (March 1966), p. 143.
21 *Ibid.,* p. 143, as cited from Kenneth Culp Davis, *Administrative Law,* 1951,
    p. 97.
22 Arvid Anderson, *op. cit.,* p. 274.
23 The Montreal Police Strike of 1969 was the first open defiance of an award in
    more than 25 years of experience with various arbitration systems in
    Canada. The Montreal police worked without a contract for over one year.
    Protracted negotiations failed to produce a settlement largely because
    government negotiators lacked the authority to bargain over wages. Little
    or no progress toward a settlement was achieved in subsequent meetings
    with the head of the City Executive Committee and with a conciliator. Re-
    course to arbitration did not, in this instance, terminate the dispute but in-
    stead, provoked a strike. The arbitrator apparently gave little consideration
    to the extensive testimony and evidence on economic issues presented by the

Policemen's Brotherhood. Only a token increase in compensation was awarded to the police. Even then Prime Minister Pierre Trudeau sympathized with the financial plight of the Montreal police although not with their strike against the award. An important lesson can be learned from this episode that there is no safeguard against a strike when the arbitrator is inept. *Report Submitted to the Commission on Inquiry into Labor Relations Between the City of Montreal and the Montreal Policemen's Brotherhood,* April 27, 1970, 87 pp. and "$108-a-week Constable says 'we'll sweat it out',' *London Daily Star,* October 9, 1969, pp. 1–2.

24 J. Joseph Loewenberg, *op. cit.,* p. 32.

25 The City of Marquette, Michigan, filed a legal appeal from an award. The action was withdrawn when the police engaged in a brief strike. Adopting a different approach, the City of Shelby, Michigan, filed suit against the impartial arbitrator. The case was dropped when the state attorney general intervened to defend the arbitrator. *City of Shelby* v. *Arbitration Board,* (Macomb Cir. Ct. Case No. s-70-2666, (1970).

26 J. Joseph Loewenberg, *op. cit.,* p. 32.

27 Jean T. McKelvey, "Factfinding in Public Employment Disputes: Promise or Illusion?" *Industrial and Labor Relations Review,* Vol. 22, No. 4 (July 1969), p. 530.

28 Statement by Morris Sackman, Industrial Relations Specialist, Division of Public Employee Labor Relations, Department of Labor, July 10, 1972, personal interview, Washington, D.C.

29 Philip E. Garber, "Compulsory Arbitration in the Public Sector: A Proposed Alternative," *The Arbitration Journal,* Vol. 26, No. 4 (1971), p. 230.

30 Carl M. Stevens, "Is Compulsory Arbitration Compatible with Bargaining?" *Industrial Relations,* Vol. 5, No. 2 (February 1966), p. 52.

31 "Teachers and Power," *The New York Times Book Review,* May 28, 1972, p. 3.

32 The issue of whether the experience of neutrals trained in the private sector is transferable to the public sector has been prominent since the first legislated arbitration statutes were enacted in the 1960s. More recently, both the rights and interest arbitration processes have been criticized for being too legalistic, costly, and lengthy; problems which are all directly related to the background and supply of arbitrators in the United States. See, for example, "Usery Diagnosis Ills of Arbitration Process, Prescribes Some Treatments," *GERR,* No. 533, December 10, 1973, pp. B-1, B-2.

33 "The Forgotten Service," *The Washington Post,* September 23, 1972.

FOR DISCUSSION AND REVIEW

1 Define legislated arbitration.
2 Explain the concept that government authority is public property. What bearing does this have on the discussion in the article?
3 How has the magnitude of the legal barriers to legislated arbitration for police and fire fighters been exaggerated?
4 Why is it difficult to enforce legislated arbitration? What are the practical issues?
5 Discuss the meaning the author attaches to "face-saving."

INTERVIEW WITH JERRY WURF

Jerry Wurf is president of the 750,000-member American Federation of State, County and Municipal Employees (AFSCME), the fastest-growing union of the 105 AFL-CIO affiliates. In 1969, Wurf was elected a vice-president of the AFL-CIO and a member of its Executive Council. He was founder and is a director of the Coalition of American Public Employees (CAPE), which includes AFSCME, the National Education Association, and other independent public employee associations.

In addition to serving on several executive boards, Wurf also is a member of the Visiting Committee on Economic Studies Program of the Brookings Institution and a member of The American Committee on U.S.-Soviet Relations.

Q Could you please begin by explaining your organization's function? Are there others like it?

A The American Federation of State, County and Municipal Employees (AFSCME) is the nation's leading public employee union. AFSCME has more than 750,000 members and, when we sit down to negotiate wages, hours, and working conditions, we represent at least 1.4 million public employees. Most of our members work for state and local governments, but we also represent employees of nonprofit, charitable institutions that are largely dependent upon public funds, and also some federal employees.

In a sense, AFSCME is an industrial union in the public sector. Our members run the entire gamut of occupations in the public service—blue-collar and white-collar; clerical, professional, and paraprofessional; engineers, highway workers, hospital workers, mental-health technicians, prison guards, child-care workers, social workers, tax examiners, police officers, school aides, cafeteria workers, architects, city planners, computer programmers, zoo keepers, and nurses, to name just a few. You name it—we've got it. There is no other national union dedicated solely to representing the entire range of state and local government employees.

Q In what way is your organization different from and similar to unions in the private sector or trade associations?

A AFSCME performs the same services for workers in the public sector that unions in private industry perform for their members.

The fundamental difference is that we usually function without any legal recognition at all, or else with only inadequate legal recognition of the right of public employees to organize and to bargain collectively with their employers. Nonetheless, we negotiate contracts, handle grievances, provide legal assistance when necessary, and deal with day-to-day problems on the job.

Unlike, say, the glass-bottle-blowers' union, we deal with what is essential a political environment. Day-to-day political decisions involving the scope of public services—such as the size of a state's budget for mental health, welfare, child care, or corrections—impact directly upon the employees who provide these services. So do legislative decisions concerning the fairness and adequacy of the tax structures which support public services. For that reason, AFSCME is very active in Congress, the state houses, city halls, county boards, and wherever else the decisions are made that determine whether there will be an adequate level of public service.

Public employees are also citizens, just like anyone else, so we have another reason to be concerned about the scope and quality of public services. We pay taxes, too. We live on the same streets, drink the same water, and send our children to the same schools as other people. We're concerned about the liveability of our communities, and the fairness of the tax structures that support public services.

One problem that particularly distresses us—as taxpayers, as citizens, and as public employees—is the generally poor quality of public management. In most states and cities, public officials reward their political supporters with top-level management jobs, regardless of their usually negligible administrative backgrounds and lack of expertise in the service that they're administering. As a union, we have no direct impact on the competence of management, but we do work to insulate public work forces from political manipulation.

There really is no basis of comparison between AFSCME and trade associations. They work to improve the business climate for their enterprises, which is a worthy-enough goal.

Q   Not too long ago a great deal was heard regarding the associational activities of public employees. This was when several strikes of police, firefighters, and others providing services in cities were occurring at a higher frequency than they seem to be now. What is your feeling regarding the organizing of public employees? Is there a moral or ethical issue related to the term "public servant" at issue?

A   For more than a quarter century, I've been working to organize public employees, but I'm not certain that the success of public employee unionism is entirely a tribute to my organizing skills.

Like other American workers, public employees have the right to join together, in organizations of their own choosing, to deal with problems on the job. This "associational activity," as you call it, has evolved into bona fide trade unionism and collective bargaining. This development is above all a comment on conditions in public employment and on the attitudes and practices of public management. Public employees must be aware that they have problems on the job—problems which require unions, and collective bargaining. Otherwise, they wouldn't have chosen unions and collective bargaining—in the face of hostile management, and an inadequate legal structure which frowns upon public employee unionism.

As for the appropriateness of the term "public servant," that's an interesting question. I can recall that, some time ago, when I was Director of our union's District Council 37, a leader in our union named John Boer made a particular issue of the insulting nature of the phrase "civil servant." Now, John Boer was a dedicated public employee and a skilled professional, just as he was, and is, a dedicated trade unionist. He pointed out that public employees serve the public, but that doesn't mean that they're "servants." The term "servant" implies servility; it implies that one is denied the rights enjoyed by other workers. We reject this concept, and, in large measure, the entire history of our union has been the struggle by public employees to shed the stigma of servitude and to attain the dignity enjoyed by other workers.

Q Have public employee unions been as successful as their counterparts have been in the private sector? What major issue have they emphasized?

A According to the U.S. Department of Labor, more than 51 percent of state and local government employees are represented by unions or by associations that function as unions. In contrast only 29 percent of the workers in private industry are unionized. This is particularly noteworthy because collective bargaining is recognized by law for almost all workers in private industry, but public employees do not enjoy a comparable legal protection of their most basic rights.

I take no pleasure in reporting that public employee unionism has been growing at a time when the trade union movement, as a whole, has been losing ground. During the period 1970–1972, public employee unions signed up an additional 143,000 members. The entire labor movement grew by only 50,000 during that period—or, in other words, unions in private industry suffered a loss of about 93,000 members which was offset by the growth in public employee unions. More recently, during the two-year period ending in 1976, the labor movement lost about 767,000 members. AFSCME grew during that period at a rate of about 1,000 members a week, so, apparently, without the growth of public employee unions, labor's retreat would have been a rout. As I've said, I find this distressing.

If there is a major issue that has been emphasized in our organizing, it's dignity—the demand by workers for some voice in their working conditions. A sanitation worker in Memphis and a welfare worker in New York City would use different words to describe the same impulse. I think the sanitation workers in Memphis said it best, with the famous picket sign from their strike in 1968—"I am a man."

Public employees have rejected the old, unilateral systems dominated by employers. Whether they're called merit systems, civil service systems, personnel codes or whatever, these are simply the employers' management tools, and they allow for no input by the employees. We work for the most basic protections of employees' rights such as a grievance system where an impartial arbitrator rather than management has the last word; promotions on the basis of objectives criteria, not favoritism; and bona fide hearings, with union representation of the employee, in the event of discipline or discharge. With a contract, there's no more mystery about the more basic working conditions and policies. Items like job classifications, caseload sizes, pay rates, seniority rules and the like are spelled out on paper, and apply to everyone.

Of course, money is an issue, too. Traditionally, the public employee was underpaid, compared to a comparable worker in private industry. We made some advances during the 1960s, but it was all catch-up—and we didn't quite catch up. Since the onset of the Nixon recession—two presidents ago—mayors and governors have tried to make public employees pay for the flight of industry from the cities, the impact of unemployment upon inadequate tax systems, the bankers' avarice and the politicians' own irresponsibility. Now, it's a battle just to keep pace with inflation.

Q Has the organizing of many groups of public employees changed the nature of the role of unions in this country?

A There has definitely been a change, now the unions know that public employees exist and have the same aspirations as other workers.

Unlike labor movements in other countries which have a much more ambitious view of their missions, the American labor movement has always had a tendency to reconcile itself to the supposed unorganizability of whole classes of workers. The craft workers used to say that the industrial workers were unorganizable; the native-born said the immigrants were unorganizable; the whites looked down on the blacks, and the men looked down on the women. Of course, the conventional wisdom was that you couldn't organize public employees.

Now, that's all changed. Faced with declining work forces in many industries, or with the difficulties of organizing in the South and Southwest, many unions from private industry have seen their salvation in organizing public employees. Unions that were originally confined to janitors, or hod carriers, or truck drivers have set up public employee divisions. Another union—which originally restricted itself only to teachers—has announced, with some fanfare, that it's going to try to sign up the full range of public employees. Other unions are getting into the act, too.

In a sense, this is a healthy development if it makes the entire labor movement aware of the urgency of issues such as public employee collective bargaining rights, or—indirectly—the importance of budgets for public services, and the fairness and adequacy of tax systems.

Q What specific differences exist between unions' interactions with management in the public sector and in the private sector?

A In most of private industry, except for the hospitals or the grape fields, the relationships between the employers and the unions have become formalized. Collective bargaining in private industry is protected by the National Labor Relations Act, and the employers have learned that they can survive the ordeal of sitting down at the bargaining table with a union representing their employees. Nowadays, even the president of a traditionally antiunion corporation such as General Electric won't indulge in the kind of antiunion rhetoric that has become fashionable among the "new breed" of liberal politicians, not to mention the old breed of conservatives.

In contrast, labor relations in the public sector have no such structure of legality and acceptability. In some states, we have the legal right to bargain with the employer over a full range of issues, and to negotiate a collective bargaining agreement. But almost inevitably, once the bargaining has finished, a third party—the legislature or a city council —comes into the act to provide the funds. And on occasion a legislature will refuse to make good on a contract negotiated in good faith between the union and a governor, or a mayor.

The essential difference is that workers in the private sector deal with an employer who can and does make binding agreements covering the entire range of working conditions. In the public sector, workers deal with administrators and managers who can never have the final say on some of the most critical pieces of the contract—wages and other cost factors.

Q Much has been written regarding unions' response to job enrichment —the use of internal rewards such as autonomy and discretion. Most seem to say union leadership is still economically oriented. How does your organization stand on this issue? Are noneconomic gains, such as better, more challenging positions, objectives of interactions with management? Are public employees' jobs in need of "enrichment" as people say is true of, for example, many manufacturing industry jobs?

A Job enrichment may sound just a little bit esoteric to a hospital worker, or a sanitation worker, or a clerical employee who is being paid much less than the minimum necessary to support a family. First of all, an underpaid employee wants an enriched paycheck. Then, he or she wants the basic protections provided under a union contract—a fair grievance system, the right to look at one's personnel file, a fair promotion procedure, a clearly defined job description, pay for work performed in a higher classification, and so on.

Much of what we fight for at the bargaining table could be called "job enrichment" although we prefer words like "rationality" and "dignity." Social workers want a rational limit on the size of their caseloads, so that they can treat their clients like people. Hospital workers want a career ladder, so they won't have to spend their lives emptying bedpans. Workers in mental health or correctional facilities want some kind of staff/inmate standard so that they won't risk their lives and safety every day in the ward or the cell block. A clerical employee doesn't want to have to clean the coffee pot and run errands for the boss, in addition to typing and filing.

To be sure, employees also have more profound aspirations—for dignity, for advancement, or what you call job enrichment. Despite their lofty rhetoric, public managers usually resist these aspirations. For example, we recently completed arduous negotiations for the first contract for more than 25,000 clerical, professional and paraprofessional employees in Illinois. The professionals demanded a voice in setting professional standards in their departments, so that, for example, a psychologist wouldn't have to approve the discharge of a mental patient who wasn't ready to leave the hospital. The clericals demanded a largely symbolic clause in their contract recognizing that clerical work is "vital and necessary." These issues were raised early in the negotiations, but management resisted both demands almost as fiercely as they would later resist our economic demands. To be meaningful, job enrichment represents a sharing of power between employer and employee, and management is very reluctant to part with its authority, even if it's the power to deny a clerical employee his or her dignity as a person, or to compel a professional employee to violate professional standards.

Q What is the role of employee organizations in regard to affirmative action plans? Have unions themselves adopted equal employment opportunity (EEO) laws and guidelines effectively?

A Unlike the construction industry or the docks in Brooklyn or San Francisco, public employment doesn't have a hiring hall or a shape-up; the union plays no role in hiring the employees.

It's the employer's responsibility to uphold standards of equity not only in hiring employees, but in promotions and day-to-day treatment on the job. A good union has to bring people together—regardless of race, sex, or religion—to fight for equity on the job, and we make sure that the politicians live up to the fair employment standards that they themselves write. When the employer makes an effort to practice fair employment, we do our best to cooperate—and, in some instances, such as the tense prison system in Illinois, our local union leadership and staff took some heat for helping to bring in more black and Hispanic prison guards. More frequently, the employer discriminates against employees—and we fight back with grievances, picket lines, back-pay suits, or complaints with the federal or state authorities.

Much of what our union fights for, such as career ladders or objective standards for promotions, could be considered an affirmative action program. A standard clause in our contracts is an antidiscimination clause, prohibiting discrimination on the basis of race, sex, religion, or political affiliation.

As for the internal life of our union, I'm not sure that we've done enough yet to achieve full participation by everyone, including groups that traditionally haven't had their fair share of power in the unions. But I'd match our record against any other union—and certainly against management in public service, or private industry. In large measure, our union has grown with the civil rights movement and the women's movement. Our battles are intertwined, and none of them has yet been completely won.

Q What do you forecast to be the impact of organizations such as yours on labor relations in the future? What impact do you foresee on the personnel departments of municipalities, states, and federal agencies?

A Our goal is to ensure that a public hospital worker, a welfare worker, a sanitation worker, or a highway worker has the same rights as a worker in private industry.

As AFSCME becomes stronger and more effective in communities throughout the nation, we anticipate—and we hope—that management will also become more sophisticated.

We're eager to undertake all kinds of experiments in public labor relations. First of all, we want to experiment with new ways of resolving deadlocked negotiations without strikes. We have endorsed voluntary binding arbitration in all public services and compulsory binding arbitration in emergency public services, such as police and fire protection. For the most part, public officials haven't taken us up on our offer; apparently, they're more afraid of allowing an impartial third party to enter labor relations than they are of disrupting essential public services.

Further down the road, we're anticipating innovations such as multiemployer, regional bargaining, which has proved successful in the apparel industry.

As of now, we're professionalizing our operations, improving our union's capacity to deal with the full range of bargaining issues around the country. We yearn to deal with more professional, more competent people on the other side of the table.